HANDBOOK OF CHARACTER STUDIES

HANDBOOK OF CHARACTER STUDIES: PSYCHOANALYTIC EXPLORATIONS

edited by

Manfred F. R. Kets de Vries
Sidney Perzow

INTERNATIONAL UNIVERSITIES PRESS
Madison   Connecticut

Library of Congress Cataloging-in-Publication Data

Handbook of character studies : psychoanalytic explorations / edited
   by Manfred F. R. Kets de Vries, Sidney Perzow.
      p. cm.
   Includes bibliographical references (p.   ) and index.
   ISBN 0-8236-2295-9
   1. Personality disorders.   2. Psychoanalysis.   I. Kets de Vries,
Manfred F. R.   II. Perzow, Sidney.
RC544.H36   1991
616.89′17—dc20   91-7878
                                                                         CIP

Manufactured in the United States of America

CONTENTS

Section III:
CONTEMPORARY CHARACTER TYPES

Section IV:
LESS CONVENTIONAL TYPES

Section V:
THERAPEUTIC CONSIDERATIONS

ACKNOWLEDGMENTS

We gratefully acknowledge the permission of the authors to reprint their works. We sincerely thank Christine Mead, Christina Davis, Natalie Rubin, and Catherine Tsagaroulis for their editorial assistance. We also like to thank the Montreal General Hospital, Department of Psychiatry for its support. Daphna Zevadi deserves our special gratitude, especially for her help in putting such a large manuscript into a readable form. We would also like to express our appreciation to Richard Nilan and Nadine Wiewior for their patience in typing the final draft. INSEAD's department of research, in particular, Diane Mitchell, has been extremely helpful in supporting our effort to make this book possible. Finally, we very much appreciate the encouragement from our publisher, Martin Azarian, for his willingness to sponsor a project of this type.

Manfred F. R. Kets de Vries, Paris
Sidney Perzow, Montreal

CONTRIBUTORS

Karl Abraham, M.D. (1877–1925), was the first German psycho-analyst. He was a member of Freud's inner circle and the founder (1910) of the Berlin Psychoanalytic Society and Institute. He made significant contributions to the study of manic depressive states, schizophrenia, and the pregenital stage of the personality.

Jacob A. Arlow, M.D., is a training and supervising analyst in New York and a lecturer at many universities and psychoanalytic institutes. He has been the editor of the *Psychoanalytic Quarterly* and the president of the American Psychoanalytic Association. He is the coauthor of *Psychoanalytic Concepts and Structural Theory* and the author of numerous articles.

Francis Baudry, M.D., is a training and supervising analyst at the New York Psychoanalytic Institute. He is an associate clinical Professor of Psychiatry at the Albert Einstein College of Medicine, New York.

Charles Brenner, M.D., is a training and supervising analyst at the New York Psychoanalytic Institute. He is a clinical professor of psychiatry at the State University of New York and a lecturer in psychiatry at Yale University College of Medicine. He is the former president of the New York Psychoanalytic Society and the American Psychoanalytic Association, as well as an honorary member of the New Jersey and Long Island Psychoanalytic Societies. He is the author of *An Elementary Textbook of Psychoanalysis, Psychoanalytic Technique and Psychic Conflict,* and *The Mind in Conflict.* He is the coauthor of *Psychoanalytic Concepts and the Structural Theory.*

Helene Deutsch, M.D. (1884–1982), was a psychoanalyst in private practice and a training analyst at the Boston Psychoanalytic Society and Institute. She studied medicine at the University of

Vienna and became a member and later the director of the Training Institute of the Vienna Psychoanalytic Society. Her special contribution to psychoanalysis has been in the area of female psychology. She is the author of *Psychoanalysis of the Neuroses, Psychology of Women, Confrontations with Myself: An Epilogue,* and many scientific papers.

Ruth Easser, M.D. (1922–1975), studied medicine at the University of Toronto and was trained at Columbia Institute of Psychoanalysis where she became a training supervising analyst. Eventually she settled in Toronto where she was a Staff Psychiatrist at the Mount Sinai Hospital and associate professor at the University of Toronto.

Otto Fenichel, M.D. (1899–1946), was a psychoanalyst in private practice. Originally a member of the Berlin Psychoanalytic Society, he became a training analyst at the same institute. He moved to Los Angeles in 1938 where he remained for the rest of his life. He is author of *Problems of Psychoanalytic Technique, The Outline of Clinical Psychoanalysis, The Psychoanalytic Theory of Neuroses,* and numerous psychoanalytic papers.

Sigmund Freud, M.D. (1856–1939), was the founder of psychoanalysis. He studied medicine at the University of Vienna and became a neurologist and psychiatrist, and eventually, a professor at the University of Vienna. In 1930 he received the Goethe Prize for literature. He was the author of innumerable books and papers.

Peter L. Giovacchini, M.D., is a clinical professor in the department of psychiatry, University of Illinois, College of Medicine. He is a former director of the Chicago Psychoanalytic Study Group and the Center for Psychoanalytic Studies. He is the editor of *Tactics and Techniques in Psychoanalytic Therapy;* author of *A Clinician's Guide to Reading Freud, Treatment of Primitive Mental States,* and *Character Disorders and Adaptive Mechanisms;* and coauthor of *Psychoanalytic Treatment of Schizophrenic, Borderline and Characterological Disorders* and *Technical Factors in the Treatment of the Severely Disturbed Adolescent.*

Harry Guntrip, M.D. (1901–1975), was a member of the British Psychological Society, and educated at the University of London.

He was a psychotherapist and a lecturer in the Department of Psychiatry, Leeds University. Among his books are: *Clinical Studies of the Schizoid Personality; Schizoid Phenomena, Object Relations and the Self; Psychoanalytic Theory, Therapy and the Self.*

Otto F. Kernberg, M.D., is Medical Director of the New York Hospital–Cornell Medical Center and Professor of Psychiatry at the Cornell Medical College. He is also training and supervising analyst of the Columbia University Center for Psychoanalytic Training and Research. He is the author of *Borderline Conditions and Pathological Narcissism, Object Relations Theory and Clinical Psychoanalysis, Internal World and External Reality, Severe Personality Disorders,* and numerous articles.

Manfred F. R. Kets De Vries, D.B.A., is the Raoul de Vitry Professor of Human Resource Management at the European Institute of Business Administration (INSEAD), France. He studied at the University of Amsterdam and Harvard University, Graduate School of Business Administration. He has been a professor at McGill University, Ecole des Hautes Etudes Commerciales, Montreal and the Harvard Business School. He is a member of the Canadian Psychoanalytic Society and a founding member of the International Society for the Psychoanalytic Study of Organizations. He is the author of *Organizational Paradoxes: Clinical Approaches to Management* and *Prisoners of Leadership,* the editor of *The Irrational Executive,* and coauthor of *The Neurotic Organization, Power and the Corporate Mind, Unstable at the Top,* and numerous articles.

Heinz Kohut, M.D. (1913–1981), was a lecturer in psychiatry at the University of Chicago. He received a medical degree from the University of Vienna and trained in neurology and psychiatry at the University of Chicago. He was a graduate of the Institute for Psychoanalysis in Chicago where he served as faculty member and training analyst. He was president of the American Psychoanalytic Association, vice president of the International Psychoanalytic Association, and vice president of the Sigmund Freud Archives. He wrote *The Analysis of the Self, The Restoration of the Self, How Does Analysis Cure, Self Psychology and the Humanities,* and many professional papers.

Stanley Lesser, M.D. (1917–1986), was a staff psychiatrist at the Mount Sinai Hospital and Associate Professor at the University of Toronto. He studied medicine at the Long Island College of Medicine and trained at the Columbia Institute of Psychoanalysis where he became a training analyst prior to settling in Canada.

Joyce McDougall, D.Ed., is a psychoanalyst in private practice and a supervising and training analyst at the Paris Society and Institute of Psychoanalysis. She had her psychoanalytic training in London and Paris and studied at the Hampstead Child Training Centre. She is the author of *Plea for a Measure of Abnormality, Theaters of the Mind, Theaters of the Body,* and coauthor of *Dialogue with Sammy*.

William W. Meissner, S.J., M.D., is a psychiatrist and psychoanalyst in private practice. He is training and supervising analyst at the Boston Psychoanalytic Institute. He was formerly clinical professor of psychiatry at Harvard Medical School and is now University Professor of Psychoanalysis at Boston College. He is the author of thirteen books including *The Paranoid Process* and numerous articles.

Karl Menninger, M.D. (1893–1990), was the chairman of the trustees of the Menninger Foundation. He was a psychiatrist and psychoanalyst. He was the founder of the Karl Menninger School of Psychiatry and Mental Health Sciences. He was president of the American Psychoanalytic Association. Among his many awards were the Medal of Freedom given by the President of the United States, the Distinguished Service Award, and the Founder's Award of the American Psychiatric Association. He was the author of fourteen books, including *The Human Mind, Man Against Himself, The Vital Balance,* and many articles.

Sidney M. Perzow, M.D., is a former McLaughlin Fellow trained at McGill Medical School and the Tavistock Clinic, London, England. He is currently an associate psychiatrist at the Montreal General Hospital, director of its individual psychotherapy training unit, and assistant professor at McGill

University. He is a member of the Canadian Psychoanalytic Society.

Wilhelm Reich, M.D. (1897–1957), was a psychotherapist in private practice. He studied medicine at the University of Vienna and worked at the Vienna Neuropsychiatric Institute. At one time he was a member of the Vienna Psychoanalytic Society. A Marxist, he tried to build a bridge between psychoanalysis and the social sciences. He established a work democracy at Orgonon. He is the author of *Character Analysis, The Mass Psychology of Fascism, The Function of the Orgasm,* and *The Sexual Revolution.*

Arnold Rothstein, M.D., is a psychoanalyst in private practice and a member of the New York Psychoanalytic Association. He is the founding editor of the *Workshop Series* of the American Psychoanalytic Association. He is the author of *The Narcissistic Pursuit of Perfection* and *The Structural Hypothesis: An Evolutionary Perspective.*

Charles Rycroft, M.D., is a psychoanalyst and psychotherapist in private practice. He was educated at Trinity College, Cambridge where he read economics and history. He studied medicine at University College, London. He has been a consultant in psychotherapy at the Tavistock Clinic. He is the author of *Anxiety and Neurosis, Imagination and Reality, Clinical Dictionary of Psychoanalysis, Reich, The Innocence of Dreams, Psychoanalysis and Beyond,* and the editor of *Psychoanalysis Observed.*

Roy Shafer, Ph.D., is a training and supervising analyst at the Columbia University Center for Psychoanalytic Training and Research. He is the recipient of the American Psychological Association's award for Distinguished Professional Contribution to Knowledge. He is the author of *Aspects of Internalization, A New Language for Psychoanalysis, Language and Insight, The Analytic Attitude,* and numerous psychoanalytic articles. He is in the private practice of psychoanalysis in New York City.

David Shapiro, Ph.D., is a psychotherapist in private practice. He studied psychology at the University of Southern California. He has been the chief of Psychotherapy at the Austen Riggs Center. He is visiting professor of psychology at the graduate faculty, New School of Social Research, New York City. Among his books are *Neurotic Styles* and *Autonomy and Rigid Character*.

Martin H. Stein, M.D., is a training and supervising analyst at the New York Psychoanalytic Institute. He is a graduate of Cornell Medical College and the New York Psychoanalytic Institute. He is a member and former chairman of the Educational Committee of the New York Psychoanalytic Institute. He was the former chairman of the Board of Professional Standards American Psychoanalytic Association.

Donald W. Winnicott, M.D. (1896–1971), was a pediatrician and a training psychoanalyst. He read biology at Cambridge. He was a physician on the staff of the Paddington Green Children's Hospital in England. He has been president of the British Psychoanalytic Society, chairman of the Medical Section of the British Psychological Society, and president of the Pediatric Section of the Royal Society of Medicine. Among his books are: *The Child, the Family and the Outside World, The Family and Individual Development, Therapeutic Consultations in Child Psychiatry, The Piggle, Playing and Reality,* and *The Maturational Processes and the Facilitating Environment.*

Elizabeth R. Zetzel, M.D. (1907–1971), was a training analyst at the Boston Psychoanalytic Institute, an associate clinical professor of psychiatry at the Harvard Medical School, and the director of the Psychotherapy Study Center at the Massachusetts Mental Health Center. She was a graduate of the London Institute of Psychoanalysis and completed her psychiatric training at the Maudsley Hospital. She is the author of *The Capacity for Emotional Growth.*

INTRODUCTION

> In general a human being cannot bear opposed extremes in
> juxtaposition, be they in his personality or in his reactions. It
> is this endeavour for unification that we call character. In
> regard to persons near to us extremely opposed emotions
> may be so strong as to become completely unbearable.
>   Sigmund Freud quoted by Jones (1953)

The word *character*, according to the *Oxford English Dictionary*,
derives from the Greek word to engrave, imprint, or inscribe.
This derivation indicates the centrality of deeply embedded, consistent, and relatively durable behavior patterns in elucidating
the term. In everyday language when we think of these aggregate
or distinctive features of a person we include qualities which
identify him or her as an unusual personality or an eccentric, and
also include such things as reputation and moral qualities.
Character represents and delimits the individual's uniqueness,
highlighting strengths and distortions. When disturbing to others
it is often labeled as pathological.

Translated into psychoanalytic terminology, Moore and Fine
(1968), define character as reflecting "the individual's habitual
modes of bringing into harmony his own inner needs and the
demands of the external world . . . [C]haracter . . . has a
permanent quality that affects the degree and manner of drive
discharge, defenses, *affects*, specific *object relations*, and adaptive
functioning in general" (p. 25). This description indicates how
character refers to the singularities in the person's cognitive,
affective, and behavioral functioning as those singularities are
observed by another.

From the point of view of definitions, character has been a
very ambiguous concept. A principal reason has been that terms
such as *character*, *temperament*, *mood*, *personality*, *identity*, the *self*, and
even the *ego* have been used interchangeably. Character, says
Schafer, "has never been provided with either a satisfactory con-

1

ceptualization or a definite place in psychoanalytic theory . . .
character overlaps the concept *ego* . . . the concept *self* . . .
and the free-floating concept *style*" (chapter 10, p. 169). Terms
such as *mood, temperament, personality*, and *identity* have also been
used interchangeably. Adding to this confusion we note that
there are approximately 27,000 terms in the English language
that concern aspects of personality, of which 3,000 refer to common traits, and that as many as 810 character types have been
"identified" (Goldberg, 1982).

Apart from problems of definition, other controversies have
arisen around the use of the concept of character and passionate
negative reactions have been common. There is pain involved in
the process of characterization. Classification has been considered
dehumanizing. Associations with sickness and hospitalization are
evoked. Some have looked at classification as an attack on the person's integrity and uniqueness. Others have expressed concern
about the self-fulfilling nature of using classification schemes at all,
feeling that persons who are typified in a certain manner may start
to behave accordingly. In general, it can be said that it proves easier
to agree on the existence of character than to agree on its identification in a specific instance.

Why Study Character?

In spite of all this, the concept has relevance and is important.
The debate on the topic continues and interest in it is growing.
But what is the source of its appeal?

A significant factor contributing to the contemporary interest
in character has been a changing patient population which increasingly complains about the dysfunctional effects of maladaptive
ways of thinking, feeling, and behaving. The majority of complaints are about "problems with living," not merely about getting rid of specific symptoms. Looking at whole structures instead
of parts is taking an ever more central position in clinical practice,
a reality which makes the analysis of character more pertinent.

Since character disorders do indeed constitute the bulk of
analytic practice (Stone, 1954; Lampl-De Groot, 1963; Baudry,
1983), it behooves the analyst to be familiar with the concept.
Baudry (chapter 9) emphasizes that a working familiarity with it
has become essential to diagnosis and assessment of potential for

analyzability, as well as to the working through process. To use his words: "It is hard to imagine a concept of more everyday concern to our work than character" (p. 149). The concept's appeal, according to McLaughlin, resides in its "beguiling near-to-experience resonance—the quality of being at the heart of what we sense to be central to our intuitive experiencing of ourselves" (quoted in Boesky, 1983, p. 240). For Schafer (chapter 10), character is a powerful concept that allows one to talk holistically and to take into account the fluid boundary between form and content while at the same time being a congenial alternative to the "more austere and confining terms of metapsychology" (p. 170).

The understanding of character—its origins, components (e.g., modes, traits, attitudes, habits, moods, styles), formation, and disruptions, along with the identification of character types and prototypes (Millon and Klerman, 1986)—is essential to communication (inter- as well as intradisciplinary), teaching, treatment, and research.

How do we go about studying character? How do we decipher man's operational code? What approach will provide the greatest insight and further therapeutic interventions? What will be our "text"? Do we study bodily signs, dress, demeanor, speech, overt behavior, or other signifiers? How "deep" do we go? Do we look at surface manifestations or deep structures? What "tools" do we have at our disposal to codify, objectify, and improve our understanding? What is our orientation going to be: will it be intuitive, impressionistic, humanistic, or scientific? Which theoretical models will provide most insight? What are the paradigms? It is our contention that of the many conceptual models used in the study of character, psychoanalysis, in spite of all its flaws, is the most promising in providing insight into this fascinating but elusive focal point of body, psyche, soul, and society.

Historical Context

The study of character has a long and turbulent history. Character has been looked at from many different perspectives. Poets, novelists, philosophers, and the like have been no strangers to the topic. As early as the fourth century B.C., Plato alluded to the fact that people may be of various types. Actually, the argument can be made that an early version of Freud's tripartite theory can be found in Plato's conceptualization of character. Plato speculated that the mind consists of three parts which individuals possess in different degrees. One element he called desire or appetite, meaning the instinctive desires in their simplest forms; the second he called reason, implying the ability to understand and think before acting—the faculty of calculation, foresight, and decision making. The third element was *thumos* or *thumoeides*, a concept difficult to translate, which stands for self-regard, self-respect, spirit, and enterprise (Plato, *The Republic*, 1955, pp. 185–193).

Another early precursor in the study of character was Theophrastus, a pupil of Aristotle and his successor as head of the Lyceum. Theophrastus wrote a notable treatise called *Characteres* which consisted of thirty brief character sketches based on Aristotle's teachings. In a satirical way—describing humankind with all its foibles and virtues—he presented a classification of different types such as the garrulous man, the stupid man, the superstitious man, and so on.

A classification which has lingered on until the present day was made, however, by a contemporary of Plato, Hippocrates. His assessment of character was based on the imbalance of bodily humors, which were the embodiments of earth, water, fire, and air. In Hippocrates' model (centuries later adopted and modified by Galen, probably the greatest physician of Roman times), there were four basic temperaments: the choleric, with its irascibility; the melancholic, with its tendency toward sadness; the sanguine, with its optimistic stand; and the phlegmatic, with its disposition toward apathy. Excesses of yellow bile, black bile, blood, and phlegm were considered responsible for the existence of each type (Mora, 1985).

In more recent times constitutional theories have focused on the visible body rather than on its supposed contents. The beginnings of a more scientific approach saw the light of day. Gall (1758–1825) attempted to correlate character with variations in the surface of the skull. His "science" of phrenology inspired a great deal of research that went on for decades before phrenology fell into disrepute. Some hundred years later, Kretschmer (1925) and Sheldon (1940, 1945), carrying the scientific torch further, brought some credibility to the constitutional approach in their studies of the correlation between body, physique, and personality. For example, Kretschmer (1925) identified four basic physical types, the pyknic, athletic, asthenic, and dysplastic, which corresponded respectively to extraverted, epileptic, schizoid, and ineffective behavior, though the last category was rather vaguely defined. Using Kretschmer's works as a basis, Sheldon (1940, 1945) also proposed a relationship between body, physique, and character. He referred to endo-, meso-, and ectomorphic builds, which supposedly were associated with three psychological types indicating visceral interests, activity and muscular interests, and intellectual interests, respectively.

Although the respectability of the study of character increased, interest in it evaporated. A different approach was called for and eventually found in the newly developing behavioral and psychological sciences. The work of two little-known turn-of-the-century Dutch psychologists, Heymans and Wiersma (1906–1909), represented the dawn of the nondynamic psychological approach to character as well as providing a conceptual link between the writings of the ancient Greeks and those of Freud. Basing their work on sophisticated, empirical dimensional studies, Heymans and Wiersma identified three "fundamental criteria" for evaluating character: activity level, emotionality, and susceptibility to external versus internal stimulation. Combinations of these led to eight types including the phlegmatic, the choleric, and the sanguine. Their "fundamental criteria" were very similar to Freud's "three great polarities" described in "Instincts and Their Vicissitudes" (1915a), namely, active–passive, ego–object, and pleasure–pain.

The Psychoanalytic Orientation

The real inspiration for the study of character as a concept began with the development of psychoanalysis. By providing a body of theory or a number of conceptual tools and a method of investigation far richer than anything preceding it, psychoanalysis allowed character to be explored as never before. Furthermore, because of these conceptual breakthroughs, the possibility of character repair could be considered seriously.

Psychoanalytic contributions to character obviously began

with Freud. In this context, a number of points must be emphasized. First, as a general psychology, psychoanalysis is by its nature involved in the study of character. In this capacity it adds a dynamic unconscious dimension to man. It links the surface of man's character to an underlying and unconscious structure (Baudry, 1983). Second, Freud's interest in character was partially "forced" upon him. His inclination was toward the study and treatment of the neuroses. Character existed as resistance—something to be avoided. Eventually, however, he approached resistance differently, leading to the discovery of the transference and the structural model. Third, Freud wrote only three articles on the subject of character (see Section I): his revolutionary paper on "Character and Anal Erotism" (1908) (chapter 1); "Some Character-Types Met With In Psycho-Analytic Work" (1925) (chapter 2); and his rarely cited paper "Libidinal Types" (1931) (see chapter 3).

Finally, and most importantly, many pertinent insights can be found in Freud's writings as scattered comments to more central theoretical expositions. Significant examples include: *The Interpretation of Dreams* (1900), the very first reference where character was linked to unconscious childhood memories; "Three Essays on the Theory of Sexuality" (1905a), which tied infantile sexuality, sublimations, and construction to character formation for the first time; "The Dynamics of Transference" (1912a), which discussed the repetition compulsion and the formation of stereotyped behavior; "The Disposition to Obsessional Neurosis" (1913a), in which he contrasted symptom and character formation; "Remembering, Repeating and Working Through" (1914a), which talked about the characterological absorption of memories; "Instincts and Their Vicissitudes" (1915a), in which he discussed the three mental polarities as described above; "Mourning and Melancholia" (1915c), for its introduction to identification; "The Ego and the Id" (1923a), in a class of its own with respect to the impact it made on characterology; "New Introductory Lectures on Psycho-Analysis" (1933), where Freud located character in all three systems of the psychic apparatus, giving pride of place to the superego; and finally, "Analysis Terminable and Interminable" (1937), where he discusses congenital ego determinants of defense selection.

The first real sign of Freud's interest in the concept of character can be observed in his article "Character and Anal Erotism" (1908), where he associated character traits with constitutional predispositions (see chapter 1). Freud suggested that early bodily experiences could be viewed as precursors of later psychological ones. He supposed that such character traits as orderliness, parsimony, and obstinacy were drive derivatives of the anal, erotogenic zone. Freud gradually recognized not only the importance of the study of character but also the problems associated with the concept. While symptoms had an ego-alien quality, character traits, in contrast, were ego-syntonic, which made them much harder to deal with. He also struggled with the question of how to distinguish symptoms from character traits. In dealing with these dilemmas, Freud noted that:

> In the field of the development of *character* we are bound to meet with the same instinctual forces which we have found at work in the neuroses. But a sharp theoretical distinction between the two is necessitated by the single fact that the failure of repression and the return of the repressed—which are peculiar to the mechanism of neurosis—are absent in the formation of character. In the latter, repression either does not come into action or smoothly achieves its aim of replacing the repressed by reaction-formations and sublimations. Hence the processes of the formation of character are more obscure and less accessible to analysis than neurotic ones [Freud, 1913a, p. 323].

In his later writings we can see how Freud began to broaden his outlook on character, going beyond mere component instinct analysis. His paper "Some Character-Types Met With In Psycho-Analytic Work" (chapter 2) exemplified this changing perspective in that he identified certain themes and patterns which characterized some of his patients (see chapter 2). However, with a better understanding of the meaning of resistance and transference, Freud's interest in character really flourished (Baudry, 1983). It became increasingly clear to him that patients had stereotyped, consistent ways of dealing with their analysts, patterns based on childhood struggles with authority and obedience. It dawned on Freud and others that they were dealing with much wider phenomena than mere symptoms. Through the analysis of resistance and transference, psychoanalysts moved away from the investigation of symptoms to that of character, seeing symptoms only as a part of it. They began to recognize that the distinction between symptoms and character traits was not necessarily a sharp one.

The development of Freud's tripartite structural model as introduced in "The Ego and the Id" (1923a) set the stage for a greater recognition of the forces of reality and a move away from a purely constitutional view of character. Freud's new view was that character was formed by both instinctual drives and historical experience. This evolution in his thinking was reflected in the paper "Libidinal Types" (chapter 3), where both constitutional factors and object relations were considered as contributing variables in character development. Character was looked at as a sort of contingency whereby some people were governed by instinctual demands, others by the forces of the superego, and yet others by those of the ego. Object relations began to been seen as playing an increasingly important role in the development of character. This point of view we find emphasized in Freud's "New Introductory Lectures on Psycho-Analysis" (1933):

> You yourselves have no doubt assumed that what is known as "character," a thing so hard to define, is to be ascribed entirely to the ego. We have already made out a little of what it is that creates character. First and foremost there is the incorporation of the former parental agency as a super-ego, which is no doubt its most important and decisive portion, and, further, identifications with the two parents of the later period and with other influential figures, and similar identifications formed as precipitates of abandoned object-relations. And we may now add as contributions to the construction of character which are never absent the reaction-formation which the ego acquires—to begin with in making its repressions and later, by a more normal method, when it rejects unwished-for instinctual impulses [p. 91].

Freud moved from lack of interest in character per se to seeing it in ever more complex ways: beyond transformed libido, he focused on characterological themes in the context of the tripartite model. However, libido theory dominated his work and had the strongest immediate impact on the other two pioneers of character theory, Karl Abraham and Wilhelm Reich.

Karl Abraham (1921, 1924, 1925), one of the original ten members of Freud's inner circle, brought Freud's work on the component instinct model of character to its apogee in three classical, sparsely written articles. In expanding libido theory he explored the relationship between the various erotogenic zones and oral, anal, and genital character types. He was the first to move away from symptoms and identify the central position of character. He also paid more attention to preoedipal factors in the genesis of character. In addition, his writings hinted at the object-relations developments that were soon to be elaborated by Melanie Klein and her followers. For Abraham, character was defined as "the sum of [the person's] instinctive reactions towards his social environment [coming to completion when] libido has reached the capacity for object-love" (1925, p. 408).

What Abraham did for component instinct analysis of character Reich did for the defense side of the drive–defense equation. Moreover, his work, captured in a brilliant and controversial text, moved character analysis into the foreground (Stone, 1954)—symptom analysis was on the way out. Reich's ideas were to have a major impact on subsequent generations of analysts, evoking strong positive or negative reactions (Sterba, 1951, 1953; Boesky, 1983).

According to Reich the individual uses stereotyped ways of interacting to protect himself against dangers, whether instinctually or externally derived. These patterns of behavior emerge as defensive solutions to the Oedipus complex and are embedded in the total psychic structure as character armor. This accounts for the characteristic ways analysands deal with the analyst. Pathology is related to the degree of rigidity in these forms of reaction. Reich suggested that we can speak of character disorders when patterns are fixed, rigid, and automatic whatever the situation encountered.

Waelder corrected the flaws in Reich's unidimensional approach. Rather than seeing character as an outcome of defensive reactions of the ego, he clarified the evolving psychoanalytic position in his paper on "The Principle of Multiple Function" (1936) where he confirmed that character was increasingly considered to be a compromise solution of the ego intersystemic struggle created by the conflicting demands of id, superego, and reality. He argued that a "future psychoanalytic theory of character . . . must be at least two-dimensional according to the dominant drive and specific methods of [task] solution" (Waelder, 1936, p. 79).

Otto Fenichel in his *Psychoanalytic Theory of Neurosis* (1945), the "bible of psychoanalysts," provided the most complete summary of the psychoanalytic theory of character as it then existed. One can easily recognize the influence of Reich and Waelder in his description of character as "the habitual mode of bringing into harmony the tasks presented by internal demands and by the external world . . . [It is] . . . a function of the constant, organized, and integrating part of the personality which is the ego . . ." (1945, p. 467). It was Fenichel's misfortune that in relating character so closely to the ego he had great difficulty in distinguishing one concept from the other—a problem that is still with us today.

But ego psychology as a separate area of endeavor grew rapidly and pushed the frontiers of character analysis forward. As a central figure in the development of ego psychology, Heinz Hartmann (1939) argued that the origin of character may be found in instinctual energies independent of conflicts and their resolution. Another innovator, Erik Erikson (1959), emphasized the role of social reality in the formation of character. In his conceptualizations identity stood for the experience of continuity and coherence of the organization of self vis-à-vis others and the influencing of the social environment. His ideas brought home the point that, with respect to character, consideration must be given to a person's development throughout the life cycle. According to him, psychopathology was strongly associated with developmental problems, not just instinctual conflicts. It should be noted how, in Erikson's terminology, identity and character became almost interchangeable entities, both describing an individual's way of organizing ongoing experience. He stressed the consolidation of character as a central task of adolescence.

Peter Blos (1968), another developmental researcher, argued that the cardinal achievement of adolescence was the transition and modification of childhood character traits into character. In the process of this formation, character takes over the homeostatic function from the regulatory agencies of childhood and stabilizes the residue of inevitable and unavoidable childhood traumata. The relentless push for actualization by this residue contributes to character's compelling nature. Whether it will become defensive or autonomous depends on the success with which adolescent developmental tasks are handled.

Thus, the evolution of the psychoanalytic understanding of character development involved a gradual change from taking character as simple drive derivatives to it being the consequence of intersystemic conflict and then a combination of genetic endowment, biological factors, and life experiences. Thus character took over the originally central position of symptoms.

At present, the analysis of symptoms can be viewed more as a preliminary to the analysis of character. Character pathology has become a primary indicator for psychoanalytic treatment. Moreover, it can be said in a metaphorical way that the original emphasis on Oedipus has been replaced by emphasis on Narcissus, meaning that greater attention is currently being given to preoedipal themes in the understanding of character. This development is part and parcel of the widening scope of psychoanalysis as borderline and narcissistic disorders and the role of the first years of life in their pathogenesis take a more central position.

However, in spite of the increased sophistication in understanding character, controversies continue. Many (Boesky for one [1983]) feel more comfortable studying character traits which are less abstract, less highly inferential, and therefore empirically closer to hand. While this approach is eminently sensible, it does have one drawback: it does not do away with the need to study character as a whole. It is clear that the whole is more than the sum of its parts. This point of view is well articulated by Blos who said that "we certainly ascertain in character formation integrative processes, structurings and patternings that belong to a different order than a mere bundling together of traits, attitudes, habits and idiosyncracies" (1968, p. 249). According to him, character formation is "an integrative process and as such aims at the elimination of conflict and anxiety arousal" (1968, p. 251).

Diverging Approaches to Character Pathology

In the meantime, despite all of these developments in the study of character, the notion of typologies had fallen on hard times. In many instances, clinically derived assessments were labeled unscientific because they were deemed insufficiently rigorous. In order to attain greater precision in diagnosis, more atomistic approaches were advocated. To use Millon's words, "the personality configuration was segmented into its ostensive constituents, construed as S-R bonds by some, statistical factors by others, dimensional traits elsewhere, and so on" (1984, p. 452). But with this shift in orientation, the richness implicit in clinical diagnosis, whole configurations, and dynamic interpretations was lost.

Moreover, the deteriorating partnership between psychiatry and psychoanalysis added to the decline in interest in character. The reasons for this development are numerous and beyond the scope of this *Handbook* (Sabshin, 1985, p. 474). Competing theories, alternative therapies, the growth of psychopharmacology, the need to maintain the purity and/or identity of psychoanalysis as a medical discipline, and disillusionment with psychoanalytic treatment, all played a part. The subsequent parting of paths has brought about some unfortunate consequences. One significant area of conflicts concerns the diverging approaches to character pathology and its classification and investigation.

It would be a mistake to believe that the loss has only been psychiatry's—that psychiatry has suffered doubly by losing the "royal road" and by being misled by spurious, theoretically anemic, and/or flash-in-the-pan concepts, models, and approaches. Psychoanalysis has lost out as well, being notoriously poor in the area of classification (category formation), identification (assigning new entities to a given category), and taxonomy (theoretical study of classification) (Blashfield, 1986, p. 363). It could indeed benefit from the advances made in this area by psychiatry and psychology.

One other aspect worth noting is that less overt functional impairment is conveyed by the psychoanalytic diagnosis of character disorder rather than by the psychiatric counterpart. For example, at the low end of the spectrum a psychiatrist may deem an individual healthy, where the psychoanalyst would note significant difficulties which need attention. This is not a question of seeing trouble where there is none but of having a greater sensitivity to issues which can seriously impair the quality of life without producing gross manifestations of functional disturbance.

Nevertheless, while the psychoanalytic study of character has become increasingly rich and sophisticated, psychiatry has retreated from a dynamic approach by arguing about the "elusive complexity" of character. Fear of making inferences and of "soft" concepts has led to a search for "hard" data, and, unfortunately, to hard times for the understanding of character disorders.

Over the last thirty years psychiatry has increasingly taken a purely organic Neo-Kraeplinian point of view in the area of psychopathology, first articulated in the influential textbook by Meyer-Gross, Slater, and Roth (1954) and strongly critical of psychoanalysis and psychotherapy. This Neo-Kraeplinian "invisible college" has led the way in developing the paradigm embodied by the *Diagnostic and Statistical Manual of Mental Disorders* (DSM-III) and its revision, DSM-III-R (American Psychiatric Association, 1987). This model emphasizes empirical attitudes and a heavy reliance on psychometric and quantitative approaches to psychopathology, as well as an operational methodology. It is hard to fault these interests and it would be folly to belittle or underestimate the serious and brilliant developments which have emerged with increasing regularity since the publication of the Washington University criteria for operational diagnoses, forerunner of DSM-III (Klerman, 1986, pp. 15–17).

While these orientations are certainly to be applauded, the results in the area of personality disorders are disappointing. The axis devoted to personality disorders in DSM-III and DSM-III-R is committee designed and politically sculpted. As Gunderson (1983) argues, "for most of the personality disorder categories there was either no empirical base . . . or no clinical tradition, thus their disposition was more subject to the convictions of individual Advisory Committee members" (1983, p. 30). Stein (Panel, 1983a) points out that "it is doubtful that one can classify any body of data without a theory upon which that classification is based" (p. 225). The failure of DSM-III has been in its inability to consider data regarding unconscious mental functioning. Without such data it is impossible to make a fully meaningful diagnostic assessment of and statement about any patient. Unconscious conflict is universal whether or not it is currently amenable to psychometric measure or capable of being operationalized. In addition, it is not the province of one particular theory. Reluctance to use psychoanalytic theory which "furnishes us with a valuable tool for observing, organizing and interpreting clinical data" (Panel Report, 1983a, p. 226) is to be regretted, as is waning attention to predisposing factors and the history of the disorder.

We can now see that the pendulum is swinging in the other direction. Alternative approaches have not lived up to their original promise and the vacuity of many of these orientations has become increasingly clear. Clinical behaviorism and psychopharmacological approaches to the study of character have proved to be overly simplistic and sterile. Hence, we can observe that attitudes toward the analysis of character have been changing. As pure empiricism and positivism have not given the answers, we can see how part function analysis is being replaced by the study of whole structures once again. In moving in that direction, however, emphasis must be put on a synthesis of psychoanalytic, cognitive, and behavioral approaches. And here psychoanalysis furnishes a unique body of data and theory not easily found elsewhere and well able to stimulate this development.

Rationale and Organization of the Handbook

Given the increasing interest in the study of character and its pathology in psychoanalysis, psychiatry, psychology, the mental health professions, and the lay community, a need exists for a body of knowledge which will stimulate and promote that interest. As much of psychoanalytic writing on the subject of character has been scattered through the literature, it has been difficult for anyone to study the subject in depth without expending considerable effort in tracking down and selecting appropriate readings. This *Handbook of Character Studies* fills the gap by bringing together a wide range of original, classical, and representative articles by leading and innovative psychoanalytic theoreticians.

The contents of the volume reflect some of the major contributions to the psychoanalytic study of character. They reveal how character shapes and is shaped by the course of life. They grapple with controversial and undecided issues, old and new, from a variety of psychoanalytic orientations: drive-structure, developmental, ego-psychological, object-relational, and phenomenological.

The *Handbook* is divided into five sections. Section I, "Pioneers," presents the groundbreaking formulations about character. Many if not most of the insights developed retain a large measure of their original vigor and need to be incorporated into newer formulations rather than simply being replaced by them.

In Section II, "Theoretical Considerations and Controversies," several different conceptual frameworks are introduced and questions are raised about possible problem areas. Section III, "Contemporary Character Types," presents a number of common character constellations found in clinical work. In Section IV, "Less Conventional Types," some less traditional character patterns are introduced. Finally, in Section V, "Therapeutic Considerations," there are articles offering different ways of looking at treatment.

The *Handbook of Character Studies* is designed to be a reference source for the practicing clinician and the scholar interested in the total personality. Ideally, it will also serve as a catalyst for future research on character, thereby ultimately aiding the individual in finding more tolerable ways of living.

Section I
PIONEERS

Psychoanalytic characterology began in 1908 with Freud's article "Character and Anal Erotism" (chapter 1 of this present work), at that time a very controversial publication for a neuropsychiatric weekly. This first and foremost of only three articles Freud devoted to character, had its foreshadowings in a letter to Jung two years earlier where Freud describes neat, stingy, and obstinate traits as sublimations of anal erotism (McGuire, 1974, p. 8). It is a conceptual development found earlier in "Three Essays on the Theory of Sexuality" (1905a) and coincidental to insights from Freud's analysis of the "Rat-Man" (1909a).

In this component instinct approach to character, Freud describes as anal characters people with features of orderliness, parsimony, and obstinacy and a history of unusual bowel behavior. He suggests that this behavior originates from a constitutionally derived anal erotism. Abstracting from these particulars Freud made his first major statements about character, echoes of which continue to be heard today: "character in its final shape is formed out of the constituent instincts: the permanent character-traits are either unchanged prolongations of the original instincts, or sublimations of those instincts, or reaction-formations against them" (chapter 1, p. 26).

In "Some Character-Types Met With In Psycho-Analytic Work" (chapter 2), character is not seen in terms of developmental sexuality but rather in terms of its emergence as an unwelcome participant in the treatment of the patient. This resistance is expressed through subtle or not directly obvious peculiarities and attitudes of the patient. Freud examines three of these "surprising" traits, all related to matters of guilt and injustice, and illustrates them with the distorted life orientations of literary figures and patients. King Richard III is characterized as an "exception," Lady Macbeth and Ibsen's Rebecca are counted

17

among those who are "wrecked by success," and, finally, some patients are described as becoming "criminals out of a sense of guilt."

In the final and most obscure but also most meaningful article on psychoanalytic taxonomy, "Libidinal Types" (chapter 3), Freud applies structural theory to a classification of normal personality. Erotic, obsessional, and narcissistic types (as well as composites of the three) are described and ascribed to dominance of one or another of the three psychic agencies—id, ego, or superego. Speculations are made as to which kind of psychological illness each type is vulnerable.

Abraham continued Freud's work on characterological derivatives of libido and gave the approach its definitive stamp. The paper chosen for this section is a development of his brilliant earlier study on orality (Abraham, 1916) and the second of three contributions to the study of character formation from the perspective of libidinal transformation. "The Influence of Oral Erotism on Character-Formation" (chapter 4) exemplifies (albeit in a highly concise way) how powerful an explanatory tool libido theory can be. Abraham describes the two substages of the oral stage (a benign sucking one and a later sadistic biting one) and the many traits such as garrulousness, generosity, envy, leechlike clinging, vampirelike draining, optimism, and pessimism that emerge from them whether as the result of formative mishandling or otherwise. He shows how traits of the anal character "are built on the ruins of oral erotism." Also noteworthy are his terse references to ambivalence, jealousy, curiosity, and the object of the instincts.

Reich's article "On Character Analysis" (chapter 5) published several years before his classic text on the subject, shifts the focus of the analytic task from attacking the symptom to undoing its source, namely, the underlying neurotic character structure. This structure is manifested more in the patient's form and manner than in the content of the material. It represents a narcissistic armoring of the ego and accounts for the resistance described by Freud in chapter 2. Resistance, particularly in the beginning phase, is a result of this armor. Reich argues that character analysis, while fraught with difficulty and danger, is a prerequisite for the successful analysis of symptoms and their infantile sources.

In the next paper, "Some Circumscribed Character Forms" (chapter 6), Reich provides clinical accounts of character armor in two well-established character types, the hysterical and the compulsive, and a third, newly introduced type, the phallic-narcissistic. According to him, the shy, coquettish, hysterical character is fixated at the genital level and suffers from surplus sexual energy. Character armoring takes the form of genital sexuality; that is, sexuality in the service of defense. The compulsive character's armor is understood as an affect block, the dissociation of affects from ideation which is produced by a "spasm of the ego" to ward off anal tendencies and possible phallic strivings. The vigorous, aggressively courageous phallic–narcissistic character is fixated at the phallic stage. Here phallic sadism and exhibitionism serve as a defense against regression to passivity and anal tendencies.

In his work on the "Psychoanalysis of Character" (see chapter 7), Fenichel argues that depth psychology should include as part of its task that "which governs the mind of the normal person during the day" (p. 108). Character, he notes, first gained attention as the cause of resistance to analytic work and later as the presenting complaint of the patient (which is still true today). Like symptoms, traits can be understood as compromise formations. They can be classified as "sublimatory" or "reactive formations" depending on whether they "satisfy" instinct or "defend" against it. The latter results in the ego becoming increasingly rigid and impoverished. Analysis aims to convert these restricting traits into "living conflicts," making the patient aware of certain behavior patterns and thereby amenable to analytic work.

Chapter 1

CHARACTER AND ANAL EROTISM

SIGMUND FREUD

Among those whom we try to help by our psycho-analytic efforts we often come across a type of person who is marked by the possession of a certain set of character-traits, while at the same time our attention is drawn to the behaviour in his childhood of one of his bodily functions and the organ concerned in it. I cannot say at this date what particular occasions began to give me an impression that there was some organic connection between this type of character and this behaviour of an organ, but I can assure the reader that no theoretical expectation played any part in that impression.

Accumulated experience has so much strengthened my belief in the existence of such a connection that I am venturing to make it the subject of a communication.

The people I am about to describe are noteworthy for a regular combination of the three following characteristics. They are especially *orderly, parsimonious* and *obstinate*. Each of these words actually covers a small group or series of inter-related character-traits. 'Orderly'[1] covers the notion of bodily cleanliness, as well as of conscientiousness in carrying out small duties and trustworthiness. Its opposite would be 'untidy' and 'neglectful'. Parsimony may appear in the exaggerated form of avarice; and obstinacy can go over into defiance, to which rage and revengefulness are easily joined. The two latter qualities— parsimony and obstinacy—are linked with each other more

This chapter originally appeared in *Standard Edition*, 9:167–176. London: Hogarth Press, 1959. Reprinted by permission of the publisher.

[1][*Ordentlich* in German. The original meaning of the word is *orderly;* but it has become greatly extended in use. It can be the equivalent of such English terms as *correct, tidy, cleanly, trustworthy,* as well as *regular, decent,* and *proper,* in the more colloquial senses of those words.]

closely than they are with the first—with orderliness. They are, also, the more constant element of the whole complex. Yet it seems to me incontestable that all three in some way belong together.

It is easy to gather from these people's early childhood history that they took a comparatively long time to overcome their infantile *incontinentia alvi* [faecal incontinence], and that even in later childhood they suffered from isolated failures of this function. As infants, they seem to have belonged to the class who refuse to empty their bowels when they are put on the pot because they derive a subsidiary pleasure from defaecating;[2] for they tell us that even in somewhat later years they enjoyed holding back their stool, and they remember—though more readily about their brothers and sisters than about themselves—doing all sorts of unseemly things with the faeces that had been passed. From these indications we infer that such people are born with a sexual constitution in which the erotogenicity of the anal zone is exceptionally strong. But since none of these weaknesses and idiosyncracies are to be found in them once their childhood has been passed, we must conclude that the anal zone had lost its erotogenic significance in the course of development; and it is to be suspected that the regularity with which this triad of properties is present in their character may be brought into relation with the disappearance of their anal erotism.

I know that no one is prepared to believe in a state of things so long as it appears to be unintelligible and to offer no angle from which an explanation can be attempted. But we can at least bring the underlying factors nearer to our understanding by the help of the postulates I laid down in my *Three Essays on the Theory of Sexuality* in 1905.[3] I there attempted to show that the sexual instinct of man is highly complex and is put together from contributions made by numerous constituents and component instincts. Important contributions to 'sexual excitation' are furnished by the peripheral excitations of certain specially designated parts of the body (the genitals, mouth, anus, urethra), which therefore deserve to be described as 'erotogenic zones'.

---

[2] Cf. Freud, *Three Essays on the Theory of Sexuality* (1905a), *Standard Edition*, 7, 186.

[3] [The material in the present paragraph is derived mainly from section 5 of the first essay and section 1 of the second (*Standard Edition*, 7, 167–169 and 176–179).]

But the amounts of excitation coming in from these parts of the body do not all undergo the same vicissitudes, nor is the fate of all of them the same at every period of life. Generally speaking, only a part of them is made use of in sexual life; another part is deflected from sexual aims and directed towards others—a process which deserves the name of 'sublimation'. During the period of life which may be called the period of 'sexual latency'—i.e. from the completion of the fifth year[4] to the first manifestations of puberty (round about the eleventh year)—reaction-formations, or counter-forces, such as shame, disgust and morality, are created in the mind. They are actually formed at the expense of the excitations proceeding from the erotogenic zones, and they rise like dams to oppose the later activity of the sexual instincts. Now anal erotism is one of the components of the [sexual] instinct which, in the course of development and in accordance with the education demanded by our present civilization, have become unserviceable for sexual aims. It is therefore plausible to suppose that these character-traits of orderliness, parsimony and obstinacy, which are so often prominent in people who were formerly anal erotics, are to be regarded as the first and most constant results of the sublimation of anal erotism.[5]

The intrinsic necessity for this connection is not clear, of course, even to myself. But I can make some suggestions which

[4][In the German editions before 1924 this read "from the completion of the fourth year."]

[5]Since it is precisely the remarks in my *Three Essays on the Theory of Sexuality* about the anal erotism of infants that have particularly scandalized uncomprehending readers, I venture at this point to interpolate an observation for which I have to thank a very intelligent patient. 'A friend of mine', he told me, 'who has read your *Three Essays on the Theory of Sexuality*, was talking about the book. He entirely agreed with it, but there was one passage, which—though of course he accepted and understood its meaning like that of the rest—struck him as so grotesque and comic that he sat down and laughed over it for a quarter of an hour.' This passage ran: 'One of the clearest signs of subsequent eccentricity or nervousness is to be seen when a baby obstinately refuses to empty his bowels when he is put on the pot—that is, when his nurse wants him to—and holds back that function till he himself chooses to exercise it. He is naturally not concerned with dirtying the bed, he is only anxious not to miss the subsidiary pleasure attached to defaecating' [*Standard Edition*, 7, p. 186]. The picture of this baby sitting on the pot and deliberating whether he would put up with a restriction of this kind upon his personal freedom of will, and feeling anxious, too, not to miss the pleasure attached to defaecating,—this caused my friend the most intense amusement. About twenty minutes afterwards, as we were having some cocoa, he suddenly remarked without any preliminary: 'I say, seeing the cocoa in front of me has suddenly made me think of an idea that I always had when I was a child. I used always to pretend to myself that I was the cocoa-manufacturer Van Houten' (he pronounced the name Van Hauten' [i.e. with the first syllable rhyming with

may help towards an understanding of it. Cleanliness, orderliness and trustworthiness give exactly the impression of a
reaction-formation against an interest in what is unclean and disturbing and should not be part of the body. ('Dirt is matter in the
wrong place.')[6] To relate obstinacy to an interest in defaecation
would seem no easy task; but it should be remembered that even
babies can show self-will about parting with their stool, as we
have seen above [p. 2], and that it is a general practice in
children's upbringing to administer painful stimuli to the skin of
the buttocks—which is linked up with the erotogenic anal zone—
in order to break their obstinacy and make them submissive. An
invitation to a caress of the anal zone is still used today, as it was in
ancient times, to express defiance or defiant scorn, and thus in
reality signifies an act of tenderness that has been overtaken by
repression. An exposure of the buttocks represents a softening
down of this spoken invitation into a gesture; in Goethe's *Götz von
Berlichingen* both words and gesture are introduced at the most
appropriate point as an expression of defiance.[7]

The connections between the complexes of interest in
money and of defaecation, which seem so dissimilar, appear to
be the most extensive of all. Every doctor who has practised
psycho-analysis knows that the most refractory and long-
standing cases of what is described as habitual constipation in

---

the English word *cow*]) and that I possessed a great secret for the manufacture of this
cocoa. Everybody was trying to get hold of this secret that was a boon to humanity but I
kept it carefully to myself. I don't know why I should have hit specially upon Van
Houten. Probably his advertisements impressed me more than any others.' Laughing,
and without thinking at the time that my words had any deep meaning, I said: 'Wann
haut'n die Mutter?' ['When does mother smack?' The first two words in the German
phrase are pronounced exactly like 'Van Houten'.] It was only later that I realized that
my pun in fact contained the key to the whole of my friend's sudden childhood recollection, and then I recognized it as a brilliant example of a screen-phantasy. My friend's
phantasy, while keeping to the situation actually involved (the nutritional process) and
making use of phonetic associations ('Kakao'['cocoa'.—"Kaka" is the common German
nursery word for faeces—cf. a dream at the end of Section IX of Freud, 1923, p. 119] and
'Wann haut'n'), pacified his sense of guilt by making a complete reversal in the content of
his recollection: there was a displacement from the back of the body to the front, excret-
ing food became taking food in, and something that was shameful and had to be concealed became a secret that was a boon to humanity. I was interested to see how, only a
quarter of an hour after my friend had fended the phantasy off (though, it is true, in the
comparatively mild form of raising an objection on formal grounds), he was, quite
involuntarily, presented with most convincing evidence by his own unconscious.'
    [6][This sentence is in English in the original.]
    [7][The scene occurs in Act III, when Götz is summoned by a Herald to surrender. In
the later acting version of the play the words are toned down.]

neurotics can be cured by that form of treatment. This is less surprising if we remember that that function has shown itself similarly amenable to hypnotic suggestion. But in psychoanalysis one only achieves this result if one deals with the patients' money complex and induces them to bring it into consciousness with all its connections. It might be supposed that the neurosis is here only following an indication of common usage in speech, which calls a person who keeps too careful a hold on his money 'dirty' or 'filthy'.[8] But this explanation would be far too superficial. In reality, wherever archaic modes of thought have predominated or persist—in the ancient civilizations, in myths, fairy tales and superstitions, in unconscious thinking, in dreams and in neuroses—money is brought into the most intimate relationship with dirt. We know that the gold which the devil gives his paramours turns into excrement after his departure, and the devil is certainly nothing else than the personification of the repressed unconscious instinctual life.[9] We also know about the superstition which connects the finding of treasure with defaecation,[10] and everyone is familiar with the figure of the 'shitter of ducats [*Dukatenscheisser*]'.[11] Indeed, even according to ancient Babylonian doctrine gold is 'the faeces of Hell' (Mammon = *ilu manman*[12]). Thus in following the usage of language, neurosis, here as elsewhere, is taking words in their original, significant sense, and where it appears to be using a word figuratively it is usually simply restoring its old meaning.[13]

---

[8][The English *filthy* as well as the German *filzig* appears in the original. Freud had already commented on the usage mentioned here, in a letter to Fliess of December 22, 1897 (Freud, 1950, Letter 79), and, later, in the first edition of *The Interpretation of Dreams* (1900), p. 200.]

[9]Compare hysterical possession and demoniac epidemics. [Freud discussed this at considerable length in Part III of his paper 'A Seventeenth Century Demonological Neurosis' (1923b). The legendary transformation of witches' gold into faeces and the comparison with the *Dukatenscheisser* below had already been mentioned by Freud in a letter to Fliess of January 24, 1897 (1950, Letter 57).]

[10][Numerous examples of this derived from folklore are given in Freud and Oppenheim's paper on "Dreams in Folklore" (1911), p. 187.]

[11][A term vulgarly used for a wealthy spendthrift.]

[12]Cf. Jeremias (1904, *Das alte Testament im lichte des alten Orients*, Leibzig, 115n.). ' "Mamon" ("Mammon") is "Manman" in Babylonian and is another name for Nergal, the God of the Underworld. According to Oriental mythology, which has passed over into popular legends and fairy tales, gold is the excrement of Hell.'

[13][For the occurrence of this in dreams, see a passage added in 1909 to *The Interpretation of Dreams* (1900), p. 407.]

It is possible that the contrast between the most precious substance known to men and the most worthless, which they reject as waste matter ('refuse'[14]), has led to this specific identification of gold with faeces.

Yet another circumstance facilitates this equation in neurotic thought. The original erotic interest in defaecation is, as we know, destined to be extinguished in later years. In those years the interest in money makes its appearance as a new interest which had been absent in childhood. This makes it easier for the earlier impulsion, which is in process of losing its aim, to be carried over to the newly emerging aim.

If there is any basis in fact for the relation posited here between anal erotism and this triad of character-traits, one may expect to find no very marked degree of 'anal character' in people who have retained the anal zone's erotogenic character in adult life, as happens, for instance, with certain homosexuals. Unless I am much mistaken, the evidence of experience tallies quite well on the whole with this inference.

We ought in general to consider whether other character-complexes, too, do not exhibit a connection with the excitations of particular erotogenic zones. At present I only know of the intense 'burning' ambition of people who earlier suffered from enuresis.[15] We can at any rate lay down a formula for the way in which character in its final shape is formed out of the constituent instincts: the permanent character-traits are either unchanged prolongations of the original instincts, or sublimations of those instincts, or reaction-formations against them.[16]

---

[14][In English in the original.]

[15][The connection between urethral erotism and ambition seems to find its first mention here. Freud occasionally returned to the point, for example, in a sentence added in 1914 to *The Interpretation of Dreams* (1900, p. 216) and in a footnote added in 1920 to the *Three Essays* (1905a, p. 239). In a long footnote to section III of *Civilisation and its Discontents* (1930, p. 21), he brought the present finding into connection with his two other main lines of thought concerning enuresis—its symbolic association with fire and its importance as an infantile equivalent of masturbation. See also the still later paper on 'The Acquisition and Control of Fire' (1932, p. 22).]

[16][There are not many accounts by Freud of the nature of "character" and the mechanism of its formation. Among them may be mentioned a passage near the end of the *Three Essays* (1905a, pp. 238–239), some remarks in the paper on "The Disposition to Obsessional Neurosis" (1913a, pp. 323–324), and especially a discussion in the first half of chapter 3 of *The Ego and the Id* (1923a), the gist of which is repeated in Lecture XXXII of the *New Introductory Lectures* (1933).]

Chapter 2

SOME CHARACTER-TYPES MET WITH IN PSYCHO-ANALYTIC WORK

SIGMUND FREUD

When a doctor carries out the psycho-analytic treatment of a neurotic, his interest is by no means directed in the first instance to the patient's character. He would much rather know what the symptoms mean, what instinctual impulses are concealed behind them, and are satisfied by them, and what course was followed by the mysterious path that has led from the instinctual wishes to the symptoms. But the technique which he is obliged to follow soon compels him to direct his immediate curiosity towards other objectives. He observes that his investigation is threatened by resistances set up against him by the patient, and these resistances he may justly count as part of the latter's character. This now acquires the first claim on his interest.

What opposes the doctor's efforts is not always those traits of character which the patient recognises in himself and which are attributed to him by people round him. Peculiarities in him which he had seemed to possess only to a modest degree are often brought to light in surprisingly increased intensity, or attitudes reveal themselves in him which had not been betrayed in other relations of life. The pages which follow will be devoted to describing and tracing back a few of these surprising traits of character.

I

The 'Exceptions'

Psycho-analytic work is continually confronted with the task of

This chapter originally appeared in the *Standard Edition*, 14:309–336. London: Hogarth Press, 1957. Reprinted by permission of the publisher.

inducing the patient to renounce an immediate and directly attainable yield of pleasure. He is not asked to renounce all pleasure; that could not, perhaps, be expected of any human being, and even religion is obliged to support its demand that earthly pleasure shall be set aside by promising that it will provide instead an incomparably greater amount of superior pleasure in another world. No, the patient is only asked to renounce such satisfactions as will inevitably have detrimental consequences. His privation is only to be temporary; he has only to learn to exchange an immediate yield of pleasure for a better assured, even though a postponed one. Or, in other words, under the doctor's guidance he is asked to make the advance from the pleasure principle to the reality principle by which the mature human being is distinguished from the child. In this educative process, the doctor's clearer insight can hardly be said to play a decisive part; as a rule, he can only tell his patient what the latter's own reason can tell him. But it is not the same to know a thing in one's own mind and to hear it from someone outside. The doctor plays the part of this effective outsider; he makes use of the influence which one human being exercises over another. Or—recalling that it is the habit of psycho-analysis to replace what is derivative and etiolated by what is original and basic—let us say that the doctor, in his educative work, makes use of one of the components of love. In this work of after education, he is probably doing no more than repeat the process which made education of any kind possible in the first instance. Side by side with the exigencies of life, love is the great educator; and it is by the love of those nearest him that the incomplete human being is induced to respect the decrees of necessity and to spare himself the punishment that follows any infringement of them.

When in this way one asks the patient to make a provisional renunciation of some pleasurable satisfaction, to make a sacrifice, to show his readiness to accept some temporary suffering for the sake of a better end, or even merely to make up his mind to submit to a necessity which applies to everyone, one comes upon individuals who resist such an appeal on a special ground. They say that they have renounced enough and suffered enough, and have a claim to be spared any further demands; they will submit no longer to any disagreeable necessity, for they are *exceptions* and, moreover, intend to remain so. In one such patient this claim was magnified into a conviction that a special providence watched over him, which would protect him from any painful sacrifices of the sort. The doctor's arguments will achieve nothing against an inner confidence which expresses itself as strongly as this; even *his* influence, indeed, is powerless at first, and it becomes clear to him that he must discover the sources from which this damaging prepossession is being fed.

Now it is no doubt true that everyone would like to consider himself an 'exception' and claim privileges over others. But precisely because of this there must be a particular reason, and one not universally present, if someone actually proclaims himself an exception and behaves as such. This reason may be of more than one kind; in the cases I investigated I succeeded in discovering a common peculiarity in the earlier experiences of these patients' lives. Their neuroses were connected with some experience or suffering to which they had been subjected in their earliest childhood, one in respect of which they knew themselves to be guiltless, and which they could look upon as an unjust disadvantage imposed upon them. The privileges that they claimed as a result of this injustice, and the rebelliousness it engendered, had contributed not a little to intensifying the conflicts leading to the outbreak of their neurosis. In one of these patients, a woman, the attitude towards life which I am discussing came to a head when she learnt that a painful organic trouble, which had hindered her from attaining her aims in life, was of congenital origin. So long as she looked upon this trouble as an accidental and late acquisition, she bore it patiently; as soon as she found that it was part of an innate inheritance, she became rebellious. The young man who believed that he was watched over by a special providence had in his infancy been the victim of an accidental infection from his wet-nurse, and had spent his whole later life making claims for compensation, an accident pension, as it were, without having any idea on what he based those claims. In his case the analysis, which constructed this event out of obscure mnemic residues and interpretations of the symptoms, was confirmed objectively by information from his family.

For reasons which will be easily understood I cannot communicate very much about these or other case histories. Nor do I

propose to go into the obvious analogy between deformities of
character resulting from protracted sickliness in childhood and
the behaviour of whole nations whose past history has been full
of suffering. Instead, however, I will take the opportunity of
pointing to a figure created by the greatest of poets—a figure in
whose character the claim to be an exception is closely bound
up with and is motivated by the circumstance of congenital
disadvantage.

In the opening soliloquy to Shakespeare's *Richard III,* Glouces-
ter, who subsequently becomes King, says:

> But I, that am not shaped for sportive tricks,
> Nor made to court an amorous looking-glass;
> I that am rudely stamp'd, and want love's majesty
> To strut before a wanton ambling nymph;
> I, that am curtail'd of this fair proportion,
> Cheated of feature by dissembling Nature,
> Deform'd, unfinish'd, sent before my time
> Into this breathing world, scarce half made up,
> And that so lamely and unfashionable,
> That dogs bark at me as I halt by them;
>
> * * * * *
>
> And therefore, since I cannot prove a lover,
> To entertain these fair well-spoken days,
> I am determined to prove a villain,
> And hate the idle pleasures of these days.

At a first glance this tirade may perhaps seem unrelated to
our present theme. Richard seems to say nothing more than: 'I
find these idle times tedious, and I want to enjoy myself. As I cannot play the lover on account of my deformity, I will play the
villain; I will intrigue, murder and do anything else I please.'
Such a frivolous motivation could not but stifle any stirring of
sympathy in the audience, if it were not a screen for something
much more serious. Otherwise the play would be psychologically
impossible, for the writer must know how to furnish us with a
secret background of sympathy for his hero, if we are to admire
his boldness and adroitness without inward protest; and such
sympathy can only be based on understanding or on a sense of a

possible inner fellow-feeling for him.

I think, therefore, that Richard's soliloquy does not say everything; it merely gives a hint, and leaves us to fill in what it hints at. When we do so, however, the appearance of frivolity vanishes, the bitterness and minuteness with which Richard has depicted his deformity make their full effect, and we clearly perceive the fellow-feeling which compels our sympathy even with a villain like him. What the soliloquy thus means is: 'Nature has done me a grievous wrong in denying me the beauty of form which wins human love. Life owes me reparation for this, and I will see that I get it. I have a right to be an exception, to disregard the scruples by which others let themselves be held back. I may do wrong myself, since wrong has been done to me'. And now we feel that we ourselves might become like Richard, that on a small scale, indeed, we are already like him. Richard is an enormous magnification of something we find in ourselves as well. We all think we have reason to reproach Nature and our destiny for congenital and infantile disadvantages; we all demand reparation for early wounds to our narcissism, our self-love. Why did not Nature give us the golden curls of Balder or the strength of Siegfried or the lofty brow of genius or the noble profile of aristocracy? Why were we born in a middle-class home instead of in a royal palace? We could carry off beauty and distinction quite as well as any of those whom we are now obliged to envy for these qualities.

It is, however, a subtle economy of art in the poet that he does not permit his hero to give open and complete expression to all his secret motives. By this means he obliges us to supplement them; he engages our intellectual activity, diverts it from critical reflection and keeps us firmly identified with his hero. A bungler in his place would give conscious expression to all that he wishes to reveal to us, and would then find himself confronted by our cool, untrammelled intelligence, which would preclude any deepening of the illusion.

Before leaving the 'exceptions', however, we may point out that the claim of women to privileges and to exemption from so many of the importunities of life rests upon the same foundation. As we learn from psycho-analytic work, women regard themselves as having been damaged in infancy, as having been undeservedly cut short of something and unfairly treated; and the embitterment of so many daughters against their mother derives, ultimately, from the reproach against her of having brought them into the world as women instead of as men.

II
Those Wrecked By Success

Psycho-analytic work has furnished us with the thesis that people fall ill of a neurosis as a result of *frustration*.[1] What is meant is the frustration of the satisfaction of their libidinal wishes, and some digression is necessary in order to make the thesis intelligible. For a neurosis to be generated there must be a conflict between a person's libidinal wishes and the part of his personality we call his ego, which is the expression of his instinct of self-preservation and which also includes his *ideals* of his personality. A pathogenic conflict of this kind takes place only when the libido tries to follow paths and aims which the ego has long since overcome and condemned and has therefore prohibited for ever; and this the libido only does if it is deprived of the possibility of an ideal ego-syntonic satisfaction. Hence privation, frustration of a real satisfaction, is the first condition for the generation of a neurosis, although, indeed, it is far from being the only one.

So much the more surprising, and indeed bewildering, must it appear when as a doctor one makes the discovery that people occasionally fall ill precisely when a deeply-rooted and long-cherished wish has come to fulfilment. It seems then as though they were not able to tolerate their happiness; for there can be no question that there is a causal connection between their success and their falling ill.

I had an opportunity of obtaining an insight into a woman's history, which I propose to describe as typical of these tragic occurrences. She was of good birth and well brought-up, but as quite a young girl she could not restrain her zest for life; she ran away from home and roved about the world in search of adventures, till she made the acquaintance of an artist who could appreciate her feminine charms but could also divine, in spite of what she had fallen to, the finer qualities she possessed. He took

---

[1] [See "Types of Onset of Neurosis" (1912b, p. 12).]

her to live with him, and she proved a faithful companion to him, and seemed only to need social rehabilitation to achieve complete happiness. After many years of life together, he succeeded in getting his family reconciled to her, and was then prepared to make her his legal wife. At that moment she began to go to pieces. She neglected the house of which she was now about to become the rightful mistress, imagined herself persecuted by his relatives, who wanted to take her into the family, debarred her lover, through her senseless jealousy, from all social intercourse, hindered him in his artistic work, and soon succumbed to an incurable mental illness.

On another occasion I came across the case of a most respectable man who, himself an academic teacher, had for many years cherished the natural wish to succeed the master who had initiated him into his own studies. When this older man retired, and his colleagues informed him that it was he who was chosen as successor, he began to hesitate, depreciated his merits, declared himself unworthy to fill the position designed for him, and fell into a melancholia which unfitted him for all activity for some years.

Different as these two cases are in other respects, they yet agree in this one point: the illness followed close upon the fulfilment of a wish and put an end to all enjoyment of it.

The contradiction between such experiences and the rule that what induces illness is frustration is not insoluble. It disappears if we make a distinction between an *external* and an *internal* frustration. If the object in which the libido can find its satisfaction is withheld *in reality,* this is an external frustration. In itself it is inoperative, not pathogenic, until an internal frustration is joined to it. This latter must proceed from the ego, and must dispute the access by the libido to other objects, which it now seeks to get hold of. Only then does a conflict arise, and the possibility of a neurotic illness, i.e. of a substitutive satisfaction reached circuitously by way of the repressed unconscious. Internal frustration is potentially present, therefore, in every case, only it does not come into operation until external, real frustration has prepared the ground for it. In those exceptional cases in which people are made ill by success, the internal frustration has operated by itself; indeed it has only made its appearance after an external frustration has been replaced by fulfilment of a wish. At first sight there is something strange about this; but on closer consideration we shall reflect that it is not at all unusual for the ego to tolerate a wish as harmless so long as it exists in phantasy alone and seems remote from fulfilment, whereas the ego will defend itself hotly against such a wish as soon as it approaches fulfilment and threatens to become a reality. The distinction between this and familiar situations in neurosis-formation is merely that ordinarily it is internal intensifications of the libidinal cathexis that turn the phantasy, which has hitherto been thought little of and tolerated, into a dreaded opponent; while in these cases of ours the signal for the outbreak of conflict is given by a real external change.

Analytic work has no difficulty in showing us that it is forces of conscience which forbid the subject to gain the long hoped-for advantage from the fortunate change in reality. It is a difficult task, however, to discover the essence and origin of these judging and punishing trends, which so often surprise us by their existence where we do not expect to find them. For the usual reasons I shall not discuss what we know or conjecture on the point in relation to cases of clinical observation, but in relation to figures which great writers have created from the wealth of their knowledge of the mind.

We may take as an example of a person who collapses on reaching success, after striving for it with single-minded energy, the figure of Shakespeare's Lady Macbeth. Beforehand there is no hesitation, no sign of any internal conflict in her, no endeavour but that of overcoming the scruples of her ambitious and yet tender-minded husband. She is ready to sacrifice even her womanliness to her murderous intention, without reflecting on the decisive part which this womanliness must play when the question afterwards arises of preserving the aim of her ambition, which has been attained through a crime.

> Come, you spirits
> That tend on mortal thoughts, unsex me here
> . . . Come to my woman's breasts,
> And take my milk for gall, you murdering ministers!
> (Act I, Sc. 5.)

> . . . I have given suck, and know
> How tender 'tis to love the babe that milks me:
> I would, while it was smiling in my face,
> Have pluck'd my nipple from his boneless gums,
> And dashed the brains out, had I so sworn as you
> Have done to this.
>
> (Act I, Sc. 7.)

One solitary faint stirring of reluctance comes over her before the deed:

> . . . Had he not resembled
> My father as he slept, I had done it . . .
>
> (Act II, Sc. 2.)

Then, when she has become Queen through the murder of Duncan, she betrays for a moment something like disappointment, something like disillusionment. We cannot tell why.

> . . . Nought's had, all's spent,
> Where our desire is got without content:
> 'Tis safer to be that which we destroy,
> Than by destruction dwell in doubtful joy.
>
> (Act III, Sc. 2.)

Nevertheless, she holds out. In the banqueting scene which follows on these words, she alone keeps her head, cloaks her husband's state of confusion and finds a pretext for dismissing the guests. And then she disappears from view. We next see her in the sleep-walking scene in the last Act, fixated to the impressions of the night of the murder. Once again, as then, she seeks to put heart into her husband:

> Fie, my lord, fie! a soldier, and afeard? What need we fear
>   who knows
> it, when none can call our power to account?
>
> (Act V, Sc. 1.)

She hears the knocking at the door, which terrified her husband after the deed. But at the same time she strives to 'undo the deed which cannot be undone'. She washes her hands, which are blood-stained and smell of blood, and is conscious of the futility of the attempt. She who had seemed so remorseless seems to have been borne down by remorse. When she dies, Macbeth, who meanwhile has become as inexorable as she had been in the beginning, can only find a brief epitaph for her:

> She should have died hereafter;
> There would have been a time for such a word.
> (Act V, Sc. 5.)

And now we ask ourselves what it was that broke this character which had seemed forged from the toughest metal? Is it only disillusionment—the different aspect shown by the accomplished deed[2]—and are we to infer that even in Lady Macbeth an originally gentle and womanly nature had been worked up to a concentration and high tension which could not endure for long, or ought we to seek for signs of a deeper motivation which will make this collapse more humanly intelligible to us?

It seems to me impossible to come to any decision. Shakespeare's *Macbeth* is a *pièce d'occasion,* written for the accession of James, who had hitherto been King of Scotland. The plot was ready-made, and had been handled by other contemporary writers, whose work Shakespeare probably made use of in his customary manner. It offered remarkable analogies to the actual situation. The 'virginal' Elizabeth, of whom it was rumoured that she had never been capable of child-bearing and who had once described herself as 'a barren stock',[3] in an anguished outcry at the news of James's birth, was obliged by this very childlessness of hers to make the Scottish king her successor. And he was the son of the Mary Stuart whose execution she, even though reluctantly, had ordered, and who, in spite of the clouding of their relations by political concerns, was nevertheless of her blood and might be called her guest.

---

[2] [An allusion to a line in Schiller's *Die Braut von Messina,* III, p. 5.]
[3] Cf. *Macbeth,* Act III, Sc. 1.:
Upon my head they placed a fruitless crown,
And put a barren sceptre in my gripe,
Thence to be wrenched with an unlineal hand,
No son of mine succeeding . . .

The accession of James I was like a demonstration of the curse of unfruitfulness and the blessings of continuous generation. And the action of Shakespeare's *Macbeth* is based on this same contrast.[4]

The Weird Sisters assured Macbeth that he himself should be king, but to Banquo they promised that his children should succeed to the crown. Macbeth is incensed by this decree of destiny. He is not content with the satisfaction of his own ambition. He wants to found a dynasty—not to have murdered for the benefit of strangers. This point is overlooked if Shakespeare's play is regarded only as a tragedy of ambition. It is clear that Macbeth cannot live for ever, and thus there is but one way for him to invalidate the part of the prophecy which opposes him—namely, to have children himself who can succeed him. And he seems to expect them from his indomitable wife:

> Bring forth men-children only!
> For thy undaunted mettle should compose
> Nothing but males. . . .
>
> (Act I, Sc. 7.)

And equally it is clear that if he is deceived in this expectation he must submit to destiny; otherwise his actions lose all purpose and are transformed into the blind fury of one doomed to destruction, who is resolved to destroy beforehand all that he can reach. We watch Macbeth pass through this development, and at the height of the tragedy we hear Macduff's shattering cry, which has so often been recognized to be ambiguous and which may perhaps contain the key to the change in Macbeth:

> He has no children!
>
> (Act IV, Sc. 3.)

There is no doubt that this means: 'Only because he is himself childless could he murder my children.' But more may be implied in it, and above all it might lay bare the deepest motive which not only forces Macbeth to go far beyond his own nature, but also

---

[4][Freud had already suggested this in the first edition of *The Interpretation of Dreams* (1900, *Standard Edition*, p. 266).]

touches the hard character of his wife at its only weak point. If one
surveys the whole play from the summit marked by these words
of Macduff's, one sees that it is sown with references to the
father–children relation. The murder of the kindly Duncan is little else than parricide; in Banquo's case, Macbeth kills the father
while the son escapes him; and in Macduff's, he kills the children
because the father has fled from him. A bloody child, and then a
crowned one, are shown him by the witches in the apparition
scene; the armed head which is seen earlier is no doubt Macbeth
himself. But in the background rises the sinister form of the
avenger, Macduff, who is himself an exception to the laws of
generation, since he was not born of his mother but ripp'd from
her womb.

It would be a perfect example of poetic justice in the manner
of the talion if the childlessness of Macbeth and the barrenness of
his Lady were the punishment for their crimes against the sanctity
of generation—if Macbeth could not become a father because he
had robbed children of their father and a father of his children,
and if Lady Macbeth suffered the unsexing she had demanded of
the spirits of murder. I believe Lady Macbeth's illness, the transformation of her callousness into penitence, could be explained
directly as a reaction to her childlessness, by which she is convinced of her impotence against the decrees of Nature, and at the
same time reminded that it is through her own fault if her crime
has been robbed of the better part of its fruits.

In Holinshed's *Chronicle* (1577), from which Shakespeare
took the plot of *Macbeth,* Lady Macbeth is only once mentioned as
the ambitious wife who instigates her husband to murder in
order that she may herself become queen. There is no mention of
her subsequent fate and of the development of her character. On
the other hand, it would seem that the change of Macbeth's
character into a bloodthirsty tyrant is ascribed to the same
motives as we have suggested here. For in Holinshed *ten years* pass
between the murder of Duncan, through which Macbeth becomes
king, and his further misdeeds; and in these ten years he is shown
as a stern but just ruler. It is not until after this lapse of time that
the change begins in him, under the influence of the tormenting
fear that the prophecy to Banquo may be fulfilled just as the prophecy of his own destiny has been. Only then does he contrive the

CHARACTER-TYPES MET WITH IN PSYCHO-ANALYTIC WORK   39

murder of Banquo, and, as in Shakespeare, is driven from one crime to another. It is not expressly stated in Holinshed that it was his childlessness which urged him to these courses, but enough time and room is given for that plausible motive. Not so in Shakespeare. Events crowd upon us in the tragedy with breathless haste so that, to judge by the statements made by the characters in it, the course of its action covers about *one week*.[5] This acceleration takes the ground from under all our constructions of the motives for the change in the characters of Macbeth and his wife. There is no time for a long-drawn-out disappointment of their hopes of offspring to break the woman down and drive the man to defiant rage; and the contradiction remains that though so many subtle interrelations in the plot, and between it and its occasion, point to a common origin of them in the theme of childlessness, nevertheless the economy of time in the tragedy expressly precludes a development of character from any motives but those inherent in the action itself.

What, however, these motives can have been which in so short a space of time could turn the hesitating, ambitious man into an unbridled tyrant, and his steely-hearted instigator into a sick woman gnawed by remorse, it is, in my view, impossible to guess. We must, I think, give up any hope of penetrating the triple layer of obscurity into which the bad preservation of the text, the unknown intention of the dramatist, and the hidden purport of the legend have become condensed. But I should not subscribe to the objection that investigations like these are idle in face of the powerful effect which the tragedy has upon the spectator. The dramatist can indeed, during the representation, overwhelm us by his art and paralyse our powers of reflection; but he cannot prevent us from attempting subsequently to grasp its effect by studying its psychological mechanism. Nor does the contention that a dramatist is at liberty to shorten at will the natural chronology of the events he brings before us, if by the sacrifice of common probability he can enhance the dramatic effect, seem to me relevant in this instance. For such a sacrifice is justified only when it merely interferes with probability,[6] and not when it

[5]Darmesteter (1881, p. lxxv).
[6]As in Richard III's wooing of Anne beside the bier of the King whom he has murdered.

breaks the causal connection; moreover, the dramatic effect would hardly have suffered if the passage of time had been left indeterminate, instead of being expressly limited to a few days.

One is so unwilling to dismiss a problem like that of *Macbeth* as insoluble that I will venture to bring up a fresh point, which may offer another way out of the difficulty. Ludwig Jekels, in a recent Shakespearean study,[7] thinks he has discovered a particular technique of the poet's, and this might apply to *Macbeth*. He believes that Shakespeare often splits a character up into two personages, which, taken separately, are not completely understandable and do not become so until they are brought together once more into a unity. This might be so with Macbeth and Lady Macbeth. In that case it would of course be pointless to regard her as an independent character and seek to discover the motives for her change, without considering the Macbeth who completes her. I shall not follow this clue any further, but I should, nevertheless, like to point out something which strikingly confirms this view: the germs of fear which break out in Macbeth on the night of the murder do not develop further in *him* but in *her*.[8] It is he who has the hallucination of the dagger before the crime; but it is she who afterwards falls ill of a mental disorder. It is he who after the murder hears the cry in the house: 'Sleep no more! Macbeth does murder sleep . . .' and so 'Macbeth shall sleep no more'; but we never hear that *he* slept no more, while the Queen, as we see, rises from her bed and, talking in her sleep, betrays her guilt. It is he who stands helpless with bloody hands, lamenting that 'all great Neptune's ocean' will not wash them clean, while she comforts him: 'A little water clears us of this deed'; but later it is she who washes her hands for a quarter of an hour and cannot get rid of the bloodstains: 'All the perfumes of Arabia will not sweeten this little hand'. Thus what he feared in his pangs of conscience is fulfilled in her; she becomes all remorse and he all defiance. Together they exhaust the possibilities of reaction to the crime, like two disunited parts of a single psychical individuality,

---

[7][This does not appear to have been published. In a later paper on *Macbeth,* Jekels (1917, p. 170) barely refers to this theory, apart from quoting the present paragraph. In a still later paper, on "The Psychology of Comedy," Jekels (1926, p. 328) returns to the subject, but again very briefly.]

[8]Cf. Darmesteter (1881, p. lxxv).

and it may be that they are both copied from a single prototype.

If we have been unable to give any answer to the question why Lady Macbeth should collapse after her success, we may perhaps have a better chance when we turn to the creation of another great dramatist, who loves to pursue problems of psychological responsibility with unrelenting rigour.

Rebecca Gamvik, the daughter of a midwife, has been brought up by her adopted father, Dr. West, to be a freethinker and to despise the restrictions which a morality founded on religious belief seeks to impose on the desires of life. After the doctor's death she finds a position at Rosmersholm, the home for many generations of an ancient family whose members know nothing of laughter and have sacrificed joy to a rigid fulfilment of duty. Its occupants are Johannes Rosmer, a former pastor, and his invalid wife, the childless Beata. Overcome by 'a wild, uncontrollable passion'[9] for the love of the high-born Rosmer, Rebecca resolves to remove the wife who stands in her way, and to this end makes use of her 'fearless, free' will, which is restrained by no scruples. She contrives that Beata shall read a medical book in which the aim of marriage is represented to be the begetting of offspring, so that the poor woman begins to doubt whether her own marriage is justifiable. Rebecca then hints that Rosmer, whose studies and ideas she shares, is about to abandon the old faith and join the 'party of enlightenment'; and after she has thus shaken the wife's confidence in her husband's moral integrity, gives her finally to understand that she, Rebecca, will soon leave the house in order to conceal the consequences of her illicit intercourse with Rosmer. The criminal scheme succeeds. The poor wife, who has passed for depressed and irresponsible, throws herself from the path beside the mill into the mill-race, possessed by the sense of her own worthlessness and wishing no longer to stand between her beloved husband and his happiness.

For more than a year Rebecca and Rosmer have been living alone at Rosmersholm in a relationship which he wishes to regard as a purely intellectual and ideal friendship. But when this relationship begins to be darkened from outside by the first

---

[9][The quotations are based on William Archer's English translation.]

shadow of gossip, and at the same time tormenting doubts arise
in Rosmer about the motives for which his wife put an end to herself, he begs Rebecca to become his second wife, so that they may
counter the unhappy past with a new living reality (Act II). For an
instant she exclaims with joy at his proposal, but immediately
afterwards declares that it can never be, and that if he urges her
further she will 'go the way Beata went'. Rosmer cannot understand this rejection; and still less can we, who know more of
Rebecca's actions and designs. All we can be certain of is that her
'no' is meant in earnest.

How could it come about that the adventuress with the 'fearless, free will', who forged her way ruthlessly to her desired goal,
should now refuse to pluck the fruit of her success when it is
offered to her? She herself gives us the explanation in the fourth
Act: '*This* is the terrible part of it: that now, when all life's happiness is within my grasp—my heart is changed and my own past
cuts me off from it.' That is to say, she has in the meantime
become a different being; her conscience has awakened, she has
acquired a sense of guilt which debars her from enjoyment.

And what has awakened her conscience? Let us listen to her
herself, and then consider whether we can believe her entirely. 'It
is the Rosmer view of life—or your view of life at any rate—that
has infected my will. . . . And made it sick. Enslaved it to laws
that had no power over me before. You—life with you—has
ennobled my mind.'

This influence, we are further to understand, has only become
effective since she has been able to live alone with Rosmer: 'In
quiet—in solitude—when you showed me all your thoughts
without reserve—every tender and delicate feeling, just as it came
to you—*then* the great change came over me.'

Shortly before this she has lamented the other aspect of the
change: 'Because Rosmersholm has sapped my strength. My old
fearless will has had its wings clipped here. It is crippled! The
time is past when I had courage for anything in the world. I have
lost the power of action, Rosmer.'

Rebecca makes this declaration after she has revealed herself
as a criminal in a voluntary confession to Rosmer and Rector
Kroll, the brother of the woman she has got rid of. Ibsen has
made it clear by small touches of masterly subtlety that Rebecca

does not actually tell lies, but is never entirely straightforward. Just as, in spite of all her freedom from prejudices, she has understated her age by a year, so her confession to the two men is incomplete, and as a result of Kroll's insistence it is supplemented on some important points. Hence it is open to us to suppose that her explanation of her renunciation exposes one motive only to conceal another.

Certainly, we have no reason to disbelieve her when she declares that the atmosphere of Rosmersholm and her association with the high-minded Rosmer have ennobled—and crippled—her. She is here expressing what she knows and has felt. But this is not necessarily all that has happened in her, nor need she have understood all that has happened. Rosmer's influence may only have been a cloak, which concealed another influence that was operative, and a remarkable indication points in this other direction.

Even after her confession, Rosmer, in their last conversation which brings the play to an end, again beseeches her to be his wife. He forgives her the crime she has committed for love of him. And now she does not answer, as she should, that no forgiveness can rid her of the feeling of guilt she has incurred from her malignant deception of poor Beata; but she charges herself with another reproach which affects us as coming strangely from this freethinking woman, and is far from deserving the importance which Rebecca attaches to it: 'Dear—never speak of this again! It is impossible! For you must know, Rosmer, I have a—a past behind me.' She means, of course, that she has had sexual relations with another man; and we do not fail to observe that these relations, which occurred at a time when she was free and accountable to nobody, seem to her a greater hindrance to the union with Rosmer than her truly criminal behaviour to his wife.

Rosmer refuses to hear anything about this past. We can guess what it was, though everything that refers to it in the play is, so to speak, subterranean and has to be pieced together from hints. But nevertheless they are hints inserted with such art that it is impossible to misunderstand them.

Between Rebecca's first refusal and her confession something occurs which has a decisive influence on her future destiny. Rector Kroll arrives one day at the house on purpose to humiliate Rebecca by telling her that he knows she is an illegitimate child, the daughter of the very Dr. West who adopted her after her mother's death. Hate has sharpened his perceptions, yet he does not suppose that this is any news to her. 'I really did not suppose you were ignorant of this, otherwise it would have been very odd that you should have let Dr. West adopt you . . .' 'And then he takes you into his house—as soon as your mother dies. He treats you harshly. And yet you stay with him. You know that he won't leave you a halfpenny—as a matter of fact you got only a case of books—and yet you stay on; you bear with him; you nurse him to the last.' . . . 'I attribute your care for him to the natural filial instinct of a daughter. Indeed, I believe your whole conduct is a natural result of your origin.'

But Kroll is mistaken. Rebecca had no idea at all that she could be Dr. West's daughter. When Kroll began with dark hints at her past, she must have thought he was referring to something else. After she has gathered what he means, she can still retain her composure for a while, for she is able to suppose that her enemy is basing his calculations on her age, which she had given falsely on an earlier visit of his. But Kroll demolishes this objection by saying: 'Well, so be it, but my calculations may be right, none the less; for Dr. West was up there on a short visit the year before he got the appointment.' After this new information, she loses her self-possession. 'It is not true!' She walks about wringing her hands. 'It is impossible. You want to cheat me into believing it. This can never, never be true. It cannot be true. Never in this world!—' Her agitation is so extreme that Kroll cannot attribute it to his information alone.

'KROLL: But, my dear Miss West—why in Heaven's name are you so terribly excited? You quite frighten me. What am I to think—to believe—?

'REBECCA: Nothing. You are to think and believe nothing.

'KROLL: Then you must really tell me how you can take this affair—this possibility—so terribly to heart.

'REBECCA (*controlling herself*): It is perfectly simple, Rector Kroll. I have no wish to be taken for an illegitimate child.'

The enigma of Rebecca's behaviour is susceptible of only one solution. The news that Dr. West was her father is the heaviest blow that can befall her, for she was not only his adopted daughter, but had been his mistress. When Kroll began to speak, she thought that he was hinting at these relations, the truth of which she would probably have admitted and justified by her emancipated ideas. But this was far from the Rector's intention; he knew nothing of the love-affair with Dr. West, just as she knew nothing of Dr. West's being her father. She *cannot* have had anything else in her mind but this love-affair when she accounted for her final rejection of Rosmer on the ground that she had a past which made her unworthy to be his wife. And probably, if Rosmer had consented to hear of that past, she would have confessed half her secret only and have kept silence on the more serious part of it.

But now we understand, of course, that this past must seem to her the more serious obstacle to their union — the more serious crime.

After she has learnt that she has been the mistress of her own father, she surrenders herself wholly to her now overmastering sense of guilt. She makes the confession to Rosmer and Kroll which stamps her as a murderess; she rejects for ever the happiness to which she has paved the way by crime, and prepares for departure. But the true motive of her sense of guilt, which results in her being wrecked by success, remains a secret. As we have seen, it is something quite other than the atmosphere of Rosmersholm and the refining influence of Rosmer.

At this point no one who has followed us will fail to bring forward an objection which may justify some doubts. Rebecca's first refusal of Rosmer occurs before Kroll's second visit, and therefore before his exposure of her illegitimate origin and at a time when she as yet knows nothing of her incest — if we have rightly understood the dramatist. Yet this first refusal is energetic and seriously meant. The sense of guilt which bids her renounce the fruit of her actions is thus effective before she knows anything of her cardinal crime; and if we grant so much, we ought perhaps entirely to set aside her incest as a source of that sense of guilt.

So far we have treated Rebecca West as if she were a living person and not a creation of Ibsen's imagination, which is always directed by the most critical intelligence. We may therefore attempt to maintain the same position in dealing with the objection that has been raised. The objection is valid: before the knowledge of her incest, conscience was already in part awakened

in Rebecca; and there is nothing to prevent our making the
influence which is acknowledged and blamed by Rebecca herself
responsible for this change. But this does not exempt us from
recognizing the second motive. Rebecca's behaviour when she
hears what Kroll has to tell her, the confession which is her
immediate reaction, leave no doubt that then only does the
stronger and decisive motive for renunciation begin to take
effect. It is in fact a case of multiple motivation, in which a deeper
motive comes into view behind the more superficial one. Laws of
poetic economy necessitate this way of presenting the situation,
for this deeper motive could not be explicitly enunciated. It had
to remain concealed, kept from the easy perception of the spectator or the reader; otherwise serious resistances, based on the
most distressing emotions, would have arisen, which might have
imperilled the effect of the drama.

We have, however, a right to demand that the explicit motive
shall not be without an internal connection with the concealed
one, but shall appear as a mitigation of, and a derivation from,
the latter. And if we may rely on the fact that the dramatist's conscious creative combination arose logically from unconscious
premises, we may now make an attempt to show that he has
fulfilled this demand. Rebecca's feeling of guilt has its source in
the reproach of incest, even before Kroll, with analytical per-
spicacity, has made her conscious of it. If we reconstruct her past,
expanding and filling in the author's hints, we may feel sure that
she cannot have been without some inkling of the intimate
relation between her mother and Dr. West. It must have made a
great impression on her when she became her mother's successor with this man. She stood under the domination of the
Oedipus complex, even though she did not know that this
universal phantasy had in her case become a reality. When she
came to Rosmersholm, the inner force of this first experience
drove her into bringing about, by vigorous action, the same
situation which had been realized in the original instance
through no doing of hers—into getting rid of the wife and
mother, so that she might take her place with the husband and
father. She describes with a convincing insistence how, against
her will, she was obliged to proceed, step by step, to the removal
of Beata.

'You think then that I was cool and calculating and self-possessed all the time! I was not the same woman then that I am now, as I stand here telling it all. Besides, there are two sorts of will in us, I believe! I wanted Beata away, by one means or another; but I never really believed that it would come to pass. As I felt my way forward, at each step I ventured, I seemed to hear something within me cry out: No farther! Not a step farther! And yet I *could* not stop. I *had* to venture the least little bit farther. And only one hair's-breadth more. And then one more—and always one more. And then it happened.—That is the way such things come about.'

That is not an embellishment, but an authentic description. Everything that happened to her at Rosmersholm, her falling in love with Rosmer and her hostility to his wife, was from the first a consequence of the Oedipus complex—an inevitable replica of her relations with her mother and Dr. West.

And so the sense of guilt which first causes her to reject Rosmer's proposal is at bottom no different from the greater one which drives her to her confession after Kroll has opened her eyes. But just as under the influence of Dr. West she had become a freethinker and despiser of religious morality, so she is transformed by her love for Rosmer into a being of conscience and nobility. This much of the mental processes within her she herself understands, and so she is justified in describing Rosmer's influence as the motive for her change—the motive that had become accessible to her.

The practising psycho-analytic physician knows how frequently, or how invariably, a girl who enters a household as servant, companion or governess, will consciously or unconsciously weave a day-dream, which derives from the Oedipus complex, of the mistress of the house disappearing and the master taking the newcomer as his wife in her place.[10] *Rosmersholm* is the greatest work of art of the class that treats of this common phantasy in girls. What makes it into a tragic drama is the extra circumstance that the heroine's day-dream had been preceded in her childhood

---

[10][Cf. the case of Miss Lucy R. in the *Studies on Hysteria* (Breuer and Freud, 1895, pp. 116–121).]

by a precisely corresponding reality.[11]

After this long digression into literature, let us return to clinical experience—but only to establish in a few words the complete agreement between them. Psycho-analytic work teaches that the forces of conscience which induce illness in consequence of success, instead of, as normally, in consequence of frustration, are closely connected with the Oedipus complex, the relation to father and mother—as perhaps, indeed, is our sense of guilt in general.[12]

III
Criminals From a Sense of Guilt

In telling me about their early youth, particularly before puberty, people who have afterwards often become very respectable have informed me of forbidden actions which they committed at that time—such as thefts, frauds and even arson. I was in the habit of dismissing these statements with the comment that we are familiar with the weakness of moral inhibitions at that period of life, and I made no attempt to find a place for them in any more significant context. But eventually I was led to make a more thorough study of such incidents by some glaring and more accessible cases in which the misdeeds were committed while the patients were actually under my treatment, and were no longer so youthful. Analytic work then brought the surprising discovery that such deeds were done principally because they were forbidden, and because their execution was accompanied by mental relief for their doer. He was suffering from an oppressive feeling of guilt, of which he did not know the origin, and after he had committed a misdeed this oppression was mitigated. His sense of guilt was at least attached to something.

Paradoxical as it may sound, I must maintain that the sense of

---

[11]The presence of the theme of incest in *Rosmersholm* has already been demonstrated by the same arguments as mine in Otto Rank's extremely comprehensive *Das Inzest-Motiv in Dichtung und Sage* (1912, Leipzig and Vienna, pp. 404–405).

[12][Some twenty years later, in his Open Letter to Romain Rolland describing his first visit to the Acropolis at Athens (1936), Freud compared the feeling of something being 'too good to be true' with the situation analyzed in the present paper.]

guilt was present before the misdeed, that it did not arise from it, but conversely—the misdeed arose from the sense of guilt. These people might justly be described as criminals from a sense of guilt. The pre-existence of the guilty feeling had of course been demonstrated by a whole set of other manifestations and effects.

But scientific work is not satisfied with the establishment of a curious fact. There are two further questions to answer: what is the origin of this obscure sense of guilt before the deed, and is it probable that this kind of causation plays any considerable part in human crime?

An examination of the first question held out the promise of bringing us information about the source of mankind's sense of guilt in general. The invariable outcome of analytic work was to show that this obscure sense of guilt derived from the Oedipus complex and was a reaction to the two great criminal intentions of killing the father and having sexual relations with the mother. In comparison with these two, the crimes committed in order to fix the sense of guilt to something came as a relief to the sufferers. We must remember in this connection that parricide and incest with the mother are the two great human crimes, the only ones which, as such, are pursued and abhorred in primitive communities. And we must remember, too, how close other investigations have brought us to the hypothesis that the conscience of mankind, which now appears as an inherited mental force, was acquired in connection with the Oedipus complex.

In order to answer the second question we must go beyond the scope of psycho-analytic work. With children it is easy to observe that they are often 'naughty' on purpose to provoke punishment, and are quiet and contented after they have been punished. Later analytic investigation can often put us on the track of the guilty feeling which induced them to seek punishment. Among adult criminals we must no doubt except those who commit crimes without any sense of guilt, who have either developed no moral inhibitions or who, in their conflict with society, consider themselves justified in their action. But as regards the majority of other criminals, those for whom punitive measures are really designed, such a motivation for crime might very well be taken into consideration; it might throw light on some obscure points in the psychology of the criminal, and furnish punishment with a new psychological basis.

A friend has since called my attention to the fact that the 'criminal from a sense of guilt' was known to Nietzsche too. The pre-existence of the feeling of guilt, and the utilization of a deed in order to rationalize this feeling, glimmer before us in Zarathustra's sayings[13] 'On the Pale Criminal'. Let us leave it to future research to decide how many criminals are to be reckoned among these 'pale' ones.

[13][In the editions before 1924, "obscure sayings." A hint at the idea of the sense of guilt being a motive for misdeeds is already to be found in the case history of Little Hans (1909b, p. 42), as well as in that of the Wolf Man (1918, p. 28), which, though published later than the present paper, was in fact mostly written in the year before it. In this latter passage the complicating factor of masochism is introduced.]

Chapter 3

LIBIDINAL TYPES

SIGMUND FREUD

Observation teaches us that individual human beings realize the general picture of humanity in an almost infinite variety of ways. If we yield to the legitimate need to distinguish particular types in this multiplicity, we shall at the start have the choice as to what characteristics and what points of view we shall take as the basis of our differentiation. For that purpose physical qualities will doubtless serve no less well than mental ones; the most valuable distinctions will be those which promise to present a regular combination of physical and mental characteristics.

It is doubtful whether we are as yet in a position to discover types to fulfil this requirement—as we shall no doubt be able to do later, on some basis of which we are still ignorant. If we confine our effort to setting up purely psychological types, the libidinal situation will have a first claim to serve as a basis for our classification. It may fairly be demanded that this classification should not merely be deduced from our knowledge or our hypotheses about the libido, but that it should be easily confirmed in actual experience and that it should contribute to the clarification of the mass of our observations and help us to grasp them. It may at once be admitted that these libidinal types need not be the only possible ones even in the psychical field, and that, if we proceeded from other qualities, we might perhaps establish a whole set of other psychological types. But it must be required of all such types that they shall not coincide with clinical pictures. On the contrary, they must comprehend all the variations which according to our practical judgement fall within the limits of the normal. In their extreme developments, however, they may well

This chapter originally appeared in *Standard Edition,* 21:215–222. London: Hogarth Press, 1961. Reprinted by permission of the publisher.

approximate to clinical pictures and in that way help to bridge the gulf that is supposed to lie between the normal and the pathological.

According, then, as the libido is predominantly allocated to the provinces of the mental apparatus, *we can distinguish three main libidinal types.* To give names to these types is not particularly easy; following the lines of our depth-psychology, I should like to call them the *erotic,* the *narcissistic* and the *obsessional* types.[1]

The *erotic* type is easily characterized. Erotics are those whose main interest—the relatively largest part of whose libido—is turned towards love. Loving, but above all being loved, is the most important thing for them. They are dominated by the fear of loss of love and are therefore especially dependent on others who may withhold their love from them. Even in its pure form this type is a very common one. Variants of it occur according as it is blended with another type and in proportion to the amount of aggressiveness present in it. From the social and cultural standpoint this type represents the elementary instinctual demands of the id, to which the other psychical agencies have become compliant.

The second type is what I have termed the *obsessional* type— a name which may at first seem strange. It is distinguished by the predominance of the super-ego, which is separated from the ego under great tension. People of this type are dominated by fear of their conscience instead of fear of losing love. They exhibit, as it were, an internal instead of an external dependence. They develop a high degree of self-reliance; and, from the social standpoint, they are the true, pre-eminently conservative vehicles of civilization.[2]

The third type, justly called the *narcissistic* type, is mainly to be described in negative terms. There is no tension between ego and super-ego (indeed, on the strength of this type one would scarcely have arrived at the hypothesis of a super-ego), and there is no preponderance of erotic needs. The subject's main interest is directed to self-preservation; he is independent and not open to intimidation. His ego has a large amount of aggressiveness at

[1][Freud had approached this classification of types in chapter 2 of *Civilisation and its Discontents* (1930), pp. 83–84.]
[2][Cf. chapter 2 of *The Future of an Illusion* (1927a, p. 11).]

its disposal, which also manifests itself in readiness for activity. In his erotic life loving is preferred above being loved. People belonging to this type impress others as being "personalities"; they are especially suited to act as a support for others, to take on the role of leaders and to give a fresh stimulus to cultural development or to damage the established state of affairs.

These pure types will hardly escape the suspicion of having been deduced from the theory of libido. But we feel ourselves on the firm ground of experience when we turn to the mixed types, which are to be observed so much more frequently than the unmixed ones. These new types—the *erotic–obsessional,* the *erotic–narcissistic* and the *narcissistic–obsessional*—seem in fact to afford a good classification of the individual psychical structures which we have come to know through analysis. If we study these mixed types we find in them pictures of characters with which we have long been familiar. In the *erotic–obsessional* type it appears that the preponderance of instinctual life is restricted by the influence of the super-ego. In this type, dependence, at once on contemporary human objects and on the residues of parents, educators and exemplars, is carried to its highest pitch. The *erotic–narcissistic* type is perhaps the one we must regard as the commonest of all. It unites opposites, which are able to moderate one another in it. One may learn from this type, as compared with the two other erotic ones, that aggressiveness and activity go along with a predominance of narcissism. Finally, the *narcissistic–obsessional* type produces the variation which is most valuable from a cultural standpoint; for it adds to the independence of the external world and a regard for the demands of conscience a capacity for vigorous action, and it strengthens the ego against the super-ego.

One might think one was making a jest if one asked why no mention has been made here of another mixed type which is theoretically possible—namely the *erotic–obsessional–narcissistic* type. But the answer to this jest is serious. Such a type would no longer be a type at all: it would be the absolute norm, the ideal harmony. We thus realize that the phenomenon of types arises precisely from the fact that, of the three main ways of employing the libido in the economy of the mind, one or two have been favoured at the expense of the others.

The question may also be raised of what the relation is of these libidinal types to pathology—whether some of them have a special disposition to pass over into neurosis, and if so, which types lead to which forms of neurosis. The answer is that the setting-up of these libidinal types throws no new light on the genesis of the neuroses. Experience shows that all these types can exist without any neurosis. The pure types, marked by the undisputed preponderance of a single mental agency, seem to have a better chance of manifesting themselves as pure charac-terological pictures, while we might expect that mixed types would provide a more favourable soil for conditions leading to a neurosis. But I think we should not make up our minds on these matters till they have been submitted to a careful and specially directed examination.

It seems easy to infer that when people of the erotic type fall ill they will develop hysteria, just as those of the obsessional type will develop obsessional neurosis; but these inferences, too, share the uncertainty which I have just stressed. People of the narcissistic type who are exposed to a frustration from the exter-nal world, though otherwise independent, are peculiarly dis-posed to psychosis; and they also present essential preconditions for criminality.

It is a familiar fact that the aetiological preconditions of neurosis are not yet known with certainty. The precipitating causes of it are frustrations and internal conflicts: conflicts between the three major psychical agencies, conflicts arising within the libidinal economy in consequence of bisexual disposition and conflicts between the erotic and the aggressive instinctual com-ponents. It is the endeavour of the psychology of the neuroses to discover what makes these processes, which belong to the nor-mal course of mental life, become pathogenic.

Chapter 4

THE INFLUENCE OF ORAL EROTISM ON CHARACTER-FORMATION

KARL ABRAHAM

According to the usual view the formation of character is to be traced back partly to inherited disposition, and partly to the effects of environment, among which particular significance is ascribed to upbringing. Psycho-analytical investigation has for the first time drawn attention to sources of character-formation which have not hitherto been sufficiently considered. On the basis of psycho-analytical experience we have come to take the view that those elements of infantile sexuality which are excluded from participation in the sexual life of the adult individual undergo in part a transformation into certain character-traits. As is well known, Freud was the first to show that certain elements of infantile anal erotism undergo a transformation of this kind. Some part of this anal erotism enters into the final organization of mature sexual life, some becomes sublimated, and some goes to form character. These contributions to character from anal sources are to be regarded as normal. They render it possible for the individual to adapt himself to the demands of his environment as regards cleanliness, love of order, and so on. Apart from this, however, we have learnt to recognize an 'anal character' in the clinical sense, which is distinguished by an extreme accentuation of certain character-traits; but it is to be noted that the excessive addiction to cleanliness, parsimony, and similar tendencies found in such characters never succeeds completely. We invariably find the opposite extreme more or less strongly developed in them.

This chapter originally appeared in *Selected Papers on Psychoanalysis*, pp. 393–406, trans. D. Bryan and A. Strachey. New York: Basic Books, 1968. Reprinted by permission of the publisher.

Now experience teaches us that not all deviations from the final character-formation of the genital stage originate in the anal sources just mentioned. We find that oral erotism is a source of character-formation as well. Here, too, we can see that the supplies from this source can fall within the normal or can greatly exceed it. If our observations are correct, then we can speak of oral, anal, and genital sources of character-formation; in doing so, however, we quite consciously neglect one aspect of the problem, since we are only taking into consideration those contributions to the formation of character which are derived from the erotogenic zones, and not those coming from the component-instincts. This neglect is, however, more apparent than real; for example, the close connection of the component of cruelty in infantile instinctual life with oral erotism will become evident in the character-formation of the individual as elsewhere, so that it is hardly necessary to draw special attention to it.

What I shall be able to say about character-traits of oral origin will perhaps be disappointing in some respects, because I cannot offer a picture comparable in completeness to that of the anal character. I shall therefore begin by pointing out certain differences between the two which should not be lost sight of, and which will moderate our expectations as regards the oral character to more suitable proportions.

In the first place, it should be remembered that of the pleasurable tendencies that are connected with intestinal processes only a small part can come to form part of normal erotism in an *unrepressed* form; whereas an incomparably greater part of the libidinal cathexis of the mouth which characterizes infancy can still be employed in later life. Thus the oral elements of infantile sexuality do not need to be changed into character-formation or sublimated to the same extent as the anal ones.

In the second place, we must bear in mind that a retrograde transformation of character, such as is connected with the outbreak of certain nervous disturbances, in the main comes to a stop at the anal stage. If it proceeds further and a pathological intensification of oral traits, such as will be described later, ensues, then these latter will show an admixture of traits belonging to the anal stage; and we should in that case expect to find a combination of the two kinds of character-traits rather than a pure culture of oral ones.

If we proceed to study these mixed products of two different sources of character-formation more deeply we make a new discovery, namely, that the origin of the anal character is very closely connected with the history of oral erotism, and cannot be completely understood without reference to it.

Clinical experience has led Freud to the view that in many people the particular libidinal emphasis that attaches to the intestinal processes is a constitutional factor. There can be no doubt that this is so. We need only call to mind how in certain families positive phenomena of anal erotism as well as anal character-traits are everywhere observable in the most different members. Nevertheless, correct as this view is, the facts admit of further explanation in the light of the following psychoanalytic observations.

In infancy the individual has an intense pleasure in the act of sucking, and we have familiarized ourselves with the view that this pleasure is not to be ascribed entirely to the process of taking food, but that it is conditioned in a high degree by the significance of the mouth as an erotogenic zone.

This primitive form of obtaining pleasure is never completely abandoned by the individual but persists under all kinds of disguises during the whole of his life, and even experiences a reinforcement at certain times and in particular circumstances. Nevertheless, as it grows up both physically and mentally, the child does effect a far-reaching renunciation of its original pleasure in sucking. Now observation shows that every such renunciation of pleasure only takes place on the basis of an exchange. It is this process of renunciation and the course it takes under different conditions which merits our attention.

First of all there is the process of the irruption of teeth, which, as is well known, causes a considerable part of the pleasure in sucking to be replaced by pleasure in biting. We need only call to mind how during this stage of development the child puts every object it can into its mouth and tries with all its strength to bite it to pieces.

In the same period of development the child begins to have ambivalent relations to external objects. It is to be noted that the friendly as well as the hostile aspect of its attitude is connected with pleasure. At about the same period a further displacement of pleasurable sensation to other bodily functions and areas occurs.

What is of particular significance is that the pleasure in sucking undertakes a kind of migration. At about the time that the child is being weaned it is also being trained in habits of cleanliness. An important prerequisite for the success of this latter process lies in the gradually developing function of the anal and urethral sphincters. The action of these muscles is the same as that of the lips in sucking, and is obviously modelled on it. The original unchecked voiding of bodily excretions was accompanied by stimulation of the apertures of the body which was undoubtedly pleasurable. If the child adapts itself to the demands of training and learns to retain its excretions this new activity also gets to be accompanied by pleasure. The pleasurable sensations in the organ connected with this process form the foundation upon which the mental pleasure in retention of every kind of possession is gradually built up. More recent investigations have shown that the possession of an object originally signified to the infantile mind the having incorporated it into its own body. Whereas to begin with, pleasure was only associated with taking in something coming from without or with expelling bodily contents, now there is added the pleasure in retaining bodily contents, which leads to pleasure in all forms of property. The relation in which these three sources of physical and mental gratification stand to one another is of the greatest practical significance for the later social conduct of the individual. If the pleasure in getting or taking is brought into the most favourable relation possible with the pleasure in possession, as well as with that in giving up, then an exceedingly important step has been made in laying the foundations of the individual's social relations. For when such a relationship between the three tendencies is present, the most important preliminary condition for overcoming the ambivalence of the individual's emotional life has been established.

In what has so far been said we have only called attention to single features of a multiform developmental process. For the purpose of our investigation it is sufficient to make clear that the first and therefore perhaps the most important step the individual makes towards attaining a normal attitude in his final social and sexual relationships consists in dealing successfully with his oral erotism. But there are numerous ways in which this important process of development may suffer disturbance. In order to understand this we must bear in mind that the pleasure of the sucking period is to a great extent a pleasure in taking, in being given something. It then becomes apparent that any quantitative divergence from the usual degree of pleasure gained can give rise to disturbances.

Given certain conditions of nourishment the sucking period can be an extremely displeasurable one for the child. In some cases its earliest pleasurable craving is imperfectly gratified, and it is deprived of the enjoyment of the sucking stage.[1] In other cases the same period is abnormally rich in pleasure. It is well known how some mothers indulge the craving for pleasure in their infants by granting them every wish. The result is that it is extraordinarily difficult to wean the child, and it sometimes takes two or three years to do it. In a few cases the child persists in taking food by sucking from a bottle until it is almost grown up.

Whether in this early period of life the child has had to go without pleasure or has been indulged with an excess of it, the effect is the same. It takes leave of the sucking stage under difficulties. Since its need for pleasure has either not been sufficiently gratified or has become too insistent, it fastens with particular intensity on the possibilities of pleasure to be got from the next stage. In doing this it finds itself in constant danger of a new disappointment, to which it will react more readily than the normal child with a regression to the earlier stage. In other words: In the child who has been disappointed or over-indulged in the sucking period the pleasure in biting, which is also the most primitive form of sadism, will be especially emphasized. Thus the formation of character in such a child begins under the influence of an abnormally pronounced ambivalence of feeling. In practice such a disturbance of the development of character expresses itself in pronounced characteristics of hostility and dislike. It accounts for the presence of the abnormally over-developed envy which is so common. Eisler has already referred this character-trait to an

---

[1] Freud made it clear long ago that stomach and bowel troubles in infancy can have a harmful effect on the mental development of the child.

oral source.[2] I fully agree with his view, but would like to
emphasize its relation to the later oral stage. In many cases an
elder child, who is already at the stage of taking food by biting and
chewing, has an opportunity of observing a younger child being
suckled. In such cases the characteristic of envy receives a special
reinforcement. Sometimes it is incompletely overcome by being
turned into its opposite; but the original feeling is easily seen to
persist in various disguises.

But if the child escapes the Scylla of this danger, it is
threatened by the Charybdis of another. It attempts to resume
the abandoned act of sucking in an altered form and in another
locality. We have already spoken of the sucking activity of the
sphincters at the excretory apertures of the body, and have
recognized that an inordinate desire to possess, especially in the
form of abnormal parsimony and avarice, stands in close relation
to this process. Thus we see that those traits, which belong to the
clinical phenomena of the anal character, are built up on the
ruins of an oral erotism whose development has miscarried. In
the present paper I shall only describe this one path of defective
development. The preceding remarks will suffice to show how
dependent is our understanding of the anal character on an adequate knowledge of the preceding stages of development.

We will pass on to consider the direct contributions rendered by oral erotism to the formation of character, and will
begin with an example taken from ordinary psycho-analytical
observation.

Neurotic parsimony, which may be developed to the point
of avarice, is often met with in people who are inhibited from
properly earning a livelihood; and the anal sources of character-
formation provide no explanation of it. It is in fact connected
with an inhibition of the craving for objects, and this indicates
that the libido has undergone some special vicissitude. The
pleasure in acquiring desired objects seems in this case to have
been repressed in favour of pleasure in holding fast to existing
possessions. People in whom we find this inhibition are always
haunted by a fear lest they should lose the smallest part of their

[2]M. J. Eisler, "Pleasure in Sleep and Disturbed Capacity for Sleep," *International Journal of Psycho-Analysis,* vol iii, 1922.

possessions. This anxiety prevents them from trying to earn money, and renders them in many ways helpless in practical life. We shall understand this type of character-formation if we go on to examine related symptoms.

In certain other cases the person's entire character is under oral influence, but this can only be shown after a thorough analysis has been made. According to my experience we are here concerned with persons in whom the sucking was undisturbed and highly pleasurable. They have brought with them from this happy period a deeply-rooted conviction that everything will always be well with them. They face life with an imperturbable optimism which often does in fact help them to achieve their aims. But we also meet with less favourable types of development. Some people are dominated by the belief that there will always be some kind person—a representative of the mother, of course—to care for them and to give them everything they need. This optimistic belief condemns them to inactivity. We again recognize in them individuals who have been over-indulged in the sucking period. Their whole attitude towards life shows that they expect the mother's breast to flow for them eternally, as it were. They make no kind of effort, and in some cases they even disdain to undertake a bread-winning occupation.

This optimism, whether it is allied to an energetic conduct in life or, as in the last-mentioned aberration, to a care-free indifference to the world, stands in noteworthy contrast to a feature of the anal character that has not been sufficiently appreciated up to the present. I refer to a melancholy seriousness which passes over into marked pessimism. I must point out, however, that this characteristic is to a great extent not directly of anal origin, but goes back to a disappointment of oral desires in the earliest years. In persons of this type the optimistic belief in the benevolence of fate is completely absent. On the contrary, they consistently show an apprehensive attitude towards life, and have a tendency to make the worst of everything and to find undue difficulties in the simplest undertakings.

A character thus rooted in oral erotism influences the entire behaviour of the individual, as well as his choice of profession, his predilections, and his hobbies. We may cite as an instance the type of neurotic official who is only able to exist when all the circumstances of his life have been prescribed for him once and for all. To him the necessary condition of life is that his means of sustenance should be guaranteed to him up to the day of his death. He renounces all ideals of personal success in favour of receiving an assured and regular income.

So far we have dealt with people whose entire character is explained on the supposition that their libido has been fully gratified in the oral stage of their development. In psycho-analytic work, however, we observe other individuals who are burdened throughout their whole life with the after-effects of an ungratified sucking period. In them there is no trace of such a development having taken place.

In their social behaviour these people always seem to be asking for something, either in the form of a modest request or of an aggressive demand. The manner in which they put forward their wishes has something in the nature of persistent sucking about it; they are as little to be put off by hard facts as by reasonable arguments, but continue to plead and to insist. One might almost say that they "cling like leeches" to other people. They particularly dislike being alone, even for a short time. Impatience is a marked characteristic with them. In some cases, those in which psycho-analytic investigation reveals a regression from the oral–sadistic to the sucking stage, their behaviour has an element of cruelty in it as well, which makes them something like vampires to other people.

We meet certain traits of character in the same people which can be traced back to a peculiar displacement within the oral sphere. Their longing to experience gratification by way of sucking has changed to a need to *give* by way of the mouth, so that we find in them, besides a permanent longing to obtain everything, a constant need to communicate themselves orally to other people. This results in an obstinate urge to talk, connected in most cases with a feeling of overflowing. Persons of this kind have the impression that their fund of thought is inexhaustible, and they ascribe a special power or some unusual value to what they say. Their principal relation to other people is effected by the way of oral discharge. The obstinate insistence described above naturally occurs chiefly by means of speech. But that function serves at the same time for the act of giving. I could, moreover, regularly establish the fact that these people could not control their other activities any more than they could their speech. Thus one frequently finds in them a neurotically exaggerated need to urinate, which often appears at the same time as an outburst of talking or directly after it.

In those features of character-formation which belong to the oral–sadistic stage, too, speaking takes the place of repressed impulses from another quarter. In certain neurotics the hostile purpose of their speech is especially striking. In this instance it serves the unconscious aim of killing the adversary. Psychoanalysis has shown that in such cases, in place of biting and devouring the object, a milder form of aggression has appeared, though the mouth is still utilized as the organ of it. In certain neurotics speaking is used to express the entire range of instinctual trends, whether friendly or hostile, social or asocial, and irrespective of the instinctual sphere to which they originally belonged. In them the impulse to talk signifies desiring as well as attacking, killing, or annihilating, and at the same time every kind of bodily evacuation, including the act of fertilization. In their phantasies speaking is subject to the narcissistic valuation which their unconscious applies to all physical and psychical productions. Their entire behaviour shows a particularly striking contrast to reticent people with anal character-formation.

Observations of this kind most emphatically draw our attention to the varieties and differences that exist within the realm of oral character-formation, and show that the field which we are investigating is anything but limited or poor in variations. The most important differences, however, are those which depend on whether a feature of character has developed on the basis of the earlier or the later oral stage; whether, in other words, it is the expression of an unconscious tendency to suck or to bite. In the latter case we shall find in connection with such a character-trait the most marked symptoms of ambivalence—positive and negative instinctual cravings, hostile and friendly tendencies; while we may assume on the basis of our experience that the character-traits derived from the stage of sucking are not as yet subjected to ambivalence. According to my observations, this fundamental difference extends to the smallest details of a person's behaviour. At a meeting of the British Psychological Society (Medical Section)

Dr. Edward Glover recently read a paper in which he gave these differences particular consideration.[3]

The very significant contrasts found in the character-formation of different individuals can be traced psycho-analytically from the fact that decisive influences on the process of formation of character have been exercised in the one case by oral impulses, and in the other case by anal ones. Equally important is the connecting of sadistic instinctual elements with the manifestation of libido flowing from the various erotogenic zones. A few examples may roughly illustrate this point. In our psycho-analyses we are able to trace phenomena of very intense craving and effort back to the primary oral stage. It need hardly be said that we do not exclude other sources of impulse as factors in those phenomena. But the desires derived from that earliest stage are still free from the tendency to destroy the object—a tendency which is characteristic of the impulses of the next stage.

The covetous impulses which are derived from the second oral stage are in strong contrast to the unassuming character of the anally constituted person. But we must not forget that the weakness of the acquisitive tendency in the latter is balanced by his obstinate holding fast to things which he has already got.

Characteristic, too, are the differences in the inclination to share one's own possessions with others. Generosity is frequently found as an oral character-trait. In this, the orally gratified person is identifying himself with the bounteous mother. Things are very different in the next, oral–sadistic stage, where envy, hostility, and jealousy make such behaviour impossible. Thus in many cases generous or envious behaviour is derived from one of the two oral stages of development; and in the same way the inclination to avarice corresponds to the succeeding anal–sadistic stage of character-formation.

There are noteworthy differences in the person's social conduct, too, according to the stage of his libido from which his character is derived. People who have been gratified in the earliest stage are bright and sociable; those who are fixated at the oral–sadistic stage are hostile and malicious; while moroseness, inaccessibility, and reticence go together with the anal character.

---

[3]"The Significance of the Mouth in Psycho-Analysis" (1924).

Furthermore, persons with an oral character are accessible to new ideas, in a favourable as well as an unfavourable sense, while the anal character involves a conservative behaviour opposed to all innovations—an attitude which certainly prevents the hasty abandonment of what has been proved good.

There is a similar contrast between the impatient importunity, haste, and restlessness of people with oral character-formation, and the perseverance and persistence of the anal character, which, on the other hand, tends to procrastination and hesitation.

The character-trait of ambition, which we meet with so frequently in our psycho-analyses, has been derived long ago by Freud[4] from urethral erotism [see chapter 1]. This explanation, however, does not seem to have penetrated to the deepest sources of that characteristic. According to my experience, and also that of Dr. Edward Glover, this is rather a character-trait of oral origin which is later reinforced from other sources, among which the urethral one should be particularly mentioned.

Besides this, it has to be noted that certain contributions to character-formation originating in the earliest oral stage coincide in important respects with others derived from the final genital stage. This is probably explicable from the fact that at these two stages the libido is least open to disturbance from an ambivalence of feeling.

In many people we find, beside the oral character-traits described, other psychological manifestations which we must derive from the same instinctual sources. These are impulses which have escaped any social modification. As examples a morbidly intense appetite for food and an inclination to various oral perversions are especially to be mentioned. Further, we meet many kinds of neurotic symptoms which are determined orally; and finally there are phenomena which have come into being through sublimation. These latter products deserve a separate investigation, which, however, would exceed the limits of this paper, hence I shall only briefly give a single example.

The displacement of the infantile pleasure in sucking to the intellectual sphere is of great practical significance. Curiosity and

---

[4] "Character and Anal Erotism" (1908), *Standard Edition,* 9 [see chapter 1].

the pleasure in observing receive important reinforcements from this source, and this not only in childhood, but during the subject's whole life. In persons with a special inclination for observing Nature, and for many branches of scientific investigation, psycho-analysis shows a close connection between those impulses and repressed oral desires.

A glance into the workshop of scientific investigation enables us to recognize how impulses pertaining to the different erotogenic zones must support and supplement one another if the most favourable results possible are to be achieved. The optimum is reached when an energetic imbibing of observations is combined with enough tenacity and ability to "digest" the collected facts, and a sufficiently strong impulse to give them back to the world, provided this is not done with undue haste. Psycho-analytical experience enables us to recognize various kinds of divergences from this optimum. Thus there are people with great mental capacity for absorbing, who, however, are inhibited in production. Others again produce too rapidly. It is no exaggeration to say of such people that they have scarcely taken a thing in before it comes out of their mouths again. When they are analysed it often proves that these same persons tend to vomit food as soon as they have eaten it. They are people who show an extreme neurotic impatience; a satisfactory combination of forward-moving oral impulses with retarding anal ones is lacking in the structure of their character.

In conclusion, it seems to me particularly important to allude once more to the significance of such combinations. In the normal formation of character we shall always find derivatives from all the original instinctual sources happily combined with one another.

It is important, moreover, to consider the numerous possibilities of such combinations because it prevents us from over-estimating any one particular aspect, important though it may be. If we consider the problems of character-formation from the one large unifying point of view which psycho-analysis affords us, from that of infantile sexuality, then it is obvious how everything weaves itself into a whole in the characterological sphere. The realm of infantile sexuality extends over two quite different fields. It covers the entire unconscious instinctual life of the mature human being. It is likewise the scene of the very important mental impressions of the earliest years of the child, among which we have to reckon prenatal influences. Sometimes we may feel dismayed in face of the mass of phenomena which meets us in the wide field of human mentality, from the play of children and other typical products of the early activity of phantasy, through the first development of the child's interests and talents, up to the most highly valued achievements of mature human beings and the most extreme individual differentiations. But then we must remember that Freud has given us in the practice and theory of psycho-analysis an instrument with which to investigate this wide subject and to open up the road to infantile sexuality, that inexhaustible source of life.

Chapter 5

ON CHARACTER ANALYSIS

WILHELM REICH

I

It is seldom that our patients are from the outset accessible to analysis; few indeed are disposed to follow the fundamental rule of analysis and to 'open up' fully to the analyst. In addition to the fact that they are not immediately able to feel the necessary degree of confidence in a total stranger, there are their years of illness, their long subjection to the influence of a neurotic *milieu,* their unfortunate experiences with neurologists and psychiatrists— in sum, an entire secondary warping of the personality—all conspiring to create a situation unfavourable to analysis. The overcoming of this obstacle becomes a precondition of analytic work, and might be accomplished fairly easily were it not for the support it receives from the individual make-up of the patient—from, as we may permit ourselves to say, his character, which itself is part and parcel of his neurosis and has been developed on a neurotic basis. There are in the main two methods of meeting these difficulties, particularly that of the evasion of the fundamental rule. One of these, that commonly practised, consists in direct education for analysis by means of instruction, reassurance, persuasion, admonition, and the like. In this case the attempt is made through the establishing of a positive transference to influence the patient in the direction of analytic candour. Extensive experience has shown, however, that this educational or active

Translated from the original: Über Charakteranalyse: *Internationale Zeitschrift für Psychoanalyse,* XIV, 1928, p. 180. (The author wishes the information to be added that this, and the following two articles, were incorporated "in *Charakteranalyse,* 1933, and in *Character-Analysis,* second (English) edition. New York, Orgone Institute Press, 1945.")

This chapter originally appeared in *The Psychoanalytic Reader,* pp. 106–123, ed. R. Fliess. New York: International Universities Press, 1948. By permission of the publisher.

method is very uncertain in its results, is at the mercy of uncontrollable chance factors, and lacks any sound basis of analytic clarity; the analyst is too greatly handicapped by the fluctuations in the transference situation and finds himself treading uncertain ground in his attempt to render the patient accessible to analysis.

The other method is a more complicated one, and although not thus far applicable to all patients is much more certain in its operation; it consists in the attempt to *substitute for educational measures analytic interpretations.* Certainly this is not by any means always possible; nevertheless it is still the ideal toward which analytic efforts should strive. Thus, instead of inducting the patient into analysis by means of advice, admonition, transference manoeuvres, and so forth, the analyst's attention is focused, more passively, on the *immediate* meaning of the bearing and attitude of the patient: *why* he doubts, or is unpunctual, or talks in a haughty or confused manner, or communicates only one thought in three, or criticizes the analysis, or produces a super-abundance of too abstruse material. Hence, for example, the analyst may deal with a narcissistic patient whose patronizing speech is couched in technical terms by attempting to convince him that this habit of his is prejudicial to the analysis, that in the interest of its progress he would do better to avoid the use of technical terminology, to abandon his attitude of haughty aloofness. Or, on the other hand, the analyst may renounce any such attempt at persuasion and, instead, wait until he has gained some inkling of why the patient behaves in just this way and not in some other. He may then perhaps discover that the patient is compensating in this way for a feeling of inferiority in relation to the analyst, and he may be able to influence him through consistent interpretation of the meaning of his behavior. This second method of procedure, in contrast to the first, is in complete accord with analytic principles.

From this attempt to replace educational or other active measures, such as the particular behavior of the patient seemed to necessitate, by purely analytic interpretation, there resulted— as unsought as it was unexpected—an approach to the analysis of *character*.

The foundation of character analysis was laid when Freud sponsored the cardinal change in analytic technique which consisted in denoting as the most important task of analysis the over-coming of resistances, in place of the direct interpretation of the patient's symptoms—the technique in use up to the time in ques-tion, but now adhered to only by Stekel and his followers. The technique consisting of the analysis of the resistances fully deserves, as developed up to the present date, the designation of character analysis. There would be no justification, however, for superseding with the latter term the other, more customary one of analysis of the resistances, if it were not for a particular circumstance which makes the term 'character analysis' the preferable one.

As we review our clinical experience, the necessity becomes clear for distinguishing from among the various resistances which we encounter in the course of treating our patients a par-ticular group of these—a group which may be termed *character resistances*. These acquire their specific imprint, not from their content, but from the patient's individual mode of behavior. The compulsive character, for example, develops resistances differ-ing specifically in form from those of the hysterical character, as the latter, in turn, from those of the genital–narcissistic, the 'impulse-ridden' or the neurasthenic character. The *form* taken by the reactions of the ego—a form which in the face of similarity of experiential content differs according to the character—*is just as much determined by infantile experiences as is the content of symptoms and fantasies.*

II. *From What Do Character Resistances Derive?*

Recently Glover has worked on the problem of differentiating character neuroses and symptom neuroses. Alexander, also, has operated on the basis of this distinction. In my earlier writings I, too, observed it; but a closer examination of case material has made it apparent that this distinction means no more than that there are neuroses with concrete, circumscribed symptoms, and neuroses which are lacking in these; the former were therefore called 'symptom neuroses', the latter 'character neuroses'; in the former, it goes without saying, symptoms are more conspicuous, in the latter, neurotic character traits. But is there, after all, such a thing as a symptom without a basis in a neurotic reaction pattern—in other words, without a neurotic character? The difference between character neuroses and symptom neuroses is simply that in the latter the neurotic character has produced symptoms as well—that the neurotic symptoms are, so to speak, a concentrate of the neurotic character. That the neurotic character suffers an exacerbation in the form of specific symptoms, on the one hand, and, on the other, is able to find other means for the discharge of damned-up libido, poses a problem for further investigation. But if the fact is recognized that a neurotic character is invariably the underlying basis of a symptom neurosis, then it is clear that in *every* analysis we have to do with 'character-neurotic' resistances—with resistances having their roots in the neurotic character; individual analyses will differ only in the varying importance which is attributed to character analysis in the individual case. But to look back upon one's analytic experience is to be warned against underestimating this importance in any case whatsoever.

From the standpoint of character analysis, the distinction between neuroses which are chronic, i.e. which have existed since childhood, and those which are acute, that is of recent development, loses all meaning; for it is not so important whether the symptoms have made their appearance earlier or later as it is that the neurotic character, the soil from which the symptom neurosis springs, was already formed—at least in its essentials—at the time of the passing of the oedipus phase. I will merely remind you of the invariable clinical experience that the boundary line which the patient draws between health and the outbreak of his illness inevitably vanishes in analysis.

Since the onset and occurrence of symptoms leave us in the lurch as regards a valid criterion, we must cast about for others. Let us consider first of all in this respect *insight* and *rationalization.*

Deficient insight is by no means an absolutely reliable characteristic but is nevertheless an important sign in character neurosis. The neurotic symptom is felt as a foreign body and gives rise to a feeling of being ill. The neurotic character trait, on the contrary, such as the exaggerated orderliness of the compulsive character or the anxious timidity of the hysterical character, is something organically built into the character. The subject may perhaps complain of his shyness or timidity, but he does not feel ill on this account. It is only when the characterological shyness rises to the pitch of pathological blushing or the obsessive orderliness to a compulsive ceremonial—i.e. when the neurotic character undergoes exacerbation to the point of the development of symptoms—that its subject feels ill.

There are also symptoms, it is true, into which little or no insight exists and which the patient regards in the light of bad habits or mere idiosyncrasies (such as for example chronic obstipation, mild *ejaculatio praecox,* etc.); yet there are a number of character traits which occasionally are felt to be pathological, such as violent outbursts of rage, gross untidiness, a tendency to lie or drink or squander money, and the like. In spite of exceptions of this sort, insight is an important characteristic of the neurotic symptom, its absence the hallmark of the neurotic character trait.

The second difference of practical importance consists in the fact that the symptom is never so completely and plausibly rationalized as in the neurotic character. Neither hysterical vomiting nor abasia, neither compulsive counting nor obsessive thinking, lend themselves to rationalization. The symptom appears to be meaningless, whereas the neurotic character is sufficiently rationally motivated as not to appear either pathological or meaningless. For neurotic character traits a reason is often put forward which would immediately be rejected as absurd if it were applied to symptoms, such as: 'He just is that way'—with its implication that he was born so, that this 'happens to be' his character, which cannot be altered. This view is certainly incorrect, for analysis shows that for definite reasons the character had to develop as it did and not otherwise, and that like a symptom it is, in principle, analysable and alterable.

It sometimes happens that in the course of time symptoms become so interwoven into the total personality as to be tantamount to character traits. Thus, for example, a counting compulsion may manifest itself within the compass of a general orderliness or a compulsive system subserve the daily routine; this sort of thing is especially true of the compulsion to work. Such modes of behavior then pass for peculiarities, for excesses, rather than for anything pathological or of the nature of illness. It can readily be seen, therefore, that the concept of illness is an entirely fluid one—that every possible gradation exists from the symptom as an isolated foreign body, via the neurotic character trait and the 'bad habit', to reality-adapted behavior. Since we cannot use these in-between conditions as a point of departure, however, the distinction between symptom and neurotic character commends itself with regard to rationalization also, despite the artificiality of all such distinctions.

With this reservation in mind, there is nevertheless a distinction to be drawn between the symptom and the neurotic character with regard to their structure. Analytic dissection demonstrates that, as far as its meaning and origin are concerned, the symptom is of far simpler structure than the character trait. Certainly it is true that the symptom is overdetermined; but the more deeply we penetrate into its determinants, the further we get from the field of symptomatology proper and the more does the characterological substratum come to the fore. Thus from any symptom we can—theoretically—arrive at its characterological 'reaction basis'. The symptom has its immediate source in only a limited number of unconscious constellations; hysterical vomiting, for example, has as its root a repressed fellatio wish and a wish for a child. Both of these are also expressed characterologically—the former in a certain infantilism, the latter in a maternal attitude; but the hysterical character underlying the hysterical symptom is determined by a multitude of largely antagonistic strivings, and is generally expressed in a specific *attitude* or *mode of behavior*. The latter is less simple to dissect than the symptom, yet in principle it is, like the symptom, to be derived and understood from infantile strivings and experiences. While the symptom corresponds essentially to a definite experience or a specific wish, the character, the specific mode or pattern of behavior of a person, represents the expression of his entire past. Hence it is possible for a symptom to develop with suddenness, while each individual trait of character requires years for its development. In this connection we must not forget that the symptom could not have made a sudden appearance if its characterological 'reaction basis' had not been already in existence.

The neurotic character traits in their totality manifest themselves in analysis as a compact *defence mechanism* against our therapeutic efforts; analytic exploration of the origin and development of this characterological 'armour shows that it has also a definite economic function, namely, it serves on the one hand as a protection against stimuli from the outer world and on the other as a means for retaining mastery over the libidinal impulses constantly welling up from the id by using up libidinal and sadistic energies in neurotic reaction formations, compensations, and so on. In the processes which underlie the forming and maintaining of this 'armour, anxiety is constantly being bound, in the same way for example, according to Freud's description, anxiety is bound in compulsive symptoms. But since the means which the neurotic character makes use of to bind anxiety, as for example reaction formations and pregenital gratifications, have no permanence, the excessive anxiety, or the dammed-up libido, sooner or later breaks through, and there then arise symptoms indicative of the struggle of the ego to maintain control over this excess. Thus the symptom is explicable from the economic standpoint also as the expression of an 'exacerbation' of the neurotic character.

Since in its economic function as a protecting armour the neurotic character has established a certain *equilibrium,* even though a neurotic one, analysis signifies a danger to this equilibrium. It is from this narcissistic protective apparatus of the ego, accordingly, whence proceed the resistances which give to the analysis of the individual case its particular stamp. But if the attitude, the behavior and the reaction pattern of the patient represent the analysable and alterable resultant of his total development, there then exists the possibility of evolving there from a technique of character analysis.

III. *The Technique of the Analysis of the Character Resistance*

In addition to the dreams, associations, slips of the tongue and the rest of the communications of the patient, his attitude and behavior, that is to say, the manner in which he relates his dreams, commits these slips, produces associations and communicates other material, deserves special attention. The patient who follows the fundamental rule is a rarity; ordinarily it requires

months of work of the character-analytic sort to bring him to even
a half-way sufficient degree of honesty in his analytic work. The
patient's manner of speech, the way in which he looks at the
analyst and greets him, the way he lies on the couch, the inflec-
tion of his voice, the measure of his conventional politeness, and
so on—all these are valuable criteria for estimating the hidden
resistances with which the patient opposes the fundamental rule,
and their understanding is the most important means of overcoming them through interpretation. The *how* is just as important
as the *what* the patient says, as 'material' to be interpreted. Often
one hears analysts complain that the analysis does not go forward,
that the patient does not produce any 'material'. What is referred
to here is usually the content of the patient's associations and
communications. But in the manner in which the patient keeps
silence or indulges in sterile repetition, for example, is equally
'material' to be evaluated. Indeed, there is hardly a situation in
which the patient brings 'no material', and we must realize that it
is our own fault if we are unable to utilize the behavior of the
analysand as 'material'.

That the manner and the form of the patient's communications have analytic significance is certainly nothing new.
But that these open up an avenue of approach to the analysis of
character in a very definite and relatively complete manner is the
subject of the present discussion. Unfavourable analytic experiences with a large number of neurotic characters have taught us
that in such cases it is primarily much more the form than the
content of the patient's communications which is important. We
need only mention in this connection the hidden resistances
manifested by the effect-poor, the 'good', the over-polite and
punctilious, likewise by those patients whose transference is
invariably a deceptively positive one, or who are violent in their
monotonous and stereotyped demand for love, or who take
analysis as a game, and those who are always 'armoured', and
those with an inward smile for everything and everybody. Such
an enumeration could be continued indefinitely, but makes the
more obvious the amount of painstaking work necessary to solve
the innumerable individual problems of technique involved.

In the interest of a general orientation, and to bring out more
fully the contrast between character analysis and symptom analysis,

let us take two pairs of patients for comparison. Let us suppose that we have under analytic treatment two patients with *ejaculatio praecox*—one of them a passive–feminine, the other a phallic–aggressive character. We have also two women with a disturbance of eating—one with a compulsive character, the other with a hysteria. Let us further suppose that the *ejaculatio praecox* of both male patients has the same unconscious meaning: fear of the (paternal) penis fantasied as in the woman's vagina. Both patients develop in the analysis a negative father transference, on the basis of the castration anxiety which underlies their symptom. Both hate the analyst (the father) because they regard him as the enemy who frustrates their pleasure, and both have the unconscious wish to do away with him. In this situation the phallic–sadistic character will ward off the danger of castration by means of insults, depreciation and threats, while the passive–feminine character will become increasingly submissive and friendly. In both patients the character has become a resistance; the former fends off the danger aggressively, the latter avoids it by the sacrifice of his own attitude and a deceptive submission. Obviously, the character resistance of the passive–feminine patient is the more dangerous, because he works by secret means; he brings wealth of material, he recollects infantile experiences, he seems in short to cooperate splendidly, but he thereby covers over a fundamental, secret spite and hatred; as long as he maintains this attitude, he lacks entirely the courage to exhibit his true self. If, disregarding this manner of behavior, the analyst deals only with *what* he brings, no analytic effort or interpretation will bring about any change in his condition. The patient may perhaps even recollect his hatred for his father, but he will not *experience* it unless the analyst interprets in terms of the transference the meaning of his deceptive attitude and behavior *before* undertaking to interpret the deeper meaning of his father hatred.

In the case of the second two patients, let us suppose that an acute positive transference has developed. The central content of this positive transference is in both patients the same as that of the symptom, namely, an oral fellatio fantasy. But although the positive transference has the same content in either case, there results a transference resistance entirely different in form: the hysteric will perhaps manifest *anxious* silence and shy behavior, the patient

with compulsion neurosis a *spiteful* silence and a cold, haughty
demeanour towards the analyst. The defence against the positive
transference makes use of various means for the purpose—in one
case aggressiveness, in another anxiety. In these two instances the
id-wish is the same, but the defence instituted by the ego differs.
Further, the form of this defence will always be the same in the
same patient; the hysteric will always set up a defence of anxiety,
the compulsive one of aggressiveness, whatever the content of
the unconscious which is ever on the point of breaking through.
That is to say, *in any given patient the character resistance remains always
the same, and disappears only with the very roots of the neurosis.*

What follows from these facts, having bearing upon the
technique of character analysis? Are there essential differences
between it and the customary analysis of resistances? There are
such differences, and they have to do with

(a) the choice of the order in which the material is to be
interpreted;

(b) the technique of the interpretation of resistances itself.

With reference to (a): if we speak of 'choice of material', we
have to expect a serious objection; it will be said that any selection
runs counter to basic psychological principles, that the analyst
must follow the patient and let himself be guided by him, and
that any selection on the analyst's part invites the risk of his falling
prey to his own inclinations and tendencies. To this it may be said
in the first place that in such a selection it is not a question of passing over analytic material, but simply of preserving a logical
sequence in interpretation, corresponding to the structure of the
particular neurosis. All material is eventually interpreted; it is
only that at a particular moment one detail is more important
than another. It should be clear, indeed, that the analyst is always
selecting, anyhow, for he has already made a selection when he
omits interpreting a dream but instead chooses this or that detail
to emphasize. One has also made a kind of selection, obviously, if
one pays attention only to the content of the patient's communications and not to their form. Thus the very fact that the
patient brings into the analytic situation material of the most
varied description compels the analyst to make a selection of the
material to be interpreted; what alone is important is that he
makes in relation to the given analytic situation a *correct* selection.

Only during phases free from resistance can the guidance be left to the patient; his compulsion to confess is not to be too much relied upon; in general, patients tend to bring to the fore only the most harmless material—a tendency which when unmasked is revealed, of course, as a resistance.

In patients who because of a particular kind of character development are unable to follow the analytic rule consistently, or in the case of any characterological obstacle to the progress of the analysis, the analyst will be under the ever-present necessity of *isolating the character resistance from the total material and of dealing with it analytically by interpreting its meaning*. This does not mean, of course, that the analyst passes over or pays no attention to all other material; on the contrary, every bit of material is valuable and welcome which throws light on the meaning and origin of the disturbing character trait; the analyst merely postpones the dissection and in particular the interpretation of whatever material is without immediate bearing upon the transference until the character resistance, at any rate in its essential features, is understood and broken down. The dangers attendant upon giving 'deep' interpretations in the presence of unresolved character resistances I have already attempted to indicate in my *Zur Technik der Deutung und der Widerstandsanalyse*.[1]

As to (b): We will now turn to some special problems of the technique of character analysis. First of all, we must forestall a possible misunderstanding. We said that character analysis begins with the isolating out and consistent analysis of the character resistance. This does not mean that one asks the patient, for instance, not to be aggressive, not to cheat, not to talk in a confused manner, to follow the fundamental rule, and so on. To do so would be not only unanalytic but fruitless. It cannot be sufficiently emphasized that what we are describing has nothing to do with education or the like. In character analysis we put to ourselves the question why the patient cheats, speaks in a confused manner, is emotionally blocked, etc.; we try to arouse his interest in his character traits, in order with his help to clarify analytically their meaning and origin. Thus we simply raise the character trait which constitutes the cardinal resistance above the level of the

---

[1] *Internationale Zeitschrift für Psychoanalyse,* XIII, 1927, p. 141.

personality, and shows the patient if possible the superficial relationships between the character and the symptoms, while it is naturally left to him whether or not he wants to utilize his knowledge to change his character. In principle we proceed no differently than in the analysis of a symptom; what is added in character analysis is merely that we isolate the character trait and confront the patient with it repeatedly, until he has attained objectivity towards it and experiences it like a distressing compulsive symptom. The neurotic character thus takes on the nature of a foreign body, and becomes an object of the patient's insight.

Through gaining such a perspective of the neurotic character a change is surprisingly brought about—at first a temporary one—in the personality; and with the further progress of the analysis of character, that instinctual force or personality trait which had given rise to the character resistance in the transference automatically emerges undisguised. To continue with the example of the passive–feminine character: the more thoroughly the patient achieved an objective attitude towards his tendency to passive submission, the more aggressive he became. This was so because his feminine behavior and attitude of deceit were an energetic reaction against repressed aggressive impulses. But with the aggressiveness we also have a reappearance of the castration anxiety which in infancy had determined the change from active to passive–feminine. Thus the analysis of the character resistance led directly to the centre of the neurosis, the oedipus complex.

One should not be under any illusions, however. The isolation and objectifying of such a character resistance, as well as its analytic working through, usually needs many months and demands unceasing work and above all unflagging patience. Yet once it has been possible to break through, the analytic work usually proceeds rapidly, to the accompaniment or *effectively* charged analytic experiences. If, on the contrary, such character resistances are allowed to go undealt with, while the analyst simply follows the patient in his material, constantly interpreting its content, such resistances form in the course of time a ballast which will be difficult if not impossible to remove. One then increasingly gains the impression that every interpretation of content was wasted, and that the patient never ceases to doubt everything or to pretend acceptance or inwardly to ridicule everything. If the elimination of these resistances was not embarked upon at the very beginning, one finds oneself helpless against them in the later stages of the analysis at a time when the most important interpretations of the oedipus complex have already been given.

In the paper already referred to I have attempted to meet the objection that it is impossible to cope with resistances before knowing what their *infantile* determinants are. The essential thing is first to see through the *present* meaning of the character resistance; for this the infantile material is not always necessary. This latter is needed for the *dissolution* of the resistance. If first one is content to demonstrate the resistance to the patient and to interpret its current or present-day meaning, then very often the infantile material with the aid of which we can then overcome the resistance makes its appearance.

If we emphasize a hitherto neglected fact, we possibly create the unintended impression of depriving everything else of significance. If we here underscore so heavily the analysis of the mode of behavior, this implies neither a neglect of content nor a modification of the hitherto existing technique; to the latter we only add something that up to now has received too little regard. Our experience shows that the analysis of characterological resistances must be put ahead of everything else; but this does not mean that one analyzes only the character resistance up to a certain date, and then begins with the interpretation of content. The two phases, the analysis of resistances and the analysis of early infantile experiences, overlap for the most part; it is solely a matter of a preponderance of character analysis in the beginning, of 'education *for* analysis *by* analysis'—while in the later stages the main emphasis is upon content and the infantile. This is of course no rigid rule but depends on the behavior of the individual patient. In one, the interpretation of infantile material will be undertaken earlier, in another, later. It is a basic rule which must be emphasized, however, that 'deep' analytic interpretations are to be avoided, even though the material itself is perfectly perspicuous, so long as the patient is not advanced enough to assimilate them. This again is nothing new, but it is evident that differences in analytic technique depend considerably on what the analyst understands by 'ready for analytic interpretation'. In this connection we have certainly to distinguish between content which has an immediate bearing upon character resistance and that which pertains to other spheres. The usual situation is that the analysand is in the beginning ready to take cognizance of the former but not of the latter. In general our attempt at character analysis simply represents an effort to achieve the greatest possible certainty in the matter of preparing the patient for analysis and of the interpretation of infantile material. This leads to the important task of studying and describing systematically the various forms of characterological transference resistances. Their technique then derives self-evidently from their structure.

IV. The Interpretation of the Ego-Defences

It is not difficult to align what we have here described as character analysis with Freud's theory of the forming and resolving of resistances. We know that every resistance consists of an id-impulse which is warded off, and of an ego-impulse which wards it off. Both of these impulses are unconscious. Theoretically, it would seem immaterial whether one interprets the id-striving first, or the ego-striving. Let us take an example. If a homosexual resistance in the form of keeping silent appears at the very outset of analysis, one may approach the id-striving by telling the patient that he is now occupied with affectionate thoughts about the analyst; one has then interpreted his positive transference, but, supposing that he does not take to his heels, it will be a long time before he reconciles himself to this forbidden idea. Hence one must preferably first approach the aspect of the resistance which is more closely related to the conscious ego, the *ego defence,* by only telling the patient at first that he is keeping silent because *for some reason or other*—thus without touching upon the id-striving—he rejects the analysis, presumably because it has become in some way dangerous to him. In the former instance one has attacked interpretatively the id aspect (in this case an erotic impulse) of the resistance, in the latter its ego aspect, the rejection.

By such a proceeding we come to comprehend at the same time both the negative transference in which every defence ultimately ends and likewise the character, the armour of the ego.

Elsewhere I have tried to bring out that the superficial and more nearly conscious layer of *every* resistance must necessarily be a negative attitude towards the analyst, regardless of whether the id-impulse that is warded off is one of hate or love. The ego projects its defence against the id-impulse on to the analyst, who has become dangerous, an enemy, because by means of the disagreeable fundamental rule he has provoked id-strivings and disturbed the neurotic equilibrium. In defending itself the ego makes use of very primitive forms of negative behavior for its protection; it summons hate impulses from the id to its assistance, even when it is a positive erotic impulse which is to be warded off.

If therefore we adhere to the rule of approaching resistances from their ego side, we thereby always resolve as well a certain amount of negative transference, a certain amount of hate, and in so doing avoid the danger of overlooking destructive tendencies, extremely well concealed as they so often are; and at the same time the positive transference is strengthened. Furthermore, the patient grasps ego interpretations more easily, because they are more in accord with conscious experience than are id interpretations, and he is thereby better prepared for the latter upon their advent.

The form of ego defence, no matter of what nature the repressed id-striving may be, is always the same, and befitting the patient's personality; and likewise, the same id-striving is warded off or defended against in different patients in different ways. Thus we leave the character untouched if we interpret only the id-striving, but we draw the neurotic character into analysis if we approach the resistance from the standpoint of the defence which they represent, that is, from the ego side. In the former case we say immediately *what* the analysand is warding off; in the latter, we first make it clear to him that he is warding off something, then how he is doing it, what means he employs for this purpose (character analysis), and only finally, when the analysis of the resistance has progressed far enough, is he told, or finds out for himself, against what the defence is directed. On this long detour to the analysis of the id-strivings all the attitudes of the ego connected with these have been analysed, and the great danger of the patient's being told something too early or remaining without effect and without participation is obviated.

Analyses in which so much analytic attention is centered upon the attitudes of the patient take no less long than others; so that we cannot boast of having indicated a means of shortening analytic treatment; but comparison shows that they take a more orderly and purposeful course, while theoretical investigation does not suffer in the least. One merely learns important infantile experiences later than otherwise; but this is more than made up for by the effective freshness with which infantile material comes forth *after* analytic work on the character resistances.

Yet we should not leave unmentioned certain disagreeable aspects of a consistent character analysis. The analysis is a far heavier burden for the patient; he suffers much more than when the character is left out of consideration. This has the advantage, to be sure, of a winnowing process: those who cannot bear it would not have achieved success anyhow, and it is better that this lack of promise should become evident after four or six months than after two years. Experience shows that if the character resistance does not give way, a satisfactory result is not to be expected; that is particularly true of cases with hidden resistances. Overcoming the character resistance does not mean that the character has been altered; naturally that is possible only after the analysis of its infantile sources. It only means that the patient has gained an objective attitude towards his character and an analytic interest in it; once this is the case, favourable progress of the analysis is probable.

V. The Undermining of the Narcissistic Protective Apparatus

As we have said, the essential difference between the analysis of a symptom and of a neurotic character trait consists in the fact that the symptom is from the beginning isolated and objectified, whereas the character trait has continually to be pointed out to the patient in order that he may attain to the same attitude towards it as towards a symptom. It is only rarely that this is easily achieved. Many patients exhibit in only slight degree any aptitude for regarding their character in an objective way; these patients have in exaggerated degree a fear of finding out about themselves. For this, in fact, involves the undermining of the narcissistic protective mechanisms and the unbinding of the anxiety which is bound up with it. If the interpretation of this attitude is unavailing, it is then necessary to present to the analysand the alternative of giving up the analysis, or of expressly agreeing to the analyst's pointing out continually and again and again the character trait in question—a thing which in the course of time will become very disagreeable to the patient.

If, for example, a patient remains affectless and indifferent, regardless of the material he is producing, one has then to do with a dangerous blocking of affect, the analysis of which must be put before everything else if one is not to run the risk of having all the material and all one's interpretations go to waste, while the patient becomes a good analytic theorist but otherwise remains the same. Unless one prefers to give up the analysis of such a case because of 'too great narcissism', one may make an agreement with the patient to the effect that one intends to confront him continually with his affectlessness, but that he, of course, may discontinue the analysis at any time he wishes. In the course of time—usually, in my experience, a number of months (in one case it took a year and a half)—the patient begins to find irksome the constant pointing out of his affectlessness and its reasons; for in the meantime one has gradually obtained sufficient clues for the undermining of the protection against anxiety which the blocking of affect represents. Eventually the patient rebels against the danger with which the analysis now threatens him— the danger of losing the protection of his psychic armour and of being confronted with his instinctual impulses, particularly his aggressiveness. But in this rebellion against analytic 'chicanery' his aggressiveness is activated, and presently the first emotional outburst, in the sense of a negative transference, in the form of an attack of hatred occurs. This achieved, the game is won. When aggressive impulses make their appearance, the blocking of affect has been broken through, and the patient becomes analysable. The analysis then proceeds as ordinarily. The difficulty consists in eliciting the aggressiveness.

The same is true when narcissistic patients, in conformity with their characterological make-up, live out their resistance in their manner of speech—when they talk in a haughty or bombastic manner or in technical terms, for example, or when they speak in carefully chosen words or in a confused manner. Modes of speech of this sort form an impenetrable wall, and no genuine experiencing in the analysis is possible until one makes the manner of speech itself the subject of analysis. Here, too, the consistent interpretation of behavior provokes the patient's narcissism to revolt, for he is loath to hear that his carefully chosen speech, his haughty utterance, his parade of technical terms, are his means of concealing his inferiority feeling from himself and the analyst, or that he talks in a confused manner because he wants to appear particularly intelligent but is unable to express his ideas in simple form. In this manner one breaches the solid ramparts of the neurotic character at a critical point, and creates an avenue of approach to the infantile origins of the character and the neurosis. Naturally it is not sufficient to point out the nature of the resistance now and again; the more stubborn the resistance, the more consistently must it be interpreted. If simultaneously the negative attitudes towards the analyst which are thus provoked are analysed, the danger of the patient's breaking off the analysis is a negligible one.

In other cases the character has been set up as a solid protecting wall against the experiencing of (infantile) anxiety and has served well in this capacity, although at a heavy cost in the enjoyment of life. If such a person then enters analysis on account of some symptom, this protecting wall serves equally well in the analysis as a character resistance, and one very soon realizes that nothing can be accomplished until this characterological armour which covers and absorbs the infantile anxiety is destroyed. This is the case, for example, in 'moral insanity' and in manic, narcissistic–sadistic characters. In such cases one is often confronted with the difficult question as to whether the symptom complained of justifies a deep character analysis. For it must be borne in mind, particularly in cases with a relatively good characterological compensation, that if the character analysis destroys this compensation a condition is temporarily created which amounts to a breakdown of the ego. Indeed, in more extreme cases such a breakdown is inevitable before a new ego structure, one readily adapted to reality, can develop. Even though one must concede that the breakdown would have taken place sooner or later anyway, the symptom in question being merely its first indication, still one will hesitate to undertake the great responsibility involved unless the need is urgent.

In this connection we must not omit to mention that in every case in which it is applied, character analysis gives rise to violent emotional outbursts, often indeed to dangerous situations, so that one must always be technically master of the situation. (Hence beginners should not attempt a character analysis.) A collection of analytic experiences of this description will be published in another place. On this account many analysts will perhaps reject the method of character analysis; in that case they will have to relinquish hope of success in no small proportion of cases. Many neuroses are not accessible to mild measures. The method of character analysis, the consistent emphasis upon the character resistances and the persistent interpretation of its forms, modes of expression and motives, are as potent as they are unpleasant for the patient. This has nothing to do with education; rather, it represents a strict analytic principal. One does well, however, to bring to the patient's attention at the beginning the various forseeable difficulties and unpleasantnesses involved in analysis.

To what extent is an alteration of the character necessary in analysis? And to what extent can it be brought about?

To the first question there is, in theory, only one answer: The neurotic character must be altered to the extent to which it forms the characterological basis of neurotic symptoms, and to the extent to which it conditions disturbances in the capacity for work and for sexual gratification.

To the second question the answer can only be an empirical one. The degree to which the actual result approximates the desired one depends in each case on a large number of factors. Qualitative changes of character cannot be directly achieved by present-day analytic methods. A compulsive character will never become a hysterical character, a paranoid character will never become a compulsive one; a choleric temperament will never change into a phlegmatic one, nor a sanguine into a melancholy. What can be achieved are quantitative changes which if of sufficient degree are tantamount to qualitative changes. Thus, for example, the only slightly feminine attitude and behavior of our compulsive female patient underwent a steady increase during analysis, while her masculine–aggressive tendencies became less apparent.

In this way the whole being of the patient becomes 'different'—a difference which is often more noticeable to outsiders who see the patient only at intervals than it is to the analyst. The inhibited and self-conscious person becomes freer, the anxious and fearful more courageous, the over-conscientious less beset by scruples, the unscrupulous more conscientious; yet a certain indefinable 'personal note' never disappears, but continues to gleam through whatever changes in the personality may have taken place. Thus, the formerly over-conscientious compulsive character becomes a realistic and conscientious worker, yet the impulse-ridden character, when cured will nevertheless act with more freedom than the former compulsive; the person cured of 'moral insanity' will never take things too seriously and always will be able to get through easily, while the cured compulsive character, owing to his lack of flexibility, will always have a somewhat difficult time. But after successful character analysis these characteristics remain within limits that do not restrict freedom sufficiently to impair the capacity for work or for sexual gratification.

One has every reason to be distrustful of therapeutic endeavours, including one's own. It will require objective criticism and verification to determine whether the assumption is justified that systematic character analysis constitutes a perhaps not insignificant augmentation of our analytic powers.

Chapter 6

SOME CIRCUMSCRIBED
CHARACTER FORMS

Wilhelm Reich

1. The Hysterical Character

Our investigation of the differentiation of character types proceeds
from two facts: First, no matter what the form of the character, its
basic function is an armoring against the stimuli of the outer world
and against the repressed inner impulses. Second, the external
form of this armoring has its specific historical determination. We
found that perhaps the most important conditions for character
differentiation are the character of the persons who exert the main
educational influence, and the stage of development at which the
decisive frustrations occur. There must be definite relationships
between the external manifestations of the character, its inner
mechanisms and its specific history of development.

The hysterical character—as complicated as the corresponding symptoms and reactions may be—represents the
simplest type of character armoring. Its most outstanding
characteristic is an *obvious sexual behavior,* in combination with a
specific kind of *bodily agility* with a definitely sexual nuance. This
explains the fact that the connection between female hysteria and
sexuality has been known for a very long time. In women, the
hysterical character type is evidenced by disguised or undisguised coquetry in gait, gaze and speech. In men, there is, in
addition, softness and over-politeness, feminine facial expression and feminine behavior.

The traits mentioned appear together with a more or less
outspoken apprehensiveness. This becomes particularly evident

This chapter originally appeared in *Character Analysis,* pp. 189–207. New York: Farrar,
Straus & Giroux, 1970. Reprinted by permission of the publisher.

when the sexual behavior seems close to attaining its goal; then the hysterical character regularly retreats or assumes a passive, anxious attitude. As violent as the hysterical action was before, just so intense is the passivity now. In the sexual act, there is often increased activity without corresponding sexual experience. This activity is an attempt to overcome intense anxiety.

In the hysterical character, facial expression and gait are never hard and heavy as in the compulsive character, or self-confident and arrogant as in the phallic–narcissistic character. In the typical case, the movements are soft, more or less rolling, and sexually provocative. The total impression is one of easy excitability, in contrast, for example, to the self-control of the compulsive character.

While coquetry paired with apprehensiveness as well as bodily agility are immediately evident, the other specific hysterical character traits are hidden. Among these are inconstancy of the reactions, that is, a tendency to unexpected and unintended changes of behavior; a strong suggestibility, always together with a strong tendency to disappointment reactions: as quickly as a hysterical character—in contrast to the compulsive character—lets himself be convinced even of what is most unlikely, as quickly will he give up the conviction and replace it by others which are just as easily acquired. Compliance then is quickly replaced by the opposite: quick depreciation and groundless disparagement. The suggestibility of the hysterical character predisposes him to passive hypnosis, but also to flights of the imagination. It has to do with the extraordinary capacity to form sexual attachments of an infantile character. The vivid imagination easily gives rise to pathological lying because imagined experiences may be conceived of and narrated as actual experiences.

Just as the hysterical character is strongly expressed in bodily behavior, so it tends to represent psychic conflicts in somatic symptoms. This can easily be understood from the libido structure.

The hysterical character is determined by a fixation on the genital phase of infantile development, with its incestuous attachment. From this fixation the hysterical character derives its strong genital aggression as well as its apprehensiveness. The genital incest wishes are repressed but have retained their full cathexis; they are not replaced by pregenital drives as is the case in the compulsive character. To the extent to which, in the hysterical character, pregenital, that is, oral, anal or urethral strivings, play a role, they are representations of genitality or are at least combined with it. In the hysterical character, mouth as well as anus always represent the female genital while in other character forms these zones retain their original pregenital function. As Ferenczi put it, the hysterical character genitalizes everything; the other forms of neuroses replace genitality by pregenital mechanisms or let the genital function as breast, mouth or anus, a mechanism which I called the flooding of the genital with pregenital libido. Since the hysterical character always suffers from a severe sexual disturbance, and since the stasis of genital libido has the most pronounced effects, the sexual agility must be as intensive as the anxiety reactions. The hysterical character, unlike the compulsive character, suffers from direct sexual tension.

This leads us to the nature of the character armor. The armor is much less solidified, much more labile than in the compulsive character. It is simply an apprehensive defense against the genital incest strivings. It seems paradoxical but is a fact that here genital sexuality is in the service against itself: the more apprehensive the total attitude, the more pronounced is the sexual behavior. The meaning of this function is the following: the hysterical character has strong and unsatisfied genital strivings which are inhibited by the general anxiety; thus he feels constantly exposed to dangers which correspond to his infantile fears; the original genital striving is then utilized for the purpose of feeling out, as it were, the nature and magnitude of the threatening dangers. Thus, when a hysterical woman makes particularly active sexual advances it would be erroneous to assume that this is genuine sexual readiness. On the contrary, with the first attempt to take advantage of this seeming readiness one will find that her behavior immediately turns into the opposite: anxiety or any kind of defense, including motor flight. The sexual behavior, then, serves the purpose of finding out whether and from where the expected dangers will realize. This is quite obvious in the transference reactions during treatment. The hysterical character is always ignorant of the meaning of his sexual behavior, fights against taking cognisance of it, becomes highly indignant at such "suggestions"; in brief, one soon realizes that what appears to be a sexual striving is sexuality in the function of defense. Only after one has unmasked this and has analytically dissolved the infantile genital anxiety does the genital striving for an object appear in its original function; to the same extent to which this happens the patient also loses the exaggerated sexual agility. The fact that this sexual behavior also expresses other, secondary strivings, such as primitive narcissism, or the wish to dominate or to make an impression, is not important in this context.

To the extent to which other than genital mechanisms are found in the hysterical character they no longer belong specifically to this character type. For example, one often finds depressive mechanisms. In these cases one finds that the genital–incestuous fixation was in part replaced by a regression to oral mechanisms. The marked tendency of hysterics to oral regressions is explained by the sexual stasis at this zone and by the fact that the mouth, having assumed the role of the genital, absorbs much libido ("displacement from below upwards"). In this process, melancholia-like reactions which belong to the original oral fixation are also activated. The hysterical character, then, presents itself in pure form if it is agile, nervous and lively; if it is depressive, retiring and autistic it shows mechanisms which are no longer specifically hysterical. Nevertheless, one is justified in speaking of hysterical depressions in contrast to melancholic depressions. The difference lies in the extent to which genital libido and object relationships are present together with the oral attitudes. This accounts for gradual transitions at the extreme ends of which we find pure melancholia and, where genitality is predominant, pure hysteria.

The hysterical character has little tendency to sublimation and intellectual achievement and a much lesser tendency to reaction formations than other character types. This is also due to the fact that the libido is neither discharged in sexual gratification which would reduce the hypersexuality nor do the sexual energies become extensively anchored in the character; rather, they are discharged in somatic innervations or in anxiety or apprehensiveness. The mechanisms of hysteria are often used to prove the alleged antithesis of sexuality and social achievement. What is overlooked is the fact that the outspoken inability to sublimate is a result precisely of the sexual inhibition in the presence of genital libido, and the fact that only the establishment of the capacity for gratification liberates social interest and achievement.

With regard to sex-economy and the prevention of the neuroses one has to ask why it is that the hysterical character cannot somehow transform his genital stasis as other characters do with their pregenital strivings. The hysterical character does not utilize the genital libido for reaction formations or sublimations; more than that, there is not even the formation of a solid character armor. The fact is that fully-developed genital excitations do not lend themselves to anything but direct gratification; their inhibition severely impairs the sublimation of other libidinous strivings also because it endows them with an excess of energy. One might assume that this has to do with a specific quality of genitality; more likely, however, it is because of the quantity of libido involved in the excitation of the genital zone. The genital apparatus can provide *orgastic* discharge, a mechanism which does not exist for any other partial impulse; for this reason, it is vital from the point of view of libido-economy. This may be in conflict with certain ethical concepts but cannot be changed. The aversion against these facts can be readily understood: their recognition would be revolutionary.

2. The Compulsive Character

The most general function of the character being the defense against stimuli, and the maintenance of psychic equilibrium, it must be particularly easy to demonstrate in the compulsive character, for this is one of the best-studied psychic formations. There are fluid transitions from the well-known compulsion symptoms to the corresponding character attitudes. The neurotic orderliness compulsion may be absent but a *pedantic concern for orderliness* is a typical trait of the compulsive character. His whole life, in all its major and minor aspects, runs according to a preconceived, inviolable program. Any change in the program is experienced unpleasurably, in more pronounced cases it even arouses anxiety. This character trait, because of its accompanying thoroughness, may help the individual to get much done; on the other hand, it also reduces the working capacity considerably because it precludes any rapid change and adaptation to new situations. It may be valuable for the official, but detrimental for the individual trying to engage in creative work or work which depends on new ideas. Thus one will rarely find compulsive characters among great statesmen; they are more likely to be found among scientists. But since pedantry paralyzes all speculation this trait will also make pioneering discoveries impossible. This leads us to another character trait which is never missing: the tendency to *circumstantial, ruminative thinking*. There is an inability to concentrate more here and less there, according to the rational significance of an object; attention is always divided more or less evenly; unessential things are thought through no less thoroughly than others which are in the center of professional interest. The more rigid and pathological this trait is, the more is thinking and attention concentrated on unessential things, the more are the rationally important things excluded from thinking. This is the result of a displacement of unconscious cathexes; that is, ideas which have become unconsciously important are replaced by far-fetched insignificant ideas. It is part of the general process of repression and is directed against repressed ideas. Usually, there are infantile ruminations about forbidden things which are never allowed to penetrate to the real concern. These ruminations also take place according to historically determined schemas; in intellectual workers, they impair intellectual motility considerably. In many cases, this is made up for by an above-average ability for abstract logical thinking. The critical abilities are better developed than the creative ones.

Another character trait which is never absent is *thriftiness* if not *avarice*. Pedantry, circumstantiality, tendency to rumination, and thriftiness derive all from one instinctual source, anal eroticism; they are reaction formations against those tendencies which played a major role during the phase of toilet training. To the extent to which these reaction formations have not been successful one finds traits of exactly the opposite nature which, together with the traits mentioned, are also typical of the compulsive character. More correctly, these are breakthroughs of the original tendencies. Then we find extreme sloppiness, incapacity for dealing with money, etc. The great tendency to *collect* things completes the list of the characterological derivatives of anal eroticism. While the connection here with the interest in the functions of evacuation is obvious, the connection between rumination and anal eroticism remains obscure. Though we always find a connection with the ruminations about where the babies come from, the transformation of the interest in defecation into a specific kind of thinking is difficult to understand. What we know here is found in the relevant articles of Freud, Abraham, Jones and Ophuijsen.

There are other character traits which derive not from the anal but from the sadistic impulses of that particular age period. Compulsive characters always have strong *reactions of sympathy and guilt feelings*. This does not contradict the fact that their other traits are by no means pleasant for other people; more than that, in the exaggerated orderliness, pedantry, etc., hostile and aggressive impulses are often directly gratified. Corresponding to the fixation of the compulsive character on the anal-sadistic stage of libido development, these traits are reaction formations against opposite tendencies. The fact should be emphasized that we can speak of compulsive character only when these traits are present in their totality but not if somebody is merely, say, pedantic, without showing any other traits of the compulsive character. If, for example, a hysterical character also shows tendencies to pedantry or rumination, he cannot be called a compulsive character.

While the character traits mentioned thus far are direct derivatives of certain partial impulses, there are other typical traits which show a more complicated structure and result from the interaction of various forces. Among these are *indecision, doubt and distrust*. In his outward appearance, the compulsive character shows marked *restraint* and *control;* his affective reactions, negative as well as positive, are lukewarm; in extreme cases, this becomes a *complete affect-block*. These latter traits are already of a formal nature, bringing us to our real subject, the dynamics and economy of the character.

The restraint and evenness in living and thinking, coupled with indecision, form the point of departure of our analysis of the character form. They cannot be derived from individual impulses like the contents of character traits; they give the individual his particular stamp; they form, in analysis, the core of the character

resistance. Clinical experience shows that the traits of doubt,
mistrust, etc., act as resistance in the analysis and cannot be
eliminated as long as one does not succeed in breaking through
the affect-block. This, therefore, deserves our special attention.
We shall limit ourselves essentially to the formal elements since
the others are well known while here we are in new territory.

We shall have to recall first what is known about the libido
development of the compulsive character. There was a central
fixation on the anal-sadistic level, that is, at about the age of two
or three. Toilet training took place too early which led to strong
reaction formations such as extreme self-control, even at a very
early age. The strict toilet training called forth a strong anal stub-
bornness which also mobilized the sadistic impulses. In the typical
compulsion neurosis, the development proceeds, nevertheless,
into the phallic phase. That is, genitality was activated but soon
relinquished again, partly because of the strong inhibitions set
up at a very early age, partly because of the antisexual attitude of
the parents. To the extent to which genitality was developed, it
was, corresponding to the previous development of anality and
sadism, in the form of phallic-sadistic aggression. It goes without
saying that a boy will repress his genital impulses all the more
quickly the more aggressive his acquired sexual constitution and
the more inhibitions and guilt feelings from an earlier phase of
development make themselves felt. Thus it is typical of compulsion neurosis that the repression of genitality is followed by a
regression to the earlier stage of anal interests and of aggression.
During the so-called latency period[1]—which is particularly well-
developed in compulsive characters—the anal and sadistic reaction formations are intensified and form the final character.
During puberty, under the influence of the increased sexual
urge, the process is repeated in abbreviated form. Usually there
are at first violent sadistic impulses toward women (phantasies of
rape, of beating, etc.), accompanied by a feeling of affective weakness and inferiority; these call forth narcissistic compensations in
the form of ethical and esthetic reaction formations. The anal and
sadistic fixations are intensified or—after a brief and usually

[1]The sexual development among children of primitive peoples shows that the latency
period is not a biological phenomenon, but a sociological one created by sexual
suppression.

unsuccessful move in the direction of genital activity—reactivated, which causes a further elaboration of the corresponding reaction formations. As a result of these processes in the depth, the puberty of the compulsive character takes a typical course. There is, first of all, a progressive flattening of affective reactions which may impress the untrained observer as a particularly good social "adjustment" and may be experienced as such by the patient himself. But together with this affect-block there is a feeling of inner emptiness and an intense desire to "start life anew" which is often attempted with the most absurd means. One such patient developed a highly complicated system according to which he was going to carry out every major and minor task in his life. Everything was figured out down to the second so that he would start his new life exactly at a given date. Since he was never able to fulfill the self-imposed conditions of his system, he always had to start all over again.

The best object for a study of the formal disturbances in the compulsive character is the affect-block. It is by no means the passive attitude of the ego which it appears to be. On the contrary, there is hardly any other character formation in which analysis reveals such an active and intense defense work. What, then, is warded off, and by what means? The typical mode of repression in the compulsive character is the dissociation of the affects from the ideas, so that very often highly censorable ideas can appear in consciousness. One such patient dreamed and talked openly about incest with his mother, even about violent rape, but he remained entirely unmoved. Genital as well as sadistic excitation was completely absent. If one analyzes such patients without concentrating on the affect-block, one gets, it is true, further unconscious material, perhaps even an occasional weak excitation, but never the affects which would correspond to the ideas. Where do they keep hidden? To the extent to which they are not absorbed by symptoms, they are to be found in the affect-block itself. This is proved by the fact that when one succeeds in breaking through the affect-block, the affects spontaneously reappear, usually at first in the form of anxiety.

It is noteworthy that at first no genital impulses are liberated but only aggressive impulses. The superficial layer of the armor, then, consists of aggressive energy. What binds it? The aggressive energy is bound with the help of anal-erotic energies. The affect-block is one great spasm of the ego which makes use of somatic spastic conditions. All muscles of the body, but particularly those of the pelvis and pelvic floor, of the shoulders and the face, are in a state of chronic hypertonia. Hence the "hard," somewhat mask-like physiognomy of compulsive characters, and their physical awkwardness. The ego takes over anal holding-back tendencies from the repressed layers and utilizes them for the defense against the sadistic impulses. While, thus, anality and aggression go together in the unconscious, they assume an antithetical function in the defense against aggression, and vice versa. That means that we do not liberate the anal energies either unless we dissolve the affect-block. We are reminded of our affect-blocked patient who, every time he rang my doorbell, would recite the Götz quotation three times. It is as if he said: "I would like to kill you, but I must control myself; therefore, you can. . . ."

The passive-feminine character also wards off his aggression by means of anal tendencies, but in a different manner. Here, anality works in the original direction as an object-libidinous impulse; in the compulsive character, however, in the form of anal holding back, that is, as a reaction formation. Correspondingly, passive homosexuality in the compulsive character is not as superficial and relatively unrepressed as in the passive-feminine which belongs to the type of the hysterical character.

How is it possible that the anal holding back in the character can be so powerful that the patients become living machines? Not only because of the anal reaction formation. The sadism which is bound up in the affect-block is not only its object but also its means in the defense against anality. That is, an interest in the anal function is also warded off by means of aggressive energy. Every affective and lively utterance provokes in the unconscious the old unresolved excitations so that there is a conscious fear that an accident may happen, that self-control may be lost. It can readily be seen that this opens the way to the whole infantile conflict between urge to let go and necessity for self-control because of fear of punishment. Correct analysis of the affect-block leads to a breakthrough into this central conflict and the displacement of the corresponding cathexes back to the original positions.

This, however, is synonymous with the dissolution of the armor.

From the affect-block one also arrives at the affective anchorings of the first identifications and the super-ego: The demand for self-control, originally imposed from the outside on a resisting ego, was internally accepted. More than that, it became a rigid, chronic, unalterable mode of reaction; this could be achieved only with the aid of repressed id energies.

Systematic resistance analysis leads to the separation of two different sadistic impulses which are contained in the affect-block. What is usually liberated first is *anal* sadism with the goals of beating, kicking, squashing, etc. After these are worked through and the anal fixations are dissolved, *phallic*-sadistic impulses, such as stabbing and piercing, come more and more to the fore. That is, the regression is eliminated and the cathexis of the phallic position begins. At this point, castration anxiety makes its first appearance in an affective manner, and the analysis of the genital repressions begins. In compulsive characters, the old infantile phobia often reappears at this stage.

We find, then, two layers of repressions in the compulsive character: more superficially, the sadistic and anal, more deeply, the phallic ones. This corresponds to the reversal of direction in the process of regression. What was more recently invested with affect in the process of regression lies closer to the surface; the object-libidinal genital impulses are most deeply repressed and covered up by layers of pregenital positions. These structural relationships make clear how erroneous it would be to try to make the patient understand affectively the weak manifestations of genital object-strivings *before* having worked through the pregenital layers. If one were to try to do this, everything would be accepted coldly or warded off with doubt and distrust.

In this connection, we have to say a few words about ambivalence and doubt. They are the most difficult obstacles unless one succeeds, from the beginning, in separating from each other the different impulses which make up the ambivalence. The ambivalence represents a conflict between love and hatred for the same person, in a deeper layer an inhibition of the libidinal as well as the aggressive strivings by the fear of punishment. If one analyzes all manifestations simultaneously, without discrimination, one cannot master the ambivalence and may arrive at the assumption of a biological, that is, unalterable ambivalent "anlage." If, on the other hand, one proceeds according to structural and dynamic considerations, the hatred soon becomes predominant; after its analysis, the libidinal strivings become crystallized out. The best means for this *splitting up of the ambivalence* is a painstaking analysis of the distrust right from the beginning of the analysis.

It goes without saying that we could do no more here than point out the most essential traits of the compulsive character.

3. The Phallic–Narcissistic Character

The formulation of a "phallic–narcissistic character" resulted from the necessity of defining character forms which stand in between compulsion neurosis and hysteria. They manifest circumscribed forms which differ sharply, both in manifestation and genesis, from the two others. The term "phallic–narcissistic character" or, less correctly, "genital–narcissistic character," has found its way into psychoanalytic terminology during the past few years. I first described this type in a hitherto unpublished paper read before the Vienna Psychoanalytic Society in October, 1926.

Even in outward appearance, the phallic–narcissistic character differs from the compulsive and the hysterical character. While the compulsive character is predominantly inhibited, self-controlled and depressive, and while the hysterical character is nervous, agile, apprehensive and labile, the typical phallic–narcissistic character is self-confident, often arrogant, elastic, vigorous and often impressive. The more neurotic the inner mechanism, the more obtrusive are these modes of behavior. As to bodily type, they belong most frequently to Kretschmer's athletic type. The facial expression usually shows hard, sharp masculine features, but often also feminine, girl-like features in spite of athletic habitus. Everyday behavior is never crawling as in passive–feminine characters but usually haughty, either cold and reserved or derisively aggressive, or "bristly," as one of these patients put it. In the behavior toward the object, the love object included, the narcissistic element always dominates over the object-libidinal, and there is always an admixture of more or less disguised sadistic traits.

Such individuals usually anticipate any expected attack with an attack on their part. Their aggression is very often expressed not so much in what they say or do as in the manner in which they say or do things. Particularly to people who do not have their own aggression at their disposal they appear as aggressive and provocative. The outspoken types tend to achieve leading positions in life and resent subordination unless they can—as in the army or other hierarchic organizations—compensate for the necessity of subordination by exerting domination over others who find themselves on lower rungs of the ladder. If their vanity is hurt, they react either with cold reserve, deep depression or lively aggression. In contrast to other characters, their narcissism expresses itself not in an infantile manner but in the exaggerated display of self-confidence, dignity and superiority, in spite of the fact that the basis of their character is no less infantile than that of others. The comparison of their structure with that of, say, a compulsive character, clearly shows the difference between pregenital and phallic narcissism. In spite of their narcissistic preoccupation with their selves they often show strong attachments to people and things outside. In this respect, they resemble most closely the genital character; they differ from it, however, in that their actions are much more intensively and extensively determined by irrational motives. It is not by accident that this type is most frequently found among athletes, aviators, soldiers and engineers. One of their most important traits is aggressive courage, just as the compulsive character is characterized by cautious hesitation and the passive–feminine character by an avoidance of dangerous situations. The success in achievement is little influenced by the fact that the courage and enterprise of the phallic narcissist differs from that of the genital character by being also compensatory, having to ward off opposite strivings.

The phallic–narcissistic character differs from the compulsive character in the absence of reaction formations against his openly aggressive and sadistic behavior. We will have to show that this aggressive behavior itself fulfills a defense function. In relatively unneurotic representatives of this type, social achievement, thanks to the free aggression, is strong, impulsive, energetic and usually productive; the more neurotic the character, the more peculiar and one-sided the achievement; from here there is every transition to the formation of paranoid systems. The achievement differs from that of the compulsive character by greater boldness and lesser attention to details.

Phallic–narcissistic men show a high erective potency, although they are orgastically impotent. Relationships with women are disturbed by the contempt for the female sex which is rarely lacking. In spite of this, they are highly desired sexual objects because in their appearance they show all the traits of masculinity. In women, the phallic–narcissistic character occurs much less frequently. The definitely neurotic forms are characterized by active homosexuality and clitoris sexuality; those who are genitally healthier are characterized by great self-confidence, based on physical vigor and beauty.

The phallic–narcissistic character comprises almost all forms of active homosexuality, male and female; most cases of so-called moral insanity, paranoia and allied forms of schizophrenia; also many cases of erythrophobia and manifestly sadistic male perverts. Many productive women also belong to this type.

Now as to the structure and genesis of this character type. Here we must distinguish those impulses which find direct gratification in the phallic–narcissistic behavior from those which form the narcissistic protection apparatus. Typically, analysis reveals an identification of the total ego with the phallus, in women the phantasy of having a penis; also, a more or less open display of this ego. In erythrophobia, this impulse is repressed and breaks through in the form of a strong neurotic feeling of shame, and blushing. These cases have in common a fixation to that phase of infantile development in which the anal-sadistic position had just been left while the genital object-libidinal position had not yet been reached and which, therefore, is characterized by a proud, self-confident concentration on the own genital. This, however, is not a sufficient explanation. The phallic narcissist is characterized not only by this phallic pride, but even more by the motives which force him to remain at this stage of development.

The pride in the real or fantasied phallus goes hand in hand with a strong phallic aggression. To the unconscious of the man of this type, the penis is not in the service of love but is an instrument of aggression and vengeance. This is the basis of his strong erective potency as well as of his inability to experience the orgasm. The infantile history regularly reveals serious disappointments in the object of the other sex, disappointments which occurred precisely at the time when attempts were made to win the object through phallic exhibition. In men, one often finds that the mother was the stronger of the parents, or the father had died early or was otherwise out of the picture.

The frustration of genital and exhibitionistic activity at the height of their development by the very person toward whom the genital interest is displayed results in an identification with that person on the *genital* level. That is, the boy will give up and introject the female object and will turn to the father in an active (because phallic) homosexual role, while the mother is retained as an object with only narcissistic attitudes and impulses of sadistic revenge. In such men, the sexual act has the unconscious meaning of again and again proving to the woman how potent they are; at the same time it means piercing or destroying the woman, in a more superficial layer degrading her. In phallic–narcissistic women, conversely, the leading motive is that of taking vengeance on the man, of castrating him during the act or of making him impotent or of making him appear impotent. This is in no way at variance with the strong sexual attraction which these strongly erotic characters exert on the other sex. Neurotic polygamy, active creating of disappointments for the partner, and passive flight from the possibility of being left alone are very often found. In other cases, where narcissistic sensitivity disturbs the compensation mechanism, erective potency is unstable, a fact which the patient is unwilling to admit to himself. The more disturbed potency is, the more labile is the general mood, and there is often a rapid alternation of hypomanic, self-confident phases and phases of severe depression. In such cases, the ability to work is also severely disturbed.

The phallic–exhibitionistic and sadistic attitude serves also as a defense against opposite tendencies. The compulsive character, after the genital frustration, regresses to the earlier phase of anality and there forms his reaction formations. The phallic character does not regress. He remains at the phallic stage; more than that, he exaggerates its manifestations *in order to protect himself against a regression to passivity and anality.* In the course of the analysis of such characters, strongly warded-off anal and passive tendencies come more and more to the fore. They constitute the character not directly but by the defense which the ego puts up against them in the form of phallic sadism and exhibitionism. They represent the exact opposite of the passive–feminine character who wards off his genital impulses with the aid of anal and passive surrender. The phallic–narcissistic character, conversely, wards off his anal and passive–homosexual impulses with the aid of phallic aggression. Analysts often describe such characters as anal or passive–homosexual. This is incorrect. The passive–feminine character cannot be called phallic–sadistic because he wards off these tendencies; similarly, the phallic–narcissistic character cannot be described as anal–passive because he wards off these tendencies. The character is determined not by what it wards off but by the manner in which and the impulses with which the defense is effectuated.

In the case of moral insanity, of active homosexuality and phallic sadism, as well as in the sublimated forms such as the professional athlete, the defense is highly successful and the warded-off tendencies of passive and anal homosexuality are expressed only in certain exaggerations. In paranoia, the warded-off tendencies fully break through in the form of delusions. Erythrophobia is most closely associated with the paranoid form of this character; it is very frequently found in the history of paranoid schizophrenics. Here, we have a symptomatic breakthrough of the warded-off passive and anal homosexuality; the patient, due to acute castration anxiety, gives up masturbation, and the additional sexual stasis, with its vasomotor manifestations, weakens the defense function of the ego. The active homosexual and the phallic sadist, on the other hand, have a strong ego defense as long as there is effective libidinal gratification. If this, for any reason, is interrupted for any considerable period of time, the passive and anal tendency also will break through, either symptomatically or without disguise.

Among the phallic–narcissistic–sadistic characters one often finds addicts, particularly alcoholics. This is not only because of warded-off homosexuality but also because of another specific trait of this type which also derives from phallic frustration. Let us take the case of the man. The frustration of phallic exhibitionism and masturbation by the mother leads to an identification with her and a strengthening of the previously relinquished anal position and tendency to passive–feminine behavior. This is immediately counteracted by an emphasis on phallic–exhibitionistic and aggressive, that is, masculine attitudes. However, in the identification on the phallic level with the woman she was provided with a fantasied penis, and the own phallus also attained the meaning of breast. For this reason, the sexually active forms of this character in men show a tendency to passive and active fellatio, and a maternal attitude toward younger men; women show such an attitude toward younger and feminine types of women. In alcoholism, there is also a regression to orality; for this reason, the typical traits of the phallic–narcissistic character are not so clear-cut.

There are many more forms of transition from the phallic–narcissistic character to the healthy genital character as well as to the severely pathological, pregenital forms of addiction and chronic depression that can be found in other characters. A good deal has been written about the relationship between genius and criminality. The type that is meant here belongs neither to the hysterical nor to the masochistic character but predominantly to the phallic–narcissistic character. Most of the sex murderers of recent history belonged to it such as Haarmann and Kürten who had suffered the most severe infantile disappointments in love and later on realized their phallic–sadistic vengeance on the love object. Landru as well as Napoleon and Mussolini belong to the phallic–narcissistic characters. The combination of phallic narcissism, phallic sadism and simultaneous compensation of passive and anal homosexual strivings makes for the most energetic characters. Whether such a type turns into a creative genius or a large-scale criminal depends largely on the social atmosphere and the possibilities it provides for an outlet of the energy in a sublimated form. The other determining factor is the measure of genital gratification which in turn determines the amount of energy which is channeled into destructive impulses of revenge. This differentiation of social and libido–economic factors is not meant to obliterate the fact that the inability to reach genital gratification depends also on social and familial factors.

Constitutionally speaking, there seems to be, in these types, an above-average production of libidinal energy which makes possible an all the more intense aggression.

The analytic treatment of phallic–narcissistic characters is one of the most thankful tasks. Since the phallic phase has been fully reached and since aggression is relatively free, the establishment of genital and social potency, other things being equal, is easier than in other character forms. The analysis is always successful if one succeeds in unmasking the phallic–narcissistic attitudes as a defense against passive–feminine tendencies and in eliminating the unconscious tendency of revenge against the other sex. If one does not succeed in this, the patients remain in their narcissistic inaccessibility. Their character resistance consists in aggressive depreciation of the analysis and the analyst in more or less disguised forms, a narcissistic taking over of the interpretation work, and in the denial of and defense against any passive or apprehensive tendency and particularly the positive transference. The reactivation of phallic anxiety is possible only by an energetic and consistent dissolution of the reactive narcissistic mechanisms. Superficial signs of passivity and anal homosexual tendencies may not immediately be followed into deeper levels because this is apt to result in complete inaccessibility.

Chapter 7

PSYCHOANALYSIS OF CHARACTER

Otto Fenichel

As is well known, psychoanalysis started as a therapy of neuroses; therefore, the neurotic symptom was its first main subject. In a neurotic symptom something happens which the subject experiences as strange and unexplainable—either involuntary movements, or other changes of bodily functions and various sensations, as in a hysterical symptom; or an overwhelming and unjustified emotion or mood, as in attacks of anxiety or depression; or queer impulses or thoughts, as in compulsions and obsessions. It is always something which seems to break in from without upon the personality and which disturbs the continuity of the personality and appears like an invasion from something outside the usual habits of the subject, coming as a vivid proof of the limits of the conscious will. It cannot be controlled by means of the usual controlling apparatus of the mind.

Before psychoanalysis undertook to study the essence of "personality," it had to investigate the disturbances of personality and the disruptions of its continuity. It was the study of the insufficiencies of conscious control and those habitual patterns of behavior which we call "character," which enabled us later to attack the problems of character itself. The result of those preliminary studies showed that the impression that the neurotic symptoms represent an invasion from another country was correct. Their ego-alien nature can be explained by the fact that they break in from a region of the mind which the subject had previously purposefully alienated from it—viz., the unconscious. Neurotic symptoms are the outcome of forces which are always at

This chapter originally appeared in *The Collected Papers of Otto Fenichel*, second series, pp. 198–214, eds. H. Fenichel and D. Rapaport. New York: W. W. Norton, 1954. Reprinted by permission of the publisher.

work but which are usually prohibited from expressing themselves. The essence of the psychology of the neuroses is the
explanation of how this normal prohibition became insufficient.
For repressed instinctual forces which are striving for discharge
are to a certain extent present in everybody. The first proof of this
fact was given by the interpretation of dreams. Dreams, like
symptoms, are disguised expressions of the repressed, and that is
the reason why they appear to the coherent and reasonable ego to
be strange, as neurotic (or even more, psychotic) symptoms do.
Normal persons may dream, too. And so we see that the unconscious is operative in normal people also. We can understand that
it is the state of sleep itself which, with the suspension of consciousness, weakens the suppressing forces of the higher levels of
personality, and so enables the deeper parts of the mind to make
their appearance. In the case of neuroses, however, the insufficiency of the prohibiting forces proceeds from other causes
than the state of sleep. It is a consequence of a too far-reaching
suppression of instinctual satisfactions. That is not of much
interest for us today. What matters is the fact that the human
mind seems to consist of two principal parts: the so-called "continuous personality," the activities of which seem at least to be of
a suppressing nature; and unconscious instinctual forces which
usually are suppressed, but which make their appearance in
neurotic symptoms and dreams, and also—we hasten to add—in
other sudden acts, emotional feelings, or attitudes which are
experienced as strange and which have always an impulsive and
instinctual character, opposed to intellect and reason. The situation is really very analogous to brain physiology, where it was also
ascertained that the activity of the higher centers, the cortex,
partly consists in suppression of activities of deeper and more
archaic centers, and that the latter find expression whenever the
higher suppressing forces become insufficient. Sometimes it
looked, therefore, as if the two parts of the human mind might
have to be represented by two different psychologies. It has been
thought that psychoanalysis, as a "depth psychology," has to
study the unconscious and the instincts, but that other, non-
analytic psychologies, would have to study the "surface," the
personality which suppresses the instincts and which governs the
mind of the normal person during the day—the "character."

But such a viewpoint is wrong. It is the genetic point of view which shows us that the relationship of the deep instincts and the unconscious, which are studied by psychoanalysis, and the ego and the so-called character, is more complicated. We certainly do not assume that there are no other phenomena in the human mind than instinctual phenomena, but we do assume that the non-instinctual phenomena can be explained as derivatives of instinctual ones, which took shape under the influence of the outer world. Just as the cellular theory is not contradicted by the existence of bones and nerves, and bones and nerves may be studied by means of the same principles as the cells, as long as it is possible to demonstrate that the bones and nerves are derivative of cells—so, in the same way, does psychoanalysis, which first studied the unconscious and the instincts, remain competent for the whole human mind as long as it succeeds in demonstrating that the conscious and non-instinctual phenomena are derivatives of unconscious and instinctual ones.

What the "ego" undertakes with the deep unconscious forces is certainly not only their suppression. It is their organization and guidance as well. And so it becomes understandable that an apparatus whose function is suppression, guidance, and organization cannot be understood before the material which is suppressed, organized, and guided is thoroughly known. First comes the psychology of what is comprehended, then the psychology of comprehension. In the so-called "ego psychology," psychoanalysis approaches the same subject as other psychologies, but it approaches it in a different way, namely genetically. I have already anticipated that it can be shown that the whole "daytime personality" which we call the ego is to be regarded basically as being a result of conflicts between primitive instincts and inhibiting outer forces.

By taking symptoms and dreams as its first objects, psychoanalysis has succeeded in studying the nature and genesis of the unconscious instincts which find their distorted expression in them. It is not my task today to talk about this part of psychoanalytic research. I remind you only of the fact that the immense field of infantile sexuality was not known before Freud.

There are three reasons why psychoanalysis could not fail to be extended to ego psychology. To begin with, there were theoretical reasons: The repressing forces are also an object for psychological study and the preliminary study of the repressed forces enabled psychoanalysis to make the next step. In addition, there were two other, practical, reasons, the importance of which has to be estimated still higher. In the first place, when the psychoanalyst tried to get at the hidden meaning of the neurotic symptoms he met the suppressing—or, as I might say in this connection, repressing—force of the ego in the form of what we know as "resistances." To overcome these resistances became his main practical task. How was it to be done? Everything was tried in this respect, and Freud has said in his *Introductory Lectures* (1916–1917) that every means of suggestion is justified for the purpose of overcoming resistances. But if, for example, a patient did not obey the basic rule which tells him to say everything which occurs to him, a scientific mind was tempted not only to influence this unreasonable behavior by means of suggestion, but to get to understand this ego, which had hitherto figured as a reasonable ego, but which in such cases seemed not to be reasonable at all. Consciously, the man was trying to do everything to co-operate; but unconsciously a "suppressing" part of his ego was antagonistic. Here was a conflict at work inside the ego; other material, associations or dreams or sleeping states of the patient, had to be used to analyze this conflict, to make the patient aware *that* he had the resistance, *why* he had the resistance, and why he had it in that form. The principle is that this is always done by the discovery that the patient, even if he does not feel any fear today, was once afraid (or ashamed or disgusted or full of bad conscience) about certain instinctual experience, and that this fear is unconsciously still working in him, so that he develops resistances against utterances which might be connected with the instincts in question. Thus it was the necessity for analyzing the resistance which in practice started psychoanalytic ego psychology. Moreover, in this way two other things were discovered: first, that certain attitudes of the patient's which always recurred when similar instinctual dangers were mobilized served the purpose of resistances, and second that not only was that purpose fulfilled by them in the psychoanalytic treatment, but that the same behavior patterns were also used by the patient in his ordinary life, either to prevent his expressions of certain instincts or to prevent his becoming aware of them. This discovery opened the way to the first "psychoanalysis of character"—that is, to the analysis of the purpose and the historical genesis of certain characterological attitudes as repressions. In the second place, it is an interesting fact that the neuroses themselves, which the analyst had to deal with, have changed. We began today with the statement that in the classical neurosis a continuous personality was suddenly disturbed at certain points by inappropriate actions, impulses, or thoughts. In modern neuroses that is no longer the case. Here the personality does not appear to be uniform, but open, torn, or deformed, and in any case so involved in the illness that one cannot say at what point the "personality" ends and the "symptom" begins. There is a very gradual transition from neurotics to those "psychopaths" and persons with "characterological anomalies," who themselves feel their need for treatment less than do the people around them. I know that you here are especially interested in so-called "criminals," a term which I do not like as a description for psychological facts, because "criminality" is a juridical and not a psychological term. But certainly "criminals" are among such "characterologically deformed" people.

It would be a fascinating task to investigate the cause of the changes in form of neurosis. I merely wish to suggest where I should look for the answer to this question. The method and manner in which the ego admits, repels, or modifies instinctual claims depend to a large extent on the way in which it has been taught to regard them by the surrounding world. During the last decades morality, this educational attitude toward the instincts, has changed very much in our European and American cultures. Classical hysteria works chiefly with the defensive mechanism of genuine repression, which, however, presupposes a simple prohibition of talk concerning the objectionable instincts, chiefly sexual, which upbringing has consistently represented as bad. The inconsistency of present-day education, itself undecided as to which instinctual claims to allow and which to suppress, results in initial license and subsequent sudden, unexpected, and therefore more cruel, deprivation. The inconsistency of the neurotic personality corresponds to this inconsistency in education. The change in the neuroses, it seems to me, reflects the change in morality. In order to understand this, however, one would have to investigate the social changes which have taken place in our culture in the last decades. In any case, the present-day neurotic characters appear to us to possess egos that are restricted by defensive measures, and psychoanalysis has had to adapt itself to this new object—and that might be the decisive reason for the interest in "psychoanalysis of character" and the recent progress which psychoanalytic characterology has made.

Now to the next question: what have "character anomalies" and "neurotic symptoms" in common, and in what respect do they differ from each other? A neurotic symptom is, in general, as you know, a distorted expression of a repressed instinct. But sometimes it is more an expression of the repressing forces—of what safeguards an executed repression. Think, for example, of neurotic impotence or frigidity; this may perhaps occasionally express some masochistic or sadistic instincts too, but it is certainly to a much greater extent, and in all cases, a method of insuring that the subject shall not give in to sexuality, which he unconsciously holds to be dangerous. Or think of the compulsive symptom which reassures the patient against unconscious death wishes. The degree in which repressed instinct and repressing forces participate in the structure of the symptom may vary; but in principle we can say that every symptom is an expression of a conflict between an instinct and counter-forces (anxiety, feelings of guilt, shame, or disgust). The same is true for dreams—cannot the same formula be applied to attitudes or patterns of behavior?

There are some attitudes in which the possibilities for instinctual satisfaction are so obvious to the observer that it does not need psychoanalysis to discover it. Consider, for instance, the amount of sadism which can be satisfied provided the subject thinks that he does it for a higher aim. There are many more attitudes still in which the purpose to repress some instincts, or to defend the subject against an instinctual danger, is obvious. Take, for example, all attitudes of the type of "reaction formation"— that is, overstrained and rigid attitudes that hinder the expression of contrary instinctual attitudes—which nevertheless may sometimes break through in various ways. Thus it seems that in principle these attitudes which a person's ego develops toward his objects as well as his own instincts are also compromises between the instincts and the anxiety which opposes them, just as symptom and dream are. The problems which, after this discovery, are now of more interest, are:

1. What are the differences between dreams and symptoms on the one hand and ego attitudes on the other, and why are those attitudes of an "ego" nature, while dreams and symptoms are alien to the ego?

2. Are all attitudes and behavior patterns such results of instinctual conflicts, or are only a certain type of them of this sort, so that besides them there may exist attitudes which are psychologically of an entirely different character?

We can divide the "attitudes" of an individual into those which are occasional and those which are habitual. The habitual ones may be summarized as "character." Character traits may once more be subdivided in those which appear only in certain situations and those which are comparatively constantly present, suggesting that the instinctual temptation which must be repressed is continually present too. There are people who are impudent, polite, indifferent, ready to prove others at fault, etc., in all situations and to all people. Such attitudes may be called "character defenses" in the narrower sense, in contrast to other types of defense.

It would, of course, be incorrect to consider the word "character" as synonymous with the expression "defensive character attitude." The way in which a person behaves in relation to instinctual actions, how he combines his various tasks in order to find a satisfactory solution—all that too goes to make up "character." In all probability psychoanalytic characterology will have to make a fundamental distinction between character traits in which—most likely after an alliance between them and the object—the original instinctual energy is discharged, and those traits in which psychoanalysis as an "unmasking" psychology can prove that the original instinctual attitude which is contrary to the manifest attitude still exists in the unconscious. We can call the first the "sublimatory" type of character trait, and the second the "reactive formation" type. This second type is betrayed, as already mentioned, either by its forced and rigid nature, or by the occasional breaking through of that which has been repressed.

It can easily be understood why the reactive type is much better understood than the sublimatory type. It is the reactive type which forms characterological anomalies and resistances whose investigation was required of psychoanalysis for practical reasons. They show themselves as frozen residues of former vivid instinctual conflicts. Freud once wrote that "it is always possible for the ego to avoid a rupture in any of its relations by deforming itself, submitting to forfeit something of its unity, or in the long run even to being gashed and rent. Thus the illogicalities, eccentricities and follies of mankind would fall into a category similar to their sexual perversions, for by accepting them they spare themselves repressions." Since the maintenance of these eccentricities must surely correspond to the reactive type and demand an expenditure of energy, it would perhaps be more correct to say that their formation corresponds to a single definite act of repression, so that the necessity for subsequent separate repressions, which would require more energy, and for separate anxiety situations, is avoided. In this way, the ego-restricting attitudes, which act as chronic anchorages of instinctual defense, are not experienced as ego-alien but are worked into the ego. Their constant operation prevents the instinct from becoming manifest, so that we see no living conflict between instinct and defense but something rigid which does not necessarily appear to the patient himself as questionable. The problem for us lies in the relative constancy of the defensive attitude assumed by the ego when faced by different demands both from the external world and from instinctual contents.

This relative constancy could also be understood for certain kinds of attitudes of the reactive type. The special quality of those attitudes seems to depend on a number of factors. It depends partly on the hereditary constitution of the ego, partly on the nature of the instincts against which the defense is directed. (As an example of this, I may quote the classical triad of the anal character: sense of order, parsimony, and obstinacy.) It depends partly, too, on the age at which the child experienced the instinctual conflict in question. At a certain age certain defensive mechanisms and attitudes are more in the foreground than others. In most cases, however, the analysis succeeds in showing that the special attitude was forced on the individual by the external world: either it was the most suitable attitude in a given situation, or all other possible attitudes were blocked in a given situation, or this attitude was promoted by similar modes of behavior in the child's personal environment with which the child identified itself; or else the attitude was exactly the opposite of these modes, which the child was trying *not* to assimilate. In this way the ego which develops a character of a defensive type becomes more and more rigid and unelastic, reproducing the same pattern of behavior instead of reacting individually to individual stimuli. Such an ego becomes increasingly poor and loses more and more possibilities of behavior—till analysis succeeds in reawakening the old conflicts and enabling the individual to reach a better solution.

Certainly you will not expect to find that if the analysis succeeds in remobilizing the old conflicts, the once-repressed infantile instincts will come into the open immediately. The child was once afraid of those instinctual impulses, and as a rule its anxiety was actually manifest in the form of an infantile anxiety neurosis. It took time to develop the character attitude of the defensive type with which the individual, as we have seen, escaped from subsequent repressions and anxieties. Thus we can say that in the defensive attitudes anxiety has been *bound*—and we find the proof for this in the fact that in remobilizing the old conflicts the first thing we usually see is that the patient develops more or less severe attacks of anxiety. The analysis of this anxiety which follows, however, brings the instinct in question to the surface. A layer of anxiety has been laid down between the original instinct and the ensuing defensive attitude.

This view that such character attitudes serve the purpose of binding anxiety is not contradicted by what Mrs. Deri [a psychoanalyst] has recently said when she stressed the fact that probably of all the attitudes which an individual has developed, those are selected to build up the character—i.e., to become chronic—which are suited to provide satisfactions as well, though it may be in a distorted form. This apparent contradiction can be overcome if two circumstances are borne in mind. First, the defensive attitudes which we are discussing are only one half of the characterological attitudes. There are also the attitudes of the sublimatory type. These have been as yet less inquired into. It may be that the reactive type represents more anxiety, the sub-limatory type more satisfaction. The other circumstance which we have to consider is that "satisfaction" does not necessarily only mean "satisfaction of genuine instinctual desires." There exists also a "satisfaction" in the sense of "security"; and the defensive character attitudes certainly are selected because they seem to give to the individual a maximum of security, namely, an avoidance of anxiety situations.

It must be admitted that this whole discussion of character traits as results of conflicts between instincts and the judgment that giving in to the instinct might be a danger, presupposes the existence of a psychic function of judgment or of a psychic instance which is able to experience fear. The question of how the function of judgment develops and how there is gradually estab-lished in the infant an apparatus which serves the purpose of communication between the individual and his surroundings, certainly goes beyond the subject of "character analysis." But it was undoubtedly the progress of character analysis which made it possible to see more clearly into that field as well, so that it can be said that the basic functions also of the ego—perception and action—can in principle be explained by the inner actions of outer influences and primitive biological needs. Mention must be made, however, of another complication in the structure of the so-called ego—a complication which occurs much later in life, say from the second to the seventh year of age. I refer to what is known as the "superego." The new elements which are brought into the picture by this agency are of special practical and theoretical importance for character analysis.

I am presuming that you are acquainted with the Freudian conception of the superego as the psychic agency which turns fear into a feeling of guilt. We have said that the first reason why the organism, which is interested in the satisfaction of its instincts, sometimes paradoxically turns against its instincts and tries to defend itself against them—the first reason is fear, based on the judgment that the instincts are dangerous. Some of the feared dangers are real and natural—as when the child gives in to the instinctual demand to grasp at the beautiful fire and burns itself. Some are real and artificial—as when the educating adults punish the child for certain instinctual acts, or threaten to withdraw their affection from the child when it behaves in certain ways (and the child needs this affection urgently), or promise premiums of higher supplies of affection if the child suppresses certain instincts. Others of the feared dangers are imaginary, in so far as the child judges its surroundings according to its own instincts, misunderstands the world in an animistic sense, and therefore expects more dreadful punishments than ever occur in reality. However this may be, in all cases giving in to the instincts becomes connected for the child with the idea of danger. It is a danger which threatens from without, and the executors of it are, to the child's mind, its parents. The child is afraid that its parents may either punish it bodily (the so-called "castration anxiety"), or by a withdrawal of their affection. But later on there comes a time when the child begins to act as a "good child" even when the parents, who might punish it, are not present or will certainly not become aware of its behavior. Then fear has been turned into a feeling of guilt. The parents who might punish it are now, so to say, inside the child itself; they are always present and are to be differentiated from the real parents. Those "inner parents," who watch the child, who give commands and prohibitions, but also prizes and protection—they are the superego, and their "incorporation" is a result of a long instinctual development which we cannot discuss today.

Now I think you already understand why I am talking about this point at considerable length. It has to do with "character analysis," insofar as the functions of the conscience are a very important component of the character of personality. Very characteristic for a personality are (a) what he considers good and what bad; (b) whether he takes the commands of his conscience seriously or not; (c) whether he obeys his conscience or tries to rebel against it, etc. On what does that depend? It depends, as all psychic structure does, on constitution and experience, and it is the experience part which we can investigate psychoanalytically. The structure of the superego, its strength, and the way in which the ego behaves toward its "id" depend in the first place on the actual behavior of the parents (for the superego, being the incorporation of the parents, is strict when the parents are strict). They depend in the second place on the instinctual structure of the child; and this in its turn depends on the child's mental constitu-

tion and all its previous experiences. The child who unconsciously hates his parents fears retaliation—his superego might
act toward his ego in the same way as once his ego wished to act
toward his parents. But for the most part the superego depends
directly on the models which the child had before him in his
environment and on the nature of his object relationship, the
incorporations of which are represented in his superego. You
know from the analysis of so-called criminals that in all probability the most severe deficiencies of the superego are to be
observed in persons who in their childhood had no opportunity
to develop lasting object relationships because they changed
from one more or less loveless foster home to another. But it is
not only the *content* of what is to be considered good and bad—
what the father first teaches and the superego later demands—
that is transmitted from one generation to the other through the
superego structure; it is also the *idea* of good and evil itself and
the way in which this idea is thought of in our society—it is the
authority which asks obedience and promises protection if
obedience is given—which are created through this change from
fear into feelings of guilt.

We have spoken of the neurotic conflicts as conflicts between
instincts on the one side and anxiety or guilt feelings on the other.
In our structural terminology we should say that they are conflicts between the id on the one side and its ego, or an alliance
between the ego and the superego, on the other. But sometimes
there are also conflicts between the ego and the superego. Not all
egos accept the demands of the superego without contradiction,
and rebellions which were once attempted (or not attempted)
against the parents may be continued against the superego. The
extreme case of disunion between ego and superego is given in
melancholia, where the whole weight of the personality is laid on
an extreme pathological feeling of guilt which destroys the
remainder of the personality. But you know that when the subject
has a certain degree of such a feeling of guilt he may try to prove
that it is not justified or to repress and to deny it. Many character
anomalies turn out to be attempts of the ego to defend itself
against a sense of guilt. There are personalities in whom the need
to contradict the superego is so overwhelming that it overshadows
all object relationships. They need "supplies of affection" from

everybody in the same way as they needed them as little children, using the feeling of being loved as an argument against inferiority and feelings of guilt (and anxieties) into which they fall back when they feel that those supplies are denied. This continual passive asking to be loved—and in a very primitive way, asking to be loved by everybody, without evolving any real relationship to real objects, this being a regression into the ways in which the little child used to center regulation of its conflicts round its self-regard—this asking for love may either be a defense of the ego against the strong superego ("when I am loved, I cannot be as bad as that, after all"), or it may be a deficiency in the development of the superego, in the sense that the individual still is more governed by outer anxiety than by guilt feelings. Such a deficiency of supplies of affection blocks all real object relationships; and it also forms the basis for manifold secondary conflicts. The most characteristic of these is the conflict between the tendency to get by force the supplies which are denied and the tendency to repress every aggression, because the aggressed person might refuse all supplies.

I have repeatedly used the term "real object relationship," but we have not yet discussed what that means.

Love and hatred have a long history of development, and in every phase of this development disturbances may occur which are then reflected in the subject's character. The considerateness for the object which characterizes love is not present from the beginning. The infant's "love" consists only in taking and not in giving; he acknowledges the objects insofar as he needs them for his satisfaction, and when this satisfaction is attained they may disappear. The subject's first experiences in this respect, the way in which he got or did not get his satisfactions as a very small child, may be decisive for his later attitudes toward his objects. His general optimism or pessimism, his relationship to "getting," his capacity or incapacity for being patient, the dependence of his self-regard upon outer supplies, or its independence of them—all this may be determined by his earliest infantile experiences with objects. Later, in the so-called anal period, he is more obliged to take the objects and their demands into consideration. The training in cleanliness is the first occasion on which he has to give up primitive erotogenic pleasure for another

person's sake, or rather, for the sake of getting the affection which
he needs from his mother. Psychoanalytic characterology has
especially studied the different ways in which those conflicts
influence the later attitudes of the ego. Certainly here are the first
social conflicts, whose specific nature has a formative force. But it
would be an error to assume that it may be more or less a matter
of chance that those social conflicts cover the anal phase. What we
have learned is that it is precisely the anal instincts which, under
the influence of these so-called social conflicts, change their aim
or object, thus becoming incorporated into the ego. The "anal
character traits" have developed, instead of anal–erotic instincts.
It is not a "modern alchemy" that instincts may be turned into
ego attitudes, as a critical author stated a short time ago. It is a
clinical fact which can be observed again and again; and it is proved
by the experience that an analysis of the conflicts which resulted
in the development of defensive ego attitudes turns them back,
after the interposition of overwhelming anxieties, into the original
instincts once more.

The same is true for the relation between so-called "orality"
and dependence. Their connection is not an accident but an
essential one. Man is a mammal, and the human infant is born
still more helpless than other mammals and requires feeding and
care on the part of adults so that he shall not die. This undoubtedly
provides a biological instinctual basis for the fact that every
human being has a remote recollection that there were once
powerful or, as it must seem to him, omnipotent beings on whose
help, comfort, and protection he could depend in time of need.
Later the ego learns to become independent and active and to use
active means to master the world by itself. But the possibility of a
"passive oral attitude" remains as a relic of infancy. Often
enough the adult person gets into situations in which he is as
helpless once again as he was as a child. Sometimes the forces of
nature are responsible, more often social forces which have been
created by people. Then he longs for just such omnipotent protection and comfort as was at his disposal as a child. He regresses,
as we are used to saying and as we can prove by observing his
instinctual behavior, to orality. There are many social institutions which make use of this biologically predetermined longing.
To be sure, none of them promises the longed-for help without

expecting some return. The conditions that they make vary greatly in different cultures. But all of them combine the promise of comfort and help with ethical conditions. The formula "if you obey me, I will protect you" is one which all gods have in common with all earthly authorities. It is true that there are great differences between the idea of an almighty god or of a modern employer on the one side and the mother who feeds her child on the other: nevertheless it is the similarity between them, it is the instinctual bond between child and mother, which explains to us the psychological effectiveness of authority. It has been said that a man's character is formed by the social institutions in which he lives. The psychoanalytical instinct psychology does not contradict this statement in the least. On the contrary, it is psychoanalysis which makes it possible to understand how the social institutions work in detail in forming the characters of the individuals who live under their rule. The instincts are interposed between the institutions and the changes of the personalities. It is clear that the individual's character, which is the result of infantile instinctual conflicts, must depend upon the content and intensity of prohibitions and encouragements which the different instincts get in different social institutions. Actually, we see that various cultures produce various character formations.

But we must return from sociology to psychoanalytic practice. What are the basic consequences of what we have been discussing for psychoanalytic practice? It is clear that all mere talking about unconscious instincts or about reconstructions of the historical past of the patient cannot change anything, as long as the energies of those old conflicts, to liberate which is the aim of psychoanalysis, are bound in certain more or less pathological character attitudes. Where there are rigid attitudes instead of living conflicts, the latter must be remobilized. For that purpose it is necessary first to make the patient aware of the peculiarity of his behavior when he is not aware of it spontaneously. When the patient is aware of what he does, he has to become aware of the fact that he is forced to do so, that he cannot do otherwise; then he will understand that it is an anxiety which makes other behavior impossible, and that he needs the behavior in question for purposes of defense. He will learn to understand historically why these defenses were obliged to assume the form they have, and eventually what it is he is afraid of. If the mobilization succeeds he will experience anxiety; and later on, instead of the rigid and frozen attitude, there will appear once again the instinctual impulses in question, the old full emotions. I have shown elsewhere in detail that and how this procedure can be described by the formulas: we change character neuroses into symptom neuroses, and we change character resistances into living transference resistances, in order to handle them afterward as ordinary symptom neuroses and transference resistances are handled. The aim of this mobilization is the reduction of the ego attitudes to those historical situations in which they were originally formed. A special problem is the investigation of this historical situation and the so-called "defense transference"—the fact that the patient seems to "transfer" to his relation to the analyst not only his past instinctual demands but also the past situations in which he developed one particular form of defense. But the explanation of this fact is not very difficult. The character defenses in general have been developed precisely for the purpose of being applied again and again in every similar situation. The patients behave as if they were careful to make continuous application of a method which had previously proved useful against the danger, just as though they never could know when a similar danger might not reappear. What the patient is really striving for unconsciously is certainly the pleasure of instinctual satisfaction. But his past experiences (real or imaginary) force the ego to produce in every situation of temptation memories which once aroused anxiety, and against those memories the same defensive patterns have to be developed over again.

The next question is whether there are any analyses at all which are not "character analyses." And perhaps in a very strict sense there are no such analyses. A certain part of the energies which are bound in useless defensive conflicts and have to be put at the disposal of the individual once again, is always bound in certain defensive attitudes. But undoubtedly there is a difference of degree between real "character analyses" and "symptom analyses."

I should now like to attempt to illustrate by a few examples the historical genesis of character defenses and their treatment. But this is not an easy task. To demonstrate what is really meant, long case histories would be needed, for which the time is lacking. I must limit myself to relating the chief features of two cases which certainly do not offer any very special characteristics. Similar features can be found in every analysis. And since the cases are rare in which the historical circumstances that necessitated certain attitudes are easily and microscopically understandable, you will excuse me if I use examples which I have once published in a similar connection. I hope that you have not read the paper in question.

The first patient I am going to describe could be called "a Don Juan of achievement." A successful and, in his own line, prominent man, he was in fact always dissatisfied with himself, always striving after higher achievements, with external success, but no sense of inward satisfaction. In a like manner, he was always trying to increase his quite adequate income and was unable to overcome his fear that it might be insufficient. He behaved in the same way in his love life: although women ran after him and he had one success after another, he always felt inwardly dissatisfied—which is understandable, since those relationships were completely lacking in tenderness and had none of the characteristics of a real object relationship. It is clear that the man was so dominated by an overwhelming narcissistic necessity that the libidinal aims of his instincts were completely overshadowed. The man was married to a woman considerably older than himself, who, in some ways, behaved toward him as a mother does to her child; she acted, that is, in many ways as a guardian to him, so that at home he, the big, successful man, was more like a little child. He found this dependence very oppressive, it is true, and was in the habit of revenging himself on his wife by attacks of rage, and by continual unfaithfulness, and by complete lack of consideration. Thus each of them made life a torment to the other. The first defensive function of his persistently unsatisfied wish to be a great man must therefore have been to deceive himself with regard to the fact that he was a little child in so many ways—one of which was his complete lack of consideration for the person who mothered him. This impression is strengthened by the knowledge that his wife was continually goading his ambition, just as his mother was in his childhood. The realization that there was something behind his continued dissatisfaction, which persisted despite all his external successes, and the truth of which he did not wish to admit, was gained in transference analysis. As in every other province, he was very ambitious in analysis and wanted to impress both me and himself by his quick success. At the outset, after he had read Freud, he was forthcoming with theories about his childhood; he grasped comparatively quickly, however, that this was not what mattered to me, and then began to observe himself and his behavior, and to behave like a "favorite pupil," continually stressing, however, the fact that the analysis progressed too slowly and that he was not satisfied with himself. On one occasion, at the last session before the holidays, he came late, because, just as he was starting for his analysis, he had a sudden attack of diarrhea, and this for the first time shook him very much. The bowels putting in their say made him experience the reality of the analysis in an entirely new way. He realized that his continual haste only served the purpose of drowning something else in him. The analysis explained this richly overdetermined diarrhea in the first place as an anxiety equivalent; it then brought this at first incomprehensible anxiety into relation with his fear of insufficient success, insufficient sexual objects, and insufficient earnings. It was then discovered that the character formation of the patient had been complete in childhood. He had always been go-ahead, cheeky, outwardly successful; he had always been the first, even in being naughty, but had, nevertheless, always been dissatisfied with himself. In this behavior he had obeyed his mother, who had always been very ambitious for her son and had always urged him on to further deeds. When it appeared that, at bottom, his mother had despised his father, who was a tradesman, and had always said to the boy, "You must be better than your father," etc., it became clear that his behavior expressed a particular form of the return of the oedipus complex from repression; it was not yet intelligible, however, why it had taken this form—why it had this essentially narcissistic note. Various things soon became more obvious, however: his father had illegally sold certain goods, the sale of which was only permitted by special concession; the policeman, therefore, was a dreaded figure in the patient's childhood. In the eyes of the boy, this considerably reduced the power of the father; he determined not to be frightened when he was big, but to make policemen afraid of him. (He remained faithful to this intention: as a motorist he loved to get policemen to intervene unjustifiably, and then afterward prove them to be in the wrong.) The circumstances in his home, moreover, were such that at times he had to stand behind the counter and serve when he was six years old. The customers liked the little boy and chose to buy from him; he felt this to be a triumph over his father, whom he already regarded as weak.

There were also two later experiences which particularly accentuated both the patient's continuous need to show his superiority in some such way and the impossibility of satisfying that need. The first experience was that when he was fourteen he was seduced by a maid, with whom he had regular sexual intercourse from that time on. This episode had been changed in memory to make it appear that it was he who had, at this age, seduced the grown-up girl. It needed analysis to convince him that it had happened the other way round, and that the whole of his later attitude to women was an attempt to alter this to him painful memory, in accordance with his wishes. This attempt, by the way, failed in a typical manner: he intended that the large number of women whom he persuaded to have intercourse with him should convince him of his active masculinity, which he unconsciously doubted; more detailed analysis, however, showed that he arranged things so that he seduced the women into showing their willingness, and that it was only when he saw this that he was not able to resist them. The second experience was that at seventeen he had an abscess on the lung for which he was operated on several times and which kept him in bed for months and convalescent for years—so that he had to be passively nursed like a little child.

The patient gradually became afraid of the transference in analysis, afraid that he might become "enslaved" to the analyst. His transference attitude was intended from the beginning to repudiate this anxiety. He attempted, even then, to disparage the analyst and to find "policemen" who were superior to him. What he expected with fear then turned out to have been true: the six-year old salesman could not feel completely superior to his grown-up father in the role of tradesman. His father, who used to beat him a great deal, had been greatly feared by him in earlier years. His relation to him had completely overshadowed his relation with his mother and, in consequence, his being needed by his father for business purposes had an additional libidinal value. The passive-narcissistic attitude was suggested to him in his early childhood by particular circumstances including, among others, illness, strict prohibition against masturbation, which put an end to his early phallic attempts, and the strictness of his father who beat him. It was, however, owing to the same set of circumstances that he feared this attitude. In this conflict, his mother's ambition, the disadvantageous comparison of his dreaded father with the policemen, and with his own successes as a salesman showed him a way out: by a continuous outward fight against his passive–narcissistic attitude, he was able to retain it at other points. The seduction by the maid and his illness after puberty then fixated these latter defensive attitudes in his character.

Another patient, a woman, was characterized by the haste with which she always undertook every more or less indifferent enterprise. She was physically, as well as mentally, always in a state of tension, always occupied with tomorrow, never living in the present. This continual activity of the ego remained on the surface to an amazing extent. Her associations spread in every direction without ever getting any deeper. Her interests and occupations also bore the stamp of a superficiality which did not correspond to her intelligence and talents. She avoided everything which had a "serious" character. In describing her experiences she expressed a peculiar sense of inferiority: "Nothing that happens to me can be serious or real." The activity, restlessness, and continual worry about what would happen tomorrow served the purpose of forestalling any serious experience which might happen, by means of her own, superficial, ego-determined, i.e., play-like activity. This patient was passionately in love with a man. She could not leave him, although serious conflicts were aroused in her as a consequence. In all her anxiety and trouble, and in particular, at the beginning of a depression, she escaped— in the same way as a drug addict escapes by means of his drug— with the help of real or imagined experiences with this man. It soon became clear that it was not real love that drove her to him, but that he satisfied narcissistic necessities whose fulfillment repelled anxiety or depression. However, it was not clear in what way he did this. Only gradually did we realize that the chief quality of this man—and in this he was the diametrical opposite of the patient's husband—was apparently that he was humorous, frivolous, and witty, and never called things by their right names. What the patient really wanted from him was the reassurance: "I need not be afraid of sexuality, it's only fun." In a first analysis the patient had from the very beginning developed the resistance of not speaking, and no progress was made. Only later did we understand that this had happened because the analysis was "serious" and that its aim was to call things by their right names, which the patient wished to avoid at all costs. The analysis with me, on the contrary, appeared to make very rapid progress. It took us a long time to understand that this progress was only apparent and was the result of a particular resistance. I had, by chance, laughed at some remarks which the patient had made during her first sessions. This enabled her to work "in isolation." What she had with me was a "fun-analysis" (in the same way that she enjoyed "fun-sexuality") without the analysis really attacking her anxieties about her real instinctual life. When a child experiences something that shakes it deeply, or when it is afraid of some occurrence, it "plays" this occurrence afterwards. It forestalls in its fantasy what is expected, or repeats the past occurrence, so changing its own passive role into an active one, in order to practice mastering the dreaded tensions with the reduced quantities which it measures out for itself. Our patient had apparently begun this process but never ended it. Her anxiety was too great for her to make the step from playing to reality. Just as another patient continually said to herself, out of fear of reality: "It is only an imaginary story and not true," so this one said: "It is only a game and not serious." The analysis showed that the "serious" sexuality had acquired its frightening character as the result of a sadistic component aroused by the birth of a younger brother at the end of the patient's fourth year. This had evoked unconscious anxiety that, if she gave in to her real impulses, she would tear the penis from men and the child from women. It is interesting to note that the escape into "playing" which was suggested to her by various circumstances in the external world was due, among other things, to a particular incident in the nursing of this younger brother. An elder sister had suggested to the patient that she should push over the perambulator and so get rid of the intruder. From that time on the patient was very much frightened of touching her little brother, particularly after she had once noticed how her mother and the nurse had laughed over the little boy as he was micturating. Her mother, had persuaded her out of this aversion to touching him by saying: "Take him in your arms; I'm standing here; you're only playing at being his mother; you're not really his mother."

Section II
THEORETICAL CONSIDERATIONS AND CONTROVERSIES

Character, a concept claimed by astrology, religion, literature, and science over its two-thousand-or-so-year history, is a "soft" concept which has changed substantially over time. Given its complexity, offering a comprehensive theory is no easy task. The articles in this section explore difficulties, confusions, and controversies, as well as presenting clarifications to further psychoanalytic investigation.

Stein turns up several obstacles to the development of a sophisticated psychoanalytic theory of character ranging from the confusion between character traits and neurotic symptoms to the operation of denial in the analyst. For example, one problem relates to implicit or manifest value judgments, often prejudicial, which interfere with objective description, evaluation, and confrontation. Other factors derive from the lack of an agreed-upon theory of aggression and the limitations of the analytic setting. These difficulties notwithstanding, he posits the overriding strength and primacy of psychoanalysis as the scientific discipline best suited to deal with the subject.

Baudry's paper is a far-reaching attempt to define the perimeters and content of character and its relevance to psychoanalysis. The result is a wealth of thought-provoking ideas on the subject. He first looks at problems concerning the varying definitions of, and levels of abstraction about, the behavior underlying described character traits. He explores contextual matters and issues of subjectivity, as well as the question of overlapping concepts such as symptom, mood, and style. He cites a number of psychoanalytic definitions and identifies the criteria for rendering the concept of character psychoanalytic. Using Waelder's principle of multiple function (1936), he looks at

129

the libidinal and defensive object relational aspects of character and others as well. Problems of classification are tackled; normal as opposed to abnormal character is discussed. The last part of his article deals with the clinical relevance and applicability of the concept, the difficulty in confronting character (expanding on Stein as above), and, finally, the key question concerning the ability of psychoanalysis to change character.

Whereas Baudry talks of a concept without an identity, Schafer introduces character as a concept without a home. He criticizes the metapsychological conceptualization of character and proceeds to place it in his "action language" alternative linking the concept to the "person as a unitary agent." Character is the name given to the particular manner in which a person organizes his or her actions. Looking at character in this way brings it closer to observable clinical experience and data, contrary to using "confining and austere" metapsychological concepts.

Pivotal to interpretive handling of character is its quality of "ego-syntonicity": the existence of a closed personal system of self-confirming principles for constructing experience. Analyzability requires not only the presence of some diversity among these organizing principles within the individual, but also the presence of some neutral, rational experiential beliefs enabling dialogue and self-scrutiny. Analysis involves the questioning of the ways of unconsciously constructing conflictual situations which can be expected and consideration of more beneficial ways of acting.

Sandler addresses an aspect of character traits beyond "discharge/defense" and adaptation. He employs an object-relations perspective. He points out that character traits are not only the expression of instinctual wishes, defensive reactions, or combinations of the two, but also forms of communication which seek to evoke or actualize wished-for responses from present-day representatives of significant object-relationships of the past. The wish is, above all, to obtain reassurance, affirmation, and well-being. This type of evocation also involves a dialogue in an unconsciously created and perceived illusory world, man living both in a real external world and a phantom world of unconsciously perceived objects.

Thus far we have been talking about character in general.

The next two papers look at the classification of character disorders, the first when psychoanalysis was in its heyday with respect to psychiatry and the second when the pendulum had begun to swing in the other direction.

Menninger, strongly influenced by Abraham, Fenichel, and Waelder, studies and classifies character disorders in terms of disharmony between the adjustment of the id, ego, and superego and reality. He relates the disorders to infantile sexual fixations and reflects on the nature of psychotic and neurotic characters.

Thirty years later, Kernberg integrates the major psychoanalytic advances in theory (structural, ego psychology, and Kleinian object relations) to provide an alternative method for classifying character pathology. He distinguishes in some detail three levels of severity according to the attained level of structural and internalized object relations development. Particular attention is paid to the most severe level—that of the borderline personality. Kernberg reviews his elsewhere described model of the development of the psychic apparatus and concludes by stressing the importance of using structural as well as descriptive classifications (for diagnostic, prognostic, and therapeutic reasons).

Chapter 8

THE PROBLEM OF CHARACTER THEORY

Martin H. Stein

"[T]he processes of the formation of character are more obscure and less accessible to analysis than neurotic ones" (Freud, 1913a, p. 323).

Sixty years ago, the theory of symptom formation reached a stage of elegance and inclusiveness which has so far been surpassed by no other clinical theory in our field. In an eight-page paper with the deceptive title, "Hysterical Phantasies and Their Relation to Bisexuality" (1908), Freud summarized what he had discovered up to that point, and managed to anticipate most of what was to be written of symptom formation during the succeeding sixty years. His introduction to the section which embodies his ideas is worth quoting:

> For the sake of general interest I will at this point go outside the framework of this paper and interpolate a series of formulas which attempt to give a progressively fuller description of the nature of hysterical symptoms. These formulas do not contradict one another, but some represent an increasingly complete and precise approach to the facts, while others represent the application of different points of view:
>
> (1) Hysterical symptoms are mnemic symbols of certain operative (traumatic) impressions and experiences.
>
> (2) Hysterical symptoms are substitutes, produced by 'conversions', for the associative return of these traumatic experiences.
>
> (3) Hysterical symptoms are—like other psychical structures—an expression of the fulfilment of a wish.

This chapter originally appeared in longer form in the *Journal of the American Psychoanalytic Association,* 17:675–701, 1968. Reprinted by permission of the author and the publisher.

(4) Hysterical symptoms are the realization of an unconscious phantasy which serves the fulfilment of a wish.

(5) Hysterical symptoms serve the purpose of sexual satisfaction and represent a portion of the subject's sexual life (a portion which corresponds to one of the constituents of his sexual instinct).

(6) Hysterical symptoms correspond to a return of a mode of sexual satisfaction which was a real one in infantile life and has since been repressed.

(7) Hysterical symptoms arise as a compromise between two opposite affective and instinctual impulses, of which one is attempting to bring to expression a component instinct or constituent of the sexual constitution, and the other is attempting to suppress it.

(8) Hysterical symptoms may take over the representation of various unconscious impulses which are not sexual, but they can never be without a sexual significance. . . .

(9) Hysterical symptoms are the expression on the one hand of a masculine unconscious sexual phantasy, and on the other hand of a feminine one [pp. 163–165].

In these nine formulas we may recognize not only the foreshadowing of ego psychology, but even more clearly the expression of a radically new and unique psychoanalytic approach.

The symptom is seen not simply as the manifestation of a sexual drive, nor of the defenses against that drive, nor even of that conflict by itself, essential though each aspect may be. A psychological phenomenon is now to be regarded as having been determined by multiple factors and as representing multiple meanings. This antireductive, antisimplistic point of view was later elaborated by Waelder (1936) under the title "The Principle of Multiple Function." It has been of the greatest importance in psychoanalytic theory generally, especially so in our efforts to understand behavior and character.[1]

Most of what was written later on the theory of symptom formation grew out of the principles expressed in this brief paper of Freud's along with those ideas which had already been suggested

---

[1] It is unfortunately too often ignored or glossed over in attempts, critical or otherwise, to make psychoanalytic theory readily accessible by oversimplification.

in *The Interpretation of Dreams* (1900) and the Dora case (1905b). The theory was readily expanded to cover the other symptom neuroses, without fundamental modifications.

Excellent as it was, it did leave some crucial questions unanswered. The most conspicuous of these, perhaps, was that of why in response to a given set of stimuli, one person developed a hysterical paralysis while another developed a phobia or compulsion. It was clear that the patients who developed these different symptoms had been quite different from one another before, in that aspect of the personality which we denote as character.[2]

It was altogether consistent with Freud's own character that within two months of his 1908 publication of "Hysterical Phantasies and Their Relation to Bisexuality," he had published another paper of crucial importance, only seven pages long, entitled "Character and Anal Erotism" [see chapter 1]. It ended with the statement: "We can at any rate lay down a formula for the way in which character in its final shape is formed out of the constituent instincts: the permanent character-traits are either unchanged prolongations of the original instincts, or sublimations of those instincts, or reaction-formations against them" [pp. 39–40].

This was a brilliant condensation, but one hardly to be compared with those of the preceding paper. A theory of character formation, apparently, was not to be so fully developed, nor to possess the remarkable inclusiveness and elegance which had marked the theory of symptom formation. Later advances in psychoanalysis, especially ego psychology, the principle of multiple function, and child analysis, have furnished us with means which should have been adequate. But we are still lacking a comparable, well-formulated and cohesive theory of how the character of the individual becomes what it is, and how it may be understood in psychoanalytic terms.

It is my intention today to question why this is so, and to indicate some steps which may be taken to evolve a theory of

[2]Nunberg put it differently in 1956a, thus: "Why conflict is resolved, at one time, by the formation of character traits and, at another, merely appeased by symptom formation, is still unknown" (p. 45).

character comparable in elegance and scope to the theory of symptom formation. I am far more optimistic about the former task, for it is generally easier to understand difficulties than to offer solutions. But we are accustomed to proceed on the assumption that the first is half the battle.

As a beginning, let us look at the concept "character" itself. It seems to be of an order of abstraction somewhat different from the concept "symptom." Yet we should be able to treat it descriptively as a thing or set of things which can be determined through observation of the subject, with a minimum number of inferential steps between sensory perception and conclusion, the latter including some type of systematic classification.[3] We should not limit ourselves to a purely descriptive approach, but we must start somewhere; and it would seem that we have gotten into difficulties by our failure to develop a satisfactory method for recording, evaluating, and interpreting what we have observed. I suggest that the first difficulty is encountered in our attempts to observe, collect, and classify our facts in a useful way. I shall, after discussing character in general terms, illustrate this problem by using a special case: the study of differences in character related to sexual identity. I shall then go on to describe other obstacles which have impeded our efforts to develop a comprehensive and general theory of character development.

The general concept of character which I shall use here is multifaceted and takes into account all of the elements of the mental apparatus, emphasizing now one, now another, according to context. It is fluid, based essentially upon the observation of "behavior" in the broadest sense. In practice, it seems feasible to define it empirically and inductively; that is, to consider a wide range of data composing those patterns of thought, affect, and behavior which are stable and have become the "mark" of the individual. The term *character* itself, derived from the Greek verbal root meaning "to sharpen, engrave, carve," connotes

[3] I am here indebted to Waelder's (1962) very useful suggestions for grading psychoanalytic statements according to the "degree of relevance," or more strictly according to the level of abstraction; for example, observation, clinical interpretation, clinical generalizations, clinical theory, metapsychology, (Freud's) philosophy (pp. 619-620).

Most of the data discussed in the next few pages will be confined to the "lower" levels of abstraction; that is, those which require fewer inferential steps than metapsychology, for example.

both its stability and its capacity to denote the individuality of its possessor.

For the sake of making certain points, I shall treat character traits and neurotic symptoms antithetically, as if one could draw a sharp line between them. I do regard them as different and generally distinguishable in practice. Character traits and symptoms are connected, it is true, may even merge with one another, and we can trace many lines of influence between them, flowing in both directions. But it is easier to begin as if this were not so, in order to emphasize the contrast, rather than the similarity.[4] While certain chronic neurotic symptoms, such as the phobias or compulsions, may eventually acquire considerable stability and may even stigmatize their possessor, this is not an essential or even a usual feature of symptom formation.

The patient's attitude toward a character trait, too, is quite different from that with which he regards a neurotic symptom. The former is rarely a part of the chief complaint, although some of its undesirable *effects* may be. One complains infrequently of a character trait, such as belligerence, for example, unless it has gotten him into trouble with his environment. Character traits are often taken for granted, therefore, and may not even be noticed by their possessor, although they may be conspicuous enough to his friends and enemies.

The symptom, on the contrary, is generally a matter for complaint by the patient, although it may be entirely concealed from others. It is not taken for granted by the sufferer unless mild, or masked by a counterphobic reaction. It is far more often regarded as if it were a kind of foreign body, which could be thrust out if the operation were not too painful.

Third, character traits do not occupy a single, well-defined sector on the continuum from adaptive to maladaptive. They need not be pathological from any point of view. Symptoms, on the contrary, are pathological by their very essence and, if adaptive to reality in a degree, are so only by virtue of some secondary gain. To be a little hysterical is common enough, perhaps univer-

---

[4]In this I am in agreement with Stone (as reported by Ross, 1960), who stated succinctly: "In any event, it is important to preserve the distinction between symptom and character trait. The term 'character' should be reserved for general, relatively stable, ego-syntonic modes of reaction and adaptation to inner and outer demands" (p. 550).

sal in some degree; but it cannot be regarded as optimal or healthy. Character traits, however, have no fixed position on the scale; whether they are to be considered desirable or undesirable, pathological or healthy, is a much more difficult decision. So much depends on the intensity and rigidity of a trait. A character trait such as enthusiasm may be thought of as entirely consistent with ideal mental health; if it appears too regularly or with great intensity, it may come to be regarded as a defect.

Then too, in our view of personality, character traits are seen in a role essentially different from that played by symptoms. We can imagine a man without neurotic symptoms, even though we don't know one. But it is not possible for us to conceive of a man without character traits. The apparent absence of distinct stable qualities is in itself a character trait—and a disconcerting one.[5]

One group of reactions, the counterphobic, falls somewhere between the classes of symptoms and character traits, in general closer to the latter. Even though they have close dynamic and genetic connections with the phobias, and are often regarded as if they were simple defenses against them, they are in fact far more complicated. Their equivocal relation to normality and pathology, their occasional adaptive value, and their interaction with the external world give counterphobic reactions much more in common with character traits. At least we may save ourselves the trouble of attempting to distinguish between rashness and counterphobia on structural grounds, for the decision depends to a great degree on the context in which the phenomenon is observed. But an exhaustive consideration of character traits as defenses against symptoms, and symptoms as expressions of character traits, would go far beyond the present scope of this paper.[6]

Finally, there is a difference in the way we look at symptoms and character traits in the context of the analytic situation. The symptom may be regarded as if it had occurred in a closed system, bounded by the personality of the patient, and we are inclined to analyze it as the manifestation of a process which goes

[5]An interesting novelistic attempt is Musil's *The Man Without Qualities*. The protagonist is as much a "character" as Oblomov or Tom Jones.

[6]Arlow (1968) has dealt with this subject very well in a paper in which he described the relation of specific character traits to defenses against perverse drive derivatives.

on within fairly narrow boundaries. "External realities," the physical environment, the culture, are recognized as important, but may, to an extent, be treated as if they were shadows. Our interest in those people who are currently important in the life of the patient is focused on what they represent of the past and to a degree on the gratifications or frustrations they represent. Culture, while recognized as ever-present, is nevertheless treated as if it were a historical influence, and the physical environment may be regarded for the moment as a contaminant. In the analytic session we attempt to create a laboratory in which these "outside" influences are understood and taken into account, but in which they can be temporarily attenuated for the purpose of the analytic work. It requires a kind of selective attention by analyst and patient alike.

This has proved a highly satisfactory method for studying the inter- and intrasystemic conflicts and compromises which contribute to symptom formation. Even though we know the closed system is a fiction, this convention has proved its value in studying neurotic symptoms. To analyze character traits, however, we are required to view matters more broadly, and even to place special emphasis on understanding the field against which the subject is viewed. A trait such as belligerence, for example, may look quite different if we are treating a pugilist or a diplomat. And our estimate would again vary, depending on whether the former were fighting in a professional bout or merely driving his car.

We must therefore employ a model which is much more open than that which has proved so useful in the description and analysis of symptoms. To study character traits requires a considerable understanding of the world in which the individual lives: not only the people, but the physical environment and the culture, which have molded him, permitted or prohibited certain behavior and even thought, and which currently stimulate, gratify, frustrate—and, in turn, are affected more or less profoundly by his actions. In this sense the character trait bears a relation to the external world different from that of the neurotic symptom.[7]

[7]For a psychoanalytic statement of the influence of sociocultural determinants of character see, naturally, Freud (1930) and Muensterberger (1969).

I have not emphasized that view of character which regards it as an "organizing principle," a ready-made mold for the resolution of internal conflicts with a minimum of energy loss, and therefore a necessity for adaptation. This concept is of a different order than the essentially descriptive elements I have outlined. It is expressed in teleological language, and leads to a definition of character in terms of what it is expected to do, rather than in terms of what it is, bringing it even more exclusively into the domain of ego function. It is a second step, rather than a first, in approaching the problem.

Briefly then, symptoms denote modes of suffering, character traits modes of behavior. It is this fact which makes the understanding of character a matter of urgent concern, whether we consider the behavior of individuals or that of groups within society.

There seems to be a universal tendency to think about character in moralistic terms, such as *strong, weak, good, bad, reliable, unreliable,* words which are used so often in popular writing and discussion, and are not entirely absent from professional discourse. It is reasonable to suggest that attitudes toward character are marked by a heavy emphasis on superego as opposed to ego functions.

This was true, as we have seen, of Freud's writings on feminine character, at least. He wrote a great deal about the conscience and ideals of women, relatively little about their judgment and learning capacity. This was not quite so true, in an explicit sense, of the writings of W. Reich; but reading his penetrating study "On Character Analysis" (1928) [see chapter 5] gives the impression that he regarded the characterological defenses of his patients as culprits to be outwitted and beaten down. Fenichel (1945), while not explicitly moralistic, still divided character types into "sublimation" and "reactive" types; in other words, "desirable" and "undesirable." His emphasis on the superego as "decisive in forming the habitual patterns of character" (p. 468) is consistent with this way of thought.

Neurotic symptoms do not seem to evoke quite so much moralizing. For one thing, we regard them as undesirable manifestations of illness, not morally "bad." This attitude allows us to maintain a high degree of objectivity, while we and the patient take a little distance and use our energies for understanding the drives, defenses, and conflicts which produce the suffering of the neurotic patient.

We find it more difficult to achieve such an attitude when treating character, for here we are faced not so much with personal suffering as with behavior. Since character traits are egosyntonic, accepted by the patient as part of himself, we meet with far less initial cooperation in our efforts to achieve and maintain the analytic situation, and we must persuade the patient to look critically at elements which he has always regarded not as foreign bodies, but as the very core of his identity. He may even be proud of those very traits which contribute most to his misery.

Technically, we know how easy it may be to point out a symptom, and how likely it is that this confrontation will be received with good grace. But if we dare to draw the patient's attention to some idiosyncratic bit of behavior, we must be prepared to be met with the accusation that we are attacking and humiliating him. While we may have made every effort to eliminate value judgments from our remarks, the patient is very likely to react as if we had scolded him rather than interpreted his behavior. This is very often the result of projection on his part; but all too often he is at least partly correct, having detected in voice or manner a note of disapprobation on our part (Stein, 1965).

It is more difficult, then, to maintain analytic detachment about behavior. For one thing, it may have direct effects on us as well as on the patient's family and friends. When he expresses his anxiety by an increase in the severity of his phobia, for example, he suffers chiefly by himself (although it is likely to trouble us to some extent). But when he expresses himself in provocative behavior, in and outside the session, he makes us suffer as well, and it is difficult to control our initial tendency to react with disapproval.

Yet we must exert such control in order to analyze, and do so without the degree of conflict which would interfere with our efforts to understand and help. With a patient who has come to us for help, and whom we have learned to know and understand, it is usually possible to accomplish this.

Theory building, the construction of valid and useful generalities, is another matter, being much more difficult than clinical interpretation. Once outside the analytic situation, which protects us as well as the patient, a good deal of our fair-mindedness is likely to be lost under the pressure of anxiety and prejudice. We are not so successful then in maintaining the analytic stance of interested objectivity, and our ubiquitous human failings interfere with our judgment, often seriously, in dealing with so sensitive a subject as human character. We must therefore add to our list a second obstacle which may be most conveniently included under the heading of prejudice.

There is yet a third: the lack of an agreed-upon theory of aggression. The theory of symptom formation rested, as we have seen, on a foundation of libido theory, elaborated to include defense and internal conflict; but this has not sufficed for a theory of character formation. For the latter, we must understand the working of the aggressive drive to a degree not achieved up to now. Aggression and action are two aspects of the same problem; without understanding one, the other remains a mystery.

It is not that the theory of aggression has lacked attention in psychoanalytic writings. But there is nothing in this field to match the *Three Essays on the Theory of Sexuality* (Freud, 1905a) and the extensive elaborations which followed it. With all of the con-tributions of Melanie Klein (1933, 1934, 1945), Hartmann, Kris, and Loewenstein (1949), Bak (1954, 1956), Schur (1966), Brenner (1968), Stone (1968), and a host of others we still have nothing to match the organizing power of libido theory with its specific phases, fixation points, and regressive pathways. It has been attacked on many grounds, biological and behavioral, but so far the theory of the libido has maintained itself as a good working basis for clinical theory. The same cannot be said for the theory of aggression.

Meanwhile our knowledge of the *development* of the ego, as opposed to knowledge of its functions, remains a matter for con-siderable dispute. We have still failed to reach substantial agree-ment on its origins, on the identification of specific phases and paths of regression; this in spite of extremely valuable con-tributions by Anna Freud (1936), Hartmann (1939, 1950), Glover (1968), and others. I suspect that this problem will be solved only when we have established a theory of aggression which is com-parable to that of the libido.

Our fourth obstacle is inherent in the analytic setting itself and in essence is a technical one. I have on other occasions drawn attention to limitations in the analyst's access to knowledge of behavior (Stein, 1965, 1967), and will summarize them only briefly now.

Observation of behavior in the analytic setting is subject to considerable distortion resulting from regression induced by the analysis itself, character being fragmented and manifested in archaic forms. We are likely, for example, to be impressed with the derivatives of polymorphous-perverse elements rather than with those related to genitality, the latter being deemphasized for the time, at least. The same might be said of all character traits on direct view in the analysis: analytic observation is weighted in favor of the archaic.

We see the patient over a long period, it is true, but for only a few hours a week and in an atmosphere which is quite special and may easily become a bit precious. It is hardly to be expected that his behavior in analysis would do more than reflect the general pattern of his activity, subject to considerable distortion. He begins with the necessity for making a certain impression; later, as regression in its various aspects is permitted to occur, his behavior reflects previous phases, manifested by hidden urges and secret fantasies. He becomes more and more the child and the dreamer alternating, often briefly, with the wide-awake, scientific observer (Stein, 1965).

All of this has occurred during the analytic session; for the rest of the day the patient is likely to be his usual self, an amalgam of such diverse character traits and capacities, along with others we may not at first even suspect, and which are far better integrated. These may be less conflict-laden and demonstrate the influence of the autonomous ego to a much greater extent. Our patient now responds to demands and operates under conditions quite different from those of the analytic session, and were we to meet him elsewhere, we might hardly know him. Occasionally it happens that we do, and we are surprised to find a competent and urbane adult instead of the anxious, childlike person who occupied the couch a few hours before. With some patients, even as they leave the office, we observe an abrupt change from sullen negativism to bright good humor, as if they became different people at that very moment; as, in a sense, they do.

We must remind ourselves accordingly that we do not observe the whole man during the brief period of our session with him. On the one hand, we hear him describe his efficient and successful activities in a highly complex business or profession, while he behaves with us so often as if he were passive, helpless, and childlike. Or the contrary may occur, somewhat less often in the neurotic patient: during the session he is highly intelligent and apparently reasonable, yet we may become aware that he conducts most of his life's activities impulsively and without much rational control. He talks a good analysis, perhaps, but acts out his archaic fantasies wildly and without insight as soon as he is released from the self-critical observation which is the substance of the analytic situation.

In either case, we must be humble in our claim to know "all about" our patient. If we observe him with the greatest care, understand his transference reactions, listen carefully to what he describes of his life outside the office, we know a great deal about him—in a sense more than anyone else possibly could. But we do not know all, and occasionally what we fail to learn may be fairly important.

This then is our fourth problem in evolving a theory of character development; it is the result of analytic regression and the limitation of the analyst's field of view.

I have described the following obstacles encountered in evolving a theory of character development: first, the operations of denial in the analyst; second, the distorting effects of prejudicial value judgments; third, the lack of an elegant and universally agreed-upon theory of aggression; and fourth, limitations of the analyst's scope of observation.

These are the difficulties. How can they be overcome? The first, denial, arises from the personality of the observer, that is, of the analyst himself. It can be greatly ameliorated, if not altogether removed, by better and more thorough analysis of the analyst.

This does not necessarily require a longer training analysis, for many such analyses may already be too long. It should impress us rather with the necessity for an investigation into those defects in the training analysis which leave important areas of the personality especially vulnerable. Whether these consist of the failure to resolve certain key conflicts, such as castration fear, or the difficulty of effective working through of the transference neurosis is an open question. I am inclined to favor the latter, since resolving the transference is probably a more difficult task than analyzing castration fantasies in training analysis. The extent to which the transference is analyzed controls how successfully the analyst is likely to continue his self-analysis during the years after graduation, and thus how well he can, among other things, overcome the tendency to deny vital facts.

The second obstacle, arising from the need to make value judgments, offers even more difficulty, but it is often capable of being overcome. The possibility of success again lies within the analyst, and depends on his endowment and what can be done during the course of his education. But while we can manage without massive denial of facts about human biology, we cannot dispense with value judgments altogether. On the contrary, they are always with us, and we should be quite lost without them.

It becomes necessary, therefore, to draw the line between indispensable value judgments and irrational prejudice. This is difficult at best; but the analyst can accomplish a great deal in his own analysis which, with the advance of his self-understanding, should help him to become more moral and less moralistic. And while he must avoid being overwhelmed by cultural preoccupations, he has the duty of understanding how he has been influenced by his own culture, including among other things his religion, culture, and socioeconomic status. Perhaps better psychoanalytic education, especially a greater understanding of superego functions, one's own and others', would help. And a careful study of Hartmann's *Psychoanalysis and Moral Values* (1960) would do no harm.

The third task, that of evolving a comprehensive theory of the aggressive drives, is well on its way. Active research in child observation by the Child Study Centre at Yale, by Mahler and her coworkers, and by British colleagues such as Anna Freud, Winnicott, and the followers of Melanie Klein, we hope will lead to useful answers in a reasonable time. Perhaps parallel researches in animal behavior will help, but I am prejudiced in favor of children. They can, eventually, talk back and tell us where we were wrong!

The solution to our fourth problem, the limitation of the analyst's view of total behavior, is not so clearly evident. It has been suggested at various times that we observe patients in other settings, interview members of their families, and even engage ourselves more actively in their personal lives. All of this has been tried and has led to poor results if not always to catastrophe. One result of such experiments is predictable and in itself should be enough to discourage such efforts: the transference will become seriously contaminated. It is difficult enough to analyze what happens between us and our patients and what the patient tells us about himself during the analytic session; playing God leads to complications in analysis far too great for human efforts to unravel.

But if we maintain the analytic situation in order to keep the transference analyzable, how can we obtain a useful picture of the patient's character? There are several things we can do.

First, it would be worthwhile to pay even more attention to behavior within the analytic session itself, for there is still so much we fail to notice about movement, ritual, tone, and gesture. We may have hesitated to bring these observations into the analysis, because of reluctance to provoke outbursts of anger; we should be more courageous.

Second, as I have suggested elsewhere (1967), there is much to be gained by undertaking the exhaustive analysis of important symptomatic acts, or of localized incidents of acting out, which have been described by the patient. The painstaking analysis of even one such event may yield surprising revelations about the patient's character structure.

Between these two sources, directly observed transference behavior and the analysis of specific actions, we are able to form about as complete a picture of character as we are likely to obtain under any conditions. And it is more accurate and more profound than that which would be obtainable under other circumstances which permit a broader view only at the cost of superficiality and transference distortion.

Third, we can do more toward better preparation of the analysts who are to make and evaluate these observations. When we discover ourselves acting on the assumption that we know all about a patient, any patient, we should be aware that we are indulging in self-deception.

Such an error is likely to originate in unresolved fragments of infantile narcissism, manifested in fantasies of omniscience. The latter play an important role in the choice of analysis as a profession, and may therefore be inadequately explored during the training analysis. More attention should be paid to enabling analytic candidates to achieve a degree of skill in reality testing required to deal with such fantasies; in other words, to develop a sense of the limitations as well as the possibilities of knowledge. We are, after all, in a field which is knowable only in part, whether in our work with patients or in our attempts to construct general hypotheses about human behavior.

Although this lecture has been chiefly about the "resistances" to the evolution of a psychoanalytic theory of character development, I shall bring it to a close by emphasizing the opportunity open to us. We should be able to construct a theory freed of the distorting effects of denial and capable of incorporating those value judgments which we find to be essential and which can be rationally supported. It should be possible to find it on a reasonably satisfactory theory of drives, including aggression, along with sharpened understanding of ego and superego development. Lastly, although we can no more observe the totality of a single human being than an astronomer can observe the whole of the universe, our knowledge of human behavior is still more accurate and less subject to distortion than that derived from other disciplines.

It is vital that we make the most of that knowledge. If the society in which we live has one claim upon our services more urgent than any other, it is that we furnish this essential element in understanding the workings of society itself, namely, a deeper understanding of the development of man's character. This would be a long overdue, but truly magnificent social contribution by the science of psychoanalysis.

Chapter 9

CHARACTER: A CONCEPT IN SEARCH OF AN IDENTITY

Francis Baudry

It is hard to imagine a concept of more everyday concern to our work than character. It is essential in formulating a character diagnosis, and occupies the bulk of our time, particularly in the process of so-called working through. The majority of patients who come to consult us nowadays hardly ever complain of symptoms. The presenting picture is generally one of vague dissatisfactions in their professional or personal life, or various inhibitions, or an inability to "find themselves." All these are manifestations of character pathology.

In spite of its common appearance, scant reference is made to problems of character and character theory in the current psychoanalytic literature. What we may be witnessing is a process similar to what Sandler (1961), writing about the superego, refers to as the dissolution of an analytic concept.

Introduction of Character in Psychoanalysis

Freud (1908) was able to identify a common clinical picture with three outstanding character traits, dynamically related to one another [see chapter 1].·He could also identify the origin of these traits as particular vicissitudes of the anal drive and make some guesses about constitutional factors and certain early life experiences which were possibly involved. There is, unfortunately, no other clear-cut easily identifiable clinical picture based on a drive vicissitude that matches the elegance of the one described by Freud.

This chapter originally appeared in the *Journal of the American Psychoanalytic Association,* 32:455–477, 1984. Reprinted by permission of the author and the publisher.

Freud's paper illustrates very well the double contribution of the psychoanalytic concept of character—first the clinical observation of certain traits as a stable cluster, second the establishment of a relation between a superficial piece of behavior and a deep structure, in this case, an instinctual drive. Thus, character shares in common with many other psychoanalytic concepts the quality of being a bridge or relational structure. Looking at character from this vantage point will be very helpful when we examine the problem of classification.

Freud's interest in 1908 was clearly the clarification of drive theory: hence the deep structure to which behavior was related turned out to be a derivative of a drive. As psychoanalysis progressed new structures of the personality and of its functioning were gradually isolated—certain defense mechanisms (identification, reaction formation) or broader structures (superego). The development of these concepts allowed connections to be established between behavior and some deeper structure other than a drive derivative.

Conceptual Ambiguities in the Definition of Character

Unlike some other terms, character has been afflicted by an unusual degree of ambiguity: there is doubt about its data base and its relation to behavior; what is or is not included under its heading is often ill-defined. The descriptive terms applying to it are taken over from lay language, lacking precision. Character also overlaps a number of other concepts (symptoms, mood, style). Not surprisingly, this confusion is reflected in the different ways psychoanalysts have written about it. In this section, I shall examine some of these problems in greater detail.

Character has in common with many other psychoanalytic terms two levels, a clinical level close to data of observation (character traits) and a more abstract one (character organization).[1] The latter will be dealt with in another paper. On the clinical level, character traits require the isolation and identification of relatively stable patterns of behavior specific to a given individual;

---

[1] I have used the term *character* to apply to both levels. In general, the context will make it clear whether I am referring to the concrete or to the abstract level.

from these it is possible to infer character traits. The concept is close to, but not identical with the data of observation. I use the term *behavior* in its broadest possible context. This includes such concepts as attitudes. Jacobson (1964) has introduced the term *ego attitudes* as defined by "characteristic features which become manifest in the most general way in all mental areas: in a person's ideals and ideas, his feelings, and his behavior" (p. 97). It is necessary to interpret the term *ego* as referring to the individual as a whole. It would make little sense to attribute *attitudes* (i.e., a subjective, introspective term) to a structure. Fenichel (1945), likewise, refers to character attitudes and ego attitudes pretty much interchangeably.

A given piece of behavior can be the concrete expression of many different character traits. A person who on the surface appears to say just the right thing might be tactful, hypocritical, adaptable, sensitive to the feelings of others, frightened of offending people, polite, chameleonlike, deceitful. This depends on the situation and on the reconstruction of the motives of the person and some aspects of his inner experience at the time. A character trait is not directly observable; it is inferred. In fact, what is observable in the adult are certain stable, repetitive behavior patterns. Description, often more successfully carried out by a good novelist than by a clinician, has then to be organized along dynamic, structural, and genetic lines to become truly psychoanalytic. This requires extensive use of clinical observations and inferences. The subjective element in the identification of character traits has been well spelled out by Stein (1969) who alludes to the moralizing tendency, the ill-defined placement on the scale of adaptive versus nonadaptive, the confusing role of reality. A man who fails to respond to some external provocation might be described as cowardly or cool, depending on a complicated combination of external circumstances and inner motivations; a friendly person would be tempted to evaluate him differently from an unfriendly person; a value judgment is involved here as well as some appreciation of the sociocultural context of the moment. The assessment of character requires we build into the system the attitude of the person who is placed in the role of the observer. What is special about analysis is not the absence of such biases in evaluation but rather that the analyst is more aware of their existence and their role in shaping his evaluating judgment.

Part of the confusion associated with the concept of character arises from unclarity about its data base. Some authors use behavior (in the sense of activity), others use attitudes, still others refer to traits or even modes of reaction or style, even further adding to the confusion; the range of possible data from which one could infer character is very great indeed—body language, mannerisms of speech, the entire range of expressive movements, posture, gait, dress, to name but a few.

I will illustrate the historical aspects of the ambiguity of character through examples of how various authors have approached the descriptive aspect of character. Though Reich (1949) does not give a concise definition of character, he alludes to his conception of the "character of the ego" as the external manifestation of the latter, "also the sum total of the modes of reaction which are specific of this or that personality—that is, a factor which is essentially functionally determined and expresses itself in the characteristic ways of walking, facial expression, posture, manner of speaking—this character of the ego consists of various elements of the outer world of prohibitions, instinct inhibitions and identifications of different kinds" (p. 160). Reich's examples are drawn mostly from the bodily manifestations of behavior in line with his biophysiological approach to psychic energy. Alexander (1923) states, "by a character trait we mean a certain stereotyped attitude in life; those people whom we call neurotic characters show this stereotyped attitude in the whole rhythm of their lives at the most decisive moment and most important turning points" (p. 15). Fenichel (1945) writes, "The term character stresses the habitual form of a given reaction—its relative constancy" (p. 467). More recently, Greenson (1967), following Reich, wrote, "The neurotic character refers to the generally ego-syntonic, habitual attitudes and modes of behavior of the patient which serve as an armor against external stimuli and against instinctual uprisings from within" (p. 76).

The ambiguity concerning the definition of *character* has been amply demonstrated by the frequently confusing use of the term by various authors. As an example, Waelder in the paper on "Multiple Function" (1936) writes, "Identification is an attempt to solve tasks in a certain problem situation. It can be designated a character trait, when an individual, in a certain combination of instincts, superego demands, and difficulties with the outer world, regularly finds his way out through identification, as his specific method of solution in a diversity of problem situations" (p. 78). In Waelder's usage, a character trait can be an abstract complicated mental mechanism such as identification as long as this device is stable, repeated, and predictable in a given individual. Rosen (1961) writes, "The term *character* is meant to convey the sense of an over-all expressive style which determines, in ways that frequently can be predicted, how an individual will react to situations or cope with given tasks." In contrast to character, style is not a dynamic concept. It is not a bridging term. It describes broad areas of the person's functioning—more general than traits, and more abstract than observable behavior. Rosen defines it as "a progressing synthesis of form and content in an individually typical manner and according to the individual's sense of 'appropriateness' " (p. 447). There will naturally be a relation between an individual's style and character (Shapiro, 1965). Because of his special interest in *style,* Rosen chose to express character through that term. Other authors might choose a different emphasis. However, the basic core remains: character on the most descriptive superficial level refers to recurrent, identifiable, stable patterns of the person's functioning.

The ambiguity surrounding character and its delimitations extends to its demarcation from symptoms and moods. For example, the statement "X. is an anxious person" can refer to the person's proneness to develop anxiety reactions with minimal external justification, emphasizing both a symptom and a trait. However, this statement need not imply the presence of actual symptoms, but could refer to a chronic state of being on guard, expecting the worst, which would constitute a character trait. I have alluded above to the distinction between symptom and character trait. Although this distinction may at times be blurred, there is, to my mind, some value in distinguishing between ego-alien disruptive aspects of behavior (symptoms) and generally self-syntonic patterns (character). An individual is able to rationalize a character trait, whereas he will complain of a symptom or be embarrassed by it. There are exceptions to this.

There are other stable characteristics which are generally grouped under the rubric of mood rather than character. The reasons for distinguishing moods from character on a superficial level are clear; moods are primarily affective discharge patterns in contrast to character, which is much more inclusive and non-specific. Whether to consider mood an aspect of character or to grant it specific independent status is a secondary question. A statement such as, "He is an angry person" or a "sad person" and other terms of purely affective nature describe the person's basic mood. There is very little psychoanalytic literature devoted specifically to moods. Jacobson (1964) describes "generalized modifications of all discharge patterns lending to our thoughts, actions and feelings a characteristic color which finds expression in what we call our mood" (p. 133). Weinshel's (1971) description of moods as "complicated psychological configurations, organized structures which encompass behavioral and cognitive elements as well as affective ones," emphasizes the similarity of mood to character. He also remarks that descriptions of character or character traits are often related to the mood of the individual concerned—boredom, bitterness, enthusiasm, smugness, and the like (p. 313). He distinguishes certain moods referred to as cast of mind or temperament which could be included under character specifically because of a "more enduring tendency and their syntonicity with the sense of self" (p. 314). I am in general agreement with Weinshel that certain moods so infuse the personality structure that they give character its stamp. The relation between mood and character is a complex one. If the mood disturbance is pronounced and chronic, it may color whole aspects of the person's functioning. We refer to depressive, hypomanic, or cyclothymic characters. On a less abstract level, we encounter chronic optimists or chronic pessimists. Mood has to be differentiated also from affective disturbances. There may be chronic pessimists who do not suffer from a clinical depression. It is in the nature of moods to "color, or at least overstate one aspect of reality and understate or blot out differing or opposing aspects; they involve, to some extent, mechanisms of denial and distortion of reality'" (Jacobson, 1971, p. 87).

Perhaps we could say that mood is an aspect of character. Certain character traits (e.g., passivity) may predispose to certain moods (e.g., boredom). The tendency to moods can be a characteristic either of individuals, as in the expression, "he is a moody person," or of certain phases, particularly adolescence. Mahler (1966) has described the greater tendency for women to have depressive moods as a reaction to certain conflicts of the separation–individuation phase. Aggression and its vicissitudes play key roles in moods, and both self and object representations are altered.

The Ingredients of Character

Having explored the conceptual ambiguities of the term *character,* it is now time to spell out what I believe can heuristically be included under its label.

The breadth of attributes included under the descriptive heading of character traits is very great: generous, dishonest, kind, haughty, hostile, impulsive, cold, cheerful, brave, inhibited, superstitious, are all commonly cited traits. They describe generally either ways of relating to people or reacting to situations, or ways of being (attitudes). A character trait will include or be heavily influenced by defenses, but it is more than a defense. It combines references to the person's moral system (dishonest, cheat, liar), to his instinctual makeup (impulsive), to his basic temperament (cheerful, pessimistic), to complex ego functions (humorous, perceptive, brilliant, superstitious), and finally to basic attitudes toward the world (kind, trustful) and himself (hesitant).

The breadth of character is enormous, as the whole of an individual's stable functioning is included under its heading. Character traits then represent an amalgam—a synthesis that expresses under one heading a combination including derivatives of drive, defense, identifications, superego aspects, though certain traits will be more directly determined by one factor. In listing the theoretical points of view from which it is possible to examine character, I shall draw largely from Waelder's (1936) remarks in his seminal paper on the principle of multiple function. The libidinal level has to be considered the prime factor; a close second would be the major mechanisms of defense; a third would be the nature of the person's object relations; next would follow the major fashions in which the person's self-esteem is regulated; other elements would include description of the person's major identifications and an assessment of the person's moral code and values; finally, character implies an adaptive function which has a genetic aspect. The latter refers to the dilemma confronting the child for whom the character trait represents the chosen solution. The concept of character is then a way of relating in a dynamic sense many different aspects of the person's functioning. It falls just a bit short of a complete metapsychological profile.

Here we come to the first major critique of the term. We can apply to it what Glover (1966) wrote about the concept of identity. "It either means little or nothing or comprises the whole of psychoanalytic psychology—the influence of instincts, the development of ego and of object relations, the part played by a sequence of mental mechanisms and finally constitutional and environmental factors. No term that involves such a complicated interaction of factors and phases of development can lay claim to the status of a basic mental concept" (p. 188).

Although I agree with Glover's overall critique, there are certain ways of organizing character that relate it to both current and past objects and have considerable clinical value. Character often includes as one of its components certain fantasies involving the person and an outside agent. The patient's behavior is determined by these fantasies, often unconscious, which the person holds about himself (this includes his past history of object choices), the world at large, and his expectations of how he will or should be treated. The task of analysis is to uncover these fantasies and trace their origins. Seen from the point of view of object relations, the behavior of the patient involves the playing out of a scenario; for example the patient may play the part of the rebellious child, casting the analyst in the role of controlling mother. The patient is stuck in this repetition because unconscious conflict, in this instance, generally around passivity, allows for no other solution. There is, however, another crucial reason for the maintenance of such character attitudes—their adaptive value at the time of formation of the trait in question. The selection by the child of a particular attitude is often the only way for him to maintain an object tie or is seen as a precondition to being loved or paid attention to.

There is still another way of integrating the interpersonal relation with the intrapersonal of intrapsychic conflict. Character, to the degree it involves another person, can be defined as the development of interpersonal strategies to avoid internal conflict (Glover, 1926).

Problem of Classification

It must be kept in mind that no individual will ever be adequately described by a classificatory label. No two people assigned to the hysterical character category will be alike, nor is it possible to synthesize the complexity of any given character under the label. These terms are only approximate; they convey in shorthand fashion certain major aspects of a person's functioning conveniently grouped under certain headings.

Taken in broad historical perspective, the problems of classification have not altered significantly in form. Character as a concept was not invented by psychoanalysts. In the prepsychoanalytic era, it was variously shared by writers, philosophers, moralists, phrenologists, sociologists, alienists, and physiologists. The classifications adopted were as varied as they were fanciful, influenced by biases, preconceptions, nationalistic views, and class-bound prejudices. Two divergent trends appear very early—one leading to the description of a large number of characters organized around one mode of behavior. This is the so-called literary method. Some of its exponents include Theophrastus, Ben Jonson, LaBruyère, Addison, Steele, and Butler. The second route followed is that of temperament—bound up with the aim of explaining and relating each basic type of bodily humors (the sanguine, melancholic, choleric, and phlegmatic) or bodily types (Sheldon and Kretschmer are more recent examples of this trend). This same trend may be found in our current classification.

On the most concrete level, a number of classifications of traits have been suggested. Fenichel (1945) refers to traits which are all pervasive versus those traits which arise only in certain situations. In the former, the attitudes are nonspecific and indiscriminately maintained toward everybody. Another approach also described by Fenichel is to classify character traits depending on whether the person avoids (phobic attitude) or opposes (reaction formation) the original impulse. Complications arise as there may be reaction formation against reaction formation, and combinations of the two types. On a more general level, Fenichel refers to pathological behavior resulting from the ego's conflict with the id, with the superego, and with reality. More general character types are derived from this last model. Of these three possible classifications, the first is based on purely a descriptive level of observation, the second is based on a mechanism which is inferred (i.e., a dynamic level), the third is clearly a structural classification. Fenichel was dissatisfied with all his efforts. As character is such a global concept, a unilinear classification is bound to rob it of its richness.

Because character does not occupy a well-defined place on the line between health and pathology, classification becomes more complicated. Character is an aspect of the individual's functioning which implies neither health nor pathology. There is no person without a character. Ideally, one would want to develop a classification of character *types* some of which would be pathological, others not. As classical psychiatry and clinical analysis start with pathology, our classification has tended to evolve from our work with character disorders; these clearly imply a pathology of character. On the clinical level, however, the normality or abnormality of a character trait are important issues. There are several vantage points from which one evaluates this: descriptive, dynamic, functional, adaptational, and structural to name the common ones. There may be no good correlation between these approaches. Certain character traits of a narcissistic nature indicative of severe pathology may not interfere with the individual's adaptation, whereas certain traits of shyness or feelings of inferiority based on much higher-level conflicts may cripple the person afflicted with them. Abnormality is a much more ambiguous concept when it comes to character traits as it requires a consideration of sociocultural setting in which the given behavior occurs. Both internal factors (for example, flexibility of the trait), and external ones need be considered; adaptation is not identical with conforming behavior. In certain situations, rebellion may be a sign of overall strength and autonomy.

The term *character disorder* has generally been applied to chronic maladaptive patterns, inflexible in nature and generally experienced as ego-syntonic. From a psychoanalytic viewpoint, it should be apparent that a descriptive nosology is insufficient. Criteria for defining what will be considered a disorder are obviously lacking, since there is no easy clear-cut differentiation between pathology and normality in the field of character. This contrasts with neurosis in which the presence of a symptom is always pathological. Character disorders represent malformations of the ego resulting from attempted compromise formation to accommodate conflicting demands impinging on the individual from the four agencies cited by Waelder (1936)—reality, superego, the drives, and the repetition compulsion.

Another term related to character disorder is *character neurosis*. Waelder (1960) defines this as either the avoidance of an impending neurosis through character changes or the integration of a developing or developed neurosis into the personality by neurotic ego distortion. The term *character neurosis* is simply a dynamic way of referring to certain types of character disorder which have a particularly close relation to neurosis. A common example would be the integration of an obsessive neurosis into an obsessional character structure.

What do we expect from an overall classification and what are its requirements? In the neglected paper on libidinal types [see chapter 3], Freud (1931) spells out the requirements for a psychoanalytic classification:

> It may fairly be demanded that this classification should not merely be deduced from our knowledge or hypotheses about the libido, but that it should be easily confirmed in actual experience, and that it should contribute to the clarification of the mass of our observations and help us to grasp them. It may at once be admitted that these libidinal types . . . shall not coincide with clinical pictures. On the contrary, they must comprehend all the variations which . . . fall within the limits of normal [p. 51].

The multiple points of view contributed by psychoanalysis to the study of character is reflected in the confused classification of character according to libidinal type (e.g., anal), neurotic organization (e.g., phobic, hysterical), or mode of relating (e.g., passive, feminine character). Study of the superego indirectly led to the description of certain types, but with no attempt at setting up a classification; for example, the "exceptions" or "those wrecked by success" [see chapter 2] (Freud, 1916). The "fate neuroses" belongs here. Interest in the partial instincts also contributed its own nomenclature; for example, sadistic or masochistic character. Concern with affects and object relations led to further types—the depressive character and the "as-if" character. Clearly not all of these "types" are on the same level of abstraction. Phobic character is a more general category than the "exceptions."

An early attempt to integrate the findings of ego psychology into a classification of character is that by Waelder (1936). Some of the points he made bear repetition. The principle of multiple function allows for a deeper understanding of the relation between the major drive organization and the person's major preferred solution to conflict (generally a defense). Waelder demonstrates convincingly that the form chosen must in some way also allow for the satisfaction of the drive: Identification, when analyzed, has in it a form of oral drive satisfaction; projection allows for a homosexual gratification. Waelder views the drives as primary, fueling all behavior which is then secondarily contained and directed by the ego. The advantage of Waelder's approach is the undoing of the fragmentation characteristic of most other attempts at classification. His work has not been exploited fully. Yet an attempt by Glover (1932) to combine all aspects of an individual's functioning in a systematic ordering dynamically relating character, symptoms, and sexual orientation became so cumbersome and unwieldly as to lose its usefulness. This is a function of the wide scope of character.

Two facts stand out: first, almost any neurosis or syndrome or even affect disturbance of a symptomatic nature can be found to have some underlying characterological formation, dealing with similar conflicts, justifying the use of the same label; second, certain character organizations stand out from a descriptive point of view because of one outstanding feature, or again represent a fit with a well-known literary or fairy-tale figure which encompasses many of the features. More scientific precision could dislodge some of these latter types and reduce them to other terms in our nomenclature. The Don Juan type is most likely a variation on narcissistic disturbances; the Cinderalla type, a form of masochistic character. Yet there is something to be said for retaining the vividness and coloring of the literary labels.

Character and the Analytic Situation

Having examined some of the problems, ambiguities, and conceptual issues of the term *character trait,* it is time to turn to its clinical application. How does it come up in our work? What obstacles are there to its usefulness? What role does it play in our formulations?

Observation and Evaluation

Stein (1969) [see chapter 8] has described the obstacles to approaching character in our daily work. The first arises from the difficulty in observing character in the analytic situation. The regression induced by the process complicates the task. It is well known that a patient's behavior in the waiting room or after he leaves our office may be markedly different from what we see on the couch. Not all character traits can be readily observed. Some may be quite hidden or defended against, whereas others may be more on the surface. Certain individuals may be more secretive about their character, others more open.

The data we have as analysts derives from our own observations, particularly about the way the patient handles the "real" transactions with us (time, money, cancellation) and the way the patient reacts to us and to our interpretations. We also have as data (more biased) the patient's observations of his own behavior with others or reports about other people's comments about him. Finally, we have the so-called transference resistances, perhaps the most important leverage in bringing character into the analytic situation.

On the clinical level, character traits represent the way an outside observer (the analyst) classifies and organizes repetitive aspects of the behavior of the person under observation. As such, character traits are observable by others, but not easily liable to introspection. Confronting a person with some aspect of his character often arouses anxiety or anger. Patients will often hear our comments about their behavior as veiled or not so veiled criticism, implying they should change. Why should there be such a reluctance to confront one's own character? What is the dynamic significance of this fact? Do we need to postulate a resistance against becoming aware of this aspect of oneself, or is it in the nature of the beast—that is, one cannot be both inside and outside oneself? Does the traditional reluctance to see ourselves as others see us emanate from a narcissistic investment in maintaining an ideal self-image, so that comments about ourselves are heard as criticism to be shunned or praise to be embarrassed about? One aspect of the resistance to facing one's character is related to the tendency to moralize about character or to hear references to one's character as critical; this can be understood from the developmental point of view. There is an intimate connection between the process of character formation and the formation of the superego. Character traits are formed in large part in relation to parental standards and as a solution to external pressures (via submission or rebellion); character formation is not completed until a firm superego (and ego) become established. A second aspect of the difficulty patients experience in facing their character is related to the different language of inner and outer experience. Behavior is, after all, a complicated compromise— the end result of conflicting tendencies only some of which are capable of entering consciousness. The person who is stingy does not experience himself that way. His inner sense may be that he should be careful and save his money, for he is uncertain what future catastrophe might befall him—though he may be conflicted about his behavior and react with guilt or shame when it is pointed out to him. When seen from the inside, behavior is no longer character but is a reflection of self-image or self representation. Character then would represent the behavioral aspects of self representations. Only a small portion of the latter are capable of introspection, depending on their relation to conflict and the individual's ability to tolerate facing less desirable aspects of himself. Yet, after a successful analysis, we expect that a patient will have gained a good bit of insight into his behavior and will be more aware than before about his character, its rigidities, its limitations and hopefully will have been able to modify certain pathological traits.

Character Resistance and Character Analysis

Glover (1926) remarked that subjecting the seemingly banal routine of everyday life to detailed scrutiny is the best prescription for the conduct of an analysis of character. This is as true now as it was then!

Reich (1949, p. 47) introduced the term *character resistance* to refer to certain stereotypic, formal aspects of general behavior "the manner of talking, of the gait, facial expression and typical attitudes such as smiling, deriding haughtiness, overcorrectness, the manner of the politeness or of the aggression." These resistances "remain the same no matter what the material is against which it is directed." The distinction between character resistance and transference resistance which Reich introduced is a valuable one. In contrast to transference reactions to the analyst, the character resistances are general, diffuse responses of the patient to people at large and to dangers emanating from his inner world of conflict. In this type of reaction, people are treated in indiscriminate fashion, as though they were all the same. These resistances to be sure, also arise in reaction to earlier experience with significant persons. In one case, a patient had to maintain considerable emotional distance from all persons regardless of sex, age, or character type. This emotional isolation arose as a consequence of certain disturbances in early mothering. The patient's mother, a narcissistic individual, became, in addition, quite depressed following the unexpected death of a child for which the patient was unconsciously blamed. Such so-called generalized transference reactions as Greenson (1967) coins them, are "characteristic of the patient's object relations in general" (p. 257). They represent frozen residues of past conflicts.

There is an important area of character and behavior not dealt with by Reich because of his focus on character as a frozen final solution—an armour plating as it were. I have in mind aspects of character and behavior that are the resultant of currently active conflicts often dating from childhood. The classical definition of character as "a once-and-for-all resolution" would seem to disqualify them from being considered a part of character; yet in every other respect, such as stability and repetitiveness, such conflict-related traits must be included. These traits may be closer to symptoms or inhibitions. Examples might include shyness or withdrawal from competitive situations as a result of exhibitionistic conflicts which are unresolved, painfully experienced, and dynamically active in the present. Greenson (1967), in his volume on technique, writes extensively about transference and resistance without any allusion to the concept of character save in a brief passage. He agrees to the necessity of tackling the patient's character traits but does not indicate how and when. This is where the art rather than the science of our discipline enters. There are clearly no hard and fast rules, and each practitioner will develop his personal style and approach. The most difficult character traits to deal with are related to the hidden or latent resistances described by Glover (1955a). The patient will very subtly distort the analytic process, or the analyst will become numbed to the destructive effect of certain chronic attitudes. A patient of mine, behind a compliant attitude, would offhandedly refer to the fact that bosses in his institution were heavy-handed in their use of authority. He did not trust people to have his interest at heart, and played his cards close to the chest. It was very difficult for me to demonstrate the same persuasive attitude in the treatment toward me, particularly as he seemed to listen very closely to what I said yet subtly ignored the substance of my communications. This patient's reaction was almost always the same—he would feel hurt, criticized, and would desperately try to modify his behavior so as to conform to what he believed I expected of him. This trait of conforming outwardly while maintaining his inner attitudes unchanged was iron-clad. Analysis of its antecedents, its adaptive value, made little impression on this patient. In this case, severe early trauma and defective mothering had seriously impaired the flexibility of the patient's character and limited the development of nondefensive self-observation.

It is possible to describe the more obvious obstacles to analysis either in terms of traits (impulsivity, tendency to act out, inability to tolerate frustration, unreliability, excessive passivity, dishonesty) or in terms of various ego and superego functions. The former are closer to clinical observation and hence easier to validate. There are certain global qualities, such as psychological mindedness or motivation, which depend in part on the presence of certain character traits (curiosity, willingness to wait, tolerance). There are also certain attitudes such as inability to tolerate shame, embarrassment, or criticism which vastly complicate our task.

Beyond the initial screening, many pitfalls await us during the course treatment. It may not be possible to detect early which character attitudes will make or break an analysis. In one instance, a severely traumatized professional person whose life was in shambles made a dramatic recovery aided by an unusual capacity to observe himself with a wry sense of humor. He was able to take distance from his behavior. He had an unusual degree of motivation and determination to succeed—identifying with his mother who had had to overcome severe odds in her own life.

The opposite problem is illustrated by a young woman referred to analysis because of what looked like a masochistic character disturbance and difficulties in relating to men. Attractive, bright, and apparently motivated for change, she seemed an ideal analytic case. This impression remained for the first few months as she presented many dreams—too many, it seemed. Her daily life all but disappeared from the sessions. A gentle comment to this effect was greeted by shock, silence, and heralded severe narcissistic character resistances. The patient had to control the sessions, would only talk about what she wanted. Any new interpretation dealing with material she decided was inappropriate would be greeted with rage or stony silence. In spite of fairly severe symptomatology and impaired object relations which caused her pain, the treatment could not really overcome what looked like a wall of narcissistic resistances. Eventually, the treatment was terminated by mutual consent. She was then seen in psychotherapy by another analyst; a similar impasse was reached. This patient had certainly developed very intense negative transference attitudes that could not be analyzed. She often compared the task of associating to being asked to walk unaided into the cage of a tiger.

Character Change in Analysis

There is a wide range of opinion concerning the possibility of character change in analysis ranging from those analysts who feel that structural change is not possible to those who are quite optimistic about character analysis producing more than behavioral adjustments. My own view is cautious optimism. I have no question that the basic core and organization of an individual remains relatively fixed; that is, an obsessional individual will never become a hysteric no matter how long he remains, but if successful, the treatment will alter considerably the degree of his obsessionalism, enable him to make more appropriate object choices, be happier, and so on. Pathogenic fantasies will lose their grip on his behavior which should become less automatic as certain infantile danger situations lose their threatening quality. Competition does not have to entail the elimination of the rival; activity does not have to have a hostile tinge.

Often we understand something about the structure of a given pathological entity after a successful piece of analytic work leads to modification of that structure. What do we find in the domain of character analysis? First of all, it is much more difficult to pinpoint change in a given character trait. The patient may comment on it in passing, or the analyst may conclude that the patient's behavior has changed, for example, that he is less passive. The therapist might be tempted to account for the change in theoretical terms—the working through of conflicts around passivity. Such a formulation tells us very little about the actual process leading to change. Can we discover with the patient what has made a difference from the experiential point of view? Is this a stable or a temporary result dependent on some vicissitudes of the transference? Just as there is a multiplicity of influences that determine the choice of a given character trait which our theory can never fully account for, we are faced with the same problem in accounting for change. This is the problem of determinism—studied particularly by Waelder. Our explanations are shorthand ways of referring to factors influencing a given behavior or change rather than causing it. Can we say anything about the types of traits that remain impervious to analysis? I would imagine that traits which are firmly rooted in the person's constitution or basic instinctual makeup (i.e., belong to a preconflict period) are more resistant to change than those based on identifications with early parental figures. Freud observed that masochistic character had a better prognosis in those instances in which the masochism was itself the result of an identification with a masochistic parent. Characteristics related to a person's tem-

perament are probably more fixed than those which are the outcome of conflicts. A slow-to-warm-up child may turn into a
somewhat distant, aloof adult with limited capacity to change this
basic orientation. We also know that certain character types are
more flexible than others. Rigidity is a trait more commonly
encountered in obsessionals than in true hysterics. A trait that
arises in reaction to a specific situation is more readily changed
than a trait that encompasses broader issues. Conflicts around
ambition are often difficult to resolve. Pathology rooted in early
conflicts and trauma is generally considered more resistive to
structural change, yet there are obvious exceptions to this rule.
Certain oral characters who need to be needed often respond
well to analysis, better than certain anally rooted traits, thus contradicting the hypothesis that traits deriving from earlier phases
in life are more stubbornly rooted and, therefore, resistive to
change. There is an unavoidable gap then between our theoretical expectations and our clinical findings. This gap exists in other
aspects of our work—not only character analysis. However, the
relative vagueness of a character trait in contrast to the specificity
of a symptom heightens the difficulty.

Conclusion

In spite of its confused status as a term, I hope the preceding has
demonstrated the need and relevance of *character* for our theory
and our practice. In addition to the role of character in the
diagnostic assessment and evaluation of analyzability, character
continually confronts us in our daily work as a resistance and also
in its intricate relation with neurotic symptoms. From a developmental point of view, we are interested in studying antecedents of
both symptoms and character traits. In the treatment, analysis of
character traits often leads to states of anxiety and transient
symptom formation as the rigid conflict is remobilized. Character formation and neurotic symptoms are both possible paths of
conflict resolution; that is, compromise formations. Even descriptively, the borderline between symptoms and neurotic character
traits is blurred. Both are also liable to the same type of analysis—
descriptive, economic, dynamic, and adaptive. Character allows
certain issues to be redefined by relating a superficial aspect of

behavior to a deep structure derived from our theory of mind. It highlights the way in which defense, identifications, and instincts mold stable behavior. It provides the most clinical way we have of pinpointing, in clear and communicable fashion, stable attributes of the individual. It presents us with a clinical language through which we can define structure and the role of fantasy.

Chapter 10

CHARACTER, EGO-SYNTONICITY, AND CHARACTER CHANGE

ROY SCHAFER

Perhaps the first question to raise in a theoretical discussion of character is whether it is worth bothering with the concept at all. Unlike the ego, which, as a systematic concept, came after it, character has never been provided with either a satisfactory conceptualization or a definite place in psychoanalytic theory. Moreover, in an amorphous way character overlaps the concept *ego*. In other respects, character overlaps both the concept *self,* which is now very much in theoretical vogue, and the free-floating concept *style* or "neurotic style" as elaborated by Shapiro (1965). But conceptualizations of *self* and *style,* in turn, usually overlap those of the *ego*. For these reasons alone, one remains uncertain of one's theoretical ground when referring to character.

One feels better positioned with respect to character when the discussion turns to clinical or technical matters and centers on such issues as resistance, defense analysis, conflict resolution, ego-syntonicity, and subtle expressions of maladaptiveness. It is, however, questionable whether this security is any more warranted than theoretical security in regard to the concept of character. This is so because for some time there have been at hand the theoretical and technical concepts of ego analysis, defense, intersystemic and intrasystemic conflict, acting out, multiple function, the synthetic function of the ego, secondary autonomy, and others of that order, and these, far more than character, have an established place in systematic psychoanalytic discussion of clinical phenomena and methods.

This chapter originally appeared in the *Journal of the American Psychoanalytic Association,* 27:867–891, 1979. Reprinted by special permission of the author and the publisher.

It would seem, then, that one might do better to forget about a systemic approach to character and do what is so often done, discuss other matters, such as the development and analysis of the total personality, under the title *character*. As a rule, in fact, analytic writing on character has tended to deal with the development and analysis of the total personality. But one need not follow this evasive precedent, nor should one, for the concept of character seems to have so strong a hold on the psychoanalytic imagination that one is obliged to try to determine the source of its power or the good uses that have been found for it. One might even hope to discover additional work that can be done in the name of character.

There seem to be a number of important and more or less interrelated reasons why character has been such a viable concept. They include, first of all, the opportunity it affords to discuss the development and analysis of the total personality; second, the contribution it makes toward satisfying the ever present urge toward nosology, especially in relation to the problem of asymptomatic neuroses; third, the way in which it takes into account the inevitably fluid but seemingly important boundary between form and content in the understanding of human action, as in the understanding of art; and finally, the freer access to experiential aspects of human contact generally, and the clinical encounter specifically, that is provided by characterological terms as compared to the more austere and confining terms of metapsychology. Some of these reasons will be touched on in the course of the following discussion. Reference will also be made to some important theoretical problems: specifically, the tension within psychoanalytic theory between, on the one hand, persistent and unquestioned naïve empiricist or positivist attitudes and, on the other, the more sophisticated epistemological conceptions that are available today; also, the questionable status of certain theoretical assumptions which dictate that a mechanistic theory of energy and structure is required to explain both the occurrence of human activity and the continuity, consistency, and coherence of this activity.

For the general organization of my discussion I have used the following four headings: The Metapsychological View of Character; Character as Action; Ego-Syntonicity; and Character

Change. In the first section I shall state and criticize the meta-psychological conceptualization of character and shall try to show how it refers to actions. In the second section, I shall restate the concept of character in action language. In the third, I shall take up the concept of ego-syntonicity as the pivotal concept in clinical and theoretical discussions of character. Finally, I shall formulate in action terms the reasonable claims that can be made about character change through psychoanalytic treatment, and in this connection I shall discuss briefly both the usefulness and the ambiguity of the distinction between content and form or structure.

The Metapsychological View of Character

One may take as a representative instance of the metapsychological view of character the careful and extensive definition offered by Moore and Fine in *A Glossary of Psychoanalytic Terms and Concepts* (1968). It is a definition that incorporates the earlier contributions of Freud, Reich (1933–1944, 1949), and Fenichel (1945), among others, and it is altogether compatible with later discussions, such as that by Blos (1968). To quote from Moore and Fine (p. 25) incompletely, though not, I think, unfairly:

> CHARACTER: That aspect of personality . . . which reflects the individual's habitual modes of bringing into harmony his own inner needs and the demands of the external world. It is a constellation of relatively stable and constant ways of reconciling conflicts between the various parts of the psychic apparatus to achieve adjustment in relation to the environment. Character therefore has a permanent quality that affects the degree and manner of drive discharge, defenses, affects, specific object relationships, and adaptive functioning in general. . . . The integrating, synthesizing, and organizing functions of the ego are significantly involved in determining character. Through these functions stimuli and impulses are sifted and organized. Some are permitted to find expression directly while others are tolerated only in altered form. Permanent character traits are either per-petuations of original impulses in modified form, sub-

limations of them, or reaction formations against them. Thus, some character attitudes or traits are defenses, others not, but none are completely independent of instinctual conflicts. [Various forms of glossary-style emphasis deleted.]

This definition includes at least several category mistakes which seem to be consequences of the pressure toward deterministic formulation that inheres in metapsychological discussion. A category mistake confuses an abstract term and its referents. For instance, the concept of character must *include* "the degree and manner of drive discharge, defenses, affects, object relationships, and adaptive functioning in general"; yet, in the definition offered by Moore and Fine, character is said to *affect* these very features of the personality. Similarly, the concept of character must *include* the type and degree of "integrating, synthesizing, and organizing" that distinguish the individual; yet, they say that the character is *determined* by the ego functions of integration, etc. These objections are not mere quibbles; they point to confusions encountered commonly and perhaps inevitably in the most serious attempts at metapsychological precision. But let us leave these objections aside and consider the definition from the standpoint of action.

"Modes of bringing into harmony" and "ways of reconciling conflicts": These are modes of action; that is to say, these phrases refer to the ways in which people get problematic things done, whether in thought or overt deed.

"The various parts of the mental apparatus": This is a mechanistic theoretical (metapsychological) way of sorting out constituent aspects of the complex actions that people perform or would perform under safe enough circumstances. These aspects include, among others, infantile wishful actions and archaic moral actions.

"The integrating, synthesizing, and organizing functions of the ego": This is a set of biological–adaptational terms; it refers to the observation that people do attempt, with varying degrees of success, to integrate, synthesize, and organize what they do.

But these metapsychological terms no longer indicate that they pertain to symbol-using people who are engaged in human action. Instead, they convey that organismic functions play their role in the mental apparatus and that they do so under the guidance and control of higher-order functions which set priorities and rule the mind. I shall return to this point. Here I am just trying to bring out the human referents of the metapsychological terms, or, in other words, to emphasize what one sees when one observes people psychoanalytically. One does not see metapsychological entities; one sees actions being performed in various modes, some of them in the form of thinking, some in emotional form, some in motor performances, and most of them in complex forms.

It is neither *a*theoretical nor *anti*theoretical to insist on returning to the observational base of psychoanalysis, for there are many ways of designating what one observes, and one of the systematic and therefore theoretical ways of doing so is to formulate psychoanalytic data as action (Schafer, 1976, 1978a). One may go further and group these actions through the introduction of higher-order concepts, such as infantile sensual and hostile actions (id impulses, so-called), defensive actions (ego mechanisms, so-called), or synthesizing actions (ego function, so-called). Returning to one's observational base does not mean limiting oneself to atomistic descriptions. Action language can be used as abstractly as the language of psychic structure.

This systematizing project entails dropping the usual stock of nominatives and their associated adjectives from the descriptive–explanatory language of psychoanalysis and relying instead on verbs and their adverbial modifiers. That is to say, it entails giving up the idea that one understands or explains more by saying that mental entities and functions, working autonomously and in some hierarchic arrangement, somehow produce a more or less continuous, consistent, and coherent psychological existence. It is eminently theoretical to proceed on the basis of an alternative assumption, namely, that it is sufficient to state, from the specifically psychoanalytic point of view and on an appropriate level of abstraction, what people do, how they do it, and their reasons for doing so. And at the same time it is eminently clinical to proceed in this manner; it is in fact the way that analysts do proceed in practice, however figurative the manifest language used in interpretations.

It is essential at this stage of the argument to emphasize

several more points. First of all, if one notices in Moore and Fine's description how broad a scope and how determining an influence is being attributed to the "integrating, synthesizing, and organizing functions of the ego," one must realize that these are functions of so high an order that they amount to a central agency in the personality; that is, they amount to a person regulating his or her existence in some kind of continuous, consistent, and coherent fashion. This central agency is the reified and anthropomorphized ego acting as a whole person, even if a conflicted one, or else it is a functional nucleus of that ego acting as a whole person. Here, in headquarters, is what I have called "the mover of the mental apparatus" (1976, chapter 5). This problem of reification and anthropomorphism was not adequately resolved in Hartmann's great monograph on adaptation (1939), and it has never been adequately dealt with by the best of metapsychologists (see, in this regard, Shafer [1976, chapter 4]. Additionally, this "mover" must be viewed as acting freely or autonomously, whatever its history. A central and superordinate regulatory agency does not fit into the deterministic scheme of metapsychology, for if it, too, were determined in the usual way, it would amount to no more than another one of the constituents of the psychic apparatus that required regulation by yet other higher-order "integrating functions" of the free or autonomous kind. These functions would dictate when synthesizing functions, for example, would be activated. The chain of determinism snaps at this point.[1]

The second point to be considered before returning to the concept of character is this: metapsychology rests on what may be termed a quasi-physical principle of inertia. It holds that no one would ever do anything unless made to do so by some underlying force; even development depends on the force of frustrated drives. It seems that something is being explained by this idea of

---

[1]It is worth mentioning that Heinz Kohut has begun addressing these problems in his recent book (1977). Coming at them from a different but related direction—that of the introspective–empathic method and the unique reality it establishes—he too has found it necessary to reject a totally and strictly deterministic, mechanistic–functional approach. Kohut now speaks of the coherent self as *being*, as well as *being experienced as*, a center of free initiative. This self is similar to what I have been referring to for some time as the person as agent.

necessary propulsive force, when actually one is witnessing an after-the-fact introduction of an assumption masquerading as a finding; it is, moreover, an assumption whose necessity has not been demonstrated. In the terms of action language, it is sufficient to state that people perform actions for reasons, the reasons being immanent in the actions and definers of them. I am referring here to the *interpretive* principle of intelligibility of actions that is the cornerstone of Freud's method. This principle is indispensable in clinical work and daily life. It is presented here as a theoretical *alternative* to the mechanistic principle of inertia rather than, as Freud saw it, a prelude to formal theorizing.

The third theoretical point to consider is that metapsychology rests on what may be termed a quasi-physical principle of structure. It holds that some entity must exist in the mind that guarantees the continuity, coherence, and consistency of action. It leads one to take it for granted that in order to act rationally and adaptively one must have an ego that makes possible and ensures just this kind of activity. In action terms, however, whatever a person does may, *when viewed in a certain way,* be said to show more or less continuity, coherence, and consistency. I am referring here to an equally indispensable principle of seeking, specifically for purposes of psychoanalytic interpretation, the best description of the way a person organizes or patterns his or her actions. Psychoanalytic redescription is distinguished by its focus on certain aspects and implications of present actions, such as the sexual, the aggressive, the defensive, the infantile, and the unconscious; it is also distinguished by its encompassing the antecedents of these actions in the multiple and circular life-historical accounts which psychoanalysis makes possible (Schafer 1978a, 1979).

Reference was made earlier to the notion of a structured hierarchy of functions. This notion depends entirely on the fact that people can be shown, through interpretation, to be following certain complex rules in their actions and adhering to certain priorities they have set. Nothing is added to the explanation of the actions by introducing metapsychology's quasi-physical principle of structure. It is a unitary person and not a something else *within* him or her impelling action and guaranteeing its organization. Seen in this light, character cannot be an entity that determines behavior; it can only be a form of explanation through systematic redescription of action in the broad sense in which I am using the term.[2]

Character as Action

Character refers to the actions that people typically perform in the problematic situations that they typically define for themselves. It thus refers to what they regularly do when they experience danger or when they must choose between or accommodate courses of action that they view as desirable though incompatible. Character also refers to just what it is that these same people regularly define as dangerous, the conflictual courses of action they regularly envisage, and the reasons why they have established these regularities. Additionally, character refers to the typical ways in which people organize what they do, for they do not ordinarily act piecemeal; rather, they act within complex, more or less stable and coherent contexts of meaning which they develop and maintain continuously. They strive to act as consistently and as unconflictually as possible. Psychoanalysis is necessary to show how this is so, for the larger and most important part of all these actions is performed unconsciously.

It is, of course, true that many situations are encountered rather than contrived or arranged. Nevertheless, analysts are always concerned with individual subjective definitions of these "objective" circumstances. Analysis centers on psychic reality.

Character is a dispositional or predictive concept. It tells what someone may ordinarily be expected to do. The designation of this or that type of character is arrived at only through a process of selection and abstraction that is carried out by an observer who has adopted a certain point of view; for example, the Freudian psychoanalytic point of view and, within that and more narrowly, the instinctual point of view ("oral character") or the diagnostic ("obsessional character"). The point of view will reflect the theoretical, technical, and literary choices of the obser-

---

[2]See also the illuminating comments on character in the critical dictionaries by Rycroft (1968) and by LaPlanche and Pontalis (1973), and the promising approach to character as communication to self and others by Bollas (1974).

ver. (By "literary choices" I refer to such masterful designations as Freud's: "those wrecked by success" and "the exceptions" [1916]. [See chapter 2.]) Contrary to the assumption of the naïve empiricist or positivist, there are no simple characterological facts waiting to be gleaned, for each observer, too, is constructing a reality.

As a dispositional concept, character is not the name of an entity that organizes or stabilizes. It is the name given to the particular way in which a person may be said to organize and stabilize his or her actions. Consequently, character development is not the development of an entity, but a progressive change in the way someone both defines and acts in his or her problematic situations. It is the sort of change which renders previously adequate descriptive terms—for instance, infantile or unstable—no longer applicable; at least they can no longer be applied to the same extent or with no significant qualification.

As a dispositional concept, character is closely related to the concept agent or person in action language. In action terms one would say that, methodologically, the observer focuses on the actions of a unitary person. A person is defined by the appropriate description of his or her actions. The idea of a person embraces someone's typical way of constructing realistic and unrealistic situations and viewing oneself and others in these situations (e.g., an innocent dealing with anal-sadistic persecutors); it also includes typical ways of behaving emotionally (e.g., savagely beating enemies to the punch) and typical perspectives that are developed on the past, the present, and the future (e.g., a Hell behind and a Heaven ahead). As was mentioned, much action is performed unconsciously, and the many actions each person is always performing are imperfectly coordinated—if not incompatible with one another.

This relation between character and agency may account for much of the abounding popularity of the concept of character. That is to say, much of the appeal of character may stem from its closeness to clinical work, and particularly from its suggesting the chief business of clinical interpretation, which is to define how and why each person systematically makes the life that he or she does. This clinical emphasis is precisely what I have been attempting to capture theoretically by giving a central place in action language to the person as agent.

It is necessary to underscore the idea of the person as *unitary* agent and to repeat that "unitary" does not imply perfectly coordinated actions or the absence of contradictory actions—what we are used to calling conflict (Schafer, 1978b). One speaks of the unitary agent in order to avoid positing the existence of a mental apparatus and then attributing to it a multiplicity of more or less independent constituent agencies. As soon as the idea of multiple agencies is invoked, one is inevitably committed to a mechanistic view of human psychology, and it does not then matter much whether those constituents are called different mental structures, such as the id, ego, and superego, or different selves or fragments of self. In the mechanistic conception, people are lived by their parts acting more or less autonomously, each according to its nature (e.g., the cruel superego or the grandiose self); here it is very much as if each of these parts is some kind of single-minded person who at best will accept some compromises. It is this conception that is epitomized in Freudian metapsychology.

Many analysts find it difficult to accept the idea of the unitary person as agent. This view of agency seems to deny conflict, that most central of all psychoanalytic concepts. But this is a mistaken understanding of action language. What is being urged is a different way of conceiving of conflict; it is being proposed that this way makes more theoretical and clinical sense (Schafer, 1978b). The proposed change requires one to give up thinking on the model of an energetically driven physical system with parts (drives, structures, etc.) that conflict with one another more or less autonomously and produce resultants; instead, one now must think of a person pursuing incompatible and contradictory courses of action or wishing to do so, experiencing distress in this regard, and attempting to carry out renunciations or develop compromises or highly synthesized solutions of the dilemmas being both created and confronted.

Among the many reasons why analysts find the unitary agent a difficult concept is their own responsiveness to what I have termed disclaimed action (Schafer, 1976 [chapter 7]; 1978a). Disclaimed action takes many forms, but what runs through all these forms is the exclusion of certain actions from the concept of oneself and others as active and responsible beings. Typical disclaimers in the verbal realm include such statements as "The impulse overwhelmed me," "His feeling slipped away," and "My thoughts are running away with me." Each such statement is a condensed narrative. Each narrative is a construction of experience rather than a factual introspective report of events in an inner world. Disclaimers are deeply rooted in our metaphoric language, and they are highly useful for certain adaptive as well as defensive purposes. Analysts and analysands alike have learned to think in these terms from the time of their earliest acquisition of language, and, for analysts, this way of thinking has been reinforced by the terms of metapsychology.

But metapsychology repeats rather than explains these narratives of a self that, far from always being the agent of its own experience, is often merely a helpless, passive observer of mental activity.[3] And yet, contrary to the language of metapsychology, good interpretations do not ever basically incorporate these disclaimers. Who would be proud of having said to a patient *in an interpretation,* "Your impulses overwhelmed you"? Although one might say such a thing quite usefully during preliminary empathic exploration of reports of subjective experience, especially if these are the disclaiming terms in which the analysand begins to give access to painful matters, one would not say it in a good interpretation. One way or another, a good interpretation conveys the idea that the impulse and the person are one, that the analysand cannot accept the insight that he or she wished to do the very action that is being disclaimed or to take a certain view of a traumatic experience, and that there are intelligible reasons why this is so. Ultimately, psychoanalytic interpretation is not *analysis* in the sense of decomposing material into its elements. Although it is true that such teasing apart of themes of issues does take place along the way, fundamentally, analytic interpretation is *synthesizing* in that it demonstrates the analysand's participation in every action, including the very action of disclaiming. In psychoanalytic work, synthesis does not follow analysis into parts; synthesis and resynthesis is inherent in interpretation.

[3]It is *always* the agent of its experience, for it always gives one or another set of meanings to those circumstances that are encountered rather than actively brought about (e.g., economic depression and loss of job viewed alternatively as "hard times," "persecution," or "proof of unworthiness").

On the basis of these considerations, it may be claimed that action language elucidates the messages conveyed by traditional analytic interpretation; it does not amount to a new, strange language of clinical intervention and certainly not to a hectoring attitude toward the analysand. The present attempt to elucidate the concept of character, long familiar and useful in clinical work, is being made in the same spirit.[4]

Ego-Syntonicity

For purposes of clinical interpretation, the key constituent of the concept of character is ego-syntonicity. This is so because the psychoanalytic modification of character depends on transforming activity that is, or at least seems to be, nonconflictual into conflictual activity.

Ego-syntonicity must not be conceived either superficially or in a biased manner. It will be conceived *superficially* whenever it is simply equated with what is consciously self-syntonic. This equation cannot hold, first, because too many important aspects of self are maintained unconsciously (e.g., the grandiose self of many narcissistic characters) and, second, because what is consciously self-syntonic may, unconsciously, be exceedingly dystonic. And ego-syntonicity will be conceived in a *biased* manner whenever it is simply equated with what is syntonic in relation to one aspect of the ego system, such as the defensive ego or the adaptive ego or the relatively autonomous ego functions. When Moore and Fine (1968), in their definition of "character disorder" (p. 26), explain ego-syntonicity on the basis of rationalization, idealization, and adaptive realistic gains, they manifest both of the biases I just mentioned, for even though they recognize that they are referring to conflictual matters with major unconscious elements, they overemphasize conscious experience and certain interests of the ego as against others. In this way they misrepresent a part as the whole, and they seem to say that there is unity when that is not what they mean. It is indeed difficult to know just how to conceptualize this key constituent of the concept of character, ego-syntonicity.

---

[4]Rado (1954), among others, approached the idea of the unitary person as agent, but his other theoretical commitments blocked his way to an adequate development of it.

I want now to propose a way out of this difficulty. I suggest that the concept of ego-syntonicity has always referred to those principles of constructing experience which seem to be beyond effective question by the person who develops and applies them. There seems to be virtually no way in which these principles can come into question, and this for two reasons: first, they are applied mostly unconsciously and pervasively, and so require extensive interpretation and working through before they can become a significant part of the analytic dialogue; and second, these principles are so fundamental that the mere raising of a question about them will itself be understood in their very terms. They are the person's fundamental grounds of understanding and certainty. Metaphorically, they are the eye that sees everything according to its structure and cannot see itself seeing.

A simple, common example of these characterological certainties is the basic, unconsciously pervasive conviction that one is unlovable and undeserving of love. The person who holds this conviction consistently constructs all possibly relevant experience in its terms and thus is always confirming its correctness and adequacy. That person not only assiduously collects obvious signs of dislike, but interprets actions of others that are indifferent in this regard, or even loving, as being other than they are, seeing them, for example, as exploitative seduction or as overestimation of his or her true self. Similarly, paranoid persons construct experience in terms that confirm grandiose and persecutory expectations, and they view anyone who dares raise a question in this regard mistrustfully as a deliberately or unwittingly dangerous enemy; in this context, an interpretation of a fear of being poisoned will be experienced unconsciously as a poisonous act or substance. One might say that these principles are beyond question in so far as the person treats the relevant questions about them not as questions but as evidence. In this way, questions are not allowed to exist outside the system of fundamental beliefs. The person's unquestioning and pervasive application of these principles thereby establishes a personal closed system.

On this view of ego-syntonicity it would seem a hopeless task to attempt modification of character. And there are, of course, those who maintain that fundamental character change is never achieved, not even by the best of analyses. An obsessive character once is an obsessive character forever: ambivalence, anal-sadism,

passive homosexuality, isolation of affect, and reaction formation continue always to be hallmarks of the obsessive character's
activity. Change can only be quantitative, never qualitative; one
may therefore only become *less* extremely obsessive, *less* self-
destructively and painfully obsessive, and the like. I shall return
to the question of how best to conceive of character change; for
now, I want only to link this conservative view of the matter to the
apparent implication of my preceding remarks that ego-syntonicity
implies a closed, perpetually self-confirming system of basic
principles for constructing experience.

I speak of the *apparent* implication of my remarks, for I
believe that in practice we encounter many characterological
actions whose organizing principles are not perfectly uniform or
integrated and whose heterogeneous composition is therapeutically accessible, the result being that during the course of analysis
these analysands do get to be seen, and to see themselves, as constructing different types of experience simultaneously. Further,
we come to recognize that at least some of these types of
experience are of a more neutral kind or developmentally more
advanced; of these developments we say that they show good
reality testing. It is this heterogeneous composition that provides
the fulcrum with the help of which it is possible to move the subjective world. The system is not closed, except perhaps under
conditions of great stress, which, when they abate, no longer preclude the development of more realistic perspectives. The
analysands of whom this is true can hear an interpretation as
such, at least some of the time, however else they hear it (e.g., as
criticism). Those who can't, are unanalyzable—at least during
that attempt at analysis. Any theory of effective interpretation or
therapeutic effect must allow for an interpretation's being heard
in more than one way.

In undertaking the analysis of a character problem, one
counts on there being some diversity of experiential principles,
even if the nature of this diversity is not clear at the time and will
not become clear until some point of access to them is discovered
by the analyst. The point of access may be some well-guarded
form of thinking hopefully, some shrugged-off way of esteeming
oneself realistically, or some shyly hidden but stable kind of loving. Here, by the way, is where variations among analysts in skill,

patience, compassion, sensitivity, and imagination make a therapeutic difference, and also variations in the goodness of fit between particular analysands and analysts.

It is important to be clear on one point especially: not just any diversity of experiential principles will do. This is so because in analytic work one always encounters some diversity of primitive principles, such as, archaic oral, anal, and phallic ways of constructing experience for instance, and also archaic defensive and superego ways. And, if this were all that there was to encounter, as might be the case in certain borderline conditions, one would have an unanalyzable person shifting around among equally irrational constructions—for instance, between feedings and enemas or between gross indulgences and cruel punishments. What is required of the analysand, therefore—and analysts have always known this—is some degree of development of neutral, rational experiential principles. The analysand need not be acting manifestly and consciously according to these more realistic principles; some analysands desperately guard against this possibility owing to their fear that terribly destructive consequences will ensue if they manifest accurate and neutral reality testing. It is especially the borderline patients who are likely to repress, project, negate or represent in dreams their truest perceptions of their analysts and their families; in these cases it is correct to say that character analysis must be constantly focused on the way these patients consistently and violently attack their own sense of reality and at the same time express it in obscure forms.

Another common type of diversity is encountered in analysands who seem so thoroughly narcissistic in their construction of experience that they never show concern for others except as the doings of these others bear directly on narcissistic issues. However, as Ruth Easser (1974) has already argued, this is not a true picture of the state of affairs. Rather, it is often the case that these analysands go to defensive extremes in order to obscure the extent to which they do or might concern themselves with others empathically. Much of their activity in analysis only becomes fully understandable when one takes into account that actual or prospective involvement with others is a danger situation in which they live constantly. Additionally, their blatantly unconcerned, egocentric activity must be viewed in part as a form of vigorous assault on the analyst's empathic participation in their subjective experience; this is an assault that is intended to forestall the dreaded recognition of mutual concern. Their relatedness to other people, far from being exclusively one of the fruits of the analysis, is a large part of the problem to be analyzed.[5] The analysis of the narcissistic character disorder requires a slow, patient approach to this diversity within an apparently monolithic closed system.

My conclusion with respect to ego-syntonicity is that any effective character analysis depends on some ego-dystonic features of the pathological character-actions. These actions must be performed conflictually. Metapsychologically speaking, some rational ego or ego functions must be collaborating with the analyst if any analysis of character is to be effected and any character change accomplished. In action terms, the person must be applying incompatible principles simultaneously— using more than one eye, so to speak—and must be able, by way of some of these principles, to recognize an interpretation as just that.

Character Change in Analysis

It is more a matter of definition than anything else whether or not one may speak of character change through analysis. A definition that stresses broad stylistic aspects makes it difficult, if not impossible, to speak of fundamental character change. In contrast, a definition that stresses the constituent actions that are subsumed by the term *character* gives one more latitude in this regard, for these constituents surely do often change to an appreciable degree. And an appreciable quantitative change may also be described as a qualitative change even when there is no precise or generally accepted convention specifying at what point quantity becomes quality.

Certain quantitative changes in action are seen commonly enough. For example, analysands no longer imagine their infantile danger situations as readily, for as a long time, and in such

---

[5]Kernberg (1975) recognizes this, in a way, in his emphasis on defensive splitting, while Kohut (1971, 1977) seems either to bypass the issue or to deny it.

extreme terms as they did earlier; they show that this is so by their dream reports, the errors they commit, their speaking frankly about an ever greater range of troublesome issues in the transference relationship, their moderating their defensive measures, and their manifesting and reporting fewer actions performed in severely anxious, guilty, or ashamed modes. Nor are effective functioning, secure relationships, and pleasurable and joyful actions so consistently excluded from their activity and from their experience of their activity and the activity of others. On these grounds they may be said to become appreciably less hysterical, obsessive, masochistic, or narcissistic, enough so to warrant speaking of their having achieved change of character. What was regularly disturbed or pathological before is no longer so; the expectations of the analytic observer concerning action are now different, even if the analysand's initial style of action remains recognizable. That style will, of course, be particularly recognizable in stressful situations.

But there is a better way of addressing the question of character change. It depends on the discussion of ego-syntonicity in the preceding section of this paper, and especially on the emphasis put there on the diversity of principles by which experience is organized. For it is possible on the basis of this diversity to modify the more archaic, less neutral principles in such a way that they no longer seem to lie beyond effective question. The analysand gets to experience them as conflictual after all. And the analysand no longer consciously fears and disclaims other well-defined ways of constructing experience to such an extent that he or she never undertakes such constructions long enough to make a real difference. It is this kind of change that is meant when one speaks of genuine insight and of the development through analysis of a continuing capacity for self-analysis. Thus, late in effective analyses and in postanalytic sessions, one sees analysands still beginning to create or accept crises of the old sort and then catching themselves in the act, questioning what they are up to—that is, asking themselves how they are threatened and why—and then going on to consider alternative views of their situations and the courses of action open to them—all of which, taken together, would have been unthinkable during early stages of their analyses. What seemed then to be closed systems and were, in fact, pretty closed, are now evidently and often much more agreeably open systems.

Character change lies, then, in the analysand's now living in vastly more complex worlds with vastly more complex repertoires of action, including the actions of representation of self and others in relation. They give different accounts of their lives and prospects. They believe in nonincestuous sexuality, in vaginas that are neither cloacal nor containers of teeth or hidden penises, in love that is not devouring, etc. And at the same time they know or, when necessary, they rediscover that they still employ the old contradictory principles and that they still revert to them, for example, when dreaming and when beginning to feel seriously endangered. Shouldn't these changes be granted the name of character change? To deny them this name would be to mistake a part (the remains of the past) for the whole (the new, enlarged context) and thus to commit a reductionistic error. It would also be to set up a simplistic and perfectionistic ideal, adherence to which can only becloud the most interesting and significant analytic issues.

This conception of character change in action terms might seem to be mistaking change of content for change of structure in that it puts so much emphasis on subjective experience. One cannot take up the topic of character change for long without introducing the long-familiar analytic distinction between change of content and change of structure. Change of content is exemplified by a swing from predominantly submissive modes of action to predominantly tyrannical modes of action; this is a change of content *only* in that the prevailing orientation of action and its representation remains authoritarian or sadomasochistic. Another frequently observed change of this sort is from manic to depressive or depressive to manic modes of action; here, the prevailing orientation remains oral-devouring, reparative, and focused on guilt, whether by proclamation or vehement denial. Analysts have learned not to be impressed by such changes of content; for more convincing signs of enduring and adaptive change, they have looked to change of structure.

Change of structure may be defined in traditional metapsychological terms as change in pattern of ego functions. This change includes lasting modification of preferred defensive measures, the direction being from more to less archaic and ego-limiting defense; more command on the ego's part over modes of activity previously dominated by the id and superego trends; decreased inter- and intrasystemic conflict; improved efficiency of such ego functions as reality testing and synthesis; the attainment of stable and gratifying relations with others; also, increased reserves of neutralized energy and improved capacity for neutralizing the energies of the id and superego, as manifest in reduced regression-rate and decreased power of infantile instinctual fixations. Reference might also be made now to maturer forms of narcissism and the completion of separation–individuation and the attainment of object constancy. If one recalls the typical traditional definitions of character, one readily recognizes that these features of *structural* change also imply *character* change in a progressive developmental direction.

I tried to show earlier that the metapsychological account of character is translatable into action terms, and I shall not extend that demonstration now in connection with the closely allied concept of structural change. But I do want to show that there are complexities concealed and ignored in the distinction between structure and content as it has usually been made. The complexities are these: thematic analysis of content is a form of structural analysis, and the tripartite structural classifications have always depended on prior appraisal of content. One does not, after all, see the ego or superego; nor does one see systems in conflict or mechanisms of defense coping with impulses. Rather, the analyst defines different types of content in the ideational and emotional aspects of action, including action in fantasy. As analysands change, analysts find them developing certain themes less often, less extremely, and with less distress, and they are able to define new themes in their analysands' actions; these are themes that imply a more stable, differentiated, and unified sense of self and others, a more consistent and coherent defensive strategy, and so on. These themes are, of course, defined both verbally and non-verbally. The metapsychological structures that have always been referred to in discussions of change of structure are formalized and abstract theoretical accounts of the changes of action and the experience of action, and these changes imply that different principles of constructing experience ("content") are being employed by the person under study.

Whether one calls it structure or content thus depends not on what one observes or can observe, but on the kinds of questions one is asking, the kinds of things one wants to say, and, ultimately, the kind of psychological reality one wants to define and work in. All change of content is redescribable as change of structure and vice versa. On this account, it is closer to clinical interpretation and the clinical situation generally to attempt to describe or name those changes of content that may safely be taken to indicate change of a stable and beneficial sort. And for theoretical purposes, it is best to remain as close as possible to the clinical. For example, when a fantasy of exalted power replaces a fantasy of utter helplessness, one is observing a change of content with little gain in adaptiveness and long-range stability; so our experience tells us, and so our way of making sense of human beings tells us. In contrast, when an analysand steadily maintains and implements ideals of realistic appraisal of what he or she can and will do reliably, when earlier that analysand communicated only fantasies of helplessness or of grandiose power or swings between the two, one is observing a change of content with considerable and observable adaptive consequences. In the same way one may observe a change in both the construction and content of the predominant danger situations and of preferred modes of gratification, and one may then justifiably speak of structural or character change.

The preceding account of change of content and structure is relevant to the broad principles of action language in the following way. Action language takes account of the fact that each action lends itself to multiple descriptions. It may be described on various levels of abstraction (e.g., as a simple act or as an expression of a broad pattern), and it may be described from different points of view (e.g., as transferential, resistant, adaptive). Although the formalistic description of actions in terms of id, ego, and superego has some uses for purposes of generalization, it is only one kind of account of actions, and it is tied to a mechanistic view of people as mental apparatuses. Consequently, it is useful to develop other, more clinically anchored, accounts of people as agents.

The account I favor is this: Character change is change of action such that descriptions which earlier were reliable, comprehensive, and therapeutically very much to the point, no longer apply or at least are no longer adequate. Thus, one must still describe a tyrant in very much the same authoritarian or sadomasochistic terms as one uses to describe a slave or a mouse; however, one cannot justifiably continue to describe an analysand in some same set of terms when he or she has begun reliably to include loving others relatively consciously, unanxiously, and pleasurably, in an overall scheme of living. Character change, then, is a required change in the psychoanalytic description of the analysand's typical, expectable ways of unconsciously constructing conflictual situations, of acting in these situations, and of developing experiential reports of these situations and their correlative actions.

Chapter 11

CHARACTER TRAITS AND OBJECT RELATIONSHIPS

JOSEPH SANDLER

As Nunberg (1956b) once remarked, "character is an elusive phenomenon." It is generally accepted that the term is often used synonymously with "personality," referring, as the psychiatric dictionary puts it, to "the characteristic . . . behavior-response patterns that each person evolves, both consciously and unconsciously, as his style of life" (Hinsie and Campbell, 1940, p. 556). The early writers on character and character traits, beginning with Freud, who shocked his readers in 1908 with his paper, "Character and Anal Erotism" [see chapter 1], were primarily concerned with understanding particular character traits as surface manifestations of instinctual wishes of one sort or another. This view reflects what can be called a "discharge" theory of character. As Freud put it in that paper: "the permanent character-traits are either unchanged prolongations of the original instincts, or sublimations of those instincts, or reaction-formations against them" (p. 26).

The idea that character can reflect defensive compromise was given particular emphasis by the work of Wilhelm Reich (1933), who saw character as arising from infantile instinctual conflict, reflecting in particular the mastery of such conflict by the use of defenses, leading ultimately to the so-called character-armor (*Charakterpanzerung*). Although Reich did not explicitly take into account the way in which adaptation to early social reality contributed to the development of character, this was later remedied by Hartmann, Erikson, Fenichel, and others. An important consequence of Reich's approach was that *character*

This chapter originally appeared in *Psychoanalytic Quarterly*, 50:694–708, 1981. Reprinted by special permission of the author and the publisher.

tended to be equated with *ego*. Thus, in 1945, Fenichel commented that "the dynamic and economic organization of its positive actions and the ways in which the ego combines its various tasks in order to find a satisfactory solution, all of this goes to make up character" (p. 466). Small wonder, then, that he went on to say that his (Fenichel's) "description of *character* is nearly identical with that previously given for the *ego*" (p. 467). It should be noted that for Fenichel, as for others before him, character traits differed from symptoms in that symptoms were seen as ego-dystonic and character traits ego-syntonic, a distinction which, from a present-day perspective, is clearly not entirely valid. It is safe to conclude, however, that with the burgeoning of ego psychology, interest in character traits declined. But the same has not been true for so-called character neurosis, or character disorder. The notion of character disturbance has been used, from the beginning, for a whole range of clinical pictures which do not manifest symptoms but "modes of behavior leading to recurrent or permanent difficulty in the patient's relation to his environment" (as Laplanche and Pontalis put it in 1973). In recent years particular attention has been paid to the narcissistic character disorders, in which the pathology is seen as radically different from that which occurs in the neuroses, and in which the patient is usually severely disturbed; so much so that it is often difficult for authors to differentiate between narcissistic character disturbance and borderline psychotic disorders. Here, too, character traits, as organized units of behavior, or as relatively fixed characteristics or dispositions of the individual, have dropped out of the picture, perhaps because we can now have a fuller view of the structural organization underlying the surface picture.

This paper is concerned with a particular theme, that of the connection between certain idiosyncracies or traits of character and the theory of object relationships. The general theory of character traits will not be discussed, and it should not be thought that the ideas put forward here apply to all traits of character or personality. There does, however, seem to be a fruitful area of psychoanalytic investigation still open to us in relation to the function and meaning of certain aspects of character.

The topic can be approached somewhat obliquely from the starting point of a consideration of certain aspects of countertransference. In a paper on countertransference and role-responsiveness

(Sandler, 1976) I put forward the idea that concepts such as transference, projection, and externalization could be widened to include the patient's attempts to manipulate or to provoke the analyst into responding in a particular way. The comment was made that:

> In the transference, in many subtle ways, the patient attempts to prod the analyst into behaving in a particular way and unconsciously scans and adapts to his perception of the analyst's reaction. . . . [We can make the assumption] that a relationship or, to say the least, an interaction, develops between the two parties to the analytic process. . . . this is in large part (though, of course, not wholly) determined by what I shall refer to as the intrapsychic role-relationship which each party tries to impose on the other. . . . I want to emphasize . . . that the role relationship of the patient in analysis at any particular time consists of a role in which he casts himself, and a *complementary* role in which he casts the analyst at that particular time. The patient's transference would thus represent an attempt by him to impose an interaction, an interrelationship . . . between himself and the analyst. . . . The patient's unconscious wishes and mechanisms with which we are concerned in our work are expressed intrapsychically in (descriptively) unconscious images or fantasies, in which both self and object in interaction have come to be represented in particular roles. In a sense the patient, in the transference, attempts to *actualize these in a disguised way,* within the framework and limits of the analytic situation [pp. 44–45].

In this formulation what was said applied not only to unconscious instinctual wishes, but *"to the whole gamut of unconscious . . . wishes related to all sorts of needs, gratifications and defences"* (p. 45). The term *actualization* was used in the dictionary sense of the term as "a making actual"; a "realization in action or fact."[1]

---

[1]Arlow (1969a), in referring to a patient who responded traumatically to a brother's death, said: "The actual death of his brother constituted an actualization of his fantasy wish to have been born without a twin" (p. 17). Actualization in that context referred to the perception of a real event which corresponded to the fantasy wish. In the present paper, the concept is used in the more active sense of bringing an event about, of acting on and modifying reality so that changes in that reality are perceived by the individual concerned.

One of the examples given to illustrate what can be called
role-evocation in the analysis was the following:

> This patient, aged 35, had not had any previous analysis and
> had very little knowledge of the analytic process. He was
> referred to me because of extreme anxiety about making
> public presentations of his work, although he felt absolutely
> competent and at ease in private and informal discussions.
> He had had a very narrow education, was the son of Eastern
> European immigrants, but because of his great financial and
> organizational skills had risen to a very high position in an
> extremely large financial organization. In the initial inter-
> view I found that he responded extremely well to trial inter-
> pretations, and I felt that work with him was going to be
> rewarding and a pleasure. During the first week or two of his
> analysis I found that I was talking very much more than I
> usually do. I should say that I am not an unduly silent analyst.
> After a little while I felt that something was making me
> anxious in regard to this patient, and some self-analytic
> reflexion on my part showed me that I was afraid he would
> leave, that I was anxious to keep him, to lower his anxiety
> level so that he would stay in analysis and that I was talking
> more than usual in order to avoid the aggressive side of his
> ambivalent feelings. When I saw this, I felt relieved and reverted
> to my more usual analytic behavior. However, I noticed at
> once the urge to talk during the session and became aware
> that the patient, by a slight inflexion of his voice, succeeded in
> ending every sentence with an interrogation, although he did
> not usually formulate a direct question. This gave me the
> opportunity to point out to him what he was doing (he was
> quite unaware of it, just as I had been unaware of it in him)
> and to show him how much he needed to have me reassure
> him by talking. He then recalled how he would feel extremely
> anxious as a child when his father returned home from work,
> and would completely engage his father in conversation, ask-
> ing him many questions in order to be reassured that his
> father was not angry with him. His father had been a pro-
> fessional fighter, was very violent, and the patient was
> terrified of him but needed his father's admiration and love,
> to be the preferred child. (Later in the analysis we were, as one
> might expect, to see his fear of his own hostility to his father.)
> He told me that his father had the habit of not listening and

not responding, and how frightening this was. The patient then realized that from early childhood onwards he had developed the trick of asking questions without directly asking them, and this had become part of his character, being intensified in situations where he feared disapproval and needed supplies of reassurance from authority figures [Sandler, 1976, pp. 45–46].

It became clear from cases like this, and others, that "the analyst will often respond overtly to the patient in a way in which he feels indicates *only* his own (the analyst's) problems. . . .[But] very often the irrational response of the analyst . . . may . . . be usefully regarded as a compromise-formation between his own tendencies and *his reflexive acceptance of the role which his patient is forcing on him*" (Sandler, 1976, p. 46). And what occurs in the analytic relationship, in what can, broadly speaking, be called the transference–countertransference interchange, also occurs outside it, and it seems evident that the dimensions of transference–countertransference are identical with those of object relationships.

The example of this patient has been quoted at some length because his way of speaking can be regarded as reflecting a mechanism, developed in his childhood, which would certainly merit the designation of being a "characteristic" if not a character trait. It had the specific function of *actualizing* a particular object-related wishful fantasy by evoking appropriate responses in those around the patient. This is very different from the "discharge" view of a character trait, mentioned earlier in this paper, in which the surface expression is an end-result, reflecting either an instinctual derivative or a defensive operation, or a compromise between the two. Rather, it is a view of certain fixed personality characteristics as "evocative," in the sense which has been described. It is such traits of character which are responsible for what have been called "character transferences" (Sandler, Holder, Kawenoka, Kennedy, and Neurath, 1969), described in the analyses of children, and which refer to:

[Those] aspects of the patient's relationship to people (or to special groups of people) [which] are not in any way specific to the therapist, but are rather in the nature of character traits.

Such reactions . . . very often are seen in the *earliest* sessions
of treatment [and later become transference, in a stricter
sense]. Typical of such manifestations is the occurrence in the
analysis of a habitual tendency to placate or appease, or
habitual demandingness, or a sadomasochistic tendency
[p. 641].

An example would be the case of a child who is frightened of
policemen or doctors, or anyone in uniform or authority, and
who begins treatment by being frightened of the analyst. This
might occur, for example, when a patient, who habitually exter-
nalizes onto adults critical aspects of his superego, relates to the
analyst in the same way as to any other adult. This would be a
"character transference." The distinctive features of this form of
relating can be brought out further by considering the example
of an adult patient who appears late for an analytic session. This
may be the consequence of a specific transference situation arising in treatment, in which, for example, an anxiety about a
homosexual attachment to the analyst has been activated. On the
other hand, the lateness might reflect a characteristic tendency in
the patient to be late.

It is possible to speculate on whether the analyst's responses
(including countertransference responses in the broad sense of
the term) to "character transference" from the side of the patient
are different in quality from the range of his normal countertransference responses to transference proper. I suspect that
there are important differences which might merit closer study.

Perhaps the most striking constellations of character traits
which frequently show themselves in "character transference"
are those which relate to sadomasochistic tendencies within the
individual. Every analyst knows of the provocative and evocative
capacities of patients with such tendencies, which have been cari-
catured in various ways. Patients with sadomasochistic character
tendencies are often adept in enticing the analyst (and others in
the extra-analytic world) to react critically in a way which
immediately evokes the most damning criticism and condemnation of the analyst by the patient. Such sadomasochistic character
tendencies are more than a simple tendency to express a wish or
constellation of wishes coming from the depths to the surface.
What we see is a mechanism which *entices* others to give a par-

ticular sort of response, a response which must be wish-fulfilling in the sense that all object relationships involve wishes, not only for instinctual gratification, but also for particular sorts of affirmation. The sadomasochistic patient needs the sadomasochistic dialogue, not only to gratify his sadistic and masochistic wishes, but also to secure the good feelings and safety which accompany the actualization of a wished-for childhood relationship.

The relationship of the unconscious wish to object relationships needs some amplification. In a previous paper (Sandler and Sandler, 1978), it was argued that:

> [W]ish-fulfillment is a far broader concept than that of the gratification of instinctual drives or their derivatives. . . . We can assume that what we call object relationships . . . represent the fulfillment of important needs in the developing child as well as in the adolescent and adult. Such needs may show themselves in the form of wishes, which may or may not be predominantly instinctual. . . . The wish may be . . . motivated by the need to restore feelings of well-being and safety. . . . Wishes are aroused by changes in the object world as much as by internal pressures. . . . The individual is constantly obtaining a special form of gratification through his interaction with his environment and with his own self, constantly providing himself with . . . something which in the object relationship we can refer to as "affirmation." Through his interaction with different aspects of his world, in particular his objects, he gains a variety of reassuring feelings. We put forward the thesis that the need for this "nourishment," for affirmation and reassurance, has to be satisfied constantly in order to yield a background of safety [p. 286].

The further comment was made that:

> [T]he patient in analysis tends to *actualize* the particular role relationship inherent in his current dominant unconscious wish or fantasy, and . . . he will try to do this (usually in a disguised and symbolic way) within the framework of the psychoanalytic situation. People also do this outside analysis, and it is not a great step to say that *the striving towards actualization is part of the wish-fulfilling aspect of all object relationships* [p. 289].

The view was taken that the particular content of the self-object dialogue is heavily influenced by the child's earliest experiences in interaction with his objects, influenced both from the side of the child and from that of the object. It is abundantly clear that the idiosyncrasies of the interchange between child and parent, even in the earliest period of life, remain as part of the object relationship. Moreover, the child learns to initiate wish-fulfilling responses from the object by the use of various mechanisms and signals which are involved in the dialogue. It should be stressed that even painful and distressing relationships can be safety-giving, reassuring, and affirming for many different reasons, as well as instinctually satisfying, and the typical sadomasochistic type of relationship exemplifies this extremely well. At this point it can be said that many of the techniques used by the child in the dialogue with his objects can be regarded as object-related character traits, or as the precursors of these, which are neither instinctual derivatives nor defenses, nor even combinations of the two, *but devices elaborated in order to evoke specific wished-for responses in others*. The example of the man who ended all his sentences with a question mark is pertinent here.

Thus far the role of character traits in evoking responses from others has been considered. Such evoked responses enable the wished-for and valued dialogues or role relationships which constitute object relationships to be realized or actualized by prompting real objects to respond in particular ways. This occurs in ordinary life and in the psychoanalytic situation in the transference, whether this be character transference, so-called transference manifestations, or transference neurosis. Within this framework we can see, I believe quite clearly, how character traits can have an essential function in the present in helping to bring about (or attempting to bring about) the wish-fulfillment inherent in object relationships. However, everything that has been discussed so far is in the realm of *actual* interpersonal relationships, of "transactions" between people, and in order that our argument be truly psychoanalytic, we need to expand it further. This is perhaps best done by a reference to a further example.

My patient, a man of forty, was a brilliant nuclear physicist whose capacities were well known to his superiors, but who had suffered all his life from a habitual tendency to procrastinate. He would delay writing his reports, or preparing papers for presentation, although he usually managed to succeed in getting them done at the last moment. He told me, "I can't 'produce' until I feel that a catastrophe might happen. It is as if I have to wait until just before some awful explosion might occur, and then I can usually force myself to sit down and work." In a previous analysis this tendency had been linked with the gaining of erotic pleasure through anal retentiveness, as witnessed by his childhood constipation, and with the satisfaction which he obtained through his sadistic control of his own feces. It had also been connected with his fantasies of being able to control his world in an omnipotent fashion.

During his analysis with me he described many problems connected with his delaying and holding back, and there is no doubt that this particular character trait of his had a distinctly "anal" quality. However, after about a year of analysis, he found that he had kept postponing paying my account for some weeks, finding one reason or another to delay payment. At the beginning of the session, when he had confessed that he had once again postponed writing a check, he told me that he was sure that I was extremely angry with him. He told me that I had looked angry when he saw me, and that he was sure now that I would explode with rage if he went on postponing any longer. He added that I must be so full of rage that I could surely think of nothing else. I was able to show him that he had used delaying payment as a way of bringing about a situation in which he felt that I was on the point of exploding and at the same time had all my attention focused on him. There was ample evidence that this repeated a situation which had occurred over and over again in his childhood, in which he would not do things which his mother had asked him to do, and she would respond to his provocation by nagging him, getting angrier and angrier. While she nagged him, he told me, she would turn her attention away from the other children and from her husband. He had learned to recognize just how far he could go and would finally do what she had wanted just before she "exploded." I should mention that this patient had a brother, some two-and-a-half years his junior, who, as a sickly child from birth, had "stolen," as the patient put it, his mother's attention from the moment of his birth. He went on to tell me that at times when he found it difficult to work, he could "almost hear the voice of his mother nagging at him."

It is possible to see that the tendency to delay had, in this patient, a dimension additional to those usually described for this typically "anal" character trait. This dimension is that of the specific object relationship involved. A major function of this patient's delaying was certainly to bring about the equivalent of "being nagged by mother." However, although it was possible to see the operation of this mechanism as it developed in the transference, this patient was not a provoker of others to be angry with him, or even to "nag" at him. He managed to deal with his colleagues in a more or less adequate way, and the symptom for which he had come to analysis was not connected with the trait of character we are considering. His dialogue with his mother occurred, for the most part, in his unconscious fantasy life, although he had to enact his *delaying* in reality in order to reexperience in fantasy the relationship with his mother in which she attended to him by nagging. The "transaction" he had with his mother was more of an intrapsychic transaction than those I have considered earlier. This patient's dialogue with his mother, which was reassuring and gratifying to him, took place in fantasy rather than reality, and when it emerged in the transference, it was more than a simple "character transference."

If we assume that his character trait involved the provoking of an object, and was in itself useless without the appropriate response from the object; that is, it was a method of bringing about a wish-fulfilling actualization, then we have to ask how this is possible with an object *in fantasy*. We would have no difficulty in answering this if we were dealing with a psychotic patient who hallucinated the mother and her nagging. One could simply say that the patient actualized the wished-for interaction with the object by a hallucinatory perception of the object, just as occurs in the dream; one could then speak of the various disguises and transformations which occur in the hallucination as being the hallucination work, just as one speaks of the dream work. It can be assumed that the maternal introject consists of a structural organization, based upon the experiences in childhood of interaction with the mother and distorted by a great variety of the patient's projections and externalizations during the course of his development. The relationship to this introject would be the basis for the nagging-and-being-nagged dialogue with the mother, which would occur in the hallucinatory experience of which we are speaking. But this patient did not hallucinate; in fact, he was largely unconscious of what was happening. Nevertheless, the difficulty can be circumvented by introducing the concept of *subliminal, unconscious,* or *preconscious* illusion. This is a difficult idea to formulate and probably a rather implausible one at first sight, because it seems to involve a contradiction. How can we have an illusion that something or someone is present and not see them? And yet, on reflection, the idea is not implausible. We are all aware that we can perceive below the threshold of conscious perception, that information can reach us subliminally and affect us profoundly. And indeed we must all have become aware, one way or another, of the degree to which we carry on our fantasy lives just below the level of conscious awareness. Of course, the term *unconscious* is used here in a purely descriptive sense. Possibly, *preconscious* would be better, and it would certainly be quite in order to describe the phenomenon we are discussing as a preconscious illusion. What is suggested is that we can, and do, create illusions in order to actualize our unconscious wishes, and that the illusions of this sort are normally kept below the threshold of normal perception. They hover just beneath it, so to speak, but the capacity for reality testing makes all the difference here between normality and psychosis.[2]

What has just been described applies to the patient who habitually procrastinated, who used a specific technique (or, if you like, a character trait) which he had developed as part of the object-relationship dialogue with his mother, as a way of recreating her presence below the threshold of conscious awareness. But he established more than her unconscious presence. He recreated a dialogue with her which was a central part of his wished-for interaction with her. By experiencing her nagging, albeit below the threshold of conscious awareness, he could feel that he could obtain her exclusive attention. He could obtain a

[2]The relation between (descriptively) unconscious fantasies and reality is delicately traced by Arlow (1969a,b) in two papers relating fantasy to disturbances of conscious experience, as well as to memory and reality testing.

sort of reassurance and affirmation, as well as satisfy libidinal and aggressive rivalrous wishes. His habitual postponing, although it may have had its roots in the anal phase of development, was a technique for evoking the subliminal, intrapsychically real experience of the transaction with mother.

The notion of mental "presences" is, of course, not new. In the 'thirties, Edoardo Weiss (1936) described a phenomenon which he called "psychic presence." We can extend this to the concept of unconscious psychic presence and relate the creation of such presences, with whom we interact, to the structures which we call introjects (Schafer, 1968). But we can go still further and speak of the unconscious relationship, interaction, and dialogue with the unconscious phantom presence as a source of the wish-fulfillment inherent in the individual's central object relationships. There is an attempt here to be more specific than one would be by referring in a general way to unconscious fantasies, by labeling the interaction with the phantom presences as unconscious fantasy. In the first place, the term has a variety of meanings. Secondly, the process of unconscious illusory interaction alluded to here is quite different from the ego function of thinking; and fantasy as a "split-off" form of thinking (Freud, 1911a) is quite different from the interaction with unconscious illusory presences in the way it has been described here. This interaction is, of course, stage-managed by that part of the psychic apparatus which we refer to as the unconscious ego, and it is not possible here to go into the difficult conceptual problems involved in the question of why and how one part of the ego can be busy deceiving another part. But it can be added, at this point, that the idea of phantom presences may also be of use in conceptualizing our relationship to those introjects which enter into the superego as well as in understanding the gains we obtain from conforming to ideals of one sort or another.

It should be clear by now that the message of this paper is that we can approach the study of such phenomena as character traits by asking ourselves first what the function of the character trait is, and next, how it operates to fulfill that function. It can then be seen how such traits are not only the expression of instinctual wishes, the product of defenses against such wishes, or combination of the two, but are also ways of evoking responses from our significant objects, or rather their present-day representatives. These latter are either actual persons in the real world, or phantom objects in a world of unconscious reality, in an illusory world which is unconsciously created and unconsciously perceived. They may be part of transactions with people who actually exist outside ourselves, or unconscious transactions with phantom objects. Such transactions are not, of course, simple repetitions of early relationship dialogues. They are affected by all the displacements and modifications which result from the operation of our defenses; and such object-related dialogues, although always wish-fulfilling, may be as much defensive as instinctually gratifying. Above all, they function to provide safety, affirmation, and well-being.

This presentation has intentionally been limited to some aspects of character, but the arguments put forward here can be developed in a number of different directions. What is true for so-called character traits may also be true for many symptoms, or for a variety of aspects of behavior. And the role of character development in relation to techniques for obtaining narcissistic supplies is another important area for exploration. But, perhaps above all, what these considerations may lead us toward is the detailed study of both overt and covert aspects of personality and character from the point of view of their relation to the dialogues which constitute our object relations. Man is a social animal, but as psychoanalysts we must know that man lives simultaneously in two societies—one we know as the people in the real external world, and the other a phantom world in which the objects are equally real but unconsciously perceived. We interact with our objects in both these worlds and spend much of our waking life trying to modify ourselves and our environments so that the discrepancy between the two is minimized. From this flow transference, projection, rationalization, and a great many other familiar everyday phenomena.

Chapter 12

CHARACTER DISORDERS

Karl Menninger

The Scope of the Problem of Character Disorder

In the category of character disorder we include a great many individuals whom the layman would consider simply queer or mean or unhappy or vicious or wicked. We include other individuals who seem superficially to be quite well adjusted but in whom on closer observation we find some disbalance or lack of proper integration between the various constituent parts of the self. Until recently such individuals were looked on as problems for the clergyman if their character defect was relatively mild or for the police court and the penologist if their character defect was severe. The normal individual is one in whom there is a proper balance between the forces of ego, superego, and id and in whom the ego has a proper relationship to outside physical and social reality.

Recently it has been shown that disbalance in these functions, which is not marked or severe enough to create actual psychosis, psychoneurosis, or perversion, creates character disorders or character neurosis. Psychoanalytic characterology, as this branch of the theory is called, is the least systematically developed. There is considerable confusion concerning the terminology which is to be applied to the various character types, with undoubted repetitions under different names of very similar character syndromes. Many points of the theory of character disorder remain to be worked out. However, with its development we may say that the last group of abnormal behavior types which previously could not be explained scientifically are beginning to be understood in a scientific manner.

This chapter originally appeared in *The Psychodynamics of Abnormal Behavior,* pp. 384–403, ed. J. F. Brown. New York: McGraw-Hill, 1940. By permission of the publisher.

Before we go on to the detail of the psychoanalytic characterology and attempt a systematic classification of the various forms of defective character, it may be well to say something of the history of the problem and to give some examples of character disorders. Although laymen have for years considered such individuals simply as morally degenerate people, or as markedly unhappy people, professional psychiatrists have for some time realized that certain character defects should be studied psychologically. Kraepelin introduced the problem to psychiatry. He used the concepts of "original morbid states" and "psychopathic personalities." The concept of original morbid states has been given up in modern psychiatry. *Psychopathic personality,* however, became a widely used nosological classification. By such a term Kraepelin referred in general to the individuals we now classify as behavior problems. In this group he placed the sexually perverse, the unstable, the litigious, alcoholics, narcotic addicts, fraudulent people like swindlers, and some criminals. It is easy to see that this included only individuals whom the layman considers morally or ethically degenerate and vicious, or in other words, individuals whose behavior if mild was treated by moral exhortation and if severe by the criminal court. It was certainly an advance to consider these individuals psychiatrically. Besides Kraepelin's concept of the psychopathic personality other similar concepts like those of "moral imbecile," "moral idiot," and "moral insanity" are found in the literature. The term *psychopath* or *psychopathic personality* is, however, misleading. Etymologically it means "mentally sick," as in the word psychopathological, where actually the sickness of these individuals is usually concerned with alloplastic rather than autoplastic behavior problems. The disordered character seldom is mentally sick in the sense of being neurotic or psychotic; rather the internal disharmony in his personality is projected into action. He gets drunk and ends in the police court, he forges checks, he repeatedly insults his employers, he cannot tell the truth, or he seduces any girl under any circumstances. He does not have delusions or hallucinations or depressions or phobias. To call these individuals "moral imbeciles" is also misleading, because actually they often have very superior intelligence and insight into their behavior difficulties. No matter how clearly they foresee the consequences of their behavior, however, this has but little regulating influence on their actions. Psychoanalysis has shown that there are disordered characters who are in no way "morally degenerate" but who still present psychiatric problems in that they are unhappy or misfits or cannot make friends or hold jobs. By persons with character disorder we consequently mean those individuals whose internal unconscious conflicts lead them to become maladjusted without becoming psychotic, neurotic, or perverse. We have seen that the neurotic and perverse personalities merge gradually into what we must call normal personalities. Between the normal individual and the defective character there is even less of a definite dividing line.

The damage done to the personality of the individual by the character disorders is sometimes even greater than that done by the psychoses. For this reason Bleuler (1924) writes, "Many psychopaths are really only in the social sense not 'insane,' before the forum of natural science they suffer from the same anomalies as many insane, only in a slighter degree. They are paranoid, schizoid, latent epileptics, cyclothymic, etc." He might also have added that some of these vary from the perverse only in degree, so that they are related to the sexually perverse. Others are related to the various stages of infantile development and remain infantile. The disordered character is often so near to the layman's idea of normal, however, that a few examples are in order before we describe the psychoanalytic theory of the structure of the personality of the disordered character.

All of us have known individuals with character disorders. Some years ago the author had occasion to interview a young woman student of eighteen. She had been drinking and going to beer parlors since she was twelve. She had had sexual relationships with nearly twenty men. She had had two abortions within the last two years. At the time of the interview she was having sexual relationships with two individuals, mutual friends, often in the same evening. She was insulting and sharp-tongued about the house. One might think this young woman was a child of the gutter, but actually she came from upper-class parents who were well educated and had the highest ethical ideals. Everything had been done for her. Most individuals have met persons of this kind and have considered them simply "bad" or morally irresponsible. To the person trained in modern psychodynamic theory the young woman in question was a neurotic character, who, despite her high intelligence, could not control her underlying erotic and aggressive urges. Psychiatric examination of the girl and her parents indicated that the superficially moral and perfect family life had actually been marred by brutal scenes and lack of affection between parents and child. The young woman was not a "happy sinner" but rather an unhappy individual driven to seek the love she should have had from her father in every man whom she met and, similarly, working out the resentment she felt against her father with her aggressive infidelity to her various lovers.

Take the case of the similar type of personality in the male. Mr. X. has three times in his career been worth more than a million dollars, has had three beautiful young wives, all of whom have had to divorce him, and, at the age of forty, is drinking himself to death. He is good-looking and intelligent. He used to work hard as an investment banker. He would work hard to get rich, fall in love, marry, and have what to all his friends seemed a perfect economic, social, and emotional adjustment. It was, however, as if he could not stand success. He would begin drinking, become maritally unfaithful, start neglecting his business, and be back where he started, usually considerably scarred in the psychological sense from the rise and fall. His first wife divorced him when he began to bring prostitutes into the home and flaunt his behavior before both wife and children. His second wife divorced him when in a drunken rage he broke a chair over her back. His third wife divorced him when he began to spend on chorus girls the insurance he was building up for his children's education. Most of his friends looked on him as a happy-go-lucky, daredevil sort of a fellow who occasionally fell into bad luck in his business, began to dissipate for that reason, and who, as a result, got into marital difficulties. To the psychiatrist he was quite obviously trying to destroy himself.

But not all disordered characters are of the "wild" sort. Many of them seem all too inhibited, too "goody-goody." The author recently interviewed a young man who had been an excellent student of physics and had nearly completed work for a doctor's degree in this subject. Suddenly he began to lose interest and wished to withdraw from the university. In this connection he consulted the writer. One might have thought from his attitude that the young man was going to develop a schizophrenic psychosis, but he showed absolutely no pathology of the cognitive processes. Despite the fact that he was intelligent and really rather handsome, this individual at the time had no friends nor had he ever had any. He was twenty-two years of age and had never had a date with a girl. He was living on a campus where there were some two thousand other young men and he knew none of them intimately. He had neither admiration nor affection for his parents nor for any of his relatives. His only activity outside studies had been reading literature and occasionally going alone to the moving pictures. He spent a great deal of time in daydreaming but not of a psychotic sort. He was perfectly rational about the daydreaming, knew that it was fantasy, and had considerable insight into the role it played in his psychological adaptations. He lost interest in study when it came close to his graduation, that is, when he might have had to use his knowledge in contact with other individuals. Whereas most of his acquaintances probably thought him shy, backward, a bookworm, to the psychiatrist he was an example of a schizoid personality. Undoubtedly many of our mathematicians and other theoreticians in science are just as shy and withdrawn as this young man, and their scientific activity may be looked on, just as this young man's, as a sublimation. They are, however, engaged in socially useful work and for that reason are not to be looked on as having character disorders. This young man was schizoid in his character because he could not allow himself the possibility of giving away anything of himself, even to society at large in the impersonal form of scientific achievement. The basic emotional pattern of his life was that he loved himself so much he could give love to no one else.

Disordered characters are not only the "wild" and "queer" ones, but include also the antisocial, the criminals, and the gangsters, and even such anomalies as the chronic practical joker or those who establish queer philanthropies. Many of the bandits and gangsters we are constantly reading of in the newspapers are examples of disordered characters. Dillinger was such a disordered character; so are Al Capone and the numerous other

American gangsters. Don Quixote and Tyl Eulenspiegel and Robin Hood are literary or historical figures that fall in this category.

The Psychoanalytic Theory of Character Disorder

According to psychoanalysis the psychopathic personality or character disorder represents a disharmony between the adjustment of the ego, the id, and the superego, and reality, or an inharmonious combination of these factors. The character disorder differs from the psychosis or psychoneurosis in that although external conflict leads to regression and unconscious conflict this conflict is worked out on the environment rather than within the self. The symptoms are thus *alloplastic*. The disordered character differs from the perverse in that the ego will not accept the infantile libidinal and aggressive urges in their original form. It is, of course, impossible to draw any strict dividing line between normality, psychosis, perversion, and the character disorder. Thus the young woman whom we described above as being a neurotic character would have been psychotic had her actual sexual adventures been imagined in the form of schizophrenic delusions. She would have been classified as perverse if the sexual behavior in which she had indulged had been either homosexual or of a form other than normal coitus, and we might even have considered her normal if instead of the many love affairs she had had but few. She could, of course, be classified as a nymphomaniac in certain aspects of her behavior. Similarly, the young physicist would have been a paranoid schizophrenic if he had developed a new and irrational mathematical theory of the universe and had suspected that other people were attempting to steal his inventions. He would have been considered perverse if his narcissistic libidinal urges had forced him to be homosexually seduced by other men or if he had engaged in a great deal of compulsive masturbation. Had he been willing to go on to his degree and accept a research or teaching position in society, we might even have considered him normal. In Table 12.1 and Figure 12.1, we give a schematic representation of the personality structure in disordered characters. Again these will best be understood by a comparison with the earlier schemata, which are also included. Since character disorders are related to infan-

TABLE 12.1

	Nature of internal conflict	Social nature of resultant behavior	Degree of regression	Relation of basic urges of love object	Resolution of conflict results in
Character disorder	Extremely inharmonious balance as in psychosis and neurosis. The break with reality is in motor rather than cognitive spheres	Behavior socially unacceptable. Impulses break through as behavior problems in a disguised form	Regression to various stages but cognitive ego not regressed	Ambivalent	Alloplastic symptoms, particularly destructive behaviors
Normal	Harmonious balance between ego, superego, id, and outside reality	Behavior in all spheres constructive and socially acceptable	None. Genital stage reached	Postambivalent. Some urges gratified, others sublimated	No conflict
Psychosis	Extremely inharmonious balance in ego, superego, id, and outside reality. Ego powerless or weak against id and breaks with reality. Superego projected or taken over by ego or oversevere	Socially unacceptable behavior in both motor and cognitive spheres. Id impulses break through in a disguised form	To at least the early anal, thus beyond the level of reality testing	Objectless or extremely ambivalent	Severe symptom formation in cognitive and motor spheres
Psychoneurosis	Inharmonious balance in ego, superego, id, and reality. Ego in conflict with superego and id but ego on side of reality	Behavior only partially acceptable. Destructive in both motor and cognitive spheres but id impulses checked	To late anal or phallic; thus not beyond the level of reality testing	Ambivalent	Autoplastic symptoms, particularly anxiety
Sexual perversion	Balance may be either harmonious or inharmonious; no break with reality, but with sexual mores	Behavior socially unacceptable but person "normal" except in sexual sphere	Unless combined with psychosis, neurosis, or genius, there is fixation rather than regression	May be postambivalent in homosexuality. Other cases ambivalent	Perverse sexual practices

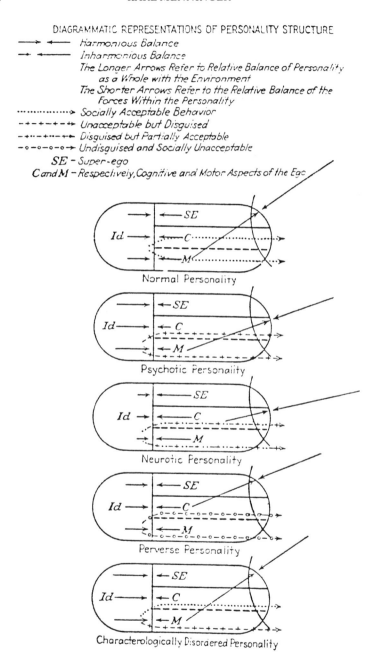

Figure 12.1. Comparing a character disorder with the other personality types.

tile fixations, to the psychoses and neuroses, and to perversion, their definition is difficult in terms of the concepts we have used for the other types. Table 12.1 and Figure 12.1 describe the "neurotic character" as an example.

Character Disorders Related to Infantile Sexual Fixation

Certain "normal" character traits are established in the earlier period of psychosexual genesis. The normal character is thus "determined" in the earliest years. We all have similar infantile experiences, and most of us in one respect or another have certain weaknesses of character. The person who technically has a character defect, however, is one who is in need of psychiatric treatment either because his character defect makes him and his family miserable or because through his character defect he comes into conflict with organized society. One might gain the idea from all this that the psychiatrist only considered as "normal" and "well-adjusted" the extremely mediocre personality. This is in a sense true, but, since the psychiatrist is not concerned with moral evaluation but rather with attempting to lead people into socially adjusted personal interrelationships, the accusation loses most of its meaning. Most of the difficult work in the world is, as a matter of fact, done by people who are in some way abnormal in the technical psychiatric sense.

Since the literature on character disorder is so new and also covers such a wide range of behavior problems, it will be obvious that we cannot deal with it in any detail here. Various nosological schemata have been devised in recent years and each of these has some methodological weakness. We shall attempt a new schema of classification of the character defects,[1] which seems the best we can do at the present time. We shall divide character defects into those primarily related to infantile sexual fixations, those primarily related to psychosis and neurosis, and those primarily related to perversion. The character disorders primarily related to infantile sexual fixation include those individuals whose sickness consists basically in the fact that, while they have gone through the various phases of normal development, certain fac-

---

[1] This schema was first suggested to the author by Dr. Robert P. Knight.

tors in the oral or the anal or the phallic period have been unduly emphasized. Among the character disorders related to psychosis and neurosis belong individuals whose behavior approaches that of the actually psychotic or psychoneurotic without actually falling into these categories. They will include characters whose individual behavior approaches mental disease but who still retain cognitive contact with reality. In the character disorders related to perversion we shall be concerned with individuals who have strong perverse sexual impulses, which, however, remain unconscious but find an outlet in the antisocial acts of the individual. Of course, since both the perversions and the mental illnesses are in themselves closely connected with infantile sexual fixations, this devision is rather arbitrary. In general we can think of these character types as individuals who simply exaggerate the normal traits that are in all of us.

We have already seen how many of the normal adult reaction forms are determined respectively in the oral, anal, and phallic periods. The characterological defects primarily related to infantile sex fixations hence represent simply an exaggeration of some of these behaviors. Thus, for instance, individuals who are never "weaned," who are never able to stand on their own feet, who think that the world owes them a living, have an overemphasis in the oral sucking stage and so what one may call the early oral or *parasitic character* is evolved. Similarly, individuals whose over-devotion to ideas of duty make them relentlessly severe in carrying out the dictates of conscience, to the extent that their acts become cruel to others and destructive to themselves, may be said to have fixations of the late anal period. In this sense individuals who seek applause and adulation to an abnormal extent have strong fixations at the phallic level. Let us deal with these various types in more detail.

The oral–dependent character type is the individual so dependent that he never stands up for himself. His character is chiefly formed in the preambivalent oral sucking period, and his world outlook is that of the unweaned infant. He is inclined to be happy-go-lucky, optimistic, and emotionally immature in that the serious things of life never affect him. Undoubtedly many of the ne'er-do-wells and many alcoholic addicts belong in this category. The type has also been called the infantile type in that the whole behavior of the personality is dominated by the pleasure principle and no sense of reality is ever established. Naturally enough a great deal of the real life behavior of these individuals is at an adult level. Sometimes they are intellectually quite brilliant, but they still drift through life without actually accomplishing much because their basic attitude is more or less that of passive dependence upon the world. Such individuals are in no way mentally disturbed, and the layman is inclined to look on them as either morally deficient or pathologically lazy. The usual treatment of such individuals through punishment and threat avails very little because these oral–dependent characters are actually sick. The concept of the oral–dependent character accounts for the many individuals who go through life without any ambition and fail to obtain the goals their families and friends expect from them.

If the fixation or traumatic experience is connected with the late oral–sadistic stage the personality is quite different. In the late oral stage the sadistic element of oral behavior develops. And this sadism in place of passive dependence makes the late oral–sadistic character in many ways the characterological opposite of the early oral character. The basic reaction is one of pessimistic distrust of the world. The world still owes the individual a living but instead of viewing it optimistically he is inclined to blame the world for everything unpleasant which happens to him. Instead of being easygoing, he is cantankerous, contemptuous, petulant. Instead of feeling that everything is right with the world, he is inclined to find everything wrong with it. Such individuals go through life making enemies instead of friends and constantly blame the other fellow for their shortcomings in accomplishment. Their social attitude is overdemanding and they are emotionally soured with the real world. These individuals are primarily narcissistic and still infantile in their reactions because at the late oral period no sense of social responsibility has been established. They become the perpetually discontented, moody people of unhappy temperament. This they certainly are, but moral exhortation does little for them.

Certain character disorders are determined by a strong fixation at the anal expulsive period. The so-called anal character was the one early (first) studied by Freud (1908) [see chapter 1] and his followers, particularly Abraham (1921), and is undoubtedly the one for which we have the clearest theoretical conceptions. Again, anal characters are quite phenotypically different in their behavior, depending upon whether the fixation is in the anal expulsive period or in the anal retentive period. The character traits of the anal expulsive period are chiefly those of megalomania and suspiciousness, coupled usually with an undue interest in money. The individual who constantly is extremely conceited, very ambitious, and makes unwarranted claims upon his own abilities but who is inclined to attribute his failures to the jealousy of rivals is a personality determined chiefly by fixations in the anal expulsive period. Such individuals are closely related to the paranoid characters, on the one hand, and to homosexual characters, on the other. They are the individuals who develop peculiar theories or peculiar hobbies and who not only bear grudges against other individuals in the field but who also believe that the true reason their real worth is not realized is the jealousy of others. Psychoanalysts derive these character traits from the megalomania connected with early consciousness of sphincter control and from the reaction formation against the homosexuality of this period.

The late anal or anal retentive character is marked usually by overmeticulousness to the extent of hair-splitting pedantry. This usually leads to a devotion to the written line of duty no matter what the cost in personal or social happiness. These individuals are usually petulant, cantankerous, and quick to rage, and many of them have an undue interest in collecting things, quite often money, so that they have been called parsimonious. This character comes at about the time of reality testing and these are individuals who are always torn between strong components of the pleasure principle and the emerging components of the superego and reality principle. Their hair-splitting doubting and pedantry come from their inability to mediate between these two types of impulses. These are of course related to the compulsion neurotics. Fenichel (1934), has described these individuals as in a constant conflict between, "I want to be naughty" and "I must be good." The petulance and cantankerousness in their behavior come from the resentment against the world which has made them give up these infantile modes of sex gratification, and their tendency to hoard comes from their unconscious substitution of money for feces. As examples we find many individuals who are petty tyrants in industry, schoolmasters who are overzealous in their demand on rigid discipline, individuals in all walks of life who must have things done in a very precise way and consequently seem rigid characters to their fellow men. Such individuals are looked on by the layman as queer, unhappy personalities, but to the psychiatrist they are sick. Actually, the anal expulsive and anal retentive stages overlap, and we seldom find clear-cut anal retentive or anal expulsive characters but rather a mixture of both.

The final stage of psychosexual development is also divided into two phases. The phallic phase is the period of narcissistic sexuality where, as we have already seen, the libidinal relationships are concerned with a sexual partner of the opposite sex but in a narcissistic, selfish fashion. The individual who must be the leader under any circumstances, who must always stand out before any group, who reacts unduly badly in the face of the slightest defeat is the individual with strong phallic fixations. The phallic character thus described is related to the hysteroid character, on the one hand, in that he is inclined to have the temper tantrums of hysteria and may develop certain conversion symptoms and to the neurotic character, on the other, in that he is inclined to demand gratification of his id impulse and may be close to sexual perversion. Such individuals are, of course, so close to normal that their sickness is rarely detected by the layman. To the layman they may be simply overambitious, exhibitionistic braggarts. Usually, however, on closer psychological examination it is found that they, too, are unhappy and sick.

The true genital character need not concern us much because it gives rise to theoretical normal behavior. It is an ideal personality in actuality seldom encountered.

We seldom find pure character disorders of the types of which we have spoken. Usually there are present in the same individual strong orally determined personality character disorders with less striking anal- and phallic-determined ones, or strong anally determined character defects with the others less striking. The transition to perversion or mental illness, on the one hand, and to complete normality, on the other, is also a gradual one. Only in extreme cases is psychiatric treatment indicated for these individuals. Although the world could get along well without the oral–dependent characters, these individuals themselves are often happy. Perhaps the world could not get along without the cranks and petty tyrants and psychological exhibitionists. At all events, the cranks and exhibitionists sometimes really accomplish a great deal, and even if they do not accomplish much they make the world a more colorful place to live in. In the more extreme cases these characterologically disordered individuals are so personally unhappy or make their associates so unhappy or perform such antisocial acts that they should receive psychiatric treatment.

Character Defects Related to Psychosis and Psychoneurosis

We have already seen that schizophrenia is the most frequent and most severe of the major functional psychoses. Many individuals who are not actually schizophrenic are nevertheless so queer, so withdrawn from reality, so isolated from normal libidinal relationships with others that, although their contacts with reality on the surface remain undisturbed, their emotional reactions to real situations are so inadequate that they closely approach schizophrenia. Such individuals we call schizoid characters. Thus, as we have seen, the case of the young physicist who had never had a close friend and who had never had libidinal relationship with a girl is an example of a schizoid character. We do not have to spend a great deal of time in describing the schizoid character because what it amounts to is a mild or attenuated form of schizophrenia. The individual has an emotional schizophrenia without any disturbance in the cognitive and perceptual processes. He may correctly *perceive* the nature of the world but he never correctly *feels* the nature of the social world. The individuals without friends, without normal libidinal and social relationships, without real interest in people may be said to be schizoid characters. Sometimes they break down into a real schizophrenia, but otherwise they go through life simply being isolated, queer, and schizoid. They still may accomplish quite a great deal. Many writers, mathematicians, and research workers in science belong in this category. Although some of them make successful adjustments others remain very unhappy. These cases can undoubtedly be helped by psychiatric treatment and psychoanalysis.

By the *cycloid character* we mean those characters who show the emotional symptoms of the manic–depressive psychosis in an attenuated form. Just as the schizoid character was to be looked on as a mild or attentuated form of schizophrenia, the cycloid character represents an attenuated manic–depressive psychosis. All of us to a great or lesser extent have fluctuations in moods of elation or depression, and in but few of us are these fluctuations completely connected with the objective life situation. But the cycloid character suffers fluctuations of mood much more severe than those of the normal individual. He will have periods of time when he is very productive, very gay, very happy, able to work with a great deal of push, when his objective life situation is really quite unfavorable, and he will have other periods when the life situation may be very favorable where he is continually depressed, feels the future has little to offer, feels he can accomplish nothing. We know the cycloid character is related to the manic–depressive psychosis, because in the cycloid character these deviations in mood follow in sequence.

One also finds individuals who are close to paranoia but who do not become psychotic. These are individuals who suffer from *ideas* of grandeur and *ideas* of persecution rather than *delusions* of grandeur and *delusions* of persecution. In other words, they have a sure belief in their own extreme competence and also a marked hostility toward other individuals which they project onto the other individuals and rationalize the idea that the others are hostile to them. Perhaps of all the character defects related to psychosis the *paranoid character* is the most frequent, and it is the most difficult to draw the line between the paranoid character and paranoia. We saw that owing to the systematized nature of delusions in paranoia the detection of paranoiacs was a very difficult matter. It is furthermore also hard to draw the line between delusions of grandeur and persecution and ideas of grandeur and persecution. The paranoid character is the person with a pet idea who is unduly suspicious of others. Many paranoid characters are individuals who engage in unnecessary lawsuits, who are inclined to go to court on the slightest provocation. Legal history abounds with cases of individuals who have destroyed their personal fortunes in fighting for crank causes in the courts. Sometimes judges realize the nature of such a psychopathological process, but probably more frequently they do not. The many overly contemptuous individuals, the individuals who are always getting into fights for what are very often minor causes, are paranoid characters. In fact, most of the cranks, most of the faddists, most individuals who are realized to be a little "crazy" about one thing or another on examination are found to be paranoid characters. Undoubtedly from paranoid characters has come much of the systematic research in science and much of the first-rate work in art and literature, and certainly all of them are by no means problems for psychiatry. Insofar as they become antisocial or unhappy, however, they become psychiatric problems.

Individuals suffering from the *compulsive character* are individuals who suffer from a mild form of compulsion neurosis. As in the compulsion neurosis the individual is driven to perform acts and to entertain ideas which he realizes are morbid and out of contact with reality, so the compulsive character is driven to entertain ideas and to perform acts which may or may not be socially useful. When the acts are socially useful we have the very productive workers in the arts, the sciences, and in industry. When the acts are completely meaningless with regard to social reality we have the compulsion neurotic. The compulsive character then covers the range of compulsive behavior from that of the individual who has to count every fence post on his walks and who has to notice the numbers of every bank note that comes into his hands and who has always to walk in the middle of the street, to the individual who has to work overtime in his position and who consequently makes good. The behavior similarly ranges from that of the deeply neurotic individual to that of the very successful productive individual. Almost always present in the compulsive character besides the compulsion to do things is the presence of obsessive doubting. Doubts about the correctness of this action, whether he should do this, that, or the other thing at a certain time, etc. This hair-splitting doubt of the compulsive character is related of course to the feeling, "I want to be bad, but I must be good" of the anal character and of the true compulsion neurotic. This obsessive doubting also arises from the ambivalence of the late anal period and from the uncertain sexuality of the late anal period. The inability to decide what activity to undertake is connected with the inability to decide on one's sexuality.

Similarly, we have *hysterical characters*, who tend to develop hypochondriasis and infantile behavior similar to real hysteria, without developing an overt neurosis. If the outstanding symptoms are closer to actual hysteria than to the phallic character as we have described it or to the neurotic character which we shall next describe, the individual is to be classified as a hysterical character.

The reader will see that there is no sharp break between the disordered character and the normal character, and perhaps an even less well-defined break between character disorders related to infantile sexual fixation and those related to psychosis and neurosis. For practical purposes the exact diagnosis makes no difference. It should be clear by this time that from the standpoint of modern psychiatry diagnostic categories in general represent differences in degree and not in kind. This is particularly true in the newly developed field of character disorders.

Character Disorders Related to Perversion

Of particular psychiatric importance is the group of character disorders which seem most closely related to abnormalities of the libidinal and hostile urges. This group most nearly approaches that of the older conception of "psychopathic personality" and most frequently engages in behaviors which are immoral or degenerate from the layman's standpoint. These individuals make wrecks of their own lives and cause great damage to their friends and loved ones and even to society at large. We saw that this group is related to perversion only in the sense that psychoneuroses are related to perversion, namely, that the symptoms of both arise as protections against the consciousness of internal conflict which arises in the pregenital development. This is what led Freud (1930) to define a neurosis as a negation of a perversion.

The concept of the *neurotic character* as it was first introduced by Alexander is perhaps the one most thoroughly developed in this field. Following examples by Freud (1908) [see chapter 1] and Abraham (1935), Alexander (1930a) was able to show how behavior disorders are closely allied to the neuroses. In the neuroses autoplastic symptoms are developed. In the neurotic character alloplastic behavior disorders are developed. When Alexander originally set up the concept it was broadly applicable to nearly all character disorders. As generally used today the neurotic character refers to the individuals who "act out" upon the environment the unconscious internal conflicts. Thus the unconscious libidinal impulses tend to seek constant sexual gratification, and the unconscious guilt and introjected hostile impulses lead the individual to indulge in behaviors for which he is punished. Neurotic characters include the two types which we used as examples in beginning this chapter. They also include "people who cannot stand success," those people who always fail after success because the strong sense of guilt in connection with infantile sexuality does not allow them to succeed. In this category fall many "criminals out of a sense of guilt." These individuals perpetrate crimes in order to be punished and thus assuage internal guilt feeling. In some ways these supposedly immoral people are overmoral but, of course, in an irrealistic sense. They sin and commit immoral acts not because they enjoy immorality but because through it they gain revenge and receive punishment. These individuals usually have disordered sexual lives. This makes us believe that they are close to perversion. The neurotic character refers to a large group of individuals whose "neuroses" consist in engaging in antisocial behavior rather than in neurotic symptoms. The same conflicts, however, underlie both the neuroses and the neurotic character, namely conflicts between the ego and id, where regression threatens to break down and where behavior and symptom protect the individual from the anxiety created by unconscious conflict.

Neurotic characters are closely related to criminals, impostors, sexual perverts, alcohol and narcotic addicts, nomads, pathological spenders and liars, and individuals with a mania for gambling. In fact, many of these individuals are neurotic characters and the nature of symptomatic acting out is quite obvious.

Since neurotic characters present such an important psychiatric problem, the question of prognosis and therapy is important. Moral exhortation and punishment are completely unsuccessful. Actually the conflicts which the subject is acting out are *unconscious* conflicts. Psychotherapy is hence indicated. Alexander (1930b) feels that psychoanalysis should be particularly successful here because of the lack of autoplastic neurotic suffering and the ability of the patient to react to reality. Other authorities, for instance, Fenichel, disagree with him rather sharply here. The nature of the individual case is important. There are many good descriptions of neurotic characters in the psychoanalytic literature. Freud (1908) [see chapter 1], Abraham (1935), and Alexander (1930b) are all worth reading on this topic. K. Menninger's book *Man Against Himself* (1938) gives many good case histories of neurotic characters.

Closely related but not identical to the conception of the neurotic character are the concepts: impulse-ridden character, the fraudulent character, and the inhibited character. An exact description of these would take us beyond the limits set for this book, and the interested reader must go to the original literature which is referred to at the end of this chapter.

Alcohol Addiction

Related to neurotic characters but having also specific etiological factors are the chronic alcohol addicts. In contemporary America these individuals present a particularly challenging psychiatric problem. Of the many alcoholics only a few develop psychoses and get psychiatric care. Still, nearly 5 percent of all new admissions to state hospitals are individuals suffering a psychosis due to alcoholism and an additional 7 percent suffer from chronic alcoholism. It is very difficult to get figures on chronic alcohol addiction, but there is no doubt that it is a very frequent disease. In some social classes—the upper bourgeois and the lower proletariat—there is small doubt that a very large percentage of the males and a fairly large percentage of the females are alcoholic. Alcoholism leads to both economic and social maladjustments which are so well known that we need not go into them.

Psychiatrists are not concerned with the social and moderate use of alcohol. For many individuals the moderate use of alcohol is really advisable and for others even its occasional abuse offers a necessary psychological analgesic, nor does the psychiatrist consider everyone who drinks or everyone who drinks too much a psychiatric problem. Some individuals who drink every day lead happy and successful lives. The alcoholic in the psychiatric sense is one who through his drinking creates unhappiness for himself and other individuals and whose drinking is compulsive. In other words, he is an individual who has a conflict as to whether he shall drink or not and sometimes he has to have a drink when his better judgment tells him to refrain. He also tends to use alcohol in increasingly large doses. From his alcoholism or rather with his alcoholism his efficiency in economic and social relationships is diminished. He loses jobs and quarrels with his friends and family.

The alcoholic fits into the general category of neurotic character. The drinking and drunken behavior is an alloplastic behavior maladjustment which arises from internal unconscious conflict. There are specific factors in the etiology of alcoholism which have been worked out most precisely by Knight (1937a, b). There are strong oral-demanding character traits. Thus alcohol represents unconsciously the mother's milk. There are definite self-destructive and self-punitive motives in the behavior. Karl Menninger (1938) has shown how these work. The alcoholic is also related to the sexually perverse in that he has strong unconscious homosexual components in his libido. Actually attenuated forms of homosexuality come out in all stag drinking parties.

Since the use of alcohol is socially permissible in some circles and socially demanded in others, in alcoholism social factors are of great importance. This must be considered in discussion of the prognosis. As long as drinking is considered the thing to do, alcoholics will not look on themselves as sick.

Concerning the prognosis for the psychological treatment of alcoholics, like all neurotic characters, there is much doubt. Durfee (1937) claims exceptional results. Knight (1937a, b) is more conservative. Here again the individual case varies greatly, and with some individuals the alcoholism seems to be the basic maladjustment and with others the alcoholism is simply a reaction against other neurotic conflicts. This second group probably respond more favorably to psychoanalytic treatment. For a more extended treatment of alcoholism the reader is referred to Durfee (1937) and Knight (1937a, b). The existent literature is reviewed by Crowley (1934).

Criminality

Modern psychiatry has recently considered the criminal. Although psychiatrists realize the problem is complicated by both legal and penological factors, they believe the psychology of the criminal furnishes psychiatric problems. To develop adequately the psychiatric theory of criminality would require a separate book. In this section we shall simply point out one or two problems and refer to some of the literature.

That punishment fails to eradicate crime is a banal statement. Recently criminologists have even come to the conclusion that it is the original incarceration that makes the first offender a hardened criminal. Psychoanalysts can understand this. The superego is recriminatory and we all have need for punishment. The punishment, however (*cf.* the theory of the manic–depressive psychosis), wipes out the guilt and the individual is free to sin again. Refusing to punish them might deter some criminals from further crimes. Even the most adjusted of us, however, harbor criminal—even murderous—impulses. Since we cannot condone them in ourselves, we cannot permit them to others. Consequently, the law becomes the superego of society and we demand law and order. Reform in criminal procedure is of necessity very slow, and perhaps it can never be completely accomplished. Gregory Zilboorg has made important studies in the field of the social psychology of criminal, particularly murder, trials which will be published shortly.

There are undoubtedly occasional crimes committed under economic pressure or for other rational (to the individual) reasons. These criminals are not the concern of the psychiatrist. There are also "normal" criminals—those individuals in whom criminality is a profession of choice, whose fathers were criminals, and whose superego comes from a criminal identification. These are problems for the sociologist. In American cities the gangsters often represent this type.

Probably the majority of criminals are neurotic characters. Crime does not pay economically, at least if one is caught. These individuals repeat crimes as alcoholics repeat sprees and Don Juans repeat seductions. They are criminals out of an unconscious sense of guilt or from unconscious antisocial impulses.

This is particularly true of performers of criminal acts against persons (murderers, rapists, etc.) and even of large numbers of crimes against property rights. Menninger, Alexander and Staub, and Alexander and Healy have written a great deal in this field. Students of sociology will find their works well worth studying.

Chapter 13

A PSYCHOANALYTIC CLASSIFICATION
OF CHARACTER PATHOLOGY

OTTO F. KERNBERG

This paper is a proposal for a classification of character pathology which integrates recent developments in our understanding of severe forms of character pathology, especially the so-called "borderline conditions," with recent developments in psychoanalytic metapsychology. This classification attempts (1) to establish psychoanalytic criteria for differential diagnoses among different types and degrees of severity of character pathology; (2) to clarify the relationship between a descriptive characterological diagnosis and a metapsychological, especially structural, analysis; and (3) to arrange subgroups of character pathology, according to their degree of severity. This system of classification should help in the diagnosis of character pathology by providing the clinician with more systematic information about the descriptive, structural, and genetic–dynamic characteristics of the different forms of character pathology. It should also help in the treatment of patients suffering from character pathology by singling out the predominant constellations of character defenses and other defenses peculiar to the categories of character pathology, which I propose to describe. Last, but not least, this proposed classification should help in determining the prognosis for psychological treatment in these conditions by differentiating types of character pathology with varying degrees of indication for psychoanalytic treatment and for psychoanalytically oriented psychotherapy.

This chapter originally appeared in longer form in the *Journal of the American Psychoanalytic Association,* 18:800–822, 1970. Reprinted by special permission of the author and the publisher.

227

Freud (1908, 1931) [see chapters 1 and 3] and Abraham (1921–1925) described character pathology in psychoanalytic terms and suggested the first classifications of character pathology. These early classifications were based on their understanding of instinctual, especially libidinal, motivations. Fenichel (1945), after criticizing these and other attempts to develop a psychoanalytic typology of pathological character types, and after incorporating W. Reich's findings (1933), suggested a classification combining dynamic and structural explanations.

From a dynamic viewpoint, Fenichel classified character traits into "sublimation" and "reactive" types, depending on whether the instinctual energy was discharged freely as part of the character trait or whether it was checked by some countercathectic measure forming part of that character trait. The sublimatory type of character trait, Fenichel stated, was mostly normal, and did not lend itself easily to further typing. In contrast, the reactive type of character traits reflected pathological developments of the personality. Fenichel suggested the subdivision of reactive character traits into attitudes of avoidance (phobic attitudes) and of opposition (reaction formation).

From the structural viewpoint, Fenichel defined character as "the ego's habitual modes of adjustment to the external world, the id, and the superego, and the characteristic types of combining these modes with one another." Accordingly, character disturbances were "limitations or pathological forms of treating the external world, internal drives, and demands of the superego, or disturbances of the ways in which these various tasks are combined."

Combining the dynamic and structural viewpoints, he proceeded to classify the reactive character traits into pathological behavior toward the id (including here among others the classical oral, anal, and phallic character traits 5); pathological behavior toward the superego (including here moral masochism, apparent lack of guilt feeling, criminality, and acting-out characters); and pathological behavior toward external objects (including pathological jealousy, social inhibitions, and pseudosexuality). Fenichel, however, appeared not to be fully satisfied by his proposed classification. He acknowledged that every person shows traits of both sublimatory and reactive types, and he suggested that the reactive characters may be "most satisfactorily subdivided by analogy to the neuroses, for the simple reason that mechanisms similar to the various forms of symptom formation are likewise operative in the formation of character traits." Following this statement, he described phobic and hysterical characters, compulsive characters, cyclic characters, and schizoid characters, as the characterological equivalents of the respective symptomatic neurosis (and psychosis).

Prelinger, Zimet, Schafer, and Levin (1964), in their comprehensive review of psychoanalytic concepts of character, comment that Fenichel's attempt to classify character types "is generally accepted in psychoanalytic theory today."

Because I believe that a reexamination of Fenichel's classification is in order due to the development of psychoanalytic understanding of the pathology and treatment of character disorders since the publication of Fenichel's classic work (Friedlander, 1947; Johnson and Szurek, 1952; Eissler, 1953a; Erikson, 1956; Stone, 1954; Greenson, 1958; Rosenfeld, 1964), as well as the broadening of psychoanalytic understanding of borderline character pathology (Deutsch, 1942 [see chapter 21]; Knight, 1953a; Frosch, 1964, 1970; Boyer and Giovacchini, 1967; Zetzel, 1968 [see chapter 19]), I shall attempt to incorporate recent findings regarding the degree of severity and the prognosis of character disorders into a psychoanalytic classification of character pathology. In so doing, I shall emphasize recent findings regarding the structural consequences to the ego and superego of pathological object relationships in these patients (Fairbairn, 1952; Van der Waals, 1952; Sutherland, 1963; Giovacchini, 1963; Jacobson, 1964; Kernberg, 1966), and I shall expand my earlier analyses of the structural disturbances in patients with borderline conditions (Kernberg, 1967, 1968).

My proposed classification will incorporate three major pathological developments: (1) pathology in the ego and superego structures; (2) pathology in the internalized object relationships; and (3) pathology in the development of libidinal and aggressive drive derivatives.

I shall describe three levels on the continuum from less severe to more severe character pathologies; for convenience, I have termed these as a *higher level,* an *intermediate level,* and a *lower level* of organization of character pathology. What follows is an outline of the assumptions underlying the proposed classification of character pathology.

The Assumptions Underlying the Proposed Classification

Regarding Instinctual Development. In contrast to earlier attempts at psychoanalytic classification of character pathology on the basis of the stages of libidinal development, the proposed classification assumes that, clinically, three main levels of instinctual fixation can be encountered: a "higher" level, at which genital primacy has been reached and predominates; an "intermediate" level, at which pregenital, especially oral regression and fixation points predominate; and a "lower" level, at which a pathological condensation of genital and pregenital instinctual strivings takes place with a predominance of pregenital aggression. This proposed classification incorporates the findings regarding instinctual developments in patients with borderline personality organization reported in an earlier paper (Kernberg, 1967).

Regarding Superego Development. The proposed classification assumes that a relatively well-integrated although excessively severe superego characterizes the "higher" level of organization of character pathology only, and that the "intermediate" and "lower" levels of organization of character pathology reflect the presence of varying degrees of lack of superego integration as well as the predominance of sadistic superego forerunners over other superego components. Jacobson's comprehensive analysis of normal and pathological stages of superego development (1964) constitutes the basis for these propositions.

Regarding Defensive Operations of the Ego and, in Particular, the Nature of Pathological Character Traits. In concordance with the structural model elaborated on in an earlier paper (Kernberg, 1966), two overall levels of defensive organization of the ego are assumed: (1) a basic level at which primitive dissociation or "splitting" is the crucial mechanism for the defensive organization of the ego; and (2) a more advanced level at which repression becomes the central mechanism, replacing splitting. In the proposed classification, the "higher" level of organization of character pathology presents the advanced level of defensive organization, repression being the main defensive operation of the ego, together with related mechanisms such as intellectualization, rationalization, undoing, and higher levels of projection. The same is true for the "intermediate" level of organization of character pathology, except that, in addition, the patient shows some of the defense mechanisms which, in an even stronger, clearly predominant way, characterize the "lower" level. At that "lower" level, primitive dissociation or splitting predominates with a concomitant impairment of the synthetic function of the patient's ego, and the presence of the related mechanisms of denial, primitive forms of projection, and omnipotence. The proposed classification assumes a continuum of pathological character traits, ranging from the sublimatory type of character traits at the one extreme, through inhibitory or phobic character traits, reaction formation type of character traits, to instinctually "infiltrated" character traits at the other extreme. The implication is that the lower the level of defensive organization of the ego, the more there is a predominance of pathological character traits in which defense and direct impulse expression are linked, so that the primal impulse expression shows through the defense. The normal character shows a predominance of sublimatory character traits; the "higher" level of organization of character pathology presents a predominance of inhibitory and reactive character traits; in the "intermediate" level of organization of character pathology, character defenses combining reaction formation against instinct with yet a partial expression of the rejected instinctual impulses make their appearance; and at the "lower" level, instinctually infiltrated character defenses predominate.

Regarding the Vicissitudes of Internalized Object Relationships. No particular pathology of internalized object relationships is present at the "higher" level, at which ego identity and its related components, a stable self concept and a stable representational world, are well established; the same is true at the "intermediate level with the exception of more conflictual object relations than at the "higher" level. At the "lower" level, severe pathology of the internalization of object relationships is present. Object relationships have a "partial" rather than "total" character, and "object constancy" has not been firmly established. Object constancy represents the child's capacity to retain his attachment to a loved person and to the internal representation of that person in spite of frustration and hostility in that relationship (Arlow, Freud, Lampl-De Groot, and Beres, 1968). Object constancy also reflects the capacity for a total object relationship, that is, a relationship in which good and bad aspects of the object and of the self (and of their respective representations) can be tolerated and integrated. This capacity is missing in these patients, and the lack of integration of the self concept, as well as of the related object representations or representational world, is reflected in the syndrome of identity diffusion (Erikson, 1956; Kernberg, 1967).

What follows is an outline of the structural characteristics of the "higher," "intermediate," and "lower" levels of organization of character pathology, and the type of pathological character formation that belongs to each level. Bibliographic references will indicate sources describing these characterological types and their differential diagnosis.

Higher Level of Organization of Character Pathology

At the higher level, the patient has a relatively well-integrated, but severe and punitive superego. The forerunners of his superego are determined by too sadistic impulses, bringing about a harsh, perfectionistic superego. His ego, too, is well integrated; ego identity (Erikson, 1956) and its related components, a stable self concept (Jacobson, 1964), and a stable representational world (Sandler and Rosenblatt, 1962) being well established. Excessive defensive operations against unconscious conflicts center around repression. The character defenses are largely of an inhibitory or phobic nature, or they are reaction formations against repressed instinctual needs. There is very little or no instinctual infiltration into the defensive character traits. The patient's ego at this level is somewhat limited and constricted by its excessive use of neurotic defense mechanisms, but the patient's overall social adaptation is not seriously impaired. He has fairly deep, stable object relationships and is capable of experiencing guilt, mourning, and a wide variety of affective responses (Winnicott, 1955). His sexual and/or aggressive drive derivatives are partially inhibited, but these instinctual conflicts have reached the stage where the infantile genital phase and oedipal conflicts are clearly predominant and there is no pathological condensation of genital sexual strivings with pregenital, aggressively determined strivings in which the latter predominate.

Most hysterical characters (Abraham, 1920; Easser and Lesser, 1965 [see chapter 14]; Shapiro, 1965), obsessive–compulsive characters (Fenichel, 1945), and depressive–masochistic characters (Laughlin, 1956) are organized at this level.

Intermediate Level of Organization of Character Pathology

At the intermediate level, the excessively punitive nature of the patient's superego is even stronger than that of the higher level disorders, but the superego is less integrated. His superego tolerates contradictory demands between sadistic, prohibitive superego nuclei on the one hand, and rather primitive (magical, overidealized) forms of the ego ideal on the other hand (Jacobson, 1964). These latter, primitive types of internal demands to be great, powerful, and physically attractive coexist with strict demands for moral perfection, and they can be observed in the patient's partially blurred superego–ego delimitations. Deficient superego integration can also be observed in the partial projections of superego nuclei (as expressed in the patient's decreased capacity for experiencing guilt and in paranoid trends), contradictions in the ego's value systems, and severe mood swings. These mood swings are caused by the primitive nature of the superego's regulation of the ego (Jacobson, 1964). The poor integration of the superego, which is reflected in contradictory unconscious demands on the ego, also explains the appearance of pathological character defenses combining reaction formations against instincts with a partial expression of instinctual impulses. At this level, the patient has fewer inhibitory character defenses than the person at the higher level, reaction formations are more prominent, and his character traits are infiltrated by instinctual strivings as seen in dissociated expressions of unacceptable sexual and/or aggressive needs, and a "structured impulsivity" in certain areas. Repression is still the main defensive operation of the ego, together with related defenses such as intellectualization, rationalization, and undoing. At the same time, the patient shows some dissociative trends, some defensive splitting of the ego in limited areas (that is, mutual dissociation of contradictory ego states) (Freud, 1938a; Kernberg, 1966), and projection and denial. Pregenital, especially oral conflicts come to the fore, although the genital level of libidinal development has been reached. While pregenital, especially oral features predominate in the clinical picture, such features reflect to a major extent regression from oedipal conflicts; further, the aggressive components of pregenital conflicts are of a "toned down" quality, in contrast to the primitivization of aggression at the "lower level" of organization of character pathology.

Object relationships at this level are still stable in the sense of a capacity for lasting, deep involvements with others, and of a capacity to tolerate the markedly ambivalent and conflictual nature of such relationships.

Most "oral" types of character pathology (Abraham, 1921–1925) are organized at this level, especially what is now designated as the "passive–aggressive" (Brody and Lindbergh, 1967) personality type. Sadomasochistic personalities (Frank, 1952), some of the better functioning infantile (or "hysteroid") personalities (Easser and Lesser, 1965 [see chapter 14]; Zetzel, 1968 [see chapter 19], and many narcissistic personalities (Rosenfeld, 1964; Kernberg, 1969) are at this intermediate level. Many patients with a stable, crystallized sexual deviation (Fenichel, 1945) and with the capacity to establish, within such a deviation, relatively stable object relationships are also at this level.

Lower Level of Organization of Character Pathology

At the lower level, the patient's superego integration is minimal and his propensity for projection of primitive, sadistic superego nuclei is maximal. His capacity for experiencing concern and guilt is seriously impaired (Winnicott, 1955), and his basis for self-criticism constantly fluctuates. The individual at this level commonly exhibits paranoid traits, stemming both from projection of superego nuclei and from the excessive use of rather primitive forms of projection, especially projective identification (Klein, 1946) as one major defensive mechanism of the ego. The delimitation between ego and superego is completely blurred:

primitive, narcissistically determined forms of the ego ideal are practically indistinguishable from primitive forms of narcissistic ego strivings for power, wealth, and admiration (A. Reich, 1953). The synthetic function of the patient's ego is seriously impaired, and he uses primitive dissociation or splitting (Fairbairn, 1952; Jacobson, 1957; Kernberg, 1967) as the central defensive operation of the ego instead of repression. The mechanism of splitting is expressed as contradictory ego states alternating with each other, and this dissociation is reinforced by the patient's use of denial, projective identification, and unconscious fantasies of omnipotence (Klein, 1946). This omnipotence reflects a defensive identification of the patient's self-concept with forerunners of his ego ideal, namely, idealized, condensed primitive self and object images. His pathological character defenses are predominantly of an "impulsive," instinctually infiltrated kind; contradictory, repetitive patterns of behavior are dissociated from each other, permitting direct release of drive derivatives as well as of reaction formations against these drives. Lacking an integrated ego and the capacity to tolerate guilt feelings, such patients have little need for secondary rationalizations of pathological character traits.

These patients' capacity for encompassing contradictory ("good" and "bad") self and object images is impaired, mainly because of the predominance of pregenital aggression as part of both ego and superego identifications. Excessive pregenital aggression also causes a pathological condensation of pregenital and genital conflicts with predominance of pregenital aggression (Kernberg, 1967); and is evidenced by sadistically infiltrated, polymorphous perverse infantile drive derivatives which infiltrate all the internalized and external object relationships of these patients. Thus, their oedipal strivings appear intimately condensed with pregenital sadistic and masochistic needs, and there may be direct expression of oedipal impulses such as in masturbatory fantasies involving the original parental objects.

Their inability to integrate libidinally determined and aggressively determined self and object images is reflected in their maintaining object relationships of either a need-gratifying or a threatening nature. They are unable to have empathy for objects in their totality; object relationships are of a part-object type, and object constancy has not been reached. Their lack of integration of self representations is reflected in the absence of an integrated self concept. Their inner world is peopled by caricatures of either the good or the horrible aspects of persons who have been important to them; and these exaggerated representations are not integrated to the extent that the person could feel that one of his inner objects had a "good side" and a "bad side." By the same token, his inner view of himself is a chaotic mixture of shameful, threatened, and exalted images. The absence of both an integrated world of total, internalized objects and of a stable self-concept determine the presence of the syndrome of identity diffusion (Erikson, 1956). In fact, identity diffusion is an outstanding characteristic of this lower level of character pathology. The lack of integration of libidinal and aggressive strivings contributes to a general lack of neutralization of instinctual energy (Hartmann, 1950, 1955), and to a severe restriction of the conflict-free ego.

All these factors, in addition to the disintegrating effects of the predominant mechanisms of splitting and related defenses, and the lack of crucial ego organizers such as an integrated self-concept and an integrated superego, contribute to severe ego weakness. Ego weakness is reflected especially in the patient's lack of anxiety tolerance, of impulse control, and of developed sublimatory channels as evidenced by chronic failure in work or creative areas (Kernberg, 1967). Primary process thinking infiltrates cognitive functioning and, although not always evident on clinical contacts, it is especially manifest on projective psychological testing (Rapaport, Gill, and Schafer, 1945–1946).

Most infantile personalities (Greenson, 1958; Easser and Lesser, 1965 [see chapter 14]; Kernberg, 1967; Zetzel, 1968 [see chapter 19]) and many narcissistic personalities (Rosenfeld, 1964; Kernberg, 1970) are organized at this level of organization of character pathology. All patients with antisocial personality structure are at this level (Friedlander, 1947; Johnson and Szurek, 1952; Cleckley, 1964). The so-called "chaotic" impulse-ridden character disorders (Reich, 1933; Fenichel, 1945), the "as-if" (Deutsch, 1942 [see chapter 21]) characters, the "inadequate personalities" (Brody and Lindbergh, 1967), and most "self-mutilators" (Kernberg, 1967) belong to this group. Patients with multiple sexual deviations, or a combination of sexual deviation with drug addiction or alcoholism, and with severe pathology of object relationships such as reflected in the strangeness or bizarreness of their sexual needs, are organized at this level (Frosch, 1964; Kernberg, 1967). The same is also true for the so-called "prepsychotic personality structures," that is, the hypomanic, schizoid, and paranoid personalities (Shapiro, 1965; Brody and Lindbergh, 1967).

The next "step down" along this continuum would carry us to the field of the psychoses. The lower level of organization of character pathology which I have been describing consists, in effect, of the group of patients who are generally included in the field of borderline disorders or "psychotic characters" (Frosch, 1964), or present "borderline personality organization" (Kernberg, 1967). The differential diagnosis between patients in the borderline field and the psychoses centers around the persistence of reality testing (Weisman, 1958; Frosch, 1964) in borderline patients, while reality testing is lost in the psychoses. This difference depends, in turn, on the differentiation between self and object representations (Jacobson, 1954a&b, 1964) and its derived delimitation of ego boundaries: these are present in lower level of organization of character pathology, lost or absent in the psychoses.

The earlier-mentioned assumptions underlying the proposed classification outlined above are related to each other in a model of development of the psychic apparatus, a model centered on the development of internalized object relationships which has been spelled out in earlier papers (Kernberg, 1966, 1967, 1968, 1970). What follows is a brief summary of these propositions regarding the development of the psychic apparatus and the mutual relationships of the four kinds of assumptions enumerated before.

The Mutual Relationships of the Stated Assumptions:
An Object-Relations-Centered Model of Development

The internalization of object relationships represents a crucial organizing factor for both ego and superego development. Introjections, identifications, and ego identity formation represent a progressive sequence in the process of internalization of object relationships. The essential components of internalized object relationships are self images, object images, and specific affect states or dispositions linking each self image with a corresponding object image. Two essential tasks that the early ego has to accomplish in rapid succession are: (1) the differentiation of self images from object images; and (2) the integration of self and object images built up under the influence of libidinal drive derivatives and their related affects with their corresponding self and object images built up under the influence of aggressive drive derivatives and related affects.

The first task is accomplished in part under the influence of the development of the apparatuses of primary autonomy: perception and memory traces help to sort out the origin of stimuli and gradually differentiate self and object images. This first task fails to a major extent in the psychoses, in which a pathological fusion between self and object images determines a failure in the differentiation of ego boundaries and, therefore, in the differentiation of self from nonself. In the "lower" level of organization of character pathology, that is, the case of borderline personality organization, differentiation of self from object images has occurred to a sufficient degree to permit the establishment of integrated ego boundaries and a concomitant differentiation between self and others.

The second task, however, of integration of libidinally determined and aggressively determined self and object images fails to a great extent in borderline patients, mainly because of the pathological predominance of pregenital aggression. The resulting lack of synthesis of contradictory self and object images interferes with the integration of the self concept and with the establishment of "total" object relationships and object constancy. The need to preserve the good self and good object images, and good external objects in the presence of dangerous "all bad" self and object images leads to a defensive division of the ego, in which what was at first a simple defect in integration is then used actively for keeping "good" and "bad" self and object images apart. This is, in essence, the mechanism of splitting, an essential defensive operation of the borderline personality organization which is reinforced by subsidiary defensive operations (especially projective mechanisms) and thus determines an overall type of ego organization different from the more advanced type of ego organization that is normally reached in the "intermediate" and "higher" levels of organization of character and ego development and where repression and related mechanisms replace splitting and its subsidiary mechanisms.

The presence of "all good" and "all bad" self and object images interferes seriously with superego integration because under these circumstances, overidealized self and object images can create only fantastic ideals of power, greatness, and perfection, and not the more realistic demands and goals of an ego ideal constructed under the influence of more integrated, "toned down" ideal self and object images. Projection of "bad" self and object images determines, through reintrojection of distorted experiences of the frustrating and punishing aspects of the parents, a pathological predominance of sadistic superego forerunners, and a subsequent incapacity to integrate the idealized superego components with the sadistically threatening ones. All of this leads to a lack of superego integration and a concomitant tendency to reproject superego nuclei. Thus, dissociative or splitting processes in the ego are now reinforced by the lack of the normal integrative contribution of the superego, and contradictory internalized demands together with the insufficiency of the ego's repressive mechanisms contribute to the establishment of contradictory, instinctually infiltrated, pathological character traits. This development is maximally true at the "lower" level of organization of character pathology, and to some extent also is present at the "intermediate" level of organization of character pathology.

In contrast, when sufficient integration of "good" and "bad" internalized object relationships (involving self images, object images, ideal self images, ideal object images) takes place so as to permit an integrated self concept and a related integrated "representational world" to develop, a stable ego identity is achieved. At this point, a central ego core is protected from unacceptable drive derivatives by a stable repressive barrier, and the defensive character traits that develop have the characteristics of reaction formations or inhibitory traits. The development of this level of integration within the ego also creates the precondition for the integration of the sadistically determined superego forerunners with the ego ideal, and the subsequent capacity to internalize the realistic, demanding, and prohibitive aspects of the parents. All of this fosters further superego integration and, eventually, depersonification and abstraction within the superego. The superego may now act as a higher level organizer of the ego, providing further pressures for a harmonious integration of any remaining contradictory trends within the ego. The "toning down" of such an integrated, more realistically determined superego permits a more flexible management of instinctual drive derivatives on the ego's part, with the appearance of sublimatory character traits. At the "higher" level of organization of character pathology the integration of the superego is still excessively under the influence of sadistic forerunners, to the extent that the superego, although well integrated, still remains excessively harsh and demanding. Repressive and sublimatory handling of pregenital drive derivatives, especially of pregenital aggression, is possible to a sufficient extent so that there is less infiltration of genital drive derivatives with pregenital, especially aggressive trends, and the oedipal–genital level of development clearly predominates. At this, the "higher" level of organization of character pathology, excessive severity of the superego centers around excessive prohibition and/or conflicts around infantile sexuality. Object constancy, a capacity for stable and deep object relationships, and a stable ego identity have all been reached at this level.

Normality represents a further, and final progression along this continuum, with a well-integrated and less severe and punitive superego, a realistically discriminating set of superego demands, ego ideal, and ego goals which permit an overall harmony in dealing with the external world as well as with the instinctual needs. The predominance of sublimatory character traits reflects such an optimum expression of instinctual needs, of adaptive and sublimatory integration of pregenital trends under the primacy of genitality, in the context of mature, adult object relationships. A firm repressive barrier against a residuum of unacceptable, infantile instinctual needs is complemented by a large sector of a conflict-free, flexibly functioning ego, and the capacity to suppress some realistically ungratifiable needs without excessive stress.

Diagnostic, Prognostic, and Therapeutic Implications

From a diagnostic point of view, the proposed classification of character pathology may help to differentiate types of character pathology which, at first, may present diagnostic difficulties in individual cases. Thus, for example, the differential diagnosis between hysterical and infantile character pathology is greatly helped by utilizing structural as well as descriptive considerations. The presenting pathological character traits may at first seem hysterical; however, a thorough examination of those traits in terms of what they reveal regarding the superego structure, the predominant defensive operations of the ego, and the kind of conflicts the patient is struggling with, may point to the fact that the predominant pathological character constellation is of an infantile rather than a hysterical type. Also, while certain types of character pathology typically coincide with a certain level of severity of character pathology, this may not be true in every case. Thus, for example, a patient with infantile personality may, on the basis of a structural analysis, appear to be functioning at the "intermediate" rather than the "lower" level of organization of character pathology, with consequences for the prognosis and treatment recommendations. One additional diagnostic advantage of the proposed classification of character pathology is the possibility, on the basis of the structural characteristics of the patient, to predict the kind of defensive operations that will predominate in the treatment, especially as transference resistances.

From the viewpoint of overall prognosis, the proposed classification reflects three levels of severity of characterological illness. The prognosis for psychoanalytic treatment of patients in the "higher" level of organization of character pathology is very good; these patients respond very well to psychoanalysis. The prognosis is less favorable at the "intermediate" level; these patients usually require lengthier psychoanalytic treatment, and the goals of analysis must at times be less ambitious. The prognosis for the "lower" level of organization of character pathology is always serious; at this level classical, nonmodified psychoanalytic treatment is usually contraindicated or a preparatory period of expressive psychotherapy is required (Eissler, 1953a; Stone, 1954; Zetzel, 1968 [see chapter 19]).

Some therapeutic implications of the proposed model have already been mentioned as part of the prognostic considerations. For patients at the "higher" level of organization of character pathology, psychoanalysis is the treatment of choice. These patients may seek treatment for symptoms of a rather recent, minor, or situationally determined type, which may improve with brief psychotherapy. Ideally, however, they should be treated with psychoanalysis rather than one of the modified psychotherapeutic procedures because at this level the maximum improvement in personality functioning can be expected from analytic treatment. For patients functioning at the "intermediate" level of organization of character pathology, psychoanalysis is still the treatment of choice unless there is some special contraindication. These patients, however, will usually require lengthy psychoanalysis, and it may well be that in some selected cases a modified treatment is preferable either to start with or even as the only mode of treatment. For patients with the "lower" level of organization of character pathology, psychoanalysis is usually contraindicated. A special, modified psychoanalytic procedure with the introduction of parameters of technique (Eissler, 1953a) is the treatment of choice at this level. (I have discussed this issue in detail in my 1968 paper [see chapter 26].) A few patients at this level may still require or may be able to benefit from nonmodified, classical psychoanalysis. However, even in the case of these patients, the proposed classification may be useful, in that it highlights, in addition to the prognostic "warning," the typical defensive operations of these patients which are so predominant in their transference reactions, and the particular, severe pathology of their superego which may present extremely difficult treatment problems.

Section III
CONTEMPORARY CHARACTER TYPES

As a group, psychoanalysts are poor nosologists. They often appear to be merely inspired namers or borrowers from literature and psychiatry. Thus we have the phallic–narcissist, the imposter, the as-if, ocnophiles and philobats, the neurotic character, the psychotic character, the fool, the Don Juan, the Don Quixote, the wishy-washy personality, the passive–feminine, the psychopath—the list goes on—the alexithymic, the impulsive, the antisocial, and other character types.

The papers in this section include those types whose impact has been major and enduring (hysterical, obsessional, and masochistic character disorders) and/or types which have been dominating psychoanalytic attention over the last fifteen to twenty years (narcissistic and borderline character disorders). One other important character type, the paranoid, is presented in Section V.

Easser and Lesser summarize the changes in the psychoanalytic approach to hysteria over the past forty years as a preliminary to applying a more rigorous definition and formulation of the disorder (inspired by Knapp and the Boston Group) based upon the analytic study of six hysterical personalities. They identify developmental trends, conflicts, and character traits typical of this group and distinguish it from a larger group of "hysteroids" who also use hysterical mechanisms, but function at pregenital to psychotic levels.

Shapiro's article on the obsessive–compulsive style (a forerunner of the chapter in his well-known text, *Neurotic Styles* [1965]) offers a broader, phenomenological look at aspects of "character configuration"; that is, modes or styles of thinking, acting, and experiencing. By incorporating cognitive attitudes and social factors he extends the dimensionality of the anal character as described in Section I.

For Shapiro, the obsessional character is distinguished by its rigid, compulsive activity, the sense of "should," and the loss of reality. This person is intense, joyless, and doubtful due to an impaired sense of autonomy. Feeling pressured, driven to be busy, he seems to be responding to a higher authority. Fearful of losing control, he is unable to have hunches, act spontaneously, or make decisions based on preference. Lacking conviction, he becomes doubtful and dogmatic. His narrow perception of the world prevents him from seeing things in their real perspective.

Many of the papers selected for this book not only contain insights about the aspect of character under discussion but also reveal something of the author's general orientation and perspective as well—his or her "brand" of psychoanalysis as it were. This is exemplified particularly well in Brenner's excellent review, critique, and contribution to the psychoanalytic understanding of the masochistic character (a slightly abbreviated version is used in the *Handbook* because of space restrictions).

Clearly and methodically, Brenner shows how our understanding of masochism has evolved in response to psychoanalytic discoveries and attendant theoretical advances. Masochism is seen as a normal component of the human personality arising out of infantile sexual conflict and serving multiple functions such as defense against infantile fears and gratification of the need and wish for punishment. The masochistic (more appropriately labeled sadomasochistic) character is regarded as differing from the normal individual not in kind but in degree. Masochistic inclinations can be associated with many sorts of neurotic symptoms and a variety of character disorders.

Over the last twenty years interest in narcissism has grown immensely with two major figures, Otto Kernberg and Heinz Kohut, dominating the field. Rothstein's paper provides us with a critical summary and clarification of their respective positions and tries to lessen the confusion resulting from their using similar new terminology in different ways and perhaps dealing with different patient groups. He reviews the evolution of the concept, touching upon the writings of Sigmund Freud, Wilhelm Reich, and Annie Reich.

Rothstein argues that the narcissistic disorder should be understood as a defensive attempt to preserve illusions of one's primary narcissism. According to him, "Narcissistic personality disorders are defined by their preferred *mode* of attempting to restore a sense of narcissistic perfection to their self-representation and by the *state of integration* of narcissism by their egos." He suggests that the difference between neurotics and narcissistic personality disorders is one of degree. The latter are more preoccupied with reliving a sense of narcissistic perfection.

Meissner's article is one of the many responses that have inundated the literature following publication of Kernberg's *Borderline Conditions and Pathological Narcissism* (1975). His contribution provides the reader with an extensive and concentrated review of psychoanalytical views on the psychopathology of the borderline character type. Meissner notes that, largely as the result of Kernberg's efforts, considerable progress has been made in identifying a group of patients neither neurotic nor psychotic, but somewhere in between, who have to be dealt with in their own terms. They can be related to the as-if personality of Deutsch (chapter 21) and the "so-called good hysteric" described by Zetzel (chapter 19). Despite Kernberg's outstanding contribution, Meissner notes that much uncertainty and ambiguity remain and there are many reasons for dissatisfaction. In an effort to clarify the field he explores eight areas of deficit found in various theoretical accounts of the condition. These include instinctual defects, defensive impairment, ego defects, developmental defects, defective object relationships, identity diffusion, the false self, and narcissistic deficits. He discusses the different concepts in considerable detail, listing the strengths and weaknesses of each. He concludes that there may be a number of forms of borderline pathology that defy theoretical integration.

Chapter 14

HYSTERICAL PERSONALITY:
A REEVALUATION

BARBARA RUTH EASSER and STANLEY R. LESSER

Through the study and treatment of hysterical symptoms, psychoanalysis as a science was born. The psychoanalytic technique, including the use of dream and free association, and its theoretical foundations as well, such as the concepts of repression, conscious–unconscious, early traumata, wish-fulfillment, symptoms as compromise wish-fulfillment, etc., derived from the study and treatment of these hysterical phenomena. The trend of psychoanalytic interest has over the past forty years shifted far from these roots. Some of the factors involved in this shift are:

1. The general course of psychoanalytic thinking has always been merged with the clinical. Repeated inconsistency in the ability of the method to reverse the course of the hysterical symptoms has led to uncertainty, discouragement, disinterest, and, in Freud's words, "affords us a good reason for quitting such an unproductive field of enquiry without delay" (Freud, 1926).

2. There have been, over the years, changes in the presenting problems of patients seeking to be psychoanalyzed. No longer are we presented with the florid conversion reactions, fugues, massive amnesias, and so on. Today our more sophisticated, urbanized patients complain of chronic maladaptation in living; that is, in working, loving, and playing. The characteristic modes which predetermine these maladaptations have been designated "character neuroses" or "character disorders." The character traits relating to the obsessive modes of dealing with neurotic conflict have been formulated, organized, and more generally

This chapter originally appeared in the *Psychoanalytic Quarterly,* 34:390–405, 1969. Reprinted by permission of the publisher.

validated as a distinct clinical entity. Freud (1908) [see chapter 1] and Abraham (1953) originally described the basic character traits of the obsessive character but there has been almost no attempt to systematize the concept of the hysterical personality. Freud (1931) has suggested some relationship between it and what he called the "erotic personality," whose major goal in life is the desire to love or above all to be loved [see chapter 3]. Even here Freud is most careful not to make a simple correlation between this personality type and a tendency to develop hysterical neurosis. Fritz Wittels (1930), Wilhelm Reich (1949), Sandor Rado (1949–1950), and others have attempted a description of the hysterical character.

3. The shift in interest from the single traumatic event to the complex mechanisms used by the psyche to cope with anxiety has resulted in a concomitant shift of psychoanalytic emphasis from fantasy content to defensive ego maneuvers. Moreover the hysteric is, if anything, characterized by fantasy, capriciousness, inconstancy and whimsy, and the intellectualized, scientific, methodologically bound investigator has been more at ease in the study of patients characterized by rigid, intellectual, and definitive ego maneuvers, namely, obsessives.

4. Not only are the hysterics, in the psychoanalytic discipline, caught in their own history but the name itself is enmeshed within its popular, even idiomatic meaning. The rubric connotes the hysterical woman, hysterical attacks, in short, "a caricature of femininity" (Chodoff and Lyons, 1958). Hysterics are wont to live up to, in fact, to exaggerate their role. They apply themselves to whatever name one may call them. The psychoanalyst in his countertransference can be aroused by the contagion of the exaggerated affect. He finds himself "holding the bag" emotionally, provoked into overplaying his role as therapist, while his patient changes course and heads down a new emotional alley, perhaps a blind one. These experiences are common to all therapists and their frustrating consequences lead analysts to exert caution, not only in regard to specific patients, but to the entire category.

5. This therapeutic chagrin may be a cause of an interesting paradoxical dissociation. On the one hand, the hysteric theoretically is considered to have achieved the highest libidinal level for neurotic fixation, that is, phallic–oedipal, and on the other hand,

the sufferers are regarded as frustrating, provocative, infantile, teasing, suggestible, irresponsible, nonintuitive, egocentric, nonproductive citizens. As such they are regarded with contempt and disparagement (Sullivan, 1956; Chodoff and Lyons, 1958; Abse, 1959; Wisdorn, 1961).

We should not be surprised to find that the hysterical personality falls victim to every possibility of misdiagnosis and skewed prognosis. Frequently within one author's list (Glover, 1959; Knapp, Levin, McCarter, Wermer, and Zetzel, 1960), we find hysteria allocated to every point on the prognostic range. To quote Knapp: "our follow-up reports so far tend to indicate that hysterical patients are, to put it simply, very good or very bad patients. . . ." In the above authors' study of twenty-five patients entering analysis, of the nine considered most suitable, the diagnosis of hysteria was made in the majority; in the eight "moderately" suitable, the diagnosis of obsessive–compulsive neurosis was made in the majority; in the least suitable, four of the six most disturbed patients had presented symptoms of hysteria at the time of intake. Moreover, in a companion study of the same research team, there were eight cases which differed appreciably in analytic results from their original expectations. "Two results were better than expected and six worse. Five of the latter six could be regarded as predominantly hysteric in character structure, but the two patients who had done extraordinarily well were also hysterical."

Evidently investigators such as the Boston Group (Knapp et al., 1960) have highlighted the need for greater diagnostic precision and evaluative formulation. It is well known that psychoanalytic theory faces difficulty when it attempts to relate either character modes or symptom complexes to any one diagnostic entity. The terms *hysteria, hysterical character,* and so on, are so loosely defined and applied so promiscuously that their application to diagnostic categories has become meaningless. The use of these labels for evaluation, analyzability, or prognosis has become tantamount to predicting a throw of the dice.

This confusion has moved the authors to review their own clinical experiences. Hysteria encompasses conversion hysteria, phobic reaction, fugue states, and hysterical character. We are limiting ourselves to a scrutiny of the hysterical character. We feel that hysterical character neurosis can be differentiated from other clinical syndromes which use hysterical mechanisms. It is our hope that we may, by so doing, clarify and delineate hysterical character as a more specific clinical entity.

We shall use material from the study and analysis of six female patients who fall within the diagnosis of hysterical personality.[1] Later we shall differentiate this group from a larger patient group who use hysterical mechanisms but diagnostically should not be classified as hysterics. For the purpose of this paper we shall refer to this latter group as "hysteroid."

The patients with hysterical personality ranged in age from twenty-one to thirty-one years; three were married and three were single. All showed good to superior performances academically and occupationally. All followed usual female pursuits; two teachers, one actress, one secretary, one personnel manager, and one housewife. They were buoyant, sprightly, lively, and energetic. While varying greatly in appearance, they were all feminine and attractive. Their charm was not dependent upon overt flamboyance or drama. This group of patients in no way displayed the provocative, seductive, exhibitionistic, high-styled attire usually attributed to the hysterical patient.

The presenting problems revolved in the main around sexual behavior and the real or fantasied sexual object. They all complained of disillusionment and dissatisfaction with their lovers. This followed the shattering of a romantic fantasy.

Although the patients showed varying degrees of sexual inhibitions and malfunctions, from total inhibition to seemingly normal sexual functioning, all expressed concern over their passionate sexuality and their fear of the consequence of such passion. The fear of their sexual passion was multidetermined. Unconsciously they were motivated to compete with women, to seduce and conquer men, and to achieve security and power vicariously through the passionate engagement of the man with themselves. These goals and the means by which they were reached were contained within their rich fantasy life. The fan-

---

[1] We have excluded male hysterics from this presentation because of a lower incidence and because in the male, at least in Western society, hysteria is most often associated with effeminate characteristics. This proneness to effeminacy and homosexuality complicates and adds other dimensions to the personality.

tasies usually involved an irresistible, magnetic body that was to be exhibited to conquer the male and exclude all other women. The burlesque queen, the *femme fatale,* the diva served to portray this image. These fantasies tended to be pure wish-fulfillment and did not contain painful, masochistic elements (as did fantasies of the more pregenitally oriented "hysteroid" patients).

The other major presenting complaint was a sense of social shyness and apprehensiveness which contrasted with active social involvement. Not one of this group lacked long-term friendships, social and cultural interests. Although all were apprehensive with strangers and in strange situations, they became rapidly and successfully involved. Nonetheless, they failed to gain confidence after repeated success. This continued apprehensiveness was associated with severe humiliation and shame should rejection occur. They obtained pleasure in entertaining others and assumed the role of hostess with graciousness, so long as they held the center of the stage, through ingratiation and seductiveness as a rule, through temper tantrums when necessary. These traits make the hysteric a warm but often trying friend.

The sense of family and family relations was strong in all. There was a marked difference in their behavior within the family group and outside it. At home, especially with their mothers, a marked regression occurred. Self-reliance, assertion, and competitiveness diminished and inhibition replaced social vigor. Their families regarded these women as juvenile, inefficient, dependent, cute, and lovable. One patient kept the nickname "Baby" until marriage.

Each had been and remained profoundly involved with her father in actuality and/or in fantasy. These fathers were all seductive. Most were dominant, arbitrary, excitable, volatile, controlling, and imaginative. Within the family, the father wrote the family comedies and tragedies. He was the inspirer and the director. Two fathers differed in that they were moderate alcoholics, soft and submissive. Through their romantic fantasy they created the expectation of future drama and adventure captured so well in the portrayal of the father in *A Tree Grows in Brooklyn*. An important characteristic of the father–daughter pair was the stimulation and seduction abruptly changing to condemnation of sexual and romantic interest when the daughters reached puberty. One father insisted that his ten-year-old daughter accompany him in a lengthy search for a strange man who purportedly had invited her for a stroll. Another, overhearing his eleven-year-old daughter's exuberant laughter as she was walking down the street holding hands with a classmate, exploded into a fury, saying, "you were holding hands, it's disgusting." Femininity, charm, and seductiveness were not only tolerated but admired and elicited as long as their physical aspects could be held in oblivion. With the budding of puberty, the attraction of the social world, and the appearance of suitors these fathers reversed their attitudes in order to preserve their pleasure in their little girls.

The mothers in this group were consistent and responsible. All were engrossed in their children and their homes. They wanted their daughters to live out their own frustrated, romantic fantasies, but they maintained their social and community interests. The patients' later social aptitudes, feminine interests, as well as their social anxiety, stemmed from identification with their mothers and from active promotion by them.

Typical of this relationship was a mother who devoted herself to the prettifying of her little daughter and spent many hours making clothing for her. This behavior continued throughout the daughter's adolescence, marriage, and even after her divorce. Following the patient's divorce, the mother sent her an elaborate and inappropriate hostess gown that signified the mother's reestablishment of her own fantasy of her child.

The major psychic conflict occurs when the gratification of physical sexuality is inhibited and repressed. Romance then preoccupies and invades every area of functioning. Since these women remain fixated to their fathers into their adult lives, the mother must be perceived as uninteresting sexually, frigid, and ridiculous in her pretense toward desirability, and observed with scorn or benign condescension for her housewifely, female pursuits. The patients are not aware of their extensive identification with and envy of the same attributes they so heartily condemn.

The conflict with the father revolves about the inability to relinquish the infantile fixation. The early demand for love and affection, dominance in other relationships of the unchanged romantic image of the father, and an envy of and desire for the father's purported physical attributes (penis envy) substitute for the forbidden sexuality. The later heterosexual relationships are typically marked by overintensity and by a fearful adulation of the partner.

We consider then the following traits to be those most intimately associated with the hysterical personality:

Labile Emotionality. The predominance of the use of feelings rather than thought in crises and conflicts.

Direct and Active Engagement with the Human World. The overt and covert need to love and more especially the need to be loved (Freud, 1931 [see chapter 3]) result in hypersensitivity to others. The patients are concerned with their own emotional reactivity, are self-absorbed, and show "an exorbitant degree of affectionate interest in self" (Rado, 1949–1950). Their egocentric need to test love through interaction with others accounts for the variety of their emotional upheavals, from enthusiastic crowing to weeping, wailing, anger, and panic, depending on the real or fancied response of their audience.

The Hysterical Patient Responds Badly Not Only to Frustration but Also to Overexcitability even though she herself may have been its main instigator. Both the pursuit of excitement and the defense against its realization result from constant proneness to distort environmental stimuli into sensual, often sexual, contexts. These distorted perceptions then feed back into the existing excitement. As tensions mount the sensual excitement terrifies the patient who responds with overt anxiety and flight.

A Close Relationship Exists Between Excitability and Its Derivative Fantasy. These fantasies are almost always concerned with romance and romantic sexuality. They are also used to "embroider, heighten, and sexualize the existing relationships" (Wisdom, 1961).

Suggestibility has, from the time of Charcot, been emphasized as a major, often the major, trait of the hysteric. The preeminence of suggestibility has been doubted more recently (Chodoff and Lyons, 1958). In the patients that we are designating as hysterical personalities we have been impressed not by manifest suggestibility but by the strength of the defense against suggestibility. Rather, suggestibility occurs more often in the object toward whom the emotionality of the hysteric is directed. The interpersonal transaction often results in the hysteric's receiving the suggestion she has assiduously implanted. More simply, she receives the suggestion she has wanted all along.

Dislike and Avoidance of the Exact, the Rote, and the Mundane. These characteristics account for such labels as irresponsible, inconsistent, self-indulgent, and rebellious. Nevertheless, although the hysteric never does a job for a job's sake, she is capable of proficiency when the tasks have sufficient scope to inspire her and to allow her to express her real or fantasied sense of drama. Despite the irresponsibility for details, the capacity to fulfill the overall task may be present. In our group of patients superior performance was the rule rather than the exception.

Closely Related to This Seemingly Irresponsible, Flighty Quality Is the Maintenance of Her Self-Presentation as a Child–Woman. Part and parcel of this child–woman façade is a denial of the unpleasant, the distasteful, the forbidden, the actual or fantasied transgression, through insouciance, naïveté, and inexperience.

The hysterical mechanism is a major psychic defensive mode. In this sense it is used by all personalities, from the normal to the most pathological. The basic hysterical mechanism involves the substitution of emotions, one for the other, or a shift in the quality of an emotional response so that it becomes, paradoxically, a substitute for itself. Any emotion may serve as a signal analogous to the use of anxiety as a warning signal against anticipated body damage or intrapsychic tension. Thus, an emotional reconnaissance is, as it were, sent forth in lieu of true, meaningful reactivity. One observes an impressive array of emotional behavior, emotional thought, emotional interrelatedness, and emotional use of the body. Despite its intensity, this emotionality always remains peripheral and a shield for the core affect. A tantrum can ward off the awareness of sexual excitement, of competitive triumph, and of feared rage in anticipation of rejection. This mechanism perpetuates vicarious and fictitious satisfactions without requiring confrontation of the primary underlying desire. Fantasy replaces actions, the implications of behavior are discounted. This may be accomplished through minimizing the behavior as play, reducing it to emotional absurdity, or exaggerating the psychic actions. The substitutive emotionality and emotional maneuvers are overdetermined as in the formation of a neurotic symptom. They serve, at once, adaptation and security, disguised and distorted gratification, secondary gains, as well as the primary defensive purpose of concealing from consciousness the basic motivating conflict.

In order to delimit the hysterical personality it is necessary to differentiate our group from other patients who also employ hysterical mechanisms. These patients range widely diagnostically from the infantile dependent to the borderline, and the psychotic. For the purpose of this discussion we shall designate these latter groups as "hysteroids."

In many instances the hysteroid would appear to be a caricature of the hysteric, much as the hysteric has been said to be a caricature of femininity. Each characteristic is demonstrated in even sharper dramatic relief. The bounds of social custom and propriety are breached. The latent aggressivity of the exhibitionism, the competitiveness and the self-absorption becomes blatant, insistent, and bizarre. The chic becomes the mannequin; the casual, sloppy; the bohemian, beat. Thus, a hysterical patient was able to enjoy the pleasures of the beauty parlor only after analysis had broken through her defense against exhibitionism while a hysteroid patient changed the color of her hair one to two times a week to keep pace with her rapidly shifting moods.

The adaptational functioning of the hysteroid is erratic. Inconstancy and irresponsibility cause the patient to suffer realistic rebuffs, injuries, and failures. By contrast, the hysteric often voices desperation and provokes concern in others but rarely is in actual danger. Historically, in the hysteroid, academic and vocational patterns usually reflect the same erratic quality of attainment, alternating with periods of serious dysfunction.

In object relationships, the hysteric has difficulty within the relationship, the hysteroid with the relationship. Friendships are maintained over long periods by the hysteric. These are characterized by much affectionate display, much ingratiation, and many emotional storms. The hysteroid starts friendships with great hopes and enthusiasm. The friendship commences with idolatry and ends in bitterness when the expectation of the rescue, nurture, and care is not fulfilled. These relational ruptures are often succeeded by detachment, isolation, depression, and paranoidlike trends. The hysteric uses emotional relationships to copulate symbolically, to hold her partner as guardian over her own erotism, to contain her own physical impulses. Since emotional engagement for the hysteroid embodies the impulse to engulf and incorporate the object, this in turn is viewed as a reciprocal threat of self-depletion. The defensive movement of detachment becomes a psychic imperative.

The hysteroid's family life is often much more disturbed, disorganized, and inconsistent. In contrast to the hysteric, the core of the hysteroid's problem lies with the mother or maternal object. There may be actual affect deprivation with such traumata as the mother's early death, or her prolonged physical or emotional illness. The mother may have been unable to provide sufficient affective care as a result of absence, passivity, depression, or disinterest. This includes the group who have had an egocentric, disinterested, hysteroid mother.

During childhood these hysteroid patients show emotional maladaptations and symptom–formation. Infantile fixations, such as prolonged thumb-sucking, enuresis, and infantile fetishism are common. Most striking is the tendency of these patients to have created a fantasy world and to have lived within it. The tendency often starts early with imaginary companions and later expands into complex portrayals of roles within the imaginary world. Of importance is the substitution of the fantasy for relationships and cooperative pleasures with contemporaries.

In preadolescence the hysteric becomes a member of the "club" and the "gang." The hysteroids increase their tendency to isolate and withdraw, viewing themselves as loners, different, superior, aloof, and so on.

Unfortunately, despite careful clinical evaluation, differentiation may not be possible without clinical trial. The difficulty in diagnostic assessment is hardly surprising when one considers that there is no sharp differentiating line but rather a continuum, and that within this continuum the hysteroid often shows the hysterical mechanism more clearly and dramatically.

Grosser fluctuations of the hysteroid personality are to be anticipated from the more infantile fixation and the consequent weaker integration and synthesis of the ego. Thus we encounter less emotional control, a lessened ability to hold and tolerate tension, and more proneness to action and depression. Generally these patients are prone to substitute analysis for life or conversely to avoid analysis through overintense involvement in life. For example, a cablegram notifies the therapist that the patient has managed to get an overseas assignment. Such behavior can be

expected whenever there is a danger that the therapist may confront the patient with her unconscious conflicts. If an overseas
assignment cannot be managed, this patient is likely to arrive
late, hung over, separated from the therapist by dark glasses, a
headache, and "defensive" guilt. Another patient managed to
lose, give away, or squander her salary whenever she was tempted
to enter the adult feminine world. Thus for her to plan the
purchase of a new dress would herald a sudden, mysterious
financial crisis.

The hysteroid moves widely, quickly, and grandly, threatening both life-functioning and therapeutic relationships. The hysteric reacts more subtly and symbolically. The hysteric will often
regress. The content of such regression may show oral and other
pregenital trends and is used to defend against the developing
sexual feelings and the erotic transference. Conversely, the hysteroid, to defend against feared passivity and primitive orality,
tends to go into action and reaction, which activity may include
the use of erotic (more exactly pseudo-erotic) transference and
sexual acting out.

Two female schoolteachers were both severely sexually
inhibited. Neither engaged in heterosexual nor masturbatory
activity. One patient sought therapy because of nonconsumma-
tion of her marriage. She insisted the difficulty was her husband's. From her associations it became clear that she would shy
away from her husband's approach. With growing awareness of
the extent of her own inhibitions she began to disparage the
eight-year-old girls in her class for their overconcern with and
enjoyment of their bodies. She also associated with anger to a
period in her own childhood when her mother stimulated her
interest in femininity. Her mother's interest, she felt, reenforced
her own sense of unattractiveness and her need to reject her own
body. She began to reexplore her body, thus evoking past
memories of pleasure from body stimulation. A period of
body experimentation ensued, and an attempt at gratification
through thumbsucking was made and rejected, while breast
stimulation proved more exciing and acceptable. This gradually led to a reversal of her negative body image and to vaginal
masturbation. With the overcoming of her inhibition of masturbation her femininity and sexuality expanded, allowing

greater exhibitionism, flirtatiousness, and eventually heterosexual relations, with orgasm. In this way, through identification and competition with her eight-year-old pupils, and on
account of her fear of sexuality and genital stimulation she had
recourse to an oral mode, thumbsucking, and then breast play, a
transitional oral–genital mode. It was necessary for this young
woman to recapitulate body-pleasure development in order to
remove sexual repression and restore her feminine self-image.

The second patient, a hysteroid, lent a quixotic, volatile
quality to all her experiences. She avoided heterosexual contact
through a diverse series of maneuvers. She lived in the smallest,
cheapest room of a woman's residence and dressed shabbily and
carelessly. Whenever her friends attempted to introduce her to
men she would forget the appointment, become angry at some
fancied slight, develop headaches, or become intoxicated on the
first drink. As the meaning of these ego maneuvers became
clearer, the turbulence and overemotionalism increased. To
cope with the resultant crises, the patient moved into activity
rather than into analysis. She looked for improved living quarters
and set about acquiring a new wardrobe. She insisted that this
was the necessary prerequisite to her entrance into the sexual
arena. Subsequently, after repeated backing and filling, she precipitously entered into an affair with a young man. She supposed
him unattainable. However, he committed the indiscretion of
falling in love with her. She reacted with rage and panic, and fear-
ing that he would trap her through impregnation, she fled. In this
patient action replaced insight. Sexual activity was used defensively to avoid becoming related either to the therapist or to the
lover. Thus, she was able to use sexuality to defend against pregenital needs, and, interestingly, she relinquished much of her
florid, irresponsible, infantile behavior in order to avoid the
more dreaded dependent therapeutic relationship.

For both the hysteric and the hysteroid, dreams are the
"royal road to the unconscious." Along this road the differences
in the level of fixation, self-image, and the defense systems
become manifest. Both are frequent dreamers and recall their
dreams with ease. The symbolic content in the hysteric tends to
be simpler, more easily deciphered, more universal, and less
individualistic. The hysteric's dreams reflect a greater ego

integration, basic trust and hope in object relations, more frankness in the underlying wish-fulfillment, less primitive, archaic imagery, both human and nonhuman. The dreams of the hysteroid are filled with vast empty spaces, scenes of desolation, destruction, and impoverishments. Surrealistic imagery abounds. These differences can be illustrated by the juxtaposition of the dreams of two patients, both from an early period of analysis and both involving transference and sexuality.

> I was the favorite wife of the Shah of Iran. An older wife was trying to shoot me. There were shots and someone was killed.

> I found myself living in a decrepit slum. Everything was broken, dirty, and messy. Suddenly some Bowery bums seemed to be clutching and trying to grab me.

The grandiose, dramatic, glamorous, successful (favorite wife) quality of the hysteric seems clear. The transference had aroused the oedipal conflict. This dream, through its lack of resolution, demonstrates the typical hysterical indefiniteness as to the outcome. The second dream is also in response to the transference. The hysteroid reacts to the arousal of transference by using more primitive defenses. The disgusting, impoverished environs mirror her self-image. The wish and the hope are deeply hidden as she visualizes her desire for a relationship in terms of an overwhelming threat.

The following two dreams will indicate a further example of the parallel but dissimilar modes by which these same two patients revealed their attitudes toward their self-images as sexual objects.

> A bull was chasing me. I noticed that I was wearing a red dress. I kept thinking it's not my red dress, it's my movements that are enraging him.

> Harry (a current beau) was starting to make love to me when suddenly he vomited all over me. I said, "that's all right, I'm menstruating anyway."

The first dream demonstrates the impulse for self-exhibition and the feeling of her own magnetism. The dream contains the hysteric's concern with rape. Within the dream she deals with the defense against her own active provocation. The symbols and their use are common and clear. In the latter dream, once more the hysteroid patient demonstrates her need to depict herself as a rejected, disgusting, and depreciated object. She relates self-loathing to her menses, a symbol of her despised femaleness, rather than to her sense of her hopelessness in regard to attainment of a relationship. Similarly, her lover is depicted as displacing and reversing his sexual impulses into oral disgust and defilement of the object, herself.

Summary

We have attempted to define clinically the hysterical character, to present the major developmental trends, and to describe the basic dynamic conflicts and defenses. To delineate this entity further we have juxtaposed descriptions and examples from a larger clinical group which we have designated as hysteroid.

Clinical practice and psychiatric literature have increasingly challenged and modified the earlier psychoanalytic formulation of hysteria. Increasing stress has been placed upon oral fixations and their resultant dependency strivings (Marmor, 1953; Chodoff and Lyons, 1958; Rangell, 1959), with the implicit discounting of oedipal conflict as "the core of the neurosis." We feel that one can err as much in the direction of emphasizing early fixation as to assume that all hysteria is oedipal in origin. It is preferable to divide these patients into two separate diagnostic classifications for the purpose of improving therapeutic selectivity and validity. We have reserved the term *hysterical personality* for the more mature and better integrated and have termed the large group that extends from the pregenital to the psychotic as *hysteroid*.

Chapter 15

ASPECTS OF
OBSESSIVE–COMPULSIVE STYLE

David Shapiro

This paper undertakes to examine certain typical aspects of obsessive-compulsive functioning. These will be broad aspects of functioning, including areas of cognitive function, overt behavior, and subjective experience. As I shall explain, these ways of functioning represent aspects of style, and therefore aspects of character. The observations on which this material is based are drawn from experience with psychological tests, from therapeutic work, and from general observation. Diagnostic testing, especially with the Rorschach test, particularly favors the development of a view of the broad style features of psychopathology and character. My interest here is in abstracting from these specific sources of observation in order to arrive at some principles of obsessive-compulsive style.

Clinical understanding of neurotic conditions usually revolves around the content of dynamic issues and specific defense mechanisms, particularly as these express themselves in conspicuous symptoms and traits. At the same time, there is general recognition that neurotic syndromes—and the dynamic issues and specific defense mechanisms that may be involved in them—exist only within much broader configurations. These configurations must include, for example, both pathological and nonpathological attitudes, modes of cognition which allow for many sorts of reality assessment as well as distortions of reality, configurations of intellectual endowment, patterns of overt behavior, sorts of subjective experience, and so on. This, of course, says only that defense mechanisms, dynamic tendencies, symptoms, or traits are not interchangeable from one character

This chapter originally appeared in *Psychiatry*, 25:46–49, 1962. Reprinted by permission of the author and the publisher.

context to another, but are aspects of a pervasive character organization.

It is not yet possible to describe such character configurations in very great detail. This insufficiency has certain outstanding consequences. It implies, first of all, an insufficient understanding of the basis of much of the consistency and stability of individual behavior and life, psychopathological or not. Knowledge of the nature of character configurations would help in understanding not only the stability of general trends of behavior but also the stability—or, from a therapeutic point of view, the persistence—of specific symptoms or pathological traits. A whole dimension of the stability of a specific symptom may derive from its consistency with and, as it were, support of the aims and principles of the character organization as a whole.

Two other points follow as corollaries to this main one. First, without sufficient understanding of the broad principles of character functioning, it is difficult to understand the relationship, in an individual, between one pathological condition and another, as when a neurotic condition decompensates into a more severe or psychotic one. Second, it is similarly difficult to understand the relationship between pathological and nonpathological aspects of individual functioning. In both cases the reason is the same: it is precisely the broad principles of character functioning which comprise the relationships in question in any one person—that is, the tie between one pathological condition and another, or the tie between pathological and nonpathological aspects of functioning.

An interest in characterological functioning must essentially lead, I believe, to a search for concepts or principles which are capable of describing general *forms* of behavior or experience, whose specific contents may be quite varied—that is, concepts such as *style* or *mode*. A concept of this sort implies a mental structure or structures which give shape—presumably a special shape for each individual—to expressions, cognition, and experiences in general, whether symptom or nonsymptom, defense against impulse or adaptive expression of impulse, pathological behavior or nonpathological behavior. Of course, I do not mean to say that any single mode or style will be reproduced in all areas of functioning, but rather that styles can be found which are capable of describing large areas of function and which can themselves be related and organized. Since such styles are relatively enduring and slow to change even when the specific contents of behavior or experience change quite sharply, it is possible to credit to them the individual's relative stability over periods of time as well as his relative consistency, at any given time, in different areas of functioning. This is illustrated in the following observation by Escalona and Heider (1959), contained in their recent developmental study: "As one notes behavioral alterations from infancy to—in the case of our study—later preschool ages, one knows that not a single behavior has remained the same, yet one is struck with the inherent continuity of behavioral style and of the child's pattern of adaptation" (p. 9).

The early psychoanalytic interest in anal–erotic character (Freud, 1908 [see chapter 1]; Jones, 1918; Abraham, 1921), whose subject matter overlaps that of this paper, was not essentially directed toward such broad forms of functioning. It was, rather, directed toward the understanding of specific traits, or clusters of traits, as relatively direct derivatives of anal–erotic impulses (unchanged perpetuations of them, sublimations of them, or reaction formations against them). It is true that those early papers of Freud, Jones, and Abraham indicate the persistence of some relatively general forms of behavior and experience, not always clearly tied to symbolic representations of their original objects and sometimes possessing considerable adaptive power (sublimation). But one may doubt, from the present-day standpoint, whether it would be feasible to derive broad forms or styles of adult behavior from this source alone. Reich (1933), later, expressed this doubt clearly and made as well a clear distinction between the content of specific traits and broad characteristic forms of behavior. In the obsessive-compulsive character, for example, he refers to the *pervasive* characteristics of emotional restraint and evenness in living, which, he says, "form the point of departure of our analysis of the character form. They cannot be derived from individual impulses like the contents of the character traits; they give the individual his particular stamp . . ." (p. 196). Unfortunately, Reich's analysis of the obsessive-compulsive character was very brief and essentially did not go beyond this particular feature of emotional restraint or, in extreme form, "affect block."

There is, nowadays, considerable psychoanalytic interest in broader dimensions of psychological functioning than those that can conveniently be encompassed by concepts of impulse and defense. Erikson's (1950) developmental concept of *modes* of functioning (incorporative, retentive, and so forth), generalized from their original organ zones and then coordinated with social possibilities or opportunities, is one important instance. Brenman (1952), in connection with the clinical problem of masochism, represents a widespread interest when she points out the necessity for an understanding which can include pathological and adaptive aspects of such ways of functioning. On the experimental–theoretical side, Klein (1954), and Gardner, Holzman, Klein, Linton, and Spence (1959) have studied modes of cognition, perception particularly, with the aim of discovering organization principles or styles which may ultimately have application to wide areas of function.

The examination of obsessive–compulsive functioning which I will undertake here is suggested by the consideration that styles of behavior may be more observable in the continuous, perhaps mundane, ordinarily unremarkable dimensions of experience and activity than in dramatic symptoms or conspicuous, isolated traits. These continuous ways of living are dimensions of pathology whose existence is known full well, but which are not often observed seriously. Yet, I believe, their study may bring one closest to principles of functioning which ultimately comprise character. I have selected four aspects of obsessive–compulsive functioning for examination: (1) rigidity; (2) compulsive activity; (3) the sense of "should"; and (4) the loss of reality.

The first and fourth areas refer primarily to cognition, although rigidity has secondary reference also to posture and body experience. The second area refers primarily to overt behavior and certain sorts of conscious experience associated with it. The third area refers to a specific content of thought and subjective experience which, though strictly speaking not on the same level of generality as the other three, I have included as an independent section because of its significance and pervasiveness. It throws light particularly on the obsessive-compulsive style of motivation-experience. I have selected these areas not because I believe them to be necessarily of greater importance than any other aspect of functioning or in any sense definitive, but because they seem to me to be typically of importance and likely to be informative.

Rigidity

The term *rigidity,* used very frequently to describe obsessive-compulsive people, refers to a number of characteristics. It may refer, for example, to a stiff body posture or social manner, or to a general behavioral quality of persistence in a course of action that is irrelevant or even absurd. But, above all, this term describes a style of thinking, and it is this that I would like to concentrate on.

What exactly is meant by rigidity of thinking? Consider as a commonplace example the sort of thinking that one may meet in a discussion with the kind of compulsive rigid person who is also called dogmatic or opinionated. Discussion, even casual conversation, with such a person is often exceedingly frustrating, and it is so for a particular reason. It is not simply that one meets with unexpected opposition, as might at first appear to be the case. Typically such discussion is frustrating because one experiences neither real disagreement nor agreement. Instead, there is no meeting of minds at all; the impression is that one is not being heard, not arousing interest in new information or other points of view, and not receiving any but perfunctory attention. The following excerpt from a conversation will illustrate the point.

Two friends, K. and L., are discussing the buying of a house in which K. is interested.

K.: So you think I shouldn't buy it?

L.: Never buy a house with a bad roof. It will cost you its price again in repairs before you're finished.

K.: But the builder I hired to look it over did say it was in good condition otherwise.

L.: The roof is only the beginning. First it is the roof and then comes the plumbing and then the heating and then the plaster.

K.: Still, those things seem to be all right.

L.: And after the plaster, it will be the wiring.

K.: But the wiring is—

L.: (Interrupts with calm assurance). It will cost double the price before you're finished.

In this illustration, L.'s inattention to K.'s points is obvious. This inattention of the rigid, compulsive person has, however, a special quality. It is not, for example, the inattention of fatigue or stupidity. On the contrary, it appears to have an active and, as it were, a principled quality. It is in just such inattention to new facts or a different point of view that what we call rigidity seems to manifest itself in the obsessive–compulsive person. I will say tentatively, therefore, that restriction of attention is one crucial and defining feature of obsessive–compulsive rigidity.

In order to clarify this and the other features of the compulsive's rigidity, it is valuable to consider the thought rigidity often observed in quite dramatic forms in cases of organic brain damage. This comparison may seem a strange one, yet it does not seem to be just a semantic accident that the trait of rigidity is described in these two pathological groups far more frequently than in any others. I would like to digress briefly to examine certain features of thought rigidity in organic cases, in which it is more vivid and on the whole perhaps better understood than in obsessive–compulsives.

Goldstein and Scheerer (1944) have shown that the rigidity of the organically brain-damaged is related to the concrete, "stimulus-bound" quality of their cognition and general mode of approach. The brain-damaged person's attention appears to be gripped or compelled by an immediately manifest functional or even visual aspect of a situation; unable to detach himself, unable to shift even though logical considerations may suggest a shift, he will behave repetitiously or perseveratively—that is, his behavior will be rigid. In contrast, the normal person has the capacity *not* to be gripped, the capacity to detach himself from the most immediately manifest features of a situation and to shift his attention, smoothly and rapidly, now to this aspect, now to that aspect. Obviously, such shifting is, at the least, a precondition for separating out what is relevant for abstraction. What I am describing here is, of course, what is called flexibility. I am suggesting that cognitive flexibility may be described as an *autonomous mobility of attention,* in that, not being gripped by aspects of the situation which are irrelevant to his essential aims, the subject is free to pursue what is pertinent to his interests. It is clear that the impairment of this autonomous mobility of attention in the organically damaged person is a critical feature of his cognitive rigidity. This conclusion can be compared with the tentative conclusion, stated above, that limitation of attention is a critical feature of obsessive–compulsive rigidity. It appears that, notwithstanding the obvious disparity between the two kinds of rigidity, particularly with respect to their severity, this essential feature of impairment (in the one case) or restriction (in the other) of free mobility of attention is common to both.

It is instructive, also, to look at one other commonly reported feature of the rigidity of the brain-damaged, namely, the special subjective experience which ordinarily accompanies it (Weigl, 1941). This experience is essentially one of passivity or surrender. It involves, as many observers have noted, a marked impairment in the sense of deliberateness, of active choice, or of will. I will consider later the type of subjective experience which seems to be associated with obsessive–compulsive rigidity, but it may be noted at this point that the capacity for autonomous mobile attention is very likely a condition for the subjective experience of autonomy or will, as it is also for cognitive flexibility or what Goldstein has called the "abstract attitude."

While the obsessive–compulsive's attention cannot be described as stimulus-bound or unable to shift, as in the brain-damaged, neither is it altogether free and mobile. Typically, his attention is quite sharply focused. On the Rorschach test, this is evident in his affinity for small details and precise delineation of them; much the same affinity is observable in his everyday life. But his attention is also, in certain respects, markedly limited in range. Specifically, it seems poorly equipped for, and tends to avoid, what might best be described as the more immediate *impression,* the more casual or passive sort of cognitive experience, which may include also what is peripheral to its intended focus. And the obsessive–compulsive seems to avoid the more passive or impressionistic sorts of cognitive experience exactly by his sharp and narrowed focus. Thus, these people will rarely be *surprised* or, as it were, *struck* by anything. They will, in fact, refer with pride to their imperturbability and single-mindedness. They will go after and get the facts, but they will often miss those aspects of a situation which give it its flavor or its impact. Although the rigid obsessive–compulsive's attention is far from being gripped and virtually immobilized, as in the brain-damaged, the fact that wide areas of cognitive experience are ruled out on the basis of their form, and not because of lack of pertinence to the individual's interests, means that this style of attention must be considered seriously limited in its mobility and autonomy as well as its range.

The sharp and narrowed focus, then, avoids certain aspects of the world even while it engages others. One further essential aspect of this style of attention—in contrast to sharply focused but more flexible styles—is that it must be maintained with a consistently high level of intensity and activity—one might say with fixity. This may be made more clear by an analogy. In shooting an arrow, the greater the tension of the bow and the speed of the arrow, the less susceptible it will be to extraneous forces such as incidental winds. Similarly, the casual impression, the element on the periphery of the focus of attention, the more passive cognitive experiences, which for someone with a smoothly mobile attention attracts interest briefly and releases it with a greater or lesser gain, is for the compulsive's attention at best only potential distraction, and he avoids it most successfully when he is most intensely focused on the small detail.

Thus, in place of the wide-ranging and mobile attention which is a condition of flexibility, the obsessive–compulsive's attention is sharply focused, narrowed, intense, and fixed. These conditions, I believe, describe the obsessive–compulsive's cognitive rigidity. And it will be understandable from this point of view that this cognitive style often combines excellent technical facility with extreme anxiety or incompetence in creative tasks.

The obsessive–compulsive does not ordinarily experience the sense of helplessness and surrender that is found in organic patients. However, he does experience an impairment of the sense of autonomy or volition. Along with the active but rigid mode of cognition described, he experiences himself as actively operating, concentrating, but not fully self-directing. He feels machinelike, or like an automaton that runs effectively, but without volition. For example, one person likened his life to a train, running well, fast, on time, and without will along a pre-determined course.

It is clear enough that certain contents—that is, certain interests of life circumstances—will be consistent with and con-genial to this style of functioning, while others will be uncongenial and will tend to disrupt or undermine the machinelike experience. It is likely, however, to be the act of shifting or change itself which is most uncongenial to the fixed, narrow attention of the obsessive-compulsive person. Change or movement, whether it is to enter-tain a new point of view or simply to move the body, ordinarily involves by its nature the greatest likelihood of a vivid awareness of free choice or autonomy—in other words, the sort of subjec-tive experience which is sharply antithetical to the machinelike obsessive–compulsive experience. It is not surprising, therefore, that various mental operations appear in obsessive–compulsive people at moments of change or movement which have the con-sequence of attenuating that experience in one way or another. The actual change itself, although it may be surrounded by a great deal of obvious hesitancy and discomfort, is often charac-terized by a staccato, exceedingly abrupt quality, as in the quick, abrupt shift from one body position to another.

One additional point in this connection is the familiar obsessional experience of "fear of loss of control." It is often assumed that this experience necessarily reflects a weakness of defense and an actual pressure of impulse of great intensity. Although sometimes this is no doubt the case, it is by no means invariably so. This "fear" seems to arise in obsessive–compulsive people when, for whatever reason, their machine-automaton experience is shaken. For the rigid person, the actual moment of change, movement, or decision, however insignificant the mat-ter at hand may look to someone else, is a moment of leap from one stable position to another. These are moments which, for the more flexible and autonomous person, are, first, not so abrupt and attenuated, and, second, filled by the experience of volition as it is related to the external interest at hand. But, given the absence of flexibility and such volitional experiences, the rigid person does feel in the small leaps which make up the moments of change and decision in everyday life a type of surrender (or loss) of control. While these everyday experiences may be tolerable because they are so attenuated, I believe that they provide a model for the rigid person of the moment-in-between, a model of loss of control which offers itself to him in the face of any inclination to abandon or relax his machine-automaton style of existence.

While I have referred mainly to the problem of cognitive rigidity, I believe that a good deal that has been said—for example, about the maintenance of the machine-automaton subjective experience—has some application to other sorts of rigidity, such as postural.

Activity

Typically, as mentioned above, the obsessive–compulsive person is intensely and more or less continuously active, and I have suggested that his attention style can be maintained only with continuous activity. However, another aspect of obsessive–compulsive activity is equally distinctive—the quality of effortfulness. For the obsessive–compulsive person, everything involves a special sense of *trying*.

The compulsive's effortfulness and trying cannot be considered simply a greater measure of the experience of effort felt by anyone engaged in an activity which in some way taxes his capacities. For the compulsive person the quality of effort is present in every activity, whether it taxes his capacities or not. Nor can this effortfulness, though it is associated with the intensity of compulsive activity, be correlated with the effectiveness of work or even with its ultimate quantity. It is true, of course, that in the area of work this quality is generally more expected and less noticeable, and work is, typically, the compulsive's preferred area of existence. But the effortfulness extends, also, into what is ordinarily play or fun. The compulsive tries just as effortfully to enjoy himself at play, and even tries just as hard to be "spontaneous." One can only conclude from all of this trying that effort is here not an incidental accompaniment to an interest or an activity, but that it is a significant and at times even dominating interest in itself. One must conclude that the compulsive's interest is typically divided between, on the one hand, the ostensible aim or activity—for example, getting the work out, cleaning the table—and, on the other hand, the achievement of a special sort of experience of effort.

The activity of the obsessive–compulsive is also aptly described as *driven,* a term which refers in part to its quantity and intensity, but also captures another aspect. This is its look of actually being pressed by, or deriving its motive force from, something outside the acting person himself. The genuine interest of the person does not seem to account for the intensity of his activity, and a discrepancy between these two becomes apparent. It is in this connection that one notices the effortful "trying" that is described above. It is evident that the effortfulness of obsessive–compulsive activity is related to its drivenness and that it reflects a subjective experience of burden or requirement imposed from the outside which the acting subject is at pains to show he is *trying* to satisfy. It is for these reasons that the compulsive person's activity is called driven. It does look as though it were in some way pressed or directed by something external, and it does in a certain sense feel so to its subject. Of course, one cannot consider this peculiar quality of compulsive activity without asking what the quasi-external pressure actually consists of, this pressure which the compulsive person appears to be at such pains to satisfy. The obvious answer, that it is a pressure which he himself applies and to which he is at the same time subjected, does not make this mode of behavior any less peculiar.

Characterizing the activity of the obsessive–compulsive and the subjective experience that is associated with it as effortful or driven implies another, complementary, aspect of this particular way of functioning. Along with the drivenness, there is also a driver. A special sort of self-awareness is never altogether absent in the experience of the obsessive–compulsive person, a watching over himself, a giving himself commands and directives. This special kind of self-consciousness, this sitting behind himself and directing, is apparent in all areas of the compulsive's life and activity. It is apparent, for example, in his continuous role-playing. It is important for the compulsive person always to be aware that he is a *this* or *that.* Once his role is established to his

own satisfaction, he guides himself accordingly. Compulsive
people are ordinarily especially aware, in this way, of their professional role, their marital or parental role, and so on. The compulsive person is even aware of the role of himself, and plays
it—that is, he has an awareness, in certain respects, of what he is
like, and directs his behavior accordingly.[1] This is the quality that
is often identified as the pompousness or stuffiness of such persons. In all these ways, the compulsive person directs himself,
and then, feeling always under a pressure that is to some degree
alien to him, executes the given activity. This special style of
activity, with its two aspects of overseer and servant mechanically
and effortfully executing directions, characterizes his life and
experience in general. Although each aspect is absolutely essential to the other, sometimes one aspect will be more evident, as
when he commands himself to "get a grip" on himself, and
sometimes the other aspect, as when he dutifully slaves over
washing his hands or doing a job perfectly.

One important and interesting example of this general style
of activity and experience is made up of what is called "willpower,"
a subject which deserves some further comment, particularly
regarding its relationship to autonomy–experience. There is no
reason to imagine that autonomous functioning necessitates any
special self-awareness. The subjective experience most characteristic of autonomous behavior is probably an experience of
freedom of choice, an experience which itself merges with or
even disappears in an un-self-conscious interest in an activity or
an object (in a broad sense) or a goal. The obsessive–compulsive
person's characteristic experience of "willpower" is far from
being identical with such an experience of freedom or of *will*. For
him, willpower is clearly an experience of command, on the
one hand, and effortful service, on the other. It is a neurotic compromise with real experience of autonomy. Or, to put it another
way, the obsessive–compulsive style *substitutes* the experience of

---

[1]Fenichel (1945) gives a good example of this, though without indicating its generality:
"A patient felt well only as long as he knew what 'role' he was supposed to 'play.' When at
work he thought, 'I am a worker,' and this gave him the necessary security; when at
home, 'Now I am the husband who comes home from work to his beloved family' "
(p. 530).

willpower, or a variant of it, for a genuine autonomy–experience in that one tends to occupy those areas of psychological life which might otherwise be occupied by the other.

There are, of course, areas of activity for which this style is perfectly well suited; for others it is inadequate. Among the latter, there is perhaps none for which the style is less suited than the process of decision making. Willpower, for example, has no application to the process of making a decision, nor does the general mode of driven activity. But how, then, does such a person make his decisions? First, as I have suggested before, although the decision may be surrounded by all sorts of hesitation and doubt, it is nevertheless in its essentials usually an exceedingly attenuated process, a leap. For all his stewing, the obsessive-compulsive person will finally decide abruptly, if he acts at all. He will say or feel something like, "What the hell!" or "I've got to do something!" and abruptly pick the next suit that the salesman happens to offer, or quickly *sign* the contract. Second, as soon as the choice is made—and the leap is done—though there may have been a few abrupt reversals in between—the decision is then transformed into a new command. From this point, no evidence is admitted, and he prefers to feel that the situation will not allow of any modification. Once he can experience this, he can devote himself with relief to the narrower and more accustomed task of executing the directive; willpower and the driven mode of activity once again find application. Thus, the interplay between decision and new data which continuously become available *in the course of action,* an interplay which is central to the activity of a more flexible person, hardly exists for the compulsive. He feels and he operates not like a free agent, but like a soldier in drill; and, of course, it is to this kind of operation or activity, and not to decision making, that his active, narrowly focused, rigid style of attention and cognition is tuned. He prefers to devote his intelligence to tactical matters and to technical virtuosity and ingenuity in pursuit of preestablished aims, and his satisfactions are not those of autonomous direction but rather those of fulfilling duty and functioning efficiently.

It is necessary to add a few remarks concerning the relationship of the doubting and worry, which often play such a conspicuous part in decision making, to the more general style. The abrupt leap which comprises the obsessive–compulsive's decision is an anxious thing. At that moment, no matter how attenuated, the most rigid, mechanical person must contend with or only narrowly avoid an experience of personal autonomy. And it is often necessary, in bridging these moments, for the obsessive–compulsive person to reavow his sense of duty and of service. He does this with his stewing and worrying—that is, with his *driven and effortful trying* to find the "right" solution. This stewing and worry, which has little in common with a flexible person's scrutiny of pertinent facts, appears, then, to be a special transformation of the general style which facilitates the leap from one more stable position of driven and effortful activity to another. This is one of several processes which facilitate decision making for the obsessive–compulsive.

It is clear that in functioning under a pressure that feels in some way external, the obsessive–compulsive not only issues these commands himself, but also is quite aware of this fact. To understand this, it is necessary to take into account one additional aspect of this mode of functioning. In every instance, I believe, the obsessive–compulsive person, though fully cognizant that he is giving commands to himself, still does not feel that they altogether *originate* with him or that he has *primary* responsibility for them. Indeed, if he did so, commands would hardly have a function, and the whole structure would be other than what it is. He feels, rather, in the capacity of an agent, a representative to himself of an entirely external office. In addition to feeling like a soldier in drill, he feels like that soldier's noncommissioned officer; his function is to keep the soldier at his duty, to execute established policy, perhaps to make tactical decisions in pursuit of preestablished aims, but certainly not to establish such general aims himself.

Thus, every decision that the obsessive–compulsive makes, the direction of every nonroutine or nontechnical activity, will be referred ultimately to some higher authority with whom responsibility for the decision is at least shared. He will invoke morality, "logic" ("Of course, I *had* to do it—it was the only logical thing"), "common sense," what is socially "appropriate," the expectations of this one or that one, rules and regulations, and so on. These and many more sources of higher authority will be experienced by him as pressing him (and backing him) in his decision or the direction of his activity. Any rule, principle, or personal statement can fulfill this function to the extent that it can be considered *authoritative*.

What may initially have been a decision based simply on his own wish, will often thereafter be erected by the obsessive-compulsive person into an authoritative principle. Sometimes a simple decision will later combine with an authoritative principle, and sometimes, if all else fails, the act of having made the decision will become sufficient principle in itself, as expressed in such slogans as, "I must stick to my decision!" "Vacillation is weak," and so on. A good example, and a typical one, of this process is the place of a special sense of *purpose*—beyond the simple purpose, living—in the obsessive-compulsive's life. What may have begun as an ordinary aim or interest becomes transformed, under the name of *purpose,* into another rigid and enduring directive under which he can mechanically and dutifully serve. Here again, the obsessive-compulsive's interest in achieving the specific content of such purpose, the ostensible goal, cannot be measured by the intensity with which he appears to pursue it. For in establishing this sense of *purpose,* as with his other activities, he does not simply experience the aims of the normal person to a greater degree; he has another, additional interest, an interest in the experience of external pressure or directive which *purpose* can offer, quite aside from its content.

Let me summarize. The effortful, mechanical, intense, and "driven" activity of the compulsive is experienced as being in a measure directed by something external and to some degree alien to his own wants. Although he is at the same time overseer, he issues commands to himself only as the representative of an external directive. The mode of attention which is consistent with the experience of activity carried out under a command is precisely the active, narrowly focused, technically preoccupied cognition previously described. This rigid style is exactly suited to the obsessive-compulsive's general mode of activity and the subjective experience associated with it. Conversely, the continuous experience of strain and general overseeing of himself are necessary to the cognitive style. For without the sense of serving under direction and straining to fulfill imposed requirements, the intense, narrowed, technically preoccupied style of cognition is senseless. Thus, one aspect of the configuration is hardly imaginable without the other.

The Sense of "Should"

When another person may experience "I want to," the compulsive person experiences, in one form or another, "I should." By "I should" the compulsive person does not refer to expediency, but rather to a sense of "ought," an experience of duty, propriety, or the like. It will be apparent that certain variations of this subjective experience of "I should" or "I must" are manifest in some severe forms of obsessional and compulsive symptoms (for example, "I must wash") and perhaps implicit in others (for example, tics). However, I will turn attention here to its more general manifestations.

The subjective feeling of "I should" is usually accompanied by a certain kind of tension and by what is commonly called "worry." At first look, one might think that this tension merely reflects an awareness, perhaps a regretful awareness, of a gap between an existing situation or course of action and one that seems more desirable. But that the tension here is not so simple is made very clear by one of the most outstanding features of obsessional "worry": No step finally to dissolve the tension is taken. For the compulsive person the tension and worry that accompany the feeling of "I should" are maintained more or less continuously. Actions which might abolish them are ordinarily avoided, and if it does happen that the tension is dissolved, another content immediately appears which once again gives rise to it.

Another, related difference—perhaps the critical one—between the normal feeling of wanting to do something and the substituted obsessive–compulsive experience of "I should" has to do, again, with the sense of external pressure or direction. Some variety of the thought-content, "I should," is invariably associated with the obsessive–compulsive's experience of external pressure and is an indispensable aspect of it. It expresses exactly the representation *to himself* of a higher and more authoritative principle than his own felt wants as a guide and directive to action. Moral principles, above all, offer themselves for this purpose, and obsessive–compulsive people will find moral or quasi-moral considerations to give some substance or plausibility to their "should" even in the most remote and unlikely places. But the "should" may also refer to any sources of authority of the sort that have been mentioned—for example, social convention or the boss's expectations.

The moral aspects of the sense of "should" coincide, of course, with what has otherwise been called a superego function. In considering the superego function here, one essential fact emerges: the obsessive–compulsive experience, "I should," is a feature of the general experience of quasi-external pressure and overseeing-of-himself previously described, and its pre-dominantly moral reference is only a special content, though an exceedingly important one, of that type of experience. The "I should" may sometimes take on a slightly different and less moral meaning, as indicated above, or may be replaced by closely similar but less moral contents such as, "I must [do the job perfectly—otherwise what will people think of me?]," or, as in the willpower experience, "I will force myself to [stop smoking, read more books]." A variety of this type of experience can be found, I believe, in every aspect of the obsessive–compulsive's life; it is entirely consistent with, and hardly imaginable without, his driven and effortful mode of activity and his rigid style of cognition. For example, even the principled quality of his narrowed attention and rigid or dogmatic attitudes represents, at least implicitly, some such thought-content as, "I must not allow myself to be distracted from my line." And when the obsessive–compulsive person uses still other words than those I have indicated to describe his self-awareness, as when he reminds himself of one or another of his roles by thinking, "I *am now* a [husband, engineer]," these words are used by him in a special sense which coincides essentially with the command-meanings I have described, either the moral "I should" or one of the others. In the instance cited, for example, the "I am now . . ." does not simply refer to a statement of fact, which would be pointless, but means rather, "I must now act like a . . ."

Thus, in this general form of experience, superego function appears to lose distinctness. To be sure, one may imagine a specifically moral content as having crystallized out of the general "I should" or "I must" form of experience, or one may be willing to assign to the superego the general form as a whole, but in either case a relatively independent mental function which one may call "superego" is difficult to identify. The theoretical problems raised here are beyond the scope of this paper; however, I would like to make one additional point concerning a specific quality which is commonly attributed to the obsessive–compulsive's superego, namely, its "harshness."

The superego of the obsessive–compulsive has often been considered to be unusually harsh, and it has also, or perhaps alternatively, been described as inadequately integrated. These descriptions no doubt reflect in part the evidence of more or less continuous tension or worry associated with the sense of "should" that appears to plague these people and from which they hardly seem able to escape. Although the phenomena are clear enough, the explanation of them seems somewhat different to me. The qualities of "harshness" or "inadequate integration" are *absolutely necessary* to the whole aim and function of the mode of experience and activity of which the sense of "should" is an aspect. Experiencing a continuous pressure that feels separate from and alien to his own wishes is the very condition that allows the compulsive to feel the presence of a command under which he can serve. If such pressure were not harsh, if it tended to merge with what are experienced as wants or free choices, the reassuring presence of an external principle would vanish, and the whole sense and direction of the obsessive–compulsive organization would be contradicted. Thus, it is not surprising that the obsessive–compulsive person ultimately rejects any apparently comforting offer of relief from the "harsh" demands of his conscience, for from his point of view such relief must promise more loss than gain.

The Loss of Reality

The obsessive–compulsive person is not deluded, yet he often acts as if he were. When, for example, the compulsive person has just finished meticulously cleaning a table and then acts as though he believed that the table was filthy and required cleaning again, can this be considered delusion? Or when an obsessional person, despite repeated assurances to the contrary, talks and acts as though he believes he has cancer or had been contaminated by an obscure type of germ through some remote chain of contacts, is this not at least incipient delusion? To answer this question, that phrase, *as though he believes,* must be considered carefully. For it turns out that the obsessional person does not really *believe* these things at all. Close examination shows that he never even states that he believes these things to be *true.* He never says, "I have cancer," or, "I have been contaminated." He says, rather, that these things *might be,* that he might have been contaminated, that he could have cancer, and this is an important difference. It may be noted, furthermore, that his interest is different from the sort one might expect in a normal concern with such matters. Typically, his greatest interest is in what are essentially technical details; he tells us with great concern, for example, that such and such a person might have touched such and such a person who probably had contact with a doorknob which he has used—details which by their nature are incapable of decisively settling the important matter with which he is ostensibly concerned. Such technical details seem to replace matters of substantial truth in his interest. The same issue comes up in connection with obsessional doubting in general. One sees obsessional people doubt obvious things in circumstances where the lack of information which might give rise to normal doubt cannot possibly be held accountable. If one assumed that the sense of truth and the meaning of doubt are for the obsessive what they are from the normal point of view, one would frequently be forced to the conclusion that the obsessional person is deluded. However, such an assumption does not seem to be warranted.

The previous discussion suggests that there is a quite general shrinking of subjective experience, emotional experience particularly, for these people. The narrowly focused attention and exclusion of the casual impression, the machinelike experience, and the restriction of experience of wanting or of free choice imply such a shrinking. One might even say that as inner experience—experience of one's own feelings, impulses, decisions, or actions—broadens and becomes rich, the obsessive-compulsive mode of functioning becomes impossible. This mode of functioning seems to have one additional outstanding consequence for the obsessive-compulsive's apprehension of the external world: *the loss of the experience of conviction.*

When one observes compulsive people closely or examines their ideas or statements, it becomes clear that answers to questions such as, "Does it feel true?" or "Is it really so?" are typically avoided. Even regarding matters on which supposedly there is no doubt the obsessive-compulsive person will often seem surprised by such a question and virtually dismiss it as irrelevant to his interest. He will not say, "It is true," but something like, "It must be," or "It fits." One compulsive patient, for example, said of the girl he planned to marry, "I must be in love with her—she has all the qualities I want in a wife." In this example, one can see the preoccupation with technical details which takes the place of a recognition of and response to the real person. The obsessive-compulsive's experience can be compared in many ways to that of a pilot who flies at night or in a fog, but with accurate and well-functioning instruments. He can fly his plane *as if* he were seeing clearly, but nothing in his situation is experienced directly; only indicators are experienced, things which signify other things.

The same point may be illustrated by another patient, a lawyer, who each morning selected his clothes for the day with the aid of a color wheel. He apparently never experienced the thought or feeling, "This is nice" or "This looks good," but thought rather, "This fits—it *must* look good." A sense of conviction about the world, a sense of truth, involves a breadth of attention, an interest in and sensitivity to the shadings and proportions of things, and a capacity for direct and spontaneous response to them for which the obsessive-compulsive person is not geared. Instead, he relies on rules and principles that, once again, feel authoritative and external to his own judgment; within this framework he may then devote himself to technical concerns. Consequently, he does not say, "It is," but says instead, "It fits."

A paradox appears in the symptomatology of the obsessive-compulsive. As far as conviction is concerned, he is characterized symptomatically by two outstanding features: doubting and uncertainty, on the one hand, and dogma, on the other. Psychoanalysis has already dissolved this paradox by demonstrating a significant relationship between the two: dogma arises to overcome doubt and ambivalence and to compensate for them. Now I would like to suggest a formal relationship, in addition to this dynamic explanation.

An essential similarity between dogma and obsessional doubting is the conspicuous absence in both of a feature present in the normal person's attitude toward matters of fact—the sense of conviction, the whole dimension of interest in real truth. One may go further. Both the doubting and the dogma of the obsessional person rely in an essential way on the narrowed attention and the technical indicator style of thinking and apprehension of the world. In dogma, it is especially obvious that the narrowed and rigid attention, considering the prospect of new information as only distracting, is essential. This narrow preoccupation with technical indicators allows the dogmatic person to feel so completely satisfied with his solutions so easily. As long as certain technical requirements are satisfied, he is capable of ignoring the rough edges of his ideas, or even of ignoring facts which to another observer flagrantly and obviously contradict them. This is the basis of the obsessive-compulsive's familiar capacity for "logical" absurdities. At the same time, this narrowed, technical interest in signs and indicators also allows the obsessional person to doubt. What may be for the normal person an insignificant matter in relation to the whole can be sufficient cause for the obsessive-compulsive person to change his perception of the whole radically. His narrowed interest in technical signs and indicators, therefore, prevents him from seeing things in their real proportions, from apprehending the rich shading and the substance of the world, and makes him liable both to be satisfied too easily and to doubt too readily. Thus, it is clear that both doubting and dogma rest on and extend the obsessive-compulsive's general absence of sense of conviction and are effective additional guarantees against such an experience.

One may observe additional similarities in dogma and obsessional doubting. For example, the special self-awareness, the overseeing of himself, and the experience of representing and serving an external principle are common to both. In the case of dogma, again, these are particularly obvious; they are manifest, for example, in the moralistic way in which the dogmatic person guards himself against any temptation to stray from his line of thought or in the lofty confidence that bespeaks a feeling of being backed by a higher authority. In the case of doubting, as well, the obsessive–compulsive person serves and feels driven by quasi-external pressure. The duty to seek greater and greater certainty, the obligation to avoid satisfaction with a judgment—these are among the principles by which the doubter drives himself.

Explaining the similarities between the doubting and the dogma of obsessive–compulsive people in terms of style tendencies which are more general than either does not, I believe, contradict the dynamic view. Rather, if dynamic considerations demonstrate that dogma arises as a defense against doubt, this point of view suggests that dogma (or another psychological operation consistent with this general style) is the most likely defense against doubt, for this sort of psychological operation is available to the doubter to a greater degree than denial, repression, projection, and so forth.

I would like to mention one other symptomatic expression of this mode of thinking and the loss of sense of truth—the compulsive's great interest in ritual. Ritualistic behavior conforms in a remarkably clear way to the description of obsessive–compulsive activity as mechanical, effortful, and as though in the service of an external directive. It also depends conspicuously on the narrowly focused, indicator style of cognition and the impairment of the sense of reality. The ritualistic act must ultimately seem absurd to one whose sense of reality and interest in truth are not impaired, no matter how comprehensible the symbolic significance of its content may be. It would be no less pointless, as an act, to the obsessive–compulsive, regardless of the dynamic forces motivating him, if his sense of reality were not impaired. But his life and interests consist in good part of the apprehension and manipulation of indicators and symbols, and the discrepancy, therefore, between symptomatic ritual and apparently nonritualistic compulsive behavior is often less great than is at first evident. Unless this broad form of thinking and experience is understood, it is difficult to understand the nature of ritualistic interest for the obsessive–compulsive person, among all those for whom dynamic issues are not expressed in such forms.

Conclusions

From an examination of various areas of obsessive–compulsive functioning cognition, activity, and subjective experience, we have arrived at certain of its typical forms, aspects of its style, which may be summarized as follows:

1. A sharply but narrowly focused, fixed mode of attention.
2. More or less continuous activity, with the replacement of the normal experience of autonomy and free choice by the experience of overseeing himself, representing an external authority to himself, serving under and therefore sharing responsibility with this quasi-external authority. Authoritative principles are sought, therefore, and activity of a more technical sort in pursuit of preestablished aims is generally preferred.
3. A pervasive sense of "I should"—that is, an experience of moral or similar pressure. It necessarily feels external and "harsh," and replaces the normal experience of "I want to."
4. An impairment of the sense of conviction and truth in favor of a technical indicator style of thinking and apprehension of the world.

These and no doubt other broad forms of functioning—themselves presumably products of complex biological, developmental, and social influences—are basic to, or give rise to, the assortment of specific obsessive–compulsive symptoms and traits. In this connection, I believe that the defense mechanisms which are generally considered most characteristic of this syndrome may also be seen to reflect these general forms. The effortful, self-conscious, and driven quality which, for example, marks and identifies reaction formations, and the narrowly focused attention and special self-awareness of what is called intellectualization may be seen as special cases, or subconfigurations, of these broad forms. I have not attempted to show directly, though it is implied in various places in this material, that an understanding of these styles of functioning will make more understandable the relationship, on the one hand, between pathological obsessive-compulsive characteristics and certain adaptive proclivities (such as adaptive technical–symbolic thinking), and, on the other hand, between obsessive characteristics and more severely pathological conditions (such as paranoid ones). This approach, I believe, holds promise for such understanding; it emphasizes that a given pathological or adaptive solution can only differentiate out of a configuration which already contains or approximates its general formal requirements. This point of view will also, therefore, clearly place the question of why a dynamic issue takes a specific *form* (the classical question of "choice of neurosis") among broad developmental problems of character growth.

Chapter 16

THE MASOCHISTIC CHARACTER: GENESIS AND TREATMENT

CHARLES BRENNER

Masochism is a subject which is of interest to psychoanalysts from both a theoretical and a clinical aspect. This was first noted by Freud (1896, 1923a, 1924) who from the clinical side emphasized the unfavorable prognostic significance of a strong unconscious need for punishment and from the theoretical side pointed out the paradoxical position which masochistic phenomena occupy in human mental life and behavior: whereas we ordinarily think of man as avoiding pain for the sake of pleasure, in masochism man seems to seek pain as a source of pleasure.

I

The essence of masochism appears to consist in an intimate relationship between pleasure and pain, or more generally between pleasure and unpleasure. It may perhaps best be defined as the seeking of unpleasure, by which is meant physical or mental pain, discomfort or wretchedness, for the sake of sexual pleasure, with the qualification that either the seeking or the pleasure or both may often be unconscious rather than conscious.

Freud raised the question: How can we explain the phenomena of masochism when at the same time we maintain the existence and importance of the pleasure principle in mental functioning? His first answer to this question is contained in "Instincts and Their Vicissitudes" (1915a). He there explained masochism as a

This chapter originally appeared in longer form in the *Journal of the American Psychoanalytic Association,* 1:197–226, 1959. Reprinted by permission of the author and the publisher.

secondary phenomenon: it was sadism which had been turned back on the self. That is to say, in the first instance the masochistic individual had had sadistic impulses or wishes toward an outside object, but for one reason or another the outside object had been replaced by the self, resulting in self-directed sadism, or masochism. The commonest or best known mechanism by which this result might occur, Freud said, was the mechanism of identification with a lost object which had been both loved and hated, as described in "Mourning and Melancholia" (1915c). At the same time Freud believed that an alternative or auxiliary factor was at work in the production of masochism, a factor which was more nearly independent of environmental factors than such an instinctual vicissitude as turning against the self. This was the capacity of the organism to experience any intense stimulation, even painful stimulation, as sexually exciting (1905a). Freud suggested that this human capacity, which might well be greater in one individual than in another, could account for the fact that masochistic perverts experienced sexual excitement and even orgasm in situations in which bodily pain was inflicted upon them, in some cases by themselves, more often by a partner. Subsequent experience in analyzing patients with masochistic behavior or fantasies convinced Freud (1919) that the relationship between pain and sexual excitement in masochists is not quite so simple and that it might perhaps be more accurate to say that for masochists pain is a condition for sexual pleasure rather than to say that it gives rise to it directly. Freud (1924) therefore amended his view that painful stimuli, or other excessive tension, normally produce sexual excitement in infancy and continue to do so throughout life in masochists. In 1924 he stated that even though the capacity of pain to produce sexual excitement in infancy "dried up" or disappeared in later life, it was "the physiological substrate which is then covered by a psychic superstructure to form erogenic masochism," the type of masochism which he considered to be its basic form.

It will be appreciated that this first explanation of Freud's, based on the two factors just outlined, was one which permitted the phenomena of masochism to be subsumed under the pleasure principle. At least it was an explanation which did not expressly contradict the view that the pleasure principle was the guiding principle of the functioning of the psychic apparatus, an assumption which Freud had made as early as 1900, in chapter 7 of *The Interpretation of Dreams*. However, Freud later suggested a different explanation which was intended to contribute to the understanding not only of masochism but of the wide range of other phenomena as well which attest the importance of destructive tendencies in the human mind.

In *Beyond the Pleasure Principle* (1920) Freud advanced the hypothesis of a death instinct. According to this new hypothesis a self-directed, destructive impulse was assumed to be present in the mind from birth and to operate independently of the pleasure principle and even in contradiction to it. Masochism, or rather its infantile prototype, was thus considered to be the primary phenomenon in human psychology and sadism the secondary one which was due to deflection of the destructive instinctual drive from its primary object, the self, outward onto other objects. To be sure, the sadism which arose in this way could again be turned back upon the self by such means as identification with the hated object, in which case secondary masochism would appear.

Whether or not the death instinct is a valid hypothesis is probably a matter for biologists rather than for psychoanalysts to decide, as Fenichel (1945) and others have pointed out. However, the concept of a destructive instinctual drive as an innate component of human mental life has become an integral part of psychoanalytic theory and analysts in general seem to be content to leave unanswered the question whether this drive is originally self-directed or not. Whatever may be the answer to this particular question, it is generally accepted that there is an important connection between the destructive or aggressive drive and the phenomena which we call masochism.

As far as one can judge from his writings Freud's chief interest in masochism lay in the problems it posed with respect to the theory of drives and of the regulatory principles of the mind: the pleasure principle and the repetition compulsion. However, his occupation with these matters of psychoanalytic theory did not preclude his making the first, fundamentally important *clini-*

cal contribution to the subject which is contained in the paper "A Child Is Being Beaten" (1919). He there advanced the idea that a perversion, like a neurosis, is a consequence of infantile sexual conflicts, in particular, of oedipal conflicts. In the case of beating fantasies the perverse wishes or practices are masochistic ones. Thus masochistic fantasies of phenomena were shown to be a part of the "legacy of the oedipus complex," as Freud so aptly put it. It might be added that the wish to be beaten was considered by Freud (1924) to be a regressive representative of oedipal strivings and to stem originally from the anal–sadistic phase of libidinal organization.

In addition to relating masochism to the Oedipus complex, Freud (1924) proposed to distinguish clinically three forms of masochism. The first of these he called erogenic masochism, by which he meant essentially perverse masochism in which pain or humiliation are associated with conscious sexual excitement and gratification. He considered this form to be the basic one which was fundamental to the development of either of the other two: feminine masochism, in which suffering was the consequence of an unconscious fantasy of being a woman in either sexual intercourse or childbirth, and moral masochism or masochistic character formation.

We see, therefore, that Freud attempted to explain the phenomena of masochism in the following ways.

1. He assumed its physiological basis, what one might call its developmental sine qua non, to be the tendency of the infant to respond to any increase in psychic tension with sexual excitement; he believed that even painful stimuli produced sexual responses in infancy, that an exceptionally great tendency to respond sexually to painful stimuli in infancy would provide a constitutional basis for later masochism, and that although this tendency "dried up" or disappeared in later life (1924), it was the "physiological substrate which is then covered by a psychic superstructure to form erogenic masochism," the basic form of masochism.

2. He assumed its instinctual basis to be the death drive, which was originally self-directed, giving rise to primary masochism. He assumed that some of the death drive remained self-directed, while the rest was deflected from the self toward objects in the

outer world during the course of infantile development (1920). This outwardly deflected part of the death drive might be again self-directed as a vicissitude of later life and would then reinforce that part of the death drive which had remained self-directed from the beginning, a development which might be spoken of as secondary masochism. It might be added that in Freud's view there would have to be some degree of fusion of self-directed destructiveness and self-directed libido to account for *pleasure* from pain as distinct from a mere tendency to self-injury or self-destructiveness, since he considered the discharge of destructive energies alone to be unaccompanied by the subjective quality of pleasure.

3. He concluded that some and perhaps all of the masochistic fantasies and behavior met with in clinical practice are consequences of the psychic conflicts of the oedipal period. This would presumably be an example of the phenomenon just referred to as secondary masochism.

4. In addition, and obviously in close connection with (3), Freud (1923a, 1924) pointed to the intimate relationship between masochistic phenomena and the superego, a concept then new to psychoanalytic theory.

5. Finally, Freud proposed to distinguish three forms of masochism: erogenic, feminine, and moral, of which he considered the first to be basic to the other two.

Subsequent authors have dealt with masochism within the framework of Freud's ideas, although their conclusions have sometimes differed from his either in content or in emphasis. The contributions of recent years may be summarized briefly as follows. The emphasis will be on additions to Freud's views and modifications of them. For a more detailed review of pertinent literature the reader is referred to Loewenstein (1957).

Reik (1939, 1941) agreed with Freud as to the role of self-directed aggression and of the superego in the mental life of masochistic individuals. He reemphasized what Freud (1919) had pointed out: that the masochist did not take pleasure in pain, but only accepted pain as a necessary *condition* for pleasure. He formulated masochism as "victory through defeat" and emphasized its unconscious aggressive, provocative, and exhibitionistic elements. He also asserted that masochism was a ubiquitous phenomenon in that some degree or trace of it was to be found in everyone.

Fenichel (1945) disagreed with Freud only in rejecting the concept of primary masochism.

Berliner (1940, 1947, 1958) has attributed masochistic character formation to a particular relationship between parent and child, one in which the child experienced only rejection, humiliation, and punishment from cruel and rejecting parents and never got from them the love and affection that parents normally give their children. Such a child comes to seek similar treatment in later life from other persons as a substitute for love. One might say it is the only kind of love he knows. This view of the genesis of masochism emphasizes its role as a defense: masochism has the function of preserving important object relationships and of avoiding the danger of object loss which would overwhelm the individual with anxiety.

Eidelberg (1934, 1958) emphasized the aspect of magical control in masochism: by provoking punishment from a parent or parent substitute the masochist creates and fosters the illusion that he can control his parent. In this way he preserves or restores his infantile feeling of omnipotence and avoids the narcissistic mortification attendant upon helplessness.

Brenman (1952) performed an especially valuable service by emphasizing that masochistic character formation is not to be understood in terms of the instinctual drives alone, or of the defenses of the ego alone, or of the operations of the superego alone. The tendency to any such one-sided approach has been apparent both before and since Brenman's paper. Thus Monchy (1950) discussed masochism only from the instinctual side, while it was viewed primarily as a consequence of ego defenses by Berliner, as noted above. The extreme of this position was shown by Menaker (1953) who proposed to call masochistic character formation an ego defense. As Brenman (1952) pointed out, masochistic character formation, like any other similarly complex phenomenon, serves many functions in the economy of the mind (Waelder, 1936), not just one function. It serves the id as a source of instinctual gratification; the superego as a means of punishment, expiation, or restriction of pleasure; and the ego as a defense and even, in many instances, as a means of adapting more or less successfully to external reality. In addition, Brenman offered the following schematic outline "of the underlying drives and defenses" which were "*specific*" for masochism: (1) from the side of the drives, an unusually strong need for love, the aggression resulting from frustration of this need for love, and perhaps "an unusual disposition to anxiety"; and (2) on the side of the ego defenses, the large-scale operation of four mechanisms, denial, reaction formation, introjection, and projection.

Bromberg (1955), like Berliner and Menaker, asserted that the child's relation with its parent was the essential factor in the development of masochistic character traits. He noted that some mothers act out with a child the ambivalent feelings they unconsciously harbor toward a sibling or parent from their own childhood. Such a mother treats the child toward whom she behaves in this way cruelly, seductively, and restrictively at the same time. This both seriously interferes with the development of the child's ego and convinces it as well that it is most loved when it suffers most, a conviction which leads to seeking suffering when love is wanted.

Bernstein (1957) emphasized the role of narcissism in three cases of masochistic character formation which he presented. As with Berliner, Bromberg and Menaker, great importance was placed on the early parent–child relationship, which Bernstein summed up by saying that as infants his patients were "in the service of the parental narcissism and immature instinctual drives." In accordance with this emphasis, Bernstein stressed the role of masochism as a protection against the danger of object loss.

Loewenstein (1957) wrote a most interesting article on the psychoanalytic theory of masochism which contains many valuable original observations as well as an extensive review of the literature. In particular he suggested as a prototype of later masochistic behavior and fantasies the behavior of very small children with authority figures which he called "seduction of the aggressor." In this game the child pretends to be "naughty" or plays at being punished with the forbidding or punishing adult who in turn only plays at scolding or punishing, soon relieving the child's distress by reassuringly loving behavior.

Stein (1956) published an excellent report of a panel discussion on masochism, held at the December 1955 meeting of the

American Psychoanalytic Association. The participants were Arlow, Bak, Berliner, Eidelberg, K. R. Eissler, Loewenstein, Stein, and Waelder. To summarize the whole of the report would involve needless repetition of what has already been said in the preceding pages, but the following point seems worth mentioning. In discussing the fact, first mentioned by Freud in 1924, that masochistic behavior and fantasies in men are often an expression of unconscious feminine wishes, Waelder pointed out that such masochistic fantasies are not a representation of femininity but rather a caricature of it.[1] There was also considerable discussion of problems involved in the treatment of masochistic patients, chiefly by Berliner (1958) and Eidelberg (1958), each of whom later published a more extensive exposition of his views on the subject. It would be logical to include here a summary of these and other statements in the literature concerning treatment, but it seems more convenient to reserve them for an introduction to the last part of the paper.

Despite its brevity and its many inadequacies this summary may perhaps suffice to give some idea of the major lines of approach to the problem of the genesis and dynamics of masochism that have appeared in the psychoanalytic literature of the last several years and to make apparent the ways in which they derive from, add to, and diverge from the views of Freud himself. Some of the additions and divergences may be attributed to improvements in psychoanalytic technique over the past thirty years and to the wider experience in the treatment of all sorts of character problems, including masochistic ones, that these improvements have made possible. These changes in the technique and scope of psychoanalysis are what we generally refer to as ego analysis, though for our present purpose it might be more appropriate to say ego and superego analysis, since the unconscious operations of the superego play such a large part in masochistic character formations. As is well known, ego analysis was made possible by the theoretical revisions which Freud (1923a) proposed in "The Ego and the Id," and the subsequent

---

[1] It may be noted that the important aspect of masochism to which Waelder thus drew attention can be described in genetic terms by saying that the masochistic fantasies and practices of adults reflect the small child's sadomasochistic theories and fantasies of what happens between men and women in sexual intercourse.

advances in the understanding of the parts played in psychic conflict by anxiety and by the defenses of the ego which were contained in *The Problem of Anxiety* (1926b). The ideas in these two works formed the foundation for the whole of modern psychoanalysis, and it is not surprising therefore that the formulations of later authors concerning masochistic character disturbances have added a good deal to the formulations of Freud himself, which hardly went beyond 1924. Thus, for example, an appreciation of the defensive aspect of masochistic fantasies and behavior had to wait until after Freud had reintroduced the general concept of defense into psychoanalytic theory in *The Problem of Anxiety* in 1926.

Another source of divergence from Freud's views which may be noted has a different origin. Most analysts have adopted either a neutral or a negative view toward the theory of a death drive and do not use it, as Freud often did, to explain psychological phenomena. For this reason the concept of primary masochism plays a much less prominent part in contemporary analytic discussions of masochism than it once did.

Finally, little is said in the recent literature about Freud's hypothesis that painful stimuli in infancy are normally sexually exciting and that this is the basis for later erogenic masochism. This neglect presumably stems from the fact that in all cases of masochism which have been observed analytically, pain is the condition rather than the source of sexual pleasure (Loewenstein, 1957).[2] It will be recalled that Freud was the first to make this observation.

II

We may proceed now to some formulations concerning the genesis of masochistic character traits and their place in psychic functioning.

---

[2]In his paper Loewenstein supports the view that pain can be the source of pleasure rather than simply a necessary condition for it, even in adult life, and that this human characteristic is fundamental to erogenic masochism. He agrees with the generally prevalent view, however, that pain is usually a necessary condition for pleasure in those conditions with which we meet clinically in adults, rather than its direct source.

The first of these formulations is one which was mentioned by Reik (1941) but which otherwise has received little direct attention in the literature on the subject. It is the proposition that masochistic phenomena play a part in the loves of all of us, the normal as well as the neurotic.

The clearest and usually the most extensive evidence of this in the course of normal psychic development is afforded by the genesis and functioning of the superego. As Reik (1941) remarked, following Freud's (1924) views on the relation between moral masochism and an unconscious need for punishment, a *need* or *wish* for punishment, as opposed to a *fear* of punishment, is in itself a masochistic phenomenon. We may add that a need for punishment, whether it be a conscious or an unconscious one, is invariably a part of normal superego functioning. It follows therefore that some degree of masochism is ubiquitous.

To clarify this point let us consider, for example, what happens in the mind of a boy in the oedipal phase who fears that his father will castrate him as a punishment for his desire to castrate and kill his father and to take father's place with mother. The expected result of the boy's fear will be the development of a whole series of defensive measures, measures which will differ from one another in a variety of ways but which will have in common the purpose of avoiding the fantasied danger, castration. Now among these defensive measures we normally expect to find a tendency on the boy's part to win his father's sympathy and love by hurting or punishing himself or by making his remorse or suffering apparent to his father. Indeed, we shall not be surprised to find these tendencies linked with the boy's passive, feminine, oedipal strivings with the result that the wish to be woman and to be loved by father in mother's place comes to serve the defensive purpose of averting the fantasied danger of being castrated by father as a vengeful rival for mother to which we referred above. These oedipal conflicts and wishes and the fantasies and fears connected with them normally become unconscious as the boy grows older, but they leave their mark in that aspect of superego function to which we refer as remorse and as a need for punishment; as a wish for penance and expiation, whether the wish be conscious or not.[3]

If this view is correct, it follows that masochism is a normal component of character formation. The question then arises whether the difference between what might be called normal and pathological masochism is one of degree or one of kind.

Such a question can be answered only on the basis of clinical experience. Perhaps future observation will reveal differences in kind, that is, qualitative differences between normal and neurotic manifestations of masochism, but so far as experience goes at present it would appear that the differences are only quantitative ones. It is true that such quantitative differences may be very great ones and of the utmost practical importance. Nevertheless, the best available evidence at the present time suggests that no sharp line can be drawn between what is called a normal character and what is called a masochistic one.

This view has important clinical implications. For one thing it makes intelligible the fact that the syndrome which is called masochistic character or moral masochism is so difficult to separate diagnostically from a variety of other pathological conditions. According to the view advanced here, masochistic phenomena or tendencies are a part of every individual's mental life. They can and often do exist together with many sorts of neurotic symptoms and with a variety of other character disturbances. In other words, the diagnostic category of masochistic character, though nosologically useful, is by means an exclusive one.

Bak (1946) has drawn attention to the masochistic aspects of paranoia and Fenichel (1945) has done the same with respect to obsessional neurosis, while many analysts have commented on the fact that it is frequently difficult to decide whether a particular case is to be diagnosed as masochistic character or as depression.

---

[3]It should be noted that this is only one aspect of superego genesis and functioning, an aspect which is emphasized here because of its importance in the theory of masochism and not because it is conceived of as the prime factor in superego formation. The importance of the fear of punishment (castration or analogous genital injury) in the formation and functioning of the superego is presumed to be of principal significance in most cases in accordance with the abundant literature on the subject since Freud (1923a).

However, it is equally true, though less frequently commented upon, that masochism plays a large role in the mental lives of many other patients as well. For example, one need only think of the patients with conversion hysteria whom one sees in any large general hospital to realize how unmistakably large is the role played by masochistic trends in the unconscious mental lives of the great majority of such patients. "La belle indifférence" is a characteristic of conversion hysteria which is hallowed by long usage and enshrined in the literature, but conscious suffering and the unconscious pursuit and enjoyment of suffering are in fact far more frequently found in patients with serious conversion symptoms than is indifference. One may also find masochistic tendencies playing a large role in patients with phobias, in addicts, in patients with impulsive character disorders, in many criminals, and so on.

Two brief clinical examples may be to the point here. A thirty-five-year-old man came to analysis because of recurrent bouts of alcoholism. The importance of his masochistic problems may be indicated by the fact that his conscious masturbation fantasies from the age of eight years until well into puberty were of a naked boy being beaten in public. This patient's alcoholic bouts were regularly precipitated by the prospect of success, a prospect which had for him unconsciously the commonplace oedipal significance of competing with and supplanting his father. The drinking had a variety of unconscious meanings, as might be supposed, but the one which is apropos here is that it was self-destructive, self-castrative, and very nearly suicidal. In fact each bout of drinking was an expression of an unconscious wish to be the prodigal son who, after riotous, profligate living returned in rags and despair to be rescued by his loving father. This patient's alcoholism thus had a specifically masochistic character: a bout of drinking was a way of producing suffering, misery, and helplessness which would lead to being loved and gratified by father.

The other example is a twenty-two-year-old man whose chief complaints were that he was generally anxious and that after dark he feared and avoided empty or ill-lighted streets. It was soon apparent that his fears were a consequence of unconscious sadomasochistic fantasies in which he was the beaten and tortured partner. In adolescence he had been an overt masochistic pervert for a time, deriving sexual gratification with orgasm from being bound naked and whipped by a girl. At the time he came for treatment he was consciously bisexual without apparent conflict, but he was increasingly terrified by his unconscious wish to be beaten, tormented, and castrated by a man, a wish which had given rise to the phobias and to the anxiety state which brought him to treatment.

These clinical notes will serve to illustrate the point that masochistic trends are of importance in patients from a variety of diagnostic categories; for example, alcoholism and phobias. It may be added that for the purpose of emphasis the two cases chosen were rather extreme ones. There are many patients in whom masochistic trends are of great importance who yet give no history of conscious beating fantasies or of masochistic perversion, as did the patients just cited.

The view that as regards masochism what is pathological differs from what is normal in degree rather than in kind has the further effect of inclining one to think of infantile factors as increasing or diminishing the individual's tendency toward masochistic character formation or behavior rather than to try to discover or establish a "cause" in infancy for the development of masochistic phenomena in later life. Most of all, this view will make impossible the idea that masochistic phenomena are per se pathological.

It may be of interest to consider for a moment the question why masochism should be universal if indeed it is so. One answer to this question might be based on the dual instinct theory (Freud, 1920): the psychic state of the neonate is assumed to be one in which both the destructive and the erotic drives are self-directed. This state Freud called primary masochism. In view of the universal tendency toward repetition of earlier states during later life it might be expected that the instinctual position of the neonate would tend to be reinstated, at least partially, resulting in later or secondary masochism.

Another answer, related more closely to observable clinical data, would be that the adaptive efforts of the child during the stormy instinctual conflicts of childhood inevitably result in some degree of masochism in the child's psychic functioning. In other words, given the psychic equipment of the child, its instinctual drives and its ego capacities, on the one hand, and the child's environment on the other, including its available gratifications and inescapable frustrations, it would appear to be unavoidable that there be at least some degree of masochism, in the patterns of psychic functioning that develop in the child's mind as it lives through this period of its life.

It should be noted, by the way, that the two answers just suggested neither contradict nor exclude one another.

There is another clinically important point about the masochistic character that derives directly from clinical experience, though it is probably related to the topic just under discussion; that is, to the ubiquity of masochism. This is the fact that sadistic and masochistic tendencies are always seen together, never separately. For the problem of masochism this has the consequence that one expects a patient's behavior or fantasies to have a sadistic or hostile meaning as well as a masochistic or passive one. It is then no surprise to be told by one author that the unconscious fantasy behind a masochistic patient's behavior is one of mollifying his parent and winning his love by submission to him and to learn from another author that such behavior represents an unconscious fantasy of humiliating and triumphing over one's parent. On the contrary, one expects that there will be *both* a sadistic and a masochistic, both a submissive and an aggressive, meaning to every patient's masochism.

Moreover, the relationship between the two opposing tendencies of sadism and masochism is not simply one of polarity or competition. Each has a defensive function as well as being a means of instinctual gratification, for example. In fact the complex phenomena of masochism can be best understood and most nearly unraveled only by viewing them in the framework of the structural hypothesis, that is, in reference to the interrelated functions of ego, superego, and id. It will be remembered that Brenman (1952) was the author who most strongly emphasized the multiple function of a masochistic character formation, and rightly so. But in fact, masochistic character formation is in no way unique in this respect. On the contrary, as Waelder (1936) pointed out, *every* psychic act may be viewed as a compromise among the various parts of the psychic apparatus.

The concept of intrapsychic compromise is an old one in psychoanalysis. It was introduced sixty years ago by Freud (1924) in connection with the formation of psychoneurotic symptoms and has been a basic part of the psychoanalytic theory of symptom formation ever since. What is apparently not always so clearly kept in mind, though it certainly should be since Waelder called attention to it so explicitly in 1936, is that the concept of compromise formation or multiple function is applicable to many psychic acts and products other than neurotic symptoms. For example, and this is what is important for our present purpose, it is equally applicable to the formation of character traits, whether masochistic or otherwise, to the extent that such character traits resemble symptoms in arising on the basis of intrapsychic conflict.

If one uses the concept of multiple function as his frame of reference in viewing the clinical phenomena of the masochistic character, it is possible to observe in one's own patients that many of the apparently unrelated explanations that have appeared in the literature as constituting the unconscious motivation of masochistic behavior are indeed coexistent in the same patient and are mutually *cooperative,* if the word is permissible in such a context. A single set of masochistic fantasies and behavior will serve a great variety of functions in an individual, as the following clinical excerpt may show.

The patient was a single woman who began analysis at the age of thirty-two because of anxiety and depression. Despite these symptoms, which continued during several years of analysis, at times with considerable exacerbation, she was able to carry on her work without interruption and to function in a superior way in positions of responsibility. Actually the principal effect of her symptoms was to make her chronically unhappy and uncomfortable and to deprive her of many of the pleasures and satisfactions of life which otherwise would have been accessible to her on the basis of her real abilities and achievements.

Several factors appear to have been significant in the genesis of the masochistic character traits which were prominent in the patient's symptomatology. (1) The patient grew up in a semirural community in which there was a downtown gambling and red-light district in which her father spent every Saturday night.

There was much talk among the children of fights, prostitutes, and killings, which was both exciting and frightening. Moreover, the patient's mother was constantly fearful that her husband would be killed or seriously hurt in his drunken revels, something which in fact never happened. As might be expected, the fantasy of being herself a prostitute figured prominently among the patient's childhood fantasies as far as could be ascertained by their revival in the transference. In these fantasies coitus was represented sadomasochistically as a violent fight between man and woman. In fact the patient's parents did quarrel often and violently, though the violence was limited to verbal exchanges. The intensity of the patient's emotional involvement in these scenes may be judged from the fact that on one occasion during a quarrel between her parents at the table when she was nine years old, she threatened to stab her father with a fork. (2) The mother's generally expressed attitude was one of suffering and martyrdom. Though this attitude was often belied by the fact that the mother gave as good as she took in her battles with the patient's father, identification with her mother had for the patient the consequence of seeing herself as an abused and mistreated individual whose lot in life was to suffer at men's hands while at the same time she strove to revenge herself on them. (3) Both her father and brother died suddenly and bloodily. The former event was the more traumatic and the more significant for her masochistic character formation. It occurred when the patient was seventeen years old as the terminal event of a year's illness which was understood by the patient to be the consequence of many years of dissipation. Her father arose one morning, had a massive hematemesis, and exsanguinated before the patient's eyes. Her brother killed himself some years later. The first of these two events contributed considerably to her unconscious guilt and to her fear that her murderous wishes could really kill, attitudes which were still further reinforced by her brother's death. As a consequence of this guilt and fear it was characteristic of her in adult life that self-punishment appeared instead of anger and revenge when a man failed to love her as she would have wished.

As might be expected, this patient's transference resistance took the form of masochistic suffering: she had a strong tendency toward a negative therapeutic reaction, getting worse or at best failing to improve with each interpretation, and in addition she was miserable, complaining, reproachful, and often silent for long periods of time. By these means she unconsciously expiated her guilt for her unconscious sadistic wishes toward me at the same time that she gratified them, still unconsciously, by triumphing over me and depriving me of what she regarded as my most precious possession: my therapeutic potency. In addition, her sulkiness and suffering duplicated her mother's behavior toward her father, so that it appeared that her masochistic transference reaction was a way of unconsciously acting out the fantasy that she and I were married and living together as mother and father had done. Again, from the point of view of her conflict with her superego, it was abundantly clear that her suffering behavior served not only as a submissive expiation but also as a defense against her guilt feelings, since by her suffering she demonstrated that it was I who was the cruel and guilty one and not she, who was on the contrary quite obviously the meek and gentle victim.

It must be understood that these many unconscious meanings did not emerge all at once nor with equal ease. They became accessible only gradually and over a long period of analysis, but each of them proved to be of importance in motivating the patient's masochistic behavior. It must also be understood that in other masochistic characters the significant unconscious motives for and functions of masochism may be at least partly different. It seems unlikely, to be sure, that in any case of masochistic character an adequate analysis would fail to find convincing evidence of an unconscious need for punishment and atonement. However, other factors may vary greatly in importance from case to case. For example, separation anxiety appeared to play a relatively minor role in the genesis of the masochistic character traits in the case just outlined, while in other cases it may play a very large role indeed.

It would seem therefore that it is probable that the various authors who have emphasized one or another particular genetic factor in masochistic character formation or one or another particular motive or function in its operation have each been correct in what they have said and have erred only in what they have omitted to say. The importance of this in clinical practice is that the analyst must expect that the proper analysis of the masochistic character traits in any patient in whom they bulk large will uncover a number of unconscious motives and functions for these traits rather than one or two, and that he will find, moreover, that these motives and functions vary somewhat from case to case.

This is particularly important to bear in mind in view of a tendency in the literature during the last several years to discuss the genesis and function of masochism solely in terms of object relations. This has been done explicitly by such authors as Berliner (1940, 1947, 1958) and Menaker (1953), and has been either implied or suggested by such others as Bernstein (1957), Brenman (1952), and Bromberg (1955).

There can be no doubt that in many patients masochistic fantasies and behavior function, among other things, as a defense against fears of losing an object or the love of an object or both. However, it is equally true that these are not the only fears against which masochism serves as a defense. It may be recalled that Freud (1926b) outlined a typical sequence of infantile and childhood fears which he believed corresponded to successive stages in psychic development: fear of object loss, fear of loss of love, castration fear, and superego fear, or guilt. In a given patient, whatever his symptoms may be, one or another of these fears will play the major role, though it is rare for any of them to be really unimportant or absent. Moreover, they are often interrelated. A familiar example of this is furnished by the boy to whom his father's love is important as a guarantee against castration. In such a case the fear of loss of love and the fear of castration are hardly to be distinguished. An equally familiar example is that of the girl who equates possession of a penis with being her parents' favorite and in whom the fear of loss of love contributes in a major way to her painful mortification at being without a penis.

Such considerations concerning the origin and content of the typical fears of childhood are of general importance to the understanding of any neurotic symptoms in adult life, and masochistic fantasies and behavior are no exception. It is likely that each of the fears mentioned plays an important role in every case of masochistic character formation, with the major emphasis being on castration fear or its feminine analogues in some cases and on fear of loss of an object or of the object's love in others.

Chapter 17

AN EXPLORATION OF THE
DIAGNOSTIC TERM *NARCISSISTIC*
PERSONALITY DISORDER

ARNOLD ROTHSTEIN

The present controversy concerning patients with "narcissistic disturbances" is reflected in the many descriptive and diagnostic labels used to refer to these patients: narcissistic, narcissistic character, phallic–narcissistic character, narcissistic character disorder, narcissistic personality, or narcissistic personality disorder. In this paper I shall attempt to clarify a number of issues related to narcissism and "narcissistic disturbances" in the hope of contributing to an elucidation of the term *narcissistic personality disorder*.

The confusion seems to stem from the fact that narcissism is discussed from a number of perspectives and within different theoretical frameworks. Narcissism is studied as a normal developmental course. It is described as a defense, as well as a ubiquitous phenomenon in the human condition. Healthy and pathological integrations of narcissism in character organization are described, leading to various diagnostic considerations. In addition, the current controversy concerning diagnosis is influenced by the fact that some analysts favor strictly defined diagnostic categories, while others are less concerned with the question of classification. More specifically, different authors stress different *aspects* of the subject's integration of narcissism. Finally, various authors employ the same terms differently without explicitly stating the distinctions. After briefly summarizing the contributions of a number of major authors in this field, I shall present my own view of the issue.

This chapter originally appeared in the *Journal of the American Psychoanalytic Association,* 27:893–912, 1979. Reprinted by permission of the author and the publisher.

Most of Freud's views of narcissism were written within a dual-instinct theory of libido and the self-preservative instinct, prior to the introduction of the structural hypothesis or a theory of aggression. He considered narcissism primarily from a *developmental* perspective as "a stage in the development of the libido which it passes through on the way from auto-eroticism to object-love" (1911b, p. 60). In elaborating its ubiquitous nature and its "place in the regular course of human sexual development" (1914, p. 73), he saw it as "the libidinal complement to the egoism of the instinct of self-preservation" (1914b, pp. 73–74). In 1923, he extended this developmental perspective by describing narcissistic libido as a normal intermediary stage in the neutralization of libidinal energy (p. 30). In the energic language of 1914, Freud alluded to the role of narcissism in all character. Continuing his developmental elaboration and anticipating the structural hypothesis, Freud (1914b) described the child's preservation of his primary narcissism within the ego ideal. Finally, in describing parents' defenses against accepting the perception of their own limits and finiteness, he (1914b, pp. 90–91) presented the normal developmental concepts of narcissistic object choice, narcissistic injury, and, implicitly, narcissistic identification.

In addition to normal developmental vicissitudes of narcissism, Freud describes some of its pathological elaborations. A footnote to his "Three Essays" (1905a), written in 1910, elaborates narcissistic fixations and object choice in the genesis of homosexuality: "the future inverts, in the earliest years of childhood, pass through a phase of very intense but short-lived fixation to a woman (usually their mother), and . . . after leaving this behind, they identify themselves with a woman and take *themselves* as a sexual object. That is to say, they proceed from a narcissistic basis, and look for a young man who resembles themselves and whom *they* may love as their mother loved *them*" (p. 145).

Further references to the subject can be found in Freud's papers on metapsychology. His appreciation of the vicissitudes of object relations is clear in his description of the relationship between split and repressed object representations and their devalued–idealized counterparts. He emphasized that, "in the origin of the fetish" (1915b, p. 150), idealization occurs "precisely on account of this intimate connection with abhorrent objects." In 1914, he used the term *narcissistic neurosis* to describe patients who today would be labeled borderline psychotic and schizophrenic, and explained such symptoms of that condition as "megalomania" and "hypochondriasis" as narcissistic aberrations and fixations of libidinal cathexes. He described (1915c) the genesis of melancholia in structural terms as an alteration of the ego secondary to a narcissistic identification; this paper foreshadowed the formulation of the superego and its contribution to the regulation of self-esteem. In 1917, he defined the genesis of the character trait of defiance from a developmental perspective and in libidinal terms, as "a narcissistic clinging to anal eroticism" (p. 130).

Finally, in 1918, he presented the Wolf Man's predisposition to neurosis as related to the "excessive strength of his narcissism," which left him vulnerable to narcissistic injury; "the precipitating cause of his neurosis . . . as . . . a narcissistic 'frustration' " (p. 118). In addition, he commented on the limits of psychoanalytic treatment in such cases. Blum (1974) has further elaborated both the childhood and later adult borderline and narcissistic features of the Wolf Man's character organization, commenting on his narcissistic vulnerability and regressive loss of object constancy. He noted that Freud shifted the emphasis at the end of the case report from primal-scene trauma to narcissistic disorder.

I hope this summary succeeds in emphasizing how much of what is current and modern with reference to the theory of narcissism and its clinical elaborations may be found in Freud's writings. Freud was keenly aware of the relationship of narcissistic phenomena to the subject's experience of frustration, his perception of limits of reality, and of real or imagined object loss. The role of aggression, of anger and hostility, in response to frustration or loss seems relatively absent from his considerations (Moore, 1975, p. 254).

In 1921 Andreas-Salomé wrote an important but seldom read or quoted paper "The Dual Orientation of Narcissism." In libidinal terms she made two points having current significance. Like Freud, she emphasized the ubiquitous place of narcissism in human development: "narcissism is not limited to a single phase of the libido, but is a part of our self-love which accompanies all phases. It is not merely a primitive point of departure of development but remains as a kind of fundamental continuity in all the subsequent object-cathexis of the libido" (p. 3). She also recognized the primal object's role in the development of narcissism, describing its genesis from identifications with preindividuated self–object experiences: "It seems to me therefore to be dangerous not to emphasize the essential duality of the concept of narcissism, and to leave the problem unresolved by allowing narcissism to stand only for self-love. I should like to bring to the fore its other obvious aspect, the persistent feeling of identification with the totality" (pp. 4–5).

W. Reich (1949) discussed narcissism as it related to character formation in general, defining explicitly what Freud and Andreas-Salomé had implied, "that the character is essentially a narcissistic protection mechanism . . . against dangers . . . of the threatening outer world and the instinctual impulses which urged for expression" (p. 158). He presented the clinical category of phallic–narcissistic character from descriptive, genetic, and dynamic points of view, and elaborated a number of factors in its genesis: "On the basis of a phallic mother-identification a phallic-narcissistic character usually develops, whose narcissism and sadism is directed especially toward women (vengeance on the strict mother). . . . This attitude is the character defense against the deeply repressed original love of the mother which could not continue to exist in the face of her frustrating influence" (pp. 152–153). Reich identified the mobilization of rage in response to this frustration. He described the relationship of this rage as it is expressed in sadistic and other sexual perversions and in attitudes and behavior of these male patients to women. Today, we would broaden the spectrum and the description of the quality of disorders in maternal relatedness that these patients encountered. Reich added to the genetic description of these patients: "In men, one often finds that mother was the stronger of the parents, or the father had died early or was otherwise out of the picture" and added a further important point, which adumbrates Kohut's conceptualizations: "The infantile history regularly reveals serious disappointments in the object of the other sex, disappointments which occurred precisely at the time when attempts were made to win the object through phallic-exhibitionism" (p. 203).

Reich's rich clinical descriptions cover what is today considered a range of the ego's narcissistic character pathology. He described a spectrum of the ego's pathologic integrations of narcissism in character organization. These range from a better integrated group who "in spite of their narcissistic preoccupation with their selves . . . often show strong attachments to people and things outside" (p. 201) to a more troubled group that included "addicts, particularly alcoholics" (p. 205). The latter were described in energic terms, and he regarded them as examples of oral regressions from phallic–oedipal and anal–homosexual conflicts. His conceptualizations were limted to the theoretical emphasis on the central significance of the oedipal conflict that was prevalent in his day. While certain of these conditions might be attributed to regression from oedipal issues today, others might be considered the result of very significant preoedipal fixations or developmental interferences.

Annie Reich (1953, 1960) has written two important papers attempting to integrate Freud's energic conceptualizations with preoedipal and structural considerations, particularly those of Jacobson (1954a). These papers are rich in their appreciation of what she refers to as narcissistic issues, but I will select only those statements that deal with the question of a diagnostic category. She modified Freud's term *narcissistic neurosis* to exclude the psychoses and to include a much wider spectrum of conditions. She states: "We now even question the usefulness of a too narrowly circumscribed nosology. We are much concerned with so-called borderline conditions, and we tend to look upon the boundary between psychosis and neurosis as somewhat fluid." Of these patients she wrote: "We know overlapping of phases [of development] to be ubiquitous. There is usually a partial regression to earlier ego and libidinal states mixed with later, more highly developed structures" (p. 289).

Earlier, Annie Reich (1953) described women who suffer from a state of "narcissistic want" due to "narcissistic injury," of feeling deserted and castrated. These fixations result in disorders of internalization and idealization of their sexual ideal and ego ideal which a narcissistic object choice is intended to undo.

Men with "narcissistic disturbances" suffer similar problems of internalization and idealization related to similar
genetics. She described: "the primitive, crudely sexual quality of
the ego ideals, conditioned by a fixation on the primitive levels
where traumatization had occurred, that represents the quintessence of this pathology" (1960, p. 307).

Kernberg (1975) prefers to reserve the term *narcissistic personalities* to those whose "main problem appears to be the disturbance of their object relationships" (p. 227). He sees these
people as "a pure culture of pathological development of narcissism" (p. 227). He emphasizes the importance of "oral rage
toward the maternal object, and, like both W. and A. Reich, the
importance of "early severe frustrations in relationships with
significant early objects" (p. 231) in the defensive genesis of this
personality organization. He expands on the description of the
mothers of these patients. They are cold and hostile and use the
child narcissistically. Their behavior toward the child is characterized by "callousness, indifference, and nonverbalized, spiteful aggression" (p. 235).

He extends descriptions by Jacobson (1954), A. Reich (1953),
and Sandler and Rosenblatt (1962) to define a specific constellation of internal self- and object representations that are pathognomonic for this personality organization: "There is a fusion
of ideal self, ideal object, and actual self images" (p. 231). This
results in a personality organization characterized by, among
other things, "coldness and ruthlessness" and deficiencies of
"genuine feelings of sadness and mournful longing; their
incapacity for experiencing depressive reactions is a basic feature
of their personalities" (p. 229). Kernberg considers this group of
patients to have a poor prognosis. He states: "The prognosis
improves with patients who preserve some capacity for depression and mourning, especially when their depression contains
elements of guilt feelings" (p. 73).

In attempting a delineation of the diagnostic category,
Kernberg's primary focus is the *state of integration* of the subject's
narcissism. This integration is based on a description of drive and
structural development. His particular emphasis is the elaboration of internalized object relations and defense organization.

In attempting to develop "A Psychoanalytic Classification of

Character Pathology" [see chapter 13] he describes a "higher," an "intermediate," and a "lower level" of organization of "character pathology" (p. 232). This paper is concerned with the lower "level," which corresponds to a "borderline personality organization." In Kernberg's (1970) classification [see chapter 13] "many narcissistic personalities are organized at this lower level" (p. 236), which he describes as having the following characteristics:

> [A] predominance of pregenital aggression . . . varying degrees of lack of superego integration as well as of the predominance of sadistic superego forerunners . . . primitive dissociation or "splitting" is the crucial mechanism for the defensive organization of the ego . . . with a concomitant impairment of the synthetic function . . . and mechanisms of denial, primitive forms of projection and omnipotence, and object constancy also reflects the capacity for a total object relationship, that is, a relationship in which good and bad aspects of the object and of the self . . . can be tolerated and integrated. This capacity is *missing* in these patients [see chapter 13, pp. 230–232; emphasis added].

In addition, the "borderline personality organization" is typified by: "nonspecific manifestations of ego-weakness"—characterized by "(1) *lack of anxiety tolerance,* (2) *lack of impulse control,* (3) *lack of sublimatory channels*" (1975, p. 22).

Kernberg (1975) clarified his comparison of the "narcissistic personality" and the "borderline personality organization" by noting that their egos' "structural characteristics" and "defense organizations" are "both strikingly similar . . . and specifically different. . . . The similarity . . . resides in the predominance of . . . 'splitting' and primitive types of projection and idealization, by omnipotent control, narcissistic withdrawal, and devaluation." The difference resides in the fact that in the narcissistic personality "there is an integrated although highly pathological 'grandiose self' " (pp. 331–332).

Kernberg employs Kohut's (1968) term *grandiose self,* but defines it differently. This distinction has not been clearly noted. Kohut's (1971) patients have "in essence attained a cohesive self" (p. 4). Kernberg (1975) equates his fused representational definition of a "narcissistic personality" with Kohut's term *grandiose self,* stating: "In my thinking, this grandiose self is a pathological condensation of rudiments of the real self, the ideal self, and the ideal objects of infancy and early childhood" (1975, p. 332). A second source of confusion derives from the fact that Kernberg and Kohut employ the term *borderline* in different ways. Kernberg's definitions of a "borderline personality organization" and a "lower level" of character pathology have been outlined. Kernberg (1970; see chapter 13, p. 232) distinguishes "borderline" from "psychotic" on the basis of the maintenance of reality testing in the former condition. For Kohut (1971) "borderline" refers to unanalyzable "veiled or fended-off instances" of schizophrenic psychoses (p. 18).

A final statement of Kernberg's contribution is required. He (1975) divided narcissistic personalities into three groups derived from a description of their behavior. The third group "function[s] overtly on a borderline level and . . . presents[s] nonspecific manifestations of ego weakness" (p. 334). The first group "are narcissistic personalities whose surface adaptation is more effective" (p. 332). Their talent allows them to adapt vocationally. However, they seek help because of "chronic difficulties in intimate relations with others" (p. 333). The second group, "representing the majority of narcissistic personalities *who come for treatment,* are those with severe disturbances in object relations . . . frequently present complicating neurotic symptoms and sexual difficulties, and are disturbed by the serious defects in their capacity for establishing lasting emotional and sexual relationships and by their *chronic* feelings of emptiness" (p. 333; emphasis added). For Kernberg, despite behavioral distinctions, all three levels are borderline and possess a pathologic grandiose self. His view of prognosis is "guarded" (p. 72) and: "the prognostic considerations . . . illustrate the limitations and difficulties in the psychoanalytic treatment of patients with narcissistic personality structure" (p. 260). Because Kohut employs different diagnostic criteria, I suspect he would consider the first group larger, including within it patients Kernberg might consider neurotic.

Kohut's (1966, 1968, 1971, and 1972) contributions are well known. He proposed a theory of normal narcissistic development. He conceptualized narcissistic libido as having a normal and independent developmental course. The libido of the narcissistic cathexis of the idealized object "undergoes a transformation" and becomes "idealized libido," which he regards "as a maturational step *sui generis* in the development of narcissistic libido and differentiated from the development of object love with its own transitional phases" (1966, p. 247). Kohut stands alone in his proposition of a separate developmental course for narcissistic libido and object libido. Yet, like Andreas-Salomé (1921), his concept of "idealizing libido" includes within it pre-oedipal idealized perceptions of the self-object and object.

Factors that interfere with the normal development of narcissistic libido result in the aberrations of development he calls "narcissistic personality disorders." The patients he discussed were not necessarily psychotic or borderline, but cover a spectrum of "specific personality disturbance of lesser severity whose treatment constitutes a considerable part of present-day psychoanalytic practice" (1971, p. 1). He (1971) does not look at clinical phenomena, "according to the traditional medical model, that is, as disease entities or pathological syndromes which are to be diagnosed and differentiated on the basis of behavioral criteria" (pp. 2–3). In distinction to psychosis and borderline states, the patients he describes have "in essence attained a cohesive self and have constructed cohesive idealized archaic objects" (p. 4).

Kohut's perspective is developmental, his emphasis on the *moae of investment* of narcissism. The area of his interest is the psychoanalytic situation. The state of integration of narcissistic investments is a secondary consideration. He sees the central pathology of narcissistic personality disorders as based on "cohesive, and more or less stable narcissistic configurations which belong to the *stage of narcissism* (that is, to that step in psychological development which according to Freud's formulation follows the stage of autoeroticism)" (1971, pp. 31–32). For Kohut, the diagnosis of narcissistic personality disorder is based "not on the evaluation of the presenting symptomatology or even life history, but on the nature of the spontaneously developing transference" (p. 23). These transferences derive from fixation at the archaically elaborated, narcissistically invested cohesive self and object representations Kohut has referred to as the grandiose self and the idealized parent imago.

For Kohut, the psychoses and borderline states are characterized, in part, by patients not becoming available to the formation of narcissistic transferences (p. 30). Instead, they experience
"fragmen[tation] of the archaic grandiose self as well as . . . of
the archaic idealized object" (pp. 29–30). This is due to their fixation on a "stage of fragmented self" which "corresponds to the
developmental phase to which Freud referred as the *stage of
autoeroticism*" (p. 29).

When considered from an object-representational perspective, it seems reasonable to conclude that Kernberg and Kohut
discussed patients quite differently. In fact, they may be discussing different groups of patients. Kernberg's "pure culture" narcissistic personalities suffer from a "fusion" of self and object
representations, while the group of patients Kohut described
have more differentiated representations. Kohut's patients suffer
"from specific disturbances in the realm of the self and of those
archaic objects cathected with narcissistic libido (self-objects)"
(p. 3). In summary, for Kohut the diagnosis of narcissistic personality disorder is based upon the elaboration of specific narcissistic transferences that depend on cohesive narcissistically
invested self and object representations and are in and of themselves an indication of analyzability. These patients are considered nonpsychotic, nonborderline, and analyzable.

Kohut's contributions are of considerable heuristic and
clinical value. Yet there is some difficulty in defining a group of
patients by the form of their transference potential. This is particularly so when one considers that the narcissistic transference
potentials are perhaps ubiquitous and elements of them may
appear in analytic endeavors with patients whose narcissistic
development is more neurotically tinged. Similarly, these transferences can be seen in psychotic form.

The present ambiguity with regard to diagnosis is related to
the fact that many analysts feel that the contributions of Kernberg
and Kohut are significant and creative as well as contradictory.
Analysts attempt to integrate and preserve the contributions of
both authors. Yet each seems limited in certain respects, and that
the two are often contradictory contributes to the confusion.
Kernberg's gift for description has resulted in an accurate portrait of a severer variety of narcissistic personality disorder. His

stress on the rage in response to frustration and on the defensive denigration of objects is important.

It is my premise here that his stress on a fused infrastructure and on an underlying unity to the psychopathology of all "narcissistic personalities," based on that configuration, is not consistent with the data. It may be that I have never worked with patients of the type he describes. I have never seen a patient who meets his representational criteria; that is, a fused actual self, ideal self, and ideal object. I have, however, seen two patients who corresponded to his behavioral criteria, but it seems to be more clinically useful to understand them as people with very rigid character-defense organizations. They had an intense need to control their animate and inanimate world. Their behavior seemed to represent an organized, tenacious, and continual striving to maintain a sense that their defined actual self representation was imbued with narcissistic perfection. These efforts reflected a perpetual struggle requiring very significant expenditures of emotional energy. As long as the patient felt his self-representation was imbued with narcissistic perfection he felt safe from the annihilating vivification of ever present object representations. When these character defenses failed, when a chink in the armor appeared, these patients were vulnerable to intense anxiety, rage, and ultimately, profound depression.

I am suggesting (as Kohut has) that these patients have a defined actual self representation. Conflict can threaten this representation with regressive dedifferentiation. In response to such a threat, these patients attempt to defend themselves by restoring illusions of perfection to their self representations. More extreme examples of this diagnostic category rigidly pursue these defensive activities as a life-style. They.may perceive any frustration as a threat to the integrity of their self representation. They attempt to create the illusion that their actual self representation is imbued with idealized qualities that will protect it from the experience of any frustration and against the imagined consequence of their rage in response to frustration.

I have worked for four years in psychotherapy with a fifty-year-old man whose predominant ego integration of narcissistic investments corresponded to Kernberg's third and sicker group of narcissistic personality. At moments of intense conflict with his object world, moments when significant objects challenged his pursuit of narcissistic perfection for his self representation, he became flagrantly paranoid or withdrew. At moments when the analyst's interventions challenged his integration of narcissistic perfection in his self representation, his mirror transference was psychotically elaborated. At such moments the analyst became more than an extension of the patient's grandiose self, as Kohut (1971, pp. 114–115) describes under the merger form of the mirror transference. In a paranoid response to interventions that he perceived as a threat to his omnipotent control, he behaved as if he were the analyst. He slipped and referred to himself as the analyst and vehemently insisted upon hearing only his own associations and interpretations. Anything other than a mirroring response stimulated disorganizing affects that the patient struggled to defend against by paranoid grandiose attacks on the analyst and his object world as well as by withdrawal.

In my opinion, there is heuristic value in maintaining the diagnostic designation narcissistic personality disorder, but it should be integrated with Freud's (1914) observation of man's ubiquitous defensive attempt to preserve illusions of his primary narcissism. W. Reich (1949) explicitly elaborated this proposition in his concept of character as essentially a narcissistic protection mechanism. His diagnostic category of the "phallic–narcissistic character" (pp. 201–207) represents an exploration of a specific mode of investment of narcissism in various states of integration typically encountered in certain male patients.

The perspective presented in this paper is an extension of that proposed by Freud, W. Reich, and Kohut. What is required is a definition of the term *narcissistic personality disorder* and a complementary psychoanalytic classification of narcissism in the "character" (Freud, 1923a, p. 28) of the ego. Any classificatory schema must be limited and incomplete, for it can only be a partial reflection of what are always more complex human phenomena.

The classification proposed in this paper is based upon an extension and elaboration of Kohut's construct of two different modes of investment of narcissism. The classification being proposed attempts to *consider both the predominant mode of investment and its state of structural integration. A narcissistic personality disorder is defined by the predominant mode of investment of narcissism in the self representation*. W. Reich's phallic–narcissistic characters as well as Kernberg's narcissistic personalities would be considered narcissistic personality disorders in this classification. In contrast to Kohut, this diagnostic designation is based on *the predominant mode of investment, not on a transference phenomenon*. A secondary diagnostic statement that reflects a consideration of *the state of structural integration* of narcissism is necessary. Again, in contrast to Kohut, it is proposed that the narcissistic personality disorder can be seen in psychotic, borderline, neurotic, and "normal" states of structural integration. Following Arlow and Brenner (1964), these categories are seen as representing a spectrum within which fluidity is possible.

These diagnostic considerations are intended to be no more than organizing rubrics to facilitate the categorization of data. They are intended to facilitate *the correlation of the predominant mode of investment of narcissism with the state of the ego's integration of narcissism*.

There are patients who show a consistent and distinct preference for one or another mode of investment. Similarly, many patients display a striking consistency and stability to their ego's integration of their investments. Some patients present mixed modes of investments with or without a potential for progressive and regressive shifts in the status of their ego organization. Finally, shifts in modes of investment and states of integration occur during the vicissitudes of an analytic experience. For example, analysands may present for analysis with a character organization and adaptation that one appropriately judges to be neurotic. Regression in response to the intensity of the analytic situation and the analytic relationship may stimulate transference forms and defensive activity reflective of an underlying "narcissistic personality disorder." I believe Freud (1916) [see chapter 2] was alluding to this, in part, when he wrote: "Peculiarities in him which he had seemed to possess only to a modest degree are often brought to light in surprisingly increased intensity, or attitudes reveal themselves in him which had not been betrayed in other relations of life"(p. 27).

W. Reich, A. Reich, and Kohut seem to have described similar patients from different perspectives. W. Reich's phallic-narcissistic characters are men defined by descriptive criteria.

Genetic and dynamic factors are considered secondary. Kohut's narcissistic personality disorders are defined by the mobilization of specific narcissistic transferences. These depend upon the presence of defined archaic self and object representations cathected with narcissistic libido. A. Reich (1953) described women who, based upon descriptive criteria, might be diagnosed as neurotic or borderline with hysteric and masochistic features. Her emphasis is upon their incorporative identification with a male narcissistic object to undo their sense of narcissistic want. In Kohut's terms, the behavior of some of these women could be conceptualized as an enactment of an idealized transference potential. Similarly, the men she describes (1960) might be seen as attempting to gain a sense of synchrony between their self representation and their "grandiose self" to diminish a sense of imminent castration anxiety and more deeply repressed separation anxiety.

A borderline integration is characterized by poor anxiety tolerance, poor frustration tolerance, and poor impulse control, as well as by a predominance of defenses such as projection, denial, and splitting. The superego and ego-ideal structuralizations are incomplete and prone to chronic externalization. Many of these patients show a preference for the mode of seeking narcissistic perfection in the external object. Their quest is typified by a profound sensitivity to disappointments in the object that interferes with their maintaining relationships. Typically, their involvement is characterized by intense idealization, followed by intolerance for and rage in response to the perception of any imperfection in the object, resulting in denigration and desertion of the object.

Kernberg (1975) conceives of splitting as the "major defensive operation" of the borderline personality organization (p. 165). In this classification the designation "borderline" emphasizes those aspects of ego integration that Kernberg (1975) refers to as "nonspecific" ego weakness (p. 162). In addition, splitting as defined by Kernberg, "the active defensive separation of contradictory ego states" (p. 165), is encountered in a spectrum of less sick patients, particularly as a regressive defensive experience in response to conflict.

The majority of patients considered narcissistic personality disorders do not demonstrate nonspecific manifestations of ego weakness and will not be designated borderline in this classification. The integration of their egos falls within a spectrum bridging the borderline and neurotic diagnostic categories. Their egos possess considerable capacity for sublimation as well as for regressions with borderline features. Such regressions may occur when these subjects are confronted with a threat to their integrations of narcissistic perfection. A narcissistic injury may provoke a regression characterized by defensive activity, anxiety, fluctuation of mood, and loss of sublimatory potential. At such a moment, when the subject feels his survival is threatened, feelings of concern for others, as well as guilt and empathy, become of secondary importance. Many patients considered narcissistic personality disorders do not experience *chronic* feelings of emptiness. Rather, they experience shifts in mood, self-esteem disturbances related to emptiness that can be correlated with the success or failure of their defensive quests for illusion of narcissistic perfection. A successful middle-aged man described his perception of life as gray and bleak when he attempted to relinquish his compulsive pursuits of perfection in conquests of women and the stock market. With regard to these patients, the issue of variability of disorder at different times and under various circumstances is being stressed. Often their egos are capable of interacting with their environments to restore a sense of narcissistic perfection to their self representations resulting in a reintegration and diminution of manifest borderline features.

A. Reich (1960) has emphasized these patients' "unbearable castration fears," their need to ward off feelings of catastrophic annihilation, and their equation of castration with object loss. Her important work emphasizes the relationship between castration anxiety and anxiety that portends the destruction of the self representation, as well as the association of phallic conflicts with formative "pregenital losses and injuries" frequently experienced by these patients.

The classification delineated here stresses two perspectives: the mode of investment and the state of integration of a subject's narcissism. Because of the importance of additional features of patients considered narcissistic personality disorders, a sketch of a "typical" narcissistic personality disorder is indicated. In this description an attempt is made to distinguish differences between patients considered narcissistic personality disorders and neurotics. It must be emphasized that the differences delineated are often distinctions of degree rather than of kind. As A. Reich (1960) pointed out, "narcissistic disturbances" include *a spectrum of patients with a spectrum of characteristics;* the boundary between who is a "narcissistic personality disorder" and who is a neurotic is a vague one.

The typical patient considered a narcissistic personality disorder is characterized by less than a neurotic character integration and an associated predominant mode of narcissistic investment in the self representation. He pursues his narcissistic investments in a more frenetic manner than do neurotics. A life-felt imperative is often associated with his quests.

Summary

A review of the relevant contributions to the theory of narcissism is undertaken to clarify the diagnostic category narcissistic personality disorder. An attempt is made to delineate the significant and creative aspects of both Kernberg's and Kohut's contributions as well as to explore those aspects of their work that are contradictory and, in that sense, confusing. A definition of narcissistic personality disorder is presented that attempts to elucidate this heuristically valuable diagnostic designation while preserving an appreciation of the ubiquitous nature of narcissism in the "character" of the ego. Narcissistic personality disorders are defined by their preferred *mode* of attempting to restore a sense of narcissistic perfection to their self representation and by the *state of integration* of narcissism by their egos. This definition is proposed within the framework of a classification of narcissism within the "character" of the ego. It is intended to complement other diagnostic considerations that reflect non-narcissistic issues.

Chapter 18

THEORETICAL ASSUMPTIONS OF CONCEPTS OF BORDERLINE PERSONALITY

WILLIAM MEISSNER

The current state of thinking about the borderline personality disorders has been relatively complacent, following as it has upon a period of much chaos and confusion. Kernberg has provided considerable clarity and illumination for the diagnosis and understanding of the personality organization of borderlines in a series of important contributions (1966, 1967, 1968 [see chapter 26], 1970 [see chapter 13], 1971), finally culminating in a more or less definitive volume (1975). His formulations have a comprehensiveness and a sweep that make them seem both formidable and definitive. Uncertainties and ambiguities remain, however, and on a variety of fronts a sense of uneasy dissatisfaction has been expressed having to do with not only diagnostic uncertainties, but also theoretical understanding of the borderline syndrome (Dickes, 1974; Klein, 1975; Gunderson and Singer, 1975; Meissner, 1978b; Guze, 1975). In addition, there seem to be certain latent assumptions and ambiguities that enter into the process of identifying, diagnosing, and formulating concepts of borderline pathology.

Terminological ambiguities reflect the underlying problem of whether the borderline entities represent forms of shifting patterns of symptom and defense, or whether they are to be regarded as more or less stable personality configurations. Descriptions of borderline syndromes seem to stumble on the lack of consistency, dramatic shifts in symptoms and behaviors, and general

This chapter originally appeared in the *Journal of the American Psychoanalytic Association*, 26, pp. 559–598, 1978. Reprinted by permission of the author and the publisher.

fluidity at all levels of borderline psychopathology. This ambiguity is augmented by the need to differentiate borderline conditions from the more established realms of neurosis and psychosis. Are they *formes frustes* of psychosis, essentially psychoses with a covering neurotic façade? Descriptions of latent schizophrenias, pseudoneurotic schizophrenia (Hoch and Polatin, 1949; Hoch and Cattell, 1959; Hoch, Strahl, and Pennes, 1962), ambulatory schizophrenia (Zilboorg, 1941, 1956, 1957), or even the psychotic character (Frosch, 1964, 1970) seem to struggle with this problem. From the opposite direction is the push toward differentiating borderline conditions from the neuroses. This has been particularly true amongst analysts who were increasingly forced to confront the question of whether or not such patients were essentially neurotics and therefore in some degree analyzable (Knight, 1953a). Under the influence of the dominant dichotomy between neurosis and psychosis, what was not clearly definable as neurosis tended to be regarded as essentially psychotic.

Only gradually has the view emerged that the borderline conditions form an intermediate realm of psychopathology that is neither neurotic nor psychotic. Attempts to describe borderline conditions as both psychotic and neurotic have proved unsatisfactory and have given way to a view of such conditions as constituting persistent forms of personality organization or character structure that had to be conceptualized and dealt with in their own terms. Kernberg more than any other has served to consolidate this perspective.

Along with this shifting perspective came other realignments in thinking. It has been gradually appreciated that the occurrence of transient regressive episodes in such personalities did not necessarily argue to an underlying psychotic process. Zetzel offered a clear delineation between borderline states and borderline personality organization (Panel, 1955; Zetzel, 1971). She emphasized that the borderline states represent a group of conditions in which the patient presents, in the initial interview, a state of regression which challenges the therapist from the outset. By way of contrast, the borderline personality initially presents few or no initial disabling symptoms, but rather shows a variety of disturbances during the course of analysis which call for appropriate assessment. In later elaboration of this position (1971), she commented that the borderline states form a group of conditions that manifest both neurotic and psychotic phenomena without fitting unequivocally in either of those diagnostic categories. In fact, the diagnosis is based on an essentially negative evaluation—the patient cannot be described as overtly psychotic or as fitting under any of the generally accepted personality disorders, may manifest no specific organic disease, and the symptoms and character structure are not consistent simply with a diagnosis of neurosis or neurotic character structure. Consequently one is left by elimination with a borderline diagnosis.

Further, the discrimination between borderline states and a borderline personality has important clinical implications. The subsequent history of a patient presenting in a borderline state, including the response to appropriate treatment, may give reason to revise the diagnosis, since the patient may have been seen in an acute regressive crisis. On the other hand, the borderline patient may not always present initial symptoms that suggest a borderline diagnosis and may in fact only reveal such a personality configuration during the course of a psychoanalytic or psychotherapeutic experience. To establish the diagnosis of borderline personality and to differentiate it from such regressive manifestations (borderline states) may require an extended evaluation of the patient's response to therapy; and evaluation of the nature of the doctor–patient relation may play an essential role. In contrast to the potentially healthy or neurotic patient in an acute crisis, the borderline patient has great difficulty establishing a secure and confident relationship with the therapist. Rather, his involvement with the therapist is colored by magical expectations, the failure to distinguish adequately between fantasy and reality, episodes of anger and suspicion, and the predominance of fears of rejection. These characteristics of the borderline therapeutic relation may persist over an extended time, but in a favorable treatment situation the borderline patient gradually becomes capable of acknowledging and partially relinquishing such unrealistic and magical expectations, fears, and suspicions.

A parallel shift in emphasis has taken place diagnostically: from a phenomenological or symptomatic evaluation to a greater attention to evaluating the organization and integration of structural aspects of the personality. As Kernberg (1975) noted:

> There exists an important group of psychopathological constellations which have in common a rather specific remarkably stable form of pathological ego structure. The ego pathology differs from that found in the neuroses and the less severe characterological illnesses on the one hand, and the psychoses on the other. These patients must be considered to occupy a borderline area between neurosis and psychosis. The term *borderline personality organization,* rather than "borderline states" or other terms, more accurately describes these patients who do have a specific, stable, pathological personality organization; their personality organization is not a transitory state fluctuating between neurosis and psychosis [p. 3].

These issues and ambiguities remain alive in the attempts to describe and formulate our understanding of borderline conditions. They also reflect and contribute to diagnostic ambiguities, and this raises the possibility that variant theoretical accounts are focusing on a diagnostically heterogeneous group of entities that forms a spectrum of borderline conditions (Meissner, 1978b). This diagnostic spectrum has not as yet been well articulated or differentiated.

These considerations reflect a certain uneasiness with current approaches to the borderline pathology, even though the dissatisfaction represents a decidedly minority opinion. Moreover, despite the dominance of Kernberg's formulations, a variety of theoretical formulations regarding the basic pathology of the borderline personality are struggling for their place in the sun. It is not always clear how these various approaches relate to each other. It may be that they are addressing themselves to different segments of the pathological spectrum and expressing different aspects of a rather heterogeneous pathological grouping. The question remains to what extent these various theoretical formulations can be successfully integrated.

Consequently, in thinking about borderline formulations we must address the question of the extent to which specific theoretical formulations may tend to mask an underlying diagnostic heterogeneity. Particular conceptualizations may be focusing on only a fragment or subsection of the borderline pathology, thus raising the related questions concerning, on the one hand, the explanatory power of specific theories and their potentiality for further integration and, on the other hand, the relationship between theoretical formulations and the underlying heterogeneity of the borderline syndromes. My purpose here is to focus on a very specific dimension of these complex problems, namely to clarify the theoretical assumptions that serve as the orienting frame of reference for particular theoretical formulations regarding the borderline personality.

Psychoanalytic theory is not so much a theory as a collection of models of the mental apparatus, which, taken together, manage to span the range of modalities in which the mental apparatus can function (Gedo and Goldberg, 1973). These various models are not altogether congruent, nor are they reducible to a least common denominator. Rather they reflect different segments and perspectives of analytic experience and are effectively differentiated by their relative success in explaining one realm of analytic data and their comparative lack of success in explaining others. And so it is with theories of borderline personality. Current attempts to formulate borderline pathology frequently draw on multiple theoretical perspectives and attempt to integrate these perspectives into a coherent account (Frosch, 1964, 1970; Kernberg, 1975). Blum (1972, 1974) enlists multiple perspectives, particularly in his reconstruction of the Wolf Man's childhood. The attempts to integrate preoedipal and oedipal factors touch on complex interactions involving ego structures and defenses, object relations, narcissistic components, and so on. This diversity applies particularly in the developmental approach, in which there is a convergence of various hypotheses. Perhaps an attempt to assess the strengths and limitations of these various theoretical perspectives will allow us to better envision their potential for useful integration and application to the understanding of borderline pathology. It may also point the way toward new perspectives in terms of which integration may be possible.

Rather than deal with specific theories, we shall focus on specific areas of deficit that receive different emphases in the various accounts of borderline pathology. The areas of deficit include (1) instinctual defects; (2) defensive impairments; (3) impairments or defects in other areas of ego functioning and integration; (4) developmental defects; (5) narcissistic defects; (6) defects and impairments in object relations; (7) the organization and pathology of the false self; and (8) forms of identity diffusion.

None of the available accounts of borderline pathology would preclude any one of the above aspects; but at the same time it must be acknowledged that no two theories will grant the same place or priority to identical aspects. For example, borderline pathology is generally felt to involve significant developmental impediments. Two separate accounts may formulate the developmental deficit in somewhat different terms, so that in their description of the developmental course they may seem to differ little. However, if one account sees the process as driven from behind by inherent and biologically given drive determinants whose impact on the developing organism is programmed by a preset timetable of organically determined events, while the other account sees the same process as the result of the progressively modulating quality of the infant's object relations with significant caretaking persons, we have an entirely different theoretical account and understanding. And the theories would render their accounts of the same developmental progression from opposite sides of the radical nature–nurture dichotomy. Our effort here is to delineate these basic theoretical assumptions embedded in accounts of the borderline pathology and to place in some perspective what may be called the "primary defect" and the degree of centrality ascribed to it in various approaches.

Instinctual Defects

Formulations that center the root of borderline pathology in some form of instinctual defect inevitably get caught in the dilemma of whether the pathology can be basically attributed to an unusual titre of instinctual power, as opposed to a relative weakening or impairment of the resources of the ego to regulate, control, and modulate instinctual derivatives. The borderline ego is frequently pictured as helpless before the intensity of the onslaught of inner instinctual forces, so that to protect itself the ego is forced into a position of helpless dependency or of omnipotent control (Geleerd, 1958).

Along the same line, other theoreticians have noted the chaotic and somewhat undifferentiated state of instinctualized energies giving rise to a sense of inner chaos. Particularly noteworthy in the evaluation of borderline patients is the manifestation of material from all phases of libidinal development, presenting a rather confused and mixed picture. This lack of instinctual phase-dominance seems to reflect an interference with a normal interaction of ego and id influences which allows for the emergence of phallic trends in the oedipal situation. The bulk of the libido remains fixed in the oral and anal levels with little evidence for phallic maturation. Rosenfeld and Sprince (1963) have commented on this aspect of the borderline pathology in children: "There seems to be a faulty relationship between the drives and the ego. At no stage does the ego give direction to the drives; neither does the ego supply the component drives with the special ego characteristics and coloring. It is as if the drives and ego develop independently and as if they belong to two different people" (p. 615). Thus, the instinctual components remain fixed at a primitive level and seem unable to emerge from the domination of the pleasure principle.

An important question raised by such formulations has to do with the basic reasons for such instinctual impediments. Kernberg makes one of the most consistently elaborated attempts to answer that difficult question. A prominent element in his analysis of borderline pathology is the predominance of pregenital, specifically oral, conflicts, and the intensity of pregenital aggressive impulses (Kernberg, 1967). The predominance of primitive pregenital aggression strongly influences the nature of the oedipal conflict. There is a pathological condensation of pregenital and genital aims under the influence of these aggressive needs and, in consequence, a premature development of oedipal strivings (1967, 1968 [see chapter 26]). The condensation of pregenital and genital aims under the influence of aggressive impulses sets the stage for primarily oral–aggressive projection, particularly onto the mother, resulting in a paranoid distortion of early parental images. The projection of both oral– and anal–

sadistic impulses turns the mother into a potentially dangerous, persecutory object. Gradually, the father is also contaminated by this aggressive projection, resulting in an amalgamated image of the father and mother as somehow dangerous and destructive. This leads to a concept of sexual relationships as dangerous and colored with aggressive and destructive themes. In an attempt to deny his oral-dependency needs and to avoid the rage and fear related to them, there is a flight into premature genital strivings which often miscarries because of the intensity of the aggression that contaminates the entire experience. Kernberg comments that these primitive dynamics may serve to discolor transference paradigms as well.

It is frequently difficult to identify where Kernberg places the primary defect, whether on the level of instinctual organization or in terms of the predominance of splitting defenses or on a defect of ego capacity for synthesis or integration. Nonetheless, some unequivocal statements can be found. He comments, for example, that the ego in its early development has two essential tasks to accomplish: the differentiation of self images from object images, and the integration of both self and object images under the influence of libidinal and aggressive drive derivatives and related affects. The first task fails to be accomplished in the psychoses, but in the lower level of character organization, for example, the borderline personality organization, self and object images are sufficiently differentiated to permit an adequate integration of ego boundaries and a differentiation of self from others. With regard to the second task, however, he comments: "integration of libidinally determined and aggressively determined self and object images fails to a great extent in borderline patients, mainly because of the pathological predominance of pregenital aggression. The resulting lack of synthesis of contradictory self and object images interferes with the integration of the self concept and with the establishment of 'total' object relationships and object constancy" (1970, p. 811). The need to preserve good self and object images from the contamination of primitive aggressive influences leads to a basic defensive division of the ego, which serves as the basis for the defensive splitting which plays such an important role in Kernberg's thinking about borderline pathology (Wilson, 1971).

The degree to which the balance of constitutional as opposed to environmental factors is struck in Kernberg's theory is not clear. It is obviously not exclusively a theory of nature as opposed to nurture, but one has the impression that constitutional factors play a clear-cut and decisive role. Masterson and Rinsley (1975) have detailed the weighting in the direction of constitutional factors in Kernberg's theory. The presence of unneutralized primitive aggression produces a situation in which there is a quantitative predominance of negative introjections, which has further implications for the persistence of splitting and the diminished capacity for constructive ego growth and the integration of self-concepts. Although Kernberg leaves room for the influence of early environmental frustration, the emphasis and the central role seem to be given over to a constitutionally determined heightened aggressive drive, which reflects his predominantly heredocongenital view. Consequently his theory pays little attention to the importance of maternal or interactional factors within the early mother–child dyad—an emphasis that sets his approach off decisively against the developmental one of Mahler, which places special emphasis on the mother's libidinal availability and its role in eliciting the development of the child's intrapsychic structure (Mahler and Furer, 1968; Mahler, 1971; Masterson and Rinsley, 1975).

If this postulation of constitutionally given aggression raises a suggestion of a Kleinian motif in Kernberg's thinking, the suspicion is not without substance. Kernberg (1967) himself has commented:

> Pregenital aggression, especially oral aggression, plays a crucial role as part of this psychopathological constellation. The dynamic aspects of the borderline personality organization have been clarified by Melanie Klein and her coworkers. Her description of the intimate relationship between pregenital and especially oral conflicts, on the one hand, and oedipal conflicts, on the other, such as occur under the influence of excessive pregenital aggression, is relevant to the borderline personality organization [p. 678].

Kernberg's approach further postulates that the primitive instincts, libidinal and aggressive, function as the specific organizing principles of the earliest psychic structures, before the achievement of self–object differentiation. Thus, the central formulation of Kernberg's theory, the internalized object relation, seems to take place prior to any self–object differentiation—a formulation that seems to provide its own inherent difficulties.

There is general clinical agreement that aggression plays a primary role in the borderline syndrome (Meza, 1970; Friedman, 1970; Gunderson and Singer, 1975). The clinical facts argue unquestionably to the importance of the role of aggression in understanding borderline pathology, but they do not argue to the necessity of postulating a primary aggressive instinct or drive, nor do they force on us the theoretical conclusion that aggression is a constitutional given. Such has been the attitude of early Freudian and Kleinian instinctual theorists, but it may be that instinctual drives themselves can be conceptualized in terms of a developmental process in which certain constitutional givens are shaped and modified by the quality of interaction with significant objects (Loewald, 1971). Nor are we compelled to think of primary aggression as essentially defused and only subsequently modified in a benign direction by fusion with libidinal inputs. It may be, for example, that the destructive and relatively "unneutralized" or "defused" quality of borderline aggression is related to the underlying vicissitudes of injured narcissism, which is threatened on a variety of fronts and for the restitution of which aggression is mobilized (Rochlin, 1973).

The appeal to instinctual factors as basic to the understanding of borderline conditions focuses the concern on essentially economic–energic factors. The key issue then becomes the distribution, channeling, or transformation of basic energies, specifically aggression, and the need to protect nascent structure from overwhelming traumatic forces. This focus may have a useful application at very early stages of development or in severe psychotic regression, but it has less utility in more evolved contexts of psychic functioning. Its explanatory range is thus quite limited (Gedo and Goldberg, 1973).

Defensive Impairment

A distinct emphasis in the formulation of borderline pathology falls upon the deficits in the defensive structure of ego. Thus the emphasis in understanding shifts to the resources of the ego as a system of functions, but specifically emphasizes the defect in defensive functions as opposed to other capacities of the ego. The most dramatic failure of the defenses is seen in periods of transient psychotic regression, in which the patient decompensates and presents an apparently psychotic picture complete with helplessness, emotional collapse, and panic.

But even on less regressed levels of functioning, the borderline tends to manifest relatively primitive defenses, including splitting, projection, projective identification, primitive idealization, and denial (Adler, 1974). Perhaps the strongest emphasis on defensive modalities and their role in borderline pathology is that given by Kernberg. He makes adequate room in his description of borderline functioning for other modalities of primitive defense operations, but splitting is the essential defensive activity which underlies the others and is essential to his understanding of borderline pathology. It is the distinction between splitting as the crucial aspect of defensive organization of the ego at a lower level of character pathology, and repression as a central mechanism at more advanced levels of defensive organization that provides the basis for a diagnostic discrimination between borderline conditions and neurotic condition. Speaking of the splitting process, Kernberg (1975) observes, "It has to be stressed that I am using the term 'splitting' in a restricted and limited sense, referring only to the active process of keeping apart introjections and identifications of opposite quality. . . . Splitting, then, is a fundamental cause of ego weakness, and as splitting also requires less countercathexis than repression, a weak ego falls back easily on splitting, and a vicious circle is created by which ego weakness and splitting reinforce each other" (p. 29). Primitive organization is inseparably linked with the internalization of pathological object relationships, which persist in a relatively non-metabolized condition as a result of the continuing effects of splitting. Kernberg (1966) explicitly relates this conceptualization to the concept of splitting in Fairbairn's account of the schizoid personality.

Kernberg's position has been questioned. Atkin (1974), for example, discusses the apparent splitting in a borderline patient. He comments:

> The "cleavage" in the cognitive, thought and linguistic functions that will be demonstrated in my patient can best be understood, in my opinion, as developmental arrest. No anxiety was produced in the analysis of the dysjunction, a proof that it is not a defense. (Where no knitting into a whole has taken place there can be no "split" in Kernberg's sense.) I found that only after some maturity of the ego occurred as a result of the psychoanalysis did anxiety appear when the discrepancies were analyzed. Only then was the dysjunction used as a defense, with resistance against giving it up [pp. 13–14].

Other aspects of the defensive configuration in borderlines have received attention. Modell (1961) has discussed the role of denial in borderlines, particularly in relation to separation anxiety. His formulation does not place denial at the root of the borderline pathology, but rather sees it as another manifestation of a defect or failure in the development of a capacity for object relationship. The denial of separation creates the illusion that the object is somehow part of the self and therefore cannot be lost. This creates a condition in which individuation cannot be acknowledged, since separation becomes equivalent to loss. The borderline differs from the psychotic in that psychotic denial is more severe and leads to the development of restitutional delusions or hallucinations. Modell notes that quantitative factors determine the extent of the denial, particularly in relation to the degree of regression in object relations.

The shift to an emphasis on defenses refocuses borderline pathology in terms of the ego, but it is specifically a defensive ego that is called into play. The description of primitive defenses tends to link borderline pathology more closely to psychotic levels of functioning. The general tendency is to think in terms of clusters of primitive defensive operations, which can then be explained in terms of some other defect, whether this is seen specifically in developmental terms or not. Thus, the role of primitive defenses in the theory of borderline pathology is generally secondary. This applies also to Kernberg's formulations regarding splitting, even though splitting seems to loom large in the general scheme he provides.

A perplexing aspect of borderline pathology has been the curious mixture of postoedipal defensive functions with more primitive pregenital ones, a point Gitelson noted some years ago (cited in Panel [1955]). It can be argued that an emphasis on splitting as a primitive defensive function does not allow for the development of higher defensive capabilities. It can even be questioned whether Kernberg's formulation tends to push out of appropriate perspective the function of higher defenses in borderline personality organization. In general, the tendency to see borderline pathology as closer to the psychotic border than to the neurotic border tends to reinforce this general inclination.

An additional point that demands consideration is the extent to which defensive defects can be read back from a more differentiated and evolved state of intrapsychic organization to early primitive developmental levels. It is by no means clear, for example, how splitting as a defensive activity arises within Kernberg's theory. It takes its point of departure from the initial integration of internalized objects and their associated affects, but it is difficult to see how this state of affairs moves to the level of defensive functioning. It may be that in order to make operative such a model of the origin of borderline personality, one must postulate initial ego capacities and functions which require a greater degree of developmental maturation and intrapsychic differentiation. This is a fundamental point of divergence between theorists who base their analysis on ego functions, both defensive and otherwise, and developmental theorists.

It is worth reminding ourselves that the theoretical account of the defensive ego represents a more evolved level of ego functioning which has its reference in the topographic model. The topographic model, and, later, the structural model which was meant to replace it (Gill, 1963), were derived from clinical data having to do with intrapsychic conflict and were not intended to explain earlier prestructural phenomena.

Other Ego Defects

While the focus on defenses as the central aspect of borderline pathology stems from the point of view that conceptualized the ego in terms of its defensive functions, the emphasis on other, nondefensive, functions stems from a later and more evolved view of the ego which centers upon notions of autonomy and adaptation (Hartmann, 1939, 1964; Rapaport, 1960, 1967). In this context, borderline pathology is viewed as a relatively stable form of ego pathology (Kernberg, 1967). The common denominator is viewed as the ego defect (Blum, 1972), which distinguishes the patient from the neurotic and in which problems of adaptation take precedence over conflicts concerning unacceptable impulses (Giovacchini, 1973). The borderline ego is envisioned as weak, ineffectual, and vulnerable (Ekstein and Wallerstein, 1956; Frosch, 1970).

Kernberg's (1967, 1971) systematic treatment of aspects of ego weakness provides us with a framework for discussing these aspects of defective ego functioning. He lists, besides the predominance of relatively primitive defensive operations related to splitting, a lack of impulse control, of anxiety tolerance, of developed sublimatory channels, a tendency to primary-process thinking, and finally, the weakening of the capacity for reality testing.

The lack of the capacity to delay impulse discharge, normally regarded as a function of the ego, had been previously noted (Panel, 1955) and related to the general fluidity of borderline cathexes and the inability to establish libidinal object constancy (Frank, cited in Panel [1956]). But, as Kernberg (1966) points out, borderline pathology represents a form of selective impulsivity and an acting-out character disorder. The patient may manifest relatively good impulse control in all but one area. He suggests, however, that we may be seeing not diminished impulse control, but an alternating activation of contradictory aspects of the patient's psychic life, as, for example, in the switching back and forth between intense sexual fears and impulsive sexual acting out, both apparently ego-syntonic.

The inability to tolerate frustration, tension, or anxiety to any significant degree has also been frequently noted as a characteristic of borderline patients (Worden, 1955; Panel, 1955, 1956; Brody, 1960; Kernberg, 1967, 1971). As Kernberg says, the important variable here is, not the degree of anxiety in itself, but the extent to which any additional anxiety tends to induce an increase of symptoms or pathological regression or other forms of pathological behavior. He regards this as a highly unfavorable prognostic indicator (1971).

Ego weakness is also reflected in a lack of sublimatory channels, specifically expressed in a capacity for work and an enjoyment of living, the capacity for creative achievement, and the ability to invest oneself in activities or in a profession that reach beyond mere narcissistic satisfactions. While sublimatory capacities are frequently expressed in creative activities and achievement, it should be noted that borderline personalities often are attracted to and find narcissistically gratifying enjoyment in creative activities, but find it difficult to deal with and master the day-to-day routine of more humdrum work situations (Fast, 1975).

The tendency to primary-process thinking, an important index of ego weakness, is one of the more frequently relied on indices clinically for identifying borderline personalities (Kernberg, 1967). Patients rarely manifest a formal thought disorder on clinical examination, but quite regularly primary-process manifestations in the form of primitive fantasies or peculiar verbalizations or other idiosyncratic responses may show up on projective testing, highlighting the importance of the use of projective tests in the diagnosis of such patients. However, it is not at all clear what a regression in such thought processes may mean, since the evaluation of it as an indicator must be considered in the context of the discrimination from an underlying psychosis.

The most critical index of ego dysfunction is the weakening of reality testing or the loss of a sense of reality. This is particularly important since the capacity to maintain reality testing is one of the most useful discriminatory indices separating borderlines from psychotics (Frijling-Schreuder, 1969). Modell (1963) has noted that the loss in a sense of reality in borderlines was more subtle and less advanced than in schizophrenics. Others find that the impairment in these capacities may be either transitory or permanent (Adler, 1970; Buie and Adler, 1972; Klein, 1975).

Frosch (1964, 1970) differentiates the quality of the patient's involvement with reality in terms of the relation to reality, the feeling of reality, and finally, the capacity to test reality. All of these aspects of the reality function of the ego are impaired, but the best preserved tends to be reality testing. It is this relative preservation of the capacity to test reality which delimits the borderline syndromes from psychotic states (Frosch, 1964;

Giovacchini, 1965). Disturbances in the patient's reality function are usually relatively easily reversible and are facilitated in this by the relative intactness of the capacity to test reality. Even patients who experience hallucinations or depersonalization may still be able to recognize these phenomena as derived from their internal experience, so that their reality testing remains functional (Frosch, 1970).

Kernberg argues that a persistent impairment of reality testing in any area of psychological functioning, and/or the production of psychotic manifestations, must be taken as a manifestation of psychosis. He (1971) thinks that if these are not present the patient is not psychotic. He also notes that the frequency or intensity of the loss of reality testing is not an important prognostic indicator, since the borderline in a regressive transference psychosis usually will respond favorably to treatment and to the increase of structure either in therapy or in his life situation. This does not hold true for the psychotic loss of reality testing.

Attention has also been called to the defective capacity of the ego to control or regulate inner psychic states in borderline patients. Ekstein and Wallerstein (1954) have compared this function to a thermostat which in neurotic patients undergoes minimal fluctuations under the control of the secondary process, but in borderline and psychotic patients fluctuates widely and unpredictably. The ego is seen as being battered back and forth by fantasies and unconscious instinctual derivatives so that the ego state fluctuates rapidly and radically through the course of the day (Ekstein and Wallerstein, 1954; Blum, 1972; Dickes, 1974; Klein, 1975).

Various investigators have focused on the lack of integrative or synthetic function as central to borderline pathology, a defect related to the incapacity to integrate sensory stimuli (Rosenfeld and Sprince, 1965), the susceptibility to dedifferentiation under stress (Frosch, 1967), the uneven binding of instinctual energies and the failure of neutralization (Rosenfeld and Sprince, 1963), and the failure to coordinate perceptual stimuli, both inner and outer, with executive responses (Giovacchini, 1973). Atkin (1974) has further pointed out that the capacity for integration and synthesis, which normally creates an integrated inner world, is defective in borderline patients and brings about lapses and discontinuities in the cognitive sphere so that primary-process influences on language and thinking as well as the predominance of pregenital sexual and aggressive responses may result. The failure to integrate brings about a bland toleration for contradictory states of thought and action without any need to unify or reconcile them.

A latent issue in the discussion of defective ego functions and their relevance to borderline pathology has to do with the question of the degree to which they are considered discrete—that is to say, the extent to which they are regarded as present or absent, as functional or impaired—as against the extent to which they are seen to function on a continuum—that is, subject to various degrees of operation or levels of functioning. The synthetic function, for example, tends to be conceptualized in terms of gradations of function, while reality testing tends to be seen more in discrete terms. Consequently, reality testing is often used as a discriminator of the presence or absence of psychosis.

But reality testing itself may be conceived in terms of degrees of alteration or impairment (Modell, 1963) and thus may be subject to contextual variations, in the sense that it may be relatively impaired in specific contexts of the patient's experience but relatively unimpaired in others. The tendency to see these functions operating discretely in the borderline context tends to dichotomize thinking and to push the concept of borderline pathology in the direction of linking it with the psychoses. Conceptualizing these functions in terms of gradients offers the opportunity of a more refined conceptualization of borderline pathology as neither psychotic nor neurotic, while it forces us to a more specific and refined sense of intermediate gradations.

It somehow seems too simplistic or "neat" to be able to ascribe the multiple impairments found in borderline pathology to a single ego defect. We need to think of multiple deviations in many areas of ego functioning as possibly operating on a different level of disturbance in each area. Such ego functions, which may be subject to a series of gradations of impairments or levels of functioning, may also be subject to a partial reversibility in their level of integration of functioning which is particularly labile in the borderline pathology (Rosenfeld and Sprince, 1963).

The focus on ego defects has a certain descriptive validity, although even here the attempt to reduce the multifaceted borderline syndromes to a single defect seems weak. Not only do the specific ego defects not explain all manifestations of borderline pathology, but they stand in need of explanation themselves. These defects are either constitutionally given or they must be explained. Ego defects thus tend to serve as an intermediate explanatory concept, which must give way usually to either a developmental or a more specifically object-relations conceptualization.

Moreover, the frame of reference, the Hartmann–Rapaport ego model, tends to focus all capacities for adaptive or autonomous functioning in the ego and sets the ego over against the undisciplined and unmodified id impulses. The function of the ego, therefore, becomes one of regulation and control in the interest of adaptive functioning. The model postulates a radical dichotomy between the undifferentiated energetic and chaotic impulses of the id and the regulating, controlling, modulating, and directing capacities of the ego. The model dictates, then, that the developmental task is for the enlargement of ego capacities and the establishment of their jurisdiction over the id. Any defect in this regimen causes the ego to yield to the power of instinctual impulses. It should be noted that this is not the only developmental model that can be envisioned, nor is it the only frame of reference within which the interrelation and integration of id impulses and ego controls can be envisioned (Apfelbaum, 1966).

Developmental Defects

Within the developmental perspective, there is a decisive shift away from a reliance on specific defects, whether of an instinctual or structural nature, to explain borderline pathology. The basis for the understanding rests rather on multiple defects affecting a variety of psychic subsystems and related to the developmental failures involved in a relatively specific phase or level of the child's growing experience. While the developmental approach rests uneasily on the assumption of constitutional factors, its primary emphasis falls on the vicissitudes of the child's object relations, so that it is in essence emphasizing experiential over constitutional factors. Further, the explanatory weight falls on the quality of the infant's object-relations experience, so that developmental perspectives enjoy a significant degree of overlap with object-relations theories.

Consequently the developmental approach provides a unifying focus within which multiple perspectives can be organized. The developmental focus adds a specific and important dimension to other theoretical accounts, namely, progression through time. This allows for the emergence of certain deficits in phase-specific sequence which may undergo a variety of developmental vicissitudes in subsequent phases. In application to borderline pathology, however, as in understanding the development of any pathology, the issues of specific and primary defects remain operative. To this extent current developmental formulations work with various theoretical models and remain usefully eclectic in terms of theoretical commitments. In this degree, then, the developmental orientation shares in and reflects the general theoretical uncertainties regarding borderline pathologies.

In proposing a developmental approach to borderline pathology a few years ago, Zetzel (1971) envisioned the borderline defect in terms of the developmental failure to achieve adequate one-to-one relationships with the respective parental objects, so that borderlines were prevented from entering into and successfully resolving a triadic oedipal involvement which simultaneously included both parental objects. The borderline may thus show relative but not necessarily equal failure in specific developmental tasks. The tasks that may be affected included establishing a definitive self–object differentiation; a capacity to recognize, tolerate, and master separation, loss, and narcissistic injury; the internalization of ego identifications and self-esteem, which permit a genuine level of autonomous functioning and the capacity to maintain relatively stable object relations. The borderline's vulnerability in the differentiation of self and object is illustrated by his difficulty in maintaining the distinction between fantasy and reality, particularly under emotional stress or in a regressive transference reaction. Thus, the borderline's capacity to internalize a stable ego identification and to achieve a genuine autonomy is severely limited and quite vulnerable.

The failure to achieve satisfactory one-to-one relationships points to relatively early developmental failure. The most consistent attempt to specify this defect has been the work of Margaret Mahler (Mahler and Furer, 1968; Mahler, 1971; Mahler, Pine, and Bergman, 1975), relating developmental failure to the separation–individuation process. The failure of that process tends to result in a relatively unassimilated bad introject around which the child's inner experience is organized. Specifically, it is the upsurge of aggression in the rapprochement subphase of the separation–individuation process that provides the conditions for the organization of the borderline intrapsychic economy (Mahler, 1971).

Rapprochement is characterized by increased separation. Development is favorable when the separation reaction is characterized by modulated and ego-regulated affects and where the titre of libido is predominant over that of aggression. The child's need to separate is accomplished by a wish for a symbiotic reunion with the mother, but this wish is attended by a fear of reengulfment. The retention of intense symbiotic strivings, in the form of womb fantasies, associated with a dread of merging and a fear of annihilation were identifiable in the Wolf Man (Blum, 1974) as an expression of borderline pathology. The child's attempts to ward off maternal impingement on his recently acquired and fragile autonomy tend to mobilize the aggressive response.

The upsurge of aggression thus tends to undermine the good self and object representations and leads to an increase of ambivalence. The result is a rapid alternation of clinging and negative behavior, reflecting a split in the object world and an attempt to preserve the good object. Mahler places considerable emphasis on the child's interaction with the mother, particularly on the mother's libidinal availability and responsiveness as the determinants of the development of the child's intrapsychic structure.

As Masterson and Rinsley (1975) propose, it is the maternal withdrawal of libidinal availability in the face of the child's efforts to separate, individuate, and achieve some degree of relative autonomy that forms the leitmotif of the borderline child's development. They postulate that the mother herself manifests borderline qualities in that she derives excessive gratification from the symbiotic involvement with the child. Thus, the child's separation, especially during rapprochement, creates a crisis in which the mother is unable to tolerate the toddler's ambivalence, assertiveness, and independence. The mother is available to the child only if the child continues to cling and behave in a regressive manner. The borderline child's dilemma is that he needs maternal supplies in order to continue the process of separating, individuating, and growing, but this very process leads to the withdrawal of those supplies. Consequently, the child tries to sustain the image of the good, supportive, and nurturing mother by splitting it from the image of the bad, rejecting, withdrawing, and abandoning mother of separation.

It should be noted that the "splitting" in this developmental perspective should be distinguished from the concept of splitting advanced by Kernberg as a specific and active defensive function. Splitting here has much more the sense of a failure of developmental integration. The contrast with Kernberg's more defensively oriented view can again be seen in terms of the relative emphasis on the constitutionally determined role of aggression in one approach, as opposed to the emphasis on environmentally determined reaction to the withdrawal of maternal libidinal availability in the other.

Whereas Mahler's discussion of these issues tends to focus the impediments in the separation–individuation process somewhere in the second and third years of life, others have placed the developmental defect even further back in the symbiotic phase of development, somewhere in the first year of life (Chessick, 1966; Giovacchini, 1973). As Horner (1975) has pointed out, the splitting becomes apparent in the separation–individuation phase, but its genetic roots can be traced to earlier levels of the symbiotic merger with an ambivalent object. Moreover, there are some suggestions in Mahler's own formulations that the beginnings of splitting and the forming of good and bad centers of frustration-deprivation or satiation–gratification are taking place even before separation plays its part. Thus, the failures of the maternal symbiosis in the hatching phase of separation or earlier may set the stage for pathological introjections that underlie the borderline pathology (Mahler and Furer, 1968; Mahler, 1971).

The developmental approach tends to focus on a particular level of developmental impairment as the specific locus of pathological defect in the borderline syndrome. It must be remembered, however, that the developmental course is subject to a variety of vicissitudes and a sequential elaboration of both progressive and regressive potentialities, which tend to significantly diversify the effects of developmental impediments at any level. Thus, for example, the dilemmas of separation and individuation are critically reworked on the adolescent level so that the borderline adolescent is again trapped in the conflict between his strivings for autonomy, on the one hand, and his fear of parental abandonment, on the other (Zinner and Shapiro, 1975). Consequently, it cannot be said that a developmental failure at a specific phase, such as rapprochement, can be related with any consistency or clarity to a specific configuration or pathological characteristics in the borderline personality on an adolescent or adult level. Mahler herself has introduced a cautionary note: "My intention, at first, was to establish in this paper a linking-up, in neat detail, of the described substantive issues with specific aspects of borderline phenomena shown by child and adult patients in the psychoanalytic situation. But I have come to be more and more convinced that there is no "direct line" from the deductive use of borderline phenomena to one or another substantive findings of observational research" (1971, p. 415).

Narcissistic Defects

The emphasis on the role of narcissism in borderline pathology shifts the locus of the pathology to the self. The metapsychological status of the self is still open to considerable question and debate, but the attempt to focus borderline pathology in terms of the defects of self-structure lends a completely new emphasis to the understanding of pathological impairments and brings the function of narcissism into the center of that understanding.

Murray (1964) regards issues of pathological narcissism in terms of narcissistic entitlement, which dictates that the patient has a right to life on his own terms. A developmental fixation at narcissistic levels can reflect either excessive gratification or deprivation: either the patient's wishes were always granted so that he assumes they should be, or they were never satisfied and he feels the world should make it up to him. Such narcissistic entitlement plays a central role in borderline pathology inasmuch as the borderline sees himself as a special person with special rights and entitlements, any frustration of which tends to shatter and undermine his self-esteem.

But it must be remembered that there is more than one level of entitlement (Buie and Adler, 1972). The mother's emotional unresponsiveness and withdrawal provide a threat to the borderline patient's survival. Such survival entitlement is related to maternal abandonment and its inherent threats of destruction or annihilation and serves as the basis of the patient's terror and rage. The persistence of such archaic ego states and their early narcissistic vicissitudes is often expressed in a sense of fragmentation, confusion between self and object, coexisting or alternating grandiosity and terror, and alternating or tangled states of dread and rage, humiliation and triumph, megalomania and devastation (Moore, 1975).

Much of this approach owes its impetus to the work of Kohut (1971), but the amalgamation of primitive, pregenital object libido and narcissism was nonetheless previously appreciated. A. Reich (1953), for example, had called attention to the characteristic of early phases of object relations for objects to be used primarily for the gratification of the self, that objects exist only to the degree that they provide such gratification and are destroyed in frustrated rage when they withhold such gratification. The narcissistic omnipotent need to control such objects is often not outgrown and may be regressively revived, so that, when the narcissistically invested object fails to provide the needed gratification, problems in self-esteem arise.

The central concept on which Kohut's approach focuses is that of the "cohesive self." The narcissistic personality disorders, as he describes them, have attained a relatively stable and cohesive although precariously balanced self, but tend to temporary fragmentation in response to narcissistic injury or loss (Kohut, 1971; Ornstein, 1974). This discrimination between narcissistic personalities and borderline or psychotic patients is cast in terms of the failure of the latter group to attain a cohesive self or self–objects, so that these remain fragmented and such patients are unable to mobilize cohesive narcissistic structures to form consistent analyzable transferences. The borderline patient has a less cohesive self that is easily subject to fragmentation so that he is unable to maintain the boundaries between self and object. The threat of disintegration is more central and critical in borderlines, whereas the disruption of the narcissistic relationship plays the more prominent role in narcissistic personalities.

It should be remembered that the narcissistic vulnerability occurs in the context of the important object relation with the mother. The infant is caught between the threat of symbiotic engulfment, on the one hand, and loss or abandonment, on the other. The usual picture is that of the narcissistic mother who withdraws her love when the child attempts to define himself as somehow separate from her. She becomes emotionally unavailable when he tries to individuate and to establish his own narcissistic equilibrium independently of her. The threat of object loss and abandonment depression leads to a narcissistic oral fixation which impedes the establishment of a cohesive self (Horner, 1975). It should also be remembered that narcissistic impediments that impinge on the organization and stabilization of the self take place within a more complex family context in which the child's dependence and failure to achieve narcissistic differentiation can serve important functions in maintaining the delicate balance of narcissistic equilibrium within the family system (Zinner and Shapiro, 1975).

It should be noted that formulations in terms of the cohesiveness of the self offer little grounds for distinguishing between borderline pathology and psychotic levels of organization. In fact, Kohut's description of the temporary regressive fragmentation of the self in narcissistic personalities sounds strikingly similar to the description of borderline regression given from other orientations. It is also noteworthy that formulations in terms of the self put the basis of the pathology on a footing entirely different from that in other approaches. The potentiality of this approach is considerable because it leaves open the possibility of reasonably well-integrated functioning in the structural components of id, ego, and superego, while the pathology develops and is rooted in the organization and functioning of the self. In many borderline cases, however, such a discrimination cannot be cleanly made, and there is evidence for defects in all of the psychic systems.

The point should be emphasized that the shift to a narcissistic basis introduces a quite distinct theoretical paradigm. The understanding of the pathology is shifted from a concern with structural integrity or the autonomy of ego/superego function to the organization and stabilization of the self as the significant principle of intrapsychic integration. The shift in emphasis to the centrality of the self follows the lead of the notion of "identity theme" as proposed by Lichtenstein (1964, 1965).

The shift in perspective, however, raises the question of what defects may be primary and what defects may be secondary, as well as the interesting diagnostic question of whether certain borderline categories may involve a pathology of the self with minimal disruption of ego and superego functions. In addition, the approach through the pathology of the self may link the pathology more specifically to the object-relations context insofar as defects of the self may address themselves to one side of the self-object differentiation. Within that frame of reference, then, defects in the organization of the self and impairments in object relations may be envisioned as two sides of the same coin.

Defective Object Relations

The contextual framework within which such primitive narcissistic issues are elaborated and worked out is provided by the consideration of object relations. Object-relations theory thus enjoys considerable overlap and interdigitation with the developmental approach and that of the vicissitudes of early archaic narcissism. These various approaches tend to be mutually reinforcing and complementary within the confines of their respective emphases. The disturbance and fragility of object relations has frequently been noted (A. Reich, 1953; Knight, 1953a; Panel, 1955; Frosch, 1964, 1967, 1970; Blum, 1972); perhaps earliest of all by Helene Deutsch (1942) in her description of the "as-if" personality [see chapter 21]. The need-satisfying quality of such relationships and the intense dependence on objects for the satisfaction of narcissistic oral supplies was characteristic (Keiser, 1958; Frijling-Schreuder, 1969; Blum, 1972; Adler, 1975; Klein, 1975). Borderline patients characteristically feel empty and hungry, demanding with an overwhelming immediacy and insistence to be nurtured by new objects, so that if these demands are not met, they experience intense rage which threatens to destroy the needed good-object relation (Adler, 1970). Libidinal object constancy is fragile and vulnerable, so that object cathexis is maintained poorly and with relative instability (Rosenfeld and Sprince, 1963, 1965; Frijling-Schreuder, 1969). Following a suggestion of Anna Freud, Rosenfeld and Sprince describe these children as "constantly on the border between object cathexis and identification" (p. 619). Borderline children easily revert to identification with the object, which may lead to a sense of merging with the object. The child's incapacity to maintain an object cathexis thus threatens the integrity of the ego, and personality characteristics become merged with those of the object.

It should be noted that Kernberg's theory is explicitly and specifically a theory of pathological internal object relations. Yet Kernberg's argument concerns itself very little with object relations as such, but rather with the internalized derivatives of object relations, which he designates "internalized object relationships." They seem to come much closer to what has been described in other contexts as "introjects" (Schafer, 1968; Meissner, 1971, 1978a). Rather than a theory of object relations as such, it comes close to being a theory of object representations, addressing itself to the vicissitudes and metabolism of such internalized objects with little attention to the relationships with objects as such.

An important contribution to the object-relations approach to borderline states was based on Winnicott's (1953) formulation of the transitional object, an idea elaborated by Modell (1963, 1968) into the concept of transitional object relations and then applied to borderline pathology. While there are remnants of such object relationships in everyone to some degree, the borderline personality is characterized by an arrest of development at the stage of the transitional object, while the healthier neurotic has been able to pass beyond that stage to the experience of the loved object as somehow separate from the self. The remnants of earlier transitional phases can be found in a variety of normal experiences, including creative and imaginative processes, cultural manifestations, religious experiences, and the like. The arrest of object-relation development at this transitional phase is not due to actual loss of the significant object, but rather to a more subtle failure of mothering in which the mother is unable to make sufficient emotional contact with the child. Modell's formulation does not distinguish adequately between borderline and psychotic forms of transitional relatedness.

The object-relations approach fills an important gap in psychoanalytic theory in focusing on and articulating the early developmental experiences that lie at the root of the child's emerging psychic structure. Consequently, its risks lie in its reductionistic tendency to read the development of later and more differentiated pathology in terms of the primitive vicissitudes of object relatedness. The explanatory force of the theory borrows from the developmental perspective in terms of concepts of fixation and developmental deviation or arrest. While these concepts have their appropriate application and range of explanatory significance, their application in the more developed and structuralized context of evolved character structure and character pathology demands validation and explanation. A critical area in this frame of reference is that of internalization. The theory must explain how object relations become internalized and provide the structural components out of which adult character and its associated pathology are formed and expressed.

The False Self

I would like to make only a brief comment about the false-self concept. It is another of Winnicott's (1960a) genial contributions, but neither its theoretical underpinnings nor its relation to the borderline concept have been established. Winnicott's description seems to lie closer to the range of schizoid character pathologies, and forms a schizoid subvariant in which the real or true self is dissociated from the false self that is caught up in compliant submission to the demands of external reality.

The description of the false self is phenomenologically apt. It may be that the false-self configuration is identifiable in some borderlines, or at least in those schizoid characters who lie close to the borderline spectrum. Borderline compliance is closely related to the intense clinging dependence and seeking of narcissistic gratification from objects, but the relationship between these conditions needs to be further explored. The "as-if" compliance so often seen in borderlines is another manifestation of this phenomenon.

However, Modell (1975) has recently linked Winnicott's false-self organization with Kohut's narcissistic personality. Dynamic issues may lie in close juxtaposition, particularly the underlying narcissistic dynamics. Unfortunately, the false-self concept covers a wide range of psychopathology, all the way from the frankly schizophrenic to the relatively healthy and normal. Modell particularly addresses the illusion of self-sufficiency, by which he characterizes narcissistic personalities and which also seems to be at issue in the guardianship of the false self over the true self.

Identity Diffusion

The loss of identity has frequently been attributed to borderline pathology (Rosenfeld and Sprince, 1963; Frosch, 1970). The loss of ego identity or its vulnerability is also an aspect of Kernberg's theory, in that ego identity represents the highest level of integration of internalized object relations. However, the organization of identification systems at a level of ego functioning in which splitting is the crucial and central defensive mechanism places whatever sense of identity has been attained in a precarious position (Kernberg, 1967). Similarly, the loss of identity in borderline patients can serve as a precipitant for creating urgent emergency states as reparative maneuvers. In this circumstance, the borderline may feel a sense of inner emptiness, having nothing inside, no individuality or originality. The acute anxiety in this state of identity diffusion can give rise to feelings of depersonalization and derealization. The patient may resort to various forms of acting out or self-inflicted pain or the creation of other emergencies in order to help restore the sense of reality and the sense of self (Collum, 1972).

The original description of acute identity diffusion was given by Erikson (1956) and specifically related to the problem in adolescent turmoil and borderline psychopathology. Acute identity diffusion occurs in a context in which experience demands a commitment to adult contexts of physical intimacy, occupational choice, competition, and psychosocial self-delineation. The individual is caught between conflicting identifications such that every move may establish a binding precedent and a concretization of psychosocial self-definition. Hence, the subject avoids significant choices, with the result that he is left in a situation of outer and inner emptiness. Fast (1974) has spoken of these terms of the multiplicity of identities, whose identity characteristics stem from the period in development in which the infant is making the transition from narcissism to a commitment to objective reality. The narcissistic sense of unbounded possibility and marked libidinization are characteristic of such partial identities.

In the face of failing identity, there are regressive attempts to delineate identity by a mutual narcissistic mirroring so that the ego loses its capacity for abandoning itself to a sexual or affectionate relation with objects. The object becomes the guarantee of the continuity of identity and raises the threat of fusion with its inherent risk of engulfment and loss of identity. The subject then often retreats, distancing himself, taking a position in which he is ready to repudiate, ignore, or destroy any forces that threaten the integrity of his self. The need to repudiate lies at the basis of the fanatical embracing of causes or the merging with a "leader" in enthusiastic discipleship. This represents an attempt to restitute identity in the face of the inability to gain genuine intimacy because of an incomplete or fragmented sense of identity. The failure of this process may lead to a paralyzing borderline state, in which there is an increasing sense of isolation and withdrawal, and a sense of fragmented and diminished identity.

The conceptualization in terms of identity seems to be dealing with the outer face of what is dealt with in more internalized terms in the frame of reference of narcissism and the coherence of the self. Thus, while the external frame of reference of the issues of self-cohesion can be articulated in terms of object relations and the psychosocial engagement of the individual, the inner structure of the problems of identity and identity diffusion can be spelled out quite adequately in terms of the structuralization of narcissism and the organization of a stable coherent self-system. It should be noted that the complex of theories having to do with narcissism, object relations, the vicissitudes of false-self organization, and the vicissitudes of identity in general tends more in the direction of emphasizing the role of experiential factors over those of constitutional givens. Each of those approaches seems to be emphasizing aspects or dimensions of the complex developmental experience, particularly the experiential rather than hereditary—or nurture rather than nature—aspects. The concept of identity diffusion thus accomplishes little more than to spell out the external implications in terms of the quality of involvement with the environment and of the inner fragmentation of the self, which is defined and delineated in narcissistic terms.

Recapitulation

Respective approaches vary in their capacity for explaining different aspects of the complex symptomatology, behavior, defensive configurations, and character structure found in the borderline spectrum.

Without attempting to be exhaustive, we can draw up some sort of balance sheet showing these relative strengths and weaknesses. Instinctual theory provides a good basis for understanding the role of aggression, the lack of libidinal-phase dominance, the predominance of primitive oral motifs, the polymorphous-perverse sexual manifestations, the tendency to volatility, the frequently seen hypomaniac behavioral patterns, the sense of vulnerability, and the frequently noted overwhelming traumatic anxiety experience of the borderline. Instinctual components, however, do not provide a good basis for understanding the lack of synthetic capacity or regulatory control of inner states, the sense of entitlement and specialness so frequently found in borderlines, side by side with a sense of worthlessness and emptiness; or the frequently observed sense of fragmentation and conflictual involvement with objects.

The approach through defenses offers a strong explanation of the alternation and dissociation of ego states, the tendency to controlling behavior and to acting out, the role of traumatic anxiety, as well as the significant role of projection in the borderline clinical picture. This approach, however, is less successful in explaining the predominance of aggression, the failure of phase dominance, the defects in autonomy, the problems related to narcissism, the fragility of identity and self cohesion, and even within the consideration of defenses themselves, the peculiar mixture of pregenital and genital defensive organization.

The approach through ego defects has considerable relevance to understanding ego weakness and the lack of synthesis, the failure of control mechanisms, and the incapacity to regulate inner psychic states, as well as the loss of the capacity to test reality. This approach is also useful in understanding regression and the general impediment to autonomous functioning, as well as the pervasive sense of vulnerability. This approach however fails to allow us to understand the predominance of aggression and primitive orality, the narcissistic issues of emptiness and worthlessness standing side by side with tendencies to idealization, or, finally, the characteristic compliance so frequently found in borderline patients.

The emphasis on narcissism deals quite effectively with the concomitant tendencies to idealization and devaluation and also with the tendency to self fragmentation and narcissistic vulnerability, the sense of emptiness and worthlessness, as well as the propensity to feelings of grandiosity, specialness, and entitlement. But the narcissistic approach offers little in the direction of understanding the perverse sexuality, typical borderline volatility, and the tendency to acting out, as well as the impairment of reality testing and other ego functions.

An approach based on object relations emphasizes the early developmental experience and the more primitive layers of psychic organization. It serves well in understanding the disturbances of object relations and the quality of the patient's experience with objects, particularly the characteristic fear–need dilemma which pervades the experience with objects. It also helps to articulate the difficulties in self–object discrimination and the tendency to schizoid withdrawal with its inherent fears of annihilation and engulfment. The object-relations approach, however, is less successful in explaining the peculiar dissociation and alternation of ego states, the failures in libidinal-phase dominance, the lack of synthetic and regulatory capacity of the ego, and finally, the issues related to narcissism and narcissistic vulnerability.

The conceptualization of borderline states in terms of identity diffusion lends itself well to the consideration of issues of self fragmentation and the loss of a sense of self, the peculiar borderline emptiness, the frequent regression confusion, as well as the tendency to acting out. But the conceptualization in terms of identity offers little ground for understanding aggressive components, the alternation of dissociated ego states, the tendency to idealization and devaluation.

The developmental approach is less easy to classify or evaluate in terms of these relative strengths and weaknesses. It overlaps to a considerable degree with all the other approaches, and thus tends to assimilate itself to their relative strengths and weaknesses. Its closest ties seem to be considerations of ego deviations, narcissistic vulnerabilities, and the vicissitudes of object relations. Considering developmental ego disturbance, Blum (1974) proposed that, while not all borderline children become borderline adults, borderline adult personality emerges from a borderline childhood and adolescence.

Conclusion

Our purpose here has been to cast some faint light on the variety of theoretical underpinnings to approaches to the understanding of borderline psychopathology. In spite of the divergence and variety of these approaches, the question still remains whether these elements can be integrated into a consistent account of greater explanatory power and range. We have noted at a number of points that divergent approaches enjoy considerable overlap and tend to articulate similar aspects of the borderline pathology from their divergent perspectives. Considerably more theoretical effort will be required to advance this integration to any significant degree. Just as we may have to think in terms of a variety of forms of schizophrenia, or a variety of forms of homosexuality, so, too, we may in fact be dealing with a variety of forms of borderline pathology which resists our attempts at integral theoretical formulation.

LESS CONVENTIONAL TYPES

We continue our survey of character types, now looking at those less frequently encountered in the literature. All but Arlow's paper describe patients who are seriously disturbed in a number of areas: Zetzel's pseudogenital hysteric, Deutsch's "as-if," McDougall's alexithymic, and Guntrip's schizoid. In the case of the last three, disturbance of affect figures prominently. We find pseudoaffectivity in the "as-if," somatoaffective disturbance in the alexithymic, and intolerance of affective involvement in the schizoid.

Disagreements concerning the maturity and analyzability of the hysterical character continue time-worn arguments concerning the phenomenology of the disorder. Conventional analytic wisdom regarded this disorder as "good"; that is, highly amenable to analysis. Zetzel, working with Knapp and others, in reviewing one hundred potential patients for supervised analysis, discovered that this point of view was only partially justified, as a significant number of "hysterical" personalities fared very badly in analysis. Zetzel helps to clarify the controversy about analyzability and pregenital pathology, corroborating the findings of Easser and Lesser. She classifies four subgroups of hysteria and defines selection criteria for analysis. A central question is whether the patient has successfully negotiated the preoedipal developmental hazards which success permits a differentiation between internal and external reality. The true (good/analyzable) hysteric has had a successful preoedipal experience and thus can maintain this distinction. She (Zetzel's patients were all women) has experienced a genuine oedipal conflict and retains significant object relations with both parents. The same can be said—albeit to a lesser extent—about the potential good hysterics. Their development, symptomatology, and character structure suggest analyzability. The so-called good hysteric appears in two versions, the depressive and the pseudogenital. The latter has a preoedipal history of parental absence and/or pathology and/or significant childhood illness, a lack of sustained object relations,

351

and significant difficulty in distinguishing reality. This group is considered unsuitable for psychoanalysis.

McDougall's work on alexithymia relates to work by French psychosomatists such as Fain (1971), Marty, De M'Uzan, and David (1963) on the "pensée opératoire" (pragmatic, operational thinking in the extreme) of psychosomatic patients. It is the only paper in the *Handbook* drawing attention to the important somato-affective dimension of character. The ideas stem from her work with psychosomatic and "normopathic" patients—both "affectless" patients with traumatic relationships in infancy and childhood. These patients suffer a radical split of psyche and soma through a violent renunciation of affect. As a result meaning and experience become devitalized and the world of dreams impoverished. Psychotic fears centering around the right to exist and be a separate individual have been aroused because of the intrusive nature of the mother–child interface. Alexithymia is a defense against this desired inner liveliness—a defense which leads to delusions in the sphere of body functions and results in the adoption of a pseudonormal, affectively impoverished lifestyle. In treatment, countertransference experiences of heavy boredom and helplessness, along with the stirring up of considerable affect, are attributed to projective identification of affect. The patient must create an inner deadness to prevent feeling primitive terror concerning body integrity. Such reactions limit feelings of identity and a sense of control over one's acts.

Allusion to the schizoid character leads us to the work of Deutsch and Guntrip. Deutsch delineates another unfeeling, pseudonormal group of patients: impoverished personalities who are prepsychotic, suffer from poorly integrated multiple identifications, and are fundamentally emotionless. These "as-if" personalities seem outwardly normal and emotionally warm. They readily attach themselves to and identify with individuals and groups as a means of giving content and reality to inner emotional and moral emptiness. Deutsch interprets the etiology of this type of character as related to a devaluation of the object serving as a model for the development of the child's personality. Early deficiency in the development of affect and failure to introject authority figures reduces inner conflict, impoverishing the total personality. She distinguishes this type of personality from hysterical characters, narcissism, psychosis, and melancholia.

Deutsch's description of the "as-if" type led to a number of papers and panels on the phenomenon. Her early incorporation of developmental, structural, and object-relations theory into her work on this group of patients foreshadowed the study of narcissistic and borderline personalities. It also contributed to an understanding of a "new type of patient" that came into prominence over the next two decades: the schizoid character.

Guntrip, a former analysand, became the lucid and popular expositor for Ronald Fairbairn. Working in isolation in Scotland, Fairbairn developed a theory radically different from Freudian drive–defense theory but very similar to that of the more influential, controversial (and less coherent) pioneer of British object-relations theory, Melanie Klein. In taking the position that libido is primarily object seeking, Fairbairn brought a new perspective on human nature to psychoanalysis. Writing about Fairbairn's theory of schizoid reactions, Guntrip describes the condition of the introverted patient, a result of being love-hungry. The schizoid character believes the love he or she bears for his object is exhausting, devouring, and destructive. Projection leads to fears of being smothered and swallowed in return. As a result these patients oscillate between being "in and out" of relationships until the disruptiveness forces them to retreat to an inner world of bad internal objects where they continue the same struggles. For Guntrip, the fundamental schizoid problem consists of being unable to dissolve an infantile relationship to a rejecting mother. He concludes by describing schizoid characteristics (such as introversion, narcissism, loneliness, loss of affect, self-sufficiency, a sense of superiority, and depersonalization) in people, institutions, and ideologies. His article also includes a brief introduction to Fairbairnian theory and the meaning of the term *internal objects* for those unfamiliar with the concept.

Taking a more traditionally American psychoanalytic approach, Arlow demonstrates the strong clinical and explanatory value of the structural model and drive–defense theory as well as their contemporary relevance in the understanding of the nature of character traits. He traces the origin of three perverse traits found in a number of his patients: inability to face matters squarely; petty lying; and practical joking. The first two are linked to voyeuristic and fetishistic tendencies, the third to transvestism. Common to all is a superego weakened by anxiety and a history of traumatic exposure to the female genital. The traits are seen as attempts to master castration anxiety through the acting out of denial in fantasy.

Chapter 19

THE SO-CALLED GOOD HYSTERIC

ELIZABETH R. ZETZEL

There was a little girl
And she had a little curl
Right in the middle of her forehead.
And when she was good
She was very, very good,
But when she was bad
She was horrid.

This nursery rhyme must be familiar to most of you. It is particularly applicable to the analysis of those female patients whose presenting symptomatology and/or character structure overtly suggests an unresolved genital oedipal situation. This leads to a presumptive diagnosis of hysteria, a condition for which traditional psychoanalysis remains the treatment of choice. Follow-up studies of the analysis of such patients have not, however, been reassuring. In Boston, for example, we reported ten years ago: "Our reports so far tend to indicate that hysterical patients are, to put it simply, very good or very bad patients" (Knapp, Levin, McCarter, Wermer, and Zetzel, 1960).

This conclusion was based on a review of one hundred patients evaluated as possible patients for supervised analysis. In preparing this paper I have also reviewed the initial clinical evaluation of nearly one hundred nonpsychotic women. Of these, more than thirty had been in analysis, either conducted or supervised, over the past ten years. On this basis I hope to revise and explain our presumptive dichotomy and the distinction made by Easser and Lesser in a more recent paper between the hysteric and the hysteroid character [see chapter 14].

This chapter originally appeared in the *International Journal of Psycho-Analysis,* 49:256–260, 1968. Reprinted by permission of the publisher.

As my opening jingle suggests, I have limited myself to the discussion of hysteria in the evaluation of female patients. Although I have evaluated, analyzed, and supervised the analysis of a number of men comparable with my sample of women, the number whose presenting symptoms were hysterical is far smaller. My findings are thus in keeping with Easser and Lesser's conclusion that presenting hysterical symptomatology is less common in men than in women [see chapter 14]. In addition, I have seldom encountered the syndrome I will describe as so-called good hysteria in the initial evaluation of male patients. The pathology of this syndrome is, I believe, largely determined by developmental hazards specific to the growth and development of the feminine character. Comparable developmental failures in men frequently result, in my experiences, in so-called normality rather than overt neurotic symptoms. These are the men whose deceptive external adaptation has been achieved on the basis of minimal awareness of inner reality, with marked deficiencies in the area of affect-tolerance. Although so-called normality is also met in women, it is far less common than so-called good hysteria. This, I believe, accounts in large part for the preponderance of women initially diagnosed as hysterical characters and/or hysteric neurotics.

In place of the earlier dichotomy I would now like to suggest that women whose presenting symptomatology suggests a diagnosis of either hysterical character or hysterical neurosis tend to fall into one of four subgroups. These may be ranged from the most to the least analyzable on the basis of their response to therapeutic analysis. Although patients in each of these groups may clearly be distinguished in their most characteristic form, I do not wish to imply a rigid compartmentalization. The most analyzable hysteric is vulnerable to regression in a bad analytic situation. Conversely, certain patients who have regressed before referral may initially present a clinical picture suggestive of more serious pathology than later proves to be the case.

My four groups may be briefly defined as follows: first, true good hysterics are young women who are both prepared and ready for all aspects of traditional psychoanalysis; second, potential good hysterics are young women whose development, symptomatology, and character structure clearly suggest an analyzable hysterical disorder. They are, however, less fully prepared and/or internally ready to make the serious commitment prerequisite to the establishment of the analytic situation. Third, women with an underlying depressive character structure frequently present manifest hysterical symptomatology to a degree which disguises their deeper pathology. Fourth, there are women whose manifest hysterical symptomatology proves to be pseudo-oedipal and pseudogenital. Such patients seldom meet the most important criteria for analyzability.

My classification is based on a reconsideration of the relation between hysteria and infantile oedipal conflict. It is essential in this context to distinguish between instinctual progression and regression and the ego achievements prerequisite to the emergence, recognition, and mastery of a genuine internal danger situation. As I have suggested elsewhere (Zetzel, 1965), the story of Oedipus himself is not a good prototype for what we now mean by a potentially healthy infantile neurosis. His father was not a real person in relation to either himself or his mother. He was a stranger by whom he was waylaid. His mother, Jocasta, was not involved with his real father but was in fact a realistically available sexual object.

The myth nevertheless highlights the nature of the dilemma with which the child is most sharply confronted if and when he reaches a genuine oedipal conflict. It was not just fear that his father was stronger and might therefore castrate him which Freud emphasized in his discussion of Little Hans; it was also the fact that Hans loved his father and did not wish to lose him. Though a rival in terms of internal reality, his father was a support and an object for identification as a real person. This conflict, in brief, is the first really significant confrontation to the child of the difference between external and internal reality. It is this difference which leads to the mobilization of the signal anxiety which motivates the major defense of the future hysteric, namely, repression.

It is my thesis, in summary, that the true hysteric, whether male or female, has experienced a genuine triangular conflict. The hysteric, in addition, has been able to retain significant object relationships with both parents. Frequently, however, the postoedipal relationship has been less satisfactory and more ambivalent than the relationship established in the preoedipal period. Hysterics, in brief, have paid too heavy a price in the attempted resolution of the oedipal triangle. They have nevertheless retained the potential capacity to recognize and tolerate internal reality and its wishes and conflicts. These are distinguished from external reality. The ability to distinguish these two aspects of reality is a major criterion for analyzability. It may indeed constitute the essence of the capacity to distinguish between therapeutic alliance and the transference neurosis.

It has of course long been recognized that the ability to modify primitive instinctual responses is initiated during the preoedipal years of development. The child first learns to tolerate delay and frustration in the early mother–child relationship. During the second, third, and fourth years of life he optimally acquires certain controls and achieves some degree of independence and autonomy. During this period, moreover, he expands his capacity for one-to-one relationships, thus adding to his own ego identifications. The major developmental tasks during the preoedipal years include first, acceptance of the limitations within one-to-one relationships without feeling seriously rejected and/or devalued; second, tolerance of increasing periods of separation from important objects, with added pleasure in available substitutes; and, third, achievement of pleasure in active mastery and learning.

In all these tasks the major frame of reference is the one-to-one relationship. The emergence of defenses against primitive instinct is thus mainly initiated by the wish for approval and its negative counterpart, fear of disapproval. It is to be anticipated that the one-to-one relationship with the mother will differ significantly from that with the father. Not only are their roles significantly different, but their spontaneous responses to the child's progression and regression will obviously cover an enormous range. It is almost inevitable that the child's relation with one of his parents will be more ambivalent than that with the other. Mastery of the hostility in the less good relationship will typically result in certain reaction formations. These, I would like to suggest, form the basis of the obsessional defenses which all of us recognize as important concomitants of the character structure of the most stable hysterics.

In this very brief outline I will focus on the specific developmental hazards which appear to be determinants of the relatively high incidence of hysterical symptoms, whether true or so-called, in adult women. First, there are many reasons over and above serious pathology in the mother which increase the probability that the little girl's preoedipal relationship with her mother will be more ambivalent than that of the little boy. Moreover, the oedipal conflict specifically entails a shift of libidinal object choice for the little girl. Her first object, the mother, becomes her rival. It is thus easy to see how earlier failures will tend to impair the maintenance of a good object relationship between mother and daughter during the infantile neurosis. This may impair the girl's feminine identification and the internalization of a positive ego-ideal.

It is also to be anticipated that many fathers are less demanding and more openly affectionate to their attractive little daughters than they are to their little sons. When this has been a striking feature of the preoedipal period there may be an impairment of full genital development. The shift to the father is, moreover, immediately preceded by full recognition of sexual differences in the phase well described as both phallic and narcissistic. On the one hand, earlier failures may thus compound penis envy. On the other, the girl may respond to her increased ambivalence by a regressive magnification of earlier passive needs. During the closing phases of the preoedipal period the boy tends to reinforce his reaction-formations against such passivity. The analyzable man who has failed adequately to resolve his oedipal situation is thus likely to present, at least initially, an obsessional rather than hysterical character structure and/or symptomatology. This same finding is, however, at least relatively true of the group I have described as the most analyzable hysterical women. These, in my experience, have defensively reinforced penis envy and associated ambitions toward active achievement partly in identification, but also in order to please a father who is not only an oedipal object but also the parent with whom the preoedipal relationship was less ambivalent and more stable.

Despite characteristic differences, men and women who have been successfully analyzed share certain major developmental successes. The ability to achieve and maintain a positive therapeutic alliance and to work through the terminal phase has been optimal in patients whose analytic material has revealed substantial mastery of ambivalence in the early mother–child relationship. This usually entails the initiation and maintenance of certain reaction formations which prove to be prophylactic against significant ego regression during the establishment of the analytic situation. These patients had, in addition, consolidated genuine one-to-one relations with both of their parents before the onset of the genital oedipal situation. Their response to both the analytic situation and the transference neurosis has demonstrated the capacity to distinguish between external and internal reality. This capacity has been most crucially tested in respect to the regressive revival in the transference neurosis of a triangular oedipal conflict. They have demonstrated during the analytic process a sustained capacity to tolerate anxiety and depression. They have, finally, demonstrated the capacity to renounce without bitterness or self-devaluation the realistically unavailable and actively to approach and attempt to attain available objects and realistic ideals.

I will here give a vignette, not of any one individual patient but of the findings which would lead me to believe that a woman belongs in my first group, namely the true hysteric who is ready for analysis. She is usually well past adolescence and has thus typically completed her formal education. She is often a virgin; if not, she has been disappointed in her sexual experiences. While she may not be frigid, she has not been able to make a major sexual investment in a man she cares for as a real person. Often she has somewhere in her life, and sometimes already married, a man who is in love with her to whom she cannot respond sexually. She is often first seen after an experience which might be described as "an hour of truth." Some event or personal confrontation has at last made it clear to her that the problem lies within herself.

Most of the patients in this group have been notably successful in areas other than their heterosexual relationships. Their academic and professional achievements have often been notable. They have in addition been able to make and keep stable friendships. Many of them were the oldest, often the most gifted, and typically the father's favorite child. None in my own group was an only child. In many of these patients historical events suggest that the failure to resolve the infantile oedipal situation may have been partially attributable to realistic events. Loss or extended separation from either parent during the height of the oedipal situation has substantially interfered with mastery through neutralization, sublimation, and positive identification with the mother. Instead, massive repression has occurred, with the oedipal father still unrelinquished and a major barrier to adult heterosexual object choice. This reconstruction has been fully confirmed in the analyses of several patients included in my first group.

How does this group of almost ideally analyzable hysterics differ from my second group, the potential good hysterics? First, this group includes a somewhat wider range of symptomatology and character structure than the first group. It is not therefore possible to give a specific clinical vignette. They are usually younger, they are always less mature than my first group. They are sometimes the youngest, or they may be only children. They have failed to achieve as stable ego-syntonic obsessional defenses as the first group. They are somewhat more passive and less consistent in respect of their academic and professional achievements. Their friendships are less stable and more openly ambivalent. They are often afraid of their dependent wishes which are nearer the surface than is typically the case with the true good hysteric.

The major problem in respect of the analysis of this group of patients concerns the first phase, namely the establishment of a stable analytic situation in which an analyzable transference neurosis may gradually emerge. Some of them are quite simply too young to make a genuine commitment. Others, first seen in a state of neurotic decompensation, may respond to analysis in one of two ways, namely, flight into health through displacement of the transference, or the emergence of a transference associated with ego regression which impairs the establishment of therapeutic alliance. If, however, these pitfalls are avoided this group of patients prove able to achieve a genuine analytic result. They do not necessarily present serious difficulties in respect of either the emergence and analysis of the transference neurosis, or the working through of the terminal phase.

My last two groups comprise the vast majority of so-called

good hysterics. The first may be analyzable in a long and difficult analysis. Depressive characters are typically women who have signally failed to mobilize their active resources during every important developmental crisis. Their basic self-esteem is low, and in addition they tend to devalue their own femininity. Despite these serious drawbacks many of these patients have experienced some genuine triangular conflict, often idealizing their fathers to an excessive degree. They have usually failed to develop adequate reaction formations during the preoedipal period. While, in briefest terms, they are able to recognize and tolerate considerable depression, they have failed significantly in the area of mastery. They are not only passive; they also feel helpless. Despite these handicaps they are often attractive, gifted women whose depression is hidden by laughter and flirtation. Their manifest symptoms may be obviously hysterical.

It may therefore prove difficult to recognize depressive characters at the time of initial evaluation. Often, however, they first come to the attention of the psychiatrist or analyst at a somewhat later age than do those included in my other groups. The fact that they did not seek help earlier is seldom as attributable to lack of opportunity as it is to their basic lack of self-esteem. They may first be seen when they are practically defeated, with considerable impairment of major ego functions. Such patients typically verbalize feelings of helplessness and/or depression quite early in treatment. They tend to develop passive, dependent transference reactions which impair their capacity adequately to distinguish between therapeutic alliance and the transference neurosis. They should not be referred for traditional analysis without careful assessment, which should include their total life situation and its potential for progressive alteration. All these patients in my own clinical experience present serious problems during the terminal phases of analysis. Unless, therefore, there are positive available realistic goals they may drift into a relatively interminable analytic situation.

Fourth and last is the group of so-called good hysterics characterized by a symptomatic picture which can only be described as floridly hysterical. While, however, their symptoms may present a façade which looks genital, they prove in treatment to be incapable of recognizing or tolerating a genuine triangular situation. Such patients all too readily express intense sexualized transference fantasies. They tend, however, to regard such fantasies as potential areas of realistic gratification. They are genuinely incapable of the meaningful distinction between external and internal reality which is prerequisite to the establishment of a therapeutic alliance and the emergence of an analyzable transference neurosis.

So-called good hysterics do not, in my opinion, meet the criteria for traditional psychoanalysis. Their major pathology is attributable to significant developmental failure in respect of basic ego functions. Initially they may, however, sometimes prove difficult to distinguish from more analyzable women who have regressed during the period which preceded their referral. Extended evaluation will often prove invaluable in making the distinction. The more analyzable patients often reconstitute fairly rapidly. The so-called good hysteric will tend, conversely, rapidly to develop an intense sexualized transference even in a structured face-to-face interview situation.

These women may first been seen at almost any age. Frequently they have been seen by more than one previous therapist and/or analyst, with unfavorable results. Unlike patients in the other group, they have few available areas of past or present conflict-free interest or autonomous ego functions. They seldom present a history which includes a genuine period of latency in respect of either achievement or peer relationships. Their obsessional defenses, if present, are not directed against their own ego-alien impulses. Like the obsessional defenses of the borderline or psychotic, they are directed towards ensuring their perception and control of certain aspects of external reality.

In many cases the developmental history will reveal one or more of the following findings:

1. absence or significant separation from one or both parents during the first four years of life;
2. serious pathology in one or both parents, often associated with an unhappy or broken marriage;
3. serious and/or prolonged physical illness in childhood;
4. absence of meaningful, sustained object relations with either sex.

No one of these observations is sufficient by itself to reach the diagnosis of so-called good hysteria. Two or more of them combined with a regressive transference readiness would, however, constitute a red light, or warning signal.

The basic question I have posed in this paper may be stated quite simply. How far can we regard manifest oedipal or genital symptomatology, that is, instinctual content, as acceptable evidence that the patient in question has achieved and/or maintained a level of ego development at which the capacity for identification, object relations, and affect-tolerance permits emergence and recognition of a triangular situation which involves three whole individuals? This I regard as indispensable for the potential ability to distinguish between external and internal reality which is one major criterion of analyzability.

I have attempted in this paper to indicate certain subgroups which may be distinguished among female patients whose presenting symptoms are hysterical. All these patients initially presented a clinical picture clearly suggestive of an unresolved oedipal genital situation. Not all of them proved to be analyzable hysterics. I may thus in conclusion paraphrase my opening jingle as follows:

> There are many little girls
> Whose complaints are little pearls
> Of the classical hysterical neurotic.
> And when this is true
> Analysis can and should ensue
> But when this is false
> 'twill be chaotic.

Chapter 20

THE "DIS-AFFECTED" PATIENT: REFLECTIONS ON AFFECT PATHOLOGY

JOYCE MCDOUGALL

This paper might well have been entitled "The *Analyst's* Affective Reactions to Affectless or 'Dis-Affected' Patients." I should perhaps explain my reasons for the use of the term *dis-affected,* which, I am well aware, is a neologism. I am hoping to convey a double meaning here. The use of the Latin prefix "dis-," which indicates "separation" or "loss," may suggest, metaphorically, that some people are psychologically separated from their emotions and may indeed have "lost" the capacity to be in touch with their own psychic reality. But I should also like to include in this neologism the significance of the Greek prefix "dys-" with its implications in regard to illness. However, I have avoided spelling the word in this way because I would then have invented a malady. Although a brief might be held, in severe cases of affect pathology, for considering a total incapacity to be in touch with one's affective experience to be a grave psychological illness, such terms in the long run tend to concretize our thinking and leave it less open to further elaboration. (The word *alexithymia,* to which I shall refer later, has already been exposed to this inconvenience. Certain colleagues say, "This person is suffering from alexithymia," as though it were a definable illness rather than simply an observable but little understood phenomenon.)

I first became interested in the psychic economy of affect and the dynamic reasons for which certain patients appear to have rendered much, if not all, of their emotional experience totally lifeless as I tried to come to terms with my counter-

This chapter originally appeared in the *Psychoanalytic Quarterly,* 53:386–409, 1984. Reprinted by permission of the author and the publisher.

transference reactions to these analysands. In many cases the analytic process seemed to stagnate for long periods of time, or it failed even to have begun. The analysands themselves frequently complained that "nothing was happening" in their analytic experience, yet each one clung to his analysis like a drowning man to a life vest. Although these patients had sought analytic help for a wide variety of reasons, they had one personality feature in common: they appeared pragmatic and factual, unimaginative and unemotional, in the face of important events, as well as in relationships with important people in their lives. As time went on, these analysands made me feel paralyzed in my analytical functioning. I could neither help them to become more alive nor lead them to leave analysis. Their affectless type of analytic discourse made me feel tired and bored, and their spectacular lack of analytic progress made me feel guilty. In my first attempt to conceptualize the mental functioning of these patients, I called them "anti-analysands in analysis" (McDougall, 1972, 1978), since they seemed to me to be in fierce opposition to analyzing anything to do with their inner psychic reality. Later, in view of their conspicuous lack of neurotic symptoms, I referred to them as "normopaths"; while clearly disturbed, they seemed to shelter themselves behind or, indeed, to suffer from a form of "pseudonormality." However, I was unable to see further into this curious condition, except to conjecture that it was probably rather widespread among the population at large.

Today I have some hypotheses to propose regarding the mental functioning that contributes to the creation of the disaffected state. These hypotheses deal, on the one hand, with the dynamic reasons that may be considered to underlie the maintenance of a psychic gap between emotions and their mental representations and, on the other, with the economic means by which this affectless way of experiencing events and people functions. It is difficult to avoid the conclusion that such an iron-clad structure must be serving important defensive purposes and that its continued maintenance must involve vigorous psychic activity, even if the patients concerned have no conscious knowledge of this and the analyst has little observable material upon which to found such an opinion.

I shall summarize briefly the different stages in my theoretical exploration and elaboration of the problems of affect pathology before going on to present two clinical vignettes that illustrate the proposed theoretical conceptualizations.

One of my first research interests, again stimulated by uncomfortable transference feelings, was directed to grasping the nature of all that *eludes* the psychoanalytic process and, in so doing, contributes to the interminability of some of our analytic cases. Certain of my patients, while diligent in the pursuit of their analytic goals and reasonably in touch with their mental pain and psychic conflicts, would for long periods of time appear to stagnate in their analytic process. Insights gained one day were lost the next, and there was little psychic change. These patients resembled my "normopaths," in that in certain areas of their lives they remained totally unaware (and thus kept the analyst unaware) of the nature of their affective reactions. I came to discover that this was due in large part to the fact that any *emotional arousal was immediately dispersed in action*. In other words, these patients, instead of capturing and reflecting upon the emotional crises that arose in their daily lives or in the analytic relationship, would tend to act out their affective experiences, discharging them through inappropriate action rather than "feeling" them and talking about them in the sessions. For example, some would attempt to drown strong emotion or mental conflict through the use of alcohol, bouts of bulimia, or drug abuse. Some would engage in frenetic sexual exploits of a perverse or compulsive nature as though making an addictive use of sexuality. Others would suffer a series of minor or major physical accidents that were not entirely "accidental." Others would create havoc in their lives by unconsciously manipulating those closest to them to live out their unacknowledged crises with them, thereby making addictive use of other people. From the point of view of the mental economy, *these all represent compulsive ways of avoiding affective flooding*. I came to realize that these analysands, due to unsuspected psychotic anxieties or extreme narcissistic fragility, were unable to contain or cope with phases of highly charged affectivity (precipitated as often as not by external events). They saw no choice but to plunge into some form of action to dispel the threatened upsurge of emotion. It might be emphasized that this could apply to exciting and agreeable affects as well as to painful ones.

Like the "normopaths," the addictively structured patients either made no mention of their acting out experiences or recounted them in a flat and affectless manner, although, on occasion, they would complain of the compulsive nature of the action symptoms. Of course, it is in no way difficult for us to identify ourselves with these action patterns. To seek to dispel painful or disappointing experiences through some form of compensatory action is typically human. However, this is a serious problem when it is the dominant or, indeed, the only method of dealing with internal and external stress.

In my attempt to better conceptualize the mental processes involved in the radical dispersal or compulsive discharge of affective experience, I was considerably helped by research workers in other fields, in particular by the published papers and ongoing research of psychoanalysts who were also psychosomaticists. Curiously enough, the latter were the first people to observe and carefully document the phenomenon of affectless ways of experiencing and communicating; they were led to delineate a so-called "psychosomatic personality." The concept of *operational thinking* (i.e., of a delibidinized way of relating to people and of being in contact with oneself) was developed by the Paris school of psychosomatic research. The concept of *alexithymia* (i.e., an incapacity to be aware of emotions, or if aware, the inability to distinguish one emotion from another, as, for example, to distinguish among hunger, anger, fatigue, or despair) was developed by the Boston school of psychosomatic research. I have found the latter psychological phenomena to be equally characteristic of addictive personalities, many of whom did not suffer from psychosomatic manifestations. An alcoholic patient of mine would make such statements as: "I frequently don't know whether I'm hungry or anxious or whether I want to have sex—and that's when I start to drink." In my experience, the incapacity to discriminate among different somatic and affective sensations, allied with the tendency to plunge into familiar action symptoms, is equally characteristic of people with organized sexual perversions, drug abuse patients, and character disordered patients who tend to seek out senseless quarrels or to engage in meaningless erotic adventures during states of conflict.

Although I remained dubious about the validity of the psychosomaticists' theoretical conceptions (insofar as my own patients were concerned), their work helped me to become aware of the fact that my two groups of "dis-affected" analysands, the addictive personalities and the normopaths, would frequently tend to somatize when under the pressure of increased external or internal stress. Events such as the birth of a baby, the death of a parent, the loss of an important professional promotion or of a love object, as well as other libidinal and narcissistic wounds, when they were not worked through emotionally or otherwise effectively dealt with, would cause a sudden disturbance in the analysand's narcissistic equilibrium. This was due to a breakdown in the habitual ways of dispersing affect in addictive behavior or to an overcharge of the alexithymic devices, with their defensive function of warding off deep-seated anxieties, thus opening the way to psychosomatic dysfunctioning. In fact, it has often occurred to me that narcissistic defenses and relationships and addictive action patterns, while they may cause psychological suffering to the individuals concerned, might at the same time, for as long as they continue to function, serve as a protection against psychosomatic regression.

The extreme fragility in the narcissistic economy and the incapacity to contain and elaborate affective experience pose questions about the possible etiology of this kind of personality structure. A study of predisposing factors goes beyond the scope of this paper, centered as it is on the *hic et nunc* of the analytic relationship and process. Briefly, it might be mentioned that the family discourse has often promulgated an ideal of inaffectivity, as well as condemning imaginative experience. Over and beyond these factors of conscious recall, I have also frequently been able to reconstruct with these patients a paradoxical mother–child relationship in which the mother seems to have been out of touch with the infant's emotional needs, yet at the same time has controlled her baby's thoughts, feelings, and spontaneous gestures in a sort of archaic "double-bind" situation. One might wonder whether such mothers felt compelled to stifle every spontaneous affective movement of their babies because of their own unconscious problems. What in the intimate bodily and psychological transactions between the mother and nursling may have rendered affective experience unacceptable or lifeless can sometimes be deduced in the analytic experience of dis-affected patients. Pulverized affect comes to light as part of the discovery of a lost continent of feeling. First, the conspicuous lack of dream and fantasy material is frequently replaced by somatic reactions and sensations; then, affects, in coming back to consciousness, may express themselves in the form of transitory pseudoperceptions. These "dream equivalents" that often follow primary process thinking may also be regarded as "affect equivalents." Thus, we might deduce that dis-affected patients, unable to use normal repression, must instead have recourse to the mechanisms of splitting and projective identification to protect themselves from being overwhelmed by mental pain. This aspect of their analysands' analytic discourse often alerts the analyst—through the confused, irritated, anxious, or bored affects that are aroused in the analyst—and enables him or her to feel, sometimes poignantly, the double-bind messages and the forgotten pain and distress of the small infant who had to learn to render inner liveliness inert in order to survive.

I hope that the following clinical examples will make clearer the theoretical notions here advanced.

When searching for suitable clinical examples among the many at my disposition, I noticed, somewhat tardily, that the patients I thought of frequently had had a previous analysis or had been in analysis with me for a number of years. In other words, I realized that this kind of affect problem *may have passed unnoticed* in analytic work for many years. The patients themselves, of course, were unaware that they suffered from an inability to recognize their emotional experiences since these were either entirely split off from consciousness or, if briefly conscious, were immediately dispelled in some form of action. One dominant feature was a conscious sense of failure, of missing the essence of human living, or of wondering why life seemed empty and boring. With my dis-affected analysands, I often discovered that the initial years of analysis had been useful in overcoming a number of neurotic problems and inhibitions, but once these were out of the way, what was laid bare was a strong but undifferentiated impression of dissatisfaction with life, of which the analysands had hitherto been unaware, much as though the neurotic structures had served, among other functions, to camouflage underlying states of depression and emptiness or of unspecified anxiety. The fact that these patients had little affect tolerance was a further discovery that the ongoing analytic process brought in its wake.

Here is a brief clinical excerpt from the analysis of a forty-year-old man. I shall call him TIM, short for The Invisible Man. TIM had undergone five years of analysis before coming to see me, three years later. Although his previous analysis had made him feel less isolated from other people and his relationship with his wife had slightly improved (that is, *she* complained less about his distance and inaccessibility), he felt that none of his basic problems had been resolved. I asked what these were. TIM: "I never feel quite real, as though I were out of touch with the others. I suppose you'd call me a schizoid kind of person. I can't enjoy things. My work bores me. . . ." And he went on to give details of the two occasions on which he had changed career directions. Now it was too late to contemplate further changes. My asking him to tell me something of his private family life led to one additional observation: although TIM did not suffer from any sexual problems in the ordinary sense of the word, he mentioned that his sexual relations and the ejaculation itself were totally devoid of any sensation of pleasure. He wondered what people meant when they talked so eagerly of sexual "excitement." He seemed to me to experience sexuality as a need, but he appeared never to have known sexual desire.

Usually, his sessions resembled each other, with little change, day after day, week after week, so that the small harvest of disturbing childhood memories had become especially precious. One involved the death of his father when TIM was seven to eight years old. He recounted that he had been on holiday at the time with relatives and had had an unaccountable bowel accident one night. The following day, his aunt told the sad news of his father's sudden death. The little boy was worried for some time by the thought that his bowel accident, in some mysterious manner, had been the cause of his father's death. In adolescence, he had suffered for long periods from insomnia and, at such times, he would tiptoe around the house, seriously concerned because of the fantasy that his state of tension and restlessness might shake the walls of the house and waken or even kill his mother and older sisters if the house were to fall down! I was touched by

these memories. They showed me a little boy profoundly convinced of, and terrified by, his hidden power to mete out death
and destruction to those nearest and dearest to him. TIM, on the
other hand, felt completely devoid of feeling about these
childhood recollections. He remained literally "un-affected" by
either the memories or my interpretation of them. He, in fact,
denied that he had ever really felt sad or anxious as a child. The
recovered memories were an object of intellectual, rather than
emotional, interest, and as such, they brought no psychic change
in their wake.

It was not in any way surprising that TIM complained of an
utter lack of transference feeling toward either his analysis or his
analyst. Explaining carefully that he neither wished nor expected
to experience any emotional attachment to his analytical enterprise, he nevertheless complained of the lack, because friends
and colleagues in analysis talked with such enthusiasm about
their transference affects that he began to wonder if there were
something wrong with him.

TIM frequently arrived twenty minutes late, and often he
missed sessions altogether. He gave no specific reason, except
that he just hadn't felt like coming or that some minor complication had made it easier not to come. He agreed intellectually that
his absenteeism could be regarded as the expression of a need to
keep a certain distance between us and that this might be due to
anxious or hostile feelings, but he was unaware of having captured any affects of this nature, even briefly. A further complication, equally typical of dis-affected patients, was that TIM
consistently failed to remember what had arisen in the previous
sessions. As with most of my analysands who suffer from an
inability to become aware of their affective experience, to the
point of believing that they had none, I intuitively felt that the
expectant silence, which is both containing and reassuring to the
"normal neurotic," was in some way dangerous for TIM. It had
nothing to do with a countertransference difficulty in supporting
silence; on the contrary, it was as though one had to fight the
temptation to give in to deathlike forces. Often such patients
drive the analyst into a countertransference corner where it is
easier to sit back in bored silence. Therefore, with TIM, after
more than a year's analytic work, I began to make longer and

more complicated interventions, often involving my own feelings and puzzlement, in the hope of rendering him more emotionally alive (although I must admit that my countertransference wish to just daydream or think of other things had many a time to be forcibly overcome!).

On one such occasion I told TIM that everything he had recounted in the two years we had spent together made me keenly aware of the existence of a sad and embittered little boy inside him who doubted whether he really existed or whether his existence was meaningful for other people. His mother, his wife and children, and his analyst were felt to be indifferent to the psychic survival of this unhappy child. After a short silence he replied: "This idea that maybe I don't really exist for other people affects me so strongly that I am almost unable to breathe." I had the feeling that he was choking back sobs.

I eagerly awaited the next day's session. After a customary ten minutes silence, TIM began: "I'm tired of this analysis and your eternal silence. Nothing ever happens, since you never say a word. I should have gone to a Kleinian!" Later I was able to understand that at the very moment TIM had begun to have difficulty in breathing, he was already engaged in eliminating all traces of my words and of their profound affective impact. Perhaps even before the session had ended, there had been no feelings left to color his thoughts. This kind of psychic repudiation or foreclosure is of a quite different order from that of either repression or denial of affectively toned ideas and experiences. In other words, although my Invisible Man took in my interventions and presence during the sessions, once he crossed the threshold on his way out, my image and my interpretations were simply evacuated from his inner world, like so many valueless fecal objects.

I do not use the anal metaphor lightly insofar as TIM is concerned since most of his fears and fantasies, when he was able to capture them long enough to communicate them, invariably revealed a consistent preoccupation with anal-type dramas and relationships. The fantasy of having killed his father through fecal expulsion was but one outstanding example. Sometimes he was convinced that he had brought mud into my building and at other times he could not free his mind of the obligation to tell me

that he had once again squashed out his cigarette butt on the car-
peted stairway leading to my apartment. Later he wondered if he
had left dirt in my entrance hall, and on one occasion he was
hampered by the obsessive thought that my consulting room
smelled of feces and that he had caused it by bringing dog drop-
pings in on his shoes. "I hope I'm not polluting the air you
breathe," he mumbled. I pointed out at various times that all this
fantasied shit seemed to be working its way farther and farther
into my living quarters, as symbolic representations of my body
and myself: into the building, my entrance, my office, and,
finally, my lungs. On each occasion, TIM thought these interpretations might be intellectually valid, but he felt nothing,
invariably went on to forget that they had ever been formulated,
and had difficulty recalling the material on which they had been
based. He nevertheless conceded that perhaps forbidden fantasies of exciting or dangerous fecal exchanges were responsible
for the fact that, since starting his analysis with me, he dressed
better and had even taken to shining his shoes. I suggested that
this gift could also be clean "cover-up," so that he might continue with impunity to find pleasure in the fantasy of filling me up
with his anal products. He burst into laughter, a rare occurrence
for TIM, and said: "I'm sure that's right. While you were talking
of the possible significance of all this, I thought to myself 'Too
bad for her!' "

It is no doubt evident from these few examples that TIM
scarcely fits into the conception of a patient with an obsessional
neurotic structure, in spite of certain similarities. While it was
true that he had many unresolved oedipal problems, his deepest
anxiety was less related to conflicts about his adult right to enjoy
sexual and professional pleasures than it was to conflicts about
his right to exist without being threatened by implosion or explosion in his contact with others.

In the course of TIM's attempts to overcome his narcissistic
and psychoticlike anxieties, we were able to discover, albeit very
slowly, that his anxiety had been dealt with by rendering himself
feelingless and to a certain extent lifeless (which gave him the
impression that he was a "schizoid" personality). In the place of
obsessional defenses and object relations, TIM displayed a more
primitive mode of mental functioning that depended less on

repression than on foreclosure from psychic awareness of all that was conflictual or was in other ways a source of mental pain. Processes of splitting and projective identification had to do duty in place of repression. Repressive mechanisms, of course, were present, but they were difficult to uncover because of TIM's terror of his own psychic reality, which had finally put him out of contact with it.

I could only guess, during the early stage of our work, that this ironclad system of eliminating from memory all of my interpretations and other interventions, as part of his dis-affected way of experiencing himself and others, must have been constructed to keep unbearable mental pain at bay, in all probability archaic anxieties concerned with feelings of rage and terror. It seemed to me that what had amounted to a struggle against any transference affect whatsoever, as well as his continual fight against the analytic process and against the libidinal temptation to let himself enjoy giving himself up to the luxury of free association, had enclosed him in an anal fortress of almost impregnable strength that might well continue to prevail for years to come.

Instead of fighting with constipated silence or with rapid elimination of any affective arousal, other patients with affect disturbance similar to that of my Invisible Man would have recourse to more "oral" means of attack and defense. Far from remaining silent, they would throw out words and imprecations, like so many concrete weapons. In spite of this apparently lively form of communication, I came to discover that these analysands were also severely dis-affected.

Here is a brief excerpt from the analysis of Little Jack Horner. In nine years of analysis, although Jack often arrived, as he put it, "deliberately fifteen minutes late because the analysis is of no value," he never once missed a session. He had had twelve years of analysis with two male therapists before coming to see me. From the first week of our work together, he expressed the conviction that I was unable to understand him and was incompetent to help him. "I cannot imagine where you get your good reputation from," he would proclaim. After a couple of years, this plaint changed slightly: "Maybe you are able to do things for the others, but I can tell you right now, *it's never going to work with me!*" When I asked him how he felt about such a situation, he remembered something he had heard about Doberman guard dogs. He said that these animals apparently suffer from character problems. They become passionately attached to their first master and are even capable of transferring this affection to a second, but should they be unfortunate enough to find themselves with a third master, they might just tear him to pieces. I said, "And I am your third analyst." There followed a moment of heavy silence before Jack Horner could gather his plums together again: "Really! You and your little analytic interpretations!" As can be imagined, the analysis of transference affect was no simple matter. Indeed, he often cut me off in the middle of a sentence, just as though I had not been speaking at all. When I once pointed this out to him, he said that I was there to listen to him and there was nothing he wished to hear from me.

I noted some years ago with my dis-affected antianalysands that if one does not remain vigilant to the countertransference affects in the analytic relationship, one runs the risk of simply remaining silent or even of disinvesting the work with them. Instead of being pleased by analytic discoveries, patients like Jack Horner tend to be narcissistically wounded by them. Sadly enough, they sometimes finish by paralyzing our analytic functioning and rendering us, like themselves, alexithymic and lifeless. The point I am trying to make here is that *this is the essential message*. It is a primitive communication that is intended, in a deeply unconscious fashion, to make the analyst *experience* what the distressed and misunderstood infant had once felt: that communication is useless and that the desire for a live affective relationship is hopeless.

To return to Jack, it can be said that I was not a fecal lump destined to be evacuated in the ways practiced by TIM; metaphorically, I was more a defective "breast" that, in consequence, needed to be demolished. The fact that one is constantly denigrated or eliminated as imaginary feces or breasts, without embodying any of the potentially valuable aspects of these part objects, is not the problem. On the contrary, these unconscious projections are a sign that something is happening in the analytic relationship. In spite of their continuing negativism, I was rather fond of the two patients in question, even though I frequently felt fed up with both of them. My discouragement with them arose from the fact that, in spite of vivid signs of suppressed affect, the analyses stagnated. It is the quasi-total lack of any psychic change in such analysands that evokes, as far as I am concerned, the more painful countertransference feelings. The constant attack upon the analytic setting or upon the relationship and the process itself, is profoundly significant and can potentially give valuable insight into the patient's underlying personality structure, but its meaning holds no interest whatever for the patients involved. It is actively either forgotten or denied.

Although many features of the psychic structure of patients like TIM and Jack Horner might be taken into consideration, I wish here to emphasize mainly the profound affective disturbance. Such analysands are out of touch with their psychic reality, insofar as emotional experience is concerned. In their dis-affected way, they also have as much difficulty in understanding other people's psychic realities, including the analyst's. The upshot is that *the others* become strongly "affected" instead!

The fundamental problem is of a preneurotic nature. It is as though such individuals had been crushed by an inexorable maternal law that questioned their right to exist in a lively and independent way. My clinical experience leads me to the conviction that this deeply incarnated "law" was one of the first elements to develop in their sense of self and that it was transmitted, in the beginning, by the mother's gestures, voice, and ways of responding to her baby's states of excitement and affect storms. She alone had decided whether to encourage or restrain her infant's spontaneity. However, it is not my intention to explore, in this presentation, the personal past or the phallic and archaic oedipal organizations of the patients in question. I wish to limit my research to the present-day factors in the analytic experience, from the point of view of the psychic economy.

In stating that the problems are preneurotic, I am not suggesting that neurotic manifestations are lacking. They are clearly evident, but their existence either is not recognized by the analysands or fails to elicit any interest on their part. When neurotic features are accessible to analysis, we frequently come to find that they have served as an alibi for the more profound psychic disturbances I have described. Jack Horner, for example, brought to his first interview with me, like a present, a couple of

classical, "good neurotic symptoms." He had managed to maintain, throughout forty years of life, including the twelve previous
years of analysis, a certain form of sexual impotence and a
recalcitrant insomnia that had dogged him since his adolescence.
Both these symptoms disappeared after three years of analysis,
but Jack was in no way happy about these changes. If anything, he
resented this passage in his analytic adventure. "No doubt, you
congratulate yourself on the disappearance of my two problems.
But nothing's really changed. It's perfectly normal to sleep at
nights, and as for making love, you might as well know that, as far
as I'm concerned, it's something like cleaning my teeth. I feel it's
necessary, and sometimes I feel better afterwards. But as for *me,* I'm
more unhappy than ever before. My symptom, my real symptom,
is that *I don't know how to live!*" Behind the evident pathos of such a
statement, we might also wonder who "me" is for Jack Horner. It
is the person who sleeps soundly? Or is it the one who makes love
without difficulty? In a sense this is not "him." His true "me," as
he understands it, suffers from an inner deadness for which he
feels there is no cure, as though a part of him had never come
alive. *Moreover, should it threaten to come to life, it must immediately be
rendered lifeless, feelingless, and therefore meaningless.*

Our analytic work up to this point would seem to have
shown that his former neurotic symptoms were a mere alibi that
served to camouflage the background scene; once gone, they left
behind a dis-affected, empty depression that laid its imprint on
his sleep, devoid of dreams, and on his sexual life, devoid of love.
His sense of identity seemed rather like a faded photograph, to
which he nevertheless clung as a sign of psychic survival. Have I
become the frame in which the sepia-tinted portrait can be
guaranteed a place? Jack Horner says that he cannot leave me in
spite of his conviction that I can do nothing to bring him to life.
How are we to understand his impression of inner death that
paralyzes each vital impulse? It is as though it were forbidden to
Jack, for impalpable reasons, to enjoy life, to delight in his own
experience of being alive in each important facet of his existence.

TIM, although a very different kind of personality, functions
with the same narcissistic affective economy. He, too, constantly
attacks each affective link that might bring him into closer contact
either with others or with his own inner psychic reality. It seems

clear that such continual psychic activity must be imbued with important defensive value. TIM and I needed five years to be able to put his symptoms into words. (As already mentioned, he did not denigrate and destroy the meaning of interpretations as did Jack Horner, but simply evacuated them from his memory.) For years, I had the feeling that I had expended considerable effort to render TIM more sensitive to his lack of contact with his affective life, yet there was little change in his detached way of feeling and being. One day, he said: "I simply don't know what an emotion really is. Wait a minute, I recognize one—those moments when I have cried here. As you well know, I would do anything in the world to avoid such a feeling, and yet sometimes it makes me feel more real. I wish I could read a book about emotion; maybe Descartes would help me. I know. There are two emotions: sadness and joy. I guess that's the lot." I wonder to myself how TIM managed to remain unaware of his rage, anger, guilt, anxiety, terrors, and feeling of love, to mention only a few common human emotions. I have limited myself to the remark that sadness and joy were valuable psychic possessions.

In the following session, to my delight, TIM had not gotten rid of his discovery. He said that he had felt deeply moved after the session and, once in his car, had found tears in his eyes. He had said to himself that he must at all costs try to formulate the emotion that flooded him and that it had taken this form: "Incredible! My analyst is concerned about me. She worries about my lack of emotion." On the way home, the tears again had come to the surface. This time he had said: "But why is it she and not my mother who taught me this?"

In the following months we became able to understand that expressions of emotion had been felt to be despicable in his family milieu and that behind this pathological ego ideal had lain other anxieties, in particular, the fear of going crazy, of exploding, of losing one's grasp of external reality if one should let oneself be invaded by emotion. Later on, TIM gained insight into his need to maintain a desertlike solitude around him for fear of melting into others and becoming confused with *their* psychic realities, as well as the recognition that he feared that were he to be invaded with emotion he would no longer be able to cope with catastrophic events (such as car accidents) with his habitual alexithymic or, as he would say, his "schizoid calm," a character trait of which he was proud. In other words, his Cartesian motto might have been: "I am not really there; therefore I am," or it might have been "I am unmoved; therefore I can function." I regard this kind of mental functioning, which manages to pulverize all trace of affective arousal, as an attempt at psychic survival in the face of near-psychotic anxieties of disintegration and loss of identity.

What happens to inaccessible affect in this case? Clearly, it does not follow the economic and dynamic paths described by Freud in hysteria, obsessional neurosis, and the so-called actual neuroses. With the analysands mentioned in this presentation, there is, on the contrary, a serious deficiency of protective defenses and of effective action in the face of mental pain, whether this is connected with narcissistic- or object-libidinal sources. The fear of being overwhelmed, or of implosion or explosion in relationships with others, often obliges the individual to attack not only his perception of his affects but also any external perceptions that run the risk of arousing emotion. In the course of analysis, we are sometimes the privileged observers of this kind of attack upon emotionally charged perceptions and can discover what actually happens to the stifled affect. This may take the form of fleeting moments of distorted external perceptions. These might be regarded as affect equivalents.

To illustrate this, here is a further fragment from the analysis of Jack Horner. For years, he had arrived ten to fifteen minutes late, proclaiming that, in any case, he was better off in the waiting room than on the couch. As a result of my prodding, he eventually became curious about the meaning of his unpunctuality and told me that he would come right on time for the following session. In fact, he came ten minutes early. Due to unforeseen and unavoidable circumstances, however, I myself was ten minutes late. Given the context, I found this most unfortunate, and I told him so. As he lay down on the couch, he said: "Good God, I couldn't care less! I was very happy there alone. The time passed quickly because I was reading an interesting article. In fact, when you came to the door, I didn't even see you—that is, I got a vague impression that you were unusually small. Actually, I was aware that you aren't dressed with your usual elegance. Seems to me you are wearing a sort of dirty grey thing. [My dress was in fact of apricot-colored suede.] Oh yes, and you didn't have any head. That's it—you looked shrunken and colorless."

In trying to examine the significance of these perceptions, he deduced, in what sounded like an exercise in logic, that perhaps he could have been a little hostile toward me because of the long wait—but he felt absolutely nothing of the kind and doubted that he could be capable of such emotion. From here, he went on to a chain of associations that included screen memories from the past, some key matters we had discussed in the course of his long analysis (recent "screen memories," so to speak, that belonged to our analytic work together), and certain constructions we had made.

Jack took up a fantasy (that had become a certitude for him over the years) that something disastrous and irrevocable had happened between him and his mother when he was four months old. He then thought of a photograph of himself as a little boy of about fifteen months, which he called the photograph of "the baby sitting alone in the snow." In reality, the snapshot, which he had once brought to show me, showed him sitting in sunshine on white sand. (My own free-floating thoughts in response to his associations went as follows: "There's Jack Horner, 'baby-alone-in-the-snow,' sitting in my waiting room, determined to know nothing of his feelings in this situation.") Without making any link, Jack went on to remember a moment, in the second year of treatment, in which he had expressed the wish to break off the analysis. Since he had often described the tempestuous manner in which he had broken off his first two analyses, I had suggested that, this time, we should make space to examine his wish to leave analysis instead of repeating an old pattern. From that time on, Jack consistently reproached me for not understanding the supreme importance of his spontaneous wish to leave me and claimed that I have permanently destroyed his chances of experiencing a true desire: "You know, I would never have left in any case. But you spoiled everything. It's ruined forever."

Here, then, was little Jack Horner, picturing himself, four to fifteen months old, full of life, making spontaneous and mean-ingful gestures toward me, but perceiving me as an implacable mother who forcefully communicates to him with my lateness that he cannot aspire to personal freedom, vitality, excitement, and desire, except at the price of losing his mother's love. His reaction was to attack his perception of the mother he perceived as rejecting and hurting him: his mother had no head; she becomes small and colorless, a desiccated, devitalized image from which he pulls away as he internalizes her in order to become his own mother.

For the infant he feels himself to be cannot give up his mother; he would rather give up his own internal vitality than lose her. He would rather freeze himself forever into the "baby-sitting-in-the-snow," playing the simultaneous, dual roles of the rambunctious child vigorously restrained by the disapproving, unresponsive, uncomprehending mother.

In his book, *Le Discours Vivant*, André Green (1973), speaking of psychotic modes of experiencing affect, writes: "Paradoxical affectivity expresses itself in action and in impulsive behavior of an explosive and unexpected kind. The link between affect and representation can be glimpsed in the relationship between acts and hallucinatory activity. The affect is acted out and its representation no longer obeys reality." Green then goes on to quote Bion's view that, for certain psychotic patients, reality as such is hated, with resulting inhibition of affective experience by the ego. At the same time, there are destructive attacks on all psychic processes. There are attacks upon the object, upon the subject's own body, and above all, upon his own thought processes. Affects not only are infiltrated with hatred, but are hated as such.

The patients of whom I am speaking do indeed use psychotic defense mechanisms, but they do not suffer from psychotic thought processes. TIM referred to himself as "schizoid," and Little Jack Horner said on a couple of occasions that he regards himself as an "autistic child"; but in either case, it is the adult part of the personality that is observing and commenting on the distressed and traumatized child within. The countertransference difficulties with such analysands do not reside in inability to identify with the nursling hidden in their inner psychic worlds. They derive instead from their utter inability to cope with the distress they feel or even to listen to it in a meaningful way. In other words, such patients lack identification with an inner, "caretaking," maternal figure. This is painfully evident in the analytic relationship, where the analyst is thrust into the role of the inadequate, incompetent, or even totally absent mother, with whom the analysand has to settle accounts from the past. Over and beyond this complicated projection, the analyst also has to accept being made into the father who has failed in his task. Not only is this father felt to forbid any attachment to the "breast-mother," but in addition he is thought to offer no compensation for the renunciations involved. Sometimes this may be expressed in the use of an addictive substance; with the patients who concern us here, the analyst and the analysis itself can become an archaic addictive substance, that is, a substitute mother, felt, as with a drug, *not to be an object of desire but of need*. The archaic father becomes a figure who refuses the nursling the right to live, in an oedipal organization in which sexuality is interwoven with oral and anal fusion wishes. Thus, it is Narcissus rather than Oedipus who implores us to rescue him. This means that the analyst is asked to support the blows of an enraged child who is struggling, with whatever means he has at his disposal, for the right to exist.

From the standpoint of the countertransference, our own "Narcissus" is sorely tried. We are tempted to ask ourselves: "Why should this child need so much more understanding, care, nourishment, than the others?" A great deal of patience, of "holding," is required. We ourselves must manage to restrain and elaborate our affective reactions while we wait for the birth of a true desire in the other. This is more difficult than it might sound, because much of the time we are faced with a death-seeking factor that tends to paralyze our own inner vitality as well as that of the analysand. The phrase that somebody "just bores us to death" is a telling one in this connection. The analysand's disinvestment of inner vitality, which is undoubtedly on the side of death, runs the risk of becoming installed within the analyst as well. The latter needs to believe that some psychic change is possible, as well as to believe that the analysand, one day, will have the courage to give up his survival techniques and begin truly to live.

One final question, also concerning our countertransference reactions, needs to be raised. Why do we accept patients into analysis who resist the analytic process as though their lives were in danger—patients whose personalities are characterized by continual acting out, continual attacks upon the analytic setting or the analytic relationship, and continual elimination from memory of every insight that comes to the surface? Why do we accept patients with an incapacity to cope with the feelings, thoughts, and fantasies that, for the first time, they are able to put into words? Why do we choose to work with people who refuse to interest themselves in the painful past and present experiences that might enlighten the mysteries of their infantile past, who intuitively and methodically destroy each potentially valuable acquisition? Why do we take into analysis analysands whose primary aim is to show us that we can do nothing for them? "Please help me, but you will see that I am stronger than you" is the credo of these patients.

Although we are frequently unaware of the difficult analytic path ahead of us when we engage ourselves in such analyses, we are also conscious, looking back on the first interviews, that we might well have forecast some of the difficulties. We have a tendency to project onto each future analysand considerable potential to undertake an analytic adventure. We tend to believe that he will be capable of making good use of us and to convince ourselves that, even in our preliminary meetings, we are able to perceive positive dimensions of his psychic being of which he is unconscious, so that we think we can be optimistic about uncovering a latent workable discourse beyond the conscious unworkable one he proffers. This is, of course, a problem of countertransference and unrealistic, hopeful expectation. There is a Dr. Knock hidden inside each of us, who wishes to believe that anyone who asks for analysis is potentially analyzable and that every analytic adventure is worth undertaking. I know that, as far as I am concerned, when I listen to patients who wish to undertake analysis, so long as they seem to be in contact with their psychic suffering and show themselves willing to search further for the causes of their psychic distress, I should like to take them all! To the extent to which they demonstrate a wish to make discoveries about their inner world, they evoke in me a similar desire. Even those who have already spent long years in analysis yet wish to continue their quest evoke in us the desire to know more about their analytic adventure and to discover what remains to be brought out from inside them, as though it were a challenge to us and our capacity for analytic understanding.

Can the countertransference pitfall perhaps be our desire to know *too much*? Bion once remarked that an analyst is someone who prefers to read a person rather than a book.

But suppose we are fooling ourselves? What if there is no readable story in this book or all the chapters are repetitive and identical? Perhaps the end of the story may even be merely the beginning, with little hope that we can do more than go around in circles. Once we start, we must assume responsibility for the mutual enterprise. Admittedly, we do this at a certain price. The analysands who are the most difficult, who cannot allow us to read their history because they have never dared to turn the first page themselves, paralyze our "reader–analyst" functioning and arouse in us terrible feelings of malaise, anxiety, frustration, guilt, and, even worse, boredom and fatigue. How can we give life to these patients who ask us only to keep their prison walls intact and to keep our affect reactions to ourselves? How are we to deal with the feeling of total impotence, of inability to help them become less dis-affected and more alive, so that they can truly develop the desire to leave us and to live? Above all, what are we to do with our own feelings of dis-affection and despair?

It is said that if one looks at anything for a long enough time, it becomes interesting. Although we are always alone with our difficult dis-affected patients, and although we well know that nobody is going to come and help us, we at least have the possibility of sharing our disquiet, our incomprehension, and our sense of incompleteness. This is one of the reasons we gather together to share our clinical experiences and our theoretical conceptualizations with one another. If we have the impression that these difficult analysands have led us into an interminable analytic experience, at least they have opened a field of research before us.

Little Jack Horner once said to me, after some eight years of analysis: "I have neutralized you completely. It doesn't matter what you do or what you say; you will never get anywhere with me. This analysis is utterly useless, but no doubt you will manage to make an article out of it!"

Chapter 21

SOME FORMS OF EMOTIONAL
DISTURBANCE AND THEIR
RELATIONSHIP TO SCHIZOPHRENIA

HELENE DEUTSCH

Psychoanalytic observations of a few types of emotional disturbances are presented in this paper, and a series of cases reported
in which the individual's emotional relationship to the outside
world and to his own ego appears impoverished or absent. Such
disturbances of the emotional life take various forms. For example, there are the individuals who are not aware of their lack of
normal affective bonds and responses, but whose emotional disturbance is perceived either only by those around them or is first
detected in analytic treatment; and there are those who complain
of their emotional defect and are keenly distressed by the disturbance in their inner experiences. Among the latter, the
disturbance may be transitory and fleeting; it may recur from
time to time but only in connection with certain specific situations
and experiences; or it may persist and form a continuous, distressing symptom. In addition, the emotional disturbance may
be perceived as existing in the personality or it may be projected
onto the outside world. In the one case the patient says, "I am
changed. I feel nothing. Everything seems unreal to me." In the
other, he complains that the world seems strange, objects
shadowy, human beings and events theatrical and unreal. Those
forms of the disturbance in which the individual himself is conscious of his defect and complains of it belong to the picture of

This publication is a combination of a paper published in the *Internationale Zeitschrift
für Psychoanalyse,* 20:323–335, 1934, under the title "Über einen Typus der Pseudoaffektivät
('als ob')" and of a lecture given at the Chicago meeting of the American Psychoanalytic
Society, 1938. It originally appeared in the *Psychoanalytic Quarterly,* 11:301–321, 1942.
Reprinted by permission of the publisher.

"depersonalization." This disturbance has been described by many authors. In the analytic literature the reader is especially referred to the studies of Oberndorf (1934, 1935), Schilder (1939), and Bergler and Eidelberg (1935).

Most of the psychoanalytic observations in this paper deal with conditions bearing a close relationship to depersonalization but differing from it in that they were not perceived as disturbances by the patient himself. To this special type of personality I have given the name "as if." I must emphasize that this name has nothing to do with Vaihinger's system of "fictions" and the philosophy of "As if." My only reason for using so unoriginal a label for the type of person I wish to present is that every attempt to understand the way of feeling and manner of life of this type forces on the observer the inescapable impression that the individual's whole relationship to life has something about it which is lacking in genuineness and yet outwardly runs along "as if" it were complete. Even the layman sooner or later inquires, after meeting such an "as if" patient: what *is* wrong with him, or her? Outwardly the person seems normal. There is nothing to suggest any kind of disorder, behavior is not unusual, intellectual abilities appear unimpaired, emotional expressions are well ordered and appropriate. But despite all this, something intangible and indefinable obtrudes between the person and his fellows and invariably gives rise to the question, "What is wrong?"

A clever and experienced man, a patient of mine, met another of my patients, a girl of the "as if" type, at a social gathering. He spent part of his next analytic hour telling me how stimulating, amusing, attractive, and interesting she was, but ended his eulogy with, "But something is wrong with her." He could not explain what he meant.

When I submitted the paintings of the same girl to an authority for his criticism and evaluation, I was told that the drawings showed much skill and talent but there was also something disturbing in them which this man attributed to an inner restraint, an inhibition which he thought could surely be removed. Toward the end of the patient's not too successful analysis, she entered this critic's school for further instruction in painting and, after a time, I received a report in which her teacher spoke in glowing terms of her talent. Several months later I received a less enthusiastic report. Yes, the girl was talented, her teacher had been impressed by the speed with which she had adopted his technique and manner of artistic perception, but, he frankly had to admit, there was an intangible something about her which he had never before encountered, and he ended with the usual question, "What is wrong?" He added that the girl had gone to another teacher, who had used a quite different teaching approach, and that she had oriented herself to the new theory and technique with striking ease and speed.

The first impression these people make is of complete normality. They are intellectually intact, gifted, and bring great understanding to intellectual and emotional problems; but when they pursue their not infrequent impulses to creative work they construct, in form, a good piece of work but it is always a spasmodic, if skilled, repetition of a prototype without the slightest trace of originality. On closer observation, the same thing is seen in their affective relationships to the environment. These relationships are usually intense and bear all the earmarks of friendship, love, sympathy, and understanding; but even the layman soon perceives something strange and raises the question he cannot answer. To the analyst it is soon clear that all these relationships are devoid of any trace of warmth, and that all the expressions of emotion are formal, that all inner experience is completely excluded. It is like the performance of an actor who is technically well trained but who lacks the necessary spark to make his impersonations true to life.

Thus the essential characteristic of the person I wish to describe is that outwardly he conducts his life as if he possessed a complete and sensitive emotional capacity. To him there is no difference between his empty forms and what others actually experience. Without going deeper into the matter I wish at this point to state that this condition is not identical with the coldness of repressed individuals in whom there is usually a highly differentiated emotional life hidden behind a wall, the loss of affect being either manifest or cloaked by overcompensations. In the one there is flight from reality or a defense against the realization of forbidden instinctual drives; in the other, a seeking of external reality in an effort to avoid an anxiety laden fantasy. Psychoanalysis discloses that in the "as if" individual it is no longer an act of repression but a real loss of object cathexis. The apparently normal relationship to the world corresponds to a child's imitativeness and is the expression of identification with the environment, a mimicry which results in an ostensibly good adaptation to the world of reality despite the absence of object cathexis.

Further consequences of such a relation to life are a completely passive attitude to the environment with a highly plastic readiness to pick up signals from the outer world and to mold oneself and one's behavior accordingly. The identification with what other people are thinking and feeling is the expression of this passive plasticity and renders the person capable of the greatest fidelity and the basest perfidy. Any object will do as a bridge for identification. At first the love, friendship, and attachment of an "as if" person have something very rewarding for the partner. If it is a woman, she seems to be the quintessence of feminine devotion, an impression which is particularly imparted by her passivity and readiness for identification. Soon, however, the lack of real warmth brings such an emptiness and dullness to the emotional atmosphere that the man as a rule precipitously breaks off the relationship. In spite of the adhesiveness which the "as if" person brings to every relationship, when she is thus abandoned she displays either a rush of affective reactions which are "as if" and thus spurious, or a frank absence of affectivity. At the very first opportunity the former object is exchanged for a new one and the process is repeated.

The same emptiness and the same lack of individuality which are so evident in the emotional life appear also in the moral structure. Completely without character, wholly unprincipled, in the literal meaning of the term, the morals of the "as if" individuals, their ideals, their convictions are simply reflections of another person, good or bad. Attaching themselves with great ease to social, ethical, and religious groups, they seek, by adhering to a group, to give content and reality to their inner emptiness and establish the validity of their existence by identification. Overenthusiastic adherence to one philosophy can be quickly and completely replaced by another contradictory one without the slightest trace of inward transformation—simply as a result of some accidental regrouping of the circle of acquaintances or the like.

A second characteristic of such patients is their suggestibility, quite understandable from what has already been said. Like the capacity for identification, this suggestibility, too, is unlike that of the hysteric for whom object cathexis is a necessary condition; in the "as if" individual the suggestibility must be ascribed to passivity and automatonlike identification. Many initial criminal acts, attributed to an erotic bondage, are due instead to a passive readiness to be influenced.

Another characteristic of the "as if" personality is that aggressive tendencies are almost completely masked by passivity, lending an air of negative goodness, of mild amiability which, however, is readily convertible to evil.

One of these patients, a woman, and the only child of one of the oldest noble families in Europe, had been brought up in an unusual atmosphere. With the excuse of official duties, and quite in accordance with tradition, the parents delegated the care and training of their child to strangers. On certain specified days of the week she was brought before her parents for "control." At these meetings there was a formal check of her educational achievements, and the new program and other directions were given her preceptors. Then after a cool, ceremonious dismissal, the child was returned to her quarters. She received no warmth and no tenderness from her parents, nor did punishment come directly from them. This virtual separation from her parents had come soon after her birth. Perhaps the most inauspicious component of her parents' conduct, which granted the child only a very niggardly bit of warmth, was the fact—and this was reinforced by the whole program of her education—that their sheer *existence* was strongly emphasized, and the patient was drilled in love, honor, and obedience toward them without ever feeling these emotions directly and realistically.

In this atmosphere, so lacking in feeling on the part of the parents, the development of a satisfactory emotional life could scarcely be expected in the child. One would expect, however, that other persons in the environment would take the place of the parents. Her situation would then have been that of a child brought up in a foster home. In such children we find that the emotional ties to their own parents are transferred to the parent substitutes in relationship to whom the oedipus complex develops with greater difficulty perhaps but with no significant modifications.

This patient, in accordance with ceremonial tradition, always had three nurses, each of whom wanted to stand first in the eyes of the parents and each of whom continually sought the favor of the child. They were, moreover, frequently changed. Throughout her whole childhood there was no one person who loved her and who could have served as a significant love object for her.

As soon as she was able to conceptualize, the patient immersed herself intensively in fantasies about the parents. She attributed to them divine powers through which she was provided with things unattainable to ordinary mortals. Everything she absorbed from stories and legends she elaborated into the myth about her parents. No longing for love was ever expressed in these fantasies; they all had the aim of providing a narcissistic gain. Every meeting with the real parents separated them further from the heroes of her imagination. In this manner there was formed in the child a parental myth, a fantasmic shadow of an oedipus situation which remained an empty form so far as real persons and emotions were concerned. Not only did reality which denied her parent relationships lead to narcissistic regression into fantasy, but this process gained further impetus from the absence of any substitutive object-libidinous relationships. The frequent change of nurses and governesses and the fact that these persons were themselves subjected to strict discipline, acted on orders, and used all available measures to make the child conform to the demands of reality, measures in which a pseudo tenderness was consciously used as a means to attain didactic ends, precluded this possibility. The child was trained very early to cleanliness and strict table manners, and the violent outbreaks of anger and rage to which she was subject in early childhood were successfully brought under control, giving way to an absolutely pliant obedience. Much of this disciplinary control was attained by appeal to the parents so that everything the child did which was obedient and proper she referred to the wish or command of the mythical father and mother.

When she entered a convent school at the age of eight, she was completely fixed in the "as if" state in which she entered analysis. Superficially, there was no difference between her life and that of the average convent pupil. She had the customary attachment to a nun in imitation of her group of girls. She had the most tender friendships which were wholly without significance to her. She went devoutly through the forms of religion without the slightest trace of belief, and underwent seduction into masturbation with quasi feelings of guilt—simply to be like her comrades.

In time, the myth of her parents faded and disappeared without new fantasies to take its place. It disappeared as her parents became clearer to her as real persons and she devaluated them. Narcissistic fantasies gave way to real experiences in which, however, she could participate only through identification.

Analysis disclosed that the success of her early training in suppressing instinctual drives was only apparent. It had something of the "trained act" in it and, like the performance of the circus animal, was bound to the presence of a ringmaster. If denial of an instinct was demanded, the patient complied, but when an otherwise inclined object gave permission for the satisfaction of a drive, she could respond quite without inhibition, though with little gratification. The only result of the training was that the drive never came into conflict with the external world. In this respect she behaved like a child in that stage of development in which his instinctual drives are curbed only by immediate external authority. Thus it happened that for a time the patient fell into bad company, in unbelievable contrast to her home environment and early training. She got drunk in low dives, participated in all kinds of sexual perversions, and felt just as comfortable in this underworld as in the pietistic sect, the artistic group, or the political movement in which she was later successively a participant.

She never had occasion to complain of lack of affect for she was never conscious of it. The patient's relationship to her parents was strong enough to enable her to make them heroes of

her fantasy, but for the creation of a warm dynamic oedipus constellation capable of shaping a healthy future psychic life in both
a positive and a negative sense the necessary conditions were
obviously lacking. It is not enough that the parents are simply
there and provide food for fantasy. The child must *really* be
seduced to a certain extent by the libidinous activity of the parents
in order to develop a normal emotional life, must experience the
warmth of a mother's body as well as all those unconscious
seductive acts of the loving mother as she cares for his bodily
needs. He must play with the father and have sufficient intimacy
with him to sense the father's masculinity in order that instinctual
impulses enter the stream of the oedipus constellation.

This patient's myth bore some similarity to the fantasy which
Freud called the "family romance" in which, however, the libidinal
relation to the parents though repressed is very powerful. By
repudiating the real parents, it is possible partly to avoid strong
emotional conflicts from forbidden wishes, feelings of guilt, etc.
The real objects have been repressed, but in analysis they can be
uncovered with their full libidinal cathexis.

But for our patient there was never a living warm emotional
relationship to the parents or to anyone else. Whether after weak
attempts at object cathexis the child returned to narcissism by a
process of regression or never succeeded in establishing a real
object relation as the result of being unloved is, for all practical
purposes, irrelevant.

The same deficiency which interfered with the development
of the emotional life was also operative in the formation of the
superego. The shadowy structure of the oedipus complex was
gradually given up without ever having come to an integrated
and unified superego formation. One gains the impression that
the prerequisites for such a development also lie in strong oedipal
object cathexes.

It is not to be denied that at a very early age some inner prohibitions are present which are the precursors of the superego
and are intimately dependent on external objects. Identification
with the parents in the resolution of the oedipus complex brings
about the integration of these elements. Where this is absent, as it
was in our patient, the identifications remain vacillating and transitory. The representatives which go to make up the conscience

remain in the external world and instead of the development of inner morals there appears a persistent identification with external objects. In childhood, educational influences exerted an inhibitory effect on the instinctual life, particularly on the aggressions. In later life, in the absence of an adequate superego, she shifts the responsibility for her behavior to objects in the external world with whom she identifies herself. The passivity of this patient as the expression of her submission to the will of another seems to be the final transformation of her aggressive tendencies.

As the result of this weak superego structure, there is little contact between the ego and the superego, and the scene of all conflicts remains external, like the child for whom everything can proceed without friction if he but obey. Both the persistent identification and the passive submission are expressions of the patient's complete adaptation to the current environment, and impart the shadowy quality to the patient's personality. The value of this link to reality is questionable because the identification always takes place with only a part of the environment. If this part of the environment comes into conflict with the rest, naturally the patient is involved. Thus it can come about that the individual can be seduced into asocial or criminal acts by a change in his identifications, and it may well be that some of the asocial are recruited from the group of "as if" personalities who are adapted to reality in this restricted way.

Analysis of this patient revealed a genuine infantilism, that is, an arrest at a definite stage in the development of the emotional life and character formation. In addition to particularly unfavorable environmental influences, it should be noted that the patient came from a very old family overrun with psychotics and invalid psychopaths.

Another woman patient had a father who had a mental illness and a mother who was neurotic. She remembered her father only as "a man with a black beard," and she tried to explain as something very fascinating and wonderful, his absences as he was moved to and from a sanitarium and an isolated room at home, always under nursing care. Thus she built a myth around her father, replacing him in fantasy by a mysterious man, whom she later called an "Indian" and with whom she had all sorts of experiences, each of which served to make her a superhuman being. The prototype for the Indian was the father's male nurse, whom the little girl saw mysteriously disappearing into her father's room. The education and upbringing of the child were relegated to nurses, but despite this she succeeded in establishing a strong libidinous attachment to the very abnormal mother. Her later relationships had elements of object-libidinal attitudes, sometimes warmer, especially in homosexual directions, but never sufficiently to change their "as if" quality. The failure to develop an adequate object cathexis was, in this patient, related to the birth of her brother toward whom she developed an unusually aggressive envy. Comparisons of genitalia led the little girl to scrutinize her body for hours on end in a mirror. Later this narcissistic activity was gradually sublimated. At first she tried to model parts of her body in clay in order to facilitate her mirror studies. In the course of years she developed great skill in modeling and was for a brief time under the tutelage of a sculptress. Unconsciously, it was the fantasy of displaying repeatedly her body to the world. In later years she created only large, very voluptuous, matronly female figures. These proved to be weak attempts to recreate the mother she had lost in childhood to her brother. Ultimately she abandoned sculpture for music simply because she believed her teacher failed to appreciate her sufficiently.

Most conspicuous in her childhood was a monkeylike imitation of her brother with whom she was for years completely identified, not in fantasy but by acting out. Disastrously for both, the brother quite early betrayed unmistakable signs of a psychosis which culminated in a catatonic excitement. The sister imitated all her brother's bizarre activities and lived with him in a world of fantasy. Only her partial object-libidinal cathexis and a displacement of the process from the brother and identification with more normal objects saved her from being institutionalized. I was inclined at first to regard her condition as the result of an identification with her psychotic brother; only later did I recognize that the etiology of her condition lay deeper.

I believe this patient is similar to the first despite the differences in their development. In the second, it seems that a disappointment shattered the strong relationship with the mother, that the mysterious absence of the father made it impossible for the little girl to find in him a substitute when her relationship to her mother was shaken, and that further relationships to objects remained at the stage of identification. By such identification she averted her intense hatred of her brother and transformed her aggression toward him into an obedient passivity in which she submissively identified herself with him. She developed no other object relationships. Her superego suffered the same fate as that of the first patient. The myth of the father and the very early devaluation of the mother prevented integration of her superego and left her dependent on persons in the external world.

A third patient, a pretty, temperamental woman of thirty-five with many intellectual and artistic talents, came to analysis because she was "tired" after a long series of adventures. It soon became clear that, as the result of a certain combination of circumstances, her interest in psychoanalysis was actually an interest in the analyst, especially in her profession. While she frequently spoke of her tremendous interest in child psychology and in Freud's theory and read widely on these subjects, her understanding of them was extraordinarily superficial and her interest entirely unreal. More careful observation disclosed that this was true not only for all her intellectual interests but for everything she did or had ever done. It was surprising to recognize in this woman, who was so indefatigably active, a condition so closely related to the pseudo affectivity of the "as if" patient. All her experiences too were based on identifications, though her identifications were not so straightforward as were those of the other type of patient which is, one might say, more monogamous and adheres to but one person or one group at a time, while this patient had so many concurrent identifications—or symbolic representations of identifications—that her conduct appeared erratic. She was, in fact, considered "crazy" by those who knew her. Her friends, however, had no notion that her apparently rich life concealed a severe lack of affect. She had come to me because of a wish to change her character, that is, to create more peace and harmony in her life by identifying herself with a "particularly solid" professional personality.

After six months the analysis appeared to be unusually successful. The patient learned to understand many things about herself and lost her eccentricities. She determined to become an analyst and when this was denied her, she collapsed. She was completely lacking in affect and complained, "I am so empty! My God, I am so empty! I have no feelings." It transpired that prior to analysis she had got into serious financial difficulties by breaking off various friendships and love relationships and had realized that she would soon have to work. It was with this intention that she came to analysis. Her plan was to become an analyst by identification with her analyst. When this proved impossible, this seemingly very able and active woman changed into a completely passive person. From time to time she had extraordinarily violent fits of childish weeping or outbursts of rage, flung herself on the floor, and kicked and screamed. Gradually, she developed a progressive lack of affect. She became completely negativistic and met all interpretations with, "I don't understand what you mean by that."

At two points in this patient's development she had suffered severe trauma. Her father was an alcoholic, and the patient often witnessed his brutal mistreatment of the mother. She sided vehemently with the latter and, when she was only seven, had fantasies in which she rescued her mother from her misery and built a little white cottage for her. She saved every penny and worked hard in school to attain this aim, only to discover that her mother was not merely a passive victim of her husband but took pleasure in being brutalized. The consequent devaluation of her mother not only deprived her of her only object of love but also arrested the development of a feminine ego ideal of an independent, adequate personality. She spent the rest of her life trying to make up for this lack by creating a whole series of identifications, in the same way as the "as if" patients.

Deprived of tenderness and affection in her childhood, her instincts remained crudely primitive. She vacillated between giving these instincts free rein and holding them in check. She acted out prostitution fantasies, indulged in a variety of sexual perversions, often giving the impression of hypomania. She emerged from these debauches by identification with some conventional person and achieved by this means a kind of sublimation, the form dependent on the particular object. This resulted in a frequent shifting of her occupation and interests. So long as it was possible for her either to retain such a relationship or to allow herself the gratification of very primitive drives she was not aware of her lack of affect.

The following cases of emotional disturbances bear close similarity with the "as if" group but differ in certain respects.

A seventeen-year-old boy of unusual intellectual ability came for analysis because of manifest homosexuality and a conscious lack of feeling. This lack of emotion included his homosexual objects, about whom he created all sorts of perverse fantasies. He was obsessionally scrupulous, modest, exact, and reliable. He was passively oral and anal in his homosexuality. The analysis was extremely rich in material but progressed in an emotional vacuum. While the transference was frequently represented in his dreams and fantasies, it never became a conscious, emotional experience.

One day I gave him a ticket to a series of lectures in which I was taking part. He went to my lecture and had severe anxiety on the stairs leading to the lecture hall. By thus mobilizing his anxiety in the transference, the analysis began to progress.

An only child from a highly cultured environment, with a father who was strict and ambitious and a mother who dedicated her life to this handsome and talented son, he nevertheless suffered the fate of affective deficiency. The fact that he grew up in an atmosphere in which he never needed to seek for love, that he was overwhelmed with tenderness without having to make any effort to obtain it paralyzed his own active strivings for tenderness. He remained bound to primitive instinctual impulses, and because there were few infantile anxieties which were not warded off with scrupulous care, there was no motive in him to build up defense mechanisms.

He underwent the trauma of the depreciation of his ego ideal when he discovered that his admired father was uncultivated and limited. This realization threatened to depreciate his own value, for he was like his father, bore his name, and heard his resemblance to him repeatedly stressed by his mother. Through rigidity and strictness, in ethical and intellectual demands, he strove to become better than the self which was identified with the father. In contrast to the previous patients, he did not identify himself with a series of objects. Instead of having emotional relationships to people, he was split into two identifications: one with his beloved mother and the other with his father. The first was feminine and sexualized; the second was overcompensatory, rigid, and narcissistic.

Unlike the "as if" patients, he complained of lack of feeling. He completely lacked the tender emotions which would have given warmth to his emotional life. He had no relation to any woman, and his friendships with men were either purely intellectual or crudely sexual. The feelings he had were of a character he would not let himself express. These were very primitive aggressions, the wildest, most infantile sexual drives, which were rejected with the declaration, "I feel nothing at all." In one way he told the truth; he was really lacking in any permissible feelings, that is, in the tender, sublimated emotions.

The tendency to identification is characteristic also of this type of affective disturbance. Even though this patient did not completely sink his personality in a series of identifications, the strongest section of his ego, his intellect, lacked originality. Everything he wrote and said in scientific matters showed great formal talent but when he tried to produce something original it usually turned out to be a repetition of ideas which he had once grasped with particular clarity. The tendency to multiple identifications occurred on the intellectual level.

Another patient of this group, a thirty-year-old married woman who came from a family in which there were many psychotics, complained about lack of emotion. In spite of good intelligence and perfect reality testing, she led a sham existence and she was always just what was suggested to her by the environment. It became clear that she could experience nothing except a completely passive readiness to split into an endless number of identifications. This condition had set in acutely after an operation in her childhood for which she had been given no psychological preparation. On recovery from the anesthesia she asked if she were really herself, and then developed a state of depersonalization which lasted a year and turned into passive suggestibility which concealed a crippling anxiety.

Common to all these cases is a deep disturbance of the process of sublimation which results both in a failure to synthesize the various infantile identifications into a single, integrated personality, and in an imperfect, one-sided, purely intellectual sublimation of the instinctual strivings. While critical judgement and the intellectual powers may be excellent, the emotional and moral part of the personality is lacking.

The etiology of such conditions is related, first, to a devaluation of the object serving as a model for the development of the child's personality. This devaluation may have a firm foundation in reality or be traceable, for example, to shock at discovery of parental coitus at a period of development when the child is engaged in his last struggles against masturbation and needs support in his efforts toward sublimation. Or, as in the case of the boy described above, the successful sublimation may be interfered with by a sexualization of the relationship to an object who should serve the child as a model for his ego ideal, in this instance, a grossly sexual identification with his mother.

Another cause of this kind of emotional disturbance is insufficient stimulus for the sublimation of the emotions, as the result either of being given too little tenderness, or too much.

Infantile anxiety may suffer a similar fate. Too harsh or too indulgent treatment may contribute to failure in the economic formation of defense mechanisms resulting in remarkable passivity of the ego. It will be recalled that in the case of the boy reported, an attack of anxiety not only mobilized the transference but also opened the way to his recovery.

The question must be raised as to how the tendency of "as if" personalities to identification with current love objects differs from the same tendency in hysteria. The great difference between the latter and the "as if" disturbance lies in the fact that the objects with which the hysterics identify themselves are the objects of powerful libidinal cathexes. Hysterical repression of affect brings freedom from anxiety and so represents a way out of the conflict. In "as if" patients, an early deficiency in the development of affect reduces the inner conflict, the effect of which is an impoverishment of the total personality which does not occur in hysteria.

The patients described here might make one suspect that we are dealing with something like the blocking of affect seen especially in narcissistic individuals who have developed loss of feeling through repression. The great fundamental difference, however, is that the "as if" personality tries to simulate affective experience, whereas the individual with a blocking of affect does not. In the analysis of the latter it can always be shown that the once-developed object relationships and aggressive feelings have undergone repression and are not at the disposal of the conscious personality. The repressed, affectively toned segment of the personality is gradually uncovered during the analysis, and it is sometimes possible to make the buried part of the emotional life available to the ego.

For example, one patient had completely repressed the memory of his mother who died when he was four, and with whom, it was clear, the greater part of his emotions had been involved. Under the influence of a very weak but nonetheless effective transference, isolated memories gradually emerged. At first these had a negative character and denied all tenderness. During analysis this patient showed also another form of emotional disturbance, namely, depersonalization. Before analysis his self-satisfaction had been unshaken. He defended himself against the transference with all his power. In the analytic hours, when clear signs of a transference *in statu nascendi* were perceptible, the patient would complain of sudden feelings of strangeness. It was clear that in him the depersonalization corresponded to the perception of a change in cathexis. It remained a question whether this was due to a new libidinal stream emerging from repression, or to a suppression of feelings connected with transference. The inner conflict in such an instance of repression of affect has little similarity to that of an "as if" patient. The analogy rests only on the affective impoverishment in both.

The narcissism and the poverty of object relationships so characteristic for an "as if" person bring to consideration the relationship of this defect to a psychosis. The fact that reality testing is fully maintained removes this condition from our conception of psychosis.

Narcissistic identification as a preliminary stage to object cathexis, and introjection of the object after its loss, are among the most important discoveries of Freud and Abraham. The psychological structure of melancholia offers us the classical example of this process. In melancholia, the object of identification has been psychologically internalized, and a tyrannical superego carries on the conflict with the incorporated object in complete independence of the external world. In "as if" patients, the objects are kept external and all conflicts are acted out in relation to them. Conflict with the superego is thus avoided because in every gesture and in every act the "as if" ego subordinates itself through identification to the wishes and commands of an authority which has never been introjected.

From the beginning, both the personal impression given by the patients themselves and the psychotic disposition in the family, especially in the first two analytically observed cases, make one suspect a schizophrenic process. The tracing of the severe psychic disturbance directly back to the developments of early childhood seems to me completely justified, and whether this speaks against the diagnosis of a schizophrenic process must, for the time being, be left undecided. My observations of schizophrenic patients have given me the impression that the schizophrenic process goes through an "as if" phase before it builds up the delusional form. A twenty-two-year-old schizophrenic girl came to me after a catatonic attack, oriented for time and place but full of delusional ideas. Until the onset of the confusional state she had led an existence almost indistinguishable from "as if" patients. Her bond to objects with whom she identified herself, and who were always outstanding women, was extremely intense. As a result of rapid shifting of these relationships, she changed her place of residence, her studies, and her interests in an almost manic fashion. Her last identification had led her from the home of a well-established American family to a Communistic cell in Berlin. A sudden desertion by her object led her from Berlin to Paris where she was manifestly paranoid and gradually developed a severe confusion. Treatment restored her to her original state, but despite warnings, her family decided to break off the analysis. The girl was not able to summon enough affect to protest. One day she bought a dog and told me that now everything would be all right; she would imitate the dog and then she would know how she should act. Identification was retained but was no longer limited to human objects; it included animals, inanimate objects, concepts, and symbols, and it was this lack of selectivity which gave the process its delusional character. It was the loss of the capacity for identification with human objects which made possible the erection of a new, delusional world.

Another schizophrenic patient for years had had a recurrent dream in which in great pain and torment she sought her mother but could not find her because she was always faced with an endless crowd of women, each of whom looked like her mother, and she could not tell the right one. This dream reminded me of the stereotyped, recurrent mother figures in the sculpture of the second "as if" patient.

Freud (1923) speaks of "multiple personality" as the result of a process in which numerous identifications lead to a disruption of the ego. This may result in manifest psychopathology, or the conflicts between the different identifications can assume a form which need not necessarily be designated as pathological. Freud refers to a purely inner process of ego formation, and this does not apply to the "as if" identifications with objects in the outer world. However, the same psychological process will also in the "as if" personality on one occasion have a more "normal" resolution and on another a pathological outcome which may be more or less severe.

Anna Freud (1936) points out that the type of pseudo affectivity observed in "as if" patients is often found in puberty. I believe that the depreciation of the primary objects (also typical of puberty) who served as models for the ego ideal plays an important role in both. Anna Freud describes this type of behavior in puberty as incurring the suspicion of psychosis. I believe that the reflections which I have presented here will also serve for puberty. At one time the process will lie within the bounds of the "normal" and at another it bears the seeds of a pathological condition. The type justifies the designation "schizoid," whether or not schizophrenia later develops.

Whether the emotional disturbances described in this paper imply a "schizophrenic disposition" or constitute rudimentary symptoms of schizophrenia is not clear to me. These patients represent variants in the series of abnormal distorted personalities. They do not belong among the commonly accepted forms of neurosis, and they are too well adjusted to reality to be called psychotic. While psychoanalysis seldom succeeds, the practical results of treatment can be very far reaching, particularly if a strong identification with the analyst can be utilized as an active and constructive influence. In so far as they are accessible to analysis, one may be able to learn much in the field of ego psychology, especially with regard to disturbances of affect, and, perhaps, make contributions to the problems of the "schizoid" which is still so obscure.

In the great delusional formations of the psychoses we see primitive and archaic drives returning from the depths of the unconscious in a dramatic manner. Regression takes place because the ego has failed. We speak of this as a "weakness of the ego" and assume that the reasons for this failure are psychological, constitutional, or organic. Psychoanalysis can investigate the first of these, especially in prepsychotic conditions to which these cases belong.

Chapter 22

A STUDY OF FAIRBAIRN'S THEORY OF SCHIZOID REACTIONS

HARRY GUNTRIP

The Schizoid Condition

The psychotherapist must be greatly concerned with those states of mind in which patients become inaccessible emotionally, when the patient seems to be bodily present but mentally absent. A patient, A., recently said "I don't seem to come here" as if she came in body but did not bring herself with her. She found herself in the same state of mind when she asked the young man next door to go for a walk with her. He did and she became tired, dull, unable to talk; she commented: "It was the same as when I come here: I don't seem to be present." Her reactions to food were similar. She would long for a nice meal and sit down to it and find her appetite gone, as if she had nothing to do with eating. One patient, B., dreamed: "My husband and I came to see you and he explained that I wasn't here because I'd gone to hospital." Complaints of feeling cut off, shut off, out of touch, feeling apart or strange, of things being out of focus or unreal, of not feeling one with people, or of the point having gone out of life, interest flagging, things seeming futile and meaningless, all describe in various ways this state of mind. Patients often call it "depression," but it lacks the heavy, black, inner sense of brooding, of anger and of guilt, which are not difficult to discover in depression. Depression is really a more extraverted state of mind, in which the patient is struggling not to break out into angry and aggressive behavior. The states described above are rather the "schizoid states." They are definitely introverted.

This chapter originally appeared in the *British Journal of Medical Psychology,* 25:86–103, 1952. Reprinted by permission of the publisher.

407

External relationships seem to have been emptied by a massive withdrawal of the real libidinal self. Effective mental activity has disappeared into a hidden inner world; the patient's conscious ego is emptied of vital feeling and action, and seems to have become unreal. You may catch glimpses of intense activity going on in the inner world through dreams and phantasies, but the patient's conscious ego merely reports these as if it were a neutral observer not personally involved in the inner drama of which it is a detached spectator. The attitude to the outer world is the same; *noninvolvement and observation at a distance without any feeling,* like that of a press reporter describing a social gathering of which he is not a part, in which he has no personal interest, and by which he is bored. When a schizoid state supervenes, the conscious ego appears to be in a state of suspended animation in between two worlds, internal and external and having no real relationships with either of them. It has decreed an emotional and impulsive standstill, on the basis of keeping out of affective range and being unmoved.

These schizoid states may alternate with depression, and at times seem to be rather confusingly mixed with it so that both schizoid and depressive signs appear. They are of all degrees of intensity ranging from transient moods that come and go during a session, to states that persist over a long period, when they show very clearly and distinctly the specific schizoid traits.

An example of a patient, C., describing herself as depressed when she's really schizoid may be useful at this point. She opened the session by saying: "I'm very depressed. I've been just sitting and couldn't get out of the chair. There seemed no purpose anywhere, the future blank. I'm very bored and want a big change. I feel hopeless, resigned, no way out, stuck. I'm wondering how I can manage somehow just to get around and put up with it." (Analyst: "Your solution is to damp everything down, don't feel anything, give up all real relationship to people on an emotional level, and just 'do things' in a mechanical way, be a robot.") Her reaction brought out clearly the schizoid trait: "Yes, I felt I didn't care, didn't register anything. Then I felt alarmed, felt this was dangerous. If I hadn't made myself do something I'd have just sat, not bothered, not interested." (Analyst: "That's your reaction in analysis to me: don't be influenced, don't be moved, don't be lured into reacting to me.") Her reply was: "If I were moved at all, I'd feel very annoyed with you. I hate and detest you for making me feel like this. The more I'm inclined to be drawn towards you, the more I feel a fool, undermined."

The mere fact of the analyst's presence as another human being with whom she needed to be emotionally real, that is, express what she was actually feeling, created an emotional crisis in her with which she could only deal by abolishing the relationship. So her major defense against her anxieties is to keep herself emotionally out of reach, inaccessible, and keep everyone at arm's length. She once said: "I'd rather hate you than love you," but this goes even further. She will neither love nor hate, she won't feel anything at all, and outwardly in sessions often appears lazy, bored at coming, and with a "laissez faire" attitude. This then is the problem we seek to understand. What is really happening to these patients and why?

Fairbairn's Theory of Schizoid Reactions

The purpose of this paper is to state Fairbairn's theory of schizoid reactions and to illustrate it by clinical material. His revolutionary rethinking of psychoanalytical theory was first presented as a recasting of the classic libido theory and as a revised psychopathology of the psychoses and psychoneuroses. Only two points in his theory need be mentioned here.

1. First he laid it down that the goal of the individual's libido is not pleasure, or merely subjective gratification, but the object itself. He says: "Pleasure is the sign-post to the object" (1941, p. 255). The fundamental fact about human nature is our libidinal drive toward good object relationships. The key biological formula is the adaptation of the organism to the environment. The key psychological formula is the relationship of the person to the human environment. The significance of human living lies in object-relationships, and only in such terms can our life be said to have a meaning.

Quite specially in this region lie the schizoid's problems. He is driven by anxiety to cut off all object relations. Our needs, fears, frustrations, resentments and anxieties in our inevitable quest for good objects are the real problem in psychopathology, because they are the real problem in life itself. When difficulties in achieving and maintaining good object relations are too pronounced, and human relations are attended with too great anxiety and conflict, desperate efforts are often made to deny and eliminate this basic need. People go into their shell, bury themselves in work of an impersonal nature, abolish relations with actual people so far as they can and devote themselves to abstractions, ideals, theories, organizations,[1] and so on. In the nature of the case these maneuvers cannot succeed and always end disastrously, since they are an attempt to deny our very nature itself. Clearly we cannot do that and remain healthy.

The more people cut themselves off from human relations in the outer world, the more they are driven back on object-relations in their inner mental world, till the psychotic lives only in his inner world. But it is still a world of object relations. We are constitutionally incapable of living as isolated units. The real loss of all objects would be equivalent to psychic death. Karen Horney (1946) says: "Neuroses are generated by disturbances in human relationships." But Horney thinks only in terms of relations to external objects at the conscious level. The real heart of the matter is a far less obvious danger, a repressed world of internalized psychic objects, bad objects, and "bad-object situations." What is new in all this is the theory of internal objects as developed in more elaborate form by Melanie Klein and Fairbairn, and the fact that Fairbairn makes object relations, not instinctual impulses, the prior and important thing. It is the object that is the real goal of the libidinal drive. We seek persons not pleasures. Impulses are not psychic entities but reactions of an ego to objects.

What is meant by a world of internal objects may be expressed as follows: in some sense we retain all our experience in life and "carry things in our minds." If we did not, we would lose all continuity with our past, would only be able to live from moment to moment like butterflies alighting and flitting away, and no relationships or experiences could have any permanent values

[1]This does not imply that such activities are necessarily always schizoid. That depends on how much personal feeling enters into the activity.

for us. Thus in some sense everything is mentally internalized, retained, and inwardly possessed; that is our only defense against complete discontinuity in living, a distressing example of which we see in the man who loses his memory, and is consciously uprooted.

But things are mentally internalized and retained in two different ways which we call respectively *memory* and *internal objects*. Good objects are, in the first place, mentally internalized and retained only as memories. They are enjoyed at the time, the experience is satisfying and leaves no problems, and can later on be looked back to and reflected on with pleasure. In the case of a continuing good-object relationship of major importance as with a parent or marriage partner, we have a combination of memories of the happy past and confidence in the continuing possession of the good object in an externally real sense in the present and future. There is no reason here for setting up internalized objects. Outer experience suffices to meet our needs. On this point Fairbairn differs from Melanie Klein.

Objects are only internalized in a more radical way when the relationship turns into a bad-object situation through, say, the object changing or dying. When someone we need and love ceases to love us, or behaves in such a way that we interpret it as cessation of love, that person becomes, in an emotional, libidinal sense, a bad object. This happens to a child when his mother refuses the breast, weans the baby, or is cross, impatient, and punitive, or is absent temporarily or for a longer period through illness, or permanently through death: it also happens when the person we need is emotionally detached and aloof and unresponsive. All that is experienced as frustration of the most important of all needs, as rejection and desertion or else as persecution and attack. Then the lost object, now become a bad object, is mentally internalized in a much more vital and fundamental sense than memory. Bereaved people dream vividly of the lost loved one, even years afterwards, as still actually alive. A patient, beset by a life long fear of dying, was found under analysis, to be persistently dreaming of dead men in coffins. In one dream, the coffined figure was behind a curtain and his mind was on it all the time while he was busy in the dream with cheerful social activities. A fatal inner attraction to, and attachment to, the dead man threatened him and set up an actual fear of dying. The dead man was his father as he had seen him actually in his coffin. Another patient had a nightmare of his mother violently losing her temper with him, after she had been dead twelve years. *An inner psychic world* (Riviere, 1952) *has been set up duplicating the original situation, but it is an unhappy world in which one is tied to bad objects and feeling therefore always frustrated, hungry, angry, and guilty, and profoundly anxious.*

It is bad objects which are internalized, because we cannot accept their badness and yet cannot give them up, cannot leave them alone, cannot master and control them in outer reality and so keep on struggling to possess them, alter them and compel them to change into good objects, in our inner psychic world. They never do change. In our inner unconscious world where we repress and lock away very early in life our original bad objects, they remain always rejecting, indifferent, or hostile to us according to our actual outer experience. It must be emphasized that these internalized objects are not just phantasies. The child is emotionally identified with his objects, and when he mentally incorporates them he remains identified with them and they become part and parcel of the very psychic structure of his personality. The phantasies in which internal objects reveal their existence to consciousness are activities of the structures which constitute the internal objects. Objects are only internalized later in life in this radical way by fusion with already existing internal-object structures. In adult life situations in outer reality are unconsciously interpreted in the light of these situations persisting in unconscious, inner, and purely psychic reality. We live in the outer world with the emotions generated in the inner one. The fundamental psychopathological problem is: how do people deal with their internalized bad objects, to what extent do they feel identified with them, and how do they complicate relations with external objects. It is the object all the time that matters, whether external or internal, not pleasure.

2. From this point of view Fairbairn constructed a revised theory of the psychoses and psychoneuroses, the second point relevant for our purpose. In the orthodox Freud–Abraham view, these illnesses were due to arrests of libidinal development at fixation points in the first five years: schizophrenia at the oral sucking stage, manic-depression at the oral biting stage, paranoia at

the early anal; obsessions at the late anal; and hysteria at the phallic or early genital stages. Fairbairn proposed a totally different view, based not on the fate of libidinal impulses, but on the nature of relationships with internal bad objects. For him, *the schizoid and depressive states are the two fundamental types of reaction in bad-object relationships, the two basic or ultimate dangers to be escaped from.* They originate in the difficulties experienced in object relationships in the oral stage of absolute infantile dependence and he treats of paranoia, obsessions, hysteria, and phobias as four different techniques for dealing with internal bad objects so as to master them and ward off a relapse into the depressed or schizoid state of mind. This makes intelligible the fact that patients ring the changes actually on paranoid, obsessional, hysteric, and phobic reactions even if any particular patient predominantly favors one technique most of the time. The psychoneuroses are, basically, defenses against internal bad-object situations which would otherwise set up depressive or schizoid states; though these situations are usually reactivated by a bad external situation.

Thus what has to be done in deep treatment is to help the patient to drop these unsatisfactory techniques which never solve the problem, and find courage to become conscious of what lies behind these symptom-producing struggles with internal bad objects; in other words, to risk going back into the basic bad-object situations in which they feel they are succumbing to one or other of the two ultimate psychic dangers, depression or schizoid loss of affect. Naturally depressive and schizoid reactions constantly break through into consciousness, in varying degrees of severity, in spite of defenses.

3. The nature of the two ultimately dangerous situations may be simply described. When you want love from a person who will not give it and so becomes a bad object to you, you can react in either or both of two ways. You may become angry and enraged at the frustration and want to make an aggressive attack on the bad object to force it to become good and stop frustrating you: like a small child who cannot get what it wants from the mother and who flies into a temper tantrum and hammers on her with his little fists. This is the problem of hate or love made angry. It is an attack on a hostile, rejecting, actively refusing bad object.

It leads to *depression* for it rouses the fear that one's hate will destroy the very person one needs and loves.

But there is an earlier and more basic reaction. When you cannot get what you want from the person you need, instead of getting angry you may simply go on getting more and more hungry, and full of a sense of painful craving, and a longing to get total and complete possession of your love object so that you cannot be left to starve. *Love made hungry* is the *schizoid* problem and it rouses the terrible fear that one's love has become so devouring and incorporative that love itself has become destructive. Depression is the fear of loving lest one's hate should destroy. Schizoid aloofness is the fear of loving lest one's love should destroy, which is far worse.

This difference of the two attitudes goes along with a difference in appearance, so to speak, of the object. The schizoid sees the object as a desirable deserter, or as Fairbairn calls it, an exciting *needed object*[2] whom he must go after hungrily but then draw back from lest he should devour and destroy it in his desperately intense need to get total possession of it. The depressive sees the object as a hateful denier, or in Fairbairn's term a *rejecting object* to be destroyed out of the way to make room for a good object. Thus one patient constantly dreams of wanting a woman who goes away and leaves him, while another dreams of furious, murderous anger against a sinister person who robs him or gets between him and what he wants. The schizoid is hungry for a desirable deserter, the depressive is murderous against a hateful robber.

Thus the two fundamental forms of internal bad objects are, in Fairbairn's terminology, the needed object and the rejecting object. In the course of years many externally real figures of both sexes may be absorbed, by layering and fusion, into these two internal bad objects, but at bottom they remain always two aspects of the breast–mother. They are always there, and parts of the ego (split off, disowned, secondary, or subsidiary "selves") are always having disturbing relationships with them, so that the depressive is always being goaded to anger, and the schizoid always being tantalized and made hungry.

---

[2]Fairbairn now prefers simply the term *Exciting Object* (EO).

The depressive position is later and more developed than the schizoid, for it is ambivalent. The hateful robber is really an aspect of the same person who is needed and desired, as if the mother excites the child's longing for her, gives him just enough to tantalize and inflame his appetite, and then robs him by taking herself away. This was neatly expressed in patient C.'s dream. "I was enjoying my favorite meal and saved the nicest bit to the end, and then mother snatched it (the breast, herself) away under my nose. I was furious but when I protested she said 'Don't be a baby.' " There is the guilt reaction, agreeing with the denier against oneself and giving up one's own needs. Fairbairn holds that depression has occupied too exclusively the center of the picture of psychopathological states as a result of Freud's concentration on obsessions with their ambivalence, guilt, and superego problems. He believes the schizoid condition is the fundamental problem and is preambivalent.

Melanie Klein (1932, 1948) stressed how ambivalence rises to its maximum over the weaning crisis at a time when the infant has learned to bite and can react sadistically. Love and hate block each other. The infant attacks and also feels identified with, the object of his aggression, and so feels guilty and involves himself in the fate, factual or phantasied, of the object. Hate of the object involves hate of oneself, you suffer with the object you attack because you cannot give up the object and feel one with it. Hence the familiar guilt and depression after a bereavement: you feel guilty as if you have killed the lost person and depressed as if you were dying with him or her. Three patients who all suffered marked guilt and depression recovered repressed and internalized deathbed scenes of a parent.

What is the meaning of hate? It is not the absolute opposite of love; that would be indifference, having no interest in a person, not wanting a relationship and so having no reason for either loving or hating, feeling nothing. Hate is love grown angry because of rejection. We can only really hate a person if we want their love. Hate is an expression of frustrated love needs, an attempt to destroy the bad rejecting side of a person in the hope of leaving their good responsive side available, a struggle to alter them. The anxiety is over the danger of hate destroying both sides, and the easiest way out is to find two objects and love one and hate the other.

But as we have seen, the individual can adopt an earlier simpler reaction. Instead of reacting with anger, he can react with an
enormously exaggerated sense of need. Desire becomes hunger
and hunger becomes greed which is hunger grown frightened of
losing what it wants. He feels so uncertain about possessing his
love-object that he feels a desperate craving to make sure of it by
getting it inside him, swallowing it and incorporating it. This is
illustrated by patient B., who phantasied standing with a vacuum
cleaner (herself, empty and hungry), and everyone who came
near she sucked them into it. At a more normal and ordinarily
conscious level this is expressed by patient C., thus: "I'm afraid I
couldn't make moderate demands on people, so I don't make
any demands at all." Many people show openly this devouring
possessiveness toward those they love. Many more repress it and
keep out of real relations.

This dream brings out the schizoid situation. So much fear is
felt of devouring everyone and so losing everyone in the process,
that a general withdrawal from all external relationships is
embarked on. Retreat into indifference, the true opposite of love
which is felt to be too dangerous to express. Want no one, make
no demands, abolish all external relationships, and be aloof,
cold, without any feeling, do not be moved by anything. The
withdrawn libido is turned inwards, introverted. The patient
goes into his shell and is busy only with internal objects, toward
whom he feels the same devouring attitude. Outwardly everything seems futile and meaningless. Fairbairn considers that a sense
of "futility" is the specific schizoid affect. Just as the depressive is
identified with the one he attacks and so hurts himself, so the
schizoid is identified with the object he devours and loses, and so
loses himself; for example, the snake eating its own tail. The
depressive fears loss of his object. The schizoid, in addition, fears
loss of his ego, of himself.

The Schizoid's Relation to Objects (Need and Fear of Object Relations)

Active. Fear of Loss of the Object

The Object as a Desired Deserter or "Needed Object." Theory only
lives when it is seen as describing the actual relations of real peo-

ple, though the material revealing the schizoid position only becomes undisguisedly accessible at deep levels of analysis, and is often not reached when defenses are reasonably effective. In the very unstable schizoid it breaks through with disconcerting ease, a bad sign.

A headmaster, D., described himself as depressed, and went on to say, "I don't feel so worried about the school or hopeless about the future." He had said the same things the week before and regarded it as a sign of improvement, but the real meaning emerged when he remarked "Perhaps my interest in school has flagged" and it appeared that his loss of the sense of hopelessness about the future was due to his not thinking about the future. He had cut it off. He then reported a dream of visiting a camp school. "The resident head walked away when I arrived and left me to fend for myself and there was no meal ready for me." He remarked: "I'm preoccupied with what I'm going to eat and when, yet I don't eat a lot. Also I want to get away from people and am more comfortable when eating alone. I'm concerned at my loss of interest in school. I don't feel comfortable with father and prefer to be in another room. I'm very introverted; I feel totally cut off."

Here is a gradually emerging description, not of depression but of a schizoid state, loss of interest in present and future, loss of appetite for food, getting away from people, introverted, totally cut off. The situation that calls out the reaction is that of being faced with a desired but deserting object, the head in the dream who prepares no meal for him, and leaves him to fend for himself when he is hungry. The head is the father, of whom he complains that he can never get near him: also the analyst to whom he says: "you remain the analyst, you won't indulge me in a warm personal relationship, you won't be my friend. I want something more personal than analysis." The schizoid is very sensitive and quickly feels unwanted, because he is always being deserted in his inner world.

Faced with these desired deserters he first feels exaggeratedly hungry, and then denies his hunger, eats little and turns away from people till he feels introverted and totally cut off. He has withdrawn his libido from the objects he cannot possess, and feels loss of interest and loss of appetite. There is little evidence of anger and guilt as there would be in depression; his attitude is more that of fear and retreat.

The Object as Being Devoured. This entire problem is frequently worked out over food. The above patient is hungry but rejects both food and people. He can only eat alone. The patient C. says that whenever her husband comes in she at once feels hungry and must eat. Really she is hungry for him but dare not show it. The same turning away from what one feels too greedily and devouringly hungry for is shown very clearly by this same patient in other ways. Visiting friends she was handed a glass of sherry, took a quick sip and put it down and did not touch it again. She had felt she wanted to swallow it at one gulp. Her general attitude to food was one of rejection. Appetite would disappear at the sight of food, she would nibble at a dish and push it away, or force it down and feel sick. But what lay behind this rejecting attitude was expressed in a dream in which she was eating an enormous meal and just went on and on endlessly. She is getting as much as she can inside her before it is taken away as in the dream where her mother whipped it away under her nose. Her attitude is incorporative, to get it inside where she cannot be robbed of it, because she has no confidence about being given enough. The breast one is sure of can be sucked at contentedly and let go when one feels satisfied: one knows it will be available when needed again. The breast that does not come when wanted, is not satisfying when one has it because it might be snatched away before need is met. It rouses a desperate hungry urge to make sure of it, not by merely sucking at it but by swallowing it, getting it inside one altogether. The impulse changes from "taking in from the breast" into an omnivorous urge to "take in the whole breast itself." The object is incorporated. The contented baby sucks, the angry and potentially depressive baby bites, the hungry and potentially schizoid baby wants to swallow, as in the case of the vacuum cleaner phantasy. A patient who at first made sucking noises in sessions, then changed to compulsive gulping and swallowing and nausea.

Fairbairn (1941, p. 252) writes: "The paranoid, obsessional, and hysterical states—to which may be added the phobic state— essentially represent, not products of fixations at specific libidinal phases, but simply a variety of techniques employed to defend the ego against the effects of conflicts of oral origin."

Now, as Fairbairn says: "You can't eat your cake and have it." This hungry, greedy, devouring, swallowing up, incorporating attitude leads to deep fears lest the real external object be lost. This anxiety about destroying and losing the love object through being so devouringly hungry is terribly real. Thus the patient C., who has become more conscious of her love-hunger with the result that on the one hand her appetite for food has increased enormously, and on the other her anxious attitude to her husband has become more acute, says: "When he comes in I feel ravenously hungry, and eat, but towards him I'm afraid I'm a nuisance. If I make advances to him I keep saying 'I'm not a nuisance am I, you don't "not want me" do you?' I'm terribly anxious about it all, it's an appalling situation, I'm scared stiff, it's all so violent. I've an urge to get hold of him and hold him so tight that he can't breathe, shut him off from everything but me." She has the same transference reaction to the analyst. She dreamed that "I came for treatment and you were going off to America with a lot of people. Someone dropped out so I went and you weren't pleased." Her comment was "you didn't want me but I wasn't going to be thrown off. I was thinking today of your getting ill, suppose you died. Then I got in a furious temper. I'd like to strangle you, kill you." That is, get a stranglehold on the analyst so that he could not leave her, but then he might be killed. The schizoid person is afraid of wearing out, of draining, or exhausting and ultimately losing love objects. As Fairbairn says, the terrible dilemma of the schizoid is that love itself is destructive, and he dare not love. Hence he withdraws into detachment and aloofness. All intimate relationships are felt in terms of eating, swallowing up, and are too dangerous to be risked. The above patient says: "I lay half awake looking at my husband and thinking, 'What a pity he's going to die.' It seemed fixed. Then I felt lonely, no point of relationship with all I could see. I love him so much but I seem to have no choice about destroying him. I want something badly and then I daren't move a finger to get it. I'm paralyzed."

Schizoid Reactions to Food and Eating. From the foregoing we may summarize the schizoid's reactions to food and eating, for since his basic problems in relation to objects derive from his basic reactions to the breast, food and eating naturally play a large part in his struggles to solve these problems. His reactions to people and to food are basically the same. Thus patient C. says: "Two men friends make me excited but it's not even a taste, only a smell of a good meal. I'm always feeling I want to be with one or the other of them, but I can't do it or I'll lose them both. One of them kissed me and I gave him a hug and a kiss and enjoyed it and wanted more. Ought I? I've sought desperately for so long and now I feel I must run away from it. I don't want to eat these days. I couldn't sleep. I felt I'd lost him: what if he or I had an accident and got killed. It's ridiculous but I'm in a constant furore of anxiety, I must see him: nothing else matters. I knew I'd be like this if I didn't see him but I didn't go. It's funny, I don't think I'm in love with him, yet I need him desperately. I can't engage in any other activity. I felt the same way with a fellow ten years ago. He went away for a day and I was in an agony of fear; what if he were killed, an awful dread. It feels like it must happen. I don't even like mentioning it in case this present friend gets killed, and I feel I'll have an accident, too. I get desperately tired, and feel empty inside and have to buy sweet biscuits and gobble them up."

Thus she has the kind of relation with this man (and with all objects) that compromises her stable existence as a separate person when she is not with him: she goes to bits. She wants to eat him up as it were, and feels swallowed up in her relation to him, and feels the destruction of both is inevitable whether she is with him or apart from him.

The patient B., before she started analysis, was having visual hallucinations of leopards leaping across in front of her with their mouths wide open. At an advanced stage of treatment these faded into phantasies and she had a phantasy of two leopards trying to swallow each other's head. She would enjoy a hearty meal and then promptly be sick and reject it. *There is a constant oscillation between hungry eating and refusal to eat, longing for people and rejecting them.*

The Transference Situation. The necessary and inevitable frustration of a patient's libidinal needs in the analytical situation is peculiarly well adapted to bring out schizoid reactions, as we have already noted. The patient longs for the analyst's love, may recognize intellectually that a steady, consistent, genuine, concern for the patient's well-being is a true form of love, yet, because it is not love in a full libidinal sense (Fairbairn reminds us that it is *agape,* not *eros*), the patient does not "feel" it as love. He feels rather that the analyst is cold, indifferent, bored, not interested, not listening, busy with something else while the patient talks, rejective. Patients will react to the analyst's silence by stopping talking to make him say something. The analyst excites by his presence but does not libidinally satisfy, and so constantly arouses a hungry craving.

The patient will then begin to feel he is bad for the analyst, that he is wasting his time, depressing him by pouring out a long story of troubles. He will want, and fear, to make requests lest he is imposing on the analyst and making illegitimate demands. He may say "How on earth can you stand this constant strain of listening to this sort of thing day after day?" and in general feels he is draining and exhausting, that is, devouring, the analyst.

He will oscillate between expressing his need and feeling guilty about it. The patient A. says: "I felt I must get possession of something of yours. I thought I'd come early and enjoy your armchair and read your books in the waiting room." But then she switches over to: "You can't possibly want to let me take up your time week after week." Guilt and anxiety then dictate a reversal of the original relationship. The patient must now be passive and begins to see the analyst as the active devourer. He drains the patient of resources by charging fees, he wants to dominate and subjugate the patient, he will rob him of his personality. A patient, after a long silence, says: "I'm thinking I must be careful, you're going to get something out of me." The analyst will absorb or rob the patient.

This terrible oscillation may make a patient feel confused and not know where he is. Thus a patient, E., says:

> I've been thinking I might lose your help, you'll make an excuse to get rid of me. I want more analysis but you don't bother with me. Analysis is only a very small part of a week. You don't understand me. There's a part of me I don't bring into analysis. I might be swallowed up in your personality and lose my individuality, so I adopt a condescending attitude to you. What you say isn't important, you're only a bourgeois therapist and don't understand the conditions of my life, your focus of analytical capacity is tiny, you're

cabined within bourgeois ideas. But if I said what I felt, I'd make you depressed and lose your support. You ought to be able to give me specific advice to help me when I feel helpless and imprisoned. I feel much the same with my girl. In analysis I feel I should get out, and away from it I feel I should be in. This week I feel in a "no man's land."

Here the whole dilemma of "craving for" yet "not being able to accept" the needed person, comes out in transference on the analyst. The swing over in transference to the opposite, from "devouring" to "being devoured," leads to the specific consideration of the passive aspect of the schizoid's relation to objects.

Passive. Fear of the Loss of Independence

The Object as Devouring the Ego. The patients' fears of a devouring sense of need toward objects is paralleled by the fear that others have the same "swallowing up" attitude to them. Thus patient C. says: "I can't stand crowds, they swallow me up. With you I feel if I accept your help I'll be subjugated, lose my personality, be smothered. Now I feel withdrawn like a snail, but now you can't swallow me up. I get a 'shutting myself off' attitude which lessens my anxiety."

The patient B., a very schizoid married woman of thirty, has for a long time been talking out devouring phantasies of all kinds, and slowly emerging from her schizoid condition. She was thin, white, cold, aloof, frigid: often it was some time before she could start talking in session, and would arrive terrified but hiding it under an automatic laugh or bored expression. When she did start talking she would begin to look tense, and tears would roll silently down and she would say she felt frightened. Gradually she has begun to talk more freely and put on weight and color and be capable of sexual relationships with her husband. Her phantasies included those of his penis eating her and of her vagina biting off his penis. On one occasion she said: "Last night I felt excited at coming here today, and then terrified and confused. I couldn't sleep for thinking of you. I felt drawn toward you and then shot back. Then I felt I was one big mouth all over and just wanting to get you inside. But sometimes I feel you'll eat me."

A male patient, F., of forty, living in a hostel reported that he had begun to get friendly with another very decent type of man there, and commented: "I've begun to get frightened. I don't know why I feel it's dangerous and I just cut myself off. When I see him coming I shoot off up to my bedroom." Then he reported a nightmare from which he had awakened in great fear. A monster was coming after him and its huge mouth closed over him like a trap and he was engulfed. Then he burst out of its head and killed it. So the schizoid not only fears devouring and losing the love object, but also that the other person will devour him. Then he becomes claustrophobic, and expresses this in such familiar ways as feeling restricted, tied, imprisoned, trapped, smothered, and must break away to be free and recover and safeguard his independence: so he retreats from object relations. With people, he feels either bursting (if he is getting them into himself) or smothered (if he feels he is being absorbed and losing his personality in them). These anxieties are often expressed by starting up in the night feeling choking, and is one reason for fear of going to sleep.

Relationships as a Mutual Devouring.   We are now in a position to appreciate the terrible dilemma in which the schizoid person is caught in object relationships. Owing to his intensely hungry and unsatisfied need for love, and his consequent incorporating and monopolizing attitude toward those he needs, he cannot help seeing his objects in the light of his own desires toward them. The result is that any relationship into which some genuine feeling goes, immediately comes to be felt deep down, and unconsciously experienced, as a mutual devouring. Such intense anxiety results that there seems to be no alternative but to withdraw from relationships altogether, to prevent the loss of his independence. Relationships are felt to be too dangerous to enter into.

The Schizoid Retreat From Objects

The "In and Out" Program.   The chronic dilemma in which the schizoid individual is placed, namely that he can neither be in a relationship with another person nor out of it, without in various ways risking the loss of both his object and himself, is due to the fact that he has not yet outgrown the particular kind of dependence on love objects that is characteristic of infancy: namely identification in an emotional sense, and the wish to incorporate in a conative, active sense. He and those he loves feel to be part and parcel of one another, so that when separated he feels utterly insecure and lost, but when reunited he feels swallowed, absorbed, and loses his separate individuality by regression to infantile dependence. Thus he must always be rushing into a relationship for security and at once breaking out again for freedom and independence: an alternation between regression to the womb and the struggle to be born, between the merging of his ego in, and the differentiation of it from, the person he loves. The schizoid cannot stand alone, yet is always fighting desperately to defend his independence: like those film stars who spend their best years rushing into and out of one marriage after another.

This "in and out" program, always breaking away from what one is at the same time holding onto, is perhaps the most characteristic behavioral expression of the schizoid conflict. Thus a young man engaged to be married says: "When I'm with Dorothy I'm quiet, I think 'I can't afford to let myself go and let her see that I want her. I must let her see I can get on without her.' So I keep away from her and appear indifferent." He experienced the same conflict about jobs. He phantasied getting a job in South America or China, but in fact turned down every job that would take him away from home. A girl in her twenties says: "When I'm at home I want to get away and when I'm away I want to get back home." Patient A., who is a nurse residing in a hostel, says:

> The other night I decided I wanted to stay in the hostel and not go home, then I felt the hostel was a prison and I went home. As soon as I got there I wanted to go out again. Yesterday I rang mother to say I was coming home, and then immediately I felt exhausted and rang her again to say I was too tired to come. I'm always switching about, as soon as I'm with the person I want I feel they restrict me. I have wondered if I did get one of my two men friends would I then want to be free again.

The patient F., a bachelor of forty who is engaged, says: "If I kiss Mary my heart isn't in it. I hold my breath and count. I can only hug and kiss a dog because it doesn't want anything from me, there are no strings attached. I've always been like that, so I've got lots of acquaintances but no real close friends. I feel I want to stay in and go out, to read and not to read, to go to Church and not to go. I've actually gone into a Church and immediately come out again and then wanted to return in."

So people find their lives slipping away changing houses, clothes, jobs, hobbies, friends, engagements, and marriages, and unable to commit themselves to any one relationship in a stable and permanent way: always needing love yet always dreading being tied. This same conflict accounts for the tendency of engaged or married couples to phantasy about or feel attracted to someone else: as if they must preserve freedom of attachment at least in imagination. One patient remarked: "I want to be loved but I mustn't be possessed."

Giving Up Emotional Relations to External Objects. The oscillation of "in and out," "rushing to and from," "holding on and breaking away" is naturally profoundly disturbing and disruptive of all continuity in living, and at some point the anxiety aroused becomes so great that it cannot be sustained. It is then that a complete retreat from object relations is embarked on, and the person becomes overtly schizoid, emotionally inaccessible, cut off.

This state of emotional apathy, of not suffering any feeling, excitement, or enthusiasm, not experiencing either affection or anger, can be very successfully masked. If feeling is repressed, it is often possible to build up a kind of mechanized, robot personality. The ego that operates consciously becomes more a system than a person, a trained and disciplined instrument for "doing the right and necessary thing" without any real feeling entering in. Fairbairn makes the highly important distinction between "helping people without feeling" and "loving." Duty rather than affection becomes the key word. Patient A. sought temporary relief from her disruptive conflict over her man friend by putting it away and making a list of all the things she ought to do, and systematically going through them one by one, routinizing her whole life—and that had been a life long tendency. She had always had to "do things in order"; even as a child she made a notebook list of games and had to play them in order.

The patient F., a man with strongly, in fact exclusively, religious interests, showed markedly this characteristic of helping people without really feeling for them. He said: "I've no real emotional relations with people. I can't reciprocate tenderness. I can cry and suffer with people. I can help people, but when they stop suffering I'm finished. I can't enter into folks' joys and laughter. I can do things for people but shrink from them if they start thanking me." His suffering with people was in fact his identifying himself as a suffering person with anyone else who suffered. Apart from that he allowed no emotional relationship to arise.

It is even possible to mask more effectively the real nature of the compulsive, unfeeling zeal in good works, by simulating a feeling of concern for others. Some shallow affect is helped out by behavior expressive of deep care and consideration for other people; nevertheless, genuine feeling for other people is not really there. Such behavior is not, of course, consciously insincere. It is a genuine effort to do the best that one can do in the absence of a capacity to release true feeling. What looks deceptively like genuine feeling for another person may break into consciousness, when in fact it is based on identification with the other person and is mainly a feeling of anxiety and pity for oneself.

Many practically useful types of personality are basically schizoid. Hard workers, compulsively unselfish folk, efficient organizers, highly intellectual people, may all accomplish valuable results, but it is often possible to detect an unfeeling callousness behind their good works, and a lack of sensitiveness to other people's feelings, in the way they will override individuals in their devotion to causes.

The schizoid repression of feeling, and retreat from emotional relationships, may however go much further and produce a serious breakdown of constructive effort. Then the unhappy sufferer from incapacitating conflicts will succumb to real futility: nothing seems worth doing, interest dies, the world seems unreal, the ego feels depersonalized. Suicide may be attempted in a cold, calculated way to the accompaniment of such thoughts

as "I am useless, bad for everybody, I'll be best out of the way."
The patient F. had never reached that point, but he said: "I feel I
love people in an impersonal way; it seems a false position;
hypocritical. Perhaps I don't do any loving. I'm terrified when I
see young people go off and being successful and I'm at a dead
bottom, absolute dereliction, excommunicate."

The Fundamental Problem: Identification

Identification and Infantile Dependence. It has already been
mentioned that schizoid problems arise out of identification,
which Fairbairn holds to be the original infantile form of relation
to, and dependence on, objects. The criticism is sometimes made
that psychoanalysis invents a strange terminology that the layman cannot apply to real life. We may therefore illustrate the state
of identification with the love object in the words of Ngaio March
(1935), a successful writer of detective fiction. In *Enter a Murderer*
she creates the character of Surbonadier, a bad actor who
expresses his immaturity by being a drug addict and blackmailer.
Stephanie Vaughan, the leading lady, says: "He was passionately
in love with me. That doesn't begin to express it. He was completely and utterly absorbed as though apart from me he had no
reality." In other words, the man was swallowed up in his love
object, had no true individuality of his own, and could not exist
in a state of separation from her. He had never become born out
of his mother's psyche and differentiated as a separate and real
person in his own right, and identification with another person
remained at bottom the basis of all his personal relationships.

The patient E. said: "If I go away from home I feel I've lost
something, but when I'm there I feel imprisoned. I feel my destiny is bound up with theirs and I can't get away, yet I feel they
imprison me and ruin my life." The patient A. dreamed of being
"grafted onto another person." The patient F. said: "Why should
I be on bad terms with my sister? After all I am my sister," and
then started in some surprise at what he had heard himself say.
The patient B. struggling to master a blind compulsive longing
for a male relative she played with as a child, said: "I've always felt
he's me and I'm him. I felt a terrible need to fuss around him and
do everything for him. I want him to be touching me all the time.

I feel there is no difference between him and me." Fairbairn
holds that identification is the cause of the compulsiveness of
such feelings as infatuation. Identification is betrayed in a variety
of curious ways, such as the fear of being buried alive, that is,
absorbed into another person, a return to the womb; also expressed
in the suicidal urge to put one's head in a gas oven: or again in
dressing in the clothes of another person. Patient C., feeling in a
state of panic one night when her husband was away, felt safe
when she slept in his pajamas.

Dissolving Identification: Separation-Anxiety, and Psychic Birth.
The regressive urge to remain identified for the sake of comfort
and security conflicts with the developmental need to dissolve
identification and differentiate oneself as a separate personality.
This conflict, as it sways back and forth, sets up the "in and out"
program. Identification, naturally, varies in degree, but the
markedly schizoid person, in whom it plays such a fundamental
part, begins to lose all true independence of feeling, thought, and
action as soon as a relationship with another person attains any
degree of emotional reality. A single illuminating example will
suffice.

The patient C. says: "I feel I lack the capacity to go out. I can
never leave the people I love. If I go out I'm emptied, I lose
myself. I can't get beyond that. If I become dependent on you, I'd
enjoy my dependence on you too much and want to prolong
babyhood. Being shut in means being warm, safe, and not confronted with unforeseen events." But this kind of security is also a
prison, so the patient goes on to say: "I feel I'm walking up and
down inside an enclosed space. I dreamed of being a baby being
born out of a gas oven (i.e., reversal of the suicide idea). I was
struck with the danger of coming out, it was a long drop from the
oven to the floor. I feel I'm disintegrating if I go out. The only
feeling of being real comes with getting back in and being with
someone. I don't feel alone inside even if there's no one there.
Sometimes I feel like someone falling out of an airplane, or falling through water and expecting to hit the bottom and there isn't
one. I have strong impulses to throw myself out of the window."
This "birth symbolism" shows that suicidal impulses may have
opposite meanings. The gas oven means a return to the womb, a
surrender to identification with mother. Falling out of the win-

dow means a struggle to separate and be born (and also casting out the person with whom one is identified). The struggle to dissolve identification is long and severe, and in analysis it recapitulates the whole process of growing up to the normal mixture of voluntary dependence and independence characteristic of the mature adult person. One of the major causes of anxiety is that separation is felt to involve, not natural growth and development, but a violent, angry, destructive breakaway, as if a baby, in being born, were bound to leave a dying mother behind.

Schizoid Characteristics

There are various characteristics which specifically mark the schizoid personality, and the most general and all-embracing is:

1. *Introversion.* By the very meaning of the term, the schizoid is described as cut off from the world of outer reality in an emotional sense. All his libidinal desire and striving is directed inwards toward internal objects and he lives an intense inner life, often revealed in an astonishing wealth and richness of phantasy and imaginative life whenever that becomes accessible to observation; though mostly this varied phantasy life is carried on in secret, hidden away often even from the schizoid's own conscious self. His ego is split. But the barrier between the conscious and the unconscious self may be very thin in a deeply schizoid person and the world of internal objects and relationships may flood into and dominate consciousness very easily.

2. *Narcissism* is a schizoid characteristic that arises out of the predominantly interior life he lives. His love objects are all inside him, and moreover he is greatly identified with them, so that his libidinal attachments appear to be himself. This subtly deceptive situation was not recognized by Freud when he propounded his theory of autoeroticism and narcissism, and ego–libido as distinct from object–libido. The schizoid's physically incorporative feeling toward his love objects is the bodily counterpart, or rather foundation, of the mentally incorporative attitude which leads to mental internalization of objects and the setting up of a world of internal psychic objects. But these mentally internalized objects, especially when the patient feels strongly identified with them,

can be discovered, contacted, and enjoyed, or even attacked, in his own body, when the external object is not there. One patient, who cannot be directly angry with another person, always goes away alone when her temper is roused and punches herself. She is identified with the object of her aggression which leads to a depressive state, though, of course, it is a libidinal attachment at bottom. The normally so-called autoerotic and narcissistic phenomena of thumb-sucking, masturbation, hugging oneself, and so on are based on identification. Autoerotic phenomena are only secondarily autoerotic; autoerotism is a relationship with an external object who is identified with oneself, the baby's thumb deputizes for the mother's breast. Narcissism is a disguised object relation. Thus the patient B. felt depressed while bathing and cried silently, and then felt a strong urge to snuggle her head down on to her shoulder, that is, mother's shoulder in herself, and at once felt better. Again sitting with her husband one evening reading, she became aware that she was thinking of an intimate relation with him and found she had slipped her hand inside her frock and was caressing her own breast. These phenomena lead to a third schizoid characteristic:

3. *Self-Sufficiency.* The above patient was actually taking no notice of her husband as an external person: her relation with him was all going on inside herself and she felt contented. This introverted, narcissistic self-sufficiency which does without real external relationships while all emotional relations are carried on in the inner world, is a safeguard against anxiety breaking out in dealings with actual people. Self-sufficiency, or the attempt to get on without external relationships, comes out clearly in the case of patient C. She had been talking of wanting a baby, and then dreamed that she had a baby by her mother. It was suggested that having a baby meant getting something of her husband inside her, and deep down that felt to be getting something of mother inside her. But since she had often shown that she identified herself very much with babies, it would also represent being the baby inside the mother. She was wanting to set up a self-sufficiency situation in which she was both the mother and the baby. She replied: "Yes, I always think of it as a girl. It gives me a feeling of security. I've got it all here under control, there's no

uncertainty." In such a position she could do without her husband and be all-sufficient within herself.

4. *A Sense of Superiority* naturally goes with self-sufficiency. One has no need of other people, they can be dispensed with. This overcompensates the deep-seated dependence on people which leads to feelings of inferiority, smallness, and weakness. But there often goes with it a feeling of being different from other people. Thus a very obsessional patient reveals the schizoid background of her symptoms when she says: "I'm always dissatisfied. As a child I would cry with boredom at the silly games the children played. It got worse in my teens, terrible boredom, futility, lack of interest. I would look at people and see them interested in things I thought silly. I felt I was different and had more brains. I was thinking deeply about the purpose of life." She could think about life in the abstract but couldn't live it in real relationships with other people.

5. *Loss of Affect* in external situations is an inevitable part of the total picture. A man in the late forties says: "I find it difficult to be with mother. I ought to be more sympathetic to her than I can be. I always feel I'm not paying attention to what she says. I don't feel terribly drawn to anyone. I can feel cold about all the people who are near and dear to me. When my wife and I were having sexual relations she would say: 'Do you love me?' I would answer: 'Of course I do, but sex isn't love, it's only an experience.' I could never see why that upset her." Feeling was excluded even from sexual activity which was reduced to what one patient called "an intermittent biological urge which seemed to have little connection with 'me.' "

6. *Loneliness* is an inescapable result of schizoid introversion and abolition of external relationships. It reveals itself in the intense longing for friendships and love which repeatedly break through. Loneliness in the midst of a crowd is the experience of the schizoid cut off from affective rapport.

7. *Depersonalization,* loss of the sense of identity and individuality, loss of oneself, brings out clearly the serious dangers of the schizoid state. Derealization of the outer world is involved as well. Thus the patient C. maintains that the worst fright she ever had was a petrifying experience at the age of two years. "I

couldn't get hold of the idea that I was me. I lost the sense for a little while of being a separate entity. I was afraid to look at anything; and afraid to touch anything as if I didn't register touch. I
couldn't believe I was doing things except mechanically. I saw
everything in an unrealistic way. Everything seemed highly
dangerous. I was terrified while it lasted. All my life since I've
been saying to myself at intervals 'I am me.' "

Fairbairn and Freud

When one surveys the material here set out, it becomes apparent
that Fairbairn's theory of the schizoid problem represents a radical revision in psychoanalytical thinking. Freud rested his theory
of development and of the psychoneuroses on the centrality of
the Oedipus situation in the last phase of infancy. Failure to solve
the Oedipus conflict of incestuous love and jealous hate of the
parent of the same sex led to regression to pregenital levels of sexual and emotional life and a lasting burden of guilt. This now
looks rather like a pioneer's rough sketchmap of an uncharted
territory by comparison with Fairbairn's detailed ordnance survey map of infantile development which is based on, but goes a
long way beyond, Melanie Klein's discoveries about internal
objects and the depressive position. The Oedipus problem as
Freud saw it was, in fact, no more than the gateway opening into
the area of the psychopathology of infancy. Yet Fairbairn's position is essentially simple. Once stated it should be apparent that
man's need of a love relationship is the fundamental thing in his
life, and that the love hunger and anger set up by frustration of
this basic need must constitute the two primary problems of personality on the emotional level. Freud's "guilt over the incestuous tie to the mother" now resolves itself into the primary
necessity of overcoming infantile dependence on the parents,
and on the mother in particular, in order to grow up to mature
adulthood. The Oedipus conflict theory in a purely biological
and sexual sense is seen to have misrepresented and distorted the
real problem, and sidetracked inquiry. The fundamental
emotional attitude of the child to both parents is the same and is
determined, not by the sex of the parent but by the child's need
for libidinal satisfaction and protective love, and a stable

environment, and by the fact that all its relationships start off on the basis of identification. In its quest for a libidinally good object the child will turn from the mother to the father, and go back and forth between them many times. The less satisfactory the object relationships with his parents prove to be in the course of development, the more the child remains embedded in relationships by identification, and the more it creates, and remains tied to, an inner world of bad internal objects who will thereafter dwell in its unconscious as an abiding fifth column of secret persecutors, at once exciting desire and denying satisfaction. A deep-seated ever unsatisfied hunger will be the foundation of the personality, creating the fundamental danger of the schizoid state.

Cultural Expressions of Schizoid Fears

Academic psychologists are fond of accusing psychoanalysts of dealing with abnormal minds and drawing from them unjustified conclusions about normal minds. In fact psychoanalysis shows conclusively that this is an entirely misleading distinction. It would be easy to demonstrate every psychopathological process from the study of so-called normal minds alone. Nowadays many people seek analysis not for specific neurotic breakdowns but for character and personality problems, and many of them are people who continue to hold effectively positions of responsibility and who are judged by the world at large to be "normal" people. Thus psychopathology should be capable of throwing an important light on many aspects of ordinary social and cultural life. This is far too large a theme to be more than touched on here. A few hints must suffice.

1. *Common Mild Schizoid Traits.* One has only to collect up some of the common phrases that describe an introvert reaction in human relationships to realize how common the "schizoid type" of personality is. One constantly hears in the social intercourse of daily life such comments as "he's gone into his shell," "he only half listens to what you say," "he's always preoccupied," or "absent-minded," "he lives in a world of ideas," "he's an unpractical type," "he's difficult to get to know," "he couldn't enthuse about anything," "he's a cold fish," "he's very

efficient but rather inhuman," and one could multiply the list. All these comments may well describe people whose general stability in any reasonable environment is quite adequate, but who clearly lack the capacity for simple, spontaneous, warm, and friendly responsiveness to their human kind. Not infrequently they are more emotionally expressive toward animals than toward the human beings with whom they live or work. They are undemonstrative: it is not merely that they are the opposite of emotionally effervescent, but rather that their relationships with people are actually emotionally shallow. It is as well to recognize, from these schizoid types, that psychopathological phenomena cannot be set apart from the so-called "normal."

2. *Politics.* All through the ages politics has rung the changes, with monotonous regularity, on the themes of "freedom" and "authority." Men have fought passionately for liberty and independence; freedom from foreign domination, freedom from state paternalism and bureaucratic control, freedom from social and economic class oppression, freedom from the shackles of an imposed religious orthodoxy. Yet at other times men have proved to be just as willing, and indeed eager, to be embraced in, and supported and directed by, some totalitarian organization of state or church. No doubt urgent practical necessity often drives men one way or the other at different periods of history and in different stages of social change. But if we seek the ultimate motivations of human action, it is impossible not to link up this social and political oscillation of aim, with the "in and out" program of the schizoid person. Man's deepest needs make him dependent on others, but there is nothing more productive of the feeling of being tied or restricted than being overdependent through basic emotional immaturity. Certainly human beings in the mass are far less emotionally mature than they suppose themselves to be, and this accounts for much of the aggressiveness, the oppositionism, and the compulsive assertion of a false, forced, independence that are such obvious social behavior trends. The schizoid person frequently "has a bee in his bonnet" about freedom. The love of liberty has been for so long the keynote of British national life that what Erich Fromm (1942) calls "the fear of freedom" found in totalitarianism, and in political as well as religious authoritarianism seems to us a strange aberration. It is

well to realize that both motives are deeply rooted in the psychic structure of human personality.

3. *Ideology.* Much has been said of "depressed eras" in history, but when one considers the cold, calculating, mechanical, ruthless, and unfeeling nature of the planned cruelty of political intellectuals and ideologists, we may well think this to be a "schizoid era." The cold and inscrutable Himmler showed all the marks of a deeply schizoid personality and his suicide was consistent. The schizoid intellectual wielding unlimited political power is perhaps the most dangerous type of leader. He is a devourer of the human rights of all whom he can rule. The way some of the most ruthless Nazis could turn to the study of theology was significant of a schizoid splitting of personality. But if we turn to the purely intellectual and cultural sphere it is not difficult to recognize the impersonal atmosphere of schizoid thinking in Hegelianism. Its dialectic of thesis breeding antithesis seems an intellectual version of the schizoid need for unity which in turn breeds the need for separation. Still more apparent is the schizoid sense of futility, disillusionment, and underlying anxiety in existentialism. These thinkers, from Kierkegaard to Heidegger and Sartre, find human existence to be rooted in anxiety and insecurity, a fundamental dread that ultimately we have no certainties and the only thing we can affirm is "nothingness," "unreality," a final sense of triviality and meaninglessness. This surely is schizoid despair and loss of contact with the verities of emotional reality, rationalized into a philosophy; yet existentialist thinkers, unlike the logical positivists, are calling us to face and deal with these real problems of our human situation. It is a sign of the mental state of our age.

Summary

We may finally summarize the emotional dilemma of the schizoid thus: he feels a deep dread of entering into a real personal relationship, that is, one into which genuine feeling enters, because, though his need for a love object is so great, yet he can only sustain a relationship at a deep emotional level, on the basis of infantile and absolute dependence. To the love hungry schizoid faced internally with an exciting but deserting object all relationships are felt to be "swallowing up things" which trap and imprison and destroy. If your hate is destructive you are still free to love because you can find someone else to hate. But if you feel your love is destructive the situation is terrifying. You are always *impelled into* a relationship by your needs and at once *driven out* again by the fear either of exhausting your love object by the demands you want to make or else losing your own individuality by overdependence and identification. This "in and out" oscillation is *the typical schizoid behavior,* and to escape from it into detachment and loss of feeling is *the typical schizoid state*.

The schizoid feels faced with utter loss, and the destruction of both ego and object, whether in a relationship or out of it. In a relationship, identification involves loss of the ego, and incorporation involves a hungry devouring and losing of the object. In breaking away to independence, the object is destroyed as you fight a way out to freedom, or lost by separation, and the ego is destroyed or emptied by the loss of the object with whom it is identified. The only real solution is the dissolving of identification and the maturing of the personality: the differentiation of ego and object and the growth of a capacity for cooperative independence and mutuality.

Chapter 23

CHARACTER PERVERSION

Jacob A. Arlow

In this paper I intend to describe some unusual character traits I have observed in certain male patients. What is striking about these traits is the fact that they are genetically related to sexual perversions and that structurally they are reproductions, in exquisite detail, of the defensive mechanisms which characterize the specific perversions. In the history of the development of these character traits one can observe how they substituted for or were the equivalent of perverse sexual practices. On the basis of these observations, a number of general conclusions will be offered concerning the relationship between certain character traits and perversions. I would also like to introduce the concept of character perversion. The relationship between these character traits and the antecedent perversions which they replaced may be expressed in the concept of "character perversion." Here I draw an analogy to the genesis of character neurosis. In this condition what had once been a symptomatic neurosis is, in the course of development, replaced by neurotic character traits; that is, character neurosis. In the patients whom I am about to describe, an original perversion or tendency toward perversion was replaced in later life by an abnormal character trait, a perverse character trait. I propose to call such phenomena "character perversion."

Of the three character traits to be described, the first two have a very similar organization and, in fact, are seen in close association. These traits may be observed in individuals who have difficulties in relationship to reality. Such persons are often

This chapter originally appeared in *Currents in Psychoanalysis*, pp. 317–336, ed. I. M. Marcus. New York: International Universities Press, 1971. Reprinted by permission of the publisher.

437

strikingly unrealistic in their daily activities. Some of them have an additional, associated trait; they have a compulsion to tell petty lies. The third type of perverse character trait to be described demonstrates a wide range of behavior, some of which is often humorous in nature. I refer to the so-called "practical joker."

The Unrealistic Character

In psychoanalytic experience, the unrealistic character type is by no means uncommon. It escapes notice because the disturbance is usually relatively mild and the patient does not complain of it. Furthermore, it may or may not upset the observer. Some degree of this disturbance may be seen in most male patients who suffer from intense castration anxiety.

The essential feature of this type of character trait is the refusal of the individual to face reality squarely. This may extend to many areas of his life. When presented with problems he will seize upon an insignificant detail, peripheral to the main point of the argument. Such a person may be dilatory but not out of malice or hostility. He does not derive the gratification from delay which is so typical of the anal character. Although perceiving the true nature of the problem he has a need to "beat around the bush." As much as possible, he tries to ignore the demands of reality which are measured in time intervals. In fact, in one of my patients, those two inexorable accompaniments of reality, death and taxes, were characteristically ignored. When obligations accumulate and are forcibly brought to the attention of this type of person, he often responds with panic.

This type of behavior must be distinguished from the counterphobic attitude Fenichel (1939a) described. Counterphobic patients seek out dangerous situations in order to master them. The unrealistic characters *ignore* situations which they know to be dangerous. Figuratively they close their eyes to real life situations. On the couch during treatment, they literally keep their eyes closed most of the time. As one patient expressed it, he prefers to treat reality as if it were a bad dream.

In the setting of treatment, as in their daily lives, it is often hard to follow the conversation of such patients. Their speech tends to become vague and the description they give of events or people is imprecise and lacking in detail. They avoid reporting day-to-day events. When pressed for greater definition they become unsure of what they had experienced and the listener becomes confused trying to understand.

During psychoanalytic treatment the unrealistic character presents many technical problems. All the trends outlined above are aggravated and are used as resistance. The patient seems unwilling or unable to draw obvious conclusions. Sometimes the therapist feels that he is dealing with a case of pseudoimbecility. When an interpretation is offered, the patient "looks away," that is, he acts as if he had not heard what had been said or he focuses his attention on some insignificant detail, or he turns to a new subject without acknowledging the transition.

Sexually, these patients usually have some disturbance of potency, most frequently, ejaculation praecox. One patient experienced complete anesthesia during sexual relations. He felt as though he were not participating in the act at all. The same patient suffered from a mild but chronic depersonalization and derealization. (In my experience, most of these patients have a form of detachment in the analytic situation which approaches depersonalization and derealization.) Experiences which other patients would feel as real, intense, and dramatic, he treated lightly or with a feeling of estrangement. An operation, a funeral, or an accident were referred to casually and dismissed in a sentence or two. Such behavior is typical for this group of patients. It is hard for unrealistic characters to take a good look at a problem; at best, they take only a sidelong glance. They are glancers, not lookers.

In a male patient the inability to look at reality was true both in a figurative and in a literal sense. Actually, of course, he repudiated what he perceived. The data of analysis demonstrated that on one level of consciousness he was always perceiving and properly interpreting the information furnished him by his senses. In addition to the typical modes of behavior just described, this patient would make a point of "not seeing" what was in the consultation room. He could let weeks go by before noticing a new item of furniture. On several occasions he passed directly by me on the street without seeing me. He rationalized these perceptual difficulties by ascribing them to the fact that he had not been wearing his glasses. Typically, however, he would not wear glasses to the analytic sessions to insure, apparently, that he could perceive neither the analyst nor what the analyst was saying.

After this problem had been discussed for some time, the patient decided to put the interpretations to test by wearing his glasses to the sessions. He began by mentioning several of the decorative features of the office which he now actually perceived; previously he had a vague surmise that they existed. His thoughts next turned to several difficulties in his business life which he had avoided confronting directly. He had delegated responsibility for these matters to some of his subordinates and when they presented him with summaries and interpretations of their findings, he glanced through the reports very briefly. Some he put aside without reading at all, although a number of important problems pressed for solution. He lived in dread of losing certain important accounts but preferred not to think of it.

His thoughts next turned to the behavior of his three-year-old son who had been having nightmares. The boy, very articulate, had begun to ask vague questions about natural phenomena. He had been refusing to go to the park to play with certain friends whose company he had hitherto enjoyed. At night he got into bed, pulled the blanket over his head and said, "Can't see anything." The patient reported that his wife claimed that these difficulties in the little boy began after the following incident took place in the park playground: The child was playing when she suddenly noticed that "his eyes froze." He was staring at a little girl whose diaper was being changed. It took him a while before he could communicate with his mother again and when he did, he began asking all sorts of questions about playgrounds, structure of benches, etc.—nothing at all about the little girl.

The patient's mother had been staying at his home. She behaved in the household as she had when the patient was a child; she was careless of her dress. When the patient reproached her for the effect this could have on his son, his mother had answered him, "It's good for him, he has to learn the truth sometimes." Further associations continued the theme of shock connected with seeing the female genital, with recollections from many periods of his life. He reported a dream in which he saw the genital area of a woman; all details had been obliterated by a firm white girdle. The dreamer could see "nothing" and his attention focused on the very edge of the girdle where a long white garter belt dangled.

In a short essay on the nature of reality, Lewin (1948) comments on the fact that the idea "reality" as it appears in free association often stands for the female genital. The patient whose character disturbance has just been described lived out this unconscious equating of the female genital with reality. Such patients behave as if they were repetitively abreacting the traumatic confrontation with the female genital. The defense which they use represents a combination of denial in phantasy to which is added a compulsive need to focus attention on some distracting, peripheral, reassuring substitute item.

One of my patients came to understand how this reality denying part of his character was connected with his choice of professional career. He was the son of a carpenter. His training went in progressive stages from the study of electronics, to physics, and then finally to mathematics. He felt that mathematics was the "queen of sciences." It was superior to all other studies because there was no need ever to have any references to real events. "If you began with a hypothesis or an assumption, you can continue to elaborate or refine the system without ever having to turn to real facts or to deal with nature. It is an invulnerable and foolproof system." When he was a little boy he spent hours phantasying about how he could erect an invulnerable castle, one that would be invulnerable against any kind of assault. His appreciation of the defensive function of his character structure and choice of profession was revealed in the following short story which he made up about a person like himself. This material came up in the context of his fear of penetrating the female genital.

A carpenter once came home to discover that the television set was not working. He tried his hardest to find out what was wrong. After many hours of labor, he gave up because he did not know enough about electronics. Consequently, he decided to study electronics and in time became an outstanding expert. He then realized that electronics is only a form of applied physics, so he bent his mind to the study of this field and soon became an eminent physicist. After a number of years he realized that physics is based upon mathematics and, as might be expected, he went back to study. Before many years he was acclaimed one of the world's great mathematicians. Years later, after many successes and honors, he sat with his wife musing on how his professional interests had developed. "Just imagine," he said to his wife, "how it all began. From not being able to fix that television set I went from one academic study to another until I reached the pinnacle of success in mathematics." "Just imagine," his wife answered, "if I had told you that day that you had forgotten to insert the plug into the wall socket."

In the clinical examples mentioned above, one may have noted indirect references to the typical male perversions of voyeurism and fetishism. These perversions, together with the others to be mentioned below, have a common origin in the need of the male child of the Oedipus phase to ward off intense castration anxiety. The perversion represents in part an attempt in the presence of overwhelming castration anxiety to make sexual gratification possible through certain behaviors which serve to reassure the individual against the danger of castration. The most common reassurance consists of some form of denial of the perception in reality of the penisless female genital.

In my experience the voyeur and the fetishist are part of a complementary series. The voyeur is compelled to look but not to see. When he is unavoidably confronted by the truth (in the form of the penisless female genital) he will have nothing to do with it. The patient whose amusing phantasy of professions was just reported was intensely scopophilic throughout childhood and adolescence. Like most voyeurs, his scopophilic activities were pursued under conditions which guaranteed that he would never really see, at close range, a completely nude woman's body. He avoided sexual relations and marriage for a long time and although unusually intelligent, he managed to keep himself ignorant of sexual information. After marriage he had sexual relations infrequently and sustained his potency either by perverse phantasies or by some distracting preoccupation with abstract concepts connected with his work. On the day following sexual relations with his wife or after being confronted with evidence that she was menstruating, his reality-denying activity would become most pronounced. It was under such circumstances that he would be driven to some perverse voyeuristic adventure or to some inappropriate, unrealistic act. When reporting these activities he seemed pseudo-imbecilic. During sessions when the events were being interpreted to him, he would blink his eyes, close them, shield them with his palm or move his head as if he were shaking off some unbearable sight. Thereafter he would either change the subject (look elsewhere) or fasten onto some peripheral detail of what had been said.

In general, patients with this kind of problem have in common a wide repertory of eye-shielding mannerisms during sessions. One patient had long-standing voyeuristic and fetishistic impulses which he had only begun to control to some extent in recent years. For the first few years of his active sexual life it was a necessary condition for potency that his partner come into bed and get under the covers wearing a full girdle or underpants. Only under the covers would he permit her to be completely nude. He was also fascinated by garter belts, particularly by long dangling garters. He had an interest in photographs which never completely revealed a woman fully nude, and was intrigued by "see through" clothes.

Another patient of this unrealistic character type passed through a very difficult latency and adolescence in which multiple perverse activities were prominent. Outstanding among these were voyeurism, exhibitionism, and fetishistic interest in shoes and bras. This latter type of defense serves as the transition to the role of fetishism in the genesis of this character trait. The fetishist in his defensive needs goes a step further than the voyeur. Not only does he look away in order to deny the unbearable reality of the female genital, he has a compulsive need to fasten his attention onto some reassuring, peripheral object. As is well known, the item upon which he fixes his attention and which becomes the obligatory condition for sexual fulfillment, unconsciously represents an actualization of the reality-denying phantasy of the female phallus. Perceiving the external, realistic representation of a female phallus negates the earlier unnerving perception of the real truth regarding female anatomy.

What determines which item the fetishist selects to represent the female phallus? According to several authors (Freud, 1927b;

Fenichel, 1945; Lewin, 1950) the fetish is selected on the basis of some contiguous visual impression which preceded or followed immediately upon the traumatizing view of the female genital. The garter, girdle, or some other item of women's underclothes, close to or actually covering the genital, lend themselves as distracting perceptions. Upon these the frightened viewer may concentrate in order to look away from the heart of the matter. Displacing his gaze upward, the future fetishist may come upon the breast (Lewin, 1950) or the bra. Looking downward he finds the heel or the shoe. The perception of the fetishistic object thus becomes a screen obscuring the truth or concealing it completely.

Thus, in these patients, the character trait of being unrealistic derives from the need to fend off the danger of castration. In my material, the danger of castration was connected with the typical conflicts of the oedipal phase and was conditioned by traumatizing exposure to the female genital. Two mechanisms are fundamental in this particular form of defending against castration anxiety. First is the mechanism of denial; that is, the perception is acknowledged consciously but is denied unconsciously. To this is added a second factor, a factor which is common to fetishism as well. When confronted with reality the individual can feel secure only if he can turn his attention to some realistic external perception which is distracting and reassuring because it corresponds to his unconscious phantasy of a female genital with a phallus. The character trait of being unrealistic is the equivalent of a constant, repetitive abreaction to the traumatic confrontation with reality in the form of the female genital.

The Petty Liar

For some patients the fetish must have a certain gauzy, filmy quality. Such patients require an item which is neither totally opaque nor fully transparent. They would love to look, in fact they have to look, but they do not want to see what is really there. In a patient who had such a requirement, a defensive shift from passive (looking) to active (showing) helped us to understand one of his pathological character traits. He was a petty liar. He was also a "Peeping-Tom" who kept complaining of the frustrations connected with voyeurism. At the last moment some item of clothing, for example, a nightgown, would obscure his view of the object he was observing at a distance; or the window shade would come down, and so on. He managed never to quite see what he thought he was looking for. Actually, to be free from anxiety he required that something be interposed between himself and the truth of the world of anatomy. The object which excited him during masturbation had to be something insubstantial and filmy. As a youngster at camp he used to peek at staff members' wives when they were getting undressed. Several times he stole some items of lingerie, kept them near his tent, and concentrated on them while masturbating.

In his daily dealings he was always telling petty lies. As a rule these were not the kind of lies from which he obtained any material benefit. He told lies even when there was no need to conceal the truth. His productions during the session were usually unclear. He himself commented on the nebulous, *veil-like* quality of what he had to say, observing once that he never liked to tell "the naked truth." When he was able to deceive people into accepting his fabrications he felt a sense of mastery. Even if he did not tell a petty lie it was important for him to adorn or embellish what he was describing. Sometimes when he succeeded in having people accept his petty lies as real, he almost began to believe them himself. His character disturbance thus resembled the structure of certain types of imposters as well as the type of pseudologia phantastica described by Fenichel (1939b). The statement which conveys the unconscious import of this kind of behavior may be expressed in the following words: "If I am successful in preventing others from seeing the truth then I need not fear that I myself will be confronted by the shocking truth." This is an example of denial by proxy (Wangh, 1962).

A sublimation of this fetishistlike defense against castration anxiety may be seen in the choice of such occupations as hairdressing, fashion design, interior decoration, and so on. There are many references, especially humorous ones, to the "deceptive" quality of female adornment and embellishment.

To recapitulate: The petty lie is the equivalent of the fetish— it is something which is interposed between the individual and reality in order to ward off the perception of the true reality and to substitute instead perceptions which facilitate ambiguity and illusion, both of which can temper for the patient the harsh reality of female anatomy. The fetish is, in a sense, a "screen" percept.

The Practical Joker and Hoaxer

It is a short step from grasping the fetish and having phantasies about women possessing penises to dressing up in a fetishlike outfit or in women's clothes and then acting out the phantasy of being a woman with a penis. These fundamental features of the transvestite may be transformed and may become the basis of the pathological character trait of the practical joker.

The following features characterize the type of joker or hoaxer to whom I refer:

1. The need to inspire panic or anxiety in others.
2. The gratification of aggression and the sense of power which comes from perpetrating the hoax.
3. The pleasure of exposing the hoax.

The joker or hoaxer acts out the defenses used by the exhibitionist and the transvestite. Certain exhibitionist perversions have in common the mechanism of identification with the aggressor. As the unprepared little boy was frightened by the shocking sight of the woman's genitals, so he turns and shocks girls by causing them to see his genital, a sight for which they are unprepared. There is a difference however. Whereas originally he *saw nothing,* in his perversion he *shows something.* Transvestism constitutes a reassuring denial. In essence, the transvestite says, "You have nothing to fear. There is no such thing as a body without a male organ. On the surface it seems female, but get a good look underneath and you will discover that the opposite is true. You thought something was missing but it was there all the time." Correspondingly, the hoax has the meaning of, "It was foolish of you to be frightened. Once you know the underlying truth you can see that from the very beginning nothing really was amiss."

The following case illustrates the genesis and elaboration of such defensive measures in a joker and how this part of his character was shaped. This material is from the analysis of a young adult who suffered from very intense anxiety. Whenever a situation developed which represented the danger of castration to him, he would resort to playing practical jokes or perpetrating some hoax. His hoaxes had the quality of arousing fear in his victims. When their suffering reached a certain degree of intensity, he would bring the hoax to an end.

There were many ways in which he played this game. He took advantage of his massive bulk and muscular development to act tough and threatening. Sometimes he played the imposter. Acting as if he were a detective or an FBI agent, without actually saying so, he would inspire anxiety by asking questions of individuals who were potentially vulnerable to investigation. Sometimes he would use the telephone and pose as an FBI agent, without saying explicitly that he was one. At other times he would call up a teacher or a relative and tease him while concealing his identity.

One aspect of the psychology of this patient's hoaxing combines identification of the aggressor with the mechanism of mastering anxiety through a proxy. In this case, the patient used his sister as well as his classmates as proxies. The pattern for this kind of hoaxing could be traced back to early childhood. In school he used to upset his classmates by spreading false rumors. For example, he told his class that a comprehensive examination was scheduled for the next day and that this test would determine the semester's grades. With his younger sister he would act out scenarios of the latest monster pictures so effectively that she was terrified. Sometimes he dropped the play quality. When they were home alone he once awakened his sister to tell her that there was a burglar in the house and that she should be very still. He went to the door of the bedroom and behaved as if he were watching a thief, returning from time to time to report what was happening. Another time he insisted that he heard a knock at the door. He proceeded to answer the knock and had a frightening conversation with an imaginary policeman, making sure all the time that his sister heard his side of the conversation.

In the treatment, he would exaggerate his symptoms, trying to create the impression that he was going insane. He complained of feelings which could be interpreted as the beginnings of psychotic depersonalization, delusions, or hallucinations. His description of anxiety feelings was most florid.

The meaning of this hoaxing activity could ultimately be understood in terms of his childhood relationship to his mother and sister. They lived in close quarters and he frequently saw them unclothed. He was very angry with his mother for exposing herself but could not tell her how he felt. Certain childhood games which he played had the purpose of reassuring him that the dangers he imagined were not real. In one such game he would play being blind, walking along the street for a predetermined distance, and then opening his eyes and experiencing a great pleasure at being able to see again. In the same way he played being a cripple. These activities are part of a typical form of children's play which I have described elsewhere (1971). Sometimes he would come home from school limping badly, complaining of some physical symptom, or reporting some academic catastrophe. After his mother was sufficiently wrought up, he would calm her down by revealing the truth.

When this behavior was being discussed in the context of castration anxiety and a phantasy of the vagina dentata, the patient recalled an incident which had been very important to him. One day at school he found some black paper which he could wrap over his three front teeth to create the illusion that the teeth were missing. So outfitted, he came home and went about his business as if nothing were amiss. Suddenly his mother caught a glimpse of his mouth. She panicked and wanted to know what happened. At this point, with great glee, he took the paper off, revealing that the teeth were intact. He recollected that at the age of five or six he would regularly play with himself before the mirror. He would press his penis back between his thighs so that his genital area corresponded to what he had seen on his little sister. With great delight he would relax the pressure on his thighs permitting the reassuring reappearance of his penis. On several occasions in latency and adolescence he dressed up in various items of his mother's clothes, used her cosmetics, and masturbated.

The same mechanisms became clear in another patient who was a practical joker. He was a thirty-year-old man, a Don Juan, who suffered from intense castration anxiety. He had the phantasy of the dentata vagina and could be potent only when he was certain that the relationship with the woman would not last and that he was free to extricate himself at will.

The patient had the following dream the night before a date with a sexually aggressive woman. He had been avoiding her because he was afraid that he would be impotent. The last time he had seen her he aggressively said many things to shock her.

This is the dream: "I saw a cat which had been run over. It was badly mutilated and bloody. It was lying on the street under a piece of clothing. I raised the piece of clothing and exposed the cat to a woman."

The patient made the following associations: His girl friend had inadvertently crushed a mouse. Its intestines protruded but it was still alive. She was disgusted with the sight. The patient, although disgusted himself, removed the mouse.

His friend is afraid of mice. He often plays practical jokes on her by pretending he hears mice in the room. Once, as a birthday joke, he presented her with a gift package containing a live mouse. On another occasion he wanted to call her attention to a crushed animal on the street, knowing she had a horror of such sights. In bed with another girl friend he once made believe that he had died.

When he was an adolescent, his parents gave a dinner party to which they had invited some new friends. The patient made his appearance without greeting anyone. He sat down and for a long time did not say a word. Suddenly he began to distort his features and to make grimaces "like an idiot." The guests were shocked and his parents were embarrassed. Then just as suddenly, he smiled charmingly and began to talk in his normal fashion. "Everyone was relieved."

His girl friend wears no underclothes. When he drives with her he will suddenly throw up her dress and expose her.

At the party, the night before the dream, he shocked his hostess and several of the women guests by making crude comments about their clothes or appearance.

He is not afraid of menstruating women, he says. On the contrary, he often goes out of his way to have relations with them. However, when he sees blood on women's legs he is disgusted. His next association was, "The animal in the dream was bloody, all cut up. I am disgusted by the idea of the dead animal."

The character trait of practical joking was interpreted in terms of an identification with the aggressor plus the reassuring element of denial—that is, what looks so terrible is not real; it is just a joke.

The patient responded with the memory of another practical joke. At the age of fifteen he had been the guest of a family friendly with his own. Sometime after he left them he wrote a thank you note, in which he bemoaned his unhappy fate, hinting that he had either been locked up in jail or confined in an insane asylum. Shortly thereafter, his mother received a letter from these friends expressing regret at what had happened to the patient. When his mother confronted him he laughed and said that it was all a joke.

His next association was, "My mother exposed herself so much I am sure I must have seen her bleeding. She was very open and must have left her pads around." (There is considerable evidence to indicate that this was true and that the patient may have witnessed some obstetrical accident.)

The patient does not recall wearing any of his mother's clothing. However, he admitted to using her facial cream and eyelash curlers as well as some of her ski clothes and snow boots. To this information, the patient added, "those things are about the same for a man as for a woman."

At camp at the age of fifteen he used to play the game of putting his penis between his thighs to simulate the vulva. He would then separate his legs and would be amused at the sight of the penis popping out.

Confirmation of the interpretation of his hoaxing came in the form of a striking bit of acting out. At the following session, after a long holiday weekend, the patient stated that he did not have relations with the aggressive, seductive woman. The morning after the date with that woman, in the company of several friends and his girl friend, he went away for the weekend. He watched his friend putting pink curlers in her hair. As a joke he put them in his own hair and dressed in her nightgown. Thus attired, he entered a room occupied by some of his friends, sidling in backwards, whereupon he suddenly turned around and faced them fully, all the while speaking in a deep, bass voice. His friends were shocked and then they all laughed. The patient then told the analyst, "I often imitate women for short periods of time."

Discussion

In the development of these patients the element of traumatic exposure to the female genital was prominent in the data. There was intimate, repeated contact with the female genitals and early exposure to female sexual hygiene in the form of menstrual pads, douche bags, and similar items. For these patients, as young boys, the confrontation with the female genital had proved to be profoundly traumatic. The intensity of the impact was determined in large measure by the degree to which the young boy was prepared for what he saw. The fact that the child was repeatedly exposed to the female genital by an aggressive mother seemed to be of greater significance than the element of the suddenness of the exposure, although in the patient's formal organization of memory, the latter element seemed to be stressed. Vulnerability to castration anxiety, of course, must be related to the concomitant events and conflicts operative during the oedipal phase, as well as to the manner in which experiences during the prephallic phases served to shape the structure of the ego's system of defenses and its propensity to anxiety.

During the latency period and extending further into the early phases of adolescence, a trend in the direction of developing perversions could be noted. These trends were not very serious nor did they necessarily eventuate in a solidly structured perversion, that is, they did not come to dominate all sexual activity nor did they constitute a regular, unfailing concomitant of masturbation. On the contrary, there was something playful, something tentative and mobile about the perverse behavior. In some cases, relatively stable perversions did develop. In both perverse tendencies and in the organized perversions, analytic study showed the various ways in which the ego had tried to master castration anxiety. The most important methods used consisted of a combination of undoing, denial, and isolation. Through these mechanisms of defense the ego attempted to secure freedom from anxiety. Essentially the young patient tried to convince himself that the testimony of his senses had been faulty. The compelling need to deny is striking in all of these cases.

No matter how intricate the system of defenses employed, it was never completely successful in accomplishing its purpose. The inner pressure of instinctual drive and the force of external stimulation made repetition of the perverse practices imperative. The perverse practice was based upon a reassuring daydream, essentially a form of denial in phantasy (A. Freud, 1946). This phantasy was unconscious. It was, in fact, in connection with fetishism that Freud (1927) had demonstrated that the reassuring phantasy of the fetishist is characteristically unconscious. In general, the specific form which a perversion takes depends upon the defense mechanism employed by the ego in the organization of the reassuring phantasy. Essentially the perversion is the phantasy acted out. This accounts for the fact that so frequently perverse activity is connected with masturbation. The methods employed by the ego to attain reassurance against anxiety are varied and are not mutually exclusive. It is not uncommon, therefore, to find several different perverse trends existing side by side in the same person. I would suspect that this is the rule rather than the exception.

Some mention must be made of the role of the superego in the organization of the perversion. Fear of retaliation and guilt seem to play only a minor deterrent force regarding the practicing of the perversion itself. It would seem that in individuals who exhibit the character traits described above, one observes a superego corrupted not by bribery as Alexander (1930) described, but rather a superego subverted by anxiety. Frequently the model for perverse solutions to internal conflict had been suggested by significant individuals in the patient's environment, with whom the patient had identified. It is not only the possible traumatic seduction into perversion which is significant but also the insinuation by way of identification of a specific type of defense. The deterrent influence of the superego is also mitigated in these cases by the playful quality which seems to attend the practice of these perverse acts. Up to a certain point they may seem like a game and in slightly disguised form, it is easy enough for the seemingly innocent little boy to beguile an audience of adults with his pantomime of perversion. In so doing he enlists their aid in overcoming superego reproaches by casting the unsuspecting adults in the role of a permissive auxiliary superego (Arlow, 1971).

In previous communications (1953, 1969a, b) I have described the value of analyzing the details of unconscious phantasy activity in order to understand symptoms and altered ego states. The same approach may be applied to understanding the relationship among symptom, character trait, and perversion. The conflicts which grow out of the oedipal period usually find concrete expression in the form of an unconscious phantasy. Depending on how the ego defends itself against the anxiety associated with the phantasy, different forms of psychological resultants may be observed. Accordingly, out of the same conflict it is possible for the individual to develop a symptom, a character trait, or a perversion. Furthermore, it is possible for these three different kinds of solutions to exist side by side in the same person. In the patients whom I have discussed above, a number of defensive maneuvers on the part of the ego united in the form of a perverse tendency. After the passage of time, usually toward the latter period of adolescence, in some of these patients a second attempt was made to control the castration anxiety which was being fended off through the perversion. In some instances the perverse activity was given up entirely and only a miniscule token act persisted. It is my impression that this was the rule rather than the exception. Some disguised residue of both perverse activity and phantasy can usually be found if searched for carefully enough. The perverse activity may be so symbolic and so distant from any recognizable sexual expression as to give the impression that the problem, from all external indications, has been resolved. This may account for the great number of patients who report that they have daydreams of a perverse nature but no actual perversions. For some patients entertaining a perverse phantasy during intercourse becomes the obligatory condition guaranteeing potency. In other instances the perverse activity forms part of the manifest content of the dream which is dreamt after sexual relations. In any event, in many of these patients careful investigation shows that at some time during adolescence perverse activity had been practiced and then had been overcome more or less as the adult sexual identity took its final form. What appeared in consciousness was a distortion of character or

the emergence of certain unusual character traits. In this paper I
have described the origin of certain such traits. The genesis of
these unusual characteristics is analogous to the genesis of the
character neurosis. In the latter, a distortion of behavior or
character takes the place of what had once been a psychoneurosis. In the patients discussed above the distortion of behavior
or character takes the place of what had once been a perversion or
a perverse trend. Accordingly, I suggest that such distortions of
character may properly be designated as character perversion.

Conclusion

In this communication I have attempted to trace the origin of certain unusual character traits through the study of the vicissitudes
of defense directed against the emergence of unconscious phantasy. What was stressed particularly was the combination of
defense mechanisms employed by the ego to ward off the anxiety
associated with the danger situation. During latency and adolescence these unconscious phantasies were part of perverse trends
or of an organized perversion which had been practiced. All of
these patients for various reasons suffered from intense castration anxiety. Particularly traumatic was the exposure to the
female genital. The traumatic impact of this event depended in
large measure upon antecedent experiences and conflicts. The
young patients responded with intense castration anxiety which
they tried to master primarily through using the mechanism of
denial in phantasy. Acting out of these phantasies led at some
point to perverse sexual practices. These practices constituted a
concretization of the phantasy which attempted to deny the
reality of the female genital. The phantasies together with the
perversion formed the major portion of the masturbation complex during adolescence. During the latter part of adolescence a
second attempt was made to control the anxiety bound by the
perverse activity. This attempt was partially successful; for the most
part the perverse activity stopped and in some instances the concomitant phantasy disappeared from conscious mental life.
Either alongside a severely attenuated set of perverse activities or
in place of such activities, there appeared some unusual charac-

ter trait which unconsciously served the same reassuring function which previously had been vested in the perversion. Typical for these character traits was the fact that the defensive mechanisms utilized corresponded precisely to the ones typical for the perversion. Accordingly, the unusual character traits had an origin and function in common with the perverse sexual activity; both tended to fend off castration anxiety. The same could be said of symptom formation. It is possible for symptom, character trait, and perverse activity to exist side by side in the same patient representing different methods by which the ego attempts to master a danger situation. In the setting of psychoanalytic treatment, through the analysis of resistance and transference, it becomes possible to observe the defensive import of the perverse character trait and to demonstrate how both the incipient perversion and the subsequent character trait had a common structure, a common origin, and a common function.

Section V
THERAPEUTIC
CONSIDERATIONS

This final section includes papers written from the perspective of the therapist, indicating from clinical experience what types of treatment have been useful for what kinds of patients, and why that may be the case. Giovacchini and Winnicott talk broadly about character disorders in general; Kernberg and Kohut densely, specifically, and definitively about borderline and narcissistic personalities; while Rycroft movingly describes the analysis of a paranoid personality. Other references to therapeutic approaches are to be found in many of the articles in the *Handbook;* examples are, Reich in Section I, Schafer in Section II, and McDougall in Section IV.

Using simple concepts in a highly original way, Winnicott provides an elegant account of character disorders and their treatment. Environmental failure disrupts the normal maturational process and burdens the child with a persisting wish to accommodate to some degree an antisocial tendency. Acting upon the intact personality, this antisocial tendency produces a character distortion which the individual attempts to socialize in various ways. He may try to conceal it, find secondary gains for it, or fit in with social custom. The socializing efforts may lead to impoverishment of personality and failure to socialize on a more general level. Problems in this process become the basis for psychotherapy. There are three aims proper to the therapy of character disorders. The first involves reaching the illness behind the distortion—making the patient ill as it were, instead of hiding the illness. The second involves managing the emerging antisocial acting out in two ways, first, by acknowledging the patient's right to reliable love and, second, by providing an ego-supportive structure that can withstand attack. The third aim involves freeing a blocked maturational process by helping the patient become appropriately angry instead of traumatized, and helping him or her to go back to the state of affairs before the trauma occurred.

For Giovacchini, patients suffering from serious character pathology share a number of features. Having been subjected to early privation, they are unable to help themselves. They present primitive, undifferentiated psychic states—poorly structured amorphous self representations—requiring a kind of help they cannot articulate because it cannot be articulated. They frantically seek reassurance that they exist, can be cared for, and can be loved, while at the same time not believing that this is possible. Through creative listening the analyst attempts to understand and respect the patient's productions. Through judicious use of theory he or she lends form to the psychopathology and makes it communicable. Using Winnicottian concepts, Giovacchini highlights the dangers of imposing preconceived concepts and premature closure. He warns of the danger that a pseudoharmony between the analyst's false perspective and the patient's false self might hide the patient's inner core in a mutually shared delusion.

There is nothing amorphous about the borderline patients Kernberg writes about nor about the treatment he advocates. While acknowledging the importance of the Kleinian approach (e.g., Heimann, Rosenfeld, Bion, Segal) in his understanding of the borderline condition and the development of his technique, he questions their use of unmodified psychoanalysis as a form of treatment. For Kernberg, the risk of transference psychosis, a transference–countertransference stalemate, and/or acting out in therapy is too high. The ego of these patients is too weak—they cannot properly dissociate an observing from an experiencing ego or manage the high levels of tension to which their excessive oral aggression predisposes them. On the other hand he disagrees with the extreme of a supportive orientation, finding such an approach shallow, nonprogressive, and conducive to acting out outside of therapy. Kernberg favors a modified form of analysis which involves the introduction of several parameters of technique. In this way the frequent acting out in therapy can be blocked. He emphasizes the role of the strong negative transference and of borderline defenses. Partial interpretation and partial deflection of this negative transference will strengthen the therapeutic alliance. Resolving the pathological defenses, especially projective identification, allows higher level defenses to be used, thereby strengthening the ego—the main goal of treatment.

Kohut's unique views on the natural development of narcissism, the narcissistic personality, and its pathogenesis and analytic treatment are outlined in his paper. Normal narcissistic development involves a bifurcation into a grandiose self and an idealized object. Ordinarily, the former blends into normal ambition and self-esteem, while the latter gives the superego its exalted state. All this happens in an environment of phase-appropriate frustration. Various types of failure can, however, disrupt this process. As a result some psychic structures do not develop properly and remain fixated on an archaic imago. The individual hungrily searches for substitutes in the world around him. Providing he has established a cohesive, albeit grandiose self, analysis can provide him with a second opportunity to continue a more appropriate development of his narcissism.

In analysis, two types of transference characteristic of this type of personality emerge. In the idealizing transference the analyst, seen as all good and powerful, empathically helps the patient to become aware of his need to idealize without allowing a regression to archaic (primitive) grandiose self states. In the mirror transference the analyst is regarded by the analysand as a part function of him and used to reflect grandiose and exhibitionistic desires. In this central part of the analysis of the narcissistic personality, the analyst activates and assists the analysand in facing his grandiose self. Kohut identifies some pitfalls such as moralizing, excessive abstraction, intolerance of admiration, and unpreparedness for periods of minimal narcissistic gratification. Psychoanalytic technique emphasizes empathic awareness of phase-specific narcissistic demands.

Rycroft's moving and detailed account of the four-year analysis of a forceful, unsuccessful actress with an idiosyncratic manner of speaking provides the reader with a dynamic picture of how a paranoid personality changes through therapy. Miss Y. sees herself initially as a female Shakespeare with telepathic powers. She wants to be immortal and share her insights with the analytic community. During the course of the analysis Rycroft comes to see her personality as defensive—an attempt to contradict her unconscious need for object love for a mother who died when she was two years old. Her belief in the value of affective communication has been shattered. The question is whether it can be restored. Through the continuity of the analysis and the sensitive interpretations of her difficulties, Miss Y. is able to overcome her omnipotent attitude and hostile transference. This frees her to work on her sense of desolation and introverted entrapment.

Rycroft's article exemplifies the preceding more general accounts of the therapeutic encounter. For instance, we recognize Giovacchini's comments about the importance of early traumata, the building of a working language, the avoidance of premature closure (e.g., by not seeing Miss Y.'s theory of development as nonsense), steering clear of shared delusions (e.g., the risk of a folie à deux regarding her idiosyncratic manner of speaking), and the need to be rescued. Guntrip's depiction of the schizoid can be seen in Miss Y.'s need to escape the prison of her introversion. Kohut's account of the mirror transference is seen in her need to have Dr. Rycroft recognize her grief. Finally, Kernberg's discussion of the use of parameters is evidenced in the modified fee structure and visiting the patient at home. The importance of the negative transference is demonstrated in the hostility of the first phase of the analysis and in Rycroft's emphasis on the importance of hostility toward an uncomprehending mother imago.

Chapter 24

PSYCHOTHERAPY OF
CHARACTER DISORDERS

D<small>ONALD</small> W. W<small>INNICOTT</small>

Although the title chosen for this chapter is the "Psychotherapy of Character Disorders," it is not possible to avoid a discussion of the meaning of the term *character disorder*. As Fenichel (1945, p. 539) remarks, "The question may be raised whether there is any analysis that is not 'character analysis.' All symptoms are the outcome of specific ego attitudes, which in analysis make their appearance as resistances and which have been developed during infantile conflicts. This is true. And to a certain degree, really, all analyses are character analyses." And again, "Character disorders do not form a nosological unit. The mechanisms at the basis of character disorder may be as different as the mechanisms at the basis of symptom neuroses. Thus a hysterical character will be more easily treated than a compulsive one, a compulsive one more easily than a narcissistic one."

It is clear that either the term is too wide to be useful, or else I shall need to use it in a special way. In the latter case I must indicate the use I shall make of the term in this paper.

First, there must be confusion unless it be recognized that the three terms: *character,* a *good character,* and a *character disorder,* bring to mind three very different phenomena, and it would be artificial to deal with all three at one and the same time, yet these three are interrelated.

Freud wrote (1905c) that "a fairly reliable character" is one of the prerequisites for a successful analysis (Fenichel, 1945, p.

This chapter originally appeared in a longer form in *The Maturational Processes and the Facilitating Environment,* pp. 203–216. New York: International Universities Press, 1965. Reprinted by permission of the publisher.

461

537); but we are considering *unreliability* in the personality, and Fenichel asks: can this unreliability be treated? He might have asked: what is its etiology?

When I look at character disorders I find I am looking at *whole persons*. There is in the term an implication of a degree of integration, itself a sign of psychiatric health.

The papers that have preceded mine have taught us much, and have strengthened me in the idea of character as something that belongs to integration. Character is a manifestation of successful integration, and a disorder of character is a distortion of the ego structure, integration being nevertheless maintained. It is perhaps good to remember that integration has a time factor. The child's character has formed on the basis of a steady developmental process, and in this respect the child has a past and a future.

It would seem to be valuable to use the term *character disorder* in description of a child's attempt to accommodate his or her own developmental abnormalities or deficiencies. Always we assume that the personality structure is able to withstand the strain of the abnormality. The child needs to come to terms with the personal pattern of anxiety or compulsion or mood or suspicion, etc., and also to relate this to the requirements and expectations of the immediate environment.

In my opinion the value of the term belongs specifically to a description of personality distortion that comes about *when the child needs to accommodate some degree of antisocial tendency*. This leads immediately to a statement of my use of this term.

I am using these words which enable us to focus our attention not so much on behavior as on those roots of misbehavior that extend over the whole area between normality and delinquency. The antisocial tendency can be examined in your own healthy child who at the age of two takes a coin from his mother's handbag.

The antisocial tendency always arises out of a *deprivation* and represents the child's claim to get back behind the deprivation to the state of affairs that obtained when all was well. I cannot develop this theme here, but this thing that I call antisocial tendency must be mentioned because it is found regularly in the dissection of character disorder. The child in accommodating the antisocial tendency that is his or hers may hide it, may develop a reaction formation to it, such as becoming a prig, may develop a grievance and acquire a complaining character, may specialize in day-dreaming, lying, mild chronic masturbating activity, bed-wetting, compulsive thumb-sucking, thigh-rubbing, etc., or may periodically manifest the antisocial tendency (that is his or hers) in a *behavior disorder*. This latter is always associated with hope, and it is either of the nature of stealing or of aggressive activity and destruction. It is compulsive.

Character disorder, then, according to my way of looking at things, refers most significantly to the distortion of the *intact* personality that results from the antisocial elements in it. It is the antisocial element that determines society's involvement. Society (the child's family and so on) must meet the challenge, and must *like or dislike* the character and the character disorder.

Here then is the beginning of a description:

> Character disorders are not schizophrenia. In character disorder there is hidden illness in the intact personality. Character disorders in some way and to some degree actively involve society.
>
> Character disorders may be divided according to:
>
> Success or failure on the part of the individual in the attempt of the total personality to hide the illness element. Success here means that the personality, though impoverished, has become able to socialize the character distortion to find secondary gains or to fit in with a social custom.
>
> Failure here means that the impoverishment of the personality carries along with it a failure in establishment of a relation to society as a whole, on account of the hidden illness element.

In fact, society plays its part in the determination of the fate of a person with character disorder, and does this in various ways. For example:

> Society tolerates individual illness to a degree.
> Society tolerates failure of the individual to contribute-in.
> Society tolerates or even enjoys distortions of the mode of the individual's contributing-in.

or   Society meets the challenge of the antisocial tendency of an individual, and its reaction is being motivated by:

1. Revenge.
2. The wish to socialize the individual.
3. Understanding and the application of understanding to prevention.

The individual with character disorder may suffer from:

1. Impoverishment of personality, sense of grievance, unreality, awareness of lack of serious purpose, etc.
2. Failure to socialize.

Here then is a basis for psychotherapy, because psychotherapy relates to individual *suffering* and need for help. But this suffering in character disorder only belongs to the early stages in the individual's illness; the secondary gains quickly take over, lessen the suffering, and interfere with the drive of the individual to seek help or to accept help offered.

It must be recognized that in respect of "success" (character disorder hidden and socialized) *psychotherapy makes the individual ill,* because illness lies between the defense and the individual's health. By contrast, in respect of "unsuccessful" hiding of character disorder, although there may be an initial drive in the individual to seek help at an early stage, because of society's reactions, this motive does not necessarily carry the patient through to the treatment of the deeper illness.

The clue to the treatment of character disorder is given by the part the environment plays in the case of *natural cure*. In the slight case the environment can "cure" because the cause was an environmental failure in the area of ego-support and protection at a stage of the individual's dependence. This explains why it is that children are regularly "cured" of incipient character disorder in the course of their own childhood development simply by making use of home life. Parents have a second and third chance to bring their children through, in spite of failures of management (mostly inevitable) in the earliest stages when the child is highly dependent. Family life is the place therefore that offers the best opportunity for investigation into the etiology of character disorder; and indeed it is in the family life, or its substitute, that the child's *character* is being built up in positive ways.

Etiology of Character Disorder

In considering the etiology of character disorder it is necessary to take for granted both the maturational process in the child, the conflict-free sphere of the ego (Hartmann), also forward movement with anxiety drive (Klein), and the function of the environment which facilitates the maturational processes. Environmental provision must be "good" enough if maturation is to become a fact in the case of any one child.

With this in mind, one can say that there are two extremes of distortion, and that these relate to the stage of maturation of the individual at which environmental failure did actually overstrain the ego's capacity for organizing defenses:

> At one extreme is the ego hiding *psychoneurotic* symptom formations (set up relative to anxiety belonging to the Oedipus complex). Here the hidden illness is a matter of conflict in the individual's personal unconscious.
>
> At the other extreme is the ego hiding *psychotic* symptom formations (splitting, dissociations, reality side-slipping, depersonalization, regression and omnipotent dependencies, etc.). Here the hidden illness is in the ego structure.

But the matter of society's essential involvement does not depend on the answer to the question: is the hidden illness psychoneurotic or psychotic? In fact, in character disorder there is this other element, *the individual's* correct perception at a time in early childhood that at first all was well, or well enough, and then that all was not well. In other words, that there happened at a certain time, or over a phase of development, an actual failure of ego support that held up the individual's emotional development. A reaction in the individual to this disturbance took the place of simple growth. The maturational processes became dammed up because of a failure of the facilitating environment.

This theory of the etiology of character disorder, if correct, leads to a new statement of character disorder at its inception. The individual in this category carries on with two separate burdens. One of these, of course, is the increasing burden of a disturbed and in some respects stunted or postponed maturational process. The other is the hope, a hope that never becomes quite extinguished, that the environment may acknowledge and make up for the specific failure that did the damage. In the vast majority of cases the parents or the family or guardians of the child recognize the fact of the "letdown" (so often unavoidable) and by a period of special management, spoiling, or what could be called mental nursing, they see the child through to a recovery from the trauma.

When the family does not mend its failures the child goes forward with certain handicaps, being engaged in

1. arranging to live a life in spite of emotional stunting, and
2. all the time liable to moments of hope, moments when it would seem to be possible to force the environment to effect a cure (hence: acting out).

Between the clinical state of a child who has been hurt in the way that is being described here and the resumption of that child's emotional development, and all that that means in terms of socialization, there is this need to make society acknowledge and repay. Behind a child's maladjustment is always a failure of the environment to adjust to the child's absolute needs at a time of relative dependence. (Such failure is initially a failure of nurture.) Then there can be added a failure of the family to heal the effects of such failures; and then there may be added the failure of society as it takes the family's place. Let it be emphasized that in this type of case the initial failure can be shown to have happened at a time at which the child's development had made it just possible for him or her to perceive the fact of the failure and to perceive the nature of the environment's maladjustment.

The child now displays an antisocial tendency, which (as I have said) in the stage before the development of secondary gains is always a manifestation of hope. This antisocial tendency is liable to show in two forms:

1. The staking of claims on people's time, concern, money, etc. (manifested by stealing).
2. The expectation of that degree of structural strength and organization and "comeback" that is essential if the child is to be able to rest, relax, disintegrate, feel secure (manifested by destruction which provokes strong management).

On the basis of this theory of the etiology of character disorder I can proceed to examine the matter of therapy.

Indications for Therapy

Therapy of character disorder has three aims:

1. A dissection down to the illness that is hidden and that appears in the character distortion. Preparatory to this may be a period in which the individual is invited to become a patient, to become ill instead of hiding illness.
2. To meet the antisocial tendency which, from the point of view of the therapist, is evidence of hope in the patient; to meet it as an S.O.S., a *cri de coeur,* a signal of distress.
3. Analysis that takes into consideration both the ego distortion and the patient's exploitation of his or her id drives during attempts at self-cure.

The attempt to meet the patient's antisocial tendency has two aspects:

1. The allowance of the patient's claims to rights in terms of a person's love and reliability.
2. The provision of an ego-supportive structure that is relatively indestructible.

As this implies, the patient will from time to time be acting out, and as long as this has a relation to the transference it can be managed and interpreted. The troubles in therapy come in relation to antisocial acting out which is outside the total therapeutic machinery, that is to say, which involves society.

In regard to the treatment of hidden illness and of ego distortion, the need is for psychotherapy. But at the same time the antisocial tendency must be engaged, as and when it appears. The aim in this part of the treatment is to arrive at the original trauma. This has to be done in the course of the psychotherapy, or if psychotherapy is not available, in the course of the specialized management that is provided.

In this work the failures of the therapist or of those managing the child's life will be real and they can be shown to reproduce the original failures, in token form. These failures are real indeed, and especially so insofar as the patient is either regressed to the dependence of the appropriate age, or else remembering. The acknowledgment of the analyst's or guardian's failure enables the patient to become appropriately angry instead of traumatized. *The patient needs to reach back through the transference trauma to the state of affairs that obtained before the original trauma.* (In some cases there is a possibility of quick arrival at deprivation trauma in a first interview.) The reaction to the current failure only makes sense insofar as the current failure *is* the original environmental failure from the point of view of the child. Reproduction in the treatment of examples as they arise of the original environment failure, along with the patient's experience of anger that is appropriate, frees the patient's maturational processes; and it must be remembered that the patient is in a dependent state and needing ego-support and environmental management (holding) in the treatment setting, and the next phase needs to be a period of emotional growth in which the character builds up positively and loses its distortions.

In a favorable case the acting out that belongs to these cases is confined to the transference, or can be brought into the transference productively by interpretation of displacement, symbolism, and projection. At one extreme is the common "natural" cure that takes place in the child's family. At the other extreme are the severely disturbed patients whose acting out may make treatment by interpretation impossible because the work gets interrupted by society's reactions to stealing or destructiveness.

In a moderately severe case the acting out can be managed provided that the therapist understands its meaning and significance. It can be said that acting out is the alternative to despair. Most of the time the patient is hopeless about correcting the original trauma and so lives in a state of relative depression or of dissociations that mask the chaotic state that is always threatening. When, however, the patient starts to make an object relationship, or to cathect a person, then there starts up an antisocial tendency, a compulsion either to lay claims (steal) or by destructive behavior to activate harsh or even vindictive management.

In every case, if psychotherapy is to be successful, the patient must be seen through one or many of these awkward phases of manifest antisocial behavior, and only too often it is just at these awkward points in the case that treatment is interrupted. The case is dropped not necessarily because the situation cannot be tolerated, but (as likely as not) because those in charge do not know that these acting-out phases are inherent, and that they can have a positive value.

In severe cases these phases in management or treatment present difficulties that are so great that the law (society) takes over, and at the same time psychotherapy goes into abeyance. Society's revenge takes the place of pity or sympathy, and the individual ceases to suffer and be a patient, and instead becomes a criminal with a delusion of persecution.

It is my intention to draw attention to *the positive element in character disorder*. Failure to achieve character disorder in the individual who is trying to accommodate some degree of anti-social tendency indicates a liability to psychotic breakdown. Character disorder indicates that the individual's ego structure can bind the energies that belong to the stunting of maturational processes and also the abnormalities in the interaction of the individual child and the family. Until secondary gains have become a feature, the personality with character disorder is always liable to break down into paranoia, manic depression, psychosis, or schizophrenia.

To sum up, a statement on the treatment of character disorder can start with the dictum that such a treatment is like that of any other psychological disorder, namely, psychoanalysis if it be available. There must follow the following considerations:

1. Psychoanalysis may succeed, but the analyst must expect to find *acting out* in the transference, and must understand

the significance of this acting out, and be able to give it positive value.

2. The analysis may succeed but be difficult because the hidden illness has psychotic features, so that the patient must become ill (psychotic, schizoid) before starting to get better; and all the resources of the analyst will be needed to deal with the primitive defense mechanisms that will be a feature.

3. The analysis may be succeeding, but as acting out is not confined to the transference relationship the patient is removed from the analyst's reach because of society's reaction to the patient's antisocial tendency or because of the operation of the law. There is room for great variation here, owing to the variability of society's reaction, ranging from crude revenge to an expression of society's willingness to give the patient a chance to make late socialization.

4. In many cases incipient character disorder is treated and treated successfully in the child's home, by a phase or by phases of special management (spoiling) or by especially *personal* care or strict control by a person who loves the child. An extension of this is the treatment of incipient or early character disorder without psychotherapy by management in groups designed to give what the child's own family cannot give in the way of special management.

5. By the time the patient comes to treatment there may already be a fixed antisocial tendency manifest, and a hardened attitude in the patient fostered by secondary gains, in which case the question of psychoanalysis does not arise. Then the aim is to provide firm management by understanding persons, and to provide this as a *treatment* in advance of its being provided as a *corrective* by court order. Personal psychotherapy can be added if it is available.

Finally,

6. The character disorder case may present as a court case, with society's reaction represented by the probation

order or by committal to an approved school or a penal
institution.

It can happen that early committal by a court proves to be a
positive element in the patient's socialization. This corresponds
again to the natural cure that commonly takes place in the patient's
family; society's reaction has been, for the patient, a practical
demonstration of its "love," that is of its willingness to "hold" the
patient's unintegrated self, and to meet aggression with firmness
(to limit the effects of maniacal episodes) and to meet hatred with
hatred, appropriate and under control. This last is the best that
some deprived children will ever get by way of satisfactory management, and many restless antisocial deprived children change
from ineducable to educable in the strict regime of a remand
home. The danger here is that because restless antisocial children
thrive in an atmosphere of dictatorship this may breed dictators,
and may even make educationalists think that an atmosphere of
strict discipline, with every minute of the child's day filled, is good
educational treatment for normal children, which it is not.

Clinical Illustrations

A Common Type of Case

A boy in later latency (first seen at ten years) was having psychoanalytic treatment from me. His restlessness and liability to
outbreaks of rage started from a very early date, soon after his
birth and long before he was weaned at eight months. His mother
was a neurotic person and all her life more or less depressed. He
was a thief and given to aggressive outbursts. His analysis was
going well, and in the course of a year of daily sessions much
straightforward analytic work was accomplished. He became
very excited, however, as his relationship to me developed
significance, and he climbed out onto the clinic roof and flooded
out the clinic and made so much noise that the treatment had to
stop. Sometimes there was danger to me; he also broke into my
car outside the clinic and drove off in bottom gear by using the
self-starter, thus obviating the need for a car key. At the same time
he started stealing again and being aggressive outside the treat-

ment setting, and he was sent by the Juvenile Court to an approved school just at a time when the treatment by psychoanalysis was in full spate. Perhaps if I had been much stronger than he I might have managed this phase, and so have had an opportunity to complete the analysis. As it was I had to give up. (This boy did moderately well. He became a lorry [truck] driver, which suited his restlessness. He had kept his job fourteen years at the time of the follow-up. He married and had three children. His wife divorced him, after which he kept in touch with his mother, from whom the details of the follow-up were obtained.)

Three Favorable Cases

A boy of eight started stealing. He had suffered a relative deprivation (in his own good home setting) when he was two, at the time his mother conceived, and became pathologically anxious. The parents had managed to meet this boy's special needs and had almost succeeded in effecting a natural cure of his condition. I helped them in this long task by giving them some understanding of what they were doing. In one therapeutic consultation when the boy was eight it was possible for me to get this boy into feeling-contact with his deprivation, and he reached back to an object relationship to the good mother of his infancy. Along with this the stealing ceased.

A girl of eight years came to me because of stealing. She had suffered a relative deprivation in her own good home at the age of four to five years. In one psychotherapeutic consultation she reached back to her early infantile contact with a good mother, and at the same time her stealing disappeared. She was also wetting and messing and this minor manifestation of the antisocial tendency persisted for some time.

A boy of thirteen years, at a public school a long way from his good home, was stealing in a big way, also slashing sheets and upsetting the school by getting boys into trouble and by leaving obscene notes in lavatories [toilets], and so on. In a therapeutic consultation he was able to let me know that he had been through a period of intolerable strain at the age of six when he went away to boarding school. I was able to arrange for this boy (middle child of three) to be allowed a period of "mental nursing" in his own home. He used this for a regressive phase, and then went to day school. Later he went to a boarding school in the neighborhood of his home. His antisocial symptoms ceased abruptly after his one interview with me and follow-up shows that he has done well. He has now passed through a university, and is establishing himself as a man. Of this case it is particularly true to say that the patient brought with him the understanding of his case, and what he needed was for the facts to be acknowledged and for an attempt to be made to mend, in token form, the environmental failure.

Comment

In these three cases in which help could be given when secondary gains had not become a feature the general attitude of myself as psychiatrist enabled the child in each case to state a specific area of relative deprivation, and the fact that this was accepted as real and true enabled the child to reach back over the gap and make anew a relationship with good objects that had been blocked.

A Case on the Borderline Between Character Disorder and Psychosis

A boy has been under my care over a period of years. I have only seen him once, and most of my contacts have been with the mother at times of crisis. Many have tried to give direct help to the boy, who is now twenty, but he quickly becomes uncooperative.

This boy has a high I.Q. and all those whom he has allowed to teach him have said that he could be exceptionally brilliant as an actor, a poet, an artist, [or] a musician. He has not stayed long at any one school but by self-tuition has kept well ahead of his peers, and he did this in early adolescence by coaching his friends in their schoolwork, then keeping in touch.

In the latency period he was hospitalized and diagnosed schizophrenic. In the hospital he undertook the "treatment" of the other boys, and he never accepted his position as a patient. Eventually he ran away and had a long period without schooling.

He would like in bed listening to lugubrious music, or lock himself into the house so that no one could get to him. He constantly threatened suicide, chiefly in relation to violent love affairs. Periodically he would organize a party, and this would go on indefinitely, and damage was sometimes done to property.

This boy lived with his mother in a small flat and he kept her constantly in a state of worry, and there was never any possibility of an outcome since he would not go away, he would not go to school or to hospital, and he was clever enough to do exactly as he wanted to do, and he never became criminal, and so kept out of the jurisdiction of the law.

At various times I helped the mother by putting her in touch with the police, the probation service, and other social services, and when eventually he said he would go to a certain grammar school I "pulled strings" to enable him to do this. He was found to be well ahead of his age group, and the masters gave him great encouragement because of his brilliance. But he left school before time, and obtained a scholarship for a good college of acting. At this point he decided that he had the wrong-shaped nose, and eventually he persuaded his mother to pay a plastic surgeon to alter it from retroussé to straight. Then he found other reasons why he could not go forward to any success, and yet he gave no one any opportunity to help him. This continues, and at present he is in the observation ward of a mental hospital, but he will find a way of leaving this and will settle in at home once more.

This boy has an early history that gives the clue to the antisocial part of his character disorder. In fact he was the result of a partnership that foundered soon after its unhappy start, and the father soon after separating from the mother himself became a paranoid casualty. This marriage followed immediately after a tragedy, and was doomed to failure because the boy's mother had not yet recovered from the loss of her much-loved fiancé who, as she felt, was killed by the carelessness of this man whom she married and who became the father of the boy.

This boy could have been helped at an early age, perhaps six, when he was first seen by a psychiatrist. He could then have led the psychiatrist to the material of his relative deprivation, and he could then have been told about his mother's personal problem, and the reason for the ambivalence in her relationship to him.

But instead the boy was placed in a hospital ward, and from this time on he hardened into a case of character disorder, becoming a person who compulsively tantalizes his mother and his teachers and his friends.

I have not attempted to describe a case treated by psychoanalysis in this series of short case descriptions.

Cases treated by management alone are innumerable and include all those children who when deprived in one way or another are adopted, or fostered out, or placed in small homes that are run as therapeutic institutions and on personal lines. It would be giving a false impression to describe one case in this category. It is indeed necessary to draw attention to the fact that incipient character disorder is being treated successfully all the time, especially in the home, in social groups of all kinds, and quite apart from psychotherapy.

Nevertheless, it is intensive work with the few cases that throws light on the problem of character disorder as of other types of psychological disorders, and it is work of the psychoanalytic groups in various countries that has laid the basis for a theoretical statement and has begun to explain to the specialized therapeutic groups what it is that is being done in such groups that so often succeeds in the prevention or treatment of character disorder.

Chapter 25

CHARACTER DISORDERS:
FORM AND STRUCTURE

PETER L. GIOVACCHINI

Patients suffering from characterological problems are familiar to most analysts. Although there are different ways of classifying patients, one easily recognizes a group of patients who present themselves as needy persons, often tense and feeling desperate and miserable, and when they finally find themselves in analysts' offices they manage to impress them with their helplessness and vulnerability. Their behavior takes many forms, ranging from an arrogant denial of any inner need to poignant bewildering appeals for help. As therapists, we feel impelled to help, but often we find ourselves feeling as helpless as the patient.

These patients, who appear ever more frequently in our consultation rooms, afford us both a practical and theoretical challenge. When a therapist focuses upon a clinical problem, he tries to understand the patient on the basis of what he has learned from other patients and to utilize his professional orientation (his theoretical frame of reference) to determine why the patient has this particular constellation of problems and how best to deal with it. Regarding patients suffering from characterological problems, the psychodynamic model with its concentration on id–ego conflict conceptualized in defensive stages of psychosexual development has not been particularly helpful. I believe that the inadequacy of our theory to help us understand these patients has been responsible for many shifts of theoretical focus. The concentration upon ego psychology and the indiscriminate adoption of the Kleinian viewpoint in some circles may well have

This chapter originally appeared in the *International Journal of Psycho-Analysis*, 543:153–160, 1973. Reprinted by permission of the author and the publisher.

been a consequence of practical problems, confusion and ignorance regarding this enigmatic and preponderant group of patients.

In the last decade our conceptual sophistication regarding early character development and maldevelopment has increased enormously and many analysts (Klein, 1948; Winnicott, 1949a, 1954; Khan, 1960; Searles, 1965; Boyer and Giovacchini, 1967; Kernberg, 1968, among others) have striven toward an integration of therapeutic work and theoretical understanding of these extremely difficult patients.

Impact of Theoretical Focus

Our theoretical orientation determines our therapeutic style. In a well-established analytic relationship the patient finds the analyst's frame of reference understandable and he is able to respond within that frame. This may not happen immediately. Eventually, however, he will become familiar with the analyst's conceptual viewpoint and make it part of his own.

I am referring to the impact our theoretical orientations have upon *determining* the patient's adaptive and defensive behavior during analysis, as well as defining core conflicts and ego defects.

The above implies that the analyst, as Freud (1914) was so often accused, is, by suggestion, forcing his preconceived notions upon the patient and making him conform to his bias (see below). The situation is by no means that simple. I hope to demonstrate that there is a subtle interaction between analyst and patient which has a reciprocal influence, but it threatens the autonomy of neither participant. On the contrary, autonomy is enhanced. In her book, *The Hands of the Living God* (1969) Marion Milner has much to say about the form that a characterological disorder might take. Her patient, a schizoid woman referred to as Susan, brought many drawings into the analysis. Mrs. Milner interpreted them in terms of a progression from amorphous lack of form to anal structuralization. Others would certainly have made different interpretations, especially when Mrs. Milner elaborated from a picture that often did not seem to warrant such a detailed interpretation. It seemed that the therapist's opinions were incorporated by the patient and then used as points of departure for extensions of Mrs. Milner's ideas into other drawings and discussions. These discussions became the central issue of the therapeutic interaction.

Two points about the forms of therapeutic interaction have to be stressed about Mrs. Milner's patient, a highly disturbed young woman who had states of psychotic decompensation. First, the patient wanted to conduct treatment by presenting Mrs. Milner with drawings, either drawn during the session or between sessions. Second, the patient's material was characterized initially by lack of structure; its amorphous qualities were reflected in both her associations and drawings.

Primitive undifferentiated psychic states have to be thoroughly understood, since they are characteristic of this large group of patients. Mechanisms and structural concepts have to be associated with content if we are to give them verbal form. It is precisely this content that constitutes psychopathology.

In a sense, then, the therapist can be said to determine the form of psychopathology, just as he determines what frame of reference the patient will best operate in (Mrs. Milner both allowed and encouraged Susan to bring her drawings into the session). With the understanding that there is always mutuality in a smoothly equilibrated psychoanalytic relationship, the therapist's role not only in determining the mode and direction of treatment, but in structuring the patient's psychopathology, especially in patients suffering from severe characterological problems, deserves special emphasis.

At first, one might assert that such a role on the part of therapist is intrusive and contradicts the aim of fostering autonomy. The suggestive influence of the analyst has already been referred to and it would seem that such an approach would interfere with the process of self-cure and not allow the developmental drive to unfold spontaneously. However, if the therapist's theoretical orientation does not prejudge therapeutic outcome, this is only an apparent contradiction. More precisely, if the analyst's conceptual orientation includes the expectation of working with all forms and manifestations of regression as they occur, that is, the analyst does not consider his theoretical framework as important as his clinical experience, he will not intrude upon the patient's autonomy. In fact, the patient relates to the analyst as his infantile orientation dictates, and the analyst merely provides a setting in which the regression is relatively comfortable or, at least, manageable. Nonetheless, the direction and nature of the regression are determined by the patient's intrapsychic needs.

In other words, psychic processes and mechanisms—for example, projection and introjection, symbiotic fusion, reintegration of split-off parts of the self, and so on—are all elements instrumental to the self-curative process of analysis. The patient tries to teach us the therapeutic principles, such as allowing him to experience all of these processes instead of interfering with them, an activity that is sometimes rationalized as analyzing away pathogenic resistive elements.

When the analyst constructs the conceptual basis for emotional problems by clothing inchoate inner processes with words, he is in a sense constructing the patient's psychopathology. Being able to perceive in terms of concepts adds an important dimension to analytic understanding, and in many respects defines the illness. The ability to raise primitive mechanisms to abstract levels within an internally consistent theoretical system is shared with the patient, and once he is able to use the "words" the analyst provides one might acknowledge that the therapist has succeeded in *creating a setting* which makes the manifest elements of the patient's psychopathology communicable.

For example, Mrs. Milner interprets her patient's early drawings as fecal representations, concrete pictorial expressions of processes related to internal regulation and control of disruptive affects and introjects. The latter threaten the integrity of the self representation and the boundary between the inner and outer worlds. Insofar as these boundaries remain fluid, they are manifested in the patient's disturbed behavior. These are pithy statements referring to a variety of psychic processes which can be discussed in terms of feces, as Mrs. Milner chooses to do. She conceptualizes levels of anal control with their vicissitudes, development, and regression.

Possibly, another therapist might have made different interpretations of the patient's early drawings. For expository reasons, I am putting to one side the possibility that Susan might have given associations to support the form of the interpretation. If one interprets the material differently, then the subsequent formulations would, to some extent, have to be different. If the patient were then to continue to discourse in these terms, the analyst would have created a different psychopathology; different, however, *in form only*.

Consequently, I believe our biases and interests have a very large share in determining the way we view patients. This, of course, is obvious, but I am not stating this in a pejorative sense. As long as certain principles are observed, this will not interfere with the patient's self-curing processes. Indeed, it will augment them, and in this connection the therapist's enthusiasm for his viewpoint may be a relevant factor. It is a common occurrence that an analyst who is investigating a formulation seems to discover it in practically every patient, his or those of others he may be supervising. If he is expounding a thesis, every patient seems to confirm it. For example, some analysts make the schizoid core of all patients a central thesis, while others may see everything either as a defense against or a regression from the oedipal conflict. I once found it amusing and interesting to reinterpret some of Freud's clinical case histories in terms of schizoid mechanisms and characterological pathology—a task that was not difficult, and which has been done in a systematic and documented fashion by Reichard (1956).

Seeing the patient's material in a light that corresponds to our orientation can be extended as to how our own needs, not necessarily professional, also contribute to what we perceive. If the therapist has a special interest or even a personal problem, it is sometimes amazing how many patients seem to concentrate upon these interests or problems. I recall my own experience when preoccupied with a severe illness in one of the members of my family, how often the organ system in question came up in my patient's associations, and colleagues have reported similar experiences. I do not believe that it is just our increased awareness of such areas that explains this phenomenon; rather, the patient responds to certain cues the analyst unconsciously emits. Not only are we dealing with the question of creating psychopathology, but the analyst's scientific and personal orientation is significant in determining the patient's material.

The analyst's orientation can also be considered in terms of
therapeutic and investigative zeal. The former, as Freud recognized, can have negative effects on the outcome of analysis. The
analyst's goals for treatment, which include his personal standards, are imposed upon the patient; imposed because patients
suffering from severe psychopathology feel them as intrusions.
For those whose autonomy is minimal, even the wish to help him
achieve a better integration can be experienced paradoxically as
an assault upon his individuality. One particular patient complained that in ten years of supportive psychotherapy by three
psychiatrists, he was "plagued" by *their* needs to help him. No
one, according to him, cared about what he felt or tried to find
out what he might have wanted (he did not know himself).

Investigative zeal, on the other hand, is different. It does not
impose in the same way as does therapeutic zeal. Here, if one
wishes to consider the therapist's needs, one is dealing with the
need to know how the patient's mind works. In some rare instances,
this too might be disruptive and preclude analysis, but in general
the patient is able to tolerate the analyst's investigative zeal and
eventually share it, in contrast to many patients' inability to cope
with therapeutic zeal. One important factor in these different
outcomes is that investigative zeal stems from the analyst and
need not be rationalized as intrinsic to therapeutic success,
whereas therapeutic zeal is often considered a fundamental feature of the analytic process, even though it may not be consciously acknowledged. Recognizing the external source of an
attitude permits the patient either to accept or reject it as an intrusion. With therapeutic zeal, however, the patient finds himself
without a choice. He does not recognize it as an attitude stemming from someone in the external world; on the contrary, he
sees it as an essential feature of the analytic interaction and one
over which he has no control.

Thus many factors determine our therapeutic style. For
example, the content of our interchange with patients includes
many metaphors. While other metaphors possibly could have
served just as well as the ones we might choose, some would not
have been compatible with fostering autonomy, and others
would not have been appropriate to the patient's particular background and series of life experiences. The metaphors, when

applied to patients suffering from characterological problems, are often expressions of psychic processes involving fusion states, fragmented ego elements and attempts at integration and structuralization in order to achieve unity. We use such metaphors to communicate our conceptual understanding to the patient.

A theoretical framework also provides the analyst with a method of trying to find landmarks, so to speak, in the turbulent wilderness the patient presents to us. It gives the therapist the assurance of an orientation and a direction which is particularly important when dealing with patients who try to convince us that they are incapable of being understood and hopeless. At the same time, they show us what they were like in their early life, their inability to organize and make sense of their environment while experiencing a desperate need to effect an organization in order to survive.

Structural Aspects

Patients suffering from characterological problems can be conceptually understood insofar as they have many common denominators regarding their fundamental structure. Although there may be many differences between one patient and another in this category, there are, nevertheless, certain similarities. Individual differences are often quantitative rather than qualitative.

Frequently, these patients are characterized by an insistent plea for help, one which is difficult to respond to because neither therapist nor patient knows what help means. Their pleas have a desperate and agonizing quality which creates a sense of urgency in the consultation room—one which seems to demand a response. The patient's request is clearly an abrasive one. He displays a clinging demandingness, which from the very beginning appears fruitless. These patients often relate to the world in an urgent, harassed manner. They display a general and pervasive tension which is seemingly unrelated to any specific object or situation.

An interesting sidelight has been that when I refer to "this type of patient" practically every analyst knows to whom I am referring. To describe a needful person should not evoke any specific recognition, but when one describes the emergency-taut atmosphere these patients create, there is usually an immediate recollection of a case that fits this description.

Focusing upon the structural viewpoint, I described in a previous publication (Giovacchini, 1970) the needfulness of patients suffering from characterological problems in terms of a hierarchical continuum. A person's requirements were viewed as ranging from the total care required by the neonate to a person with a psychic organization that has control over his needs and is able to exercise a maximum amount of autonomy in obtaining gratification. At the primitive end of the spectrum, one finds a relatively unstructured psychic organization and primitive mental processes devoid of abstractions with communication primarily centered around physiological needs.

Many persons intuitively respond to a distressed infant, but when an adult's level of communication remains primitive, most people feel uncomfortable. The analyst has great difficulty in responding to what he cannot understand. The patient, in turn, is unable to articulate what he wants because it cannot be articulated. He wants help but he doesn't really know what he means by help. The concept of being helped is not sufficiently structured so that it can be placed in an interpersonal context. Early in the analysis, neither patient nor therapist comprehend the true nature of what is being sought.

In order to be more specific I will present a clinical vignette which I believe is typical of this group and enables us to focus upon structural characteristics.

A young housewife in her late twenties began treatment in a rather stormy fashion. She came an hour and a half early for her first appointment. When I saw her in the waiting room she looked calm and composed, but when she recognized that I was the analyst, her face became tense and anxious. When we had ascertained that she had "mistaken" the time and would have to wait in order to see me, she regained her former composure. When she entered the consulting room she was once again distressed. Still, even though there were many histrionic elements in her behavior, her anguish seemed genuine and she seemed to be suffering intensely.

Her misery took the form of physical complaints, which seemed to be an odd mixture of pain and the physiological accompaniments of anxiety. She complained of very severe stomach cramps and "butterfly" sensations. Then she described headaches, which seemed to range from severe throbbing migraines to tension headaches. She also had visual and equilibratory disturbances.

Her gait was most peculiar. She stumbled when she came into the office. Once she dropped her purse, and during the interviews she frequently lost her car keys or misplaced her gloves.

From our first moment of contact she turned to me for help. Her physical discomfort caused her tremendous anguish but she would become just as upset when she misplaced needed objects. She then would revile herself and expected me to do something to relieve this anguish. Matters reached a ludicrous extreme when she managed to flood her basement by turning a wrong valve. Not knowing what to do she called me on the telephone and told me about the situation, but this time she didn't even know what to ask of me.

Her constant demand for succor and support frequently took the form "tell me what to do." However, her urgent requests went beyond asking how to conduct herself in a problem situation, a problem that was never defined, but also involved being told "how to feel." She was asking to be supplied a sensory response, but the stimulus was not explicitly stated.

The patient created a picture of utter consternation, confusion, and helplessness. She managed to make everyone involved with her feel the same way. Her family, her husband especially, tried to avoid her because she would arouse them to utter exasperation. They did not know what to do to make her comfortable. On the other hand, her husband had severe emotional problems of his own which enabled him to put up with such a situation. The reason the patient sought treatment at the time she did was associated with certain changes that occurred in the marital equilibrium as a result of his psychotherapy.

During the course of treatment she revealed a very traumatic background, both physically and emotionally. The first three months of her life were precarious. She was not able to retain food and became marasmic. She vomited after every feeding and screamed and kicked because of colic. Her mother—a timid, schizoid, naive woman—was said to have blamed herself for her daughter's inability to thrive, but she did not consult a physician.

Finally, when she was described as dying of starvation, relatives (her father was a depressed nonparticipant) insisted that her mother seek medical help. The mother's remorse and ambivalence made her immobile; one afternoon an aunt practically kidnapped the patient and took her to the hospital. The physician diagnosed a pyloric obstruction and the patient underwent surgery. Her postoperative course was relatively smooth and she gradually improved while in the hospital. At home she continued improving but at a rate which the surgeon felt was too slow. She still had some symptoms. She vomited often but not with the same regularity or intensity as previously. She also continued having colic. It is difficult to this day to say whether it ever stopped because she still had stomach cramps when she first sought treatment.

The patient stressed her inability to be gratified. During treatment she drew a parallel between her stomach not being able to "receive" food and her psyche not being able to make experiences with the outer world "helpful." Consequently she constantly felt "empty," weak and vulnerable.

She described her mother in a similar fashion, that is, as weak and vulnerable. Furthermore, she saw both herself and her mother as hollow shells with thin egglike coverings that could crack any time.

Apparently her mother had sufficient guilt that she tried, although incompetently, to take care of her daughter. The child, in turn, was especially difficult to care for, which added to the mother's sense of inadequacy and guilt. This created a vicious cycle, causing the mother to be even more inadequate.

My patient demonstrated a reduced capacity for distinguishing between inner stimuli. She was literally unable to discriminate between various bodily sensations and at times it was difficult for her to determine whether she felt hungry or needed to urinate or defecate. Her visceral sensations were experienced merely as vague pressures.

When one's needs are poorly and imperfectly structured and have undergone, relatively speaking, a limited emotional development, they are, as mentioned above, incapable of being articulated in a sophisticated adult setting. The outer world, therefore, is incapable of giving satisfaction because it cannot understand what is required.

When a mother is unable to respond to her child because of her personal psychopathology or other factors the situation is often disastrous. One is thus faced with an impasse where adequate satisfaction that would lead to self-esteem and assurance that gratification is forthcoming is not received. Memory traces of satisfying experiences are not formed and the child is unable to structure a current situation in terms of anticipation of potential gratification.

Why then do these patients pursue gratification so avidly? My patient furnishes some valuable data to shed light on this question.

As a neonate, she literally could not be gratified. Food did not nurture and the external world was incapable of soothing her discomfort. Furthermore, her mother had both physical and emotional reasons that impeded the establishment of a nurturing, mothering relationship.

Lack of gratification and inability to make one's discomfort known cause a child to feel helpless, vulnerable, and later unloved. This problem may have been especially intense in my patient since because of her pyloric stenosis no one was capable of responding to her inner tension.

In adult life she seemed to repeat these infantile experiences when her helplessness and vulnerability became prominent features of the analytic relationship. However, this orientation was pervasive and as far as I could tell was typical of all of her relationships.

Her initial reaction to treatment was that she simply would not respond to the implicit or explicit request that she talk about whatever she might choose. She refused to make an autonomous choice and forced me to structure the relationship. This is similar to patients who cannot free associate and clingingly demand that the analyst take over completely.

She constantly emphasized that her inner discomfort could only be imperfectly soothed and it was reported that during early childhood her mood was generally listless and she seldom responded to any experience. I was reminded that *ordinarily* the infant cries and protests when the gratifying person leaves his perceptual range. It seemed that insofar as my patient had a relative lack of internalized adaptive experiences, she was unable to feel that something valuable was being threatened or lost. She withdrew, it seemed, in order not to experience further failures. It was reported that the patient seldom, if ever, cried—even in situations where she seemed to be abandoned. Perhaps she never really understood what being abandoned meant, because feeling abandoned indicates that one must have known what it was like to feel accepted (nurtured).

My patient's biological helplessness, the pyloric obstruction, must have considerably aggravated her mother's vulnerability and helplessness. *Insofar as the patient's needs had been impossible to meet, she must have wondered whether her needs were impossible.* Her ego defect may have been due to the situation that early in life neither she nor her external world had the executive techniques required to gratify her.

As she grew older she developed interpersonal techniques which seemed to have to constantly prove to herself that there were persons in the outer world who could help her. Because of her intestinal blockage and neonatal frustration she was relatively unable to internalize adaptive experiences. She had difficulty in forming stable mental representations. Later in life, she had to constantly reassure herself that others could take care of her; that she could survive and be lovable.

In general, patients suffering from characterological effects apparently do not experience very much in the way of satisfaction during their crucial formative years. Developmental studies have borne this point out. What is being emphasized here is that these patients have to develop an ability to "extract" help from the environment. Insofar as they never had corresponding helpful experiences during childhood they tend to create further frustrations, both for themselves and for those to whom they appeal for help as adults.

Thus these patients can be viewed as seeking reassurance that they can be cared for. This reassurance is also intended to prove to themselves that they are capable of being loved, that they have something inside of themselves that is worthwhile. In a fundamental sense they are trying to prove that they exist.

Many patients with characterological problems need to structure their relationship with the external world in terms that are consonant with their needs and defenses (Giovacchini, 1967). The particular patient referred to here had to construct an identity based upon the unproven premise that she could be "helped."

From a structural viewpoint, the ego defect involved executive adaptive techniques and the self representation. These patients are unable to incorporate adaptive nurturing experiences. Their memory traces lack the modalities required for satisfaction of basic needs. This has two important effects on ego integration: (1) the psyche does not develop executive techniques that enable the person to adapt efficiently to the external world in terms of autonomously seeking his own nurture (nurture, of course, is now being used in an extended sense and refers to a variety of gratifications which go beyond the oral), and (2) they are unable to relate the external world in a satisfactory and gratifying fashion. The difficulty is merely compounded when the patient finds himself unable to gain benefits from what would have been for another person a potentially helpful experience. Not knowing how to help himself or how to receive help from others leads to a state of frustration and hopelessness. The latter is reflected in the patient's lowered self-esteem, a negative self-appraisal which involves the identity system. These patients have poorly structured, amorphous self representations, and lack confidence and security.

Summary and Conclusions

Two aspects of patients suffering from characterological disorders have been stressed: (1) the patient's primitive, preverbal fixations allow the therapist to contribute to the form of the patient's psychopathology as he attempts to conceptualize psychic mechanisms and ego defects in secondary process communicable terms, and (2) the specific type of ego defect encountered in such patients leads to a frantic pursuit of reassurance that they are capable of being helped, although fundamentally they constantly prove to themselves that such a pursuit is fruitless and hopeless.

These two factors have opposite effects upon the therapeutic response. The first makes the patient more amenable to therapy if the analyst continues to respect the fundamental nature of the patient's productions, and does not distort, misunderstand, or attempt to impose his preconceived concepts. In other words, the clothing the analyst uses to dress the patient's productions must fit, although styles may vary. To use Winnicott's felicitous expression, the analyst's secondary processes must not "impinge" upon the patient's primary processes (Winnicott, 1954).

Such patients are often not easily understood, and in his need to be helpful, the analyst sometimes introduces ideas to the patient which stem from his need to do something rather than from true understanding. Creative listening, as is true of all creativity, involves a tolerance of ambiguity, an ability to wait until the analyst can understand and the patient is ready to be understood. Only then can the form of the patient's disorder be determined by nonintrusive, synthesizing elements of the analyst's psyche. Such moments, however, cannot be hurried; otherwise, one is imposing something extraneous upon the patient.

Such premature closure may cause the patient to despair further. We often hear of such situations misinterpreted as examples of the unfeasibility of the psychoanalytic method. On other occasions, the patient responds with eager acceptance but ego integration is not achieved. Again I find one of Winnicott's concepts useful in explaining this apparent harmony between patient and therapist: the patient's "false self" (Winnicott, 1949a) is relating to the analyst's false perspective, while the patient's agonizing inner core is, for the moment, submerged by a mutually shared delusion. I refer to the analyst's perspective as false because it represents the therapist's *false analytic* self. The true analytic self derives understanding from what the patient reveals rather than from elements of the analyst's value system and other aspects of his self representation. Letting the patient remain in the foreground is an inherent attribute of the analytic identity. Being assertive obliterates one's analytic identity, although other nonprofessional aspects of the self representation might be enhanced by such an active orientation. Respect for another's autonomy increases analytic autonomy.

The first factor, then, referring to the analytic setting contributing to the form the patient's psychopathology will take, is, in general, a positive therapeutic element. The second aspect discussed, the way patients suffering from characterological problems experience and express the need to be helped, creates complications and has often been responsible for failure.

Recognizing why these patients are so desperate has been of some help in dealing with them by helping us recognize why we cannot deal with them at the manifest level of their demands. If the picture of intrinsic and preordained frustration is viewed from a therapeutic perspective rather than reacted to with counterfrustration (which is also to some extent a projection of the patient's frustration) or by a reactive attempt to show him that he can be helped, there is hope for further integration. Concentrating upon the adaptive significance of the patient's characterological defenses lessens the therapist's frustrations and makes it somewhat easier for him to deal with this group therapeutically.

Chapter 26

THE TREATMENT OF PATIENTS WITH BORDERLINE PERSONALITY ORGANIZATION

Otto F. Kernberg

Many patients with borderline personality organization do not tolerate the regression within a psychoanalytic treatment, not only because of their ego weakness and their proneness to develop transference psychosis, but also, and very predominantly, because the acting out of their instinctual conflicts within the transference gratifies their pathological needs and blocks further analytic progress. What appears on the surface as a process of repetitive working through is in reality a quite stable compromise formation centered in acting out of the transference within the therapeutic relationship.

Efforts to treat these patients with supportive psychotherapy frequently fail. Supportive psychotherapy aims at reinforcing the defensive organization of the patient, tries to prevent the emergence of primitive transference paradigms, and tries to build up a working relationship in order to help the patient achieve more adaptive patterns of living. Such an approach prevents regression within the transference; transference psychosis does not develop; and the kind of therapeutic stalemate previously mentioned is avoided. However, a supportive approach frequently fails because the characteristic defenses predominating in these patients interfere with the building up of a working relationship, the "therapeutic alliance" (Sterba, 1934; Zetzel, 1966). The negative transference aspects, especially the extremely severe latent negative transference dispositions, tend to mobilize

This chapter originally appeared in longer form in the *International Journal of Psycho-Analysis*, 49:600–619, 1968. Reprinted by permission of the author and the publisher.

even further the pathological defenses of these patients. The final outcome of such an approach is often the splitting up of the negative transference, much acting out outside the treatment hours, and emotional shallowness in the therapeutic situation. The "emptiness" of the therapeutic interaction over long periods of time may be a consequence of such a supportive approach, and this emptiness also tends in itself to produce therapeutic stalemates. In this case, instead of the turbulent, repetitive acting out of the transference within the hours, a situation develops in which the therapist attempts to provide support, which the patient seems incapable of integrating.

In most patients with borderline personality organization, a special form of modified analytic procedure or psychoanalytic psychotherapy may be indicated. This psychotherapy differs both from the classical psychoanalytic procedure, and from the more usual forms of expressive and supportive psychoanalytically oriented psychotherapies. Following Eissler (1953a), this psychotherapeutic procedure can be described as representing the introduction of several "parameters of technique" into the psychoanalytic situation, without expecting them to be fully resolved. The term *modification of technique* seems preferable to that of *parameter of technique,* when such modification is introduced into a treatment situation that corresponds to a psychoanalytic psychotherapy rather than to a classical psychoanalysis (Frosch, personal communication).

The main characteristics of this proposed modification in the psychoanalytic procedure are: (1) systematic elaboration of the manifest and latent negative transference without attempting to achieve full genetic reconstructions on the basis of it, followed by "deflection" of the manifest negative transference away from the therapeutic interaction through systematic examination of it in the patient's relations with others; (2) confrontation with and interpretation of those pathological defensive operations which characterize borderline patients, as they enter the negative transference; (3) definite structuring of the therapeutic situation with as active measures as necessary in order to block the acting out of the transference within the therapy itself (for example, by establishing limits under which the treatment is carried out, and providing strict limits to nonverbal aggression permitted in the hours); (4) utilization of environmental structuring conditions, such as hospital, day hospital, foster home, and so on, if acting out outside of the treatment hours threatens to produce a chronically stable situation of pathological instinctual gratification; (5) selective focusing on all those areas within the transference and the patient's life which illustrate the expression of pathological defensive operations as they induce ego weakening and imply reduced reality testing; (6) utilization of the positive transference manifestations for maintenance of the therapeutic alliance, and only partial confrontation of the patient with those defenses which protect the positive transference; (7) fostering more appropriate expressions in reality for those sexual conflicts which, through the pathological condensation of pregenital aggression and genital needs, interfere with the patient's adaptation; in other terms, "freeing" the potential for more mature genital development from its entanglements with pregenital aggression.

Review of the Pertinent Literature

A general review of the literature on borderline conditions is included in a previous article (Kernberg, 1967). From the point of view of the treatment of borderline conditions, Knight (1953a, b) and Stone (1954) present the most comprehensive overview. The main question raised in the literature is whether these patients can be treated by psychoanalysis or whether they require some form of psychotherapy. Intimately linked with this question is the delimitation of what is psychoanalysis and what is not. Thus, for example, Fromm-Reichmann (1950), who has contributed significantly to the treatment of borderline and psychotic patients, implies that the psychoanalytic procedure may be used for such patients, but she extends the concept of what is referred to as psychoanalysis to include what many other authors would definitely consider analytically oriented psychotherapy.

Gill (1951, 1954) has attempted to delimit classical psychoanalysis from analytically oriented psychotherapies, stating that psychoanalysis, in a strict sense, involves consistent adherence by the analyst to a position of neutrality (and neutrality, he rightly states, does not mean mechanical rigidity of behavior with sup-

pression of any spontaneous responses). He believes that psychoanalysis requires the development of a full, regressive transference
neurosis and that the transference must be resolved by techniques of interpretation alone. In contrast, Gill further states,
analytically oriented psychotherapies imply less strict adherence
to neutrality; they imply recognition of transference phenomena
and of transference resistance, but they use varying degrees of
interpretation of these phenomena without permitting the
development of a full-fledged transference neurosis, and they do
not imply resolution of the transference on the basis of interpretation alone.

This delimitation is a useful one but exception can be taken
to Gill's (1954) implication that in psychoanalysis the analyst
"actively produces" the regressive transference neurosis. In
agreement with Macalpine (1950), Gill (1954) states that "the
analytic situation is specifically designed to enforce a regressive
transference neurosis." However, the analytic situation permits
the development of the regressive pull inherent in the emergence
of the repressed, pathogenic childhood conflicts. Macalpine's
description of what she calls the regressive, infantile setting of the
analytic situation seriously neglects the progressive elements
given in that situation, such as the respect of the analyst for the
patient's material, for his independence, and the implicit trust
and confidence the analyst has for the patient's capacity to
mature, and to develop his own solutions (Ticho, 1966).

To return to the main point, Gill's definition is very helpful
in differentiating psychoanalysis proper from the psychoanalytically oriented or exploratory psychotherapies. Eissler (1953a)
has further clarified this issue in his discussion of the "parameters of technique," which imply modifications of the analytic
setting usually necessary in patients with severe ego distortions.
He suggests that the treatment still remains psychoanalysis if
such parameters are introduced only when indispensable, not
transgressing any unavoidable minimum, and when they are
used only under circumstances which permit their self-elimination,
their resolution through interpretation before termination of the
analysis itself. Actually, as Gill (1954) points out, this involves the
possibility of converting a psychotherapy into analysis. Additional
clarifications of the differences between psychoanalysis and

other related psychotherapies can be found in papers by Stone (1951), Bibring (1954), and Wallerstein and Robbins (1956).

From the viewpoint of Gill's delimitation of psychoanalysis, it appears that authors dealing with the problem of the treatment of borderline conditions may be placed on a continuum ranging from those who recommend psychoanalysis, to those who believe that psychotherapy rather than psychoanalysis, and especially a supportive form of psychotherapy, is the treatment of choice. Somewhere in the middle of this continuum there are those who believe that some patients presenting borderline personality organization may still be analyzed while others would require expressive psychotherapy; and also there are those who do not sharply differentiate between psychoanalysis and psychotherapy.

The first detailed references in the literature to the therapeutic problems with borderline patients were predominantly on the side of recommending modified psychotherapy with supportive implications, in contrast to classical psychoanalysis. Stern (1938, 1945) recommends an expressive approach, with a constant focus on the transference rather than on historical material, and with constant efforts to reduce the clinging, childlike dependency of the patient on the analyst. He feels that these patients need a new and realistic relationship, in contrast to the traumatic ones of their childhood; he believes that such patients can only gradually develop the capacity to establish a transference neurosis similar to that of the usual analytic patient. He concludes that analysis may and should be attempted only at later phases of their treatment. Schmideberg (1947) recommends an approach probably best designated as expressive psychotherapy, and is of the opinion that these patients cannot be treated by classical analysis. Knight's (1953a, b) important contributions to the psychotherapeutic strategy with borderline cases lean definitely in the direction of the purely supportive approach, on one extreme of the continuum. He stresses the importance of strengthening the ego of these patients, and of respecting their neurotic defenses; he considers "deep interpretations" dangerous because of the regressive pull that such interpretations have, and because the weak ego of these patients makes it hard enough for them to keep functioning on a secondary process level. He stresses the importance of structure, both within the psychotherapeutic setting and in the utilization of the hospital and day hospital, as part of the total treatment program for such patients.

Somewhere toward the middle of the spectrum are the approaches recommended by Stone (1954) and Eissler (1953a). Stone feels that borderline patients may need preparatory psychotherapy but that at least some of these patients may be treated with classical psychoanalysis either from the beginning of treatment or after some time to build up a working relationship with the therapist. Stone also agrees with Eissler that analysis can be attempted at later stages of treatment with such patients only if the previous psychotherapy has not created transference distortions of such magnitude that the parameters of technique involved cannot be resolved through interpretation. Eissler suggested that in some cases it might be necessary to change analysts for the second phase of the treatment. Glover (1955) implies that at least some of these cases are "moderately accessible" to psychoanalysis.

At the other end of the spectrum are a number of analysts influenced to varying degrees by the so-called British school of psychoanalysis (Winnicott, 1949b, 1960b; Little, 1951; Heimann, 1955b; Bion, 1957; Rosenfeld, 1958; Segal, 1964). These analysts believe that classical psychoanalytic treatment can indeed be attempted with many, if not all, borderline patients. Some of their contributions have been of crucial importance to the better understanding of the defensive organization, and the particular resistances characteristic of patients with borderline personality organization. Despite my disagreement with their general assumption about the possibility of treating most borderline patients with psychoanalysis, I believe that the findings of these analysts permit modifications of psychoanalytically oriented psychotherapies specifically adapted to the transference complications of borderline patients: I am referring here especially to the work of Winnicott (1949b), Heimann (1955b), Little (1958, 1969a, b), Rosenfeld (1964), and Segal (1964).

My suggestions for treatment outlined in the present paper would appear in the middle zone of the continuum: in my opinion, in most patients presenting borderline personality organization a modified analytic procedure or special form of expressive psychoanalytic psychotherapy rather than classical psychoanalysis is indicated. This expressive approach should involve consistent interpretive work with those defensive operations reflecting the negative transference and contributing directly or indirectly to maintaining the patient's ego weakness. There are some patients with borderline personality organization for whom psychoanalysis is definitely indicated and I shall attempt to identify them.

Transference and Countertransference Characteristics

An important feature of the therapeutic problems with borderline patients is the development of transference psychosis. Several authors have described the characteristics of this transference regression, and a general summary about this issue can be found in a paper by Wallerstein (1967).

Perhaps the most striking characteristic of the transference manifestations of patients with borderline personality organization is the premature activation in the transference of very early conflict-laden object relationships in the context of ego states that are dissociated from each other. It is as if each of these ego states represents a full-fledged transference paradigm, a highly developed, regressive transference reaction within which a specific internalized object relationship is activated in the transference. This is in contrast to the more gradual unfolding of internalized object relationships as regression occurs in the typical neurotic patient. Clinical experience reveals that the higher levels of depersonified and abstracted superego structures are missing to an important extent, and the same is true for many autonomous ego structures, especially neutralized, secondarily autonomous character structures. Thus the premature activation of such regressed ego states represents the pathological persistence of "nonmetabolized" internalized object relations of a primitive and conflict-laden kind.

The conflicts that typically emerge in connection with the reactivation of these early internalized object relations may be characterized as a particular pathological condensation of pregenital and genital aims under the overriding influence of pregenital aggression. Excessive pregenital, and especially oral, aggression tends to be projected and determines the paranoid distortion of the early parental images, particularly those of the

mother. From a clinical point of view, whether this is a consequence of severe early frustration or actual aggression on the
mother's part, whether it reflects excessive constitutional
aggressive drive derivatives, whether it reflects a lack of capacity
to neutralize aggression or lack of constitutionally determined
anxiety tolerance, is not so important as the final result—the
paranoid distortion of the early parental images. Through projection of predominantly oral–sadistic and also anal–sadistic
impulses, the mother is seen as potentially dangerous, and hatred
of the mother extends to a hatred of both parents when later they
are experienced as a "united group" by the child. A "contamination" of the father image by aggression primarily projected onto
mother and lack of differentiation between mother and father
tend to produce a combined, dangerous father–mother image
and a later conceptualization of all sexual relationships as
dangerous and infiltrated by aggression. Concurrently, in an
effort to escape from oral rage and fears, a "flight" into genital
strivings occurs; this flight often miscarries because of the intensity of the pregenital aggression which contaminates the genital
strivings (Heimann, 1955a).

The transference manifestations of patients with borderline
personality organization may at first appear completely chaotic.
Gradually, however, repetitive patterns emerge, reflecting primitive self representations and related object representations under
the influence of the conflicts mentioned above, and appear in the
treatment as strongly negative transference paradigms. The
defensive operations characteristic of borderline patients (splitting, projective identification, denial, primitive idealization,
omnipotence) become the vehicle of the transference resistances.
The fact that these defensive operations have, in themselves, ego-
weakening effects (Kernberg, 1966, 1967) is suggested as a crucial
factor in the severe regression that soon complicates the premature transference developments.

What is meant by "ego weakness" in borderline patients? To
conceive of ego weakness as consisting of a rather frail ego barrier
which, when assaulted by id derivatives, is unable to prevent
them from "breaking through" or "flooding" the ego, appears
insufficient. Hartmann and his colleagues' (Hartmann, Kris, and
Loewenstein, 1946) and Rapaport's (1957) analyses of the ego as

an overall structure within which substructures determine specific functions, as well as being determined by them, convincingly imply that ego weakness should be conceptualized not simply as absence or weakness of such structures, but as replacement of higher-level by lower-level ego structures. One aspect of ego weakness in patients with borderline personality organization is evidenced by the "lower" defensive organization of the ego in which the mechanism of splitting and other related defenses are used, in contrast to the defensive organization of the ego around the "higher" mechanism of repression and other related defenses in neuroses (Kernberg, 1966). Also, the failure of normal integration of the structures derived from internalized object relationships (integrated self-concept, realistic object representations, integration of ideal self and ideal object representations into the ego ideal, integration of superego forerunners with more realistic introjections of parental images into the superego, etc.) interferes with the process of identity formation and individualization, and with neutralization and abstraction of both ego and superego functions. All of this is reflected in the reduction of the conflict-free ego sphere, clinically revealed in the presence of "nonspecific" aspects of ego weakness, particularly a lack of anxiety tolerance, a lack of impulse control, and a lack of developed sublimatory channels (Kernberg, 1967).

In addition, and most importantly from the point of view of psychotherapeutic intervention with these patients, "nonspecific" ego weakness is also evident in the relative incapacity of the patients with such a pathological ego organization tentatively to dissociate their ego into an experiencing and an observing part and in the related incapacity to establish a therapeutic alliance. The dynamics of borderline personality organization are much more complicated than what is conveyed by the metaphor of "flooding" the ego because of its "weak barriers," because underneath the "weaknesses" are extremely strong, rigid, primitive, and pathological ego structures.

Let us now return to the issue of transference regression in these patients. Once they embark upon treatment, the crucial decompensating force is the patient's increased effort to defend himself against the emergence of the threatening primitive, especially negative, transference reactions by intensified utilization of the very defensive operations which have contributed to ego weakness in the first place. One main "culprit" in this regard is probably the mechanism of projective identification, described by Melanie Klein (1946) and others (Heimann, 1955a, b; Money-Kyrle, 1956; Rosenfeld, 1963; Segal, 1964). Projective identification is a primitive form of projection, mainly called upon to externalize aggressive self and object images; "empathy" is maintained with the real objects onto which the projection has occurred, and is linked with an effort to control the object now feared because of this projection (Kernberg, 1965, 1967).

In the transference this is typically manifest as intense distrust and fear of the therapist, who is experienced as attacking the patient, while the patient himself feels empathy with that projected intense aggression and tries to control the therapist in a sadistic, overpowering way. The patient may be partially aware of his own hostility but feel that he is simply responding to the therapist's aggression, and that he is justified in being angry, and aggressive. It is as if the patient's life depended on his keeping the therapist under control. The patient's aggressive behavior, at the same time, tends to provoke from the therapist counteraggressive feelings and attitudes. It is as if the patient were pushing the aggressive part of his self onto the therapist and as if the counter-transference represented the emergence of this part of the patient from within the therapist (Money-Kyrle, 1956; Racker, 1957).

It has to be stressed that what is projected in a very inefficient and self-defeating way is not "pure aggression," but a self representation or an object representation linked with that drive derivative. Primitive self and primitive object representations are actually linked together as a basic units of primitive object relationships (Kernberg, 1966), and what appears characteristic of borderline patients is that there is a rapid oscillation between moments of projection of a self representation while the patient remains identified with the corresponding object representation, and other moments in which it is the object representation that is projected while the patient identifies with the corresponding self representation. For example, a primitive, sadistic mother image may be projected onto the therapist while the patient experiences himself as the frightened, attacked, panic-stricken little child; moments later, the patient may experience himself as the stern, prohibitive, moralistic (and extremely sadistic) primitive mother image, while the therapist is seen as the guilty, defensive, frightened but rebellious little child. This situation is also an example of "complementary identification" (Racker, 1957).

The danger in this situation is that under the influence of the expression of intense aggression by the patient, the reality aspects of the transference–countertransference situation may be such that it comes dangerously close to reconstituting the originally projected interaction between internalized self and object images. Under these circumstances, vicious circles may be created in which the patient projects his aggression onto the therapist and reintrojects a severely distorted image of the therapist under the influence of the projected aggressive drive derivatives, thus perpetuating the pathological early object relationship. Heimann (1955b) has illustrated these vicious circles of projective identification and distorted reintrojection of the therapist in discussing paranoid defenses. Strachey (1934) has referred to the general issue of normal and pathological introjection of the analyst as an essential aspect of the effect of interpretation, especially in regard to modifying the superego. This brings us to the problem of the influence of "mutative interpretations" (Strachey) on the establishment and maintenance of the therapeutic alliance.

It was mentioned above that one aspect of ego weakness in patients with borderline personality organization is the relative absence of an observing ego. We may now add that this factor is compounded by the patient's distortion of the therapist resulting from excessive projective operations under the influence of the negative transference. To establish a therapeutic alliance with the therapist becomes equal to submission to him as a dangerous, powerful enemy, and this further reduces the capacity for the activation of the observing ego.

A repeated observation from the Psychotherapy Research Project at The Menninger Foundation, about the psychotherapy of borderline patients, is that a high price was paid when the therapist tried to stay away from the latent negative transference and attempted to build a therapeutic relationship with the patient in an atmosphere of denial of that negative transference. Frequently, under these conditions, the results were an emotionally shallow therapeutic relationship, and a pseudosubmission by the patient to what he experienced as the therapist's demands. Serious acting out or even interruption of the treatment followed periods in which the therapist thought that the patient was "building up an identification" with him, or "introjecting value systems" of the therapist, while the patient remained emotionally detached. The implication is that a consistent undoing of the manifest and latent negative transference is an important, probably indispensable, prerequisite for a broadening of the observing ego and for solidifying a therapeutic alliance.

The gradual broadening of the conflict-free ego sphere together with a broadening of the observing ego throughout therapy facilitates the disruption of the vicious circle of projection and reintrojection of sadistic self and object images in the transference. Strachey (1934), in his description of mutative interpretations, identifies two phases of such interpretations: the first phase consists of a qualitative modification of the patient's superego; and the second consists of the patient's expressing his impulses more freely, so that the analyst can call attention to the discrepancy between the patient's view of him as an archaic fantasy object, and the analyst as a real external object. Strachey implies that first the patient permits himself to express his aggression in a freer way, as his superego prohibitions decrease; only then can the patient become aware of the excessive, inappropriate nature of his aggressiveness toward the external object and be able to acquire insight into the origin of his reaction; so the need to project such aggression once again onto the analyst gradually decreases. I would add to this description that, both in the phase of superego modification and in the phase of differentiation between the patient's fantasied object and the analyst as a different object, an observing ego is needed. Thus, the observing ego and interpretation of projective–introjective cycles mutually reinforce each other.

The discussion of projective identification leads to the issue of how the intensity of projection and reintrojection of aggressive drive derivatives in the transference interferes with the observing functions of the ego; and this interference in itself contributes to the transference regression. Yet, the most important way in which projective identification contributes to the transference regression is the rapid oscillation of projection of self and object images; this rapid oscillation undermines the stability of the patient's ego boundaries in his interactions with the therapist.

In previous papers (1966, 1967) I have commented on the differentiation between self and object representations which are part of early introjections and identifications. The organizing function of this differentiation of ego boundaries was stressed. In the psychosis, such differentiation between self and object images does not take place sufficiently and ego boundaries are therefore missing to a major extent. In contrast, in patients presenting borderline personality organization, this differentiation has taken place sufficiently, and therefore ego boundaries are more stable. The borderline patient is capable of differentiating the self from external objects, internal experience from external perception, and reality testing is also preserved to a major extent. This capacity of the borderline patient is lost within the transference regression.

Rapidly alternating projection of self images and object images representing early pathological internalized object relationships, produces a confusion of what is "inside" and "outside" in the patient's experience of his interactions with the therapist. It is as if the patient maintained a sense of being different from the therapist at all times, but concurrently he and the therapist were interchanging their personalities. This is a frightening experience which reflects a breakdown of ego boundaries in that interaction, and as a consequence there is a loss of reality testing in the transference. It is this loss of reality testing in the transference which most powerfully interferes with the patient's capacity to distinguish fantasy from reality, and past from present in the transference, and also interferes with his capacity to distinguish his projected transference objects from the therapist as a real person. Under such circumstances, the possibility that a mutative interpretation will be effective is seriously threatened. Clinically, this appears as the patient experiencing something such as, "Yes, you are right in thinking that I see you as I saw my mother, and that is because she and you are really identical." It is at this point that what has been referred to above as a transference psychosis is reached.

At this point, the therapist and the transference object

become identical, the loss of reality testing is reflected in the development of delusions, and even hallucinations may complicate the transference reaction. The therapist may be identified with a parental image: one patient felt that the therapist had become her father and would rape her. At other times the therapist may be identified with a projected dissociated self representation: one patient became convinced that his analyst carried on an affair with the patient's mother and threatened to kill him.

Transference psychosis is a term which should be reserved for the loss of reality testing and the appearance of delusion material within the transference that does not affect very noticeably the patient's functioning outside the treatment setting. There are patients who have a psychotic decompensation during treatment which is for all purposes indistinguishable from any other psychotic breakdown, and which affects their life in general as well as the therapeutic situation. It may be that regression in the transference did contribute to the breakdown, but it is questionable whether the term *transference psychosis* is always warranted under these conditions. In contrast, patients with a typical transference psychosis may develop delusional ideas and what amounts to psychotic behavior within the treatment hours, over a period of days and months, without showing these manifestations outside the hours. Hospitalization may sometimes be necessary for such patients, and at times it is quite difficult to separate a transference-limited psychotic reaction from a broader one. Nevertheless, in many borderline patients this delimitation is quite easy, and it is often possible to resolve the transference psychosis within the psychotherapy (Reider, 1957; Romm, 1957; Little, 1958; Holzman and Ekstein, 1959; Wallerstein, 1967). Control of transference acting out within the therapeutic relationship becomes of central importance.

Transference acting out within the therapeutic relationship refers to the acting out of the transference reaction in the hours, within the treatment setting itself. As part of the transference regression, any patient may tend to act toward the therapist rather than reflect on his feelings about him. For example, rather than verbally expressing strong feelings of anger and reflecting on the implications and sources of this anger, a patient may yell at the therapist, insult him, and express his emotions in what amounts to direct actions rather than verbally, over a period of weeks and months. This, of course, is not exclusive to borderline patients, but in the typical analytic treatment of neurotic patients such acting out during the hours only occurs at points of severe regression, after many months of build-up, and can usually be resolved by interpretation alone. This is not so in the case of patients with borderline personality organization, and the therapist's efforts to deal with acting out within the therapeutic relationship by interpretation alone, especially when it is linked with a transference psychosis, frequently appears to fail. This is partly so because of the loss of the observing ego by virtue of the projective–introjective cycles mentioned and because of the loss of ego boundaries and of the reality testing that goes with it. To a major degree, however, such unrelenting transference acting out is highly resistant to interpretation because it also gratifies the instinctual needs of these patients, especially those linked with the severe, preoedipal aggressive drive derivatives so characteristic of them. It is this gratification of instinctual needs which represents the major transference resistance. Two clinical examples will illustrate this point.

A hospitalized borderline patient literally yelled at her hospital physician during their early half-hour interviews, and her voice carried to all the offices in the building. After approximately two weeks of such behavior, which the hospital physician felt unable to influence by any psychotherapeutic means, he saw her by chance shortly after leaving his office. He was still virtually trembling, and was struck by the fact that the patient seemed completely relaxed, and smiled in a friendly way while talking to some other patients with whom she was acquainted. Before entering the hospital, the patient had engaged in bitter fights with her parents for many years. In the hospital, all the fightings centered on her physician, while the hospital staff was surprised by the relaxation she showed with other personnel. It gradually became clear that her angry outbursts toward her physician reflected a gratification of her aggressive needs far beyond any available to her before she entered the hospital, and that this gratification in itself was functioning as the major transference resistance. When this was conveyed to her, and the hospital physician limited the amount of yelling and insulting that would be permitted in the hours, the patient's anxiety increased noticeably outside the hours, her conflictual patterns became more apparent within the hospital, and shifting attitudes in the transference became apparent, indicating movement in the therapy.

Another patient who was seen in expressive psychotherapy demanded an increase of his hours in an extremely angry, defiant way. Over a period of time it was interpreted to him that it was hard for him to tolerate the guilty feelings over his own greediness, and that he was projecting that guilt onto the therapist in the form of fantasies of being hated and depreciated by him. It was also interpreted that his demands to see the therapist more often represented an effort to reassure himself of the therapist's love and interest in order to neutralize his distrust and suspiciousness of the therapist's fantasied hatred of him. The patient seemed to understand all this but was unable to change his behavior. The therapist concluded that the patient's oral aggression was being gratified in a direct way through these angry outbursts, and that this development might contribute to a fixation of the transference. The therapist told the patient of his decision not to increase the hours and at the same time presented as a condition for continuing the treatment that the patient exercise some degree of control over the form and appropriateness of the expression of his feelings in the hours. With this modification of technique in effect, a noticeable change occurred over the next few days. The patient became more reflective, and finally was even able to admit that he had obtained a great satisfaction from being allowed to express intense anger at the therapist in such a direct way.

The acting out of the transference within the therapeutic relationship becomes the main resistance to further change in these patients, and parameters of technique required to control the acting out should be introduced in the treatment situation. There is a danger of entering the vicious circle of projection and reintrojection of sadistic self and object images of the patient as the therapist introduces parameters of technique. He may appear to the patient as prohibitive and sadistic. This danger can be counteracted if the therapist begins by interpreting the transference situation, then introduces structuring parameters of techniques as needed, and finally interprets the transference situation again without abandoning the parameters. Some aspects of this technique have been illustrated in a different context by Sharpe (1931), who demonstrates how to deal with acute episodes of anxiety.

In many cases, the consistent blocking of the transference acting out within the therapeutic relationship is sufficient in itself to reduce and delimit the transference psychosis to such an extent that further interpretive work may suffice to dissolve it. The very fact that the therapist takes a firm stand and creates a structure within the therapeutic situation which he will not abandon tends to enable the patient to differentiate the therapist from himself, and thus to undo the confusion caused by frequent "exchange" of self and object representation projections by the patient. Also, such a structure may effectively prevent the therapist's acting out his countertransference, especially the very damaging chronic countertransference reactions which tend to develop in intensive psychotherapy with borderline patients (Sutherland, personal communication).

Chronic countertransference fixations are to an important degree a consequence of the patient's success in destroying the analyst's stable and mature ego identity in their relationship (Kernberg, 1965). In order to keep in emotional contact with the patient, analysts working with patients presenting borderline personality organization have to be able to tolerate a regression within themselves, which on occasions may reactivate the remnants of early, conflict-laden relationships in the therapist. Aggressive impulses tend to emerge in the analyst, which he has to control and utilize in gaining a better understanding of the patient. The extra effort needed for this work with the countertransference and the very tolerance and neutrality toward the patient which is part of the analyst's effort to keep in emotional touch with him, increase the stress within the therapist. At the same time, the aggressive behavior of patients with severe transference regression continuously undermines the analyst's self-esteem and self-concept in their interaction, and thus also the integrating ego function of the analyst's ego identity. Thus, the analyst may be struggling at the same time with the upsurge of primitive impulses in himself, with the tendency to control the patient as part of his efforts to control these impulses, and with the temptation to submit in a masochistic way to the patient's active efforts of control (Money-Kyrle, 1956). Under these circumstances, pathological, previously abandoned defensive operations and especially neurotic character traits of the analyst may become reactivated, and the patient's and the analyst's personality structures come to appear as if they were "prematched" to each other, interlocked in a stable, insoluble transference-countertransference bind. The establishment and maintenance of structuring parameters or modifications of technique is, then, a fundamental, protective technical requirement at that point and often has to be maintained throughout a great part of the course of the psychotherapy with borderline patients.

The issue of the indications for hospitalization, in order to provide this structure when it is not possible to provide it otherwise, is beyond the scope of this paper. I would only stress that for many patients hospitalization is indispensable to creating and maintaining an environmental structure which effectively controls transference acting out.

Does the transference psychosis also represent the reproduction of unconscious, pathogenic object relationships of the past, and thus provide further information about the patient's conflicts? Sometimes it appears difficult to find evidence in the patient's past of interactions with the parental figures characterized by the violence and primitiveness of the transference reaction at the level of a regressive transference psychosis. At other times, the transference indeed appears to reflect actual, very traumatic experiences that these patients have undergone in their infancy and early childhood (Frosch, personal communication; Holzman and Ekstein, 1959). It is probable that the transference in all of these patients originates, to a large extent, in the fantasy distortions which accompanied the early pathogenic object relationships, as well as in the relationships themselves, and in the pathological defensive operations mobilized by the small child to extricate himself from the threatening interpersonal relationships. The transference psychosis represents a condensation of actual experiences, a gross elaboration of them in fantasy, and efforts to modify or turn away from them (Klein, 1952). This brings us to the technical problems of dealing with the pathological defensive operations characteristic of borderline patients which were mentioned above. Interpretive work attempting to undo these pathological operations as they enter the transference may further serve to resolve the transference psychosis and to increase ego strength.

Because the acting out of the transference within the therapeutic relationship itself appears to be such a meaningful reproduction of past conflicts, fantasies, defensive operations, and internalized object relationships of the patients, one is tempted to interpret the repetitive acting out as evidence for a working through of these conflicts. The repetition compulsion expressed through transference acting out cannot be considered working through as long as the transference relationship provides these patients with instinctual gratification of their pathological, especially their aggressive needs. Some of these patients obtain much more gratification of their pathological instinctual needs in the transference than would ever be possible in extra-therapeutic interactions. The patient's acting out at the regressed level overruns the therapist's effort to maintain a climate of "abstinence." At the other extreme, to maintain such a rigid and controlled treatment structure that the transference development is blocked altogether, and especially the negative transference remains hidden, appears also to induce a stalemate of the therapeutic process, which is as negative in its effect as unchecked transference acting out. A "purely supportive" relationship, understood as a careful avoidance of focusing on the transference, often brings about a chronic shallowness of the therapeutic relationship, acting out outside the treatment hours which is rigidly split off from the transference itself, pseudosubmission to the therapist, and a lack of change despite years of treatment. There are patients who in spite of all efforts cannot tolerate transference regression, nor the establishment of any meaningful relationship, without breaking it off; nevertheless, the overall psychotherapeutic chances are much better when attempts are made to undo emotional shallowness and bring about a real emotional involvement within the therapy. The price is high, the danger of excessive transference regression unavoidable, but with a careful and consistent structuring of the therapeutic relationship it should be possible in most cases to prevent the development of insoluble transference–countertransference binds.

How much of a "real person" does the therapist need to appear to be in the patient's eyes? Several authors have stressed the importance of the therapist appearing as a "real person," permitting the patient to use him as an object for identification and superego introjection. Gill (1954) has stated that "we have failed to carry over into our psychotherapy enough of the non-directive spirit of our analysis." If what is meant by "real person" refers to the therapist's direct and open interventions, his providing structure and limits, and his active refusal to be forced into regressive countertransference fixations, then the therapist should indeed be a real person. However, if what is meant by "real person" is that the regressive transference reactions of borderline patients, their inordinate demands for love, attention, protection, and gifts should be responded to by "giving" beyond what an objective, professional psychotherapist–patient relationship would warrant, objection must be made to the therapist being such a "real person." What has been called the excessive "dependency needs" of these patients actually reflects their incapacity really to depend upon anyone, because of the severe distrust and hatred of themselves and of their past internalized object images that are reactivated in the transference. The working through of the negative transference, the confrontation of the patients with their distrust and hatred, and with the ways in which that distrust and hatred destroys their capacity to depend on what the psychotherapist can realistically provide, better fulfills their needs. Clinical experience has repeatedly demonstrated that the intervention of the psychotherapist as a particular individual, opening his own life, values, interests and emotions to the patient, is of very little, if any, help.

The supposition that the patient may be able to identify himself with the therapist while severe, latent, negative transference dispositions are in the way, or are being acted out outside the treatment setting, appears highly questionable. The development of an observing ego appears to depend not on the therapist's offering himself as an unconditional friend, but as a consequence of a combined focus on the pathological cycles of projective and introjective processes, on transference distortion and acting out, and on the observing part of the ego itself. In this connection, what Ekstein and Wallerstein (1956) have observed in regard to borderline children, holds true for adults also: "The maintenance of the therapeutic relationship, often made possible by interpreting within the regression, thus lays the foundation for the new development of identificatory processes rather than the superimposition of an imitative façade . . ."

A systematic focus on and analysis of the manifest and latent negative transference is essential to undo the vicious cycle of projection and reintrojection of pathological, early self and object representations under the influence of aggressive drive derivatives. This systematic analysis, together with the blocking of transference acting out and a direct focusing on the observing function of the ego, represent basic conditions for change and growth in the therapy. In addition, the interpretation of the negative transference should stop at the level of the "here and now," and should only partially be referred back to its genetic origins, to the original unconscious conflicts of the past. At the same time, the ventilation and interpretation of the negative transference should be completed by a systematic examination and analysis of the manifestations of these negative transference aspects outside the therapeutic relationship, in the patient's immediate life in all areas of interpersonal interactions.

The rationale for this suggestion is that the regressive nature of the transference reaction makes it hard enough for the patient to differentiate the therapist as a real person from the projected transference objects, and that genetic reconstructions, by further opening up regressive channels, may further reduce the reality-testing of the patient. This does not mean that the patient's past should not be drawn into the transference interpretation when that past is a conscious memory for the patient rather than a genetic reconstruction, and when it reflects realistic aspects of his past and preconscious fantasy distortions of it. Sometimes a reference to an experience from the past relating to what the patient erroneously perceives in the therapist now, may actually help the patient to separate reality from transference. The secondary "deflection" of the negative transference by incorporating its interpretation into the broader area of the patient's interactions outside the treatment and his conscious past tends to foster the patient's reality testing and to provide considerable support within an essentially expressive psychotherapeutic approach.

The question of "insight" in borderline patients deserves discussion. Unfortunately, one frequently finds that what at first looks like insight into "deep" layers of the mind and into unconscious dynamics on the part of some borderline patients is actually an expression of the ready availability of primary process functioning as part of the general regression of ego structures. Insight which comes without any effort, is not accompanied by any change in the patient's intrapsychic equilibrium, and, above all, is not accompanied by any concern on the patient's part for the pathological aspects of his behavior or experience, is questionable "insight." Findings from the Psychotherapy Research Project at The Menninger Foundation encourage a restriction of the concept of insight, especially in applying it to the description of borderline patients. "Authentic" insight is a combination of the intellectual and emotional understanding of deeper sources of one's psychic experience, accompanied by concern for and an urge to change the pathological aspects of that experience.

The differentiation of "positive" and "negative" transference requires further scrutiny. To classify a transference as positive or negative is certainly a rather crude oversimplification. Transference is usually ambivalent and has multiple aspects within which it is often hard to say what is positive and what is negative, what is libidinally derived and what is aggressively derived. Patients with borderline personality organization are especially prone to dissociate the positive from the negative aspects of the transference, and often tend to produce an apparent "pure" positive or "pure" negative transference. It is important to undo this artificial separation, which is one more example of the operation of the mechanism of splitting in these cases. It would be misleading to understand the emphasis on a consistent working through of the negative transference as implying a neglect of the positive aspects of the transference reactions. On the contrary, emphasis on the positive as well as on the negative transference is essential for decreasing the patient's distorted self and object images under the influence of aggressive drive derivatives, and for reducing his fears of his own "absolute" badness. The positive aspects of the transference have to be highlighted therefore, in combination with the ventilation of the negative aspects of the transference. It is important to deal with the here and now of the positive as well as the negative aspects of the transference of borderline patients, without interpreting the genetic implications of their aggressive and libidinal drives (Ticho, personal communication). At the same time, a good part of the positive transference disposition available to the patient may be left in its moderate, controlled expression, as a further basis for the development of a therapeutic alliance and for the ultimate growth of the observing ego (Schlesinger, 1966).

Psychotherapeutic Approaches to the Specific Defensive Operations

I referred in earlier papers (1966, 1967) to the mechanism of splitting and other related ones (primitive idealization, projective identification, denial, omnipotence), all of which are characteristic of borderline patients. Here I will limit myself to stating how these defensive operations appear from a clinical point of view, and to suggest overall psychotherapeutic approaches in dealing with them.

Splitting

It needs to be stressed once more that the term *splitting* is used here in a restricted, limited sense, referring only to the process of active keeping apart of introjections and identifications of opposite quality; and this use of the term should be differentiated from its broader use by other authors. The manifestations of splitting can be illustrated with a clinical example.

The patient was a single woman in her late thirties, hospitalized because of alcoholism and drug addiction. She appeared to make remarkably steady progress in the hospital after an initial period of rebelliousness. She started psychotherapy several months before her discharge from the hospital, and then continued in outpatient psychotherapy. In contrast to her previously disorganized life and work, she seemed to adjust well to work and social relations outside the hospital, but established several relationships, each of a few months' duration, with men who appeared to exploit her and with whom she adopted quite masochistic attitudes. The therapeutic relationship was shallow;

the patient was conventionally friendly. A general feeling of "emptiness" appeared to hide a strong suspiciousness, which she emphatically denied and only later admitted to her former hospital doctor but not to her psychotherapist. After a period of several months of complete abstinence, she got drunk, became quite depressed, had suicidal thoughts, and had to be rehospitalized. At no point did she let the therapist know what was going on and he only learned about this development after she was back in the hospital. Once out of the hospital again, she denied all transference implications and indeed all emotional implications of the alcoholic episode. It must be stressed that she had the memory of strong emotions of anger and depression during the days in which she was intoxicated, but she no longer felt connected with that part of herself and repeatedly expressed her feelings that this was simply not her, and she could not see how such an episode could possibly occur again.

This marked the beginning of a long effort on the therapist's part, over a period of several months, to bring the usual "empty," "friendly" but detached attitude of the patient together with her emotional upheaval during the alcoholic crisis, and especially with her efforts to hide that crisis from the therapist. Only after two more episodes of this kind, separated from each other by periods of apparently more adaptive behavior and good functioning over several months, did it become evident that she was experiencing the therapist as the cold, distant, hostile father who had refused to rescue her from an even more rejecting, aggressive mother. The patient, at one point, told the therapist with deep emotion how on one occasion, in her childhood, she had been left abandoned in her home, suffering from what later turned out to be a severe and dangerous illness, by her mother who did not wish her own active social life to be interfered with. The patient felt that if she really expressed to the psychotherapist–father how much she needed him and loved him, she would destroy him with the intensity of her anger over having been frustrated so much for so long. The solution was to keep what she felt was the best possible relationship of detached friendliness with the therapist, while splitting off her search for love, her submission to sadistic father representatives in her masochistic submission to unloving men, and her protest against father in alcoholic episodes during which rage and depression were completely dissociated emotionally from both the therapist and her boyfriends.

Efforts to bring all this material into the transference greatly increased the patient's anxiety; she became more distrustful and angry with the psychotherapist, the drinking reverted to her old pattern of chaotic involvements with men associated with excessive intake of alcohol, and all efforts to deal with this acting out through psychotherapeutic means alone failed. The decision was made to rehospitalize her. It should be stressed that from a superficial point of view the patient appeared to have done quite well earlier in the psychotherapy but now appeared to be much worse. Nevertheless, it was the psychotherapist's conviction that for the first time he was dealing with a "real" person. He hoped that a continuation of psychotherapy combined with hospitalization for as long as necessary might help her to finally overcome the stable, basic transference paradigm outlined above.

This case illustrates a strong predominance of the mechanism of splitting, its defensive function against the emergence of a rather primitive, predominantly negative transference, and its consequences evident in the shallowness and artificiality of the therapeutic interaction. A therapeutic alliance could not be established with this patient before the mechanism of splitting had been sufficiently overcome. Only consistent interpretation of the patient's active participation in maintaining herself "compartmentalized" finally could change the stable, pathological equilibrium. Consistent efforts had to be made to bridge the independently expressed, conflicting ego states, and the secondary defenses protecting this dissociation had to be sought out and ventilated in the treatment. With these patients it is not a matter of searching for unconscious, repressed material, but bridging and integrating what appears on the surface to be two or more emotionally independent, but alternately active ego states.

Primitive Idealization

Primitive idealization (Kernberg, 1967) manifests itself in the therapy as an extremely unrealistic, archaic form of idealization. This idealization appears to have as its main function the protection of the therapist from the patient's projection onto him of the negative transference disposition. There is a projection onto the therapist of a primitive, "all good" self and object representation, with a concomitant effort to prevent this "good" image from being contaminated by the patient's "bad" self and object representations.

One patient felt that he was extremely lucky to have a psychotherapist who represented, according to the patient, the best synthesis of the "intellectual superiority" of one country where the therapist was born, and the "emotional freedom" of another country where the patient thought he had lived for many years. On the surface, the patient appeared to be reassured by a clinging relationship with such an "ideal" therapist, and protected against what he experienced as a cold, rejecting, hostile environment by a magical union with the therapist. It soon developed that the patient felt that only by a strenuous, ongoing effort of self-deception, and deception to the therapist about himself, could he keep his good relationship with the therapist. If the therapist really knew how the patient was feeling about himself, the therapist would never be able to accept him, and would hate and depreciate him. This, by the way, illustrates the damaging effects of overidealization for the possibility of utilizing the therapist as a good superego introjection, in contrast to an overidealized, demanding one. It later turned out that this idealization was developed as a defense against the devaluation and depreciation of the therapist, seen as an empty, pompous, and hypocritically conventional parental image.

It is hard to convey in a few words the unrealistic quality of the idealization given the therapist by these patients, which gives quite a different quality to the transference from the other, less regressive idealization that may be seen in the usual neurotic patients. This peculiar form of idealization has been described as an important defense in narcissistic personality structures (Rosenfeld, 1964; Kohut, 1966b). Psychotherapists who themselves present strong narcissistic traits in their character structure may at times be quite easily drawn into a kind of magical, mutual admiration with the patient, and may have to learn through bitter disappointment how this defensive operation may effectively undermine the establishment of any realistic therapeutic alliance. To firmly undo the idealization, to confront the patient again and again with the unrealistic aspects of his transference distortion, while still acknowledging the positive feelings that are also part of this idealization, is a very difficult task because underneath that idealization are often paranoid fears and quite direct, primitive aggressive feelings toward the transference object.

Early Forms of Projection, and Especially Projective Identification

Projective identification is central in the manifestations of the transference of patients presenting borderline personality organization. Heimann (1955b) and Rosenfeld (1963) describe how this defensive operation manifests itself clinically.

One patient, who had already interrupted psychotherapy with two therapists in the middle of massive, almost delusional projections of her hostility, was finally able to settle down with a third therapist, but managed to keep him in a position of almost total immobility over a period of many months. The therapist had to be extremely careful even in asking questions; the patient would indicate by simply raising her eyebrow that a question was unwelcome and that therefore the therapist should change the subject. The patient felt that she had the right to be completely secretive and uncommunicative in regard to most issues of her life. She used the therapy situation on the surface as a kind of magical ritual and, apparently on a deeper level, as an acting out of her needs to exert sadistic control over a transference object onto which she had projected her aggression.

The acting out within the therapy hours of this patient's need to exert total, sadistic control over her transference object could not be modified. The therapist thought that any attempts to put limits on the patient's acting out or to confront her with the implications of her behavior, would only result in angry outbursts on the patient's part and in interruption of the treatment.

This raises the question of how to cope with patients who begin psychotherapy with this kind of acting out, and who attempt to distort the therapeutic situation to such a gross extent that either their unrealistic demands are met by the therapist or the continuation of the treatment is threatened. Some therapists believe that it may be an advantage to permit the patient to start out in therapy without challenging his unrealistic demands, hoping that later on, as the therapeutic relationship is more established, the patient's acting out can be gradually brought under control. From the vantage point of long-term observation of a series of cases of this kind, it seems preferable not to attempt psychotherapy under conditions which are unrealistic. If the therapist fears that an attempt to control premature acting out would bring psychotherapy to an interruption, the necessity of hospitalization should be considered and this should be discussed with the patient. One indication for hospitalization is precisely that of protecting the beginning psychotherapeutic relationship with patients in whom regressive transference acting out cannot be handled by psychotherapeutic means alone, and where the confrontation of the patient with his pathological defensive operations threatens to induce excessive regression. Hospitalization under these circumstances may serve diagnostic as well as protective functions, and should be considered even with patients who, even without psychotherapy, would most likely continue to be able to function outside a hospital. If psychotherapy is indicated, and if the psychotherapy is unrealistically limited by premature acting out, hospitalization, even though stressful for the patient, is preferable to undertaking a psychotherapy within which the necessary structuring is interfered with by the same pathology for which definite structuring is indicated.

Projective identification is a main culprit in creating unrealistic patient–therapist relationships from the very beginning of the treatment. The direct consequences of the patient's hostile onslaught in the transference, his unrelenting efforts to push the therapist into a position in which he finally reacts with counteraggression and the patient's sadistic efforts to control the therapist, can produce a paralyzing effect on the therapy. It has already been suggested that these developments require a firm structure within the therapeutic setting, consistent blocking of the transference acting out, and in the most simple terms, a protection of the therapist from chronic and insoluble situations. To combine this firm structure with consistent clarifications and interpretations aimed at reducing projective mechanisms is an arduous task.

Denial

In the patients we are considering, denial may manifest itself as simple disregard for a sector of the patient's subjective experience or a sector of his external world. When pressed, the patient can acknowledge his awareness of the sector which has been denied, but cannot integrate it with the rest of his emotional experience. It is relatively easy to diagnose the operation of denial because of the glaring loss of reality testing that it brings about. This patient acts as if he were completely unaware of a quite urgent, pressing aspect of his reality.

One patient, who had to meet a deadline for a thesis upon which his graduation and the possibility of a job depended, simply dropped the subject of the thesis in the psychotherapy sessions during the last two weeks before the deadline. He had discussed with his psychotherapist his fear of and anger toward the members of the committee in charge of examining his paper, and his denial here served the purpose, primarily, of protecting him against his paranoid fears of being discriminated against, and from those teachers whom he supposed wished to humiliate him in public. The therapist repeatedly confronted the patient with his lack of concern about finishing the paper and with his lack of effort to complete it. While interpreting the unconscious implications of this neglect, the therapist explored and confronted the patient with the many ways in which he was preventing himself from completing the paper in reality.

Denial can take quite complex forms in the transference, such as the defensive denial of reality aspects of the therapeutic situation in order to gratify transference needs.

One patient, in an attempt to overcome her anger about the analyst's unwillingness to respond to her seductive efforts, developed fantasies about the analyst's hidden intentions to seduce her as soon as she expressed her wishes for sexual intimacy with him in a submissive, defenseless way. At one point this fantasy changed to the fantasy that she was actually enjoying being raped by her father and by the analyst, and at one time intense anxiety developed in her, with a strong conviction that the analyst was actually her father, that he would sadistically rape her, and that this would bring about disaster. Out of the several implications of this transference development, the need to deny the reality of the analyst's lack of response to her sexual overtures, and her anger about this, seemed to predominate. The analyst pointed out to her that in one part of her she knew very well that the analyst was not her father, that he was not going to rape her, and that as frightening as these fantasies were, they still permitted her to deny her anger at the analyst for not responding to her sexual demands. The oedipal implications were excluded, for the time being, from his comment. The patient relaxed almost immediately and at this point the analyst commented on her reluctance to enter into an intimate relationship with her fiancé because of the fear that her unrealistic angry demands on him would stand in the way of her sexual enjoyment, and because her projection onto her fiancé of her own anger would turn the actual intimacy into a threat of sadistic rape for her. This opened the road to further insight about her denial of aggressive impulses as well as of reality.

This last example illustrates what the consistent working through of the pathological defenses which predominate in borderline patients attempts to accomplish. The working through of these defenses increases reality-testing and brings about ego strengthening, rather than inducing further regression. This example also illustrates the partial nature of the transference interpretation and the deflection of the transference outside the therapeutic relationship.

At times the patient especially needs to deny the positive aspects of the transference, because of his fear that the expression of positive feelings will bring him dangerously close to the therapist. The patient fears that such excessive closeness will free his aggression in the transference as well as the (projected) aggression of the therapist toward him. Schlesinger (1966), in illustrating this particular use of denial, has suggested that denial in the area of positive transference reaction should be respected because it may actually permit the patient to keep himself at an optimal distance from the therapist.

Omnipotence and Devaluation

These two, intimately linked defensive operations of omnipotence and devaluation refer to the patient's identification with an over-idealized self and object representation, with the primitive form of ego ideal, as a protection against threatening needs and involvement with others. Such "self idealization" usually implies magical fantasies of omnipotence, the conviction that he, the patient, will eventually receive all the gratification that he is entitled to, and that he cannot be touched by frustrations, illness, death, or the passage of time. A corollary of this fantasy is the devaluation of other people, the patient's conviction of his superiority over them, including the therapist. The projection of that magical omnipotence onto the therapist, and the patient's feeling magically united with or submissive to that omnipotent therapist, are other forms which this defensive operation can take.

This defensive operation is actually related to the primitive idealization mentioned above. The fractionating of the defensive operations which are characteristic of borderline patients into completely separate forms may clarify their functioning but it does necessarily oversimplify the issue. There are complex inter-twinings of all these defensive operations, and they present themselves in various combinations.

A patient with severe obesity and feelings of intense insecurity in social interactions eventually became aware of her deep conviction that she had the right to eat whatever she wanted and to expect that whatever her external form, she would still be admired, pampered, and loved. She paid only lip service to the acknowledgment that her obesity might reduce her capability to attract men, and became very angry with the therapist when the reality of this consideration was stressed. The patient began psychotherapy with the assumption that she could come for her appointment with the therapist at any time, take home the magazines in his waiting room, and need not care at all about leaving cigarette ash all over the furniture. When the implication of all this behavior was first pointed out to her, she smiled approvingly of the therapist's "perceptiveness," but no change occurred. It was only after the therapist made very clear to her that there were definite limits to what he would tolerate, that she became quite angry, expressing more openly the derogatory thoughts about the therapist that complemented her own feelings of greatness. The conscious experience of this patient was that of social insecurity and feelings of inferiority. Her underlying feelings of omnipotence remained unconscious for a long time.

Instinctual Vicissitudes and Psychotherapeutic Strategy

A predominant characteristic of the instinctual development of patients with borderline personality organization is the excessive development of pregenital drives, especially oral aggression, and of a particular pathological condensation of pregenital and genital aims under the overriding influence of aggressive needs. This instinctual development has direct relevance for the therapeutic approach to these patients. The therapist should remember that in the midst of the destructive and self-destructive instinctual manifestations are hidden potentials for growth and development, and especially that what appears on the surface to be destructive and self-destructive sexual behavior may contain the roots of further libidinal development and deepening interpersonal relationships.

There was a time when a typical misunderstanding of the implications of psychoanalytic theory and practice was the assumption that sexual activity in itself was a therapeutic factor. We have advanced a long way from such misunderstandings, and have learned that often what appears on the surface to be genital activity is actually in the service of aggressive, pregenital aims. With patients presenting borderline personality organization the opposite danger of seeing only their pregenital, destructive aims, to the neglect of acknowledging their efforts to overcome their inhibited sexual orientation, appears to be a frequent clinical problem.

A promiscuous, divorced, young woman, hospitalized after a psychotic regression which followed years of disorganized behavior, was restricted in the hospital from male patients. On several occasions a few minutes of unobserved time had been enough for her to have intercourse in an impulsive way with other patients, practically strangers. Over many months this patient was regularly controlled and in the sessions with her hospital doctor the implications of her behavior were discussed only in terms of her "lack of impulse control" and her "inappropriate behavior." When a new hospital doctor tried to evaluate further the implications of her sexual behavior, it evolved that her sexual activity had deep masochistic implications, and represented the acting out of her fantasy of being a prostitute. The hospital doctor took the position that not all sexual freedom implied prostitution, and in discussing these issues with her, the patient became very angry with him stating that he was "immoral," and she became very anxious and very angry with him when he eliminated the restrictions. She then became involved sexually with several other patients in a provocative manner, all of which the hospital doctor used further to confront her with the masochistic fantasies and the pattern of becoming a prostitute, and the implication of her submission to a primitive, sadistic superego which represented a prohibitive, combined father–mother image. She was finally able to establish a good relationship with one patient, with whom she fell in love, went steady for a two-year period, and whom she eventually planned to marry. During the latter part of these two years they had sexual intercourse, characterized by her being able for the first time in her life to have tender as well as sexual feelings toward just one man and by her taking precautions not to get pregnant, which was in contrast to her previous behavior.

To dissociate the normal, progressive trends within the pathological sexual behavior from its pregenital aims is easier said than done. This must be a continuous concern of the psychotherapist working with such patients.

Further Comments on the Modality of Treatment

This particular form of expressive, psychoanalytically oriented psychotherapy is a treatment approach which differs from classical psychoanalysis in that a complete transference neurosis is not permitted to develop, nor is transference resolved through interpretation alone. It is an expressive psychotherapeutic approach in that unconscious factors are considered and focused upon, especially in regard to the negative transference and to the consistent work with the pathological defenses of these patients. Parameters of technique or modifications of technique are used when necessary to control transference acting out, and although some of these parameters may be resolved during the course of the treatment itself, this is not necessarily possible nor desirable with all of them. There are also clearly supportive elements implicit in this approach. First, in the manipulation of the treatment situation, which the therapist has to undertake as part of the need to structure it. The frequency of the hours, the permissiveness or restriction in regard to out-of-hour contacts, the limits to which the patient may express himself, all may be considered as examples of factors which may be changed as the treatment demands. Second, clarifications of reality take up an important segment of the therapist's communications, and direct suggestions and implicit advice-giving are difficult to avoid under these circumstances.

The therapist should try to remain as neutral as possible, but neutrality here does not mean inactivity, and beyond certain degrees of activity on his part, the issue of whether the therapist is still neutral or not becomes academic. In general, it appears preferable to keep this kind of therapy in a face-to-face situation in order to stress the reality aspects of it, but there is nothing magical in itself about either lying on the couch or sitting in front of the therapist. There are treatments carried out on the couch which in effect are psychoanalytic psychotherapy rather than psychoanalysis.

The goal of ego strengthening is ever present in this expressive, psychoanalytically oriented treatment. The working through of the pathological defenses characteristic of the borderline personality organization permits repression and other related defenses of a higher level of ego organization to replace the ego-weakening, pathological defenses of the lower level: this in itself strengthens the ego. Conflict resolution is necessarily partial, but at times a great deal can be achieved with this kind of treatment approach.

One final and very important question remains. Are some of these patients analyzable either from the beginning of the treatment, or after a period of preparatory psychotherapy of the type suggested? The differences of opinion in this regard were referred to above in the review of the literature. There are specific patients within the large group presenting borderline personality organization who appear to benefit very little from the expressive, psychoanalytically oriented treatment approach I propose, and where nonmodified psychoanalysis is the treatment of choice from the beginning. This is particularly true for patients presenting the most typical forms of narcissistic personality organization.

Such patients present an unusual degree of self-reference in their interactions with other people, a great need to be loved and especially to be admired by others, and present an apparent contradiction between a very inflated concept of themselves and an inordinate need for tributes from others. Superficially, these patients do not appear to be severely regressed and some of them may function very well socially; they usually have much better impulse control than the average patient presenting borderline personality organization. They may be quite successful and efficient. It is only their emotional life which, on sharper focus, appears to be shallow and reflects an absence of normal empathy for others, a relative absence of enjoyment from life other than from the tributes they receive, and a combination of grandiose fantasies, envy, and the tendency to depreciate and manipulate others in an exploitative way.

These patients usually have such solidified, functioning pathological character structures that it is very difficult to mobilize their conflicts in the transference using the therapeutic approach proposed in this paper. Many of these patients appear to tolerate classical psychoanalysis without undue regression. Some of them unfortunately not only tolerate the analytic situation but are extremely resistant to any effort to mobilize their rigid characterological defenses in the transference. Ernst Ticho (1966) has suggested that there exists one group of indications for psychoanalysis which may be called "heroic indications." This indication is for patients in whom, although it seems more or less doubtful whether psychoanalysis would be of help, it seems reasonably beyond doubt that any treatment other than psychoanalysis would not be of help. Narcissistic personalities are part of this group. There are other authors who also feel that psychoanalysis is the treatment of choice for these patients, and who have contributed decisively to our understanding of the dynamics

of these patients and the technical difficulties in their analyses
(Kohut, 1966; Rosenfeld, 1964). In every patient presenting a
borderline personality organization, at one point during the
diagnostic examination the question of analyzability should be
considered and psychoanalysis should be rejected only after all
the contraindications have been carefully evaluated.

This paper attempts to outline a general psychotherapeutic
strategy with patients presenting borderline personality organization. The danger of such an outline is that it may be misinterpreted as a set of fixed rules, or that because of its necessarily
comprehensive nature, it may appear too general. It is hoped that
this outline may contribute to the overall frame of reference for
therapists who are working with these patients and who are,
therefore, well acquainted with the complex tactical therapeutic
issues that each patient presents.

Chapter 27

THE PSYCHOANALYTIC TREATMENT OF NARCISSISTIC PERSONALITY DISORDERS

Heinz Kohut

Introductory Considerations

The classification of the transferencelike structures mobilized during the analysis of narcissistic personalities presented here is based on previous conceptualizations (Kohut, 1966) of which only the following brief summary can be given. It was suggested that the child's original narcissistic balance, the perfection of his primary narcissism, is disturbed by the unavoidable shortcomings of maternal care, but that the child attempts to save the original experience of perfection by assigning it on the one hand to a grandiose and exhibitionistic image of the self: the *grandiose self,* and, on the other hand, to an admired you: the *idealized parent imago.* The central mechanisms which these two basic narcissistic configurations employ in order to preserve a part of the original experience are, of course, antithetical. Yet they coexist from the beginning and their individual and largely independent lines of development are open to separate scrutiny. At this moment it can only be pointed out that, under optimum developmental conditions, the exhibitionism and grandiosity of the archaic grandiose self are gradually tamed, and that the whole structure ultimately becomes integrated into the adult personality and supplies the instinctual fuel for our ego-syntonic ambitions and purposes, for the enjoyment of our activities, and for important aspects of our self-esteem. And, under similarly favorable circumstances, the idealized parent imago, too, becomes integrated

This chapter originally appeared in *The Psychoanalytic Study of the Child,* 23:86–113, 1968. New York: International Universities Press. Reprinted by persmission of the publisher.

into the adult personality. Introjected as our idealized superego, it becomes an important component of our psychic organization by holding up to us the guiding leadership of its ideals. If the child, however, suffers severe narcissistic traumata, then the grandiose self does not merge into the relevant ego content but is retained in its unaltered form and strives for the fulfillment of its archaic aims. And if the child experiences traumatic disappointments in the admired adult, then the idealized parent imago, too, is retained in its unaltered form, is not transformed into tension-regulating psychic structure but remains an archaic, transitional object that is required for the maintenance of narcissistic homeostasis.

Severe regressions, whether occurring spontaneously or during therapy, may lead to the activation of unstable, prepsychological fragments of the mind–body–self and its functions which belong to the stage of *autoerotism* (cf. Nagera, 1964). The pathognomonically specific, transferencelike, therapeutically salutary conditions, however, on which I am focusing, are based on the activation of psychologically elaborated, cohesive configurations which enter into stable amalgamations with the *narcissistically* perceived psychic representation of the analyst. The relative stability of this narcissistic transference–amalgamation, however, is the prerequisite for the performance of the analytic task in the pathogenic narcissistic areas of the personality.

The Narcissistic Transferences

I shall now examine the two narcissistic transferences delimited in accordance with the previously given conceptualizations: the therapeutic activation of the idealized parent imago for which the term *idealizing transference* will be employed, and the activation of the grandiose self which will be called the *mirror transference*.

Therapeutic Activation of the Idealized Parent Imago: The Idealizing Transference

The *idealizing transference* is the therapeutic revival of the early state in which the psyche saves a part of the lost experience of global narcissistic perfection by assigning it to an archaic (transitional) object, the idealized parent imago. Since all bliss and power now reside in the idealized object, the child feels empty and powerless when he is separated from it and he attempts, therefore, to maintain a continuous union with it.

Idealization, whether it is directed at a dimly perceived archaic mother-breast or at the clearly recognized oedipal parent, belongs genetically and dynamically in a narcissistic context. The idealizing cathexes, however, although retaining their narcissistic character, become increasingly neutralized and aim-inhibited. It is especially in the most advanced stages of their early development that the idealizations (which now coexist with powerful object-instinctual cathexes) exert their strongest and most important influence on the phase-appropriate internalization processes. At the end of the oedipal period, for example, the internalization of object-cathected aspects of the parental imago accounts for the contents (i.e., the commands and prohibitions) and functions (i.e., praise, scolding, punishment) of the super-ego; the internalization of the narcissistic aspects, however, form the exalted position of these contents and functions. It is from the narcissistic instinctual component of their cathexes that the aura of absolute perfection of the values and standards of the superego and of the omniscience and might of the whole structure are derived. The stream of narcissism, however, which is subsumed under the term *idealized parent imago* remains vulnerable throughout its whole early development; that is, from the stage of the incipient, archaic idealized object (which is still almost merged with the self) to the time of the massive reinternalization of the idealized aspect of the imago of the oedipal parent (who is already firmly established as separate from the self). The period of greatest vulnerability ends when an idealized nuclear superego has been formed, since the capacity for the idealization of his central values and standards which the child thus acquires exerts a lasting beneficial influence on the psychic economy in the narcissistic sectors of the personality.

The beginning of latency, however, may be considered as still belonging to the oedipal phase. It constitutes the last of the several periods of greatest danger in early childhood during which the psyche is especially susceptible to traumatization because after a spurt of development a new balance of psychological forces is only insecurely established. If we apply this *principle of the vulnerability of new structures* to the superego at the beginning of latency and, in particular, to the newly established idealization of its values and standards and of its rewarding and punishing functions, it will not surprise us to learn from clinical experience that a severe disappointment in the idealized oedipal object, even at the beginning of latency, may yet undo a precariously established idealization of the superego, may recathect the imago of the idealized object, and thus lead to a renewed insistence on finding an external object of perfection.

Under optimal circumstances the child experiences gradual disappointment in the idealized object—or, expressed differently: the child's evaluation of the idealized object becomes increasingly realistic—which leads to a withdrawal of the narcissistic idealizing cathexes from the object imago and to their gradual (or more massive but phase-appropriate) internalization, that is, to the acquisition of permanent psychological structures which continue, endopsychically, the functions which had previously been fulfilled by the idealized object. If the child's relationship to the idealized object is, however, severely disturbed, for example, if he suffers a traumatic (intense and sudden, or not phase-appropriate) disappointment in it, then the child does not acquire the needed internal structure, but his psyche remains fixated on an archaic object imago, and the personality will later, and throughout life, be dependent on certain objects in what seems to be an intense form of object hunger. The intensity of the search for and of the dependency on these objects is due to the fact that they are striven for as a substitute for missing segments of the psychic structure. These objects are not loved for their attributes, and their actions are only dimly recognized; they are needed in order to replace the functions of a segment of the mental apparatus which had not been established in childhood.

The structural defects which are the result of early disturbances in the relationship with the idealized object cannot be discussed within the confines of this essay. The following clinical illustration will instead focus on the effect of later traumatic disappointments, up to and including early latency.

Mr. A., a tall, asthenic man in his late twenties was a chemist in a pharmaceutical firm. Although he entered analysis with the complaint that he felt sexually stimulated by men, it soon became apparent that his homosexual preoccupations constituted only one of the several indications of an underlying broad personality defect. More important were periods of feeling depressed (with an associated drop in his work capacity); and, as a trigger to the preceding disturbance, a specific vulnerability of his self-esteem, manifested by his sensitivity to criticism, or simply to the absence of praise, from the people whom he experienced as his elders or superiors. Thus, although he was a man of considerable intelligence who performed his tasks with skill and creative ability, he was forever in search of approval: from the head of the research laboratory where he was employed, from a number of senior colleagues, and from the fathers of the girls whom he dated. He was sensitively aware of these men and of their opinion of him. So long as he felt that they approved of him, he experienced himself as whole, acceptable, and capable; and was then indeed able to do well in his work and to be creative and successful. At slight signs of disapproval of him, however, or of lack of understanding for him, he would become depressed, would tend to become first enraged and then cold, haughty, and isolated, and his creativeness deteriorated.

The cohesive transference permitted the gradual reconstruction of a certain genetically decisive pattern. Repeatedly, throughout his childhood, the patient had felt abruptly disappointed in the power of his father just when he had (re)established him as a figure of protective strength and efficiency. As is frequent, the first memories which the patient supplied subsequent to the transference activations of the crucial pattern referred to a comparatively late period. The family had come to the United States when the patient was nine and the father, who had been prosperous in Europe, was unable to repeat his earlier successes in this country. Time and again, however, the father shared his newest plans with his son and stirred the child's fantasies and expectations; but time and again he sold out in panic when the occurrence of unforeseen events and his lack of familiarity with the American scene combined to block his purposes. Although these memories had always been conscious, the patient had not previously appreciated the intensity of the contrast between the phase of great trust in the father, who was most confidence-inspiring while he was forging his plans, and the subsequent disappointment.

Most prominent among the patient's relevant recollections

of earlier occurrences of the idealization–disappointment sequence were those of two events which affected the family fortunes decisively when the patient was six and eight years old respectively. The father who, during the patient's early childhood, had been a virile and handsome man had owned a small but flourishing industry. Judging by many indications and memories, father and son had been very close emotionally and the son had admired his father greatly. Suddenly, when the patient was six, German armies invaded the country, and the family, which was Jewish, fled. Although the father had initially reacted with helplessness and panic, he had later been able to reestablish his business, though on a much reduced scale, but, as a consequence of the German invasion of the country to which they had escaped (the patient was eight at that time), everything was again lost and the family had to flee once more.

The patient's memories implicated the beginning of latency as the period when the structural defect was incurred. There is no doubt, however, that earlier experiences, related to his pathological mother, had sensitized him and accounted for the severity of the later acquired structural defect.

Described in metapsychological terms, his defect was the insufficient idealization of the superego and, concomitantly, a recathexis of the idealized parent imago of the late preoedipal and the oedipal stages. The symptomatic result of this defect was circumscribed yet profound. Since the patient had suffered a traumatic disappointment in the narcissistically invested aspects of the father imago, his superego did not possess the requisite exalted status and was thus unable to raise the patient's self-esteem. In view of the fact, however, that the patient had not felt equally deprived of those aspects of the father imago that were invested with object-instinctual cathexes, his superego was relatively intact with regard to those of its contents and functions that were built up as the heir to the object-instinctual dimensions of the oedipal father relationship. His nuclear goals and standards were indeed those of his cultural background transmitted by his father; what he lacked was the ability to feel more than a fleeting sense of satisfaction when living up to his standards or reaching his goals. Only through the confirmatory approval of external admired figures was he able to obtain a sense of heightened self-esteem. In the transference he seemed thus insatiable in two demands that he directed toward the idealized analyst: that the analyst share the patient's values, goals, and standards (and thus imbue them with significance through their idealization); and that the analyst confirm through the expression of a warm glow of pleasure and participation that the patient had lived up to his values and standards and had successfully worked toward a goal. Without the analyst's expression of his empathic comprehension of these needs, the patient's values and goals seemed trite and uninspiring to him and his successes were meaningless and left him feeling depressed and empty.

The Genesis of the Pathogenic Fixation on the Idealized Parent Imago

As can be regularly ascertained, the essential genetic trauma is grounded in the parents' own narcissistic fixations, and the parents' narcissistic needs contribute decisively to the child's remaining enmeshed within the narcissistic web of the parents' personality until, for example, the sudden recognition of the shortcomings of the parent, or the child's sudden desperate recognition of how far out of step his own emotional develop-ment has become, confronts him with the insuperable task of achieving the wholesale internalization of a chronic narcissistic relationship. The complexity of the pathogenic interplay between parent and child, and the varieties of its forms, defy a com-prehensive description. Yet in a properly conducted analysis, the crucial pattern will often emerge with great clarity.

Mr. B., for example, established a narcissistic transference in which the analyst's presence increased and solidified his self-esteem and thus, secondarily, improved his ego functioning and efficiency.[1] To any impending disruption of this beneficial deployment of narcissistic cathexes, he responded with rage, and with a decathexis of the narcissistically invested analyst, and a hypercathexis of his grandiose self, manifested by cold and imperious behavior. But, finally (after the analyst had gone away, for example), he reached a comparatively stable balance: he

---

[1]The episode described here concerns a patient who was treated by a colleague (a woman) in regular consultation with the author.

withdrew to lonely intellectual activities which, although pursued with less creativity than before, provided him with a sense of
self-sufficiency. In his words, he "rowed out alone to the middle
of the lake and looked at the moon." When, however, the
possibility of reestablishing the relationship to the narcissistically
invested object offered itself, he reacted with the same rage that
he had experienced when the transference—to use his own
significant analogy—had become "unplugged." At first I thought
that the reaction was nonspecific, consisting of yet unexpressed
rage about the analyst's leaving, and of anger at having to give up
a newfound protective balance. These explanations were, however, incomplete since the patient was in fact by his reactions
describing an important sequence of early events. The patient's
mother had been intensely enmeshed with him, and had supervised and controlled him in a most stringent fashion. His exact
feeding time, for example, and in later childhood, his eating
time, was determined by a mechanical timer—reminiscent of the
devices which Schreber's father employed with his children
(Niederland, 1959)—and thus the child felt that he had no mind
of his own and that his mother was continuing to perform his
mental functions long beyond the time when such maternal
activities, carried out empathically, are indeed phase-appropriate
and required. Under the impact of the anxious recognition of the
inappropriateness of this relationship, he would in later childhood withdraw to his room to think his own thoughts, uninfluenced
by her interference. When he had just begun to achieve some
reliance on this minimum of autonomous functioning, his mother
had a buzzer installed. From then on, she would interrupt his
attempts of internal separation from her whenever he wanted to
be alone. The buzzer summoned him more compellingly (because
the mechanical device was experienced as akin to an endopsychic
communication) than would have her voice or knocking. No
wonder, then, that he reacted with rage to the return of the
analyst after he had "rowed to the center of the lake to look at
the moon."

The Process of Working Through and Some Other Clinical Problems in the Idealizing Transference

Little need be said concerning the beginning of the analysis.
Although there may be severe resistances, especially those

motivated by apprehensions about the extinction of individuality due to the wish to merge into the idealized object, the pathognomonic regression will establish itself spontaneously if the analyst does not interfere by premature transference interpretations. The working-through phase of the analysis can, however, begin only after the pathognomonic idealizing transference has been firmly established. It is set into motion by the fact that the instinctual equilibrium which the analysand aims to maintain is sooner or later disturbed. In the undisturbed transference the patient feels powerful, good, and capable. Anything, however, that deprives him of the idealized analyst creates a disturbance of his self-esteem: he feels powerless and worthless, and if his ego is not assisted by interpretations concerning the loss of the idealized parent imago, the patient may turn to archaic precursors of the idealized parent imago or may abandon it altogether and regress further to reactively mobilized archaic stages of the grandiose self. The retreat to archaic idealizations may manifest itself in the form of vague, impersonal, trancelike religious feelings; the hypercathexis of archaic forms of the grandiose self and of the (autoerotic) body self will produce the syndrome of emotional coldness, tendency toward affectation in speech and behavior, shame propensity, and hypochondria.

Although such temporary cathectic shifts toward the archaic stages of the idealized parent imago and of the grandiose self are common occurrences in the analysis of narcissistic personalities, they may be precipitated by seemingly minute narcissistic injuries the discovery of which may put the analyst's empathy and clinical acumen to a severe test.

The essence, however, of the curative process in the idealizing transference can be epitomized in a few comparatively simple principles. A working-through process is set in motion in which the repressed narcissistic strivings with which the archaic object is invested are admitted into consciousness. Although the ego and superego resistances with which we are familiar from the analysis of the transference neuroses also do occur here, and although there are in addition specific ego resistances (motivated by anxiety concerning hypomanic overstimulation) which oppose the mobilization of the idealizing cathexes, the major part of the working-through process concerns the loss of the narcissistically experienced object. If the repeated interpretations of the meaning of separations from the analyst on the level of the idealizing narcissistic libido are given with correct empathy for the analysand's feelings—in particular for what appears to be his lack of emotions, that is, his coldness and retreat, for example, in response to separations—then there will gradually emerge a host of meaningful memories which concern the dynamic prototypes of the present experience. The patient will recall lonely hours during his childhood in which he attempted to overcome a feeling of fragmentation, hypochondria, and deadness which was due to the separation from the idealized parent. And he will remember, and gratefully understand, how he tried to substitute for the idealized parent imago and its functions by creating erotized replacements and through the frantic hypercathexis of the grandiose self: how he rubbed his face against the rough floor in the basement, looked at the mother's photograph, went through her drawers and smelled her underwear; and how he turned to the performance of grandiose athletic feats in which flying fantasies were being enacted by the child, in order to reassure himself. Adult analogues in the analysis (during the weekend, for example) are intense voyeuristic preoccupations, the impulse to shoplift, and recklessly speedy drives in the car. Childhood memories and deepening understanding of the analogous transference experiences converge in giving assistance to the patient's ego, and the formerly automatic reactions become gradually more aim-inhibited.

The ego acquires increasing tolerance for the analyst's absence and for the analyst's occasional failure to achieve a correct empathic understanding. The patient learns that the idealizing libido need not be immediately withdrawn from the idealized imago and that the painful and dangerous regressive shifts of the narcissistic cathexes can be prevented. Concomitant with the increase of the ability to maintain a part of the idealizing investment despite the separation, there is also an enhancement of internalization, that is, the analysand's psychic organization acquires the capacity to perform some of the functions previously performed by the idealized object.

Therapeutic Activation of the Grandiose Self: The Mirror Transference

Analogous to the idealized object in the idealizing transference, it is the grandiose self which is reactivated in the transferencelike condition referred to as the *mirror transference*.

The mirror transference constitutes the therapeutic revival of the developmental stage in which the child attempts to retain a part of the original, all-embracing narcissism by concentrating perfection and power upon a grandiose self and by assigning all imperfections to the outside.

The mirror transference occurs in three forms which relate to specific stages of development of the grandiose self:

1. An archaic form in which the self experience of the analysand includes the analyst; it will be referred to as *merger through the extension of the grandiose self*.

2. A less archaic form in which the patient assumes that the analyst is like him or that the analyst's psychological makeup is similar to his; it will be called the *alter ego transference* or *twinship*.

3. A still less archaic form in which the analyst is experienced as a separate person who, however, has significance to the patient only within the framework of the needs generated by his therapeutically reactivated grandiose self. Here the term *mirror transference* is most accurate and will again be employed. In this narrower sense the mirror transference is the reinstatement of the phase in which the gleam in the mother's eye, which mirrors the child's exhibitionistic display, and other forms of maternal participation in the child's narcissistic enjoyment confirm the child's self-esteem and, by a gradually increasing selectivity of these responses, begin to channel it into realistic directions. If the development of the grandiose self is traumatically disturbed, however, then this psychic structure may become cut off from further integrative participation in the development of the personality. Insecurely repressed in an archaic form, it is, on the one hand, removed from further external influence; yet, on the other hand, continues to disturb realistic adaptation by its recurrent intrusions into the ego. In the mirror transference, however, it may become cohesively remobilized, and a new road to its gradual modification is opened.

The central activity in the clinical process during the mirror transference concerns the raising to consciousness of the patient's infantile fantasies of exhibitionistic grandeur. In view of the strong resistances which oppose this process and the intensive efforts required in overcoming them, it may at times be disappointing for the analyst to behold the apparently trivial fantasy which the patient has ultimately brought into the light of day.

True, at times even the content of the fantasy permits an empathic understanding of the shame and hypochondria, and of the anxiety which the patient experiences; shame, because the revelation is at times still accompanied by the discharge of unneutralized exhibitionistic libido; and anxiety because the grandiosity isolates the analysand and threatens him with permanent object loss.

Patient C., for example, told the following dream during a period when he was looking forward to being publicly honored: "The question was raised of finding a successor for me. I thought: How about God?" The dream was partly the result of the attempt to soften the grandiosity through humor; yet it aroused excitement and anxiety, and led, against renewed resistances, to the recall of childhood fantasies in which he had felt that he was God.

In many instances, however, the nuclear grandiosity is only hinted at. Patient D., for example, recalled with intense shame and resistance that as a child he used to imagine that he was running the streetcars in the city. The fantasy appeared harmless enough; but the shame and resistance became more understandable when the patient explained that he was operating the streetcars via a "thought control" which emanated from his head, above the clouds.

Although the content of the grandiose fantasy cannot be further discussed here, it is important to clarify the role of the mirror transference which enables its emergence. As indicated before, the patient's major resistances are motivated by his attempt to escape from the uneasy elation alternating with fear of permanent object loss, painful self-consciousness, shame-tension, and hypochondria which is due to the dedifferentiating intrusions of grandiose fantasies and narcissistic–exhibitionistic libido into the ego. The transference, however, functions as a specific therapeutic buffer. In the mirror transference, in the narrower sense, the patient is able to mobilize his grandiose fantasies and exhibitionism on the basis of the hope that the therapist's empathic participation and emotional response will not allow the narcissistic tensions to reach excessively painful or dangerous levels. In the twinship and the merger, the analogous protection is provided by the long-term deployment of the narcissistic cathexes upon the therapist, who now is the carrier of the patient's infantile greatness and exhibitionism.

Later, especially with the aid of the very last clinical example referred to in this presentation, some of the specific, concrete clinical steps by which the mobilized infantile narcissistic demands gradually become tamed and neutralized will be demonstrated. Here, however, the general significance of the mirror transference in the context of therapy will be examined.

The rational aims of therapy could not, by themselves, persuade the vulnerable ego of the narcissistically fixated analysand to forgo denial and acting out and to face and to examine the needs and claims of the archaic grandiose self. In order to actuate, and to maintain in motion, the painful process which leads to the confrontation of the grandiose fantasies with a realistic conception of the self, and to the realization that life offers only limited possibilities for the gratification of the narcissistic-exhibitionistic wishes, a mirror transference must be established. If it does not develop, the patient's grandiosity remains concentrated upon the grandiose self, the ego's defensive position remains rigid, and ego expansion cannot take place.

The mirror transference rests on the therapeutic reactivation of the grandiose self. That the analyst can be enlisted in the support of this structure is an expression of the fact that the formation of a cohesive grandiose self was indeed achieved during childhood; the listening, perceiving, and echoing–mirroring presence of the analyst now reinforces the psychological forces which maintain the cohesiveness of the self-image, archaic and (by adult standards) unrealistic though it may be. Analogous to the therapeutically invaluable, controlled, temporary swings toward the disintegration of the idealizing parent imago when the idealizing transference is disturbed, we may encounter as a consequence of a disturbance of the mirror transference the temporary fragmentation of the narcissistically cathected, cohesive (body–mind) self and a temporary concentration of the narcissistic cathexes on isolated body parts, isolated mental functions, and isolated actions, which are then experienced as dangerously disconnected from a crumbling self. As is the case in the idealizing transference, these temporary disturbances of the transference equilibrium occupy in the analysis of narcissistic personalities a central position of strategic importance which corresponds to the place of the structural conflict in the ordinary transference neuroses; and their analysis tends to elicit the deepest insights and leads to the most solid accretions of psychic structure.

The following constitutes an especially instructive illustration of such a temporary regressive fragmentation of the therapeutically activated grandiose self.

Mr. E. was a graduate student whose psychopathology and personality structure will not be discussed except to say that he sought relief from painful narcissistic tension states by a number of perverse means in which the inconstancy of his objects and sexual goals was indicative of the fact that he could trust no source of satisfaction. This brief report concerns a weekend during an early phase of the long analysis when the patient was already beginning to realize that separations from the analyst[2] upset his psychic equilibrium, but when he did not yet understand the specific nature of the support which the analysis provided. During earlier weekend separations a vaguely perceived inner threat had driven him to dangerous voyeuristic activities in public toilets during which he achieved a feeling of merger with the man at whom he gazed. This time, however, he was able, through an act of artistic sublimation, not only to spare himself the aforementioned cruder means of protection against the threatened dissolution of the self, but also to explain the nature of the reassurance he was receiving from the analyst. During this weekend, the patient painted a picture of the analyst. The key to the understanding of this artistic production lay in the fact that in it the analyst had neither eyes nor nose—the place of these sensory organs was taken by the analysand. On the basis of this evidence and of additional corroborative material, the conclusion could be reached that a decisive support to the maintenance of the patient's narcissistically cathected self-image was supplied by the analyst's perception of him. The patient felt whole when

[2]This analysis was carried out by a senior student at the Chicago Institute for Psychoanalysis under regular supervision by the author.

he thought that he was acceptingly looked at by an object that substituted for an insufficiently developed endopsychic function: the analyst provided replacement for the lacking narcissistic cathexis of the self.

Some General Therapeutic Considerations Concerning the Mirror Transference

The analysand's demands for attention, admiration, and for a variety of other forms of mirroring and echoing responses to the mobilized grandiose self, which fill the mirror transference in the narrow sense of this term, do not usually constitute great cognitive problems for the analyst, although he may have to mobilize much subtle understanding to keep pace with the patient's defensive denials of his demands or with the retreat from them when the immediate empathic response to them is not forthcoming. Here it is of decisive importance that the analyst comprehend and acknowledge the phase-appropriateness of the demands of the grandiose self and that he grasp the fact that for a long time it is a mistake to emphasize to the patient that his demands are unrealistic. If the analyst demonstrates to the patient that the narcissistic needs are appropriate within the context of the total early phase that is being revived in the transference and that they have to be expressed, then the patient will gradually reveal the urges and fantasies of the grandiose self, and the slow process is thus initiated that leads to the integration of the grandiose self into the realistic structure of the ego and to an adaptively useful transformation of its energies.

The empathic comprehension of the reactivation of the earlier developmental stages (the alter ego transference or twinship; the merger with the analyst through the extension of the grandiose self) is, however, not achieved easily. It is, for example, usually difficult for the analyst to hold fast to the realization that the meagerness of object-related imagery with regard to current and past figures as well as with regard to the analyst himself is the appropriate manifestation of an archaic narcissistic relationship. A frequent misunderstanding of the mirror transference in general and of the therapeutic activation of the most archaic stages of the grandiose self in particular thus consists in its being mistaken for the outgrowth of a widespread resistance against the establishment of an object-instinctual transference. And many analyses of narcissistic personality disorders are either short-circuited at this point (leading to a brief analysis of subsidiary sectors of the personality in which ordinary transferences do occur while the principal disturbance, which is narcissistic, remains untouched) or are forced into a mistaken and unprofitable direction against diffuse, nonspecific, and chronic ego resistances of the analysand.

If the establishment of a mirror transference is, however, not prevented, the gradual mobilization of the repressed grandiose self will take place and a number of specific, pathognomonic, and therapeutically valuable resistances will be set in motion. The principal end of the working-through processes in the idealizing transference is the internalization of the idealized object which leads to the strengthening of the matrix of the ego and to the strengthening of the patient's ideals; the principal end of the working-through processes in the mirror transference is the transformation of the grandiose self which results in a firming of the ego's potential for action (through the increasing realism of the ambitions of the personality) and in increasingly realistic self-esteem.

An important question posed by the analysis of narcissistic personalities, especially in the area of the grandiose self, concerns the degree of therapeutic activity which needs to be employed by the analyst. In applying Aichhorn's technique with juvenile delinquents (1936), for example, the analyst offers himself actively to the patient as a replica of his grandiose self, in a relationship which resembles the twinship (or alter ego) variant of a mirror transference (see also A. Freud's illuminating summary [1951]). A delinquent's capacity to attach himself to the analyst in admiration indicates, however, that an idealized parent imago and the deep wish to form an idealizing transference are (preconsciously) present, but, in consequence of early disappointments, they are denied and hidden. It was Aichhorn's special understanding for the delinquent that led him to offer himself first as a mirror image of the delinquent's grandiose self. He was thus able to initiate a veiled mobilization of idealizing cathexes toward an idealized object without yet disturbing the necessary protection of the defensively created grandiose self and its activities. Once a bond is established, however, a gradual shift from the omnipotence of the grandiose self to the more deeply longed-for omnipotence of an idealized object (and the requisite therapeutic dependence on it) can be achieved.

In the analytic treatment of the ordinary cases of narcissistic personality disturbance, however, the active encouragement of idealization is not desirable. It leads to the establishment of a tenacious transference bondage, bringing about the formation of a cover of massive identification and hampering the gradual alteration of the existing narcissistic structures. But a spontaneously occurring therapeutic mobilization of the idealized parent imago or of the grandiose self is indeed to be welcomed and must not be interfered with.

There are two antithetical pitfalls concerning the form of the interpretations which focus on the narcissistic transferences: the analyst's readiness to moralize about the patient's narcissism; and his tendency toward abstractness of the relevant interpretations.

The triad of value judgments, moralizing, and therapeutic activism in which the analyst steps beyond the basic analytic attitude to become the patient's leader and teacher is most likely to occur when the psychopathology under scrutiny is not understood metapsychologically. Under these circumstances the analyst can hardly be blamed when he tends to abandon the ineffective analytic armamentarium and instead offers himself to the patient as an object to identify with in order to achieve therapeutic changes. If lack of success in areas that are not yet understood metapsychologically is tolerated, however, without the abandonment of analytic means, then the occurrence of new analytic insights is not prevented and scientific progress can be made.

Where metapsychological understanding is not entirely lacking but is incomplete, analysts tend to supplement their interpretations with suggestive pressure and the weight of the personality of the therapist becomes of greater importance. There are thus certain analysts who are said to be exceptionally gifted in the analysis of "borderline" cases and anecdotes about their therapeutic activities become widely known in analytic circles. But just as the surgeon, in the heroic era of surgery, was a charismatically gifted individual who performed great feats of courage and skill, while the modern surgeon tends to be a calm, well-trained craftsman, so also with the analyst. As our knowledge about the narcissistic disorders increases, their treatment becomes the work of analysts who do not employ any special charisma of their personalities but restrict themselves to the use of the tools that provide rational success: interpretations and reconstructions. There are, of course, moments when a forceful statement is indicated as a final move in persuading the patient that the gratifications obtained from the unmodified narcissistic fantasies are spurious. A skillful analyst of an older generation, for example, as asserted by local psychoanalytic lore, would make his point at a strategic juncture by silently handing over a crown and scepter to his unsuspecting analysand instead of confronting him with yet another verbal interpretation. In general, however, the psychoanalytic process is most enhanced if we trust the spontaneous synthetic functions of the patient's ego to integrate the narcissistic configurations gradually, in an atmosphere of analytic–empathic acceptance, instead of driving the analysand toward an imitation of the analyst's scornful rejection of the analysand's lack of realism.

The second danger, namely, that interpretations regarding the narcissistic transference might become too abstract, can be much diminished if we avoid falling victim to the widespread confusion between object relations and object love. We must bear in mind that our interpretations about the idealizing transference and the mirror transference are statements about an intense object relationship, despite the fact that the object is invested with narcissistic cathexes, and that we are explaining to the analysand how his very narcissism leads him to a heightened sensitivity about certain specific aspects and actions of the object, the analyst, whom he experiences in a narcissistic mode.

If the analyst's interpretations are noncondemnatory; if he can clarify to the patient in concrete terms the significance and the meaning of his (often acted-out) messages, of his seemingly irrational hypersensitivity, and of the back-and-forth flow of the cathexis of the narcissistic positions; and especially, if he can demonstrate to the patient that these archaic attitudes are comprehensible, adaptive, and valuable within the context of the total state of personality development of which they form a part—then the mature segment of the ego will not turn away from the grandiosity of the archaic self or from the awesome features of the overestimated, narcissistically experienced object. Over and over again, in small, psychologically manageable portions, the ego will deal with the disappointment at having to recognize that the claims of the grandiose self are unrealistic. And, in response to this experience, it will either mournfully withdraw a part of the narcissistic investment from the archaic image of the self, or it will, with the aid of newly acquired structure, neutralize the associated narcissistic energies or channel them into aim-inhibited pursuits. And over and over again, in small, psychologically manageable portions, the ego will deal with the disappointment at having to recognize that the idealized object is unavailable or imperfect. And, in response to this experience, it will withdraw a part of the idealizing investment from the object and strengthen the corresponding internal structures. In short, if the ego learns first to accept the presence of the mobilized narcissistic structures, it will gradually integrate them into its own realm, and the analyst will witness the establishment of ego dominance and ego autonomy in the narcissistic sector of the personality.

Reactions of the Analyst

Reactions of the Analyst During the Mobilization of the Patient's Idealized Parent Imago in the Idealizing Transference

Some time ago I was consulted by a colleague concerning a stalemate which seemed to have been present from the beginning of the analysis and to have persisted through two years of work. Since the patient, a shallow, promiscuous woman, showed a serious disturbance of her ability to establish meaningful object relationships and presented a history of severe childhood traumata, I tended initially to agree with the analyst that the extent of the narcissistic fixations prevented the establishment of that minimum of transferences without which analysis cannot proceed. Still, I asked the analyst for an account of the early sessions, with particular attention to activities on his part which the patient might have experienced as a rebuff. Among the earliest transference manifestations several dreams of this Catholic patient had contained the figure of an inspired, idealistic priest. While these early dreams had remained uninterpreted, the analyst remembered—clearly against resistance—that he had subsequently indicated that he was not a Catholic. He had justified this move by her supposed need to be acquainted with a minimum of the actual situation since in his view the patient's hold on reality was tenuous. This event must have been very significant for the patient. We later understood that, as an initial, tentative transference step, she had reinstated an attitude of idealizing religious devotion from the beginning of adolescence, an attitude which in turn had been the revival of awe and admiration from childhood. These earliest idealizations, as we could conclude later, had been a refuge from bizarre tensions and fantasies caused by traumatic stimulations and frustrations from the side of her pathological parents. The analyst's misguided remark, however, that he was not a Catholic—that is, not an idealized good and healthy version of the patient—constituted a rebuff for her and led to the stalemate, which the analyst, with the aid of a number of consultations concerning this patient and his response to her, was later largely able to break.

I am focusing neither on the transference nor on the effect of the analyst's mistake on the analysis, but on the elucidation of a countertransference symptom. A combination of circumstances, among them the fact that I observed other, similar incidents, allows me to offer the following explanation with a high degree of conviction. An analytically unwarranted rejection of a patient's idealizing attitudes is usually motivated by a defensive fending off of narcissistic tensions, experienced as embarrassment and leading even to hypochondriacal preoccupations, which are generated in the analyst when repressed fantasies of his grandiose self become stimulated by the patient's idealization.

Are these reactions of the analyst in the main motivated by current stress, or are they related to the dangerous mobilization of specific repressed unconscious constellations?

In a letter to Binswanger, Freud (1913b) expressed himself as follows about the problem of countertransference: "What is given to the patient," Freud said, must be "consciously allotted, and then more or less of it as the need may arise. Occasionally a great deal . . ." And later Freud set down the crucial maxim: "To give someone too little because one loves him too much is being unjust to the patient and a technical error."

If a patient's incestuous object-libidinal demands elicit an intense unconscious response in the analyst, he may become overly technical vis-à-vis the patient's wishes or will not even recognize them—at any rate, his ego will not have the freedom to choose the response required by the analysis. A parallel situation may arise in the analysis of a narcissistic personality disturbance when the remobilization of the idealized parent imago prompts the analysand to see the analyst as the embodiment of idealized perfection. If the analyst has not come to terms with his own grandiose self, he may respond to the idealization with an intense stimulation of his unconscious grandiose fantasies and an intensification of defenses which bring about his rejection of the patient's idealizing transference. If the analyst's defensive attitude becomes chronic, the establishment of a workable idealizing transference is interfered with and the analytic process is blocked.

It makes little difference whether the rejection of the patient's idealization is blunt, which is rare; or subtle (as in the instance reported), which is common; or, which is most frequent, almost concealed by correct, but prematurely given, genetic or dynamic interpretations (such as the analyst's quickly calling the patient's attention to idealized figures in his past or pointing out hostile impulses which supposedly underlie the idealizing ones). The rejection may express itself through no more than a slight over-objectivity of the analyst's attitude; or it may reveal itself in the tendency to disparage the narcissistic idealization in a humorous and kindly way. And finally, it is even deleterious to emphasize the patient's assets at a time when he attempts the idealizing expansion of the ingrained narcissistic positions and feels insignificant by comparison with the therapist—appealing though it might seem when the analyst expresses respect for his patient. In short, during those phases of the analysis of narcissistic personalities when an idealizing transference begins to germinate, there is only one correct analytic attitude: to accept the admiration.

*Reactions of the Analyst During the Therapeutic Mobilization of the
Patient's Grandiose Self in the Mirror Transference*

The mirror transference occurs in different forms which expose
the analyst to different emotional tasks. In the mirror transference in the narrower sense the patient reacts to the ebb and
flow of the analyst's empathy with, and response to, his narcissistic needs, and the presence of the analyst is thus acknowledged.
Even these circumstances, however, may elicit reactions in the
analyst which interfere with the therapeutic reactivation of the
grandiose self since the analyst's own narcissistic needs may
make him intolerant of a situation in which he is reduced to the
role of mirror for the patient's infantile narcissism. In the
twinship (alter ego) and merger varieties of the remobilization of
the grandiose self, however, the analyst is deprived of even the
minimum of narcissistic gratification: the patient's acknowledgment of his separate existence. While in the mirror transference
the analyst may become incapable of comprehending the patient's
narcissistic needs and of responding to them, the most common
dangers in the twinship or merger are his boredom, his lack of
emotional involvement with the patient, and his precarious
maintenance of attention. A theoretical discussion of these
failures must, however, be omitted here. On the one hand, it
would require an examination of the psychology of attention in
the absence of stimulation by object cathexes; on the other hand,
one would have to study certain aspects of the vulnerability of
empathy in analysts which are genetically related to the fact that a
specific empathic sensitivity, acquired in an early narcissistic
relationship, often contributes decisively to the motivation for
becoming an analyst. Instead of a theoretical discussion, however, the attempt will be made to illuminate the subject matter
with the aid of a clinical example.

Miss F., age twenty-five, had sought analysis because of diffuse dissatisfactions. Despite the fact that she was active in her
profession and had numerous social contacts, she was not
intimate with anyone, and felt different from other people and
isolated. She had a series of love relationships but had rejected
marriage because she knew that such a step would be a sham. She
was subject to sudden changes in her mood with an associated

uncertainty about the reality of her feelings and thoughts. In metapsychological terms the disturbance was due to a faulty integration of the grandiose self which led to swings between states of anxious excitement and elation over a secret "preciousness" which made her vastly better than anyone else (during times when the ego came close to giving way to the hypercathected grandiose self) and states of emotional depletion (when the ego used all its strength to wall itself off from the unrealistic, grandiose substructure). Genetically, the fact that the mother had been depressed during several periods early in the child's life had prevented the gradual integration of the narcissistic–exhibitionistic cathexes of the grandiose self. During decisive periods of her childhood the girl's presence and activities had not called forth maternal pleasure and approval. On the contrary, whenever she tried to speak about herself, the mother deflected, imperceptibly, the focus of attention to her own depressive self-preoccupations, and thus the child was deprived of that optimal maternal acceptance which transforms crude exhibitionism and grandiosity into adaptably useful self-esteem and self-enjoyment.

During extended phases of the analysis, beginning at a time when I did not yet understand the patient's psychopathology, the following progression of events frequently occurred during analytic sessions. The patient would arrive in a friendly mood, settle down quietly, and begin to communicate her thoughts and feelings: about current topics; the transference, and insights concerning the connection between present and past, and between transferences upon the analyst and analogous strivings toward others. In brief, the first part of the sessions had the appearance of a well-moving self-analysis when the analyst is, indeed, little else than an interested observer who holds himself in readiness for the next wave of resistances. The stage in question lasted much longer, however, than the periods of self-analysis encountered in other analyses. I noted, furthermore, that I was not able to maintain the attitude of interested attention which normally establishes itself effortlessly and spontaneously when one listens to an analysand's work of free associations during periods of relatively unimpeded self-analysis. And, finally, after a prolonged period of ignorance and misunderstanding during which I was inclined to argue with the patient about the correctness of my interpretations and to suspect the presence of stubborn, hidden resistances, I came to the crucial recognition that the patient demanded a specific response to her communications, and that she completely rejected any other. Unlike the analysand during periods of genuine self-analysis, the patient could not tolerate the analyst's silence, but, at approximately the midpoint of the sessions, she would suddenly get violently angry at me for being silent. (The archaic nature of her need, it may be added, was betrayed by the suddenness with which it appeared—like the sudden transition from satiation to hunger or from hunger to satiation in very young children.) I gradually learned, however, that she would immediately become calm and content when I, at these moments, simply summarized or repeated what she had in essence already said (such as, "You are again struggling to free yourself from becoming embroiled in your mother's suspiciousness against men." Or, "You have worked your way through to the understanding that the fantasies about the visiting Englishman are reflections of fantasies about me"). But if I went beyond what the patient herself had already said or discovered, even by a single step only (such as: "The fantasies about the visiting foreigner are reflections of fantasies about me and, in addition, I think that they are a revival of the dangerous stimulation to which you felt exposed by your father's fantasy-stories about you"), she would again get violently angry (regardless of the fact that what I had added might be known to her, too), and would furiously accuse me, in a tense, high-pitched voice, of undermining her, that with my remark I had destroyed everything she had built up, and that I was wrecking the analysis.

Certain convictions can only be acquired firsthand and I am thus not able to demonstrate in detail the correctness of the following conclusions. During this phase of the analysis the patient had begun to remobilize an archaic, intensely cathected image of the self which had heretofore been kept in repression. Concomitant with the remobilization of the grandiose self, on which she had remained fixated, there also arose the renewed need for an archaic object that would be nothing more than the embodiment of a psychological function which the patient's psyche could not yet perform for itself: to respond empathically to her narcissistic display and to provide her with narcissistic sustenance through approval, mirroring, and echoing. The patient thus attempted, with the aid of my confirming, mirroring presence, to integrate a hypercathected archaic self into the rest of her personality. This process began at this stage with a cautious reinstatement of a sense of the reality of her thoughts and feelings; it later moved gradually toward the transformation of her intense exhibitionistic needs into an ego-syntonic sense of her own value and an enjoyment of her activities.

Due to the fact that I was at that time not sufficiently alert to the pitfalls of such transference demands, many of my interventions interfered with the work of structure formation. But I know that the obstacles that opposed my understanding lay not only in the cognitive area; and I can affirm, without transgressing the rules of decorum and without indulging in the kind of immodest self-revelation which ultimately hides more than it admits, that there were specific hindrances in my own personality which stood in my way. There was a residual insistence, related to deep and old fixation points, on seeing myself in the narcissistic center of the stage; and, although I had of course for a long time struggled with the relevant childhood delusions and thought that I had, on the whole, achieved dominance over them, I was not up to the extreme demands posed by the conceptually unaided confrontation with the reactivated grandiose self of my patient. Thus I refused to entertain the possibility that I was not an object for the patient, not an amalgam with the patient's childhood loves and hatreds, but only, as I reluctantly came to see, an impersonal function, without significance except insofar as it related to the kingdom of her own remobilized narcissistic grandeur and exhibitionism. For a long time I insisted, therefore, that the patient's reproaches related to specific transference fantasies and wishes on the oedipal level—but I could make no headway in this direction. It was ultimately, I believe, the high-pitched tone of her voice which expressed such utter conviction of being right— the conviction of a very young child; a pent-up, heretofore unexpressed conviction—which led me on the right track. I recognized that, whenever I did more (or less) than to provide simple approval or confirmation in response to the patient's reports of her own discoveries, I became for her the depressive mother who deflected the narcissistic cathexes from the child upon herself, or who did not provide the needed narcissistic echo.

The clinical situation described in the foregoing pages and, especially, the analyst's therapeutic responses to it require further elucidation.

At first hearing I might seem to be stating that, in instances of this type, the analyst must indulge a transference wish of the analysand; specifically, that the patient had not received the necessary emotional echo or approval from the depressive mother, and that the analyst must now give it to her in order to provide a "corrective emotional experience" (Alexander and French, 1946).

There are indeed patients for whom this type of indulgence is not only a temporary tactical requirement during certain stressful phases of analysis but who cannot ever undertake the steps which lead to that increased ego dominance over the childhood wish which is the specific aim of psychoanalytic work. And there is, furthermore, no doubt that, occasionally, the indulgence of an important childhood wish—especially if it is provided with an air of conviction and in a therapeutic atmosphere that carries a quasi-religious, magical connotation of the efficacy of love—can have lasting beneficial effects with regard to the relief of symptoms and behavioral change in the patient.

The analytic process in analyzable cases, however, as in the one described in the present clinical vignette, develops in a different way. Although, for tactical reasons, the analyst might in such instances transitorily have to provide what one might call *a reluctant compliance with the childhood wish,* the true analytic aim is not indulgence but mastery based on insight, achieved in a setting of (tolerable) analytic abstinence. The recognition of the specific childhood demand was only the beginning of the working-through process concerning the grandiose self. It was followed by the recall of clusters of analogous memories concerning her mother's entering a phase of depressive self-preoccupation during later periods of the patient's life. Finally, a central set of poignant memories, upon which a series of earlier and later ones seemed to be telescoped, referred specifically to episodes when she came home from kindergarten and early elementary school. At such times she would rush home as fast as she could, joyfully anticipating telling her mother about her successes in school. She recalled then how her mother opened the door, but, instead of the mother's face lighting up, her expression remained blank; and how, when the patient began talking about school and play and about her achievements and successes of the preceding hours, the mother appeared to listen and participate, but imperceptibly the topic of the conversation shifted and the mother began to talk about herself, her headache, and her tiredness and her other physical self-preoccupations. All that the patient could directly recall about her own reactions was that she felt suddenly drained of energy and empty; she was for a long time unable to remember feeling any rage at her mother on such occasions. It was only after a prolonged period of working through that she could gradually establish connections between the rage which she experienced against me, when I did not understand her demands, and feelings she had experienced as a child.

This phase was then followed by a slow, shame-provoking, and anxious revelation of her persistent infantile grandiosity and exhibitionism; the working through accomplished during this period led ultimately to increased ego dominance over the old grandiosity and exhibitionism, and thus to greater self-confidence and to other favorable transformations of her narcissism in this segment of her personality.

Concluding Remarks

The foregoing examination must, in its entirety, be considered a summarizing preview of a broader study; no retrospective survey of the findings and opinions that have been presented will, therefore, be given. It must be stressed, however, that there are some important aspects of the subject matter which either could only be mentioned briefly or had to be disregarded altogether.

Thus, as mentioned initially, it was necessary to omit almost all references to the work of others, such as, for example, the significant contributions by H. Hartmann (1953), K. R. Eissler (1953b), E. Jacobson (1964), and A. Reich (1960); furthermore, it was not possible to compare the approach toward our subject matter taken in the present study with that chosen by such important authors as Federn (1952) on the one hand and Mahler (1952) on the other; and, finally, still within the same context, it was not possible to discuss the work of Melanie Klein and her school which often appears to be concerned with disorders that are related to those scrutinized in this essay.

No attempt was made to define and delimit the area of psychopathology with which this study is dealing; the question of the appropriateness of the use of the term *transference* in the present context could not be taken up; the discussion of the role of aggression had to be bypassed; the recurrent traumatic states in which the focus of the analysis shifts temporarily to the near-exclusive consideration of the overburdenedness of the psyche could not be illuminated; many other difficulties, therapeutic limitations, and failures were not considered; and, most regrettably, it was not possible to demonstrate the specific wholesome changes that occur as the result of the transformation of the narcissistic structures and of their energies. In all: it was the aim of this contribution to give the outline of a systematic approach to the psychoanalytic treatment of narcissistic personalities; a thorough scrutiny of the subject could not be undertaken.

Chapter 28

THE ANALYSIS OF A
PARANOID PERSONALITY

CHARLES RYCROFT

I

Recently, on rereading my paper on the "Function of Words in Psycho-Analytical Treatment" (1958), I noticed for the first time that almost all my clinical examples were taken from one patient, a woman whom I had in analysis from 1948 to 1952. In this present paper I shall give some account of this patient and describe certain aspects of her analysis.

There are, of course, certain disadvantages in reporting a case six years after the end of treatment, but these will, I hope, be compensated for by my having in the meantime acquired sufficient distance to be able to present both her and my contribution to the analytical relationship with reasonable detachment. As Miss Y. was a person who tended to evoke very strong reactions in everyone who had dealings with her, the detachment given by the passage of time is perhaps of particular value in the present instance. I have, however, made no attempt to conceal my own emotional reactions, as I believe that by including them I shall give a truer account of the dynamics of the analytical process than I should were I to present myself as having been a detached observer throughout.

This chapter originally appeared in the *International Journal of Psycho-Analysis*, 41:59–69, 1960 and in *Psychoanalysis and Beyond*. London: Chatto & Windus; Chicago: University of Chicago Press. Reprinted by permission of the author and the publishers.

II

The story of Miss Y.'s analysis begins two years before she came to me for treatment. She was at that time in her midthirties, an unsuccessful actress living an insecure and Bohemian existence. Quite suddenly she became depressed and withdrew completely from her previously very sociable life. During her "breakdown," as she called it, she experienced various peculiar changes in her moods and perception of reality. These she observed and recorded, using them as the material for a self-analysis which she conducted for the next year. As her only guides she relied on the only two books on psychoanalysis she had ever read, Theodore Reik's *Ritual* (1946) and Wilhelm Reich's *Character Analysis* (1949). She also occasionally talked on the telephone with two doctors whom she had known when they were medical students and who both had shown a passing interest in psychoanalysis. On the basis of her introspective findings, and armed with what we should consider somewhat inadequate theoretical support, she undertook not only an independent self-analysis but also the construction of a new system of psychopathology. Unfortunately, she never put down on paper any definitive statement of her system, but during the first few months of her analysis with me I came to know it intimately. So far as I could see, it was entirely logical and self-consistent and, apart from its not being true, I could find only three flaws in it. First, it was based on only one case. Second, it attached no significance to any experiences after the age of three months. Third, it took no cognizance of guilt. In all other respects it conformed to the usual pattern of recognized psychopathological theories and took account of both internal and external reality, of stages of libidinal development, and of libidinal fixations and the transformation of infantile libidinal drives into nonsexual social and artistic activities. Her three stages of libidinal development were (1) uterine, in which the relation to the mother was mediated by auditory, tactile, and postural channels; (2) birth, which was a "traumatic" stage leading to "paranoid" anxieties particularly associated with visual and thermal sensations; and (3) oral, in which the relation to the mother was mediated by the mouth and all other bodily organs with the exception of the genitals. The phenomenon of love was associated with this third stage, and under ideal conditions of development played no further part in human relations after this stage was passed. This, to her mind, was her one really original contribution to psychoanalysis, the discovery that all love is "infantilistic," as she put it. In her view, really mature sexual relationships contained no trace of love, and in her own sexual relations forepleasure was only permissible as a regrettable concession to the immaturity from which her partners, all unfortunately unanalyzed, inevitably suffered. Sexual relations were, however, not purely sensual acts—sensuality was, indeed, in her view masturbatory—but were experiences of "transcendental harmony" produced by the interchange of electrical energy. It would, I think, be a mistake to dismiss these ideas of hers as nonsense. Once one has cut one's way through the semantic confusion centering round her use of the word *love,* one can see that she was struggling to formulate an insight about the qualitative difference between genital and pregenital love. Her theories had extensive ramifications, but for the moment I shall give only two other details. First, she held that all sublimations have their origin in some specific aspect of one or other of her three stages, music, for instance, being derived from the primary pleasure of listening to the pulsations of the umbilical cord. Second, she had discovered the existence of psychically real internal figures; these she called "effigies" for reasons which will become apparent later. Miss Y. had absolute conviction of the essential truth of her system, and this conviction had exactly the same basis as has ours in *our* analytical theories; her experiences during her own personal analysis.

After about a year Miss Y. came out of her depression and decided to have treatment with a psychoanalyst. She knew that analysts, like all other bourgeois professional people, charged exorbitant fees for their services, so she set to work to save money and to get a well-paid job acting, with a view to seeing an analyst during the middle of the day, when, she surmised, they probably have difficulty in filling their vacancies. After a year she had saved about £150 and had got a part for which she was paid £25 a week in a show that promised to have a long run. She then got into touch with one of the doctors I mentioned earlier, who referred her to me with a diagnosis of phobia.

Her conscious reason for seeking analytical treatment was *not* that she had realized she was seriously ill. On the contrary, she believed that she had much more to give analysis than analysis had to give her. The reasons she gave during the first few weeks of analysis were:

First, she wished to become a child analyst, believing that the insights she had obtained during her self-analysis would enable her to make original contributions to the theory and practice of child analysis.

Second, she intended to become physically immortal. She had discovered that physical illness and aging were caused by the "paranoia" engendered by a traumatizing and hostile infantile environment, and she therefore concluded that thorough analysis of her reactive sadism and conflicts would eliminate the otherwise inevitable tendency to decay and death. She rather reluctantly admitted her inability to carry out unaided the complete analysis necessary to ensure immortality, so she decided to enlist the help of a classically trained analyst, fully realizing, of course, that *his* limitations would have to be made good by what *she* taught *him*. Since the ultimate goal was physical immortality, she could afford to envisage an almost interminable analysis. However long it lasted, it would be short in comparison with the ultimate reward of life eternal—for analyst as well as herself. She had never encountered anyone who was prepared to take these ideas of hers seriously, but she did not herself consider them particularly outrageous or original. She thought she was merely drawing an obvious logical conclusion which conventional analysts, with typical bourgeois cowardice, had been too frightened to face. So far as I know, she was unacquainted with the notion of the death instinct; the pathogenic factor which she hoped to eliminate by complete analysis was the paranoia induced by the sadism of the infantile environment.

Third, she wished to be relieved of a pain she experienced during sexual intercourse. This pain was unilateral and occurred only with deep penetration. She had already been informed by a competent surgeon that it was indubitably of organic origin and that it could be relieved by a lower abdominal operation. She was not, however, prepared to accept this, the whole idea of surgery being anathema to her.

Miss Y. did not mention her ideas about physical immortality during her initial consultation, quite consciously withholding them until she felt I was fully committed to continuing her treatment. At the time I accepted the referring physician's opinion that she was a suitable case for psychoanalytical treatment without question. My first impressions of her were of her determination to have analysis, her tremendous tenseness, and her bewilderingly complex mode of speech, which last I shall describe in detail later.

III

Two details of the initial consultation proved later to have contributed significantly to the dynamics of the analytical relationship, even though at the time they passed unnoticed by me.

When we came to discuss fees she told me about the money she had saved and that she was at present earning £25 a week. I then asked her how long she expected the show to last and how much of the year she usually spent "resting," thereby using the common stage euphemism for "unemployed." She said perhaps six months a year, so I suggested we discuss fees on the assumption that she earned £12 not £25 a week. I had correctly guessed that £25 a week was considerably more than she was accustomed to earn, but I entirely failed to realize that I had confronted her with an attitude toward money which ran counter to all her preconceptions about professional people. She had assumed without question that analysts were ruthless in their pursuit of fees, and that I would fix hers without any regard to her circumstances. The fact that I enquired carefully into them and took account of them when deciding on the fee I should charge had, therefore, the effect of undercutting one of her most cherished grievances.

I became aware of another significant feature of the initial consultation when I found it necessary to investigate my own countertransference. I then realized that Miss Y. had very effectively dared me into undertaking her analysis. By presenting herself as a difficult case and as having made strenuous exertions to make treatment possible from her side, she had appealed both to my sporting instincts—a phrase, incidentally, she would have found highly offensive—and to that counterphobic tendency which makes one determined to undertake a task just because it has been presented as difficult. I learnt later that games of daring had been carried to hair-raising lengths in her childhood and that she had retained into adult life an exceptional capacity to accept physical risks. At one time she had earned her living in a circus riding on the pillion of the motor-cycle that circles the Wall of Death. By daring me in this way she evoked a determination to penetrate her defenses which, in alliance with her own determination to be analyzed at whatever cost, helped to overcome her equally great determination *not* to abandon any of her defenses. The importance of this lies in the fact that her analysis turned out to belong to the not uncommon category which raises the question of why the analyst commits himself to the treatment of a patient from whom he cannot expect the usual economic reward.

IV

Miss Y. was small and slight, but her marked presence made her appear taller than she was. She was strikingly good-looking, though the effect was marred by her tense expression and posture. She spoke in a low, harsh, or husky voice. Her clothes were either untidy to the point of sluttishness—my receptionist nicknamed her the Gypsy—or exotic to the point of being bizarre. She was intensely interested in her effect on other people, but made no attempt to appear smart or fashionable.

At first I often had considerable difficulty in understanding her highly individual mode of speech, and I had therefore to analyze it in some detail. It contained the following five peculiarities: (1) She made her own choice of prefixes and suffixes, always, for instance, saying "comatic," not "comatose." (2) She gave words private meanings that were remote from and yet obviously somehow related to their accepted meaning. "Comatic," for instance, meant lethargic, intellectually lazy, unawakened. (3) She had a number of favorite words which she used in unusual or old-fashioned senses. One of these was "reactionary," which meant sensitive or responsive. (4) She had invented new words and appropriated a number of already existing words to signify various intrapsychic phenomena she had encountered during her self-analysis and for which she had had no words in her pre-breakdown vocabulary. The most striking example of this was the word *effigy* to describe an internal object. (5) She preferred abstract to concrete modes of expression and avoided metaphor, preferring to restrict her vocabulary to words which have lost all apparent connection with any concrete object or activity. This was the crucial disturbance, and its cause became clear in the light of her reactions to the use of metaphor by myself. It then became obvious that she had difficulty in distinguishing between the literal and metaphorical meanings of words, and between words and the concrete objects they signify. If, for instance, I used the phrase "getting something off one's chest," this evoked the sensation of something on her chest weighing her down, not the idea of unburdening herself. My use of this phrase was taken as a sadistic attack, a deliberate attempt to make her feel a weight on her chest. I am not sure to what extent this difficulty existed in her everyday life or how much it was exacerbated by regression during the analytical session.

She herself tried to maintain that the difficulties in verbal communication that sometimes arose between us were due to her American upbringing and that she was unfamiliar with idiomatic English. This was quite untrue, as for various reasons I insisted confidently from the beginning, and I later learned that all the significant figures in her childhood had been brought up in England and had all clung militantly to their English middle-class accents despite long residence abroad. The real reason for her conviction that she could not understand English and that I could not understand her expatriate speech was her unconscious belief that there had been an irreparable break in the channels of affective communication between herself and mother-figures which no words, not even those of her mother tongue, could ever bridge.

Although I became in time familiar with the idiosyncrasies of her speech and knew, for instance, that "reactionary men have no sense of structure" had nothing to do with politics but meant that sensitive men are incapable of lasting personal relationships, I deliberately refrained from making more than the minimum amount of accommodation to them for fear of becoming involved in a linguistic folie à deux which might make it harder for her to work through her hostility to the uncomprehending mother-imago. I am not altogether sure that I was right in adopting this policy.

Some of her neologisms were amusing, but quite unintentionally so. A lowerarchy was a hierarchy viewed from above—those of us who are not at the top of course usually view hierarchies from below. She once, again quite seriously, said: "Annoyed? I was paranoid." I have, of course, been describing an early stage in a schizoid thought disorder, the result of a regressive disturbance in symbolic thinking and of the confusion created by her attempt to master unaided the disordered perceptions of her breakdown. This thought disorder cleared up completely during the analysis. During the period of recovery she used to make up jokes based on metaphor being taken literally. Some of them were used as captions for a volume of humorous drawings made by a friend of hers.

In line with her belief in her capacity to analyze herself without external aid was her faith in her own untrained creative powers. At the age of ten she had decided to become the female Shakespeare; at the same age she also decided to become a ventriloquist. At seventeen she wrote a poem identical with one by Verlaine and a melody identical with one by Rachmaninov. At the age of thirty she had been told, so she said, by a ballet teacher that with a few weeks' practice she could reach the standard of a ballerina. She also claimed telepathic powers. The only artistic gifts to which she made no pretensions were painting and drawing. It is not surprising that one of her reports at Dramatic School—acting was the only art for which she had any formal training—described her as exceptionally talented but quite incapable of learning from anyone. A dream she had in the first year of analysis depicted the omnipotent character of her belief in her genius. It also shows her failure to deny *completely* her need for external support.

> *Dream I.* She was demonstrating to a group of stuffy bourgeois professors her ability to dance without touching the ground. She had, however, to keep one finger touching a round tea-table in the middle of the room.

Her determination to deny any need to be dependent on others was also shown in her attitude to external dangers and difficulties. Not only was she physically fearless but she also seemed without social anxiety. She was never shy or overawed by anyone and was quite incapable of accepting any offers of patronage that might have helped her professionally. She also denied any anxiety about the economic insecurity in which she habitually lived. During a phase of the analysis in which she was penniless she refused unemployment relief and tried to persuade herself that hunger pains were psychogenic. Nor did she admit that any dangers attach to sexual promiscuity.

She would not have used the word *promiscuous* about herself, but it would be hard to find another word to describe the bewilderingly rapid series of transient encounters that made up her sexual life. In her view it was a search for an ideal partner with whom she could experience complete sexual harmony uncontaminated by either love or sensuality. Occasionally, or so she said, her search was successful, when she found a "reactionary" man, but then, alas, they always proved to have no "sense of structure." The others always proved "comatic." Rather inconsistently, I thought, she referred to her sexual partners as lovers.

It will already have become obvious that Miss Y. was counterphobic rather than phobic, and that in many ways her character was paranoid. In the last section of his paper on Schreber, Freud observes that the familiar principal forms of paranoia can all be represented as contradictions of the single proposition "I (a man) love him (a man)," and goes on to show that projection cannot be the essential mechanism in paranoia. Although Miss Y. certainly used the mechanism of projection extensively her defensive personality seemed to be based on a massive contradiction of her unconscious wishes and fears rather than on denial and projection. Her heterosexual promiscuity contradicted her underlying attachment to the mother and her fear and hatred of men. Her pretensions to genius, an example of what Freud called sexual overestimation of the ego, contradicted her unconscious need for object love, this being reinforced by her ideological rejection of love as infantile. Her imagined discovery of a means by which death could be eliminated was a contradiction not a denial of death. Similarly her conviction that almost everyone other than herself was sadistic was as much a contradiction of her need for love as a projection of her own sadism. This was shown by the fact that it was just those classes of persons whose occupation it is to care for others and whose care she needed that were in her view most sadistic. She considered all doctors, especially women doctors and psychiatrists, to be sadists. In principle psychoanalysts were not, though during the first year of analysis most of my interpretations were considered to be deliberate sadistic attacks. In charitable moods she attributed my sadism to the contamination I had suffered while acquiring a medical qualification. All mothers she met were scrutinized closely and any mistakes or awkwardnesses they showed were attributed to sadism; when possible she interpreted this to them.

Her need to love and feel loved had, however, found one outlet. She kept cats—several of them, which she had saved from being put down. She was devoted to them and fondly believed that they were dependent on her. Fortunately, she decided early in the analysis that I too was fond of cats. That cats were part of an *external* reality about which she had normal emotions and in which her usual omnipotent defenses did not operate was shown by the fact that the first open, naïve expression of anxiety in the analytical situation occurred in relation to one. One day the housekeeper's cat went to sleep under the analytic couch, from which it emerged during the middle of the session. When Miss Y. suddenly noticed it stalking towards the door, she leapt off the couch on the opposite side. I remained seated. I am convinced that if a man, not a cat, had emerged, she would not have batted an eyelid.

Another feature of her personality, which was, I think, manic rather than paranoid, was that her appearance and whole demeanour could alter so much that it was hard to believe the different characters presented to one were in fact aspects of the same person. In one character she was hard, aggressive, querulous, and argumentative, and usually sluttishly dressed. In another she was transfigured and radiant, absolutely confident in her ability to charm everyone she encountered. In such moods everyone in the street stared at her appreciatively as she passed and complete strangers came up and talked to her. It was an important step in the analysis when she compared this to the way passersby will stop to talk to a happy baby and, though still flattered, recognized it to be an intrusion on her privacy. These changes in mood at first occurred independently of the analysis and were remarked upon by others than myself; later they became associated with changes in the transference.

In describing Miss Y.'s character I have already used the terms *counterphobic, paranoid,* and *manic,* and the question arises, I think, whether she was, *psychiatrically* speaking, psychotic. She certainly displayed incongruity of affect. This was well described by one of her lovers who once remarked to her: "It's the glorious irrelevance of you. You look at the sugar-bowl with intense hatred and talk of the weather with an expression of ecstasy." I am fairly sure that at first she was terrified that I would decide she was mad and was more than relieved that I never in any way treated her as such.

Since Miss Y. often behaved and spoke in a way that in everyday life one might be inclined to dismiss as pretentious, absurd, and bizarre, I must mention explicitly that very early on I decided that she was in fact a very gifted, though profoundly disturbed, person, and, in particular, that she had an unerring aesthetic sense. It would be hard to justify such an impression by citing examples that would be generally convincing, and I shall only say that her sensibility often manifested itself negatively. No one could have hated Rembrandt as passionately as she did without a profound though denied insight into his understanding of aging and death.

So far I have presented Miss Y.'s character and ideas without relating them in any way to the childhood experiences which alone make them comprehensible. My reason for having done this is that during her analysis I had to learn to feel at home with the defensive personality she presented to the world before I could learn the bare facts of her childhood, let alone acquire any imaginative understanding of it.

V

Miss Y. was the youngest child of the only English-speaking family living in a small village in America, both her parents having emigrated from England. They were converts to Catholicism, and five children followed each other in rapid succession, first a boy and then four girls. The whole family's life was overshadowed by a series of deaths which occurred before Miss Y. was ten years old. Her mother died when she was just over two. An aunt then came to keep house and care for the children; she died when Miss Y. was four-and-a-half. The children next had a governess who was committed to a mental hospital when Miss Y. was ten and who died there soon after admission. Miss Y. had some recollection of all three deaths. In her early teens her father remarried. Her stepmother found Miss Y. unmanageable and both parents became very strict in their attempts to control her adolescent interest in boys. She reacted by becoming more and more defiant. In her late teens she was put for a while into a reformatory run by nuns and later, after failing to hold down a number of office jobs, she was shipped back to England to live with some distant relations in a small provincial town. She soon found the aspidistras and antimacassars unendurable and before she was twenty-one she ran away and got a job with a circus. From then onwards she lived a precarious, unsettled, and nomadic existence, her only contacts with her family being very occasional letters to her sisters and appeals for financial help to her brother. Under these circumstances no confirmatory external evidence about her childhood was available, while her own description of her treatment by her father and stepmother bore all the hallmarks of paranoid distortion. The idea she had at the beginning of her analysis that both her father and brother had attempted to abuse her sexually was, fairly certainly, a delusion. I suspect that her father was a moody and difficult man who was often at his wits' end as to how to handle five motherless children. They ran wild and much of their hostility and resentment was worked out on each other in bullying and spitefulness, with my patient, as the youngest, bearing the brunt of a lot of it. I think, too, that to begin with she was her father's favorite child. She owed to him her interest in poetry and acting and was the only one of the children to be infected by his passion for Shakespeare. His getting rid of her, first to a reformatory and then to England, was, I suspect, the action of a man bitterly disillusioned in his idealized favorite daughter rather than that of a crude disciplinarian. What her precise misdemeanors were I never discovered. The other children have all made conventional adjustments to the American way of life.

Although these facts about her childhood are very scanty, they are enough to make her unconscious longing for the mother, her conscious hatred of her father, and her fear of death, all imaginatively comprehensible. They offer, however, no explanation of the paranoid twist to her personality, of the fact that her infantile traumata led not to repression, impoverishment of the ego, and symptom formation, but to the development of an ego itself based on active contradiction of her pathological, unconscious impulses. One consequence of the fact that she emerged from her childhood not with a psychoneurosis but with a paranoid, manic character was that energy which in a neurotic is dissipated in symptom formation or held in leash by repression was available to her organized ego, though at the price of a partial break with reality. This was the basis of the forcefulness of personality which was one of her most striking characteristics.

VI

Miss Y.'s analysis lasted for rather over four years. I shall not attempt to describe its course fully, but shall confine myself to giving a general picture of the three phases into which the analysis fell and to describing in more detail a number of crucial episodes. Miss Y. was a prolific dreamer of remarkably undisguised dreams, which I shall use extensively as illustrative material without reporting her associations, which were in general more confusing than illuminating.

The three phases into which the analysis fell were:

1. A phase of resistance, in which Miss Y. fought to prevent disintegration of her omnipotent and narcissistic defenses.
2. A phase of regression, in which she reexperienced the despair and depression that had necessitated construction of these defenses, and
3. A phase of recovery, in which she acquired sublimations and reconstructed her defenses on a less omnipotent and narcissistic basis.

Since the phase of regression had a rapid onset and ended suddenly during one of my holidays, this division into three phases corresponds closely to the clinical facts and is not a theoretical construct introduced to facilitate exposition. The phase of regression was, however, foreshadowed more than once during the phase of resistance, and I shall describe one instance of this in some detail.

VII

The phase of resistance lasted for just under two years. The preceding sections of this paper have in the main been based on impressions and information acquired during this first phase. It was characterized by long periods of intense hostility toward me, alternating with short periods of complete harmony. During the hostile periods she attacked me on almost every possible count. I was held to be sadistic, insensitive, stupid, and ununderstanding, and to be a legitimate target for her hatred of all things English— English conventions, English snobbery, English doctors, English food, English cooking, and English weather. All attempts to interpret this hostility were taken as indicating my approval of what she was attacking and therefore as further proof of my insensitivity and stupidity. Alternatively I was thought to be deliberately provoking her by affecting to approve the obviously intolerable conditions by which she was daily traumatized. Now although most of this hostility was undoubtedly transferred, the accusation that I was being ununderstanding did at times and in certain respects have some validity. There were two reasons for this, one unavoidable, the other the result of a failure in discrimination on my part.

The unavoidable reason was the confusion created by her highly individual habits of speech. *She* used a language I had yet to understand, while *I* used a language that to her meant lack of understanding, since to her mind it was inherently incapable of describing her inner feelings and was full of phrases designed to disturb her by evocation of painful imagery. She had, furthermore, a hatred of language itself since, in her view, it only exists because human beings fail to understand each other. Her repudiation of her mother tongue and her attempt to replace it by a private language was, as I have already mentioned, an indication of her despair about the possibilities of affective communication.

The avoidable reason was that I failed to discriminate sensitively enough between different types and sources of aggression. Evidence of penis envy and oral frustration was only too obvious in her attacks on doctors and on English food and weather, and it was true that she envied me for being a man and felt frustrated by the mother country which gave her neither food nor warmth, but her dreams—as I only realized much later on when I had reason to abstract them from my notes—suggested that her envy and aggression were not primary and instinctual but were part of her defense. Her repudiation of her need for love and her attachment to internal objects from whom she derived her sense of omnipotence had imprisoned her in her internal world and her fundamental demand on me was that I should help her take the risk of abandoning her self-sufficiency and trust an external object. Having made this demand on me, having instated me as someone by whom she could hope to be rescued, her anxiety compelled her to hate and fear me. Just because I was the person she had chosen to liberate her from her internal objects I inevitably became the person who threatened to destroy her sense of omnipotence. Just because I was the person she had put into a position in which I could prove myself trustworthy and make her aware of her need for love I became the person it was most necessary to prove hateful, insensitive, and ununderstanding. Furthermore, she had to test out that I could continue to be benevolent, however venomous she might be. Interpretations of her hostility in terms of envy and oral aggression lost sight of all this and, in particular, lost sight of the fact that her whole aggressive attitude toward me was an attempt to contradict the impression she had in fact gained in the initial consultation that I was a person to whom she could trust herself.

I shall now quote some dreams which illustrate this and depict her narcissistic attachment to internal objects and her sense of imprisonment by this attachment.

I have already quoted her dream of dancing before a group of bourgeois professors.

Dream II. She was masturbating by rubbing her legs together as though there were a penis between them.

Dream III. She was trying to suck her own breast. Then she decided to masturbate but desisted when she remembered she would have to tell her analyst. . . . She was escaping from a prison.

Dream IV. She was in a medieval castle. She and an old woman walked out over the drawbridge. The moat was full of drowned "effigies," the corpses of her former lovers. Then she tried to reach the sea but her way was blocked by a wall of ice.

Dream V. She was escaping from the Soviet Union in a boat. In the middle of the sea she found a trap door. She opened it and found a Post Office Savings Book.

Dream VI. Her clitoris was elongated and tubular. She was alone on an island except for one other person, whose sex was uncertain.

These dreams depict very clearly, I think, her attempt to sustain herself by a narcissistic attachment to internal objects and the resulting sense of loneliness and imprisonment. The sense of omnipotence which constituted the illusory gain from her attachment to internal objects is strikingly presented in her dream of dancing before the bourgeois professors and also in the image of the enlarged vaginal–phallic clitoris.

During the phase of resistance there were three ways in which she could temporarily lose her sense of being trapped. One was with her cats. Another was in her sexual promiscuity. The third was in her phases of harmony with me. During these she felt that I understood her completely and absolutely, everything I said was wise and right. My consulting room was always beautifully warm and the weather perfect. All this, however, was resistance too. She came late for sessions and only welcomed my interpretations enthusiastically by reading into them her own preconceptions about herself. These ecstatic manic moods were identical with the transfigured, radiant moods I described earlier. That they were based on a phantasy of union with the analyst as mother is shown by the following dreams.

Dream VII. She and her analyst are in a studio. She is at peace.

Dream VIII. The analyst is sitting beside her as she lies on the couch. She falls asleep. When she wakes up he asks her whether all her friends are homosexual. Then he feeds her with salad.

I have already mentioned that the phase of regression was foreshadowed on more than one occasion during this first phase of resistance. The most impressive of these occurred near the end of the first year of analysis and was precipitated by circumstances external to it. She had been persuaded, partly by myself, to have a surgical operation for her dyspareunia and went into hospital during one of my holidays. The operation was planned to take place three days before I returned to work. I was therefore surprised and disturbed when she telephoned to tell me that she would be coming to her session despite having had the operation only three days previously. When she arrived she walked straight to the couch without looking at me or greeting me in any way. She lay down and went completely limp, in striking contrast to her usual very tense posture. She remained silent and uncannily motionless. I assumed, rightly, that she had discharged herself from hospital almost immediately after the operation, and knowing that she had had a lower abdominal operation feared that she might have had a hemorrhage. Her absence of color did nothing to reassure me, and I remember entertaining for a moment the idea that she had come to die on the couch. I was therefore more relieved than distressed when I noticed that she was weeping silently. After a while she tried to speak but failed, and I helped her off the couch onto a chair. She then told me what had happened. She had had the operation with much less pain and distress than she had feared and had been coping successfully with the barbarous conditions in an English hospital until a small child had been admitted to the ward. This child had cried all night and she had been as much upset by the indifference of the nursing staff as she was by the crying itself. Next morning she could endure it no longer and after a row with the ward sister and house physician had discharged herself from hospital. I hardly needed to point out that she was reexperiencing her own desolation after the deaths in her own childhood and that her indignation on the child's behalf was born of her own need for consolation.

VIII

During the months following this episode she began to change. She stopped being promiscuous and became preoccupied with her memories of a young Frenchman, half her own age, with whom she had had a short affair. She lost her job after a quarrel with the producer and then sabotaged every audition she went to by her unaccommodating attitude. Her savings were nearly exhausted. She became increasingly aware of her dependence on me and stopped attacking me incessantly. She began to have anxiety dreams in which I featured as a benevolent and protecting figure.

> *Dream IX.* She is climbing a cliff to reach the analyst. On the way she passes a thug or policeman. The analyst had become very wise and intelligent and she realized that his sadistic treatment of her had all been play-acting done for her own good.

Soon after this dream she became regressed. By this I mean that she entirely dropped her defensive attitude toward me, that instead of lying tense and overalert on the couch she became relaxed and absorbed, that instead of arguing with me and producing masses of highly intellectualized material in a loud, harsh voice she started describing simply and quietly what she felt it must have been like to have been a child and infant. She became so absorbed in the analysis that the question of her working did not arise, and she spent most of her time continuing the analysis in imagination, sleeping, or daydreaming about the young Frenchman. To my mind this Frenchman was clearly an idealized representation of myself, but interpretations to this effect were always unacceptable to her.

The actual content of the sessions during this phase is difficult to describe. With one exception her reconstruction of the experiences and emotions of infancy corresponded closely with the picture of infancy painted by contemporary analytical research. The exception was her complete rejection of the idea that an infant can feel anger or hatred toward its mother and that it can be disturbed by its own destructive phantasies. Interpretations of dreams which seemed to me to depict this aspect of infancy were either brushed aside or reacted to with such anxiety that I eventually decided to let her take her own time discovering the importance of infantile aggression.

The emotional atmosphere of this phase is even harder to convey. This is partly because it contained two elements which are logically incompatible and which yet coexisted without apparent contradiction. One was a feeling that I was bored, tired, ill and indifferent, while she was listless, despairing, and overcome with a sense of futility; it was as though she was reenacting a mother–infant relationship from which all life had been withdrawn. The other was her belief that I *could* be trusted to see her through, could be a support until she succeeded in gaining access to her own sources of vitality. At times the only evidence of hopefulness in her was the regularity and punctuality with which she attended sessions. She paid no fees during this period, living entirely on borrowed money. However, despite her helplessness and absorption in the analysis, her dependence on me and surrender to me as an introjectible good object never became fully explicit, largely, I think, owing to her fear of the destructive implications of her incorporative phantasies, her fear that she might turn me into an effigy. As a result she never asked me to lend her money and deflected some of her longings onto the Frenchman who by living abroad remained out of range of her aggression and could do nothing to disillusion her.

She dreamed much less during this phase, and I shall only quote two dreams.

> *Dream X.* A female producer did not want to give her a part. . . . She was hurt to find that there were no photographs of her in Mrs. X.'s album.

Here we see the feeling of being slighted by being unwanted and unremembered by her mother, who, as she then felt, would not have died if she had really loved her daughter, but the dream contains no hint of anger or resentment.

Dream XI. She pressed her breasts against a wall. Although her breasts were anatomically hers, they were also someone else's.

It is this dream which justifies my interpretation of Dream III, in which she was trying to suck her own breast, as an internalized object relationship and not as an autoerotic activity. This last dream depicts her acquisition of insight into the object dependence implicit in her narcissism. It also represents her primary identification with the analyst as breast.

Eventually, however, aggressive feelings began to emerge unequivocally. First, she remembered a gardener in her childhood who had always kept the vegetables locked up and how determined she had been to steal some of them. Then she had openly sadistic dreams which shocked her profoundly.

Dream XII. She is in a butcher's shop buying meat. She takes his carving knife and starts cutting up two white cats. Then she is in my consulting room, where I am analyzing a lesbian friend of hers. I look as though I am going to work off some of my aggression on the lesbian, but instead I show her (i.e., Miss Y. herself) a drawing done by a poet friend of hers. It is very chaotic, but I assure her that he has also done some very "integrated" drawings.

In the first part of this dream it was, of course, the cruelty to cats which shocked her so much. In the second part she depicts her dawning insight into the intimate connexion between creativity and aggression, but does not yet dare locate either within herself. The integrative processes which were already occurring within her have therefore to be represented as taking place off-stage, at one remove from the analytical situation.

Dream XIII. She is forced down a cul-de-sac by a lorry. Then a workman is lying unconscious on the ground. She can only presume that she herself must have attacked him.

Here she depicts the feeling that she is being forced into a position in which she will no longer be able to deny her aggression.

IX

Dream XIII was dreamt at the end of November 1950. To her first session after my Christmas holidays Miss Y. brought some drawings that she had done. I was very struck by their strict realism and classical technique: they were *integrated,* to use the word she had herself used when recounting Dream XII. I also felt there was something frightened and overcautious about them. As I put it in the notes I made at the time: "Her drawings show a fear of being too violent, e.g., very gentle lines on paper that would tear easily." The best drawings were all of cats. During the session she told me how she had come to start drawing. Over Christmas she had been with a friend to visit the friend's mother. The mother and daughter were not on good terms and the atmosphere had been tense. On one occasion her friend lost her temper with her mother. Miss Y.'s sympathies were with her friend, and she suddenly found herself wishing to murder the mother. This feeling came like an illumination, and with it many things that I had said to her about hostility and ambivalence fell into place. Later, when she got home, the idea of trying her hand at drawing occurred to her; she sat down with pencil and paper and found she had no great difficulty in drawing her cats and other objects in the room. Since then she had spent much of her spare time drawing.

Drawing was one of the few arts about which Miss Y. had had no pretensions, and her attitude toward her newly acquired aptitude was in striking contrast to her previous tendency to refuse all help and guidance and to rely defiantly on her own inner genius. She took evening classes in drawing and seemed quite prepared to learn from her teachers. Indeed, her only complaint about the art class was that she found her tendency to flirt with the male students interfered with her work. It was also very striking that she had no objection to spending hours copying the work of old masters and seemed only to acquire a realistic technique. She was quite uninterested in abstract or "advanced" forms of art.

She also began to write poetry again. Here too she expressed herself in simple traditional forms and she never showed me a poem which was not comprehensible on a single reading. In a series of poems about her childhood she worked through her grief and described her recovery of the internal image of a loving mother and the resulting loss of her inner sense of isolation. I regret that I am unable to quote any of these poems.

Miss Y.'s need to draw, and, in particular, her need to draw the external world as it is, was an expression of her drive to escape from the prison of her introversion and to reestablish contact with the world of everyday reality, which she used her hands and eyes to master and rediscover. On the same day that she first showed me her drawings she asked me how much longer I thought the analysis would last, and shortly afterwards she began to concern herself with the problem of earning a living. As she decided that acting was not her métier and had no other training and qualifications, the remaining eighteen months of the analysis were to some extent disorganized by her search for suitable work, and it was partly for economic reasons that she terminated analysis four years after beginning treatment.

I do not intend to describe in any detail this last phase of recovery. Much of it consisted in working over again material I have already presented, but with the difference that she was capable of operating the normal split in the ego which enables psychoneurotic patients to observe and reflect upon the material they present instead of becoming totally immersed in it. There were also periods in which development seemed to be occurring spontaneously and in which my function was confined to providing a setting in which insight could increase and to being ready to intervene when she seemed to be losing her way. I have no doubt that in view of the emotional insecurity of her childhood and the social insecurity of her adult life the mere continuity of the analytical relationship had a therapeutic effect. I think too that the sudden emergence of a sublimation and, with it, of a firmer grasp of reality indicates that a normal, nondefensive ego organization must have already been present when treatment began, however overshadowed it may have been by her highly defensive "personality." The last phase of her analysis was a phase of recovery, not only in the sense that she recovered from her regression, but also in the sense that she recovered certain faculties and potentialities which had previously been dissociated and therefore inaccessible. In the last resort this was based on recovery of the belief in the possibility of affective communication, a belief which had been shattered by the traumatic experiences of her childhood. The most obvious example of her becoming more in touch with, more at home in outer reality was her changed habit of speech—I remember being amazed when she first came out with such an ordinary word as *flirt*—but much more than this was, of course, involved.

In April 1951 Miss Y. received a telegram telling her that her father had died. After unsuccessful attempts to find a friend to stay with her, she rang up and asked me to come and see her. The sense of urgency was obvious in her voice and I went at once. When I arrived, almost the first thing she said was that in a sense I needn't have come at all, all she had needed was the certain knowledge that I had appreciated the urgency of her call and that I was willing to come, though of course, she added, the only way I could show this was by actually coming. What she needed was that her grief should be recognized, otherwise she was in danger of denying it. Miss Y. had realized this danger herself, hence her call to me. After talking about this for a little while she gave me a cup of tea and I returned home. My reason for reporting this incident—the only occasion on which I stepped out of the analytical role—is to give an example of the sensitivity and perceptiveness which she had kept hidden behind her narcissistic defenses, a perceptiveness which made her realize how easy it would have been to recall only the grievances of her adolescence and to maintain that she had always hated her father and recognize immediately how urgently she needed a witness for her grief. It did not, of course, require much imagination on my part to appreciate that someone who had lost three mothers in her childhood and who as an adult had had to fabricate theories denying the inevitability of death, needed endorsement of her threatened insight when confronted with the fact of her father's death.

Miss Y. had in fact identified with her father in many ways, and I have already given material, without commenting on it, which shows how extensively a phallic organization was interwoven with her omnipotent defenses. During the last months of her analysis she became markedly more feminine, a process which began shortly after she first admitted hostility toward the mother. A fortnight later she had the following dream.

> *Dream XIV.* She is in a room belonging to a beautiful girl. At first she thinks the girl is not there, but to her surprise she finds her asleep in bed.

A few days later she expressed concern on my behalf for the first time. She was worried, she said, about the aggression I must have to put up with from my other patients. During the same hour she said she had just realized how much she always wanted to be the center of attention and how hard she found it to tolerate the idea that it was unrealistic of her to expect me always to be able to understand immediately what she was getting at. A few days later she remembered how slighted she had felt following her father's second marriage. One can perhaps detect in this sequence a hint of the conflict she must have had as a girl between the *phantasy* of being her father's devoted wife, concerned about the demands made on him by all the other children, and the *knowledge* that she was still one of them herself; and then the mortification of discovering that she was not cast for the role of her father's daughter–wife.

Her earlier sexual promiscuity had been homosexual in the sense that her idea of eliminating love from sex involved denial of specifically masculine and feminine emotions. She now began to express quite simple feminine anxieties. She complained of her compulsion to flirt. She admitted to being frightened when walking alone through dark streets at night. She dreamt that a man tore open her blouse and then broke one of her vases. When she set up house with a man she was appalled at her tendency to nag him. Fairly soon before the end of the analysis she had the following dream.

> *Dream XV.* In the middle of a party a girl squats to urinate. She has a penis which she tries to push back into its proper place as a vagina. She fails to do it herself so she enlists the aid of a man, who pushes it in with his penis.

In this dream we see depicted the reversal of another of the contradictions on which her defensive "personality" was based. Instead of accepting her femininity, as a normal woman would, or denying her lack of a penis, as a hysteric would, she had tried to contradict her anxieties about being a woman and not a man by asserting that her vagina was really a penis. This contradiction involved her in an untenable break with reality, and the dream epitomizes her return to reality through analysis, depicting first her attempt to return unaided and then the acceptance of help. What it leaves out is her resistance to the required invagination, her struggle to retain her omnipotent bisexual penis–vagina, which she could only begin to relinquish after she had tested out during the phase of regression that it was safe to rely on someone other than herself, and had achieved some degree of inner security through acquiring an internal image of a mother whose "legacy of gentleness could cool her even when the fire of hatred burnt within her." I am here paraphrasing one of her poems.

This dream, which is the last that I shall quote was a wish-fulfillment, since it depicted as completed a process which in fact remained incomplete. Unlike the actual surgical operation she had, which was an outstanding success, her analysis was only partially successful. Although she became a much softer person, she remained in many ways narcissistic and schizoid, and there was, I think, a manic element in the partial recovery she made. Insofar as this can be attributed to a failure in technique rather than to limitations inherent in her pathology, the fault lay in my failure to bring certain relations directly into the transference, notably her idealization of the young Frenchman and her impulse to murder her friend's mother. As a result the dynamic changes which occurred when she recognized her hostility and found she could draw, took place by a sort of manic intrapsychic manipulation conducted under my aegis, as it were, rather than directly within the transference relationship.

Although Miss Y.'s analysis ended prematurely, she had a proper last session. During it she said: "Well, I see it all now. It wasn't their fault and it wasn't mine either," and then turning round to look at me she added, "though why in hell didn't you say so at the very beginning?" This was meant half-humorously, but perhaps she had a point. Perhaps if I had started from the assumption that she must have been through some experience too painful to be assimilated and that she was seeking a relationship secure and sensitive enough for her to abandon her protective defenses and risk suffering again, things might have been easier and quicker. But perhaps she would not have understood what I was talking about and could not have done so until she had unburdened herself of much of the aggression with which she had become overcharged.

Theoretical Discussion

I have taken the term *contradiction* from the third, theoretical, section of Freud's (1911b) paper on Schreber, where he remarks that "the familiar forms of paranoia can all be represented as contradictions of the single proposition, I (a man) love him (a man)." However, Freud himself did not regard "contradiction" as a mechanism, and he appears to have been using the idea of contradicting a proposition purely descriptively, without envisaging that it might be possible to use it to conceptualize a specific dynamic process. After showing how the four principal forms of paranoia correspond to the four different ways in which the proposition "I love a man" can be contradicted, Freud goes on to give reasons why projection cannot be regarded as the pathognomonic mechanism in paranoia and to argue that the "pathogenic factor" in paranoia is that libido which has been detached from external objects is used for aggrandizement of the ego, that is, that there is regression to the stage of narcissism. At no point does he suggest that the contradiction he has described could itself be envisaged as a specific paranoid mechanism; the emphasis is on the homosexuality, not on the process of contradicting it. Nor does he mention the concept of "denial," the defense which nowadays is commonly coupled with projection as providing the basis of paranoid disorders. For instance Heimann (1953) writes, "As is well known, delusional jealousy and fear of persecution are based on denial and projection." The reason for this omission of Freud's is, of course, historical. In 1911 the preoccupation of analysis was still with the establishment of fixation-points to the exclusion of differentiation of specific modes of defense.

Contradiction, however, is not the same thing as denial, and to my mind Miss. Y., whose character defenses showed a marked resemblance to the clinical picture of paranoia, did something more than deny and project her attachment to the mother, her hostility to men and her fear of death; she constructed an organized pattern of behavior and thought which was designed to replace her repressed wishes, feelings, and anxieties by a totally different order of experience. The development of this distorted ego could no doubt be formulated in terms of the interaction of several different mechanisms of defense—the list would certainly have to include denial, repression, regression, projection, introjection, reversal, transformation of affects, reaction formation, and rationalization—but there is, I think, something to be gained by seeing it as a single dynamic process which manifested itself both as an unconscious phantasy and as a strategy of defense.

EPILOGUE:
TOWARD AN AGENDA FOR THE STUDY
OF CHARACTER

> You would play upon me, you would seem to know my stops, you would pluck out the heart of my mystery, you would sound me from my lowest note to the top of my compass and there is much music, excellent voice in this little organ yet cannot you make it speak. 'Sblood' do you think I am easier to be played on than a pipe?
>
> Shakespeare—*Hamlet*

With this volume we have sought to acquaint the reader with a wide range of issues belonging to the domain of character studies. The various factors affecting the way in which character shapes the course of life have been examined. A number of contributors have presented different conceptual frameworks and issues, many of which are still being debated. However, the various contributions clearly illustrate that the concept of character remains a somewhat elusive phenomenon: Baudry (chapter 9) introduces character as a concept in search of an identity, while Schafer (chapter 10), refers to it as a concept without a home. Nevertheless, our purpose in organizing this *Handbook* was to attempt to remove some of the mystery surrounding character and demonstrate the potential for communality in orientation among the different theoreticians and clinicians. Given the importance of the concept of character in contemporary life, we believe that such an effort to find connections is most appropriate. To continue to neglect the study of character is no longer a tenable proposition. It would be quite ironic to be doing serious work on the nature and treatment of character disorders without really understanding what is deemed disordered.

The presentations of the various contributors to the *Handbook* make it obvious that to facilitate future research—to convert the concept of character from a loose term of convenience to one that can be studied—a more precise definition will be needed. Without less ambiguous descriptions of what we are talking about it will be difficult to use terms such as *character formation, normal character, character disorders,* and the *treatment of character*. Such a need is timely whatever point of view the user may have: that of psychology, psychiatry, psychoanalysis, sociology, anthropology, literary criticism, political science, or management.

We have seen how character follows a course of development starting at an embryonic or inchoate state and continuing throughout the lifespan. From a very young age onward, dispositional and temperamental differences can be observed. Much later, beginning in midlatency and culminating in late adolescence, the process of consolidation of the various structures of the mind takes place. The question of the degree of modification with advancing age is a more controversial one that warrants further study. We are all aware, however, of a reduction in the tolerance for new experiences as we get older.

We have seen the extent to which character appears to be the result of the interplay of dispositions, aspects of infantile sexuality not open to adult sexual expression, and the interaction with the external environment. Without experiences with others— be it of an affectionate or aggressive nature—there would be no opportunity to develop character. Character will also be reflected in the ways in which the individual manages stress and is able to deal with change. Here we have in mind the cycles and rhythms of life, the various developmental tasks, and the different hurdles and obstructions, be they anticipated or unforeseen.

Keeping these various factors in mind (but also realizing the danger of adding to the existing state of confusion), in order to further a research agenda on the study of character, we offer our own definition of the concept. For us, character stands for an adaptive, creative, organizing, and unifying entity which originates from all three psychic agencies but is especially the result of the experiences and efforts of the ego in its synthetic and identifying function. Thus, character can be viewed as the ego's highest level of integrative functioning, bringing together auxiliary organizations (such as core dispositions, temperament, psychic structure, and developmental relay mechanisms) that have emerged, are created, and/or are experienced, particularly during the formative years (Thomas and Chess, 1977; Thomas, Chess, and Korn, 1982; Abrams, 1982). The task of this structure is to attend to the demands and needs of the three agencies, along with those of external reality, in a balanced way. Accordingly, character reflects and integrates multiple identifications that have occurred during the course of life.

Taking more of an operational point of view, we can summarize by defining character as *the highest level of psychological organization achieved by the individual, crystallized in adolescence and expressing the habitual ways of how wants (wishes, needs), obligations (duties, responsibilities), opportunities, and hindrances are experienced, understood, and managed.* We believe that this definition encompasses and integrates most of the existing thoughts on the subject of character. As a more holistic definition we believe it will be helpful in furthering future studies of character.

Obstacles to the study of character have been spelled out both in the Introduction as well as in the contributions by Stein (chapter 8) and Baudry (chapter 9). Other stumbling blocks to the further understanding of character do, however, remain. First—and this is reflected in our definition—there is the immense complexity of the subject of investigation. This concern has been shared by many students of character. To give an example, Blos (1968) came to the same conclusion, observing that:

> The problem of character formation is of such a vast scope that almost any aspect of psychoanalytic theory is related to it . . . we deal with a concept of enormous complexity or with integrative processes of the highest order [p. 245].

> The more complex a psychic formation, the more elusive to the observer becomes the total configuration or organization [p. 250].

There is yet another obstacle. When talking about psychic structure, metapsychological profiles, and mental apparatus, many psychiatrists, psychologists, and psychoanalysts are of the opinion that they are really referring to character, and they are not alone in that assumption. We can already see how, in his lecture "The Dissection of the Psychic Personality" (to be found in *New Introductory Lectures* [1933]), Freud is not really addressing the total personality but is actually referring to the different agencies of the mind. Unfortunately, elaborations of such a kind result in two problems. First, they mistakenly regard character theory as coterminous with psychoanalysis. Second, they lead to the complaint that structures have been defined by their functions and a true psychoanalytic morphology is missing. This controversy would seem to suggest that we need to accept not only that different levels of conceptualization are mutually compatible but also that they are essential to one another. We shall have to reconcile ourselves to the fact that the credential necessary for a psychology to be a depth psychology is not the complexity of its concepts but the degree to which it can explain manifest behavior patterns by reaching the deeper recesses of mental functioning. If a theoretical approach cannot deal with simple reality it needs to be modified. As Charcot once said, "la théorie, c'est bon, mais ça n'empêche pas d'exister" (theory is fine, but it should not prevent us from existing). Character theory can be viewed as the morphological aspect of structural theory. This addition, which unfortunately but inevitably seems to be accompanied by the anthropomorphization and reification of the structural apparatus (a sign of a theory stretched to the limit), may be something of an answer to the problem.

Finally, there has been the protest against introducing yet another supraordinate concept to what some have woefully called a growing structural catalogue. A supraordinate concept that encompasses the three agencies of the mind is seen as a challenge to the whole notion of the well-established tripartite organization and irreconcilable with it in the view of some. After all the confusion created by the concepts identity and self, a new contender—character as organization—is not exactly welcomed with open arms.

We believe, however, that our definition of character helps overcome all of these obstacles. To be more specific, it helps clarify what students of character are really referring to. Character is no longer defined unidimensionally as defensive (the problem with Reich's definition) or as ego (the problem with Fenichel's definition), but is updated and broadened to include the important adaptive, creative, and organizational components. Our definition recognizes maturational, cognitive, and developmental aspects. Further, it reduces theoretical strain on conceptualizations of the ego (the anthropomorphizing) and responds to the criticism of a supraordinate structure. Viewing character as the morphological aspect of the ego also gives it coordinates of its own and corrects the fallacy of it being coterminous with psychoanalysis itself. As a consequence of this latter correction, its dimensions—albeit still enormous—are reduced. We believe that such an outlook helps in advancing further research agendas.

What would we like to see as future developments? First and foremost a diminution of the obstacles to further study, along with a sensitization on the part of mental health professionals to the significant characterological aspects of their work. Thus, psychoanalysis would be seen not only as a psychology of the *mind* in conflict, as Wallerstein and Weinshel (1989) would have it, but also as a dynamic psychology of the *person*—of his or her character.

Michels (1988) reminds us of what is only too apparent: whether we like it or not, not only has the scope of psychoanalysis widened but our discipline has been (and still is) in the process of perfecting its therapeutic focus on the treatment of character pathology. Such disturbances, from the "worried-well" or "problems in living" to severe borderline personality disorders (or, probably more accurately, psychotic characters), are the "bread and butter" of psychoanalytic work for most analysts. It is for this reason that such a large portion of the *Handbook* has been given over to disorders of character and their treatment. This being the case, there is room for inclusion of deficit theory alongside conflict theory and room for introducing a common language for psychoanalysis, at least as far as clinical theory is concerned.

The training of analysts and dynamically oriented psychotherapists would be a good place to begin. Arlow and Brenner (1988) note the absence of courses on technique for dealing with pathological character traits. The orientation of curricula in the various institutes needs to be modified to meet this hiatus and reflect the importance of character pathology in the assessment of potential analysands, in the therapeutic process, and in the progress accounts of training cases. Such an outlook also necessitates a greater willingness on the part of analysts to familiarize themselves with the work of colleagues in the adjacent fields. The whole area of character disorders would benefit from greater collaborative work between psychiatry and psychoanalysis. As Weinshel and Wallerstein (1969) put it, "psychoanalysis is the dynamic psychology of psychiatry" (p. 347).

The ability of analysts and dynamically oriented psychotherapists to think in terms of character results in the availability of a coin that can be used across narrow specialty interests—and, as psychoanalytic theory continues to diverge rather than converge, this applies as much within the discipline as without. Since psychoanalysis is being seen more and more as an independent psychological discipline in its own right, the solidity of this currency becomes even more important.

Next on our research list we can find a vast literature on theoretical, research, clinical, and practical issues germane to character theory and therapy which awaits being brought more closely within "working range." One example among many in this regard is the literature on narcissism, alluded to in the Introduction. Though Reich did draw attention to character as a narcissistic structure, not much has been done since his conceptualizations other than the work on narcissistic character disorders. Narcissism is currently regarded not just as a less-than-desirable aspect of the person but also as an important if not fundamental source of his or her creativity, ambition, and impetus for self-actualization. In this latter capacity it can obviously play an important role in theoretical models of character. For instance, entitlement, an element of narcissism, is partly concerned with primitive aspects of a sense of justice. It is thus a bridge from narcissism to superego functions and from there to the psychoanalytic theory of values. As such it may also help us understand more about the place of aggression in character formation. A theory of values has additional importance for the concept of normal character.

The self is the subjective side of character but, unlike the latter, more a feature of the Western Judeo-Christian mode of thinking than the Eastern one. In the age of narcissism, self representations, self-image, self-esteem are all buzzwords of the "me" generation. Does a shift of focus to the "we" generation suggest a comparable shift from "ego to wego"? We think it does. Whereas the self is self-reflective, issues of character are more context bound and require the presence of the other. The interface of character with social setting needs serious research attention.

Another poorly charted area of major significance to character studies concerns the question of normality. McDougall's (1978) plea for a certain measure of abnormality seems to reflect a common wish. The "normal character" raises eyebrows and the "wholesome character" likewise. Other terms such as *stable, well put together,* or *solid* are less offensive. It is impossible to talk of a disordered character without some standard against which to compare it. Naturally, the idea of normality and abnormality as different positions on a continuum has not helped in creating operational standards. A related difficulty is that of naming or classifying aspects of normality, all of which have a bearing on being able to identify a *standard for comparison*. While there are reams of material on the types of character disturbances, their pathogenesis, and treatment, there is comparatively little written about normality. Some steps in the right direction have been taken however. Elaborating on some of Freud's thoughts on the subject, Abraham (1953) talked about the genital character, a concept which Reich (1949) further developed. In more recent years, Hartmann (1964) has dealt with the same subject and Vaillant (1977) has also done some fine research in this area. Doubtlessly the question of a *Weltanschauung,* benevolent neutrality, and differences of opinion contribute to the difficulty. But it is not an insurmountable difficulty and must represent another high priority for our field.

Identification is a major process in character formation and pathology most dramatically in evidence in cases of multiple personality, a subject of increasing interest in the last few years. Freud considered it in terms of multiple identifications. Deutsch's "as if" character suffered from multiple and pathological caretaking leading to problems in identification. How multiple caregivers affect identification and character formation becomes a question which warrants attention. In an age of combined families and ever earlier and longer day-care settings, we can ask ourselves whether children are being exposed to too much and too little at the same time. An urgent question with immediate relevancy would be: are there too many caretakers and not enough time with any given one? Can partial identification later in life such as with one's analyst or therapist serve as an antidote?

We think that there should also be dialogue between findings from research on cognition with those from research on character. The way individuals map out their perceptions—how each person receives, stores, organizes, and uses information (i.e., how specific cognitive styles are brought into being), can definitely further our understanding of the field.

Last but not least on our future research agenda should be comprehension of the extent to which we can change or modify character at each stage of life. Without such knowledge it is impossible to evaluate the prospect for transfiguration at different points in time. Life-cycle studies help us understand how psychological structures are shaped and modified over time, how new structures are superimposed on existing ones. Developmental research, looking at cognitive, affective, behavioral, and psychological processes in infancy and early childhood and studies of disposition and temperament have helped address the issue of therapeutic "bedrock"—the absolute limits of therapeutic character modification. What happens at more mature stages of human functioning needs further clarification in order to better understand the process of eventual modification. Here, integration of findings from neurobiology and artificial intelligence can be of assistance.

Over the years analyses have taken longer and longer to reach termination. This raises a host of new questions. What are the underlying reasons, and are there grounds for concern? Are analysts attempting to affect character more than is possible or accepting patients not suitable for treatment? We would be closer to answering these questions if we addressed the matter of possible and wished-for changes in character.

We began this *Handbook* with the statement that psychoanalysis is a most powerful tool in deciphering human functioning. The various contributions have demonstrated the extent to which psychoanalytic concepts and theories can be instrumental in furthering our understanding of character. In the chapters between Introduction and Epilogue we have presented perspectives on a set of topics that seem to capture the most promising avenues for character study.

All in all, this *Handbook* demonstrates that the study of character is coming of age. In the midst of confusion there is an unquestionably greater sophistication emerging. Outside the psychoanalytic and psychiatric world, the interest in character continues to grow. Both in the world of work and in the political sphere we find an increasing number of contributions related to character. The content of journals such as *Political Psychology, Administration and Society, Human Relations,* and *Leadership Quarterly* reflect this new trend. We should keep in mind that if the lay public is interested in character studies, it is surely opportune for psychoanalysts, psychiatrists, and psychologists to help out. There seems to be a great need to transcend existing disciplinary boundaries.

To conclude, there is currently an opportunity for convergence of various research orientations both within and without our field of studies. Researchers are increasingly inclined to look beyond their own paradigms in order to arrive at a rapprochement and thus to meet the challenges of the future. To make this happen, however, it will be necessary to maintain the existing momentum in our area of inquiry and continue our search for a better understanding of the elusive concept of character.

REFERENCES

Abraham, K. (1916), The first pregenital stage of the libido. *Selected Papers of Karl Abraham,* trans. D. Bryan & A. Strachey. New York: Basic Books, 1968, pp. 248–280.

_____ (1920), Manifestations of the female castration complex. *Selected Papers on Psycho-Analysis.* London: Hogarth Press, 1927, pp. 338–369.

_____ (1921), Contributions to the theory of the anal character. *Selected Papers of Karl Abraham,* trans. D. Bryan & A. Strachey. New York: Basic Books, 1968, pp. 370–392.

_____ (1924), The influence of oral erotism on character-formation. *Selected Papers of Karl Abraham,* trans. D. Bryan & A. Strachey. New York: Basic Books, 1968, pp. 393–406.

_____ (1921–1925), Psycho-analytical studies on character-formation. *Selected Papers on Psycho-Analysis.* London: Hogarth Press, 1927, pp. 370–417.

_____ (1925), Character-formation on the genital level. *Selected Papers of Karl Abraham,* trans. D. Bryan & A. Strachey. New York: Basic Books, 1968, pp. 407–417.

_____ (1935), The history of an impostor in the light of psychoanalytic knowledge. *Psychoanal, Quart.,* 4:570–587.

_____ (1953), *Selected Papers on Psychoanalysis.* New York: Basic Books.

Abrams, S. (1982), Disposition and the environment. *The Psychoanalytic Study of the Child,* 41:41–60. New Haven, CT: Yale University Press.

Abse, D. W. (1959), Hysteria. In: *American Handbook of Psychiatry,* Vol. 1, ed. S. Arieti. New York: Basic Books, pp. 272–292.

Aichhorn, A. (1936), The narcissistic transference of the "juvenile impostor." In: *Delinquency and Child Guidance,* eds. O. Fleischmann, P. Kramer, & H. Ross. New York: International Universities Press, 1964, pp. 174–191.

Adler, G. (1970), Valuing and devaluing in the psychotherapeutic process. *Arch. Gen. Psychiat.,* 22:454–461.

_____ (1974), Regression in psychotherapy: Disruptive or therapeutic? *Internat. J. Psychoanal. Psychother.,* 3:252–264.

_____ 1975), The usefulness of the "borderline" concept in psychotherapy. In: *Borderline States in Psychiatry,* ed. J. E. Mack. New York: Grune & Stratton, pp. 29–40.

Alexander, F. (1923), The castration complex in the formation of character. *Internat. J. Psycho-Anal.,* 4:11–42.

———— (1930a), *Psychoanalysis of the Total Personality*. Washington, DC: Nervous & Mental Diseases.

———— (1930b), The neurotic character. *Internat. J. Psycho-Anal.*, 2:292–311.

———— French, T. M. (1946), *Psychoanalytical Therapy: Principles and Application*. New York: Ronald Press.

American Psychiatric Association (1980), *Diagnostic and Statistical Manual of Mental Disorders*, 3rd ed. Washington, DC: American Psychiatric Press.

———— (1987), *Diagnostic and Statistical Manual of Mental Disorders*, 3rd ed. rev. Washington, DC: American Psychiatric Press.

Andreas-Salomé, L. (1921), The dual orientation of narcissism. *Psychoanal. Quart.*, 1962, 31:1–30.

Apfelbaum, B. (1966), Ego psychology: A critique of the structural approach to psychoanalytic theory. *Internat. J. Psycho-Anal.*, 47:451–475.

Arlow, J. A. (1953), Masturbation and symptom formation. *J. Amer. Psychoanal. Assn.*, 1:45–58.

———— (1968), Character and perversions. Paper presented at the Twentieth Anniversary Meeting of the New Orleans Psychoanalytic Institute, October 5, 1968.

———— (1969a), Unconscious fantasy and disturbances of conscious experience. *Psychoanal. Quart.*, 38:1–27.

———— (1969b), Fantasy, memory and reality testing. *Psychoanal. Quart.*, 38:28–51.

———— (1971), A type of play in latency boys. In: *Separation–Individuation: Essays in Honor of Margaret Mahler*, eds. J. B. McDevitt & C. F. Seltlage. New York: International Universities Press.

———— Brenner, C. (1964), *Psychoanalytic Concepts and the Structural Theory*. New York: International Universities Press.

———— ———— (1988), The future of psychoanalysis. *Psychoanal. Quart.*, 57:1–14.

———— Freud, A., Lampl-de Groot, J., & Beres, D. (1968), Panel discussion. *Internat. J. Psycho-Anal.*, 49:506–512.

Atkin, S. (1974), A borderline case: Ego synthesis and cognition. *Internat. J. Psycho-Anal.*, 55:13–19.

Bak, R. (1946), Masochism in paranoia. *Psychoanal. Quart.*, 15:285–301.

———— (1954), The schizophrenic defence against aggression. *Internat. J. Psycho-Anal.*, 35:129–134.

———— (1956), Aggression and perversion. In: *Perversions: Psychodynamics and Therapy*, eds. S. Lorand & M. Balint. New York: Random House, pp. 231–240.

Baudry, F. (1983), The evolution of the concept of character in Freud's writings. *J. Amer. Psychoanal. Assn.*, 31:3–31.

Bergler, E., & Eidelberg, L. (1935), Der mechanismus der Depersonalization. *Internat. Zeit. für Psychanal.*, 21:258–285.

Berliner, B. (1940), Libido and reality in masochism. *Psychoanal. Quart.*, 9:322–333.

———— (1947), On some psychodynamics of masochism. *Psychoanal. Quart.*, 16:459–471.

_____ (1958), The role of object relations in moral masochism. *Psychoanal. Quart.*, 27:38–56.

Bernstein, L. (1957), The role of narcissism in moral masochism. *Psychoanal. Quart.*, 26:358–377.

Bibring, E. (1954), Psychoanalysis and the dynamic psychotherapies. *J. Amer. Psychoanal. Assn.*, 2:745–770.

Bion, W. R. (1957), Differentiation of the psychotic from the non-psychotic personality. *Internat. J. Psycho-Anal.*, 38:266–275.

Blashfield, R. K. (1986), Structural approaches to classification. In: *Contemporary Directions in Psychopathology: Toward the DSM-IV*, eds. T. Millon & G. L. Klerman, New York: Guilford Press.

Bleuler, E. (1924), *Textbook of Psychiatry*. New York: Macmillan.

Blos, P. (1968), Character formation in adolescence. *The Psychoanalytic Study of the Child*, 23:245–263. New York: International Universities Press.

Blum, H. P. (1972), Psychoanalytic understanding and psychotherapy of borderline regression. *Internat. J. Psychoanal. Psychother.*, 1:46–60.

_____ (1974), The borderline childhood of the wolf man. *J. Amer. Psychoanal. Assn.*, 22:721–742.

Boesky, D. (1983), Resistance and character theory: A reconsideration of the concept of character resistance. *J. Amer. Psychoanal. Assn.*, supplement, 31:227–246.

Bollas, C. (1974), Character: The language of self. *Internat. J. Psychoanal. Psychother.*, 34:397–418.

Boyer, L. B., & Giovacchini, P. L. (1967), *Psychoanalytic Treatment of Schizophrenic and Characterological Disorders*. New York: Science House, pp. 208–335.

Brenman, M. (1952), On teasing and being teased: And the problem of moral masochism. *The Psychoanalytic Study of the Child*, 7:264–285. New York: International Universities Press.

Brenner, C. (1968), Some problems in the psychoanalytic theory of the instinctual drives. Presented at the Twentieth Anniversary Meeting of the New Orleans Psychoanalytic Institute, October 5, 1968.

Breuer, J., & Freud, S. (1893–1895), Studies on Hysteria. *Standard Edition*, 2. London: Hogarth Press, 1955.

Brody, E. B. (1960), Borderline state, character disorder and psychotic manifestations: Some conceptual formulations. *Psychiat.*, 23:75–80.

_____ Lindbergh, S. S. (1967), Trait and pattern disturbances. In: *Comprehensive Textbook of Psychiatry*, eds. A. R. Freedman & H. I. Kaplan. Baltimore: Williams & Wilkins, pp. 937–950.

Bromberg, N. (1955), Maternal influences in the development of moral masochism. *Amer. J. Orthopsychiat.*, 25:802–809.

Buie, D. H., & Adler, G. (1972), The uses of confrontation with borderline patients. *Internat. J. Psychoanal. Psychother.*, 1:90–108.

Chessick, R. D. (1966), The psychotherapy of borderline patients. *Amer. J. Psychother.*, 20:600–614.

Chodoff, P., & Lyons, H. (1958), Hysteria, the hysterical personality and hysterical conversion. *Amer. J. Psychiat.*, 114:734–740.

Cleckley, H. (1964), *The Mask of Sanity*, 4th ed. St. Louis: C. V. Mosby, pp. 362–401.

Collum, J. M. (1972), Identity diffusion and the borderline maneuver. *Comprehen. Psychiat.*, 13:179–184.

Crowley, R. M. (1934), Psychoanalytic literature on drug addiction and alcoholism. *Psychoanal. Rev.*, 26:39–54.

Darmesteter, J., ed. (1881), *Macbeth*. Paris.

Dickes, R. (1974), The concepts of borderline states: An alternative proposal. *Internat. J. Psychoanal. Psychother.*, 3:1–27.

Durfee, C. H. (1937), *To Drink or Not to Drink*. New York: Longmans, Green.

Easser, B. R. (1974), Empathic inhibition and psychoanalytic technique. *Psychoanal. Quart.*, 43:557–580.

Eidelberg, L. (1934), A contribution to the study of masochism. In: *Studies in Psychoanalysis*. New York: International Universities Press, 1951, pp. 31–40.

———— (1958), Technical problems in the analysis of masochists. *J. Hillside Hosp.*, 7:98–109.

Eissler, K. R. (1953a), The effect of the structure of the ego on psychoanalytic technique. *J. Amer. Psychoanal. Assn.*, 1:104–143.

———— (1953b), Notes upon the emotionality of a schizophrenic patient and its relation to problems of technique. *The Psychoanalytic Study of the Child*, 8:199–251. New York: International Universities Press.

Eissler, M. J. (1922), Pleasure in sleep and disturbed capacity for sleep. *Internat. J. Psycho-Anal.*, 3:30–42.

Ekstein, R., & Wallerstein, J. (1954), Observations on the psychology of borderline and psychotic children. *The Psychoanalytic Study of the Child*, 9:344–369. New York: International Universities Press.

———— (1956), Observations on the psychotherapy of borderline and psychotic children. *The Psychoanalytic Study of the Child*, 11:303–311. New York: International Universities Press.

Erikson, E. (1950), *Childhood and Society*. New York: W. W. Norton.

———— (1956), The problem of ego identity. *J. Amer. Psychoanal. Assn.*, 4:56–121.

———— (1959), Identity and the Life Cycle. *Psychological Issues*, Monograph 1. New York: International Universities Press.

Escalona, S., & Heider, G. M. (1959), *Prediction and Outcome*. New York: Basic Books.

Fain, M. (1971), Prélude à la vie fantasmatique. *Rev. Française de Psychoanal.*, 35:291–364.

Fairbairn, W. R. D. (1941), A revised psycho-pathology of the psychoses and psychoneuroses. *Internat. J. Psycho-Anal.*, 22:250–279.

———— (1944), Endopsychic structure considered in the light of object-relationships. *Internat. J. Psycho-Anal.*, 25:70–93.

———— (1952), *An Object Relation Theory of Personality*. New York: Basic Books, 1954.

Fast, I. (1974), Multiple identities in borderline personality organization. *Brit. J. Med. Psychol.*, 47:291–300.

_____ (1975), Aspects of work style and work difficulty in borderline personalities. *Internat. J. Psycho-Anal.*, 56:397–403.

Federn, P. (1952), *Ego Psychology and the Psychoses*, ed. E. Weiss. New York: Basic Books.

Fenichel, O. (1934), *Outline of Clinical Psychoanalysis*. New York: W. W. Norton.

_____ (1939a), The counterphobic attitude. *Internat. J. Psycho-Anal.*, 20:263–274.

_____ (1939b), The economics of pseudologia phantastica. *Internat. Ztschr. f. Psychoanal.*, 24:21–32.

_____ (1945), *The Psychoanalytic Theory of Neurosis*. New York: W. W. Norton.

Fintzy, R. T. (1971), Vicissitudes of the transitional object in borderline children. *Internat. J. Psycho-Anal.*, 52:107–114.

Frank, J. D. (1952), Two behavior patterns in therapeutic groups and their apparent motivation. *Human Rel.*, 5:289–317.

Freud, A. (1936), *The Ego and the Mechanisms of Defense*. New York: International Universities Press, 1946.

_____ (1951), Obituary: August Aichhorn. *Internat. J. Psycho-Anal.*, 32:51–56.

Freud, S. (1896), Further remarks on the defence neuropsychoses. *Standard Edition*, 2:157–186. London: Hogarth Press, 1962.

_____ (1900), The Interpretation of Dreams. *Standard Edition*, 4–5. London: Hogarth Press, 1953.

_____ (1905a), Three essays on the theory of sexuality. *Standard Edition*, 7:125–248. London: Hogarth Press, 1953.

_____ (1905b), Fragment of an analysis of a case of hysteria. *Standard Edition*, 7:7–122. London: Hogarth Press, 1953.

_____ (1905c), On psychotherapy. *Standard Edition*, 7:257–270. London: Hogarth Press, 1953.

_____ (1908), Hysterical phantasies and their relation to bisexuality. *Standard Edition*, 9:159–166. London: Hogarth Press, 1959.

_____ (1909a), Notes upon a case of obsessional neurosis. *Standard Edition*, 10:153–257. London: Hogarth Press, 1955.

_____ (1909b), Analysis of a phobia in a five-year-old boy. *Standard Edition*, 10:31–152. London: Hogarth Press, 1955.

_____ (1911a), Formulations on the two principles of mental functioning. *Standard Edition*, 12:213–226. London: Hogarth Press, 1958.

_____ (1911b), Psycho-analytic notes on an autobiographical account of a case of paranoia. *Standard Edition*, 12:3–82. London: Hogarth Press, 1958.

_____ (1912a), The dynamics of transference. *Standard Edition*, 12:97–108. London: Hogarth Press, 1958.

_____ (1912b), Types of onset of neurosis. *Standard Edition*, 12:227–238. London: Hogarth Press, 1958.

_____ (1913a), The disposition to obsessional neurosis. *Standard Edition*, 12:311–326. London: Hogarth Press, 1958.

_____ (1913b), Letter to Ludwig Binswanger of February 20, 1913. In:

Binswanger, L. *Erinnerungen an Sigmund Freud*. Bern: Francke Verlag, 1956, p. 65.

———— (1914a), Remembering, repeating and working through. *Standard Edition*, 12:145-156. London: Hogarth Press, 1958.

———— (1914b), On narcissism: An introduction. *Standard Edition*, 14:69-102. London: Hogarth Press, 1957.

———— (1914c), On the history of the psychoanalytic movement. *Standard Edition*, 14:3-66. London: Hogarth Press, 1957.

———— (1915a), Instincts and their vicissitudes. *Standard Edition*, 14:109-140. London: Hogarth Press, 1957.

———— (1915b), Repression. *Standard Edition*, 14:143-158. London: Hogarth Press, 1957.

———— (1915c), Mourning and melancholia. *Standard Edition*, 14:237-260. London: Hogarth Press, 1957.

———— (1916), Some character types met with in psycho-analytic work. *Standard Edition*, 14:309-333. London: Hogarth Press, 1957.

———— (1916-1917), Introductory Lectures on Psycho-Analysis. *Standard Edition*, 15-16. London: Hogarth Press, 1963.

———— (1917), On the transformations of instinct as exemplified in anal eroticism. *Standard Edition*, 17:127-133. London: Hogarth Press, 1955.

———— (1918), From the history of an infantile neurosis. *Standard Edition*, 17:3-122. London: Hogarth Press, 1955.

———— (1919), A child is being beaten. *Standard Edition*, 17:175-204. London: Hogarth Press, 1955.

———— (1920), Beyond the pleasure principle. *Standard Edition*, 18:3-64. London: Hogarth Press, 1955.

———— (1923a), The ego and the id. *Standard Edition*, 19:3-68. London: Hogarth Press, 1961.

———— (1923b), A seventeenth century demonological neurosis. *Standard Edition*, 19:69-108. London: Hogarth Press, 1961.

———— (1923c), Remarks on the theory and practice of dream interpretation. *Standard Edition*, 19:108-121. London: Hogarth Press, 1961.

———— (1924), The economic problem of masochism. *Standard Edition*, 19:157-172. London: Hogarth Press, 1961.

———— (1926a), Inhibitions, symptoms and anxiety. *Standard Edition*, 20:77-178. London: Hogarth Press, 1959.

———— (1926b), *The Problem of Anxiety*. New York: W. W. Norton, 1936.

———— (1927a), The future of an illusion. *Standard Edition*, 21:3-58. London: Hogarth Press, 1961.

———— (1927b), Fetishism. *Standard Edition*, 21:152-159. London: Hogarth Press, 1961.

———— (1930), Civilisation and its discontents. *Standard Edition*, 21:64-145. London: Hogarth Press, 1961.

———— (1932), The acquisition and control of fire. *Standard Edition*, 22:185-196. London: Hogarth Press, 1964.

———— (1933), New Introductory Lectures on Psycho-Analysis. *Standard Edition*, 22:3-184. London: Hogarth Press, 1964.

_____ (1936), A disturbance of memory on the Acropolis. *Standard Edition*, 22:239–250. London: Hogarth Press, 1964.

_____ (1937), Analysis terminable and interminable. *Standard Edition*, 23:204–254. London: Hogarth Press, 1964.

_____ (1938a), Splitting of the ego in the process of defence. *Standard Edition*, 23:273–278. London: Hogarth Press, 1964.

_____ (1938b), Constructions in analysis. *Standard Edition*, 23:255–270. London: Hogarth Press, 1964.

_____ (1950), Extracts from the Fliess Papers. *Standard Edition*, 1:175–279. London: Hogarth Press, 1966.

_____ Oppenheim, D. E. (1911), Dreams in folklore. *Standard Edition*, 12:175–204. London: Hogarth Press, 1958.

Friedlander, K. (1947), *The Psycho-Analytical Approach to Juvenile Delinquency*. New York: International Universities Press, pp. 183–187.

Friedman, H. J. (1970), Dr. Friedman replies (Corresp.) *Amer. J. Psychiat.*, 126:1677.

Frijling-Schreuder, E. C. M. (1969), Borderline states in children. *The Psychoanalytic Study of the Child*, 24:307–327. New York: International Universities Press.

Fromm, E. (1942), *The Fear of Freedom*. London: Kegan Paul.

Fromm-Reichmann, F. (1950), *Principles of Intensive Psychotherapy*. Chicago: University of Chicago Press.

Frosch, J. (1964), The psychotic character: Clinical psychiatric considerations. *Psychiat. Quart.*, 38:81–96.

_____ (1967), Severe regressive states during analysis: Introduction. *J. Amer. Psychoanal. Assn.*, 15:491–507.

_____ (1970), Psychoanalytic considerations of the psychotic character. *J. Amer. Psychoanal. Assn.*, 18:24–50.

Gall, F. J. (1825), *Sur les fonctions du cerveau et sur celles de ses parties*. Paris: Baillière.

Gardner, R., Holzman, P. S., Klein, G. S., Linton, H., & Spence, D. (1959), Cognitive Control: A Study of Individual Consistencies in Cognitive Behavior. *Psychological Issues*, Monograph 4, 1/4:45–64. New York: International Universities Press.

Gedo, J. E., & Goldberg, A. (1973), *Models of the Mind: A Psychoanalytic Theory*. Chicago: University of Chicago Press.

Geleerd, E. R. (1958), Borderline states in childhood and adolescence. *The Psychoanalytic Study of the Child*, 13:279–295. New York: International Universities Press.

Gill, M. M. (1951), Ego psychology and psychotherapy. *Psychoanal. Quart.*, 20:62–71.

_____ (1954), Psychoanalysis and exploratory psychotherapy. *J. Amer. Psychoanal. Assn.*, 2:771–797.

_____ (1963), Topography and Systems in Psychoanalytic Theory. *Psychological Issues*, Monograph 10, Vol. 3/2. New York: International Universities Press.

Giovacchini, P. L. (1963), Integrative aspects of object relationships. *Psychoanal. Quart.*, 32:393–407.

_____ (1965), Transference, incorporation, and synthesis. *Internat. J. Psycho-Anal.*, 46:287–296.

_____ (1967), Frustration and externalization. *Psychoanal. Quart.*, 36:571–583.

_____ (1970), Characterological problems: The need to be helped. *Arch. Gen. Psychiat.*, 22:245–251.

_____ (1973), Character disorders: With special reference to the borderline state. *Internat. J. Psychoanal. Psychother.*, 2:7–36.

Glover, E. (1924), The significance of the mouth in psycho-analysis. *Brit. J. Med. Psychol.*, 4:1–24.

_____ (1926), The neurotic character. *Internat. J. Psycho-Anal.*, 7:11–30.

_____ (1932), A psychoanalytic approach to the classification of mental disorders. In: *On the Early Development of Mind*. New York: International Universities Press, 1956, pp. 161–186.

_____ (1954), Therapeutic criteria of psychoanalysis. *Internat. J. Psycho-Anal.*, 35: 95–101.

_____ (1955a), Counter-resistance and counter-transference. In: *The Technique of Psychoanalysis*. New York: International Universities Press, pp. 88–107.

_____ (1955b), The analyst's case-list (2). In: *The Technique of Psychoanalysis*. New York: International Universities Press, pp. 185–258.

_____ (1966), Metapsychology or metaphysics. *Psychoanal. Quart.*, 35:177–190.

_____ (1968), *The Birth of the Ego*. New York: International Universities Press.

Goldberg, L. (1982), From ace to zombie: Some explorations in the language of personality assessment. In: *Advances in Personality Assessment*. Vol. 1, eds. C. Spielberger & J. Butcher. Hillsdale, NJ: Lawrence Erlbaum.

Goldstein, K., & Scheerer, M. (1944), Abstract and concrete behavior: An experimental study with special tests. *Psychological Monographs*. Washington, DC: American Psychological Association, 53:239–261.

Green, A. (1973), *Le Discours Vivant*. Paris: Presses Universitaires de France.

Greenson, R. R. (1958), On screen defenses, screen hunger, and screen identity. *J. Amer. Psychoanal. Assn.*, 6:242–262.

_____ (1967), *Technique and Practice of Psychoanalysis*. New York: International Universities Press.

Gunderson, J. G., & Singer, M. T. (1975), Defining borderline patients: An overview. *Amer. J. Psychiat.*, 132:1–10.

_____ (1983), DSM-III: Diagnoses of personality disorders. In: *Current Perspectives on Personality Disorders*, ed. J. P. Frosch. Washington, DC: American Psychiatric Press, pp. 20–39.

Guze, S. B. (1975), Differential diagnosis of the borderline personality syndrome. In: *Borderline States in Psychiatry*, ed. J. E. Mack. New York: Grune & Stratton, pp. 69–74.

Hartmann, H. (1939), *Ego Psychology and the Problem of Adaptation*. New York: International Universities Press, 1958.

_____ (1950), Comments on the psychoanalytic theory of the ego. *The Psy-*

choanalytic Study of the Child, 5:74–96. New York: International Universities Press.

_____ (1953), Contribution to the metapsychology of schizophrenia. *The Psychoanalytic Study of the Child*, 8:177–198. New York: International Universities Press.

_____ (1955), Notes on the theory of sublimation. In: *Essays on Ego Psychology*. New York: International Universities Press, 1964, pp. 215–240.

_____ (1960), *Psychoanalysis and Moral Values*. New York: International Universities Press.

_____ (1964), *Essays on Ego Psychology*. New York: International Universities Press.

_____ Kris, E., & Loewenstein, R. M. (1946), Comments on the formation of psychic structure. *The Psychoanalytic Study of the Child*, 2:11–38. New York: International Universities Press.

_____ _____ _____ (1949), Notes on the theory of aggression. *The Psychoanalytical Study of the Child*, 3/4:9–36. New York: International Universities Press.

Heimann, P. (1953), Certain functions of introjection and projection in early infancy. In: *Developments in Psycho-Analysis*, ed. Melanie Klein. London: Hogarth Press.

_____ (1955a), A contribution to the reevaluation of the oedipus complex: the early stages. In: *New Directions in Psycho-Analysis*, eds. M. Klein, P. Heimann & R. E. Money-Kyrle. London: Tavistock Publications, pp. 23–38.

_____ (1955b), A combination of defence mechanisms in paranoid states. In: *New Directions in Psycho-Analysis*, eds. M. Klein, P. Heimann & R. E. Money-Kyrle. London: Tavistock Publications, pp. 240–265.

Heymans, G., & Wiersma, E. (1906–1909), Beitrage zur speziellen Psychologie auf Grund einer Massenuntersuchung. *Zeitschrift für Psychologie*, pp. 42, 46, 49, 51.

Hinsie, L. E., & Campbell, R. J. (1940), *Psychiatric Dictionary*, 4th ed. New York: Oxford University Press, 1970.

Hoch, P. H., & Cattell, J. P. (1959), The diagnosis of pseudoneurotic schizophrenia. *Psychiat. Quart.*, 33:17–43.

_____ _____ Strahl, M. O., & Pennes, H. (1962), The course and outcome of pseudo-neurotic schizophrenia. *Amer. J. Psychiat.*, 119:106–115.

_____ Polatin, P. (1949), Pseudoneurotic forms of schizophrenia. *Psychiat. Quart.*, 23:248–276.

Holzmann, P. S., & Ekstein, R. (1959), Repetition-functions of transitory regressive thinking. *Psychoanal. Quart.*, 28:228–235.

Horner, A. J. (1975), Stages and processes in the development of early object relations and their associated pathologies. *Internat. Rev. Psycho-Anal.*, 2:95–105.

Horney, K. (1946), *Our Inner Conflicts*. London: Kegan Paul.

Jacobson, E. (1954a), Contribution to the metapsychology of psychotic identifications. *J. Amer. Psychoanal. Assn.*, 2:239–262.

_____ (1954b), The self and the object world. *The Psychoanalytic Study of the*

Child, 9:75–127. New York: International Universities Press.

———(1957), Denial and repression. *J. Amer. Psychoanal. Assn.*, 5:61–92.

———(1964), *The Self and the Object World*. New York: International Universities Press.

———(1971), *Depression*. New York: International Universities Press.

Jekels, L. (1917), Shakespeare's Macbeth. *Imago*, 5:166–176.

———(1926), Zur Psychologie der Komödie. *Imago*, 12:320–332.

Johnson, A. M., & Szurek, S. A. (1952), The genesis of antisocial acting out in children and adults. *Psychoanal. Quart.*, 21:323–343.

Jones, E. (1918), Anal-erotic character traits. In: *Papers on Psycho-Analysis*. Baltimore: Beacon Press, 1967, pp. 413–437.

———(1953), *The Life and Work of Sigmund Freud*, Vol. 2. New York: Basic Books.

Keiser, S. (1958), Disturbances in abstract thinking and body-image formation. *J. Amer. Psychoanal. Assn.*, 6:28–652.

Kernberg, O. (1965), Notes on countertransference. *J. Amer. Psychoanal. Assn.*, 13:38–56.

———(1966), Structural derivatives of object relationships. *Internat. J. Psycho-Anal.*, 47:236–253.

———(1967), Borderline personality organization. *J. Amer. Psychoanal. Assn.*, 15:641–685.

———(1970), Factors in the psychoanalytic treatment of narcissistic personalities. *J. Amer. Psychoanal. Assn.*, 18:51–85.

———(1971), Prognostic considerations regarding borderline personality organization. *J. Amer. Psychoanal. Assn.*, 19:595–635.

———(1975), *Borderline Conditions and Pathological Narcissism*. New York: Jason Aronson.

Khan, M. M. R. (1960), Clinical aspects of the schizoid personality: Affects and technique. *Internat. J. Psycho-Anal.*, 41:430–437.

Klein, D. F. (1975), Psychopharmacology and the borderline patient. In: *Borderline States in Psychiatry*, ed. J. E. Mack. New York: Grune & Stratton, pp. 75–91.

Klein, G. S. (1954), Need and regulation. In: *Nebraska Symposium on Motivation*, ed. M. R. Jones. Lincoln: University of Nebraska Press.

Klein, M. (1932), *The Psycho-Analysis of Children*. London: Hogarth Press.

———(1933), The early development of conscience in the child. In: *Contributions to Psycho-Analysis 1921–1945*. London: Hogarth Press, 1948, pp. 267–277.

———(1934), On criminality. In: *Contributions to Psycho-Analysis 1921–1945*. London: Hogarth Press, 1948, pp. 278–281.

———(1945), The oedipus complex in the light of early anxieties. In: *Contributions to Psycho-Analysis 1921–1945*. London: Hogarth Press, 1948, pp. 339–390.

———(1946), Notes on some schizoid mechanisms. *Internat. J. Psycho-Anal.* 27:99–110.

———(1948), *Contributions to Psycho-Analysis 1921–1945*. London: Hogarth Press.

_____ (1952), The origins of transference. *Internat. J. Psycho-Anal.*, 33:433–438.

Klerman, G. L. (1986), Historical perspectives in contemporary schools of psychopathology. In: *Contemporary Directions in Psychopathology*, eds. T. Millon & G. L. Klerman. New York: Guilford Press.

Knapp, P. H., Levin, S., McCarter, R., Wermer, H., & Zetzel, E. (1960), Suitability for psychoanalysis: A review of one hundred supervised analytic cases. *Psychoanal. Quart.*, 29:459–477.

Knight, R. P. (1937a), The dynamics and treatment of chronic alcohol addiction. *Bull. Menn. Clin.*, 10:223–250.

_____ (1937b), Psychodynamics of chronic alcoholism. *J. Nerv. Ment. Dis.*, 86:536–548.

_____ (1953a), Borderline states. In: *Psychoanalytic Psychiatry and Psychology*, eds. R. P. Knight & C. R. Friedman. New York: International Universities Press, 1954, pp. 97–109.

_____ (1953b), Management and psychotherapy of the borderline schizophrenic patient. In: *Psychoanalytic Psychiatry and Psychology*, eds. R. P. Knight & C. R. Friedman. New York: International Universities Press, pp. 110–122.

Kohut, H. (1966a), Forms and transformations of narcissism. *J. Amer. Psychoanal. Assn.*, 14:243–272.

_____ (1966b), Transference and countertransference in the analysis of narcissistic personalities. Presented at the 2nd Panamerican Congress for Psychoanalysis, Buenos Aires, Argentina, August 1966.

_____ (1968), The psychoanalytic treatment of narcissistic personality disorders. *The Psychoanalytic Study of the Child*, 23:86–113. New York: International Universities Press.

_____ (1971), *The Analysis of Self*. New York: International Universities Press.

_____ (1972), Thoughts on narcissism and narcissistic rage. *The Psychoanalytic Study of the Child*, 27:360–400. New York: Quadrangle.

_____ (1977), *The Restoration of the Self*. New York: International Universities Press.

Kretschmer, E. (1925), *Körperbau und Character*. Berlin: Springer Verlag.

Lampl-De Groot, J. (1963), Symptom formation and character formation. *Internat. J. Psychoanal.*, 44:1–11.

Laplanche, J., & Pontalis, J. B. (1973), *The Language of Psycho-Analysis*. New York: W. W. Norton.

Laughlin, H. P. (1956), *The Neuroses in Clinical Practice*. Philadelphia: Saunders, pp. 394–406.

Lewin, B. (1948), The nature of reality, the meaning of nothing, with an addendum on concentration. *Psychoanal. Quart.*, 17:524–526.

_____ (1950), *The Psychoanalysis of Elation*. New York: W. W. Norton.

Lichtenstein, H. (1964), The role of narcissism in the emergence and maintenance of a primary identity. *Internat. J. Psycho-Anal.*, 45: 49–56.

_____ (1965), Towards a metapsychological definition of the concept of self. *Internat. J. Psycho-Anal.*, 46:117–128.

Little, M. (1951), Countertransference and the patient's response to it. *Internat. J. Psycho-Anal.*, 32:32–40.

――― (1958), On delusional transference (transference psychosis). *Internat. J. Psycho-Anal.*, 39:134–138.

――― (1960a), Countertransference. *Brit. J. Med. Psychol.*, 33:29–31.

――― (1960b), On basic unity. *Internat. J. Psycho-Anal.*, 41:377–384.

Loewald, H. W. (1971), On motivation and instinct theory. *The Psychoanalytic Study of the Child*, 26:91–128. Chicago: Quadrangle.

Loewenstein, R. M. (1957), A contribution to the psychoanalytic theory of masochism. *J. Amer. Psychoanal. Assn.*, 5:197–234.

Macalpine, I. (1950), The development of the transference. *Psychoanal. Quart.*, 19:501–539.

Mahler, M. S. (1952), On child psychosis and schizophrenia: Autistic and symbiotic infantile psychoses. *The Psychoanalytic Study of the Child*, 7:286–305. New York: International Universities Press.

――― (1966), Notes on the development of basic moods: The depression affect. In: *Psychoanalysis: A General Psychology*, ed. R. M. Loewenstein. New York: International Universities Press, pp. 152–168.

――― (1971), A study of the separation–individuation process: And its possible application to borderline phenomena in the psychoanalytic situation. *The Psychoanalytic Study of the Child*, 26:403–424. New York: International Universities Press.

――― Furer, M. (1968), *On Human Symbiosis and the Vicissitudes of Individuation*, Vol. 1. New York: International Universities Press.

――― Pine, F., & Bergman, A. (1975), *The Psychological Birth of the Human Infant*. New York: Basic Books.

Marmor, J. (1953), Orality in the hysterical personality. *J. Amer. Psychoanal. Assn.*, 7:656–671.

Marsh, N. (1935), *Enter a Murderer*. London: Penguin Books.

Marty, P., M'Uzan, M. de, & David, C. (1963), *L'investigation psychosomatique*. Paris: Presses Universitaires de France.

Masterson, J. F. (1972), *Treatment of the Borderline Adolescent: A Developmental Approach*. New York: John Wiley.

――― Rinsley, D. B. (1975), The borderline syndrome: The role of the mother in the genesis and psychic structure of the borderline personality. *Internat. J. Psycho-Anal.*, 56:163–177.

McDougall, J. (1972), The anti-analysand in analysis. In: *Psychoanalysis in France*, ed. S. Lebovici & D. Widlöcher. New York: International Universities Press, 1980, pp. 333–354.

――― (1978), *Plea for a Measure of Abnormality*. New York: International Universities Press, 1980.

McGuire, W., ed. (1974), *The Freud/Jung Letters*. Princeton, NJ: Princeton University Press.

Meissner, W. W. (1971), Notes on identification. II. Clarification of related concepts. *Psychoanal. Quart.*, 40:277–302.

――― (1978a), *The Paranoid Process*. New York: Jason Aronson.

_____ (1978b), Notes on some conceptual aspects of borderline personality organization, working paper.

Menaker, E. (1953), Masochism—A defense reaction of the ego. *Psychoanal. Quart.*, 22:205–220.

Menninger, K. (1938), *Man Against Himself*. New York: Harcourt, Brace.

Meyer-Gross, W., Slater, E., & Roth, M. (1954), *Clinical Psychiatry*. Baltimore: Williams & Wilkins.

Meza, C. (1970), Anger—A key to the borderline patient. (Corresp.) *Amer. J. Psychiat.*, 126:1676–1677.

Michels, R. (1988), The future of psychoanalysis. *Psychoanal. Quart.*, 57:167–185.

Millon, T. (1984), On the renaissance of personality assessment and personality theory. *J. Pers. Assess.*, 48/5:450–466.

_____ Klerman, G. L. eds. (1986), *Contemporary Directions in Psychopathology: Toward the DSM-IV*. New York: Guilford Press.

Milner, M. (1969), *The Hands of the Living God*. New York: International Universities Press.

Modell, A. H. (1961), Denial and the sense of separateness. *J. Amer. Psychoanal. Assn.*, 9:533–547.

_____ (1963), Primitive object relationships and the predisposition to schizophrenia. *Internat. J. Psycho-Anal.*, 44:282–292.

_____ (1968), *Object Love and Reality*. New York: International Universities Press.

_____ (1975), A narcissistic defense against affects and the illusion of self-sufficiency. *Internat. J. Psycho-Anal.*, 56:275–282.

Monchy, R. (1950), Masochism as a pathological and as a normal phenomenon in the human mind. *Internat. J. Psycho-Anal.*, 31:95–97.

Money-Kyrle, R. E. (1956), Normal countertransference and some of its deviations. *Internat. J. Psycho-Anal.*, 37:360–366.

Moore, B. E. (1975), Toward a clarification of the concept of narcissism. *The Psychoanalytic Study of the Child*, 30:243–276. New Haven, CT: Yale University Press.

_____ Fine, B. D., ed. (1968), *A Glossary of Psychoanalytic Terms and Concepts*. New York: The American Psychoanalytic Association.

Mora, G. (1985), History of psychiatry. In: *Comprehensive Textbook of Psychiatry*, 4th ed., eds., H. I. Kaplan & B. J. Sadock. Baltimore: Williams & Wilkins.

Muensterberger, W. (1969), On the cultural determinants of individual development. In: *Man and His Culture: Psycho-Analytic Anthropology after "Totem and Taboo,"* ed. W. Muensterberger. London: Rapp & Whiting.

Murray, J. M. (1964), Narcissism and the ego ideal. *J. Amer. Psychoanal. Assn.*, 12:477–528.

Musil, R. (1953), *The Man Without Qualities*, trans. E. Wilkins & E. Kaiser. Vols. 1,2,3. London: Martin Secker & Warburg.

Nagera, H. (1964), Autoerotism, autoerotic activities, and ego development. *The Psychoanalytic Study of the Child*, 19:240–255. New York: International Universities Press.

Niederland, W. G. (1959), Schreber: Father and son. *Psychoanal. Quart.*, 28:151–169.

Nunberg, H. (1956a), Character and neurosis. *Internat. J. Psycho-Anal.*, 37:36–45.

——— (1956b), *Principles of Psychoanalysis: Their Application to the Neuroses*. New York: International Universities Press.

Oberndorf, C. P. (1934), Depersonalization in relation to erotization of thought. *Internat. J. Psycho-Anal.*, 15:271–295.

——— (1935), The genesis of the feeling of unreality. *Internat. J. Psycho-Anal.*, 16:296–306.

Ornstein, P. (1974), On narcissism: Beyond the introduction, highlights of Heinz Kohut's contributions to the psychoanalytic treatment of narcissistic personality disorders. *Annual of Psychoanalysis*, 2:127–149. New York: International Universities Press.

Panel (1955), The borderline case. L. Rangell reporter. *J. Amer. Psychoanal. Assn.*, 3:285–298.

——— (1956), The borderline case. L. L. Robbins, reporter. *J. Amer. Psychoanal. Assn.*, 4:550–562.

——— (1983a), Clinical aspects of character. M. H. Stein, chairperson. M. S. Willick, reporter. *J. Amer. Psychoanal. Assn.*, 31:225–236.

——— (1983b), Theory of character. S. M. Abend, reporter. *J. Amer. Psychoanal. Assn.*, 31:211–224.

Plato, *The Republic*, trans. H. D. P. Lee. Harmondsworth: Penguin Books, 1955.

Prelinger, E., Zimet, C. N., Schafer, R., & Levin, M. (1964), *An Ego-Psychological Approach to Character Assessment*. Glencoe, IL: Free Press, pp. 11–36.

Racker, H. (1957), The meanings and uses of countertransference. *Psychoanal. Quart.*, 26:303–357.

Rado, S. (1949–1950), *Lecture Notes in Psychodynamics*. New York: Columbia University Psychoanalytic Clinic.

——— (1954), Hedonic control, action-self, and the depressive spell. In: *Psychoanalysis of Behavior: The Collected Papers of Sandor Rado*, Vol. 1. New York: Grune & Stratton, 1956, pp. 286–311.

Rangell, L. (1959), The nature of conversion. *J. Amer. Psychoanal. Assn.*, 7:632–662.

Rapaport, D. (1957), Cognitive structures. In: *Contemporary Approaches to Cognition*, ed. J. S. Bruner. Cambridge, MA: Harvard University Press, pp. 157–200.

——— (1960), The Structure of Psychoanalytic Theory: A Systematizing Attempt. *Psychological Issues*, Monograph 6, Vol. 2/6. New York: International Universities Press.

——— (1967), *The Collected Papers of David Rapaport*, ed. M. M. Gill. New York: Basic Books.

_____ Gill, M. M., & Schafer, R. (1945–1946), *Diagnostic Psychological Testing*, Vol. 1:16–28, Vol. 2:24–33. Chicago: Year Book Publishers.

Reich, A. (1953), Narcissistic object choice in women. *J. Amer. Psychoanal. Assn.*, 1:22–44.

_____ (1960), Pathologic forms of self-esteem regulation. In: *Psychoanalytic Contributions*. New York: International Universities Press, 1973, pp. 288–311.

Reich, W. (1927), Zur technik der Deutung under Widerstandsanalyse. *Internat. Ztschr. für Psychoanal.*, 13.

_____ (1933), *Character-Analysis Principles and Techniques for Psychoanalysts in Practice and in Training*. New York: Orgone Press, 1945.

_____ (1949), *Character Analysis*. New York: Farrar, Straus & Giroux.

Reichard, S. (1956), A re-examination of Studies in Hysteria. *Psychoanal. Quart.*, 25:155–177.

Reider, N. (1957), Transference psychosis. *J. Hillside Hosp.*, 6:131–149.

Reik, T. (1939), The characteristics of masochism. *Amer. Imago*, 1:26–59.

_____ (1941), *Masochism in Modern Man*. New York: Farrar & Rinehart.

_____ (1946), *Ritual: Psychoanalytic Studies*. New York: International Universities Press.

Riviere, J. (1952), The unconscious phantasy of an inner world. *Internat. J. Psycho-Anal.*, 33:160–172.

Rochlin, G. (1973), *Man's Aggression: The Defense of the Self*. Boston: Gambit.

Romm, M. E. (1957), Transient psychotic episodes during psychoanalysis. *J. Amer. Psychoanal. Assn.*, 5:325–341.

Rosen, V. (1961), The relevance of "style" to certain aspects of defence and the synthetic function of the ego. *Internat. J. Psycho-Anal.*, 42:447–457.

Rosenfeld, H. (1958), Contribution to the discussion on variations in classical technique. *Internat. J. Psycho-Anal.*, 39:238–239.

_____ (1963), Notes on the psychopathology and psychoanalytic treatment of schizophrenia. In: *Psychotherapy of Schizophrenic and Manic-Depressive States*, eds. H. Azima & L. Glueck, Jr. Washington, DC: American Psychiatric Press.

_____ (1964), On the psychopathology of narcissism: A clinical approach. *Internat. J. Psycho-Anal.*, 45:332–337.

_____ (1965), Some thoughts on the technical handling of borderline children. *The Psychoanalytic Study of the Child*, 20:495–517. New York: International Universities Press.

_____ Sprince, M. P. (1963), An attempt to formulate the meaning of the concept "borderline." *The Psychoanalytic Study of the Child*, 18:603–635. New York: International Universities Press.

Ross, N. (1960), Report of panel: An examination of nosology according to psychoanalytic concepts. *J. Amer. Psychoanal. Assn.*, 8:535–551.

Rycroft, C. (1958), An enquiry into the function of words in the psychoanalytic situation. *Internat. J. Psycho-Anal.*, 39:408–415.

_____ (1968), *A Critical Dictionary of Psychoanalysis*. New York: Basic Books.

Sabshin, M. (1985), Psychoanalysis and psychiatry: Models for potential future relations. *J. Amer. Psychoanal. Assn.*, 33:473–492.

Sandler, J. (1961), On the concept of the superego. *The Psychoanalytic Study of the Child*, 15:128–162. New York: International Universities Press.

———— (1976), Countertransference and role-responsiveness. *Internat. Rev. Psychoanal.*, 3:43–47.

———— Holder, A., Kawenoka, M., Kennedy, H. E., & Neurath, L. (1969), Notes on some theoretical and clinical aspects of transference. *Internat. J. Psycho-Anal.*, 50:633–645.

———— Rosenblatt, B. (1962), The concept of the representational world. *The Psychoanalytic Study of the Child*, 17:128–145. New York: International Universities Press.

———— Sandler, A. M. (1978), On the development of object relationships and affects. *Internat. J. Psycho-Anal.*, 59:285–296.

Schafer, R. (1968), *Aspects of Internalization*. New York: International Universities Press.

———— (1976), *A New Language for Psychoanalysis*. New Haven/London: Yale University Press.

———— (1978a), *Language and Insight*. New Haven/London: Yale University Press.

———— (1978b), Conflict as paradoxical actions. *Psychoanal. & Contemp. Thought*, 1:3–19.

———— (1979), The appreciative analytic attitude and the construction of multiple case histories. *Psychoanal. & Contemp. Thought*, 2:3–24.

Schilder, P. F. (1939), The treatment of depersonalization. *Bull. NY Acad. Med.*, 15: 258–272.

Schlesinger, H. (1966), In defense of denial. Presented to the Topeka Psychoanalytic Society, June 1966.

Schur, M. (1966), *The Id and the Regulatory Principles of Mental Functioning*. New York: International Universities Press.

Schmideberg, M. (1947), The treatment of psychopaths and borderline patients. *Amer. J. Psychother.*, 1:45–70.

Searles, H. F. (1965), *Collected Papers on Schizophrenia and Related Subjects*. New York: International Universities Press.

Segal, H. (1964), *Introduction to the Work of Melanie Klein*. New York: Basic Books.

Shapiro, D. (1965), *Neurotic Styles*. New York: Basic Books.

Sharpe, E. F. (1931), Anxiety, outbreak and resolution. In: *Collected Papers on Psychoanalysis*. London: Hogarth, 1950, pp. 67–80.

Sheldon, W. H. (1940), *The Varieties of Human Physique: An Introduction to Constitutional Physiology*. New York: Harper.

———— (1945), *Atlas of Men: A Guide for Somatotyping the Male of All Ages*. New York: Harper.

Stein, M. H. (1956), Report of panel on the problem of masochism in the theory and technique of psychoanalysis. *J. Amer. Psychoanal. Assn.*, 4:526–538.

_____ (1965), States of consciousness in analytic situation: Including a note on the traumatic dream. In: *Drives, Affects, Behavior*, Vol. 2, ed. M. Schur. New York: International Universities Press, pp. 60–86.

_____ (1967), The analysis of character. (Abstract:) *Bull. Phil. Assn. Psychoanal.*, 17:114–118.

_____ (1969), The problem of character theory. *J. Amer. Psychoanal. Assn.*, 17:675–701.

Sterba, R. (1934), The fate of the ego in analytic therapy. *Internat. J. Psycho-Anal.*, 15:117–126.

_____ (1951), Character resistance. *Psychoanal. Quart.*, 20:72–76.

_____ (1953), Clinical and therapeutic aspects of character resistance. *Psychoanal. Quart.*, 22:1–20.

Stern, A. (1938), Psychoanalytic investigation of and therapy in the borderline group neuroses. *Psychoanal. Quart.*, 7:467–489.

_____ (1945), Psychoanalytic therapy in the borderline neuroses. *Psychoanal. Quart.*, 14:190–198.

Stone, (1951), Psychoanalysis and brief psychotherapy. *Psychoanal. Quart.*, 20:215–236.

_____ (1954), The widening scope of indications for psychoanalysis. *J. Amer. Psychoanal. Assn.*, 2:567–594.

_____ (1968), Reflections on the psychoanalytic concept of aggression. The Abraham A. Brill Lecture, presented to the New York Psychoanalytic Society, November 26, 1968.

Strachey, J. (1934), The nature of the therapeutic action of psychoanalysis. *Internat. J. Psycho-Anal.*, 15:127–159.

Sullivan, H. S. (1956), *Clinical Studies in Psychiatry*. New York: W. W. Norton, pp. 203–228.

Sutherland, J. D. (1963), Object-relations theory and the conceptual model of psychoanalysis. *Brit. J. Med. Psychol.*, 36:109–124.

Thomas, A., & Chess, S. (1977), *Temperament and Development*. New York: Brunner/Mazel.

_____ Korn, J. (1982), The reality of difficult temperament. *Merrill-Palmer Quart.*, 28:1–20.

Ticho, E. (1966), Selection of patients for psychoanalysis or psychotherapy. Presented at the 20th Anniversary Meeting of the Menninger School of Psychiatry Alumni Association. Topeka, Kansas, May.

Vaillant, G. E. (1977), *Adaptation to Life*. Boston: Little, Brown.

Van der Waals, H. G. (1952), Discussion of the mutual influences in the development of ego and id. *The Psychoanalytic Study of the Child*, 7:66–68. New York: International Universities Press.

Waelder, R. (1936), The principle of multiple function. *Psychoanal. Quart.*, 5:45–62.

_____ (1960), *Basic Theory of Psychoanalysis*. New York: International Universities Press.

_____ (1962), Psychoanalysis, scientific method and philosophy. *J. Amer. Psychoanal. Assn.*, 10:617–637.

Wallerstein, R. S. (1967), Reconstruction and mastery in the transference psychosis. *J. Amer. Psychoanal. Assn.*, 15:551–583.

_____ Robbins, L. L. (1956), The psychotherapy research project of the Menninger Foundation; IV. concepts. *Bull. Menn. Clin.*, 20:239–262.

_____ Weinshel, E. M. (1989), The future of psychoanalysis. *Psychoanal. Quart.*, 58:341–373.

Wangh, M. (1962), The evocation of a proxy. *The Psychoanalytic Study of the Child*, 17:451–469. New York: International Universities Press.

Weigl, E. (1941), On the psychology of so-called processes of abstraction. *J. Abnorm. & Soc. Psychol.*, 36:3–33.

Weinshel, E. (1971), Some psychoanalytic considerations in moods. *J. Amer. Psychoanal. Assn.*, 51:313–320.

Weisman, A. D. (1958), Reality sense and reality testing. *Behav. Sci.*, 3:228–261.

Weiss, E. (1936), Presenza psichica e super-io contributo all'esplorazione psicologica della coscienza morale. In: *Saggi di Psicoanalisi in Onore di Sigmund Freud*. Rome: Cremonese Libraio Editore.

Wilson, C. P. (1971), On the limits of the effectiveness of psychoanalysis: Early ego and somatic disturbance. *J. Amer. Psychoanal. Assn.*, 19:552–564.

Winnicott, D. W. (1949a), Mind and its relation to the psyche-soma. In: *Collected Papers*. New York: Basic Books, 1958.

_____ (1949b), Hate in the countertransference. *Internat. J. Psycho-Anal.*, 30:69–75.

_____ (1953), Transitional objects and transitional phenomena. In: *Playing and Reality*. New York: Basic Books, 1971, pp. 1–25.

_____ (1954), Withdrawal and regression. In: *Collected Papers*. New York: Basic Books, 1958.

_____ (1955), The depressive position in normal emotional development. *Brit. J. Med. Psychol.*, 28:89–100.

_____ (1960a), Ego distortion in terms of true and false self. In: *Maturational Processes and the Facilitating Environment*. New York: International Universities Press, 1965, pp. 140–152.

_____ (1960b), Countertransference. *Brit. J. Med. Psychol.*, 33:17–21.

Wisdom, J. O. (1961), A methodological approach to the problem of hysteria. *Internat. J. Psycho-Anal.*, 42:224–237.

Wittels, F. (1930), The hysterical character. *Med. Rev. Rev.*, 36:186–190.

Worden, F. G. (1955), A problem in psychoanalytic technique. *J. Amer. Psychoanal. Assn.*, 3:255–279.

Zetzel, E. (1965), The use and misuse of psychoanalysis in psychiatric training and psychotherapeutic practice. In: *Proceedings of the 6th International Congress of Psychotherapy*, eds. M. Pines & T. Spoerri. Basel/New York: Karger.

_____ (1966), The analytic situation. In: *Psychoanalysis in the Americas*, ed. R. E. Litman. New York: International Universities Press, pp. 86–106.

_____ (1971), A developmental approach to the borderline patient. *Amer. J. Psychiat.*, 127:867–871.

Zilboorg, G. (1941), Ambulatory schizophrenias. *Psychiat.*, 4:149–155.

———(1956), The problem of ambulatory schizophrenias. *Amer. J. Psychiat.*, 113:519–525.

———(1957), Further observations on ambulatory schizophrenias. *Amer. J. Orthopsychiat.*, 27:677–682.

Zinner, J., & Shapiro, E. R. (1975), Splitting in families of borderline adolescents. In: *Borderline States in Psychiatry*, ed. J. E. Mack. New York: Grune & Stratton, pp. 103–122.

NAME INDEX

615

SUBJECT INDEX

Achievement, Don Juan of,
123-126
Acting out, 222. *See also*
Transference acting-out
in character disorder, 332,
468-469
in therapy, 519
Action language, 130
Actualization, 193, 197
function of, 195
wish-fulfilling, 200-201
Addictively structured patients, 368
Adolescence, formation of character
during, 10-11
Affect
blocking of, 85, 98-99
deficient tolerance of, 356
flattening of, 97
inaccessible, 379-380
loss of, 431
pathology of, in "dis-affected"
patients, 365-385
psychotic modes of
experiencing, 382
Affection, supplies of, 118-119
Affective flooding, compulsive ways
of avoiding, 367
Affectless personality, 352. *See also*
"Dis-affected" patient
Aggression
lack of agreed-upon theory of,
142
masking of, 391
and narcissistic type, 52-53

in phallic-narcissistic character,
102-103
projected onto mother, 500
Aggressive drives
inhibited, 232-233
need to evolve theory of, 145
Aggressive impulses
denial of, 522
pregenital, 327; intensity of,
325-326
Aggressive outbursts, in character
disorder, 471-472
Aggressor, seduction of, 291
Alcohol addiction
and character disorder,
223-224
masochistic character in,
296-297
Alcoholic, splitting in, 515-517
Alexithymia, 352, 365, 368,
379-380
Alloplastic symptoms, 210-213
Ambition, 65
Ambivalence
in compulsive character,
99-100
splitting of, 100
symptoms of, 63-64
Anal character, 55, 215-216
reticence of, 64
traits of, 18, 120
Anal-erotic character, early
psychoanalytic interest in,
263-264

621

phallic-narcissistic character in, 102

Working through process, 149

Worry

in obsessive-compulsive, 273–274

and sense of "should," 276